PARTY
POLITICS
IN
AMERICA

PARTY POLITICS IN AMERICA

Fifth Edition

FRANK J. SORAUF

University of Minnesota

LITTLE, BROWN AND COMPANY
Boston   Toronto

Library of Congress Cataloging in Publication Data

Sorauf, Frank J. (Frank Joseph), 1928–
    Party politics in America.

    1. Political parties—United States.   I. Title.
JK2265.S65 1984   324.273   83-24891
ISBN 0-316-80439-8

Library of Congress Catalog Card Number 83-24891

ISBN 0-316-80439-8

9 8 7 6 5 4 3 2 1

BP

Published simultaneously in Canada
by Little, Brown & Company (Canada) Limited

Printed in the United States of America

Acknowledgments begin on page 463.

For My Mother and Father

Preface

The purposes and outlooks of this book—even its eccentricities—will be apparent to readers without my alerting them in a lengthy preface. And what prefatory materials on the parties ought to be read I have included in the introductions to the six parts of the book, where they *will* be read.

The sins of commission of which I am guilty are on the pages of the book for everyone to see. I hope readers will not hesitate to call them to my attention. My sins of omission may, however, require a brief comment. With the scholarly literature on parties growing so rapidly, I have had to make difficult, even arbitrary, selections from it. In the interests of both brevity and logic, I have also resisted the temptation to dwell at length on interest groups and American voting behavior. This is a self-imposed limitation, but I think it can be defended on intellectual as well as practical grounds.

Readers familiar with earlier editions of this book will find that the basic approach and structure of the book remain the same, but there are a number of changes. I have thoroughly updated the book to reflect recent events and new developments in American politics and to draw on the scholarly literature of the last four years. I have also done some rewriting and recasting on many pages in the interest of greater clarity. Beyond these usual changes, I have more thoroughly reworked the chapters on the national parties and campaign finance. I hope the result is a clearer and more useful book.

Finally, I should like to acknowledge some of the debts I have incurred in putting this book into its fifth edition. This one bears enough similarity to the first four editions for the debts incurred in doing them to continue here. To the thanks I gave in the prefaces to those editions I should like to add a few more. Many students, friends, and colleagues continue to make useful comments about the book. I hope they will forgive such a brief and collective acknowledgment. I am especially indebted to Steven J. Rosenstone for his extended comments and observations and to Gerald R. Elliott for his help in locating materials. I am also grateful for the splendid work of my typist, Gloria Priem, and my research assistant, Stephen Ansolabehere. As usual, too, the people at Little, Brown were patient and helpful.

Contents

PARTY
POLITICS
IN
AMERICA

I
Parties and Party Systems

The open and aggressive pursuit of personal advantage will probably never win the admiration of any society. It certainly has not won the admiration of ours. Yet the things men and women want for themselves and for others—status, security, justice, and wealth, for example—are in short supply. People compete for them by trying to influence government to recognize their claims rather than those of others. This striving to win the things we think desirable—a striving we call "politics"—is therefore as widespread as those desires are.

The pervasiveness of politics is a central fact of our times. We have seen in the twentieth century an enormous expansion of governmental activity. The demands of a complex, increasingly urbanized, industrialized society, and the dictates of a world beset by international tensions, do not easily permit a return to limited government. For the foreseeable future, a substantial proportion of the important conflicts over the desirable things in American society will be settled within the political system. The really meaningful issues of our time will surely be how influence and power are organized within the political system, who wins the rewards and successes of that political activity, and to whom the people who make the decisions are responsible. It will increasingly be within the political system that we will decide, in the candid phrase of Harold Lasswell, "who gets what, when, how."[1]

In the United States, these political contestings are directed largely at the regular institutions of government. Few political scientists believe that the real and important political decisions are made clandestinely by murky, semivisible elites and merely ratified by the governmental bodies they con-

---

[1]The phrase comes from the title of Harold Lasswell's pioneering book *Politics: Who Gets What, When, How* (New York: McGraw-Hill, 1936).

1

trol.[2] It may happen, to be sure, that political decisions in a local community are made by a group of influential local citizens rather than by a city council or a mayor or a school board. Nonetheless, one is reasonably safe in looking for the substance of American politics in the legislatures, executives, and courts of the nation, the fifty states, and localities. The politics of which we have been talking consists, therefore, of the attempts to influence either the making of decisions within these governmental bodies or the selecting of the men and women who will make them.

This struggle for influence, this "politics," is not unorganized, however confusing it may seem to be. Large political organizations attempt to mobilize influence on behalf of aggregates of individuals. In the Western democracies the political party is unquestionably the most important and pervasive of these political organizations. It is not, however, the only one. Interest groups such as the American Farm Bureau Federation and the AFL–CIO also mobilize influence. So do smaller factions and cliques, charismatic individuals, and nonparty political organizations such as Americans for Democratic Action and the American Conservative Union. And so do the political action committees (PACs) that pay a substantial part of the costs of American campaigning. We cannot, therefore, use the term *politics* to refer only to the activities of the political parties. Even though a substantial portion of American politics goes on within and through the political parties, a substantial portion also goes on outside them. Interest groups rather than parties, for example, bring certain issues and policy questions to legislatures and administrative agencies. Nonparty organizations also support candidates for office with money and manpower, sometimes even more effectively than the parties do. Thus, the terms *politics* and *political* include not only the activity of the political parties but also that of other political organizers.

At this point, it may help to step back and survey the entire political system in order to understand the place of parties and other political organizations in it (Figure I.1). All these political organizations work as intermediaries between the millions of political individuals and the distant policymakers in government. They build influence into large aggregates in order to have a greater effect on the selection of policymakers and the policies they will make. At the same time, they codify and simplify information about government and politics as it moves back to the individual. In a very real sense, therefore, these political organizers are the informal agents by which individuals are represented in the complex democracies of our time. They are both the builders and the agents of majorities.

In any political system, the political organizations develop an informal

---

[2]C. Wright Mills, in *The Power Elite* (New York: Oxford University Press, 1956), offers the best-known example of such interpretations of American politics.

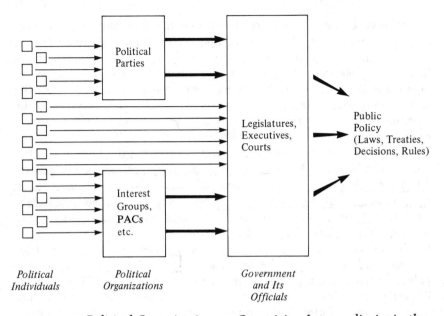

FIGURE I.1   *Political Organizations as Organizing Intermediaries in the Political System*

division of labor. The political parties concentrate on contesting elections as a way of aggregating influence. Others, especially the interest groups, pursue the avenues of direct influence on legislators or administrators. Still others seek mainly to propagate ideologies or build support on specific issues of foreign or domestic policy. Indeed, the nature of the division of labor among the various political organizations says a great deal about any political system and about the general processes of mobilizing influence within it. The division also speaks meaningfully about the political parties. It is a commonplace, for example, that among the parties of the democracies, the American political parties are occupied to an unusual extent with the single activity of contesting elections. The parties of Western Europe, on the other hand, have been more committed to spreading ideologies and disciplining legislators. And those of countries such as India have been more involved with transmitting political values and information to a citizenry that lacks other avenues of political socialization and communication.

The division of labor among political organizations is, however, neither clear nor permanent. There is always an overlapping—and hence a competition—among political organizations over the performance of their activities. That competition is most obvious when it takes place within the party system, the competition of one party against another. It also takes place, however, between parties and other political organizations—for example, in the competition of parties and powerful interest groups for the attention and support of legislators or for the right to name a candidate in a primary election. Furthermore, the extent to which any one kind of political organization controls or participates in any one kind of organizing activity may change radically over time. Certainly, no one would argue that the American political parties today control as much of the business of campaigning as they did 70 or 80 years ago.

All of this competing for a role in American politics implies another kind of competition. The political organizations compete among themselves for political resources: money, skills, expertise, the efforts of men and women. All of these resources are necessary for the fueling of organizational activity, but none of them is in particularly abundant supply in the American society. Then, with those resources at hand, they compete for the support of individual citizens—that is, they seek their support for the goals and leadership of the organization. In sum, the parties and other political organizations compete for scarce resources with which to mobilize the political influence necessary to capture the scarce rewards the political system allocates. They compete first for the capacity to organize influence and then for the influence itself.

Despite these excursions beyond the subject of political parties, however, this *is* a book about political parties. The broader survey of politics and political organizations has merely been background for two themes that will recur throughout the remainder of the book. The first is that the political party is not the unique political organization we have conventionally thought it to be. On the contrary, it is frequently similar to other political organizations, and the difficulty of coming to a clear, agreed-on definition of a political party illustrates that point only too well. When one undertakes any exercise in definition, as we do for the parties in the first chapter, the temptation is always to err on the side of the distinctiveness, even the uniqueness, of the phenomenon one is trying to define. It may well be that the distinctions between parties and other political organizations are not, after all, so great as one might imagine. Parties do have their distinctive qualities—and it is important to know them—but there is little point in denying their similarity to many other political organizations.

Second, the broad perspective is essential background for assessing the role and position of the political parties in the American democracy. American writers about the political parties have not been modest in their claims for them. They have celebrated the parties as agents of democracy and even as the chosen instruments through which a democratic citizenry governs itself. Some have gone a step further to proclaim them the originators of the democratic processes that they now serve. E. E. Schattschneider opened his classic study of the American parties this way in 1942:

The rise of political parties is indubitably one of the principal distinguishing marks of modern government. The parties, in fact, have played a major role as *makers* of governments, more especially they have been the makers of democratic government. It should be stated flatly at the outset that this volume is devoted to the thesis that the political parties created democracy and that modern democracy is unthinkable save in terms of the parties.[3]

Other scholars, and many thoughtful Americans, too, agree that the American democracy presumes the two-party system of today.

Yet the major American parties have changed and continue to change—both in the form of their organization and in the pattern and style of their activities. Political parties as they existed a century ago scarcely exist today, and the political parties we know today may not exist even a half-century from now. In this book, a vigorous case will be made for the proposition that the political parties have lost their preeminent position as political organizations and that competing political organizations now perform many of the activities traditionally regarded as the parties' exclusive prerogatives.[4] If this is indeed the case, we must face the question of whether political parties are indeed indispensable and inevitable shapers of our democratic politics.

These two suspicions—that the parties may be less distinctive and their activities less pervasive than we have thought—add up, perhaps, to no more than a plea for modesty in the study of the American political parties. It is perfectly natural for both young and experienced scholars to identify with the objects of their study and thus to exaggerate their importance. Medievalists often find the late Middle Ages to be the high point of Western civilization, and most scholars of hitherto obscure painters and philosophers find the objects of their study to have been sadly neglected or tragically underestimated. So, too, has it been with the study of political parties.

All of this is not to suggest, out of hand, that the American political parties are or have been of little importance. Their long life and their role in the politics of the world's oldest representative democracy scarcely lead to that conclusion. The plea here is merely for a careful assessment, for an abandoning of preconceptions, old judgments, and "great general truths." Assertions that political parties are essential to or the keystone of American democracy may or may not be true, but simply as assertions they advance our understanding of politics and parties very little. The proof is in the evidence, and the evidence is in a detailed knowledge of what the political parties are and what they do.

[3]E. E. Schattschneider, *Party Government* (New York: Rinehart, 1942), p. 1.
[4]See also Anthony King, "Political Parties in Western Democracies," *Polity* 2 (1969): 111–41.

1

IN SEARCH OF THE
POLITICAL PARTIES

Consider the American adults who insist, "I'm a strong Republican," and "I've been a Democrat all my life." It is unlikely that they ever worked within the party organization of their choice, much less made a financial contribution to it. They would be hard-pressed to recall its recent platform commitments, and if they did, they would not necessarily feel any loyalty to them. Furthermore, they probably never meet with the other Americans who express the same party preferences, and they would likely find it difficult to name the local officials of their party. In fact, their loyalty to the party of which they consider themselves "members" may be little more than a disposition to support its candidates at elections if all other considerations are fairly equal. Yet when the interviewers of polling organizations come to their doors, they hesitate not at all to attach themselves to that political party. And we do not hesitate to credit their word, for it is in the nature of the American parties to consider people Democrats or Republicans merely because they say they are.

Are the major American parties, then, nothing more than great, formless aggregates of people who say they are Democrats and Republicans? Are they nothing more than vague political labels that people attach themselves to? It is perilously easy to conclude so, but the American political parties are also organizations. It *is* possible to join them, to work within them, to become officers in them, to participate in setting their goals and strategies—much as one would within a local fraternal organization or a machinists' union. They have characteristics that we associate with social organizations: stable, patterned personal relationships and common goals. In other words, they are more than aggregates of people clinging in various degrees of intensity to a party label.

The act of defining the political party, and the American parties in particular, is hampered by the fact that the nature of the political party, like beauty, often rests in the eye of the beholder. The definition is often a personal perception; it seems to depend on what one is looking for, what one hopes to see, what consequences one wants parties to have. (See, for example, the range of definitions in the box.) Any one person's definition is likely to be rooted in a particular time and orientation and therefore is not likely to reflect the diversity that marks the parties. Whatever the rea-

---

A Variety of Definitions of the Political Party

Party is a body of men united, for promoting by their joint endeavors the national interest, upon some particular principle in which they are all agreed.

Edmund Burke,
*Thoughts on the Cause
of the Present Discontents* (1770)

. . . Any group, however loosely organized, seeking to elect governmental office-holders under a given label.

Leon D. Epstein,
Political Parties in Western Democracies
(New Brunswick, N.J.: Transaction, 1979), p. 9.

"Party" or "political party" means any political organization which elects a state committee and officers of a state committee, by a state convention composed of delegates elected from each representative district in which the party has registered members and which nominates candidates for electors of President and Vice President, or nominates candidates for offices to be decided at the general election."

Delaware Statutes (15 Del. C. § 101)

"Established political party" for the state shall mean a political party which, at either of the last two general elections, polled for its candidate for any statewide office, more than two percent of the entire vote cast for the office. . . .

Missouri Statutes (V.A.M.S. § 115.013)

At the local level parties have degenerated in most parts of the country to the point where they are now simply legal conveniences by which ambitious people with independent financing gain access to a ballot line.

John B. Anderson,
independent candidate for president in 1980,
in *New York Times*, October 31, 1982.

son, however, neither political scientists nor politicians have achieved any consensus on what sets the political party apart from other political organizations.

Despite the absence of consensus, however, the most common definitions fall into three main categories. Those whose approach is ideological define the parties in terms of commonly held ideas, values, or stands on issues. That approach has not engaged many observers of the American political parties, for ideological homogeneity or purpose has not been a hallmark of the major American parties. Most of the attempts at definition vacillate between two other options. One of these views the political party as a hierarchical organization or structure that draws into its orbit large numbers of voters, candidates, and active party workers. The other approach sees the political parties largely in terms of what they do—their role, function, or activities in the American political systems. Proponents of this approach frequently identify American political parties with election campaigns. We now turn to these two approaches.

THE POLITICAL PARTY AS A SOCIAL STRUCTURE

Large organizations or social structures consist of people in various roles, responsibilities, patterns of activities, and reciprocal relationships. But which people, what activities, what relationships are we talking about when we speak of the two major American parties? The party leaders and officials, the hundreds of anonymous activists who work for candidates and party causes, the people who vote for the party's candidates, the actual dues-paying members, the people who have an emotional involvement in the fortunes of the party, the men and women elected to office on the party's label? All of them? Some of them?

The major American political parties are, in truth, three-headed political giants—tripartite systems of interactions that embrace all these individuals. As political structures, they include a party organization, a party in office, and a party in the electorate (Figure 1.1).

The Party Organization

In the party organization, one finds the formally chosen party leaders, the informally anointed ones, the legions of local captains and leaders, the ward and precinct workers, the members and activists of the party—that is, all those who give their time, money, and skills to the party, whether as leaders or as followers. These are the men and women who make the decisions of the party and who do its work. The organization operates in part through the formal machinery of committees and conventions set by

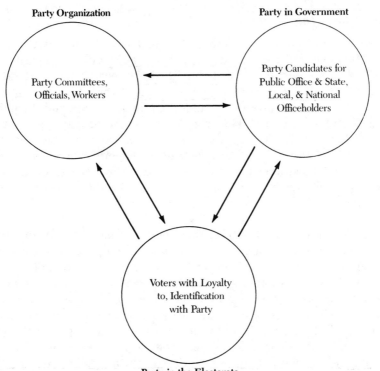

Party Organization

Party in Government

Party Committees,
Officials, Workers

Party Candidates for
Public Office & State,
Local, & National
Officeholders

Voters with Loyalty
to, Identification
with Party

Party in the Electorate

FIGURE 1.1 *The Three-Part Political Party*

the laws of the fifty states and in part through its own informal apparatus.
Here one finds the centers of party authority and bureaucracy, and here
one also observes the face-to-face contacts and interactions that bespeak
organization of any kind.

The Party in Government

The party in government is made up of those who have captured office
through the symbols of the party and of those who seek to do so. The chief
executives and legislative parties of the nation and the states are its major
components. Although in many ways they are not subject to the control
or discipline of the party organization, they do, in the broadest sense, speak
for the party. Their pronouncements are the most audible party statements and carry the greatest weight with the public. A party's president
or leader in the Congress claims more attention than its national
chairperson.

The Party in the Electorate

The party in the electorate is the party's least well defined part. It comprises the men and women who affiliate casually with it, show it some degree of loyalty, and even vote habitually for it, even though they do not participate in the party organization or interact with its leaders and activists. These individuals are not subject to the incentives and disciplines of the party organization. They are, in effect, the regular consumers of the party's candidates and appeals. As such, they make up the majorities necessary for effective political power in the American political system. Their association with the party is a passive one, however—accepting here, rejecting there, always threatening the party with the fickleness of their affections.

In their three-part structure, therefore, the major American parties include mixed, varied, and even contradictory components. Each party, for example, is a political organization with active, even disciplined participants. It is also an aggregate of unorganized partisans who may begrudge the party organization even the merest public gesture of support or loyalty. The party thus embraces the widest range of involvement and commitment. It is a reasonably well-defined, voluntary political organization and, at the same time, an open, public collection of loyalists.

Perhaps the most telling characteristic of the major American parties, therefore, is the relationship that their clientele—the party in the electorate—has to them. The other political organizations, such as interest groups and ad hoc campaign organizations, usually work to attract supporters beyond their members and workers; but this wider clientele remains outside the political organization. This is not so with the political party. The party in the electorate is more than an external group to be wooed and mobilized. State laws usually permit it a voice in the selection of the parties' candidates in the direct primary, and in many states it helps select local party officials such as ward and precinct committeepersons. Consequently, the major American party is an open, inclusive, semipublic political organization. It includes both a tangible political organization and its own political clientele (as well as the party in government, of course). In this combination of exclusive organization and inclusive clientele, of organization and electorate, the political party stands apart from the other political organizations on the American scene and apart from parties elsewhere.

Finally, each major party differs from state to state in the relationships and interactions among its three sectors. The Republicans and the Democrats are so decentralized and so diverse that virtually every state party has its own distinctive mix of the three. Party organizations, for example, differ in form from state to state; in some the party organization dominates the party in government, whereas in others the reverse is the case. Also, party electorates differ in composition and in the bases of their loyalties; in some states the two parties in the electorate divide roughly along social class lines, but in others they do not. Indeed, much of the distinctive quality of a state party is a reflection of the form and composition of each of the party sectors and of their relationships with each other.

THE PARTY AS A CLUSTER OF ACTIVITIES

From a discussion of the political parties as social structures, we move to a definition of them in terms of activities. We move from what they are to what they do. In varying degrees, the competitive political parties of every democracy perform three sets of activities: they select candidates and contest elections, they propagandize on behalf of a party ideology or program, and they attempt to guide the elected officeholders of government. The degree of emphasis that any particular political party puts on each of these individual activities varies within and between countries, but no party completely escapes the necessity of any of them.

Parties as Electors

It often appears that the American parties are little more than regular attempts to capture public office. Electoral activity so dominates the life of the American party that its metabolism follows almost exactly the cycles of the election calendar. Party activity and vitality reach a peak at the elections; between elections, the parties go into a recuperative hibernation. Party activity is goal oriented, and in American politics most of the general goals as well as the goals of the individual sectors depend ultimately on electoral victory. It is, in fact, chiefly in the attempt to achieve their often separate goals through winning public office that the three sectors of the party are brought together in unified action.

Parties as Propagandizers

Second, the American parties carry on a series of loosely related activities that perhaps can best be called education or propagandization. There is, of course, a school of thought that argues that the American parties fail almost completely to function on behalf of ideas or ideologies. The Democrats and Republicans, to be sure, do not espouse the all-inclusive ideologies of a European Marxist or proletarian party. They do, however, represent the interests of and the issue stands congenial to the groups that identify with them and support them. In this sense, they become parties of business or labor, of the advantaged or the disadvantaged. Moreover, events since the 1960s suggest that ideology in a purer sense is coming to the American parties. In presidential politics alone, one merely needs to mention the Goldwater conservatism of 1964, the McGovern liberalism of 1972, and the Reagan conservatism of 1980.

Parties as Governors

Finally, the successful candidates of the American parties organize the decision-making agencies of government. The legislatures of forty-nine states (the exception is nonpartisan Nebraska) and the United States Congress are organized along party lines, and the voting of their members shows, to varying degrees, the effects of party discipline and cohesion. To be sure, on controversial issues that cohesion is irregular, sporadic, and often unpredictable in most legislatures. The congressional Democrats, for example, divide roughly between northern liberals and more conservative southerners. Yet, in the aggregate, an important degree of party discipline does exist. In executive branches, presidents and governors depend on their fellow partisans for executive talent and count on their party loyalty to bind them to the executive programs. Only the American judiciary largely escapes the organizing and directing touch of the parties.

These, then, are the chief overt activities of democratic political parties generally and of American parties in particular. They are the activities that the parties set out consciously to perform. Large sections of this or any other book on the American parties must be devoted to them.

To list these activities of the parties, however, is not to suggest that the American parties monopolize any or all of them. The parties compete with nonparty political organizations over the ability and the right to perform them. The American parties, having organized the legislatures, battle constantly—and often with little success—against interest groups and constituency pressures in order to firm up party lines for votes on major bills. In attempting to nominate candidates for public office, especially at the local level, the party faces often insurmountable competition from interest groups, community elites, and powerful local personalities, each of whom may be sponsoring pet candidates. In stating issues and ideologies, they are often overshadowed by the fervor of the minor (third) parties, the ubiquitous interest groups, the mass media, public figures, and political action groups.

These patterns of party activity also affect the party structure and its three sectors. The emphasis on the electoral activities of American parties, for example, elevates the party in government to a position of unusual power, even dominance. It frequently competes with the party organization for the favor of the party in the electorate. In parties more closely allied with issues and ideologies—such as those of continental Europe—party organizations are often able to dictate to legislative parties.

On the other hand, individuals from all three sectors of the party may unite in specific activities. Party organization activists loyal to officeholders may unite with those persons, with other individuals of the party in government, and with individuals in the party electorate to return them to public office. When the election is won or lost, they will very likely drift apart again. Therefore, one finds within the parties these functional clusters or nuclei, these groups of individuals, drawn together in a single, concerted action.[1] Small and informal task groups cut across the differences in structure and goals that characterize the three party sectors. In American politics, alliances and coalitions are more common within the parties than between them.

THE UNPLANNED CONSEQUENCES OF PARTY ACTIVITY

The goal-seeking behavior of any individual or organization has unintended consequences. Congress, by pursuing its legislating activities, may be said to be either resolving or aggravating great areas of social conflict, depending on the judgment of the observer. Similarly, interest groups, in pursuing their particular goals in the legislative process, are also providing an informal, auxiliary avenue of representation. The same search for the unplanned consequences of party activities is an old tradition in the study of the American parties. It produces rich insights into the contributions of the parties to the American political system. Yet it can be frustrating, its findings imprecise and elusive.

When we say that a political party is picking a candidate or organizing an election campaign, we are talking about overt, intended, observable party activity. When we say that the same party is organizing consensus, integrating new groups into society, or giving voice to political opposition, however, we are describing the activities we *impute* to the parties. These statements are about the *consequences* of party activity rather than about the activity itself. As such, they depend on the meaning, results, or outcomes of action we, as individual observers, see. Some of our observations are more easily verified by empirical evidence than others are. It is surely easier to show that the parties contribute to the political socialization of young Americans than it is to demonstrate that they settle social conflict, because it is easier to observe the process and results of socialization. Regardless of these matters of degree, however, the basic truth remains: it

---

[1]On the party as a series of task-oriented nuclei, see Joseph A. Schlesinger, "Political Party Organization," in James G. March (ed.), *Handbook of Organizations* (Chicago: Rand McNally, 1965), pp. 764–801.

is much easier to prove or establish the activity itself than the results or consequences it brings about.

It is not surprising, then, that scholars of the American political parties have seen and recorded wildly differing sets of these unintended consequences. They have usually referred to them as "functions," but that semantic convention is virtually the extent of their agreement. It is perhaps foolish to compound the confusion, but what follows is a brief list of some of the most readily identifiable—and thus most frequently mentioned—of these functions or unplanned consequences of party activity.

1. The parties participate in the *political socialization* of the American electorate by transmitting political values and information to large numbers of current and future voters. They preach the value of political commitment and activity, and they convey information and cues about a confusing political system. By symbolizing and representing a political point of view, they offer uninformed or underinformed citizens a map of the political world. They help them form political judgments and make political choices, and, in both physical and psychological terms, they make it easier to be politically active.

2. The American parties also contribute to the *accumulation of political power*. They aggregate masses of political individuals and groups and thereby organize blocs that are powerful enough to govern or to oppose those who govern. For the confused and confounded citizen, they simplify, and often oversimplify, the political world into more comprehensible choices. By using his or her attachment to the party as a perceptual screen, the voter has a master clue for assessing issues and candidates. Thus, both within the individual and in the external political world, the political party operates to focus political loyalties on a small number of alternatives and so to accumulate support behind them.

3. Because they devote so much effort to contesting elections, the American parties dominate the *recruitment of political leadership*. One needs only to run down a list of the members of the cabinet or even the federal courts to see how many of them entered public service through a political party or through partisan candidacy for office. Furthermore, the orderly contesting of elections enables the parties to routinize political change, especially change of governmental leadership. More than one commentator has noted the disruptive quality of leadership changes in those countries in which no stable political parties contest in regular elections. Also, because the American parties pervade all governmental levels in the federal system, they may recruit and elevate leadership from one level to another.

4. Finally, the American parties are a *force for unification in the divided American political system*. The fragmentation of government is an in-

contestably crucial fact of American politics. To the fragmentation of the nation and the fifty states, multiplied by the threefold separation of powers in each, the two great national parties bring a unifying, centripetal force. They unify with an obviously limited efficiency; for example, they often fail to bind the president and the Congress together in causes that can transcend the separation of powers. Their similar symbols and traditions, however, are a force for unity in governmental institutions marked by decentralization and division.

There are two chief difficulties with this list of party functions. First, there is not much agreement on them, a result not only of scholars' different perceptions of the parties but also of their disagreement over what the word *function* means. Some use it to denote the obvious activities of the parties (e.g., their contesting of elections), whereas others use it, as we do in this text, to describe the unintended consequences or fortunate by-products of the intended activities of the parties. For yet another group, *function* suggests a contribution the party makes to the operation of the broader political system. Second, there is the problem of defining or formulating the functional categories so that they can be observed and measured. If, as some writers have argued, one function of political parties is to organize social conflict or to articulate important social interests, how do we verify by our own observations whether all parties or some parties do, in fact, perform those functions? For reasons having to do with both of these problems, this book will look largely at party activity itself—at the more easily observable, intended activity rather than its unintended consequences.

THE SPECIAL CHARACTERISTICS OF POLITICAL PARTIES

Perhaps it is time to end these excursions into related topics and narrow the search for political parties. Our goal is not a memorable, one-sentence definition. Rather, we seek an understanding of what characterizes the political parties and sets them apart from other political organizations. We need, in other words, a firm grasp of what the political parties are and what they do.

All political organizations exist to organize and mobilize their supporters either to capture public office or to influence the activities of those already in public office. That much, at least, they all have in common. If the term *political party* is to have any meaning at all, however, there must also be differences between parties and other political organizations.

[2]Theodore Lowi has brought together a number of descriptions of party functions in his article "Toward Functionalism in Political Science: The Case of Innovation in Party Systems," *American Political Science Review* 57 (1963): 570–83.

Far too much has been made of the differences between the major American parties and other political organizations, especially the large national interest (or pressure) groups. The differences are there, however, even if they are really only differences among species of the same genus.

Above all, the political party is distinguished from other political organizations by its concentration on the contesting of elections. Although the major American parties do not monopolize the contesting of elections, their preeminence in this activity cannot be questioned. Other political organizations do attempt to influence American electoral politics. In many localities, interest groups encourage or discourage candidates, work for them within parties, contribute to campaign funds, and get their members to the polls to support them. Other nonparty organizations may raise funds, organize endorsements, and recruit workers for some candidate's campaign for public office. The parties, however, are occupied with the contesting of elections in a way and to a degree that the other political organizations are not. Indeed, their names and symbols are the ones the states recognize for inclusion on most ballots.

Commitment not only to electoral activity but also to its organizational consequences characterizes the political party. Since the party chooses to work toward its goals largely in elections, it must recruit an enormous supportive clientele. Organizations that attempt to influence legislative committees or rule making in administrative agencies may succeed with a few strategists and the support of only a small, well-mobilized clientele. The political parties, in order to win elections, must depend less on the intricate skills and maneuverings of organizational strategists and more on the mobilization of large numbers of citizens. Party appeals must be broad and inclusive; the party cannot afford either exclusivity or a narrow range of concerns. It is at the opposite pole from the "single-issue" group or organization. To put it simply, the major political party has committed itself through its concentration on electoral politics to the mobilization of large numbers of citizens in large numbers of elections, and from that commitment flow many of its other characteristics.

Furthermore, the major American political parties and similar parties elsewhere are characterized by a full commitment to political activity. They operate solely as political organizations, solely as instruments of political action. Interest groups and most other political organizations, however, do not. They move freely and frequently from political to nonpolitical activities and back again. The AFL–CIO, for example, seeks many of its goals and interests in nonpolitical ways, especially through collective bargaining. It may, however, turn to political action—to support sympathetic candidates or to lobby before Congress—when political avenues appear to be the best or the only means to achieve its goals. Every organized group in the United States is, as one observer has suggested, a potential political organization.[3] Still, the interest group almost always maintains some sphere of nonpolitical action.

Political parties are also marked by an uncommon stability and persistence. The personal clique, the faction, the ad hoc campaign organization, and even many interest groups seem by contrast almost political will-o'-the-wisps, which disappear as suddenly as they appear. The size and the abstractness of the political parties, their relative independence of personalities, and their continuing symbolic strength for thousands of voters assure them of a far greater longevity. Both major American parties can trace their histories over a century, and the major parties of the other Western democracies have impressive, if shorter, life spans. It is precisely this enduring, ongoing quality that enhances their value as reference symbols. The parties are there as points of reference, year after year and election after election, giving continuity and form to the choices Americans face and the issues they debate.

Finally, the political parties are distinguished from other political organizations by the extent to which they operate as cues or symbols—or even more vaguely as emotion-laden objects of loyalty. For millions of Americans, the party label is the chief cue for their decisions about candidates or issues. It is the point of reference that allows them to organize and simplify the buzzing confusion and strident rhetoric of American politics. As a potent reference symbol, the party label organizes the extensive confusion of American politics *within* individual American citizens. It organizes their perceptions and structures their choices; it relates their political values and goals to the real options of American politics.

To summarize, the major American political parties exist, as do other political organizations, to organize large numbers of individuals behind attempts to influence the selection of public officials and the decisions these officials subsequently make in office. The parties are set apart by:

1. The extent to which they pursue their organizing through the contesting of elections.
2. The extensiveness and inclusiveness of their organization and clienteles.
3. Their sole concentration on political avenues for achieving their goals.
4. Their demonstrated stability and long life.
5. Their strength as cues and reference symbols in the decision making of individual citizens.

No one of these characteristics alone sets the political party apart from other political organizations, but when they are taken together and the

---

[3]David B. Truman, *The Governmental Process* (New York: Knopf, 1951).

matter of degree is considered, they do set the major political party apart from other types of political organizations.

To reemphasize a point previously made, however, the differences between parties and other political organizations are often slender. Interest groups certainly contest elections to some degree, and the larger ones have achieved impressive stability and duration and considerable symbolic status. They, too, can recruit candidates and give political clues and cues to their members and fellow travelers. Many national associations, such as those of environmentalists, differ from the parties chiefly in size and influence. They promote interests and issue positions, they try to influence and organize officeholders, and they, too, participate in elections by endorsing candidates and (through their political action committees) by contributing to their campaigns. Like the parties, they achieve symbolic status for their members and like-minded voters. They do not, however, and in most localities cannot, offer their names and symbols for candidates to use on the ballot. It is only that difference and the whole question of size and degree that separate their activities and political roles from those of the parties.

So similar are the parties to some other political organizations that they resemble them more closely than they do the minor or third parties. In other words, there are different types of political parties. The minor political parties, called minor because they are not electorally competitive, are only nominally electoral organizations. Not even the congenital optimism of candidates can lead Socialists or Prohibitionists to expect victories on the ballot. Lacking local organization, as most of them do, they resemble the major parties less than do the complex, nationwide interest groups. Also, their membership base, often related to a single issue, may be just as narrow, just as exclusively recruited, as that of most interest groups. In structure and activities, groups such as the United States Chamber of Commerce and the AFL–CIO resemble the Democrats and Republicans far more than do the Libertarians and the Socialist Workers.

THE RISE OF AMERICAN PARTIES

To see the special role and character of political parties, there is no better place to look than at their origins and their rise to importance. In the United States, their history is one of an almost 200-year alliance with an emerging popular democracy. The American parties grew up in response to the gradual expansion of the adult suffrage and to all the changes it brought to American politics.[4]

[4]There are, of course, many histories of the American political parties in general and of particular parties. Most, however, devote virtually all their pages to the candidates and

In the first years of the Republic, the vote was limited in every state to those free men who could meet the property-holding or tax-paying requirements. Furthermore, the framers of the new Constitution of 1787 had intentionally limited the power of individual voters at elections. The president was to be chosen, not by a direct vote of the electorate, but indirectly by a group of notables making up the electoral college. Also, although election to the House of Representatives was entrusted to a direct popular vote, that of the Senate was not. Its members were to be chosen by the respective state legislatures. (Those respective state legislatures, taking the same cue, also decided to select the members of the electoral college themselves.) It was, in short, a cautious and limited beginning to democratic self-government.

In their first years, the American parties grew out of and matched this politics of a limited suffrage and indirect elections. They began, in fact, largely as caucuses of like-minded members of the Congress. They involved only the men and the issues of politics in the nation's capital. These congressional caucuses nominated presidential candidates and mobilized groups of political figures supportive of or opposed to the administration of the time. Party organization back in the states and localities did not develop until about 1800, with "committees of correspondence." These were the first outreaches of the legislative caucuses to the voters "back home," and through them officeholders organized and communicated with the electorate. Early in the nineteenth century, the efforts at local organization resulted in the development of some free-standing local party organizations in a few counties and cities. The development of parties back in the states, however, went slowly and sporadically, at least until the 1820s.

So matters stayed for the first thirty or forty years of the Republic. In fact, one of the infant parties, the Federalists, virtually disappeared shortly after the defeat of its last president, John Adams, in 1800. The Jeffersonian Republicans, the new party of agrarian interests and the frontier, quickly established its superiority and enjoyed a twenty-year period of one-party monopoly. So thorough was the domination by the time of James Monroe's presidency that the absence of party and political conflict was dubbed the "Era of Good Feelings." Despite the decline of one party and the rise of another, however, the nature of the parties did not change. It was a time during which government and politics were the business of an elite of well-known, well-established men, and the parties reflected the politics of the

platforms of the parties; few discuss the parties *qua* parties. For three that do, see William N. Chambers, *Political Parties in a New Nation* (New York: Oxford University Press, 1963); Everett C. Ladd, Jr., *American Political Parties* (New York: Norton, 1970); and William N. Chambers and Walter D. Burnham (eds.), *The American Party Systems* (New York: Oxford University Press, 1967).

TABLE 1.1　*Popular Vote and Voter Turnout for Presidential Elections: 1824–40*

	1824	1828	1832	1836	1840
Total popular vote	356,038	1,155,350	1,217,691	1,505,000	2,412,000
Turnout (percentage of adult white males)	26.9	57.6	55.4	57.8	80.2

Sources　Data on the popular vote from *Historical Statistics of the United States*. The calculation of turnout percentages is reported in William N. Chambers, "Election of 1840," in Arthur M. Schlesinger, Jr., and Fred L. Israel, *History of American Presidential Elections*, Vol. 1 (New York: Chelsea House, 1971), p. 687.

time. In both of his successful races for the presidency (1816 and 1820), Monroe was the nominee only of the Jeffersonian caucus in the Congress.

The early politics of the country began, however, to undergo sharp changes in the 1820s. The states began to expand the electorate by removing the property requirements for suffrage; by the 1830s, the removal had been accomplished. The result was a tremendous increase in the electorate between 1820 and 1840. (See Table 1.1.) Simultaneously, the electoral college ceased to function as it had at first, and presidential politics were transformed. As Everett C. Ladd has written:

> The framers of the Constitution envisioned the president selected by an electoral college of wise and dispassionate men chosen by the several state legislatures; the electors, equal in number to the membership of Congress, would consider the needs of the Republic and exercise their independent judgment. The presidency was thus to be doubly insulated from the people. But one layer of intended insulation was ripped away after the election of just one president—Washington—with the pledging of electors: the majorities in the state legislatures began choosing electors pledged to a particular candidate for the presidency, thus transforming the electoral college from a body for independent judgment to a vehicle for carrying out the wishes of popularly elected state legislative majorities. Then in the 1820s another large step in democratizing the presidency was taken, as all the states except South Carolina shifted from legislative designation to popular election of the slates of electors.[5]

With these changes in the electorate and in the method of electing a president, there were bound to be changes in the politics of that election.

The impact was immediate. The caucus nominations fell under increasing criticism as the work of a narrow-based and self-perpetuating

[5]Ladd, *American Political Parties*, pp. 59–60 (emphasis removed).

elite. Quite apart from criticism, however, the caucus system began to decline from its own infirmities. The attempt of the Jeffersonians to nominate a presidential candidate in 1824 was a shambles. The chosen candidate of the caucus, William Crawford, ran fourth in the race, and since no candidate won a majority in the electoral college, it was left to the House of Representatives to choose among John Quincy Adams, Henry Clay, and Andrew Jackson. The House chose Adams over Jackson, the front-runner in the election. Jackson, in turn, defeated Adams in 1828 as the nation teetered on the edge of a new party politics.

The "new" party politics—and the modern political party—emerged in the 1830s. First, the nonparty politics of the Era of Good Feelings gave way to the two-party system that has prevailed ever since. Andrew Jackson took the frontier and agrarian wing of the Jeffersonians into what we now think of as the Democratic party. The National Republicans, whose candidate in 1832 was Henry Clay, merged with the Whigs, and bipartyism in the United States was born. Second, and just as important, the parties as political institutions began to change. The Jacksonian Democrats held the first national nominating convention in 1832—at which, appropriately, Jackson himself was nominated for a second term. (The Whig and Anti-Masonic parties had both held more limited conventions a year before.) The campaign for the presidency also became more "popular" as new campaign organizations and tactics brought the contest to more and more people. As a consequence, Jackson came to the White House for a second term with a popular mandate as the leader of a national political party. Larger numbers of citizens were voting (see Table 1.1) than had ever voted before.

At the same time, party organization in the states had a new burst of growth, and conventions increasingly replaced caucuses as the means of nominating candidates for state and local office. By the middle of the century, therefore, party organization was developing throughout the nation, and the party convention became an increasingly common way of picking party candidates. Also, by 1840, the Whigs and the Democrats established themselves as the first truly national party system, one in which both parties were established and competitive in all the states.

Modern political parties—pretty much as we know them today—had thus arrived by the middle of the nineteenth century. They were, in fact, the first modern parties in western history, and their arrival reflected, above all, the early expansion of the electorate in the United States. The comparable development of parties in Great Britain did not occur until the 1870s, after further extension of the adult male electorate in the Reform Acts of 1832 and 1867.

Just as the parties were reaching their maturity, they and American politics received another massive infusion of voters from a new source: immigration from Europe. Hundreds of thousands of Europeans—the great majority from Ireland and Germany—came to the country before the Civil War. So many immigrated, in fact, that their very coming and their entry into American politics became a political issue. The newcomers found a ready home in the Democratic party; and a nativist third party, the American party (the so-called Know-Nothing party), sprang up in the 1850s. The tide of immigration was only temporarily halted by the Civil War. New nationalities came from 1870 on, in a virtually uninterrupted flow until Congress closed the door to mass immigration in the 1920s.

The American cities offered industrial jobs to the newcomers from abroad, and they settled heavily in them. It was there in the cities that a new party organization, the city "machine," developed in response to the immigrants' problems and vulnerabilities. The machines were more than impressively efficient party organizations. They were social service mechanisms that helped the new arrivals cope with a new country and with all the threats and adventures of urban, industrial society. They softened the hard edge of poverty, they smoothed the way with government and the law, and they taught the immigrants the ways and customs of their new life. Moreover, they were in many instances indistinguishable from the government of the city; theirs was the classic instance of "party government" in the American experience. They also were the vehicle by which the new urban working class won control of the cities away from the largely Anglo-Saxon, Protestant elites that had prevailed for so long. Thus, the parties again became the instrument of the aspirations of new citizens, just as they had been in the 1830s. In doing so, they achieved the high point of party power and influence in American history.

The American parties—simply as political organizations—thus reached their zenith, something of a "Golden Age" indeed, by the beginning of the twentieth century. Party organization now existed in all the states and localities; it positively flourished in the industrial cities. Parties achieved an all-time high in discipline in the Congress and in most state legislatures. They controlled campaigns for public office—they held rallies, did door-to-door canvassing, and got the voters to the polls. They controlled access to a great deal of public employment. They were an important source of information and guidance for a largely uneducated and often illiterate electorate. Indeed, they rode the crest of an extraordinarily vital American politics; the latter half of the nineteenth century, we often forget, featured the highest voter turnouts in the history of American presidential elections. The parties suited the needs and limitations of the new voters and the problems of mobilizing majorities in the new and raw industrial society. If ever a time and a political organization were well matched, this was it.

To be sure, the democratic impetus was not spent by the turn of the century. The electorate continued to expand—with the enfranchisement of women, with the delayed securing of the vote for blacks, and with the lowering of the voting age to eighteen. The move to direct, popular elections and away from the indirection the Founding Fathers favored also continued its inexorable course. The Seventeenth Amendment decreed the direct election of senators, and by the 1970s the movement to substitute direct election of the president for the electoral college reached its greatest support and credibility. Just as important for the parties, however, were the changes wrought in them in the name of the continuing commitment to egalitarianism and popular democracy. Sleek, powerful, and even arrogant at the end of the nineteenth century, the parties fell under attack by the Progressive reformers. The reformers enacted the direct primary to give the citizenry a voice in party nominations, and large numbers of state legislatures wrote laws to define and limit party organization. The business of nominating a president was made more popular by the establishment of presidential primaries in the states, and activists within the parties reformed their national conventions. All in all, by the 1980s, Americans had a pair of parties and a party politics born and shaped in the triumph of the democratic ethos and its expectations.[6]

The reforms of the twentieth century were to some extent intended to diminish the power and position the parties had achieved by the end of the 1800s. To that extent, they succeeded. For these and a number of other reasons, the heyday of the American parties passed. The theme of the decline of the parties runs through all commentaries on the American parties these days, and it will certainly run through this one. Even so, the parties remain to a considerable extent what they were eighty or a hundred years ago: the preeminent political organizations of mass, popular democracy. They developed and grew with the expansion of the suffrage and the popularizing of electoral politics. They were and remain the invention by which large numbers of voters come together to control the selection of their representatives. They rose to prominence at a time when a new electorate of limited knowledge and limited political sophistication needed the guidance of their symbols. Thus it was that the modern American political party was born and reached its time of glory in the nineteenth century. When one talks today of the decline of the parties, it is the standard of that Golden Age against which the decline is measured.

THE PARTY IN ITS ENVIRONMENT

It is the nature of a book on political parties to treat them more or less in isolation, to lift them from their context in the political system for special scrutiny. Yet, useful as isolation is, it may give the impression that the

---

[6]On the reform of the parties, see Austin Ranney, *Curing the Mischiefs of Faction* (Berkeley: University of California Press, 1975).

political parties are autonomous structures, moving without constraint within the political system. In a search for the parties alone, there is a danger of overlooking the many forces in their environment that shape both their form and their activities.

It is possible, on the other hand, to let analysis and logic run riot and to imagine a party environment that includes virtually every other structure and process in the political system and a great deal outside it. Despite the superficial truth that every social structure or process is related to every other one, however, some influences on the party clearly are more powerful and insistent than others. It will suffice to limit this discussion to them.

Electorates and Elections

As the preceding section indicates, the expansion of the American electorate shaped the very origin and development of the parties as political organizations. Furthermore, each new group of voters that enters the electorate challenges the parties to readjust their appeals. The parties must compete for the votes and support of new voters, and the necessity of doing so forces them to reconsider their strategies for building the coalitions that can win elections.

Similarly, the fortunes of the parties are also bound up with the nature of American elections. The move from indirect to direct elections transformed both the contesting of elections and the parties that contested them. Should we finally come to direct election of the American president, that change, too, would have its impact on the parties.

The election machinery in a state may indeed be thought of as an extensive regulation of the parties' chief political activity. At least, it is often difficult to determine where the regulation of the party ends and electoral reform begins. Consider, for example, the direct primary. It is both a significant addition to the machinery of American electoral processes and a sharp regulation of the way a party selects the candidates who bear its label in an election. Even the relatively minor differences in primary law from one state to another—such as differences in the form of the ballot or the time of the year in which the primary occurs—are not without their impact on the parties. In short, the collective electoral institutions of the nation and of the fifty states set a matrix of rules and boundaries within which the parties compete for public office.

The Political Institutions

Very little in the American political system escapes the influence of American federalism and the separation of powers. No single factor seems to affect the American legislative parties, for example, so much as the separation of the legislature from the executive. Among the party systems of the world, the legislative parties in parliamentary systems have the greatest discipline in voting and the strongest ties to the party organization. The institutions of the parliamentary form lead to the legislative party's cohesive support of (or opposition to) a cabinet drawn from one legislative party or the other. The political parties in American legislatures are under much less pressure to support or oppose a completely separate chief executive. Indeed, support for and opposition to executive programs often cut sharply across party lines.

The decentralization of American federalism has also left its imprint on the American parties. It has instilled in them local political loyalties and generations of local, often provincial, political traditions. It has spawned an awesome range and number of public offices to fill, creating an electoral politics that in size and diversity dwarfs that of all other political systems. By permitting local rewards, local traditions, even local patronage systems, it has sustained a whole set of semiautonomous local parties within the two parties. The establishment of these local centers of power has worked mightily against the development of strong permanent national party organs)

Statutory Regulation

No other parties among the democracies of the world are so bound up in legal regulations as are the American parties. The forms of their organization are prescribed by the states in endless, often finicky, detail. The statutes on party organization set up grandiose layers of party committees and often chart the details of who will compose them, when they will meet, and what their agenda will be. State law also defines the parties themselves, often by defining the right to place candidates on the ballot. A number of states also undertake to regulate the activities of parties; many, for example, regulate their finances, and most place at least some limits on their campaign practices. So severe can these regulations be, in fact, that in some states the parties have tried various strategies to evade the worst of the burdens.

The Political Culture

It is one thing to specify such tangibles in the parties' environment as regulatory statutes, electoral mechanisms, and even political institutions. It is quite another, however, to pin down so elusive a part of the party environment as the political culture. A nation's political culture is the all-enveloping network of the political norms, values, and expectations of its people. It is, in other words, the people's conglomerate view of what the political system is, what it should be, and what their place is in it.

The feeling that party politics is a compromising, somewhat dirty business has been a major and persistent component of the American political culture. Since the advent of public opinion sampling, the indicators of that hostility toward partisan politics have multiplied. A number of polls have found, for example, that American parents prefer that their sons and daughters not choose a full-time political career. In their estimation, politics as a vocation compares unfavorably with even the semiskilled trades.[7] In the spring of 1975, the Gallup Poll asked a national sample of college students to rate the "honesty and ethical standards" of people in a number of vocations. Although only 2 percent rated college teachers and 5 percent rated medical doctors "low" or "very low," 53 percent gave those ratings to political officeholders. Only "advertising practitioners" scored below the officeholders, and then by only one percentage point.[8] (For another measure of the party's position in the American political culture, see the box.)

A more systematic review of American attitudes toward the party system points similarly to a low level of popular support for the parties. Furthermore, this decline began before Watergate and thus reflects more basic, perhaps more intractable, causes. In 1973, for example, a national sample of adults was asked to pick among four possibilities in identifying which "part of the government" they most often trusted "to do what's right." The Congress and the Supreme Court were each chosen by more than 30 percent of the sample, and almost 24 percent chose the president. Only 1.3 percent chose the political parties. All in all, as Jack Dennis concludes, support for the American parties has dipped to "dangerously low levels."[9]

Suspicion of things partisan is only one element, however, in a multifaceted political culture that shapes the American parties. The views of Americans are relevant on such broad points as representative democracy itself. A Burkean view of representation, which holds that the representative ought to decide public questions on the basis of his or her own information and wisdom, certainly retards the development of party discipline in American legislatures. More detailed public attitudes govern even such matters as the incentives for party activity and the kinds of campaign tactics a party or candidate chooses. Indeed, the whole issue of what we consider fair or ethical campaigning is simply a reflection of the norms and expectations of large numbers of Americans.

[7]See William C. Mitchell, "The Ambivalent Social Status of the American Politician," *Western Political Quarterly* 12 (1959): 683–99.

[8]*Minneapolis Tribune*, May 19, 1975.

[9]Jack Dennis, "Trends in Public Support for the American Party System," *British Journal of Political Science* 5 (1976): 187–230.

"The Politician Puzzle"

One measures the American political culture in all kinds of ways. Note the following bit of evidence about the status of the American politician from an article on logical puzzles and a master puzzler in the magazine of the Smithsonian Institution, the complex of galleries and museums in Washington, D.C. It would be hard to imagine such a riddle about doctors or bankers.

> A certain convention numbered 100 politicians. Each politician was either crooked or honest. We are given the following two facts:
>
> —At least one of the politicians was honest.
> —Given any two of the politicians, at least one of the two was crooked.
>
> Can it be determined from these two facts how many of the politicians were honest and how many of them were crooked? . . . A fairly common answer is '50 honest and 50 crooked.' Another rather frequent one is '51 honest and 49 crooked.' Both answers are wrong. Now let us see how to find the correct solution.
>
> We are given the information that at least one person is honest. Let us pick out any one honest person, whose name, say, is Frank. Now pick any of the remaining 99; call him John. By the second given condition, at least one of the two men—Frank, John—is crooked. Since Frank is not crooked, it must be John. Since John arbitrarily represents any of the remaining 99 men, then each of those 99 men must be crooked. So the answer is that one is honest and 99 are crooked.
>
> <div align="right">Ira Mothner, "The Puzzling
and Paradoxical Worlds of Raymond Smullyan,"
<i>Smithsonian</i> 13 (June 1982).</div>

The Nonpolitical Environment

Much of the parties' nonpolitical environment works on them through the elements of the political environment. Changes in levels of education, for example, affect the political culture, the skills of the electorate, and the levels of political information. Great jolts in the economy alter the structure of political issues and the goals of the electorate. Educational levels and socioeconomic status also seem related to elements of the political culture. The aforementioned study in Wisconsin suggests that less-educated Americans accept party loyalty and discipline more easily than the better educated do. Even general social values are quickly translated into political values. Acceptance of a Catholic candidate for the American presidency had to await changes in social attitudes about religion in general and about Catholicism in particular.

Whether the impact of the nonpolitical environment is direct or indirect, however, may be beside the point. The impact is strong and often disruptive. The advent of a recession, for example, may have important repercussions on the parties. It may make raising money more difficult; it will certainly make patronage positions more attractive and perhaps even shift the incentives for recruiting the workers on whom the party organizations rely. It will also certainly define a very important issue for the electorate. If the crisis is especially severe, as was the Great Depression of the 1930s, it may even fracture and reorganize the pattern of enduring party loyalties.

What began in this chapter as a search for the distinctiveness of the parties has thus concluded by looking at how they became what they are. To be sure, it is important to have a firm grasp of what we mean when we refer to a political party—especially to understand its peculiar three-part nature. The search for the parties, however, is, paradoxically, a search for more than the parties. It is incomplete without a grasp of the context, the environment, in which they are set and by which they are shaped.

2

THE AMERICAN
TWO–PARTY SYSTEM

The powerful personalities and the eccentric issues that often mark the American minor parties have an uncanny ability to divert our attention from the routines of American electoral politics. Amid the sometimes portentous gravity of our politics, it may lighten the spirit to reflect on a political party devoted to the moral superiority of vegetable foods. And in a politics traditionally divorced from systematic public philosophy, many Americans have understandably been attracted by the ideology and conscience of such parties as the Progressives and the Socialists. It excites us, too, that each new minor party comes as a potential David to challenge the two Goliaths of American politics.

What had been little more than colorful or interesting since the 1920s, however, became a matter of considerable seriousness in 1968. In the presidential election of that year, George C. Wallace captured almost 10 million votes and came close to throwing the entire election into the unpredictable hands of the House of Representatives. Had he not been struck down by an assassin's bullet midway in the 1972 preconvention campaign, he might well have exceeded his 1968 accomplishment. How is it, then, that we refer so glibly to the American two-party system? Why do we acknowledge only two parties and cavalierly disregard the whole array of smaller ones? Like our deceptively simple references to political parties, our references to party systems flow easily—and vaguely; but the mathematics of "two" and the components of a "system" are by no means self-evident.

The conventional terminology we use to describe party systems is based on two related major premises: that parties are primarily electoral organizations and that their electoral activities are carried out in direct competition with other electoral parties. The designation of a one-party, two-party, five-party, or any other multiparty system simply indicates the number of political parties able to compete for office with some prospect of success. This is the distinction between the competitive major parties and the noncompetitive minor parties. What we call the party system, therefore, is composed only of the electorally competitive parties.

For all its elegant simplicity (and to some extent because of it), this conventional classification of party systems has a number of significant shortcomings:

— It focuses solely on one dimension of the competition among political organizations. Consequently, it overlooks the possibility that minor parties compete ideologically or programmatically with major parties, even though they do not compete electorally.

— By focusing only on the political parties, it ignores the full range of competition among all kinds of political organizations. Even in the business of nominating candidates for public office, a party may face competition from a local interest group or political elite.

— By classifying parties exclusively by electoral competition, it ignores any differences in organization the parties may have and centers its measurement on the size of the party's electorate.

— Finally, it tends to ignore the implications of the word *system*. It overlooks the relationships and interactions one expects in any system and settles merely for the presence of competitive parties and their presumed competings in elections.

This concept of the party system is so ingrained in both everyday use and in the scholarly literature, however, that one has little choice but to work within its terms.[1]

THE NATIONAL PARTY SYSTEM

Despite local deviations to one-partyism, the American party system is and has been a two-party system for the past 150 years. Beyond all subtle variations in competition, there is the inescapable, crucial fact that almost all partisan political conflict in the United States has been channeled through two major political parties. They rise and fall, they establish their seats of strength, they suffer their local weaknesses, but they endure. Perhaps even more remarkable is the fact that one does not easily find another democracy in which two parties have so long and so thoroughly dominated pol-

---

[1]For a sophisticated critique of the traditional classification and analysis of party systems, see Giovanni Sartori, *Party and Party Systems* (Cambridge, England: Cambridge University Press, 1976).

itics. Even in Great Britain, three parties—the Conservatives, Liberals, and Labourites—have sustained some degree of competition for most of this century, and a fourth, the Social Democrats, entered competition in the 1980s.

One cannot argue, though, that the American two-party system is as old as the Republic. The period before 1836 was one of instability in the party system. The Federalists established a short period of superiority during the presidency of George Washington but faded quickly with the rise and success of the Jeffersonian Republicans (see box). The Jeffersonians rode their success to a brief period of dominance that culminated in the nonparty (or one-party) politics of Monroe's two terms. As the caucus system crumbled in the 1820s, however, new national parties emerged, and by 1836 a stable two-partyism was established. For the almost 150 years since then, one party—the Democratic party—has sustained a place in the party system. In opposition, the Whigs survived until the 1850s and were replaced almost immediately by the infant Republican party. Both the Democratic and Republican parties were briefly divided by the events of the Civil War, but old party lines and labels survived the war and, indeed, survive to this day.

Thus, the two-party drama is long but its cast of characters short. In truth, it has not been quite so cut and dried. Minor parties have briefly pushed themselves into competitiveness but, significantly, never for two presidential elections in a row. The Democratic and Republican parties have also changed, of course, in their issues and appeals and in the coalitions that are their "parties in the electorate." All of those hedges, however, do not hide the fact that for more than 125 years, the Democratic and Republican parties have together been the American two-party system.

The longevity of the two major parties, exceptional in itself, is almost overshadowed by the closeness of their competition. Of the twenty-four presidential elections from 1888 through 1980, the Republicans won thirteen and the Democrats eleven.[2] Of those twenty-four elections, only six were decided by a spread of more than 20 percent of the popular vote of the two major parties; that is, in eighteen of the elections, a shift of 10 percent of the vote or less would have given the other party's candidate the lead. Also, in only four of those twenty-four presidential elections did the winners receive more than 60 percent of the total popular vote: Warren G. Harding in 1920, Franklin Roosevelt in 1936, Lyndon Johnson in 1964, and Richard Nixon in 1972. Ten of the twenty-four elections were decided by a spread of less than 7 percent of the popular vote, and presidential elections have generally been so close that Dwight D. Eisenhow-

---

[2]The Democrats led the popular vote in twelve elections, however, losing the election of 1888 in the electoral college despite Grover Cleveland's lead in the popular vote.

The American Major Parties

The list of the American major parties is short and select. In almost 200 years of history, only five political parties have achieved a competitive position in American national politics. Three lost it; the Democrats and Republicans maintain it to this day.

1788	1816	1832	1856	1900

Federalists

Jeffersonians

Democrats →

Whigs

Republicans →

➤ 1. *The Federalists*. The party of the new Constitution and strong national government, it was the first American political party. Its support was rooted in the Northeast and the Atlantic seaboard, where it attracted the support of merchants, landowners, and established families of wealth and status. Limited by its narrow base of support, it quickly fell before the success of the Jeffersonians and the Virginia presidents.

➤ 2. *The Jeffersonians*. Opposed to the nationalism of the Federalists, it was a party of the small farmers, workers, and less privileged citi-

---

er's 57.4 percent of the popular vote in 1956 was widely called a landslide. The shade over 61 percent with which Lyndon Johnson won in 1964 also set a new record for a president's percentage of the popular vote.[3] The 1960s also saw two of the closest presidential elections in American history. In 1960, John F. Kennedy polled only 0.2 percent of the popular vote more

[3]The reader may be confused here about political record keeping. Note that this 61.1 percent vote for Lyndon Johnson was his percentage of the total popular vote. Other relevant records in presidential elections are the greatest electoral college vote—Franklin Roosevelt in 1936, with 523 votes—and the greatest percentage of two-party vote—Calvin Coolidge in 1924, with 65.2 percent.

zens who preferred the authority of the states. Like its founder, it shared many of the ideals of the French Revolution, especially the extension of the suffrage and the notion of direct popular self-government. (At various times it was known by such names as the Republican party and the Democratic-Republican party, both of which confuse it unnecessarily with contemporary parties.)

3. *The Democrats*. Growing out of the Jacksonian wing of the Jeffersonian party, it was initially Jackson's party and the first really broad-based, popular party in the United States. On behalf of a coalition of less privileged voters, it opposed such commercial goals as national banking and high tariffs; it also welcomed the new immigrants and opposed nativist opposition to them (On the post–Civil War period, see Chapter 6.)

4. *The Whigs*. This party, too, had roots in the old Jeffersonian party—in the Clay-Adams faction and in enmity to the Jacksonians. Opposed in its origins to the strong presidency of Jackson, its greatest leaders, Clay and Webster, were embodiments of legislative supremacy. For its short life, the Whig party was an unstable coalition of many interests, among them nativism, property, and the new business and commerce.

5. *The Republicans*. Born in 1854 as the great conflict approached, it was the party of northern opposition to slavery and its spread to the new territories. Therefore, it was also the party of the Union, the North, Lincoln, the freeing of the slaves, victory in the Civil War, and the imposition of Reconstruction. From the Whigs, it also inherited a concern for business, mercantile, and propertied interests. (On the post–Civil War period, see Chapter 6.)

---

than Richard Nixon; Mr. Nixon, in turn, led the popular vote by only 0.7 percent in 1968.[4]

As close as the results of the presidential elections have been, the elections to Congress have been even closer. If we move to percentages of the two-party vote for ease of comparison, we quickly note the remarkable

[4]A persuasive case can be made, in fact, that Nixon actually led Kennedy in the popular vote; the different conclusion depends on how one counts the votes cast for the unpledged electors in Alabama. For a statement of the problem, see Lawrence D. Longley and Alan G. Braun, *The Politics of Electoral College Reform*, 2nd ed. (New Haven: Yale University Press, 1975), pp. 5–6.

balance between the aggregate votes cast for Democratic and Republican candidates for the House of Representatives from all over the United States during the past 50 years (Table 2.1). From 1932 through 1982, in none of the biennial elections to the House of Representatives was there a differ-

TABLE 2.1   *Percentage of Two-Party Vote Won by Republican Candidates for the Presidency and House of Representatives: 1932–82*

	Presidential Election		House Election	
Year	Percentage Republican	Percentage Spread between Republican and Democratic Candidates	Percentage Republican	Percentage Spread between Republican and Democratic Candidates
1932	40.9	−18.2	43.1	−13.8
1934			43.8	−12.4
1936	37.5	−25.0	41.5	−17.0
1938			49.2	−1.6
1940	45.0	−10.0	47.0	−6.0
1942			52.3	4.6
1944	46.2	−7.6	48.3	−3.4
1946			54.7	9.4
1948	47.7	−4.6	46.8	−6.4
1950			49.9	−0.2
1952	55.4	10.8	50.1	0.2
1954			47.5	−5.0
1956	57.8	15.6	49.0	−2.0
1958			43.9	−12.2
1960	49.9	−0.2	45.0	−10.0
1962			47.4	−5.2
1964	38.7	−22.6	42.5	−15.0
1966			48.7	−2.6
1968	50.4	0.8	49.1	−1.8
1970			45.6	−8.8
1972	61.8	23.6	47.3	−5.4
1974			43.0	−14.0
1976	48.9	−2.2	42.8	−14.4
1978			45.6	−8.8
1980	55.2	10.6	48.7	−2.6
1982			44.2	−11.6

Sources   Data from 1932 through 1960 from Donald E. Stokes and Gudmund R. Iverson, "On the Existence of Forces Restoring Party Competition," *Public Opinion Quarterly* 26 (Summer 1962): 162. Data for 1962 through 1982 from *Statistical Abstract* (1982).

ence greater than seventeen percentage points in the division of the two-party vote. The median percentage spread between the candidates of the two parties for the House from 1932 through 1982 was 6.2; it was 10.6 for the presidential candidates in the same period. Perhaps even more telling, in every year except 1948, 1960, 1968, and 1976, the margin between congressional candidates was smaller than that between the presidential aspirants.

The fineness and persistence of party competition in national politics is apparent, therefore, in even the quickest survey of recent electoral history. Even more impressive, perhaps, is the resilience of the major parties. Although from time to time the parties have lapsed from closely matched competitiveness, in the long run they have shown a remarkable facility for restoring balance. The Democrats recovered quickly from their failures of the 1920s, and the Republicans confounded the pessimists by springing back from the Roosevelt victories of the 1930s. Also, despite the catastrophes of Watergate and the Nixon administration, the Republicans came back again in 1980.

Is this aggregate record of winning and losing in national elections what we mean by a two-party system? Well, yes and no. It does express the vote support for national candidates running on national issues under national party labels. Indeed, the struggle for the presidency every four years is undoubtedly the one occasion on which we actually do have national parties and a national party system. On the other hand, such measures are only aggregates, and they obscure the possibility of one-partyism in various parts of the country. That is, statements about national competitiveness gloss over the issue of how unevenly the competitiveness is spread over the states and localities of the nation.

THE FIFTY AMERICAN PARTY SYSTEMS

All but obscured in the incredible closeness of both presidential elections and the aggregate vote for the House of Representatives is the one-partyism not apparent when one examines only national totals. It was not until 1964, for example, that Georgia cast its electoral votes for a Republican and Vermont voted for a Democrat for the first time since the Civil War. Also, although one may talk of the aggregate closeness of the biennial elections to the House, the aura of competitiveness vanishes somewhat if one looks at the individual races. Significant numbers of candidates win election to the House of Representatives with more than 60 percent of the total vote; in 1982, in fact, 66 percent of them did. In that year, 30 of them were elected without any competition whatsoever.

If we are to discuss the varying degrees of competitiveness of the fifty state party systems, however, the practical problem of defining *compet-*

itiveness can be postponed no longer. Logically, competitiveness suggests either an assessment of the quality of past competition or a prediction of the possibilities of competitiveness in the near future. In both cases the problems are considerable. First, we must decide whether to count vote totals and percentages or simply the offices won. Do we regard a party that systematically garners 40 or 45 percent of the vote, but never wins office, any differently than we do one that hovers around the 20 to 25 percent mark? If we are to make distinctions between parties such as these, where do we draw the fine line between competitiveness and noncompetitiveness—at 30, 35, 40, or 45 percent? Many scholars settle for the 40 percent figure. Then, too, we must decide whether and how to discriminate between the party that averages 40 percent of the vote and wins office occasionally from the party that averages 40 percent and never wins.

Finally, the classifier of parties and party systems on the basis of competitiveness must determine which offices to count—the vote for presidential candidates, for governors and senators, for statewide officials (such as the attorney general), for the state legislature, or for a combination of them. A state may show strikingly different competitive patterns between its national and its state and local politics. Arizona in the 1950s, for example, voted twice for Eisenhower, elected a Republican governor in three of the five elections, and voted twice for a Republican senator, Barry Goldwater. Yet, during those years, the Arizona state senate ranged from 79 to 100 percent Democratic, and the lower house varied from 63 to 90 percent Democratic.[5]

In categorizing the party systems of the American states, one can dismiss the possibility of multiparty systems. To be sure, there are a few examples of them in the American experience. In Minnesota, Wisconsin, and North Dakota in the 1930s and 1940s, remnants of the Progressive movement—the Progressive party in Wisconsin, the Farmer-Labor party in Minnesota, and the Non-Partisan League in North Dakota—competed with some success against the major parties. In all three cases, however, the heavy pressures of the national two-party system forced them to disband and send their loyalists into the two major parties. In these and a few other instances of statewide multipartyism in the recent American past, the period of multipartyism was brief and ended with a return to two-partyism.

The range of party systems among the fifty states, then, extends only the short way from the one-party system to the competitive two-party system. Drawing on the work of others, a group of scholars recently divided the fifty state party systems into four categories: one-party Democratic, modified one-party Democratic, modified one-party Republican and two-

---

[5]These data come from *Book of the States* (Chicago and Lexington, Ky.: Council of State Governments) for the 1950s and 1960s.

party (see Table 2.2); no states fell into a one-party Republican category. The rankings are based on a composite index of (1) the popular vote for Democratic gubernatorial candidates, (2) percentages of seats held by Democrats in the state legislature, and (3) percentages of all gubernatorial and state legislative terms controlled by the Democrats. The resulting averages of these percentages yielded scores from 1.000 (complete Democratic success) to .000 (total Republican success); the scores are reported with the rankings in Table 2.2. The rankings are based wholly on state offices; they do not take into account the state's vote in presidential or senatorial elections. To some extent, therefore, they are isolated from the abnormal patterns of national politics that accompany presidential victories of the magnitude of Ronald Reagan's in 1980.[6]

Useful as they are, such indices again do not fully reveal the complexities of party competition. One rarely finds competitiveness evenly spread through the politics of any one state. In Arkansas in 1980, for example, Reagan and Carter ran almost dead even, and three of the state's four congresspersons were elected without opposition. To concentrate on variations within state politics, gubernatorial elections generally reflect a more intense competitiveness than do elections to the state legislature. Of the governors elected or reelected in 1978 or 1980, 80 percent were elected with less than 60 percent of the vote.[7] Yet the state legislatures that were elected in the same period revealed a partisan composition that belied the competitiveness in the election of governors. In only 39 percent of the houses of the state legislatures did the percentage of Democratic legislators fall between 40 and 59 percent (Table 2.3). To be sure, some of the lack

---

[6]John F. Bibby, Cornelius P. Cotter, James L. Gibson, and Robert J. Huckshorn, "Parties in State Politics" (Chap. 3), in Virginia Gray, Herbert Jacob, and Kenneth Vines (eds.), *Politics in the American States*, 4th ed. (Boston: Little, Brown, 1983). Their work is based on the measurements of Austin Ranney, whose categories were, in turn, based on those of Richard Dawson and James Robinson, "Inter-Party Competition, Economic Variables, and Welfare Policies in the American States," *Journal of Politics* 25 (1963): 265–89. For other data and measures, see Paul T. David, *Party Strength in the United States, 1872–1970* (Charlottesville: University of Virginia Press, 1972), updated with later data in the *Journal of Politics* for August 1974, May 1975, May 1976, and August 1978; Joseph A. Schlesinger, "A Two-Dimensional Scheme for Classifying the States According to Degree of Inter-Party Competition," *American Political Science Review* 49 (1955): 1120–28; David G. Pfeiffer, "The Measurement of Inter-Party Competition and Systemic Stability," *American Political Science Review* 61 (1967): 457–67; Mark Stern, "Measuring Interparty Competition: A Proposal and a Test of a Model," *Journal of Politics* 34 (1972): 889–904; and Harvey J. Tucker, "Interparty Competition in the American States: One More Time," *American Politics Quarterly* 10 (1982): 93–116. Despite the welter of measures and indices reported here, two scholars have found that there is a very high order of correlation among the results of the various measures. See Richard E. Zody and Norman R. Luttbeg, "An Evaluation of Various Measures of State Party Competition," *Western Political Quarterly* 21 (1968): 723–24.

[7]The data on the governors were drawn from *Congressional Quarterly Weekly Reports*, March 31, 1979, and November 8, 1980.

TABLE 2.2   *The Fifty States Classified According to Degree of Interparty Competition: 1974–80*

One-Party Democratic	Modified One-Party Democratic	Two-Party	Modified One-Party Republican
Alabama (.9438)	South Carolina (.8034)	Montana (.6259)	North Dakota (.3374)
Georgia (.8849)	West Virginia (.8032)	Michigan (.6125)	
Louisiana (.8762)	Texas (.7993)	Ohio (.5916)	
Mississippi (.8673)	Massachusetts (.7916)	Washington (.5808)	
Arkansas (.8630)	Kentucky (.7907)	Alaska (.5771)	
North Carolina (.8555)	Oklahoma (.7841)	Pennsylvania (.5574)	
Maryland (.8509)	Nevada (.7593)	Delaware (.5490)	
Rhode Island (.8506)	Hawaii (.7547)	New York (.5390)	
	Florida (.7524)	Illinois (.5384)	
	Connecticut (.7336)	Nebraska (.5166)	
	New Jersey (.7330)	Maine (.5164)	
	Virginia (.7162)	Kansas (.4671)	
	New Mexico (.7113)	Utah (.4653)	
	California (.7081)	Iowa (.4539)	
	Oregon (.6954)	Arizona (.4482)	
	Missouri (.6932)	Colorado (.4429)	
	Minnesota (.6680)	Indiana (.4145)	
	Tennessee (.6648)	New Hampshire (.3916)	
	Wisconsin (.6634)	Idaho (.3898)	
		Wyoming (.3879)	
		Vermont (.3612)	
		South Dakota (.3512)	

Source   John F. Bibby, Cornelius P. Cotter, James L. Gibson, and Robert J. Huckshorn, "Parties in State Politics," in Virginia Gray, Herbert Jacob, and Kenneth Vines (eds.), *Politics in the American States*, 4th ed. (Boston: Little, Brown, 1983), p. 66 (Table 3.3). Reprinted by permission.

TABLE 2.3   *Size of Democratic Contingent in Forty-nine American State Legislatures: 1978*

Percentage Democratic	Upper House	Lower House
0–19	0	0
20–39	7	8
40–59	18	20
60–79	14	12
80–100	10	9
	49[a]	49[a]

[a] The total is only 49 because Nebraska has a nonpartisan legislature.

Source   Data from *Book of the States, 1982–83* (Lexington, Ky: Council of State Governments, 1982).

of partisan balance in the American legislatures may be a result of very skillful drawing of district lines. With all allowances made, however, the patterns of competitiveness suggested by these data are not the same patterns indicated by the data from gubernatorial elections of the period.

Thus, it is difficult to speak even of a *state* party system. On close inspection, each one is an aggregate of different competitive patterns. It is not at all unusual for a party—even one that wins most statewide elections—to have trouble filling its ticket in some local elections. Powerful officeholders can use a long term and the advantage of office to build a personal following independent of party strength. For the rest of their careers, they may insulate themselves from the normally competitive politics in their states. In fact, nothing dampens two-party competition more effectively than the power of incumbency exercised in a small and homogeneous constituency.

THE CAUSES AND CONDITIONS OF TWO–PARTYISM

The rarity of the two-party system among the democracies and its dominance in American politics have stimulated a considerable explanatory effort. The question is an obvious one: Why should this one nation among so many others develop a two-party system? In the interests of an orderly attack on the problem, the most frequent explanations have been divided into four groups: institutional, dualist, cultural, and consensual.

Institutional Theories

By far the most widespread explanation of the two-party system associates it with electoral and governmental institutions. In part, it argues that single-member, plurality electoral systems produce two-party systems and that multimember constituencies and proportional representation result in multipartyism. Plurality election in a single-member district means simply that one candidate is elected and that the winner is the person who receives the largest number of votes. There are no rewards for the parties or candidates that run second, third, or fourth. In a system of proportional representation, on the other hand, a party polling 20 percent or so of a nation's votes may capture close to 20 percent of the legislative seats. Legislators are elected on party slates in multimember districts by the strength of the vote for their parties. Thus, if a district sends five members to the parliament, the breakdown might be:

Party A	39% of vote	2 seats
Party B	36% of vote	2 seats
Party C	20% of vote	1 seat
Party D	5% of vote	—
	100% of vote	5 seats

That same 20 percent would win few, if any, seats in the American electoral system.[8] The American election system offers no reward of office to any but the plurality winner and, so the theory goes, thus discourages the chronic minority parties.

Many of the institutional theorists also argue the importance of the single executive. The American presidency and the governorships—the main prizes of American politics—fall only to parties that can win pluralities. On the contrary, a cabinet in a European nation may be formed by a coalition that includes representatives of minority parties; indeed, even the prize of the premiership may go to a small party. Giovanni Spadolini, the premier of Italy in the early 1980s, came from a party that held less than 3 percent of the parliamentary seats. In countries with a single national executive, the indivisible nature of the office favors the strongest competitors. Beyond the loss of the executive office, moreover, the minor party is denied the national leadership, the focus of the national campaign, and the national spokespersons that increasingly dominate the politics of the

---

[8]Large numbers of states do have multimember districts for one or both houses of the state legislature. The fact that these districts have not altered the two-party system suggests that plurality election is more important than single-member districting in sustaining two-partyism.

democracies. The necessity to contend for a national executive, in other words, works against local or regional parties, even those that may elect candidates in their own bailiwicks.[9]

Dualist Theories

The dualists maintain that an underlying duality of interest in the American society has sustained the American two-party system. V. O. Key suggested that the initial sectional tension between the eastern financial and commercial interests and the western frontiersmen stamped itself on the parties in their incipient stages and fostered a two-party competition. Later, the dualism shifted to the North-South conflict over the issue of slavery and the Civil War, and then to the present urban-rural and socioeconomic status divisions.[10] A related line of argument points to a "natural dualism" within democratic institutions: party in power versus party out of power, government versus opposition, pro and anti the status quo, and even the ideological dualism of liberal and conservative. Thus, social and economic interests or the very processes of a democratic politics—or both—reduce the political contestants to two great camps, and that dualism gives rise to two political parties.

Cultural Theories

This school of explanation in many ways smacks of the older, largely discredited national character theories. It maintains that the United States and Britain have nurtured two-party systems because of their "political maturity" or their "genius for government." More modestly, it attributes the two-party systems to the development of a political culture that accepts the necessity of compromise, the wisdom of short-term pragmatism, and the avoidance of unyielding dogmatism. Americans and Britons, in other words, are willing to make the kinds of compromises necessary to bring heterogeneous groups of voters into two political parties. Then, as they develop the dual parties, their political cultures also develop the attitudes and norms that endorse the two-party system as a desirable end in itself.

---

[9]The institutional theorists are best represented by Maurice Duverger, *Political Parties* (New York: Wiley, 1954); and E. E. Schattschneider, *Party Government* (New York: Rinehart, 1942). On Duverger, see William Riker, "The Two-Party System and Duverger's Law," *American Political Science Review* 76 (1982): 753–66.

[10]See, for example, V. O. Key, *Politics, Parties and Pressure Groups*, 5th ed. (New York: Crowell, 1964), pp. 229ff.; and James C. Charlesworth, "Is Our Two-Party System Natural?" American Academy of Political and Social Science *Annals* 259 (1948): 1–9.

Social Consensus Theories

Finally, the American party system has been explained in terms of a wide-sweeping American social consensus. Despite a diverse cultural heritage and society, Americans early achieved a consensus on the fundamentals that divide other societies. Virtually all Americans traditionally have accepted the prevailing social, economic, and political institutions. They accepted the Constitution and its governmental apparatus, a regulated but free-enterprise economy, and (perhaps to a lesser extent) American patterns of social class and status.

In the traditional multiparty countries such as France and Italy, substantial chunks of political opinion have favored radical changes in those and other basic institutions. They have supported programs of fundamental constitutional change, the socialization of the economy, or the disestablishment of the Church. Whether it is because Americans were spared feudalism and its rigid classes or because they have had an expanding economic and geographic frontier, they have escaped the division on fundamentals that racks the other democracies and gives rise to large numbers of irreconcilable political divisions. Since the matters that divide Americans are secondary, so the argument goes, the compromises necessary to bring them into one of two major parties are easier to make.[11]

In appraising these explanations of the American two-party system, one has to ask some searching questions. Are the factors proposed in these explanations *causes* of the two-party system, or are they *effects* of it? The chances are that they are, at least in part, effects. Certainly, two competitive parties will choose and perpetuate electoral systems that do not offer entrée to minor parties. They will also channel opinion into alternatives, reducing and forcing the system's complexities into their dual channels. The two-party system will also create, foster, and perpetuate the political values and attitudes that justify and protect itself. It will even foster some measure of social consensus by denying competitive opportunities to movements that challenge the great consensus of the status quo.

Although these factors may be effects of the two-party system, they certainly are also causes. If they are, however, why has the two-party system been such a comparatively rare phenomenon? If single-member constituencies and plurality elections explain American two-partyism, why did they not produce a similar outcome in Third Republic France? Moreover, American society is not the first to have an overriding duality of interests in its politics. The socioeconomic class division between "haves" and "have-nots" has plagued many democracies without leading to a two-

[11]See Leslie Lipson, "The Two-Party System in British Politics," *American Political Science Review* 47 (1953): 337–58.

party system. The implication seems clear that no one of these theories alone can explain the virtual uniqueness of the American party system.

At the risk of fence straddling, one may venture to suggest that all four explanations illuminate the development of the American party system. No one of them need exclude the impact of any other. Their unique combination has produced a unique two-party system. At the root of the explanation lies the basic, long-run American consensus on fundamental beliefs. Traditionally, no deep rifts over the kind of economy, society, or government we want have marked our politics. More than one European observer has remarked on the resulting nonideological character of American politics. Consensus has been fostered by American education and social assimilation and has been aided by two major parties inhospitable to challenges to that consensus. If the consensus has broken down to some extent in the last generation, it has done so well after the American two-party system was established and deeply entrenched.

Lacking cause for deep ideological divisions and disagreeing on few fundamentals, Americans were easily formed into two conglomerate, majority-seeking political parties. The institutions of American government—such as single-member constituencies, plurality elections, and the single executive—were free to exert their power to limit the parties to two without having to repulse countervailing pressures of social division. So, too, in the absence of deeply felt ideologies, a pragmatic opposition to the party in power was easily able to develop a dualism of the "ins" and the "outs." Moreover, once the two-party system was launched, its very existence fostered the values of moderation, compromise, and political pragmatism that ensure its perpetuation. It also created deep loyalties within the American public to one party or the other and deep loyalties to the genius of the two-party system itself.

EXCURSIONS INTO ONE–PARTYISM

To argue the existence of only two competitive parties is not to argue that their competitiveness is spread evenly over the country. There have been substantial statewide and local pockets of one-partyism in the United States. The states of the Deep South spent very close to their own "four score and seven" years as the country's most celebrated area of one-party domination. Much the same could be said in the past of the rocklike Republicanism of Maine, New Hampshire, and Vermont. Also, scattered throughout the country today are thousands of one-party cities, towns, and counties in which the city hall or county courthouse comes perilously close to being the property of one party. Parallel to the question of the causes of the two-party system, therefore, is the question of the causes of one-partyism within it.

One-partyism set within the context of broad, two-party competitiveness often reflects a "fault" in the distribution of the electorates of the competitive parties. Since the 1930s, the major American parties, especially in national elections, have divided the American electorate roughly along lines of socioeconomic status and issues—a point that will be developed later. Suffice it here to note that Democratic loyalties have been far more common among ethnic, racial, and religious minority groups, urban workers, and lower socioeconomic status (SES) groups in general. The Republicans, on the other hand, have drawn a disproportionate number of loyalists from higher status and rural groups.

Thus, one-partyism may result from a maldistribution of the characteristics that normally divide the parties. The local constituency may be too small to contain a perfect sample of SES characteristics and thus of competitive politics—hence the noncompetitiveness of the "safe" Democratic congressional districts of the older, lower-middle-class neighborhoods of the cities and the "safe" Republican districts of the more fashionable and spacious suburbs. In other words, the more heterogeneous are its people, the more likely the district is to foster competitiveness.

Alternatively, one-partyism may result from some potent local basis of party loyalty that overrides the SES dualism. In the classic one-partyism of the American South, regional loyalties long overrode the factors that were dividing Americans into two parties in most of the rest of the country. Reaction to the Republican party as the party of abolition, Lincoln, the Civil War, and the hated Reconstruction was so pervasive, even three generations after the fact, that the impact of the SES division was precluded. It was thus a one-partyism based on isolation from the factors that normally produced two-party competitiveness.

Empirical studies of one-partyism suggest, however, that its causes are far more complex than these two logical possibilities. Competitiveness has been associated with general socioeconomic diversity in the constituency— especially with urbanism and its industrialism, higher income levels, and ethnic diversity. Yet the relationships are not always strong or dramatic, and one recent study finds no such relationships at all.[12] We are thus left

---

[12]Charles M. Bonjean and Robert L. Lineberry, "The Urbanization-Party Competition Hypothesis: A Comparison of All United States Counties," *Journal of Politics* 32 (1970): 305–21. For a further introduction to the study of the correlates of competitiveness in the American party system, see David Gold and John R. Schmidhauser, "Urbanization and Party Competition: The Case of Iowa," *Midwest Journal of Political Science* 4 (1960): 62–75; Phillips Cutright, "Urbanization and Competitive Party Politics," *Journal of Politics* 25 (1963): 552–64; and Thomas W. Casstevens and Charles O. Press, "The Context of Democratic Competition in American State Politics," *American Journal of Sociology* 68 (1963): 536–43. The reader who explores this literature should be aware both of the varying definitions of competition and urbanness and of the difference between competitiveness of states and competitiveness of subdivisions (e.g., counties) within states.

more or less to conjecture. Perhaps a homogeneous district cut from the middle range of SES factors tends to be more competitive than an equally homogeneous district at either the top or the bottom of the SES spectrum. Alternatively, in some localities the patterns of competitiveness may have little to do with patterns of national SES politics or with any other characteristics of the electorate. They may instead reflect the influences of local personages, of powerful officeholders, of local traditions, or of local political conflict, such as that between a dominant industry and its disgruntled employees.

One may also look at these pockets of one-partyism another way. The American party system is made up of two electorally competitive parties, which is really to say that it is formed by two parties competing to enlist a majority of the American electorate. If these two parties were fully competitive in every constituency in the country, they would approach a fifty-fifty division of the electorate. They must compete at various disadvantages, however; and frequently, in some area or locality, one party works at a disadvantage that it never manages to overcome. The result is the ability of the other party to maintain a one-party domination. The understanding of one-partyism, then, requires an understanding of the various kinds of competitive disadvantages a party may face.

The competitive disadvantages begin with stubborn party loyalties. Voters are not easily moved from their attachments to a party, even though the reasons for the original attachment have long passed. Also, a party trying to pull itself into competitiveness may find itself caught in a vicious circle of impotence. Its inability to win elections limits its ability to recruit resources, including manpower, because as a chronic loser it offers so little chance of achieving political goals. It may even find itself without an effective appeal to the electorate. The Republican party in the South, for example, found for many years that the Democrats had preempted the salient political issues in that region.

Today, the would-be competitive party finds disadvantage taking another form: the formation of party loyalties among lines determined by national or statewide political debate. If the Democratic party is identified nationally with the aspirations of the poor and minority groups, its appeal in a homogeneous, affluent suburb may be limited. Thus, national politics may increasingly rob the local party organization of the chance to develop strength based on its own issues, personalities, and traditions. To the extent that party loyalties and identifications grow out of national politics, competitiveness (or the lack of it) may be out of the control of the local party organizations.

There are, to be sure, other sources of competitive disadvantage. The dominant party may shore up its supremacy by carefully calculated legislative districting. In the past, southern Democrats stifled potential competitiveness by artificially restricting the electorates to middle-class whites. In other instances, majority parties have supported nonpartisanship in local elections as a way of drawing on their one-party consensus. In addition to these institutional buttresses to one-partyism, of course, powerful party organization and sedulous canvassing can maintain superiority. Finally, the normal processes of socialization and social conformity work to the disadvantage of a local party trying to become competitive. That force of conformity, a number of observers have argued, works especially against competitiveness in the closely knit, socially sensitive world of American suburbia.

THE "ALSO-RANS": THE THIRD PARTIES

Periodically, a new minor party flashes onto the national scene, getting attention from both scholars and journalists out of proportion to its electoral impact. Attention aside, however, only seven minor parties in all of American history have carried so much as a single state in a presidential election (see box). More important, perhaps, no minor party has come

---

The Big Little Parties

To put the minor parties in some perspective, we need some point of calibration; that is, we need some measure by which we can compare their electoral strength to that of the major parties and by which we can separate the stronger and weaker minor parties. If we take as a measure the ability to draw at least 10 percent of the popular vote for president, only four parties qualify (numbers 3, 4, 5, and 7 below). If we choose as a more liberal but certainly modest test of strength the ability to carry one state—just one—in a presidential election, only seven minor parties in American history qualify.

1. *Anti-Masonic party*. 1832: 7 electoral votes. A party opposed to the alleged secret political influence of the Masons; later part of an anti-Jackson coalition that formed the Whig party.

2. *American (Know-Nothing) party*. 1856: 8 electoral votes. A nativist party opposed to open immigration and in favor of electing native-born Americans to public office.

3. *People's (Populist) party*. 1892: 22 electoral votes. An outgrowth

---

close to winning the presidency. The best minor party records so far were set in 1912 by Teddy Roosevelt and the Progressives, with 17 percent of the electoral vote and 30 percent of the popular vote. That candidacy was, in fact, the only minor party candidacy ever to run ahead of one of the major party candidates in either electoral or popular vote.

Between the peaks of third-party influence are the valleys. In 1964, for example, the leading minor party—the Socialist Labor party—attracted only 45,168 voters, and the minor parties altogether polled only one-fifth of one percent of the popular vote. After the George Wallace phenomenon of 1968—almost 10 million votes for Wallace alone—minor party strength ebbed once again. The total minor party vote for president in 1980 was 1,383,608 (Table 2.4), or about 1.6 percent of the total popular vote for president. More telling, perhaps, was the independent, nonparty campaign of John Anderson, which drew more than four times the votes of the minor parties combined: 5,720,060.

The very looseness with which we customarily use the term *third party* to designate all minor parties may indicate that third place is as good (or bad) as last place in a two-party system. It would be a serious mistake, however, to treat the minor parties as indistinguishable. They differ in

---

of a movement of agrarian protest opposed to the economic power of bankers, railroads, and fuel industries and in favor of a graduated income tax, government regulation, and currency reform (especially free silver coinage).

4. *Progressive (Bull Moose) party.* 1912: 88 electoral votes. An offshoot of the Republican party, it favored liberal reforms such as an expanded suffrage, improved working conditions, conservation of resources, and antimonopoly laws.

5. *Progressive party.* 1924: 13 electoral votes. A continuation of the 1912 Progressive tradition with the candidacy of a man who had been one of its founders and leaders (Robert La Follette).

6. *States Rights Democratic (Dixiecrat) party.* 1948: 39 electoral votes. A southern splinter of the Democratic party, it ran as *the* Democratic party in the South on a conservative, segregationist platform.

7. *American Independent party.* 1968: 46 electoral votes. The party of George Wallace; traditionalist, segregationist, and opposed to the authority of the national government.

TABLE 2.4   *Popular Votes Cast for Minor Parties in 1976 and 1980 Presidential Elections*

Parties: 1976	Vote: 1976	Parties: 1980[a]	Vote: 1980
Libertarian	173,011	Libertarian	921,299
American Independent	170,531	Citizens	234,294
American	160,773	Communist	45,023
Socialist Workers	91,314	American Independent	41,268
Communist	58,992	Socialist Workers	38,737
People's	49,024	Right to Life	32,327
U.S. Labor	40,043	Peace and Freedom	18,116
Prohibition	15,934	Workers' World	13,300
Socialist Labor	9,616	Others and scattered	39,244
Others and scattered	51,404		1,383,608
	820,642		

[a] John Anderson ran in 1980 as an independent candidate rather than as the candidate of a political party; therefore, his 5,720,060 votes are not included in the table.

Source   Richard M. Scammon (ed.), *America Votes 14* (Washington, D.C.: Governmental Affairs Institute, 1981).

origin, purpose, and function, and American political history affords a rich variety of their activities to illustrate those differences.[13]

Although it is true, first of all, that most minor parties are parties of *ideology and issue*, they differ in the scope of that commitment. The narrow, highly specific commitment of the Prohibition and Vegetarian parties is apparent in their names. In the 1840s, the Liberty party and its successor, the Free Soil party, campaigned largely on the single issue of the abolition of slavery. At the other extremes are the parties that have the broadest ideological commitments—the Marxist parties and the recent profusion of conservative parties. The Libertarian party, for example— the leading minor party of 1976 and 1980—advocates a complete withdrawal of government from most of its present programs and responsibilities (see box). In the middle ground between specific issues and total ideologies, the examples are infinitely varied. The farmer-labor parties of economic protest—the Greenback, Populist, and Progressive parties—ran

[13]The literature on American third parties is rich and varied. Among the best contributions are John D. Hicks, *The Populist Revolt* (Minneapolis: University of Minnesota Press, 1931); Richard Hofstadter, *The Age of Reform* (New York: Knopf, 1955); David A. Shannon, *The Socialist Party of America* (New York: Macmillan, 1955); K. M. Schmidt, *Henry A. Wallace: Quixotic Crusade 1948* (Syracuse: Syracuse University Press, 1960); George Thayer, *The Farther Shores of Politics* (New York: Simon and Schuster, 1967); Marshall Frady, *Wallace* (New York: World, 1968); and Daniel A. Mazmanian, *Third Parties in Presidential Elections* (Washington, D.C.: 1974).

The Libertarian Alternative

Founded in 1972, the Libertarian party grew quickly to become the leading vote-getter among the minor parties in both 1976 and 1980. Its presidential candidate in 1980 was a California lawyer, Edward E. Clark. Clark had run for governor of California in 1978 and had drawn more than 5 percent of the total vote. Some of his political views were reported in a *New York Times* account of one of his press conferences in early 1980:

> "Ultimately," the Libertarian said at a news conference here today, "we believe in the complete privatization of society," with a "vastly restricted" government and a corresponding huge reduction in the taxes that finance the Government.
>
> Mr. Clark told a questioner that eventually he advocated returning highway and street systems to private ownership, "the way they used to be" under Colonial toll-road practices.
>
> In foreign affairs, the Libertarian candidate advocates a "noninterventionist policy," letting other nations defend themselves, reducing defense expenditures substantially and withdrawing from the United Nations and the North Atlantic Treaty Organization, while maintaining extensive social and cultural relations abroad.
>
> Warren Weaver, Jr., in *New York Times*,
> January 22, 1980.

on an extensive program of government regulation of the economy (especially of economic bigness) and social welfare legislation. The Progressive party of 1948—at least the part of it separate from the Communist party—combined a program of social reform and civil liberties with a foreign policy of friendship with the Soviet Union and reduction of Cold War tensions.

The minor parties differ, too, in their *origin*. Some were literally imported into the United States. Much of the early Socialist party strength in the United States came from the freethinkers and radicals who fled Europe after the failures of the revolutions of 1848. Socialist strength in cities such as Milwaukee, New York, and Cincinnati reflected the concentrations of liberal German immigrants there. Other parties—especially the Granger and Populist parties and their successors—were parties of indigenous social protest, born of social inequality and economic hardship in the marginal farmlands of America. Other minor parties began as splinters or factions of one of the major parties. The Gold Democrats of 1896, the Progressives (the Bull Moose party) of 1912, and the Dixiecrats of 1948 come to mind. So great were their objections to the platforms and candidates of their parent parties that the Progressives and Dixiecrats contested the presidential elections of 1912 and 1948 with their own slates and programs.

Recent presidential elections have seen the entry of a new variety of minor party: the "nonparty." Found chiefly in the southern states, these nonparties have been dissident movements within the Democratic party that have refused to run as separate parties on the ballot. Instead, they have exploited two other strategies. In some instances, they have attempted to run their own candidate (rather than the one chosen by the party's national convention) as the official presidential candidate of the Democratic party in the state. The only four states that J. Strom Thurmond carried in 1948 for the Dixiecrats (Alabama, Louisiana, Mississippi, and South Carolina) were those in which he, rather than Harry Truman, was the candidate of the Democratic party. George Wallace also captured the Alabama Democratic label in 1968, displacing Hubert Humphrey as the Democratic candidate in that state. In other cases, these party movements have run unpledged slates of presidential electors. In 1960, unpledged slates ran in Louisiana as a States Rights party and in Mississippi as the Democratic party (although there was another Democratic party ticket pledged to Kennedy). In 1964, another unpledged Democratic slate of electors ran in Alabama and prevented the Johnson-Humphrey ticket from appearing on the Alabama ballot.

Finally, the third parties differ in their *tactics*. For some, their mere existence is a protest against what they believe is the unqualified support of the status quo by the major parties. Operating as a political party also offers a reasonably effective educational opportunity. The publicity value of the ballot is good, and with it often goes mass media attention the party could not otherwise hope for. Indeed, many of these parties have freely accepted their electoral failures, for they have chosen, by their very nature, not to compromise ideological principles for electoral success.

Other minor parties, however, do have serious electoral ambitions. Often their goal is local, although today they find it difficult to control an American city as the Socialists did, or an entire state as the Progressives did. More realistically, today they may hope to hold a balance of power between the major parties in the manner of the Liberals in New York. In the 1965 mayoral election, for instance, John Lindsay's vote on the Republican ticket was less than that of his Democratic opponent; his vote reached the necessary plurality only with the addition of the votes he won in the Liberal party column. Or a party may, as did the Dixiecrats of 1948 and Wallace's American Independent party of 1968, play for the biggest stakes of all: the presidency. Both parties hoped that by carrying a number of states, most likely southern states, they might prevent the major party tickets from winning the necessary majority of votes in the electoral college, thus throwing the stalemated election into the House of Representatives. The Wallace effort of 1968 faltered because Richard Nixon carried an unexpected number of large states.

These parties of electoral opportunity are certainly the ones that have enjoyed the minor party successes of recent years. The more traditional, stable parties of ideology, which Norman Thomas and the Socialists typified for so long in American politics, seem to be in decline. It is more individuals than parties of electoral opportunity, however, that challenge the major parties. George Wallace's American Independent party was little more than a vehicle for his ambitions and had, perhaps, not much more than the degree of organization required by the states for a place on the ballot. With his retirement, it has slipped into ineffectuality. In fact, after running on the American Independent ticket in 1968, Wallace backed away from the party's leadership and was contesting within the Democratic party for convention delegates when he was shot in 1971. In a similar vein, Eugene McCarthy, a Democrat in 1968, flirted with third-party and independent possibilities in the 1970s. John Anderson sought the Republican presidential nomination and then ran as an independent candidate for the presidency in 1980 before founding his National Unity party in 1982. The loosening of party loyalties to the two major parties and the ease with which a popular candidate becomes known through television and the other media make such careers increasingly feasible.

Their variety is endless, but what have the minor parties contributed to American politics? For better or for worse, they have influenced, perhaps even altered, the courses of a few presidential elections. By threatening—about once a generation—to deadlock the electoral college, they probably have kept alive movements to reform it. Beyond their role as potential electoral spoiler, however, can they count any significant accomplishments? The answer, to be candid, is that they have not assumed the importance that all the attention lavished on them suggests.

One line of argument has maintained persistently that the minor parties' early adoption of unpopular programs ultimately has forced the major parties to adopt them. Its proponents point to the platforms of the Socialist party in the years before the 1930s. The issue is whether or not the Socialists' advocacy for twenty or thirty years of such measures as a minimum wage had anything to do with their enactment in the 1930s. Unfortunately, there is no way of testing what might have happened had there been no Socialist party. The evidence suggests, however, that the major parties grasp new programs and proposals in their "time of ripeness"—when large numbers of Americans have done so and when such a course is therefore politically useful to the parties. In their earlier, maturing time, new issues need not depend on minor parties for their advocacy. Interest groups, the mass media, influential individuals, and factions within the major parties may perform the propagandizing role, often more effectively than a minor party. More than one commentator has noted that the cause of prohibition in the United States was served far more effectively by interest groups such as the Anti-Saloon League than by the Prohibition party.

WHITHER THE AMERICAN TWO–PARTY SYSTEM?

George Wallace's lawyers stood before the United States Supreme Court in early October of 1968 to plead that the Court strike down Ohio's election law and permit Wallace's name to be printed on the ballot in that state as a presidential candidate. It was a scene awash in irony. Wallace had often excoriated the Court for its willingness to invalidate the laws of states, and now his attorneys were making substantially that request. The Ohio law in question had been passed in 1948 to prevent the third-party candidacy of Henry Wallace in that state. The law required that a new and unestablished party collect a number of signatures equal to 15 percent of the votes cast in the last statewide election—a percentage that required the Wallace forces to muster 433,000 signatures in 1968. In addition, the Ohio law required those petitions to be submitted in early February, a time far earlier than most campaigns are mobilized. Finally, it prohibited independent, nonparty candidates.

In its defense, the state of Ohio did not deny its intentions. The law was intended, the state freely conceded, to work to the disadvantage of any other than the two established parties. The state argued that it had a legitimate interest in preserving the existing two-party system, in preventing a division of the vote among a number of parties, and ultimately in making sure that small pluralities would not win elections. The discrimination against third parties, in other words, was the avowed policy of the state of Ohio. The argument did not sway the Supreme Court, and by a vote of six to three, the Court struck down the Ohio law for violating the equal protection clause of the Fourteenth Amendment. Justice Black, speaking for the Court, asserted that the Ohio law imposed an unconstitutional burden on the rights of voting and association and that it discriminated against supporters of minor parties. Thus, with the help of the Supreme Court, George Wallace placed his name on the Ohio ballot in November of 1968.[14]

The lessons of the story of Wallace against the State of Ohio are many. To some extent, at least, it marked the end of the argument that it is constitutionally proper to support and preserve the two-party system with electoral law that discriminates against third-party competitors. It also

[14]*Williams* v. *Rhodes*, 393 U.S. 23 (1968). In 1983 the Supreme Court also ruled that Ohio and the other states could not discriminate against independent candidates (such as John Anderson in 1980) seeking a place on the presidential ballot of the state. *Anderson* v. *Celebrezze*, 103 S. Ct. 1564 (1983).

signaled the extraordinary success of Wallace in surmounting the obstacles that separate the minor party from effective, competitive status in American politics. Victory over Ohio law gave him access to his fiftieth state ballot in November 1968. Beyond all these points, however, the success of Wallace suggests answers about the future of third parties in American politics.

The Wallace campaign of 1968 was a triumph over the two major obstacles that minor parties and independent candidates face: access to the ballot and financial health. As for the first, a number of states presented no particular barriers; a mere 300 signatures sufficed to get Wallace's name on the ballot in Colorado. Heroic efforts were necessary, however, in other states. California law, for instance, required that voters signing his petitions be registered as voters and members of the American Independent party; for most of them, that meant going through the formal step of ceasing to be Democrats or Republicans and reregistering as members of the new party. Although Wallace smoothed the way to the ballots of the fifty states, John Anderson in 1980 still spent a great deal of both time and money in assuring that his name would be before the American voters (see box).

The financial barriers were no less daunting for Wallace, and they remain serious impediments to challenges from outside the two major parties. Campaigns based on the mass media, on armies of advertising and public relations specialists, and on polls and surveys cost increasingly large sums of money. The Wallace campaign astounded observers of American political finance by raising and spending some $7 million, by far the largest sum ever spent by a minor party campaign in American history. Moreover, he was widely thought to have left the 1968 campaign with a surplus in excess of $1 million. For John Anderson, the problem had been changed by the public funding of presidential campaigns that began in the mid-1970s. By polling more than 5 percent of the popular vote, he qualified for more than $4 million in public funds. Therefore, the money came after the election, but his vote total does make him eligible for public funding during the 1984 campaign. (Campaign finance will be considered more fully in Chapter 13.)

George Wallace also solved—if only in part—the problem of a minor party's becoming a national party. Almost all the effective minor party activity of the past century has been intensely local. Each of the minor parties has been concentrated in one state or region or in a city or two. Socialists came from Germany in the middle of the nineteenth century and established Socialist enclaves in cities such as New York, Milwaukee, and Cincinnati. Regional agricultural depressions gave rise to Populism and other similar movements of the plains and prairies. Traditionally, third parties have fed on local loyalties, interests, and appeals, but those appeals increasingly have lost out in a mobile society that receives the same po-

Getting on the Ballot
Without a Party Label

A substantial part of John Anderson's independent campaign for the presidency in 1980 involved simply getting on the ballots of the states. Petitions with large numbers of signatures were required in most states, and in at least ten, formal legal action was necessary to win a place on the presidential ballot. (In some of those states, the challenge to the Anderson forces was supported by the Democratic National Committee.) The result was to give a special character to the Anderson campaign and, perhaps, to do it considerable harm. One pair of observers expanded on the latter point:

> Some of his managers in both Washington and the various state headquarters were beguiled by the unrealistic notion of using the ballot access operation to build an "organization" for the general election campaign. The result, in state after state, was that they labored to get far more signatures than were needed to qualify for the ballot, even allowing for the likelihood that many of them might be found invalid. For example, operating on the idea that numbers would be politically impressive, his supporters accumulated almost 150,000 signatures in Illinois when only 25,000 were needed. And even in conservative states where he was given no chance of winning, the same pattern was often followed. In Arizona, for instance, almost five times the required number of signatures were produced. All this yielded one-day stories in the state involved but nothing of any practical help for the general election campaign ahead. . . .
>
> One result, unsurprisingly, was that the ballot access campaign used up virtually all the money, some $2,500,000, available during the summer and left none for the equally important task of telling the country through advertising something about the candidate who was qualifying for the ballot. At one point, the campaign was supposed to be setting aside $250,000 a week from the returns on its direct mail so that David Garth would have one million dollars to spend on basic advertising in August. But when the time came, the money wasn't there, and the campaign was actually one million dollars in debt. As Anderson himself would say later, "I had a media expert without a media campaign."

Jack W. Germond and Jules Witcover,
*Blue Smoke and Mirrors: How Reagan Won
and Why Carter Lost the Election of 1980*
(New York: Viking, 1981), pp. 236–37.

litical messages via the same radio and television networks, the same magazines, and the same press services and syndicated columnists. Thus, minor parties find it hard to become national parties, and they also find it hard to maintain the regional base necessary to win state votes in the electoral college. (To be sure, the five states Wallace carried in 1968 were all from the Deep South.) In 1980, John Anderson ran a national campaign that garnered 6 percent of the national popular vote; his 15 percent in Massachusetts and Vermont, however, was as close as he came to carrying a state.

What, then, can we predict for minor parties in American politics? There will continue to be a few local third parties that reflect special local conditions, especially quirks in local election laws. The classic instance, of course, is that of the New York minor parties—the Liberals, the Conservatives, and the Right to Life party. They exist because they can nominate the candidates of a major party to run under their party labels. New York election law thus makes them important brokers in New York elections. For national impact, however, minor parties generally will ride the coattails of a well-known, charismatic candidate. That appears to be the lesson of George Wallace and John Anderson. It also appears to be the lesson of attempts to found racial and ethnic parties. Separate black parties developed in a number of southern states shortly after the passage of the Civil Rights Acts of the 1960s, but blacks in the South now increasingly organize within the Democratic party (in caucuses or conferences within it) or in nonparty citizen or community organizations. Similarly, La Raza Unida, the Chicano party, has failed to become an important electoral force.[15]

Although the future of the minor parties seems uncertain, one can point with confidence to a second general trend in the American party system: the increasing competitiveness of the major parties. It is probably safe to say that in national and statewide politics, we are in a period of the most intense, evenly spread two-party competitiveness in the past 100 years. No regions of the country, and very few states, can be thought of as one-party areas. Even the once-solid Democratic South is solid no more. Republicans Barry Goldwater in 1964 and Richard Nixon in 1972 carried Alabama, Georgia, Louisiana, Mississippi, and South Carolina; in 1980, Ronald Reagan carried every state of the Confederacy except Georgia, the home state of the Democratic candidate.

[15]On the black parties, see Hanes Walton, Jr., *Black Political Parties: A Historical and Political Analysis* (New York: Free Press, 1972). More generally, on black politics in the South, see David Campbell and Joe R. Feagin, "Black Politics in the South: A Descriptive Analysis," *Journal of Politics* 37 (1975): 129–59. For an account of the early Texas successes of La Raza Unida, see Neal R. Peirce, *The Megastates of America* (New York: Norton, 1972), pp. 558–63.

To take the longer view, presidents increasingly have been winning with popular vote percentages that vary less and less from one state to another. Table 2.5 indicates that the standard deviations from the national average of the presidential popular vote in the states have been diminishing in this century. In other words, presidents are no longer carrying some states by fat margins while losing others in a similarly lopsided way. As the overwhelming votes of the one-party states are eliminated, presidential candidates tend to amass more nearly uniform vote percentages all across the country. Competitiveness, then, is spreading increasingly across the fifty states.

This spread of major party competitiveness reflects the same nationalization of life and politics in the United States that threatens local minor parties. It is increasingly difficult for one major party to maintain its dominance on the basis of appeals and traditions quite different from those in the rest of the country—as, for example, the Democrats did in the South from 1875 to 1950. Furthermore, the social and economic conditions that support one-partyism are disappearing. Fading especially are the political

TABLE 2.5   *The Growth of National Two-Party Competitiveness: Standard Deviations of Presidential Popular Vote in the States: 1896–1980*

Year	Standard Deviation[a]	Year	Standard Deviation[a]
1896	17.5	1940	13.4
1900	14.0	1944	12.3
1904	18.8	1948	9.8
1908	14.9	1952	8.5
1912	15.8	1956	8.3
1916	13.4	1960	5.8
1920	16.1	1964	10.3
1924	16.0	1968	9.7
1928	13.5	1972	6.9
1932	14.0	1976	6.6
1936	12.6	1980	7.3

[a] The standard deviation is a measure of the distance of dispersal of items from the average. It discriminates, therefore, among the dispersals of the following three series: 3, 6, 9; 4, 6, 8; and 5, 6, 7. Even though the means (averages) and the medians of the three series would be identical (6), the standard deviations would decline in the order in which the three series are listed. The data used in the table are the percentages of the total vote in each state won by the winning candidate.

monopolies of powerful groups that once dominated the politics of a single state from a base in cotton, copper, oil, silver, or organized labor. As Americans move about the country, as industry comes to formerly agrarian states, as more and varied people move to the urban centers, each state increasingly becomes a microcosm of the diversity of life and interest that undergirds the national competition between the two parties. National mass media and national political leaders also bring the symbols and dialectics of Democratic–Republican conflict to all corners of the country. Thus, the party electorates are increasingly recruited by the appeals of national candidates and issues—regardless of whatever special appeals the local party organization makes.

Conversely, state party organizations and leaders cannot hold out against the political issues and images that engulf the rest of the country. They cannot easily set up their own competitive subsystem. As a result, a creeping competitiveness accompanies the end of one-partyism at the state level. First, the states become competitive in national elections; then the old one-party ties and fears slowly break down, and competition seeps down to local elections. Pennsylvania, for example, became competitive in presidential politics in the 1930s after forty years of domination by the GOP; by the 1950s and 1960s, the state was competitive in state and local politics. In the 1960s and 1970s, the same process was under way in a number of southern states.

Ironically, the increasing degree of two-party competition has created a set of vexing problems for the American parties. By eliminating pockets of one-party strength, the new competitiveness eliminates a source of stability in the party system. When a party holds noncompetitive strongholds of its own, it can survive even a catastrophic national loss through victories and continued officeholding in its own areas of strength. Without those one-party strongholds to fall back on, a losing party in the future may find its loss more sweeping and devastating. Furthermore, the spread of two-party competitiveness expands the scope of party competition and thus makes extra demands on the resources the parties must employ. When one-party areas could be written off in a presidential campaign and election, the area of political combat was reduced. Now the parties must mobilize and organize more resources than ever, for a presidential campaign must be fought in fifty rather than in thirty states.

Nevertheless, the reign of the existing parties and, more generally, of the American two-party system seems secure. The parties' support may not be what it was, but their resilience is still remarkable. Talk of the imminent decline of the Republicans after Watergate and the losses of 1974 and 1976 was silenced by the party's resurgence in the 1978 and 1980 elections. Changes in the parties and in their appeals, it appears, will have to take place within the party system we have known for more than a century.

II

The Political Party as an Organization

It is often easier to see the political activity than the actor. The tense excitement of a bitterly fought election, the carnival antics and revival meeting fervor of national conventions, the wrangling between partisan blocs in a state legislature—these and the other activities of the political parties could not be more obvious. There is a palpable actor behind the activity, however—a political party with characteristics not unlike those of large national corporations, trade unions, and fraternal societies. The political party is no mere bundle of activities, no disembodied ideology, no unseen hand in the political process. It is a definable, observable social structure that must itself be organized in order to organize political interests.

Within the political party, two of the sectors—the party organization and the party in government—have stable relationships and a rough division of labor and responsibility. In other words, both have the characteristics we associate with an organization of any kind. It is a bit misleading, therefore, to call only one of them the party organization, but such are the semantic vagaries of American politics. In justification of that usage, however, it is true that the party organization alone has the organizational capacity to plan and initiate the major share of party activities. It also has the most systematic network of relationships and roles of all the party sectors. It is the sector that speaks in the name of the party, governs it, and under law is responsible for it. It is the sector in which active partisans work to set the goals of the party and to mobilize and deploy its resources. In that sense, it is the part of the party most concerned with its governance and its priorities.

In concrete terms, the party organization is the formal apparatus of the precincts, wards, cities, counties, congressional districts, and state that results from the legislation of the state itself. It is the party created for the purposes of the state. In addition, each party has set up a national committee, which peaks the pyramid of committees the state has created. The party organization is thus the totality of the machinery operated by party officials, leaders, members, and activists. The three chapters that follow will describe it.

The public life and activities of the party organization—its espousal of ideas and recruitment of candidates, for instance—will receive treatment in later chapters. Party organizations have a "private life," however, in addition to their public life. It involves the kinds of internal relationships and behavior one might find in any complex organization. In considering that private life, the three chapters of this part will examine:

— *The formal structure of the organization:* its committees and machinery; the selection of its leadership.

— *The centers of power:* the relative centralization or decentralization of power within the organization; the locus of final authority within it.

— *The patterns of decision making:* the processes by which decisions are made, especially the degree of intraorganizational democracy.

— *Cohesion and consent:* the maintenance of unity, discipline, and morale within the organization.

— *The recruitment of resources:* the ability of the organization to attract people, money, and skills and the incentives it uses to do so.

— *The division of labor:* the various roles and relationships among people within the organization.

The private life of the party is far less obvious than its public life. Although we may separate them, however, the two are obviously related. To a considerable extent, the internal, organizational characteristics of the party determine its capacity to carry on its external, public activities.

A comparison with the large business organization is, if not pressed too far, a valid one. The party organization competes with other political organizations for political resources—manpower, knowledge, and money. Its rewards or incentives bring together varied groups of men and women who seek their special, and often differing, goals through the medium of party action. What are considered rewards and incentives from the "mobilizing" viewpoint of the party organization are merely the goals and ends for which their activists have come together in the party. Many of the party organization's activities, therefore, may be viewed in terms of its attempts to win those goals and thereby reward the faithful for their investment of resources, loyalties, work, and support.

Ultimately, the most important questions about the party organizations concern their effectiveness, vitality, and capacity. These characteristics can be summed up as *strength*, and the strength of the party organization has two dimensions: its ability to hold its own in its relationships with the two other sectors of the party, and its ability to function efficiently and consistently in mobilizing resources and making decisions. In other words, the party organization must be able to function successfully both within the political party and within the broader political system.

In its relationships with the party in government and the party in the electorate, the party organization rarely achieves any permanent supremacy within the American political party. All three sectors of the party struggle for control of its symbols and its political capabilities. All three have goals—at times, competing goals—and each seeks control of the party as a means to its own particular ends. Rarely is the party organization able to dictate to the party in government. It is far more common for the organization to be dependent on and even submissive to the other sector. It must also conduct an almost endless wooing of its own party electorate, most of whom are neither formal members nor unfailingly loyal voters.

In addition to these strained and often dependent relationships with the other sectors of the party, the organization confronts formidable problems in maintaining its internal vitality. Contrary to popular impression, party organizations are not unified, omnipotent monoliths. They have within them men and women of different values and goals, and they have always been plagued with dissidents and competing factions. They or parts of them often display amazing degrees of organizational apathy, ineptness, and even organizational disintegration. It is not unusual, for example, to find entire county organizations of the Democratic or Republican party in total disuse.

In both these dimensions of the problem of strength and vitality, there are many variations within the American parties. The next few chapters will illustrate the varieties of party organizations. The basic fact remains that by the standards of political parties of most Western democracies, the American party organizations are comparatively weak and insubstantial. To a considerable extent, the problem is in the very nature of the animal. The party organization is an expression of some very special qualities of the American political party.

At the risk of considerable oversimplification, one can say that, among democratic political parties, two types of organization appear most frequently: the cadre and the mass membership. In the cadre party, of which the major American parties are prime examples, the organizational machinery is run by a relatively small number of leaders and activists. These officials and activists perpetuate the apparatus of the organization, make decisions in its name, and pick the candidates and strategies that will enlist large numbers of voters. In the mass membership party, on the other hand, the party organization grows out of and is more continuously responsible to the party membership. In such parties, substantial portions of the party electorate are involved in the party organization as dues-paying members

TABLE II.1   *Comparison of Cadre and Mass Membership Party Organizations*

Organizational Feature	Cadre Party	Mass membership Party
Members	Generally few	Many dues-paying members
Activities	Predominantly electoral	Ideological and educational, as well as electoral
Organizational continuity	Active chiefly at elections	Continuously active
Leadership	Few full-time workers or leaders	Permanent bureaucracy and full-time leadership
Position in party	Usually subordinate to party in government	Generally some influence over party in government

and even as participants in year-round activities. The party organization therefore has a continuous responsibility to its membership, often providing such nonpolitical benefits as insurance and leisure-time activities. In a mass membership party, the three sectors are drawn together, with the party organization often occupying a central, dominant position. What we think of as the party in the electorate becomes an integral, even guiding, part of the party organization, with the right to pick officers and to vote on policy questions. Because of its great power in the selection of candidates—no primary elections limit it—this organization of the mass membership party exerts far greater control over the party in government. In short, the mass membership party resembles a continuous, participatory organization; the cadre party, on the other hand, is far more a momentary, pragmatic coalition of interests and people brought together in a temporary way to win elections (see Table II.1).[1]

Thus, American party organizations are what they are because American political parties are what they are. The American cadre-style party organization expresses the organizational needs of parties that are preoccupied—indeed, obsessed—with contesting elections. It reflects the organizational needs of parties that must appeal to majorities rather than to 10, 20, or 30 percent of the electorate. It reflects the needs of parties that traditionally have not been concerned with ideology, with vast political

[1]Maurice Duverger, in *Political Parties* (New York: Wiley, 1954), inaugurated the distinction between cadre and mass membership parties. (A third edition of the volume was published in New York by Barnes and Noble in 1969.) For an expansion of that analysis and an excellent comparison of the American parties with those of other Western democracies, see Leon D. Epstein, *Political Parties in Western Democracies* (New Brunswick, N.J.: Transaction, 1979).

causes, or even with taking specific stands on political issues. Finally, it reflects a political system in which the electorate is already organized by a wealth of interest groups and other nonparty political organizations. The party organization of the American parties does *not* reflect the politics of a multiparty system, the politics of a deeply ideological political system, or a political system in which the parties have monopolized the organization of political interests.

There is an insubstantial and even unimpressive quality to party organization in the American parties. Perhaps this is the reason the early, classic studies of party organization were written in Western Europe rather than in the United States.[2] The American party organizations are nonetheless there, however, and they command our attention. Despite their comparative weakness and episodic failures, they are at the very center of the political parties. More than any other sector, they control the parties' lives, their names, and their symbols. Any study of the American political parties slights them at great peril.

[2]The major examples are the Duverger book cited in the preceding footnote; Robert Michels, *Political Parties* (Glencoe, Ill.: Free Press, 1949, but first published in 1915); and Moisei Ostrogorski, *Democracy and the Organization of Political Parties*, first published in 1902 and now available in an edition of two volumes, edited and abridged by Seymour Martin Lipset (New York: Anchor, 1964).

3

THE PARTY ORGANIZATION:
STATE AND LOCAL

The semantics of American politics often reflect its most tenacious myths. The entire popular vocabulary of party organization suggests almost menacing strength. "Machines" headed by "bosses" keep the local "captains" toeing a "party line." Their power or strength has become, in a lately fashionable idiom, their "clout." Yet even the most cursory experience with American party organization suggests that all the puffery hides a vastly less imposing reality.

In many ways, the myth of monolithic party organization—and its related vocabulary—is itself a part of the greater American fear of politics and politicians. In what has become virtually a conspiratorial theory of American politics, the party organization or "machine" is the prime conspirator or corrupter in a wider net of political intrigue. The truth about American party organization is therefore difficult for many Americans to accept, for it involves not only a recognition of reality about the parties but also a modification of some dim view of politics in general. Perhaps because they carry no such preconceptions, foreign observers have found it easier to see American party organization as it really is. Recognition of the truth may surprise them, but it forces no major reorientation of political beliefs.

One in a long series of distinguished foreign commentators on the American polity, H. G. Nicholas, cut quickly through the major myth of party organization in the early 1950s:

> Englishmen who have viewed American elections from three thousand miles across the Atlantic have generally been impressed by the elaborateness of the organizations involved as well as by the magnitude and professionalism of it all. The very language of American politics suggests a planned, powerful, smooth-running and disciplined instrument. Surely, these Englishmen have decided, an American party is the counterpart in

the field of politics of the corporation in the field of American business—
a great, synthetic, efficient, productive mechanism, smoothly controlled
from above and ordering the movement of millions below.

I have discovered in the last few weeks that such an image quickly
vanishes when confronted with reality. Even a cursory inspection of the
American political scene at election time reveals a wholly different condition of affairs. Far from order, there is a rich and riotous confusion;
in place of impersonal "machines," there is every kind of spontaneous
organism. The disciplined ward heelers turn out to be an unseemly
scramble of enthusiastic volunteers; the symmetrical pyramid we have
heard about—from precinct to ward to county to state to nation—is an
untidy cairn composed of stones of every conceivable size, with mortar
either inadequate or nonexistent, and with an apex whose location shifts
according to wherever you happen to be standing at the moment. . . .

The American party organization is a phoenix, burning itself out
after each election, soaring with a new (or at least a rewelded) pair of
wings after each primary. The effort this must involve for all concerned
is something that appalls the visitor; the energy that is given to it excites
his admiration; the complexities that result therefrom befuddle his poor
comprehension.[1]

So it is that things are seldom what they seem in American party organization. Our main problem may be that we are always shifting among
three levels of reality: the party organizations as they are stipulated in state
legislation, the party organizations as they are in real life, and the party
organizations as large numbers of Americans imagine them to be. Neither
the pages of statute books nor the fears of many Americans accurately
mirror the reality of party organization.

THE FORMS AND OUTLINES OF ORGANIZATION

The constitutions and statutes of the fifty states bulge with detailed prescriptions defining the nature of party organizations and the duties they
are to perform. The states have, in fact, enacted such a kaleidoscopic variety of legislation on the parties that it defies summary or classification.
In scope and extent, the laws range from those of Oregon, which specify
party structure in detailed and full-blown provisions of more than 5,000
words, to those of some other states, which dispose of the parties in a few
sentences or paragraphs. In between are all grades and degrees of statutory
specificity—laws that permit the parties to determine the composition of
the state central committee and those that not only spell out committee
composition but set the dates and places of its meetings, those that require

[1]H. G. Nicholas, "A Briton Considers Our Bewildering Party Apparatus," *The Reporter*, November 25, 1952, pp. 28–29.

legislative district organization and those that don't, those that leave the running of the parties to the parties and those that even set the agendas of their periodic meetings.

Despite the variety of state approaches, however, the cardinal fact remains that the definition and regulation of political party organization in the United States have been left largely to the states. The United States Constitution makes no mention of parties; it does not have even an oblique reference to them in its elegant paragraphs. Nor has the Congress attempted very often to define or regulate them. Only in the 1970s legislation on campaign finance is there a substantial body of national legislation that affects the parties. For the rest, it has remained to the states to do as they wished.

This mass of state legislation on the parties covers an extensive range of subjects. Virtually every state has attempted to define the ways in which parties and their candidates are admitted to the ballot. They usually set vote minima—a few percent of the vote cast in the last gubernatorial election, perhaps—or, alternatively, they prescribe the number of signatures required on petitions for access to the ballot. Virtually all states assign specific tasks to the parties: the replacement of candidates who die during the campaign or the selection of presidential electors, for instance. Yet, in many ways, the most important statutory provisions are those that outline the organizational form the parties must assume and the procedures they must observe as they organize or reorganize.

The party organizations created by the states have one dominant characteristic in common: they match the voting districts and at least some of the constituencies of the state. They form great step pyramids of the myriad, overlapping constituencies of a democracy committed to the election of vast numbers of officeholders (Figure 3.1). At the bottom, they are usually built on the smallest voting districts of the state. The basic functionary in the party organization is the local committeeperson, representing a ward, a precinct, or a township.[2] Then, in a confusion of layers, the ward and city committees, county committees, and sometimes even state legislative and congressional districts are piled on top of each other.[3] At the apex of the pyramid there is invariably a state committee, usually called a state central committee in the idiom of these statutes. The degree to which this entire structure is actually specified by the statutes differs from state to state. State statutes generally ordain the county and the state com-

---

[2]Terminology for local party officials is in transition. A majority of party organizations seem to have replaced "committeeman" and "committeewoman" with "committeeperson." Most state statutes, however, hold to the former usages.

[3]Within the same state, the various intermediate committees may cover geographical areas of varying sizes and thus may occupy different positions in the organizational pyramid. Congressional districts, for example, may be smaller than a city or larger than a county, depending on the density of population.

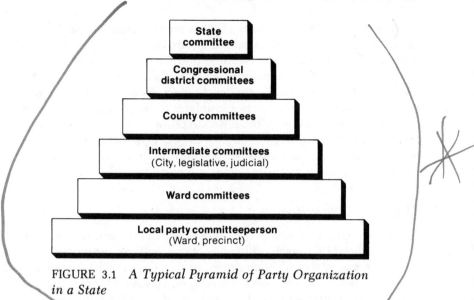

FIGURE 3.1   *A Typical Pyramid of Party Organization in a State*

mittees; some then mandate the other levels, whereas others leave the full articulation of the organizational hierarchy to the parties themselves.

The Elected Committeeperson

Usually, the local committeeperson (or captain or chairperson) is chosen from the precinct, the smallest voting district in the states. Occasionally, he or she is selected from the ward (especially in larger cities) or from the township (in rural areas). Since there are more than 100,000 precincts in the United States, a fully staffed, two-party system would assume the participation of at least some 200,000 men and women. In truth, of course, many of the local committee positions are either vacant or only nominally occupied.

The local committeepersons generally are selected in one of three ways. Most are chosen at local party caucuses or in the primary elections of the party, but in a few instances, higher party authorities appoint them. In states that choose them in the primaries, any voter may place his or her name in nomination for the party position with a petition signed by a handful of local voters. If, as often happens, there are no nominees, the committeeperson may be elected by an even smaller handful of write-in votes. In other states, the statutes direct or permit the party to hold local caucuses in the wards and precincts to which any voters of the area who declare themselves attached to the party's principles may come. These party loyalists then elect the committeepersons in the caucuses; they also generally elect delegates to county and/or state conventions.

The duties of the local party officials are not often fully spelled out in the statutes. In areas where local parties are active, the officials naturally develop organizational responsibilities that the statutes never mention. In the past, the fabled local committeemen or "ward heelers" of the American political machine knew the local voters, catered to their needs and problems, introduced the party candidates to them, and propagandized the parties' issues—all with the ultimate purpose of turning out a bloc of votes for the party on election day. In the less active local parties that are common today, the committeepersons may do little more than occasionally attend meetings and campaign for a party candidate or two.

The Local Committees

A welter of party committees rises above the local committeepersons. Collectively, they often make up the city, town, village, legislative, county, and congressional district committees, or they elect the delegates who do. In a few cases, however, these committees, or some of them, are chosen at county conventions or by the party's candidates for public office. Regardless of this profusion of committees and the various mechanics of their formation, the chief committee is generally the county committee, although in some states the congressional district committees assume a comparable importance.

The dominance of the county committee in most parts of the country is not difficult to explain. The county as a political division elects not one but a considerable number of public officials, and those officials often control the one major remaining source of political patronage—the county courthouse. Furthermore, many other constituencies—such as congressional districts, state legislative districts, and judicial districts—are defined largely in terms of counties. Then, too, in much of America, life and trade are drawn to the local county seat from the surrounding area. Finally, the statutes of most states reinforce the key position of the county committees. Often their members form other parallel committees, and often, too, they send their chairpersons or delegates to form the state central committee.

In some metropolitan areas, however, the local party structure is more complex and more diverse. In the Bronx, for example, the Democratic county committee is composed of some 3,750 local committeepersons. All of them, in each state legislative district (for the state assembly), elect district leaders, who in turn elect the county leaders. Typically, the Democrats of neighboring Brooklyn and Queens have somewhat different organizational structures. In other metropolitan centers, the city committees of the large central city assume an unusual importance.

Many states, however, do more than create the bare bones of a party structure. They also regulate the party's activities and its internal processes. Something of the detailed nature of such regulation may be seen in

Minnesota's strictures on the operation of its ward and precinct party caucuses. Its statutes specify very precisely:

— The full details of the public announcement of the caucus, which must be made at least twenty days in advance.
— The minimum length of the caucus (one hour).
— The length of time during which the caucus must receive nominations (one-half hour).
— The procedures for challenging the presence of any of the participants.
— The use of the secret ballot in all caucus elections.
— The use of *Robert's Rules of Order* (revised edition) in the caucus deliberations.

Other states spell out equally detailed standards for party operation. They may require that local committees meet within thirty or forty-five days after the primary elections, that they notify the secretary of state or the county clerk of the election of officers within a set time, that they not permit the voting of proxies, that they observe a fixed order of business at their meetings, or that they hold their conventions in certain types of public buildings. Again, the variety of rules is endless, but the point is clear: under the laws of the states, the political parties are not, in the usual sense, merely private organizations.

The State Central Committees

The state central committees of the fifty states are created in almost as many ways as human ingenuity can devise. In some states, the lawmakers have left the composition to the decision of the parties, but in most they have decided the matter themselves. Basically, the differences center on two points: the lower party unit from which the state committee members are chosen and the ways in which they are chosen. The unit represented may be the county, the congressional district, the state legislative district, the state convention, cities, or a mixture of these. The methods of choice include election in the party's primaries, election by a lower committee, ex officio representation, or selection by a party convention. The possible number of combinations of the two factors is enormous, and the states use most of them. (See, for example, the state committees outlined in the box.)

The activities of these state committees often are set down in almost painful detail. California statutes, for example, provide that the chairman of the state central committee shall serve a two-year term, that he cannot succeed himself, and that the office must be held alternatively by residents of the northern and southern halves of the state. It is common to assign the committees responsibility for calling and organizing party conventions, for drafting party platforms, for supervising the spending of party

The Composition of Six
State Central Committees

Illinois: One representative from each congressional district, chosen in the primary election.

South Carolina: One representative per county, chosen at a county convention, plus the state chairman and vice-chairman, chosen at the state convention.

California: Although the two major parties differ in the composition of state central committees, the committee is generally composed of delegates to the party's state convention, party candidates and public officials, state party representatives to the national committee, the chairperson of each county committee, and many additional members appointed by county chairpersons, party candidates and public officials, and state convention delegates.

Oregon: At least two members from each county, with additional members from counties for each 15,000 registered voters affiliated with the party.

New York: Two representatives elected in the primary from each state assembly district.

Wisconsin: At least two members from each congressional district, chosen by the state convention.

---

campaign funds, and for selecting the party's presidential electors, representatives to the national committee, and national convention delegates and alternates. Regarding the main business of running a party organization and supporting candidates in the primaries and general elections, state statutes are generally silent, except to say, occasionally, that the parties may make whatever rules are necessary for the conduct of party business. Some, however, do forbid or permit the committees to endorse candidates in the primary. State committees in New York may even designate the party candidates for governor, subject to challenge in the primary.

A number of states assign to statewide conventions many of the powers and responsibilities that other states leave to the state central committees. They may ordain that the state convention write the platform, select the national committeepersons from the state, nominate presidential electors, and choose delegates and alternates to the party's national convention. Indeed, some states provide that the state convention select the state committee itself. Furthermore, in a small number of states, the state conven-

tion of the party actually nominates candidates for some statewide offices—
a reminder of the power of conventions in the days before the direct
primary.[4]

Such, then, are the formal organizational structures created for the
parties in the states. Three general observations about them are in order.
First, state legislators view the parties almost exclusively as electoral organizations. The organizational layers relate to voting districts and to the
constituencies in which public officials are chosen, and the duties assigned
to them are almost exclusively concerned with the contesting of elections.
The political party organization—as seen in the statute books of the
states—is clearly an auxiliary to the state's regulation of nominations and
elections. Indeed, the dominant concern in its creation too often seems to
be its usefulness in helping the state administer the electoral processes,
rather than its viability as a healthy, ongoing party organization.

Second, it is clear from the statutes that state legislators have also
viewed the parties as skeletal organizations—as cadre parties—run by a
small number of party officials. There is little evidence that they have
entertained the possibility of membership parties, or even of parties that
attract the concerns and labors of many activists. Indeed, they assume the
contrary. By opening the election of local committeepersons (and of other
party officials) to the electorate in the primary election, they have defined
the parties' voters as a quasi-membership group. By legislative fiat, they
have tried to democratize the parties, to open them to the ultimate participation and authority of all voters. Thus, the party that results is not a
private association whose participating members choose its leaders and
chart its affairs; it is the semipublic, easily permeable hybrid of which we
have already spoken.

Finally, although the formal organization of the parties appears to be
hierarchical, it is not. The state party hierarchies have more aptly been
described by V. O. Key as "a system of layers of organization."[5] In some
states, for example, the state central committee's members are chosen directly by the voters; the committee, therefore, does not grow out of the
committees below it. Even when the linkage between the layers of organization is direct, the links move from bottom to top. Such a system would
hardly appear to be ideally designed to produce the centralization of power
at the apex that the very concept of hierarchy presumes. The authority of

---

[4]No genuinely comprehensive summary of state statutory provisions on party organization seems to be available. The provisions of the laws of any state can be found easily in
the state's codified statutes; the material on party organization is usually located under the
general heading "elections." For some summarization, see *State Party Structures and Pro-*
cedures: A State by State Compendium (New York: National Municipal League, 1967,
mimeographed).

[5]V. O. Key, *Politics, Parties and Pressure Groups*, 5th ed. (New York: Crowell, 1964),
p. 316.

upper levels over the lower levels is anything but secure. Basically, the party organization is a system of party committees close to and growing from the political grass roots. The result is to build into the party organization a great deal of localism and decentralization.

THE SUBSTANCE AND REALITIES OF PARTY ORGANIZATION

These elaborate statutory parties, with their many layers of committees and their armies of committeepersons, conform to the mental images most Americans have of the party organizations. They are the machines, the organizations, the bosses, the ward heelers, and the party cabals of which the great party juggernauts are said to be made. Where statutes and public expectations see active legions of committeepersons and layer on layer of impressive organization, however, there is often only sporadic activity and undermotivated party workers. Sometimes, too, there is organization and activity quite unimagined by the lawmakers of the state. In short, one often cannot accept at face value the picture of party organization in the volumes of state statutes.

Local Party Organization

Vigorous and disciplined party organization of the sort the statutes envision does exist at the local level, and the best example is the classic urban political machine. Its heyday was the turn of the twentieth century, and its promised land was the burgeoning American city. Its annals are replete with the colorful histories of Tammany Hall in New York, the knaveries of the Pendergasts in Kansas City and Frank ("I am the law") Hague in Jersey City, the cheeky threats of Chicago's "Big Bill" Thompson to punch the King of England on the nose, and the genial rascality (and mail fraud conviction) of Mayor James Curley of Boston.[6] In the last twenty years, however, urban machines have met a series of stunning defeats. The first was the triumph of Mayor Robert Wagner over the organization Democrats in New York in 1961, and the most recent was the victory of Mayor Jane Byrne over the Chicago Democratic machine's candidate to succeed Richard Daley in the 1979 primary and her subsequent loss to Harold Washington in the 1983 primary. Between those times, all manner of problems beset other urban machines. Some, such as the one in Pittsburgh, were upset by middle-class reformers; others, such as the one in Phila-

---

[6]The antics of Mayor Curley were in fact immortalized—and somewhat romanticized—in the novel by Edwin O'Connor (and its movie version), *The Last Hurrah* (Boston: Little, Brown, 1956).

delphia, were replaced by more effective practitioners of the old ethnic politics of the cities.

The recent history of the Daley organization in Chicago tells one a good deal about the present and future of the urban machine. Bolstered by control over some 35,000 patronage jobs and access to another 10,000 in the private economy, the Cook County Democratic organization and Mayor Richard Daley controlled nominations and elections and the making of public policy in the city. The key was in turning out a disciplined vote that would support the choices of the machine; conventional wisdom had it that the organization could deliver 350,000 disciplined voters, the vast majority of whom were the holders of party patronage and their families, friends, and relatives. The machine gradually lost control of that vote, however. The decline may have started with the violence surrounding the Democratic national convention in 1968 and the unflattering publicity it brought the mayor and his colleagues. Certainly, too, the machine suffered important defections, and its image was tarnished by convictions for corruption. Probably most important, however, it failed after Mayor Daley's death to sustain the level of city services. A series of electoral defeats that had begun while Daley was alive culminated after his death in the upset victory of Byrne over Michael Bilandic, chosen by the machine as Daley's successor.

Irritation over the failure of the city to remove the winter's heavy snows and to maintain other city services led, in part, to the undoing of the Chicago machine, but an assortment of accumulated grievances also contributed. The vote for Byrne was especially heavy in the black wards— a sign of the many tensions between the machine and the racial minorities in the city. Young voters also appear to have rejected the organization in large numbers. Thus, in a primary with an unusually large turnout—almost 60 percent in an off-year primary election—the machine could not turn out a vote of sufficient size for its somewhat colorless candidate. So far, Chicago's experience squares with the experiences of other city organizations. (Some of the Democratic county organizations in New York City have recently lost as many primaries as they have won.) What was different in Chicago was that Mayor Byrne at no time rejected the Democratic organization and its modus operandi. She committed herself, in fact, to lead the machine and revitalize it. That she failed became clear when she lost the Democratic primary for her own reelection to Harold Washington, a black congressman, in early 1983.[7]

Urban machines such as Chicago's depend fundamentally on the dis-

----

[7]For three pictures of the Daley-Chicago organization, see Mike Royko, *Boss: Richard J. Daley of Chicago* (New York: Signet, 1971); Milton Rakove, *Don't Make No Waves, Don't Back No Losers* (Bloomington: Indiana University Press, 1975); and Eugene Kennedy, *Himself: The Life and Times of Mayor Richard C. Daley* (New York: Viking, 1978).

tribution of patronage jobs. These appointments win the indispensable loyalty and service of the workers in the machine itself. Their efforts, in turn, produce the party vote—their own votes and those of their friends, family, and neighbors. Local party workers also win voter loyalties by coping with the problems of their constituencies (see box). Often, those problems are personal—unemployment or a delinquent child—as well as public or governmental. The machine and its workers earn political gratitude by finding social welfare agencies for the troubled, jobs for the jobless, contracts for local merchants, or even the storied Christmas baskets or deliveries of coal for the needy. Thus, the classic urban machine has always been part electoral organization, part "informal government," part social service agency, and part ladder for upward social and economic mobility. To an uncanny degree, it resembles the local organization of a European mass membership party, but there are differences, of course. The American machine has no membership base, and it has few, if any,

---

Urban Shepherd, Machine Style

In his book on Mayor Richard Daley and the Chicago machine, Milton Rakove reports at length on an evening spent with Alderman Vito Marzullo of Chicago's 25th Ward as he ministered to his flock:

> Marzullo's precinct captains were assembled in the rear room. After State Senator Sam Romano called the roll of the forty-eight precincts in the 25th Ward, Marzullo took the podium to remind the captains to maintain their efforts. "No man walks alone. Mingle with the people. Learn their way of life. Work and give service to your people."
>
> After the meeting with the captains, Marzullo moved to the front office to greet his constituents. A precinct captain ushered in a black husband and wife. "We got a letter here from the city," the man said. "They want to charge us twenty dollars for rodent control in our building." "Give me the letter. I'll look into it," Marzullo replied. The captain spoke up. "Your daughter didn't vote on November fifth. Look into it. The alderman is running again in February. Any help we can get, we can use." "I'm looking for a job," the woman said. "I don't have anything right now," said the alderman.
>
> The telephone rang. Marzullo listened and said, "Come to my office tomorrow morning." He hung up. "She's a widow for thirteen years. She wants to put her property in joint tenancy with her daughter. The lawyer wants a hundred dollars. I'll have to find someone to do it for nothing."

ideological concerns. Its focus on the immediate needs of its constituents has driven it to look almost completely inward and to ignore the issues and ideologies of the political world beyond. It is provincially concerned with the city, and its politics are almost completely divorced from the issues that agitate our national politics.[8]

Yet the machines of the big cities have never been and are not now typical of party organization in the United States. The other extreme— essentially unrepresented in the scholarly or popular literature because it

[8]The literature on the American urban machine is staggering in its size. Among the best pieces are Edward Banfield and James Q. Wilson, *City Politics* (Cambridge, Mass.: Harvard University Press, 1963); Harold Gosnell, *Machine Politics: Chicago Model* (Chicago: University of Chicago Press, 1939); Raymond E. Wolfinger, "Why Political Machines Have Not Withered Away and Other Revisionist Thoughts," *Journal of Politics* 34 (1972): 365–98; and John A. Gardiner and David J. Olson, *Theft of the City* (Bloomington: Indiana University Press, 1974).

"Some of those liberal independents in the city council, they couldn't get a dog out of a dog pound with a ten-dollar bill," Marzullo snorted. "Who's next?"

* * *

"On election day, every captain gets $50 to $200 for expenses in the precinct," Marzullo explained. . . . "We make contributions to all of our candidates and pay assessments for people running from our ward. When the mayor runs we carry the ward for him by at least five to one. He's a great family man. A great religious person. We've been together all the way. I got six married children. He came to every one of their weddings. He invited me to the weddings of every one of his kids. You don't go back on people like that."

* * *

In middle-class wards on the northwest and southwest sides of the city, precinct captains can help get tax bills appealed, curbs and gutters repaired, scholarships for students to the University of Illinois, summer jobs for college students, and directions and assistance to those who need some help in finding their way through the maze of government bureaucracy with a grievance.

Milton Rakove, *Don't Make No Waves,*
Don't Back No Losers
(Bloomington: Indiana University Press, 1975),
pp. 120, 121, 122.

---

offers so little to study—is virtual disorganization. In such cases, most of the committee positions in the party's county unit are unfilled or are held by completely inactive incumbents. A chairman and a handful of loyal party officials may meet occasionally to carry out the most essential affairs of the party. Their main activity occurs shortly before the primary elections, as they plead with members of the party to become candidates or offer themselves as candidates in order to "fill the party ticket." They are largely without influence or following, for theirs is often a chronic minority party. They meet infrequently, raise little money for election campaigns, and create little or no public attention. The extent of such organizational weakness is difficult to estimate, although it is surprisingly common in much of rural America.

Most American local party organization lies between these two extremes, but "between" encompasses a great organizational distance. It might be most accurate to say that the average local party comes closer to the pole of disorganization than to the pole of maximum organization. Often, the incentives with which to staff and maintain the most active party organization are simply not present, or the political culture of the locale does not recognize the propriety of the politics of reward and sanction on which a machine organization rests. Above all, the necessary numbers of voters may not be involved in politics, may not see the importance of a vital party organization and their role in it. Even in a state such as Minnesota—recognized widely for its open and participant politics—the party caucuses in the 1980 presidential year attracted only about 7 percent (about 140,000 people) of the citizens who voted in the subsequent elections.[9]

Although it is not easy to locate the "average" city or county organization, it probably has most of these characteristics:

1. An active chairman and executive committee, plus a few associated activists, who in effect make most of the decisions in the name of the party, who raise funds, who seek out and screen candidates (or approve the candidates who select themselves), and who speak locally for the party.

2. A ward and precinct organization in which only a few local committeepersons are active and in which there is little door-to-door canvassing or other direct voter contact.

3. Active participation in organizational matters by some of the party's elected public officials, who may share effective control of the organization with its official leadership.

---

[9]The figure is less than 5 percent if one uses as a base all adults aged eighteen years or over living in the state.

A distinctly periodic calendar of activities, marked by watchful waiting or general inactivity at other than election times.

Here one does not find the serried ranks of party foot soldiers. The leadership operates not with threats and iron discipline, but with pleading and cajoling. Few incentives and rewards remain with which to recruit all the effort and manpower the statutory structures seem to assume.

Such a sketch of the "average" local party organization cannot, of course, begin to suggest the many forms that local parties take in the United States. It takes no account, for instance, of the oligarchic rural or small-town machines, in which a few local notables (who may or may not hold party or public office) dominate a political organization with a combination of patronage, local prestige and status, friendship, kinship, and private economic power. (It is one of the most durable—and least supportable—myths of American politics that political muscle, or even corruption, is always urban.)

A sketch of the "average" organization also takes no account of urban party organizations that operate at a level of considerable effectiveness, albeit a level or two below that of the prototypical machine. A study of parties in the Detroit area defined the precinct committeeperson's three "critical" tasks to be the registration of new voters, the canvassing (by phone or personal visits) of those who are already registered, and the roundup of voters on election day. Only 17 percent of the Democratic precinct leaders and 25 percent of the Republican leaders performed all three tasks, but another 38 percent of the Democrats and 22 percent of the Republicans carried out two of the three.[10]

State Party Organization

For much of the period since World War II, the state party organizations have been buffeted on all sides. Changes in presidential politics have diminished their roles in the national conventions that choose presidential candidates. Delegates to those conventions increasingly are chosen by the voters and are pledged to a seeker after the nomination; fewer and fewer of them are selected from or by the state party organizations. Many of the state parties that enjoyed the use of state patronage jobs have lost control of them. Above all, they have lost some of their ability to control state nomination and election campaigns. Candidates find it increasingly easy

[10]Samuel J. Eldersveld, *Political Parties: A Behavioral Analysis* (Chicago: Rand McNally, 1964), pp. 349–50. David Olson made one of the few systematic attempts at categorizing county party organizations in "Toward a Typology of County Party Organizations," *Southwestern Social Service Quarterly* 48 (1968): 558–72.

to win nominations in primary elections without party organization support; they find it easier than ever to raise money for their own campaigns and thus run them without party help. The new importance of the media in politics and the rise of a new breed of campaign experts offer the candidates new ways of reaching voters that have little or nothing to do with the parties.

It is somewhat surprising, therefore, that a large national study of party organization in the United States found that the state parties not only are alive but in some respects are healthier than they were 20 years ago (Table 3.1).[11]At the least, they now are more likely to maintain a well-staffed, permanently housed party organization than they were a generation ago—but staff and organization for what purpose, for what role or activities of the state parties? The authors of the study think it likely that "the stronger, more virile state parties will be able to use their organizational resources to provide campaign services to state and local candidates (particularly those running for the state legislatures) while supplementing the role of candidate organizations geared to congressional, senatorial, gubernatorial, and presidential elections."[12] The revivified state parties are already moving in that direction. Ninety percent of them, for example, run campaigning seminars for party candidates, and a great majority of them now have mobilization programs through which to identify and turn out their party's likely voters. The state parties, it thus appears, have at last allied themselves with the new campaign skills to recapture a role in the election campaigns. It is in the best American tradition of "joining 'em if you can't beat 'em."

Most of this activity takes place, of course, not in the unwieldy state central committees, but in the bureaucracies they create. We are therefore seeing the first real signs of the "bureaucratization" of the parties—their dominance, or at least the dominance of their activity, by full-time, paid, professional staffs. These party bureaucrats cannot easily exert much influence over the party in government; nor do they exert much control over local party units in the state. Theirs is a service organization that brings useful skills and information to party candidates in the election campaigns. Their services will certainly win the appreciation and gratitude of the candidates, which leads one to wonder about the ultimate uses of state party organization strength—can the state parties convert the obligation of their successful candidates to support for party positions or programs?

---

[11]The materials in Table 3.1 and in the text here come from two of the first reports from that study. See Robert J. Huckshorn and John F. Bibby, "State Parties in an Era of Political Change," in Joel L. Fleishman (ed.), *The Future of American Political Parties* (Englewood Cliffs, N.J.: Prentice-Hall, 1982), pp. 70–100; and James L. Gibson, Cornelius P. Cotter, John F. Bibby, and Robert J. Huckshorn, "Assessing Institutional Party Strength," paper presented at the annual meeting of the Midwest Political Science Association, Cincinnati, 1981.

[12]Huckshorn and Bibby, "State Parties," p. 99.

TABLE 3.1 *Comparison of State Party Organizations:
Early 1960s and 1979*

Organizational Feature	Percentage of Democratic and Republican State Parties that Have Each Feature	
	Early 1960s	1979
Permanent state headquarters	50	91
Full-time chairman or director	63	95
Voter mobilization programs	39	70
Policy of primary endorsements	14	39

Sources Data from Robert J. Huckshorn and John F. Bibby, "State Parties in an Era of Political Change," in Joel L. Fleishman (ed.), *The Future of American Political Parties* (Englewood Cliffs, N.J.: Prentice-Hall, 1982), pp. 70–100; and James L. Gibson, Cornelius P. Cotter, John F. Bibby, and Robert J. Huckshorn, "Assessing Institutional Party Strength," paper presented at the annual meeting of the Midwest Political Science Association, Cincinnati, 1981.

Extralegal Organizations

At various times, the two major parties in various parts of the country have tried to approach a mode of organization closer to the ideological, mass membership parties of Europe. Obviously, the statutory parties of the states—the quintessential cadre parties—were not appropriate for that purpose. The alternative was exactly that—an alternative form of party organization that was developed and maintained apart from the organizational apparatus set up by the laws of the states.

In Wisconsin, for example, extralegal parties succeeded for a time in functioning as the de facto parties of the state. The conservative wing of the Wisconsin Republicans, repeatedly losers to the La Follette progressive wing in the primaries, formed the first extralegal organization in the 1920s to support its candidates in the GOP primary. When the Progressives left the Republican cover in the 1930s and formed their own party, the "regular" Republicans found it easier to operate through their informal party organization than through the heavily regulated statutory organization. The Democrats, casting about for a more effective party organization, followed suit in the 1940s and 1950s. Both parties operated through these duplicating voluntary organizations until 1974, maintaining a separate and docile statutory organization to perform the mandated statutory duties. In 1974, the Wisconsin legislature brought developments full circle by

abolishing the statutory committees and vesting in the voluntary committees the functions that state statutes require.[13]

In states such as New York and California, the extralegal parties have
never fully replaced the statutory parties. Democratic reform clubs were
originally formed in New York City to break the power of Tammany Hall.
They draw on educated, middle-class activists committed to liberal issues
to replace the traditional cadre parties—and their "bosses" and patronage—with a membership organization. As recently as 1980, the New
Democratic Coalition still included approximately 70 such reform clubs
in the city. The city's popular Democratic mayor, Edward Koch, began
his political career in the club movement. California has a history of such
membership organizations going back to the 1930s, when liberal Republicans founded the California Republican Assembly (CRA) to revive a
faltering Republican party. A conservative competitor, the United
Republicans of California, sprang up in the early 1960s to oppose the liberals of the CRA, but conservatives captured the CRA just a short time
later. In 1965, the liberal Republicans repaired to a new set of organizations, the California Republican League. On the Democratic side, the
older of the organizations, the liberal California Democratic Clubs, was
founded in 1953 with the remnants of the 1952 Stevenson supporters. In
both parties, these clubs feature some separate local organizations, a hard
core of dues-paying members, and a series of tumultuous conventions at
which the clubs' ideologists endorse candidates for support at their party's
primary. Their impact now appears to have run its course, however, and
by the early 1980s they no longer claim either substantial membership or
influence in the California parties.[14]

The development of these extralegal organizations speaks volumes
about the failure of the usual statutory organizations to accommodate the
new style of organization. The statutory organizations had little room for
the new emphasis on ideology, on avocational leadership, and on greater
participation by dues-paying members. Furthermore, the extralegal organizations reflect the problems statutory party organizations have in controlling their parties' primary elections. In Wisconsin, the old statutory
party conventions were required to convene *after* the primary; in California, the statutory party organizations are forbidden to make endorsements in the primary.

[13]For an account of the Wisconsin voluntary organizations in their flower, see Leon D.
Epstein, *Politics in Wisconsin* (Madison: University of Wisconsin Press, 1958). By the late
1950s, the two parties' voluntary organizations had enrolled some 20,000 dues-paying
members.

[14]For a brief account of the history of the California clubs (and for overviews of big
state politics generally), see Neal R. Peirce, *The Megastates of America* (New York: Norton,
1972), pp. 584–85. On the reform clubs, see James Q. Wilson, *The Amateur Democrat* (Chicago: University of Chicago Press, 1962).

Like everything else about the American parties, the reasons for the decline of these extralegal party organizations are complex. In some instances (such as Wisconsin) they succeeded in making the statutory forms more hospitable. In others, creative party leadership found that it could graft membership bodies onto existing organizations. Some of the ideologically motivated partisans began to work outside the parties, and others found the struggle on issues to be carried on more usefully through issue caucuses within the parties. (A number of state parties, for example, have acquired feminist caucuses in recent years.) Above all, the mass membership model of the vital and successful party organization has yielded once again to another model—this time that of the professional, bureaucratized service party. The ideological urges of the 1970s have yielded somewhat to a renewal of electoral pragmatism in the parties, and preferences in party organization reflect the trend.

THE LOCUS OF POWER

It remains to ask what, in reality, the locus of power is within these party organizations. Is the hierarchical chain of authority really maintained? Most scholars believe that in most states it is not, that the major locus of organizational authority is the county committee. Many state party organizations are, in fact, federations—and loose ones, at that—of semiautonomous or autonomous local baronies and baronial county chairmen. Writing about the Ohio Democratic party in the early 1960s, one observer noted:

> There was, in fact, no statewide Democratic party in Ohio. The state's Democratic party was an aggregation of city machines which had little or no interest in statewide elections unless the candidate was from their city. Ray Miller, the Cuyahoga County (Cleveland) Democratic boss, explicitly maintained that his organization was an independent entity with neither legal nor moral ties with a state Democratic party.[15]

Added to the fragmentation of this decentralization is the fragmentation of factionalism. Parties divide by regions of the state, by rural-urban differences, along ethnic and religious lines, by loyalty to local leaders, and especially by liberal and conservative preferences. Factionalism affects every state party; differences are only matters of degree and of the nature of the division.[16]

[15]John H. Fenton, *Midwest Politics* (New York: Holt, Rinehart & Winston, 1966), p. 137.

[16]On the classic liberal-conservative factionalism in the Texas Democratic party, see James E. Anderson, Richard W. Murray, and Edward L. Farley, *Texas Politics*, 3rd ed. (New York: Harper & Row, 1979), pp. 61–71.

In their recent study of state parties, Malcolm Jewell and David Olson have erected a typology of state parties, primarily according to the strength and the nature of factions within them. Leaving aside the electorally ineffective parties (the authors call them the "electorally passive" parties), they find that active party organizations fall into three categories: cohesive, bifactional, and multifactional. It is not that the cohesive parties have no factions, but that they are able to unite their partisans despite the factions.[17] To a very great extent, therefore, the cohesive parties are those of centralized power within the state. The bifactional and multifactional parties—regardless of the causes or bases of their factionalisms—inevitably are fragmented and decentralized. That, in turn, means that power and authority within them reside in the most viable of the local levels—the county organization.

Questions of centralization and decentralization or factional structures are important ultimately for what they mean for the operation of the parties. The cohesive and centralized state party organizations have vastly greater power over candidates for statewide office and far greater capacity for enforcing discipline in their parties in the state legislatures. They can control party finances and through them the conduct of election campaigns. The decentralized alternative undermines the possibility of party cohesion in the legislature and prevents the development of statewide issues or campaigns. Instead of a state politics conducted by a state party organization, the individuals of the party in government triumph at the statewide level, and locally there prevails a fragmented politics of local interests and leaders.

To build a powerful state organization is to overcome both the grassroots localism of American politics and the widespread antipathy to strong party discipline. Understandably, it is not easy. Strong and skillful personal leadership by a governor, a senator, or a state chairman helps; so do political resources. Indiana's Democratic party, for example, maintained its strength and its reputation as one of the country's most powerful state organizations by controlling a considerable amount of patronage—estimates vary from 10,000 jobs on up—and by preserving a tradition whereby the grateful patronage holders returned 2 percent of their salaries to the party coffers.[18] It also helps to have a tradition or culture that accepts the notion of a unified and effective party in the state. Similarly, it makes a difference whether or not the state parties are given important political responsibilities. It is no coincidence that central party organization has flourished in the states in which primary elections are least ex-

---

[17]Malcolm E. Jewell and David M. Olson, *American State Political Parties and Elections*, rev. ed. (Homewood, Ill.: Dorsey, 1982), pp. 56–73.

[18]Robert J. McNeill, *Democratic Campaign Financing in Indiana, 1964* (published jointly by the Institute of Public Administration, Indiana University, and Citizens' Research Foundation, 1966).

tensive—states such as Connecticut and Indiana—and in which party organization determines much more directly who the statewide and congressional candidates will be.

TRENDS AND CHANGES

Party organization reflects the political culture and the socioeconomic conditions of the time. No case better illustrates that fact than the decline of the city machine in American politics. Civil service and merit systems have gradually robbed it of the patronage jobs with which it rewarded its workers and officers. The ethnic minorities who supported it in its dominant days have been increasingly integrated into American life. Greater education and literacy have created a political awareness and sophistication that rebels at being led to the polls, sheeplike and docile, in a "delivered" vote. The values of the times demand participatory rights for individuals in all organizations. The growth of the welfare state has provided freely and openly the welfare services that the urban machine "gave" only to its deserving patrons. Also, the growth of national, ideologized politics and national candidates has helped break down the isolated localism and the essentially issueless politics of the machine.

Where something approaching the old-style urban machine persists today, it is in circumstances not unlike those the new immigrant faced in American cities at the turn of the century. The black, Puerto Rican, Indian, and Chicano newcomers to the cities face the same (or more severe) problems of poverty, discrimination, political powerlessness, ethnic isolation, and inability to cope with the life of the city. Many of the older political incentives and organizational styles work in their neighborhoods; but the shift of local party power to the new minorities has not gone smoothly. The older white groups have tried to hold on to positions of party authority in most cities. It is not surprising that the decline of the old machines in a number of cities featured the massive desertion of the vote of minorities. That was certainly the fate of Jane Byrne and the Chicago Democrats. Change and adaptation may be the rule, but party organizations may choose at their peril not to obey it.

Changes in their environments—such as changes in the populations of the cities and in the technology of campaigning—work fundamental changes in the forms of party organization. One need only look at changes in the operating party organizations of the cities and the states. Furthermore, among these environmental influences on the parties, the statutory definitions imposed by the states are only one element—indeed, one of the least flexible and changeable elements. Changes in party organizations, therefore, are much more apt to reflect changes in the nonstatutory part of the environment. For illustration, one need only look to two emerging trends that portend significant changes for state and local organizations: the increasing power of the national committees and the increasing inclination of courts to limit the states' authority over the parties.

Unquestionably, the Democratic and Republican national committees have strengthened their positions over the past decade or two. They have raised more money and have participated in setting more party priorities than ever before. They have recruited more candidates in the states and have enforced more national party rules than they did in earlier times. (The centralization in the parties will be discussed more fully in Chapter 5.) The consequences for the state parties are both clear and unclear. It is clear that the state parties will receive new advice and resources, and perhaps new directives, from the national parties. For the short run, the relationship between state and national parties may fairly be called one of "interdependence."[19] What is not so clear is whether that poise or balance between the two levels will be sustained if the national parties further increase their authority and resources. For the state organizations, the line between interdependence and dependence may well narrow.

Equally momentous changes for party organizations in the states may well come from the courts. No longer is the power of state legislatures over the parties unchallenged. Twice in the past decade, the United States Supreme Court has upheld the power of the national party (i.e., the national committee and convention of the party) against conflicting state law. In both cases, the Court sided with the rules of the national Democratic party on the selection of delegates to its national convention against Illinois and Wisconsin laws that set other procedures for the selection of delegates.[20] Moreover, it based those decisions on the point that "the National Democratic Party and its adherents enjoy a constitutionally protected right of political association."[21] If the rights of the national party are so protected, however, what of the rights of a state party vis-à-vis the legislative power of the state? At least for the moment, the Court seems not inclined to extend the point that far. It has recently held that the laws of the state of Washington do not violate the rights of party adherents in preventing them from altering by party rules what they consider to be the unworkable state committee created by state law. Speaking for the Court, Justice Stevens cited the state's legitimate interest in assuring orderly elections.[22] Lower courts, however, have appeared to be increasingly sympathetic to such suits. A federal district court in Rhode Island has recently invalidated a state statute specifying the size and selection of local party committees.[23]

[19]The word was used by Huckshorn and Bibby, "State Parties."

[20]*Cousins* v. *Wigoda*, 419 U.S. 477 (1975) and *Democratic Party* v. *La Follette*, 450 U.S. 107 (1981). The former is the Illinois case; the latter is the Wisconsin case.

[21]*Cousins* v. *Wigoda*, p. 489.

[22]*Marchiro* v. *Chaney*, 442 U.S. 191 (1979).

[23]*Fahey* v. *Darigan*, 405 F. Supp. 1386 (1975).

In short, the hitherto unquestioned power of the states in creating party organization is no longer unquestioned.

It is not easy to gauge the condition of American party organization. The Center for Political Studies of the University of Michigan reported, for example, that in the 1980 campaign, only 24 percent of American adults had been contacted by someone from one of the parties or from the presidential campaigns.[24] In other words, most of the voting electorate was reached either by other candidates or, if at all, by the mass media. Unquestionably, this revolution in campaigning reflects the diminished importance of party organizations. They are no longer the indispensable instrument for election to office. Candidates may now purchase the information and skills necessary for the campaign from pollsters and from public relations specialists. Several generations ago, they would have had no alternative but to get them from the party organizations.

It is clear, therefore, that the formal, statutory party organizations control or affect less and less of campaign politics. Membership clubs, candidates and their organizations, ambitious individuals, campaign technocrats, donors of political money, issue groups and caucuses, and even some traditional interest groups also work the election campaigns. Many of them ally themselves with a party label and, to some extent, with a party organization. Therefore, state and local party organizations are far looser and more flexible today than the words of the statutes would suggest. The local party organization is now generally a loose aggregation of:

— The statutory organization (or the active parts of it).
— The candidates and their organizations and supporters.
— Related party organizations (the clubs, the caucuses, the factional organizations).
— Active and potentially active individuals (supporters of candidates, issues, and the party itself; would-be candidates and party leaders).
— Allied nonparty organizations (local interest groups, political action committees, ideological associations).

In other words, the party is a flexible and somewhat undisciplined pool of active groups and individuals. They are recruited to the party for different reasons, and they are activated by different candidates, different issues, and different elections. A hotly contested school board election will activate one cluster of partisans, and a congressional election will activate another. What we have thought of as the party organization is really a

[24]The data come from the Center's National Election Study of 1980 and are made available, as are data from all of its national election studies, through the Inter-University Consortium for Political and Social Research.

reservoir of organizations and activists from which are drawn the shifting organizational coalitions that speak and act in the name of the local party.

In searching for change in American party organization, however, one ought not lose sight of what does not change. The American parties remain largely skeletal, cadre organizations, run by small numbers of activists and involving the great masses of their supporters scarcely at all. The shift away from the organizational forms inherent in the statutes of the states has largely been a shift from a well-defined cadre organization to a looser, more amorphous cadre organization. Despite the brave appearance of some membership clubs, the American parties are still a long way from becoming mass membership parties, and they are still some distance from achieving the continuously active, year-round tempos of parties elsewhere in the world. By the standards of those parties, American party organization continues to be characterized by unusual fluidity and evanescence, by failure to generate activity at nonelection times, and by the ease with which a handful of activists and public officeholders dominate it.

4

THE POLITICAL PARTY
OF THE ACTIVISTS

Behind the imposing facades of the statutory party structures are the living, organizational realities of the political parties. The statutes do not reckon with the men and women of the party, their goals and motives, their interactions and relationships, the contributions they make to the organizations, the price they exact for those contributions. Yet the activity and motivations of those men and women are closer to the real world of party politics than all the statutory paragraphs put together.

We may easily accept the bemused cynicism of Will Rogers about the organizational condition of the American parties: "I don't belong to an organized political party, I'm a Democrat." However disorganized the parties may be, however, they *are* purposive, goal-seeking organizations. They are vastly committed to the winning of elections. In addition, they may seek any number of short- and long-run goals: the spread of an ideology, the enactment of a set of public policies, or the easing of regulations that affect their activities.

As an organization, therefore, the major political party is a mechanism for uniting people in the pursuit of goals. It recruits and mobilizes the resources and skills for political action. In the employment of those resources, it works out a division of labor and a hierarchy of authority. Like any other complex organization, it has its leaders and followers, its own specialization of role and function, its own internal system of communication. Also, it is a decision-making apparatus in which choices must be made about the mobilization of resources, the setting of strategies, and the deployment of assets. These internal processes are what the private life of the political party is all about. They are the processes by which the party organization converts the raw materials of people, resources, and expertise into goal-oriented activity.

Goal seeking also goes on within the party organization on a personal, individual level. Individual party leaders, workers, and members are in the party organization for some identifiable, if covert or implicit, set of reasons. In other words, there must be rewards or incentives—"pay-offs" in the broadest sense of the word—for devoting one's time to party activity rather than to the service of the PTA or the improvement of one's golf game.

THE SYSTEM OF INCENTIVES

The American political parties have never operated primarily in a cash economy. They have rarely bought or hired the millions of labor hours they need. Even today, paid staffs are small or nonexistent in most party organizations, and it is a rare local chairman who draws a substantial salary from the party organization. The great number of Americans who are active in the parties receive no cash in return for their considerable time and skills. Even the earthy old custom of paying precinct workers on election day is vanishing. What is it, then, that induces party workers to lavish their hours and efforts on the affairs of the parties? If the parties' payments are not made in cash, in which coin are they made?[1]

Patronage

Patronage—the use of appointive governmental positions to reward past party work and to induce future labors—is hardly unique to the American political parties.[2] Even today, the municipal services of the Italian cities swarm with the partisans in power. Very probably, however, no other party system over its history has relied so systematically on patronage as the American system. The easy confidence of the Jacksonians that no public task was so complex that it demanded experience, and their matching conviction that "to the victors go the spoils," set the ethic early in the nineteenth century. From then to the present, a vast array of public job-holders—from elevator operators and charwomen in city halls to American ambassadors in foreign capitals—have owed their appointments to political worthiness and the right political sponsorship.

Despite the explosive growth of government bureaucracy in this century, the amount of patronage available to the parties has declined pre-

---

[1] For a somewhat different categorization of incentives, see James Q. Wilson, *Political Organizations* (New York: Basic Books, 1974).

[2] The concept of patronage here is one of appointment to governmental jobs on the basis of political criteria. Other studies use broader definitions that include at least the two categories of patronage and preferment used here. Martin and Susan Tolchin, for example, in *To the Victor* . . . (New York: Random House, 1971), work with a definition of patronage that includes "the allocation of the discretionary favors of government in exchange for political support" (p. 5).

cipitously. The expansion of civil service and merit systems has been the chief reason. What was once a flourishing federal patronage (historians write of the hordes of ill-mannered job seekers overrunning presidential inaugurations) has by now dwindled to well below 1 percent of the federal establishment. There still remain the United States marshals and attorneys, the collectors of customs, and the rural mail carriers, to mention a few of the classic federal patronage posts, but theirs is a shrinking roster.

Similar declines have come, albeit more slowly, to the states and localities. Any number of states, counties, and cities—the great majority, probably—have virtually abolished patronage, moving to merit systems of some sort. In recent years, even some of the vaunted centers of patronage have seen the merit principle making new and severe inroads. Kentucky legislation in 1960 reduced the number of year-round jobs available for patronage from 16,000 to 4000, about 75 percent of them on the highway maintenance crews.[3] Pennsylvania, which had almost 50,000 patronage positions as late as 1970, lost a sizable number in collective bargaining. In 1971, some 17,500 workers, most of them also with the highway crews, negotiated a contract in which the state agreed not to discriminate against any employee on the basis of political affiliations. The contract also forbids the state to require workers to make political contributions or to engage in political activity. Furthermore, in 1976 the United States Supreme Court held that patronage dismissals violated the Constitution of the United States. A majority of the justices thought that the dismissal of an otherwise satisfactory employee for political reasons—especially those having to do with a change in parties in power—violated the employee's freedoms of political belief and association.[4] Thus, where patronage survives, it does so under increasingly restricted conditions (see box).

The increasing unavailability of patronage, however, is only a part of the parties' problem. There are administrative problems as well. A survey of county chairpersons in Ohio found that they achieve only a partial return in party work or contributions from their patronage appointees.[5] The problems the parties encounter in using the available patronage jobs are legion. Patronage seekers may not meet the skill requirements of the job; heavy-equipment operators are hard enough to find without adding a set of political credentials. Also, the politics of patronage has always worked

[3]Malcolm E. Jewell and Everett W. Cunningham, *Kentucky Politics* (Lexington: University of Kentucky Press, 1968), p. 43.

[4]*Elrod v. Burns*, 427 U.S. 347 (1976). In late 1979, a federal district court judge in Chicago extended the logic of *Elrod* to hold that hiring (as well as firing) for political reasons violated the Constitution in that it discriminated against job applicants without the proper political credentials. Since the judge in the case had not yet filed his final order, the possibility of appeal was still uncertain in 1983.

[5]W. Robert Gump, "The Functions of Patronage in American Party Politics: An Empirical Reappraisal," *Midwest Journal of Political Science* 15 (1971): 87–107.

Patronage in Transition

The transformation of patronage by the reforms of merit systems and the courts is clearly illustrated in the counsel James D. Nowlan offers "Illinois managers" in his book, *Inside State Government.* In the chapter "Patronage and Personnel," Nowlan also draws on the experience of the state's former patronage chief, Donald A. Udstuen.

> Patronage is a term used for appointments to government jobs that are based on sponsorship by a political patron. A patron can be a county chairman for a political party, a state legislator, or an employing public official and his or her staff. Patronage considerations affect almost every vacancy that arises among the corps of 70,000 employees who work for the governor. . . .
>
> Traditionally, patronage politics meant firing employees and replacing them with persons loyal to an administration. Prior to adoption of the Personnel Code, terminations were a wholesale activity when one party replaced another in the governorship. Even after the code, which provided some protection against political firings, it was possible and legal to use the 'transfer authority' to induce persons to leave their state posts. . . .
>
> Another technique used to make room for party loyalists was simply to eliminate job classifications held by persons the new administration wanted out and then create new, but very similar classifications, for which it could get its people qualified.

best among the depressed and disadvantaged; most patronage positions do not tempt the educated, "respected" middle-class leadership the parties would like to attract. Furthermore, elected executives may use patronage to build their own political followings rather than the party apparatus. Finally, the parties may not be able to use the patronage available to them. Especially when they win power after years of failure, they do not have the necessary administrative machinery or an adequate list of job seekers.[6]

At the same time, pressures have understandably grown for patronage with which to reward the educated, middle-class activists in the parties and campaigns. One solution is the "political non-job":

> Happily, political leaders have devised ways to bestow the status symbols of high office without the job itself. At Democratic national

[6]On the problems of using patronage, see also Frank J. Sorauf, "State Patronage in a Rural County," *American Political Science Review* 50 (1956):1046–56; and Michael Johnston, "Patrons and Clients, Jobs and Machines: A Case Study of the Uses of Patronage," *American Political Science Review* 73 (1979): 385–98.

Today all that is changed. In addition to the protections of the code, union contracts . . . have made reclassifications for patronage purposes almost impossible. But the single most important impediment to traditional patronage politics has been the 1972 Shakman Decree, named after Michael Shakman, an anti-Daley machine activist. This federal [court] order permanently enjoined government officials, including those in Illinois state government, from firing public employees for political reasons. . . .

As a result, patronage considerations now focus on filling naturally occurring vacancies. Even then, the patronage chief must see that a sponsored job candidate is qualified by examination before he can get the person appointed to a position covered by the code. How then does the beleaguered patronage director ever fulfill all the demands placed on him by county chairmen and legislators?

Udstuen explains the dilemma as follows:

> The patronage chief is in a no-win situation. On one hand he has the insatiable demand for jobs by his political party, and on the other he has only so many jobs open. And there are only so many things you can do with the Personnel Code. Inevitably, as various jobs open, the type of people you are being pressured most to take care of don't quite fit. There's an awful lot of square pegs for the round holes in the patronage business.

> James D. Nowlan, *Inside State Government*
> (Urbana: Institute of Government and Public
> Affairs, University of Illinois, 1982), pp.
> 54, 55, 56.

---

headquarters in Washington, where many such split-level appointments are routinely requisitioned and cleared, the new institution is known as "the honorary." Elsewhere it has been dubbed the patronage non-job, and it can range from nomination to a White House advisory committee to an invitation to be an honored member of an Air Force civic inspection tour of California, arranged at the behest of your local Congressman.[7]

Thus, one way or another, the patronage system holds on. Where it persists in public employment, however, party and public officials are much less free to use it politically than they once were. When the considerations of merit become more and more insistent, the considerations of politics inevitably weaken.

Elected Office

Public office has the income, responsibility, prestige, and excitement—not to mention the power—that most patronage positions do not. Also, since

[7]Don Oberdorfer, "The New Political Non-Job," *Harper's* (October 1965), pp. 108ff.

the political party offers an efficient—and in some cases the only—avenue to elective office, it is inevitable that the possibility of a career in public office should recruit new party activists or sustain activity after other incentives have worn off. Robert Huckshorn, for instance, found that between 1962 and 1972, one-third of all the state party chairpersons were candidates for elective office after serving as chairperson. Moreover, the offices they sought were often important ones: governorships, other statewide office, and seats in the United States Congress.[8]

There are party organizations with such disciplined control over their primaries that they can and do "give" public office, especially at the state and local level, to loyal party workers. The candidate is offered the chance to run (it is his or her "turn") and then does little as the party organization runs up the necessary majorities. That degree of control over nomination and election to office is vanishing, however, along with patronage. Today, it is far more common for party leaders or workers to develop their own candidates. Candidates need advice, know-how, manpower, and money, and in most parts of the country the party still remains a likely source of them. Service in the party, then, yields the skill, experience, connections, approval, and resources that any candidate needs. For the partisan who already holds office, there is no easier way to ensure reelection or to move to a more attractive office than by work in the party. So sedulous are the party's officeholders in currying the support of the party organizations that speculation over their ambitions and "moves" remains a favorite intraparty recreation.

Of all the incentives for work in the parties, the incentive of public office appears to be the one that most divides men and women. According to a number of studies, it is considerably more common among men. In this special sense of the word, therefore, men in the parties are more "ambitious"; it is a finding, note the authors of one of the studies, that "comports well with recent evidence that the underrepresentation of women in elective office is more the result of a paucity of women candidates than discrimination against them at the polls."[9] We are still left to consider the sources of those gender differences, of course—early socialization, adult experiences and options, or discrimination within the party?

Preferments ~~favors~~

The tangible, material rewards of politics may take forms other than appointive or elective office. The active partisan or the financial "fat cat"

[8]Robert J. Huckshorn, *Party Leadership in the States* (Amherst: University of Massachusetts Press, 1976), p. 37.

[9]Diane L. Fowlkes, Jerry Perkins, and Sue T. Rinehart, "Gender Roles and Party Roles," *American Political Science Review* 73 (1979): 772–80, at p. 779. See also Harold G. Clarke and Allan Kornberg, "Moving Up the Political Escalator: Women Party Officials in the United States and Canada," *Journal of Politics* 41 (1979): 442–77.

may, for example, seek preference in the awarding of public contracts. In this respect, it is no accident that the leaders of the construction industry are so active politically in the states and localities that spend millions every year on roads and public buildings. Preference may take other forms: a tolerant or haphazard application of regulatory or inspection policies, unusually prompt or efficient public services (snow and garbage removal, for example), a forgiving instrument of the law (e.g., the fixed traffic ticket), or the granting of a scarce public service (admission to crowded mental hospitals, for instance). It may also involve the granting of scarce "opportunities," such as liquor licenses or franchises. By "preferment," in other words, one means special treatment or advantage, and it usually depends on the party's holding the decision-making positions in government. It is partly in this sense that parties talk of "controlling" city hall, the county courthouse, or the state capitol.

One particularly unappealing form is the preferment given to activities that operate on the shady side of the law. It may involve calculated ignoring of prostitution, bookmaking, the numbers game, or traffic in drugs in return for some form of political support. In other forms, it has involved the parties' taking a share of protection money or the proceeds from crime, vice, or the rackets. The prevalence of such an incentive to party effort is understandably difficult to estimate. Perhaps it suffices to say that it is probably less vital than the political cynics think and more important than the Pollyannas admit. The chances are, though, that what nexus there is between crime and government goes on through mechanisms other than the political party. When it touches the party and electoral politics, the influence of crime is probably felt more through campaign contributions than directly in the party organization. In 1960, Alexander Heard estimated ("a guess—that is what it is") that underworld money accounted for 15 percent of the campaign receipts at state and local levels.[10]

Socioeconomic Mobility Contacts

Political activity offers easy publicity and contacts for those who seek them: young lawyers trying to build a practice, owners of food and watering spots, insurance and real estate brokers, storekeepers, and the socially ambitious. Party activity opens up the contacts that lead to prosperity in a

---

[10]Alexander Heard, *The Costs of Democracy* (Chapel Hill: University of North Carolina Press, 1960), p. 163. Beyond Heard's estimate, it is not easy to find a serious treatment of the relationships between crime and politics. Undoubtedly, the subject itself restricts the usual scholarly inquiries. There are broader studies of corruption in government and politics, but they often suffer from a broad or imprecise definition of corruption. For a discussion and bibliography, see John G. Peters and Susan Welch, "Political Corruption in America: A Search for Definitions and a Theory," *American Political Science Review* 72 (1978): 974–84.

business or profession, to a new job or business opportunity, even to an elevated social status.

Writes one observer of the Philadelphia organization men:

> One explanation of their motivation would locate the "boys'" essential urge in the factor known as "prestige." The truth is, many intellectuals and many members of the upper class who have come in contact with politicians argue that, for the Irish, Jewish, Italian bright boys who pursue it, politics is a "status-conferring" occupation. The Bill Greens and the Victor Blancs and the Aus Meehans, they point out, could no doubt have earned wealth and even the respect of their fellow-men by selling insurance, practicing law, and the like. But one thing that they could not earn in these ways is "place" in the community. Politics gives them that.[11]

In the tired American phrase, some people join the active ranks in the parties to "get ahead," whether they define getting ahead in terms of upward social or economic mobility.

Social and Psychological Satisfactions

The personal, nonmaterial rewards of party activity are not easy to identify and certainly are not easy to measure. One can sense, however, the social rewards of politics in the camaraderie of the gang at party headquarters or the courthouse. It is evident at a party dinner as the workers press around the great and near-great of the party, hoping for a word of greeting or a nod of recognition. In the new-style political clubs, the attractiveness of the social life and friendship circle is explicit. "Many volunteers are rootless, transient newcomers searching the city for a means of associating with like-minded people." Although the parties' clubs rely on the social incentives, however, those incentives are probably secondary:

> Although many clubs in various cities offer their members reduced air fares to Europe on charter flights, a full schedule of social events, forums featuring prestigious speakers, and the opportunity to play the political game, and although some members join simply to find a mate quickly or get to Paris inexpensively, if the clubs should cease to define themselves as organizations devoted to liberalism or reformism or similar worthy causes, they could not for long sustain the interest of any but the handful who simply enjoy the company of others or like being district leader.[12]

[11]James Reichley, *The Art of Government: Reform and Organization Politics in Philadelphia* (New York: Fund for the Republic, 1959), p. 104.

[12]James Q. Wilson, *The Amateur Democrat* (Chicago: University of Chicago Press, 1962), p. 165.

Perhaps one can say more simply that party politics is a splendid vehicle for gregariousness. Almost all reported research on the motivations of party activists has found that they say they "like people" or that they "like politics."

Social satisfactions merge almost imperceptibly into the psychological. "Like the theater, politics is a great nourisher of egos," writes one observer. "It attracts men who are hungry for attention, for assurance that somebody loves them, for the soul-stirring music of their own voices."[13] Party work may also offer the individual a cause or an enterprise with which to identify, a charismatic leader to follow, a round of activities that can lift him or her above the personally unrewarding tasks of the workaday world. The party may be a small island of excitement in a sea of routine. It may even offer an occasion for the manipulation or domination of others, a chance to decide or command, even an avenue for the projection of aggression and hostilities.

Ideology and Policy Issues *stand up for your beliefs*

Even the most casual soundings of party rhetoric indicate an increasing identification of partisans as "liberals" or "conservatives." Behind these phrases lies a potent motivation to party activity: a commitment to clusters of related attitudes about government and politics, especially about the proper role of government in contemporary society. On a more modest and limited scale, the spur to activity may be concern for a single issue or interest (tax cuts, the war in Vietnam, abortions, the maintenance of local schools) or a single area of policy concern (foreign policy, civil rights, the environment). The "cause" may, indeed, be the reform or rehabilitation of the political party itself.

Just as the importance of the immediate, material, personal rewards of politics has recently declined, that of issue and ideology has increased. Even in Manhattan, long the fief of Tammany Hall, the trend has been evident:

> There is a "new look" among today's political activists. They are "respectable," solid middle-class citizens. The party "hack" of fiction, films, and the traditional literature is hard to find among the young, well-educated, affluent, and socially acceptable committeemen—and women—of the nineteen-sixties. Concomitantly, both the nature of political motivation and the character of political activity have changed. The contemporary politician considers his party organization an instrument for effectuating policy rather than a haven of personal security. He

[13]John Fischer, "Please Don't Bite the Politicians," *Harper's* (November 1960), p. 16.

tends to be more interested in social reform than in catering to individual constituents.[14]

These issue concerns in the local parties have paralleled the ideological triumphs in the national parties: the capture of the Republicans by Goldwater conservatives in 1964, the success of the liberal Democratic ideologues on behalf of Eugene McCarthy (1968) and George McGovern (1972), and the victories of Ronald Reagan in 1980 both within the Republican party and throughout the nation.

Party activists may also be drawn to the party by a more general civic commitment. A sense of obligation and duty as a citizen, a belief in the democratic values of citizen participation, may impel them. Scholars who have questioned party workers about their motives for service in the party know the familiar answers. They were asked to serve, and they assented because it was their civic duty. Often that response, in whatever words it may be couched, merely masks what the respondent feels are less acceptable motives. Often, however, it is an honest reflection of deeply ingrained civic values. Often, too, it may be combined with honest, if vague, commitments to "good government" and political reform.

The Party Itself

Two final varieties of incentive, both related essentially to the party per se, must be mentioned. First, as a party activist works within the party, the well-being of the party itself becomes an incentive for work. He or she attaches loyalties and aspirations to the party, and its health becomes an end in itself. The party's wins and losses become issues in and of themselves, and attacks on it are far more than attacks on its policies and activities. Second, it may be, as Robert Salisbury suggests in his study of St. Louis politicians, that large numbers of party activists participate "because they were brought up in a highly politicized atmosphere." The party "participant per family socialization was probably not exposed to involvement in other kinds of organizations, any more than a devout young communicant of the church would necessarily be taught to carry his devotion into other organizational settings."[15] In other words, party workers may gravitate to the party because they are accustomed to it and because, through years of socialization, they have invested loyalties in it.

No party organization depends on a single incentive, and very few partisans labor in the party for only one reason. Most party organizations

[14]Robert S. Hirschfield, Bert E. Swanson, and Blanche D. Blank, "A Profile of Political Activists in Manhattan," *Western Political Quarterly* 15 (1962): 505.

[15]Robert H. Salisbury, "The Urban Party Organization Member," *Public Opinion Quarterly* 29 (1965–66): 562, 564.

rely on a variety or system of incentives. Patronage workers may coexist with workers attracted by policy issues or by a middle-class sense of civic responsibility. The mixture of incentives may vary between urban and rural areas, or between different local political cultures. One study suggests that, at least in New York's Nassau County, issues and ideologies are a less potent incentive in the majority party than in the minority party.[16] The mix may even vary within the same party organization. Eldersveld reports that in Wayne County, Michigan, the precinct chairpersons depend heavily on the rewards of social contacts, whereas the party's higher leadership seeks a combination of immediate economic gain and ideological-philosophical rewards.[17]

For all the subtleties of the mix and variety of incentives, however, general comments about their overall frequency *are* possible. Scholarly evidence on the point comes from sporadic studies of parties in scattered parts of the country, but what evidence there is points to the dominance of ideological or issue incentives. Put very simply, the desire to use the party as a means to achieve policy goals appears to be the major incentive attracting individuals to party work these days.[18] Although similar data are unavailable for earlier periods, there is ample reason to believe that this generalization was far less true of party workers a generation or two ago.

Incentives may change, however, for any individual; that is, the incentive that recruits people to party activity may not sustain them in that activity. Several studies suggest that a shift in incentives takes place in those party activists attracted by the purposive incentives—those who seek to achieve issue, ideological, or other impersonal goals through their party activity. To sustain their involvement in party work, they tend to depend more on incentives of social contact, identification with the party itself, and other personal rewards and satisfactions.[19] Perhaps an electorally pragmatic party—one traditionally committed to the flexibilities necessary to win elections—has difficulty providing the ideological successes necessary to sustain workers whose incentives remain ideological for any length of time.

[16]Dennis S. Ippolito and Lewis Bowman, "Goals and Activities of Party Officials in a Suburban Community," *Western Political Quarterly* 22 (1969): 572–80.

[17]Samuel Eldersveld, *Political Parties: A Behavioral Analysis* (Chicago: Rand McNally, 1964), p. 278; see also all of Chap. 11.

[18]Lewis Bowman, Dennis Ippolito, and William Donaldson, "Incentives for the Maintenance of Grassroots Political Activism," *Midwest Journal of Political Science* 13 (1969): 126–39; and Charles W. Wiggins and William L. Turk, "State Party Chairmen: A Profile," *Western Political Quarterly* 23 (1970): 321–32.

[19]Among others, see M. Margaret Conway and Frank B. Feigert, "Motivation, Incentive Systems, and the Political Organization," *American Political Science Review* 62 (1968): 1159–73.

THE PROCESSES OF RECRUITMENT

The mere existence of incentives for work in the party organization will not automatically produce a full roster of active workers. In the political party, as in any other large organization, the organization must recruit actively in order to ensure for itself useful and compatible recruits. Potential activists may lack either the knowledge of the opportunity or the stimulus to act, or both. Therefore, there must be some process of recruitment that will join the opportunity and the stimulus to the incentives in order to attract the activists.

Nonetheless, the parties do not find it easy to recruit. Frequently, their incentives are not attractive enough to compete even with the modest pleasures of activity in a local service club. They lack any effective mechanism for recruiting new personnel, and they may even ignore the necessity for self-renewal. Furthermore, state statutes often take at least part of the recruitment process out of their hands; open party caucuses and the election of party officials in primaries tend to encourage self-recruitment at the expense of party initiatives and control. Above all, the chronic need for personnel of any kind disposes the parties to accept whatever help is available. Even patronage-rich organizations in job-poor communities tend not to be rigorous in recruiting new activists. Friendship and contacts within the party organization may speed the entry of the new activist more effectively than political skills or promise of performance.

In the absence of regular and rigorous recruitment by the party, opportunities for party work come in a haphazard way. Initially, a certain degree of awareness of the parties is necessary, as are strong political goals and commitments. Then, at the time of recruitment, there must also be some more immediate occasion or stimulus for the individual to enter party work. Sometimes that stimulus is internal, and the individual in effect recruits himself or herself. In other cases, the stimulus is external, most often the invitation or persuasion of some other individual. Activists tend to ascribe their initial recruitment largely to these external stimuli; two studies of local party workers have set the proportion of self-starters at only 10 and 29 percent of the interviewees.[20] In view of the favorable myth that the office seeks the individual, however, it may be that the party activists protest too much.

In sum, then, we have an extensive, informal recruitment system—a complex of interrelated factors that selects out of the American population a particular group of men and women. Its chief elements are:

[20]Phillip Althoff and Samuel C. Patterson, "Political Activism in a Rural County," *Midwest Journal of Political Science* 10 (1966): 39–51; and Lewis Bowman and G. R. Boynton, "Recruitment Patterns among Local Party Officials," *American Political Science Review* 60 (1966): 667–76.

— The motives, goals, and knowledge of the men and women whom the parties want to recruit.

— The incentives to party activity that the party can offer, and the external factors that alter the value of the incentives (e.g., the impact of employment levels on the value of patronage).

— The nature of the party's recruitment role (e.g., the election of precinct workers in primaries versus their appointment).

— The contacts, opportunities, and persuasions that are the immediate, proximate occasions of recruitment.[21]

The components of this system change constantly, and as they do, they affect the supply of personnel entering the organization. Recruitment in any form, however, is a matching of the motives and goals of the individual with the incentives and expectations of the party organization. The immediate act of recruitment is either the catalyst or the occasion for the matching.

An auxiliary recruitment system may work *within* the organization to promote especially successful party workers to positions of greater responsibility. The data we have on the political careers of party activists, however, do not suggest that party workers inch up a career ladder in the party, position by position. Only about one-third of a group of county chairpersons and cochairpersons in Oklahoma, for example, had ever held any other party office, and half of them had never held any public or party office at all.[22]

In contrast, party leadership in the Detroit area has risen exclusively through the avenues of party and public office. One group came up through the precinct positions, another came through the auxiliary organizations (i.e., the women's groups, youth organizations, political clubs), and a third and smaller group moved from the race for public office to a career within the party.[23] In general, the way stations of a political career vary with the nature of the political organization. In party organizations that have relatively open access and easy mobility, careers in the party are developed easily, almost spontaneously. In disciplined, hierarchical party organizations, party activists work up the hierarchy in carefully graded steps and expectations.

---

[21]For an alternative but similar recruitment model, see Bowman and Boynton, "Recruitment Patterns." C. Richard Hofstetter, in "Organizational Activists: The Bases of Participation in Amateur and Professional Groups," *American Politics Quarterly* 1 (1973): 244–76, also concludes that individual participation is based on considerations much broader than simple responses to incentives.

[22]Samuel C. Patterson, "Characteristics of Party Leaders," *Western Political Quarterly* 16 (1963): 343–44.

[23]Eldersveld, *Political Parties*, pp. 142–43.

THE RECRUITS: AMATEURS AND PROFESSIONALS

Since recruitment patterns both change over time and differ from locality to locality, it is not easy to generalize about the activists they recruit into the party organization. Note, for example, the differences between the local committeemen and committeewomen of the Democratic parties of Pittsburgh and Manhattan:[24]

	Pittsburgh (1970)	Manhattan (1959–60)
Patronage holders	74% of men, 42% of women	Approximately 5% "on public payroll"
Education	17% attended or graduated from college	67% attended or graduated from college
Age	15% under 40	28% under 35
Occupations	Overwhelmingly governmental	19% business executives and professional; 24% small businessmen

This is not to suggest that any single factor in the recruitment (in this case the presence or absence of the patronage incentive) fully explains the differences between the Democratic activists of these two city organizations. Differences of this sort may also reflect the kinds of personnel the organization wants and needs, differences in organizational roles and tasks (as between dominant and minority parties or between machine and club-style parties), or even differences in what the local community considers acceptable motives and incentives.

American party activists, despite all such variations, do have two characteristics in common that set them apart from the general population of adults. First, they tend, rather uniformly, to come from families with a history of party activity. Study after study indicates that large numbers of party activists had an adult party activist in their immediate family as they were growing up. Second, activists are marked by their relatively high socioeconomic status (SES), whether one measures SES by income, by years of formal education, or by occupation. The highest SES among the active partisans can be found, as one might expect, in the top leadership ranks of the parties. The parties thus attract men and women with the time and financial resources to afford politics, with the information and knowledge to understand it, and with the skills to be useful in it. Only in some local organizations have there been exceptions, especially their

[24]Hirschfield, Swanson, and Blank, "A Profile of Political Activists"; and Lee S. Weinberg, "Stability and Change Among Pittsburgh Precinct Politicians, 1954–70," *Social Science 50* (1975): 10–16.

precinct workers; in general, only in patronage-oriented, favor-dispensing machines in the center cities are the party workers at all representative of the populations with which they work.[25]

In most parts of the country, Republican activists come from higher SES groups than do their Democratic counterparts. The Republicans' higher SES undoubtedly reflects their policies and ideological sympathies for higher income and status groups over the past generation or more. One exception to the general SES ascendancy of the Republicans does appear around the country. In one-party Democratic areas, the dominant Democratic party attracts high-status leadership, probably because it is both "respectable" as the party of power and inviting as the party of opportunity.[26]

Within this overloading of high-status activists, one special dominance—that of lawyers—is too obvious to be overlooked. Lawyers are the high priests of the American political cult. Studies of county chairpersons in Oklahoma, Kansas, North Carolina, and Wisconsin show a median percentage of attorneys among county chairpersons somewhat above 20 percent. Recently, more than 40 percent of the state chairpersons around the country were attorneys.[27] To an extent unduplicated in other democracies, the lawyer in American society is the professional political careerist. Lawyers have cultivated skills in oratory and debate, and they are occupationally concerned with the actions of government, schooled in public issues, and practiced in parliamentary procedures. Naturally, to many Americans they appear ideally suited for political leadership. The major parties even reserve for them a special type of political reward: the elective or politically appointive judgeship.[28]

Workers in the two parties also tend to vary in personal characteristics. In a significant number of localities across the country, the Democratic party organizations have larger percentages of Catholics and Jews,

[25]Minor parties may also be an exception to the relatively high SES of party activists. See, for example, James M. Elden and David R. Schweitzer, "New Third Party Radicalism: The Case of the California Peace and Freedom Party," *Western Political Quarterly* 24 (1971): 761–74.

[26]Patterson, "Characteristics of Party Leaders," pp. 332–52; and William J. Crotty, "The Social Attributes of Party Organizational Activists in a Transitional Political System," *Western Political Quarterly* 20 (1967): 669–81. On the more general SES differences between workers of the two major parties, see Richard J. Heuwinkel and Charles W. Wiggins, "Party Competition and Party Leadership Attributes," *American Journal of Political Science* 17 (1973): 159–69. It is also important to note that although party leaders do come from upper SES groups, by and large they do not come from the very highest, elite SES circles.

[27]Patterson, "Characteristics of Party Leaders," p. 339; Crotty, "Social Attributes," p. 677; Wiggins and Turk, "State Party Chairmen," p. 325.

[28]One cannot even begin to summarize the literature dealing with lawyers in American politics. As an example, see Heinz Eulau and John D. Sprague, *Lawyers in Politics* (Indianapolis: Bobbs-Merrill, 1964).

and those of the Republican party have higher percentages of Protestants. Similarly (and very much related), Democratic workers more frequently than Republicans come from Irish, Southern European, and Eastern European national and ethnic stock. Republicans come more frequently from Northern European and Western European backgrounds and from old Yankee families. These interparty differences again reflect the basic voter coalitions of the two parties. Of course, there is a strong tendency for the activists of both parties to reflect the ethnic, racial, national, and religious composition of a homogeneous area. Although they are thoroughly representative of these groups, their education, income, and occupation (especially those of the Republicans) are still well above the average SES for the area. Finally, women are underrepresented in the formal committee positions in both parties; moreover, they tend to be found in the lower, nonleadership levels of party work.[29]

There remains the tantalizing and elusive question of the personalities and psyches of the party activists. On a commonsense level, one can say without fear of contradiction that party activists are often gregarious and extroverted. This is apparent almost by definition alone, for party activity is not apt to appeal to the introvert or the misanthrope. Harold Lasswell and others have argued, however, that there is a special "political personality"—that political life attracts men and women with personal tensions that can be easily projected on public objects or with personal needs that can be sublimated or satisfied in political activity.[30] No convincing evidence exists, however, that the parties attract activists with any different or more pressing personality needs than those of the American population as a whole. One study has found, in fact, that the incidence of "authoritarian personalities" is not high among party workers. (The few authoritarians tend to favor both disciplined, hierarchical party organizations and nonideological party goals and activities.)[31]

Beyond social and psychological characteristics, it also matters what goals, expectations, and skills the activists bring to the party organizations. The goals and activities of the party and the men and women it recruits reflect one another. In fact, observers of the American party organizations have developed a two-part typology of party activists, based not only on their personal characteristics but also on the role they play in the organization and the expectations they have for it. The terminology differs—

[29]See, for example, Harold G. Clarke and Allan Kornberg, "Moving Up the Political Escalator: Women Party Officials in the United States and Canada," *Journal of Politics* 41 (1979): 442–77.

[30]Harold Lasswell, *Psychopathology and Politics* (Chicago: University of Chicago Press, 1931), and also his *Power and Personality* (New York: Norton, 1948).

[31]Louise Harned, "Authoritarian Attitudes and Party Activity," *Public Opinion Quarterly* 25 (1961): 393–99.

Professionals and Amateurs: A Typology

Labels	Old Style Professional, pragmatic	New Style Amateur, purist
SES level	Above average	Well above average
Incentive	Patronage, preferment	Issue, ideology
Governing role in party	Follower	Participant
Expectations for party	Candidate, elec- tion-oriented	Concerned with issues
Locus of party loyalty	Traditional party organization per se	Officeholders, party clubs, and other auxiliaries

the old-style activist may be called the professional or the pragmatist; the new-style activist may be called the amateur or the purist (see box). Such types are abstractions, of course, rather than descriptions of specific individuals; they tend, therefore, to be purer and more extreme than one often finds in reality.

The implication of amateurs versus professionals for party organization is clear. A different party emerges with one type—or with its predominance—than with the other. Above all, the new or amateur activists are more issue-oriented and insist on participation and agenda setting within the organization in order to bring those issue concerns to the party. They are less comfortable with the traditional electoral pragmatism of the parties—that is, with making compromises in their positions in order to win elections. Indeed, they sometimes bring a new willingness to *lose* elections rather than compromise positions. To the extent that they stamp such a willingness on party organizations, they bring a profound change to the American parties. They also work a change of similar magnitude by bringing to the parties a strong impetus for reform, not only in the internal business of the party but also in its external environment, by favoring, for example, the adoption of presidential primaries and simplified voter registration.[32]

---

[32]The same dichotomy between amateurs and professionals will also be examined in the discussion of national convention delegates in Chapter 12. On amateurs and professionals generally, see Dan Nimmo and Robert L. Savage, "The Amateur Democrat Revisited," *Polity* 5 (1972): 268–76; and C. Richard Hofstetter, "The Amateur Politician: A Problem in Construct Validation," *Midwest Journal of Political Science* 15 (1971): 31–56.

VITALITY OF THE PARTY ORGANIZATION

Party organizations are apparatuses for recruiting political resources and mobilizing them in the pursuit of political goals. Some do it with strength and vitality; others are ineffective. For decades, the American model or ideal in local party organization has been the classic urban machine. Its organizational hierarchy, its full range of year-round services and activities, and its army of eager workers in the wards and precincts have traditionally represented organizational strength. It is an organizational form in which the personal attention, service, friendship, and persuasiveness of the local party worker are directed at the local electorate. All its activities throughout the year are geared to earning the support of that electorate, thus enabling the activists and office seekers of the party to deliver its vote and achieve their political goals through victory at the polls.

As the preceding chapter suggested, the ideal has never been the norm. Its chief and indispensable ingredient, the local ward or precinct worker, has too often been inactive or completely absent. Even in the American cities, evidence has begun to mount:

— Some 27 percent of the party activists in St. Louis did not perform "any significant amount of political or electioneering tasks."[33]

— Only about one-fourth of a group of workers in Massachusetts and North Carolina performed all four "critical" campaign tasks (door-to-door canvassing, telephone campaigning, transporting people to the polls, and talking to voters about the election); only one-half of them performed any three.[34]

— In the Detroit area, only 13 percent of the Democratic precinct workers and 3 percent of the Republicans met criteria of organizational efficiency close to the model of the well-organized political machine.[35]

If there were comparable data on rural and small-town party organization, they surely would suggest even greater disorganization.

The organizational problem extends, however, beyond inert or underactive committeepersons. Parties often cannot maintain the nexus of roles and relationships on which the organizational paragon depends. Eldersveld's study of the Detroit parties offers the fullest analysis. Communication lines in the parties, he found,

> were not a perfect pyramid; communication was highly voluntaristic and noncoercive. From one-fourth to two-fifths of the precinct leaders did not have contacts with their district leaders, and from 10 to 15 percent

[33]Salisbury, "The Urban Party Organization Member," p. 557.

[34]Lewis Bowman and G. R. Boynton, "Activists and Role Definitions of Grass-roots Party Officials," *Journal of Politics* 28 (1966): 132–34.

[35]Eldersveld, *Political Parties*, p. 348.

seemed almost completely isolated. Further, the content of communication in the party seemed highly preoccupied with "vote getting" and campaign tactics.

Nor were authority relationships pyramided:

> The vast majority of precinct leaders were "little oligarchs," running their operations alone or with "friends and neighbors," with limited contact and involvement in district-level operations, and with limited reasons for self-consciously adjusting their work patterns and plans to perceive district-level demands.[36]

Throughout the Detroit parties, in fact, there was diversity rather than the monolithic homogeneity the ideal assumes. Local workers entered and remained in party service for a splendid variety of motives. They carried out different tasks, even within the same party. They had differing political values and differing perceptions of political reality—even differing views of their own party and the opposing party. In addition, they differed greatly in the way they perceived their roles as precinct leaders. The parties "did not communicate one particular role conception to rank-and-file leaders. The party line, if there was one, was confused and poorly communicated." As a result, some 45 percent of these workers saw themselves chiefly as vote mobilizers, 24 percent as ideological leaders, 18 percent as welfare promoters for local residents; and 10 percent appeared to have formulated no role at all.[37]

The search for the strong, vital party organization goes on—hampered, however, by the lack of agreement on what the ideal ought to be. For many partisans and observers, the ideal remains the classic, turn-of-the-century urban machine. It is an ideal rooted in time, in the methods of campaigning, and in the electorate of a past era. Its operations are not acceptable, however, to the new activists and the reformers; furthermore, voters can be reached by means other than the ubiquitous precinct worker. What we need—but haven't found—is some common measure of strength and effectiveness for the political realities of the late twentieth century. In that search, one scholar has proposed a two-part measure: the extent of full-time staffing of the party organization, and its ability to control and limit competition for nominations to public office.[38]

Although the problem of assessing organizational strength has not been solved, the attempts to solve it go on. Although the shades of vitality in party organization are not easy to sort out, one can much more easily

---

[36]*Ibid.*, pp. 377, 408.

[37]*Ibid.*, pp. 254, 270. No roles were ascertained for 3 percent of the leaders.

[38]Ronald E. Weber, unpublished paper, quoted in Malcolm Jewell and David Olson, *American State Political Parties and Elections* (Homewood, Ill.: Dorsey, 1978), pp. 61–62.

recognize dormancy or inactivity. Thus, it is possible to generalize roughly about the conditions under which organizational strength develops.

Urban-Rural Differences

The close proximity of people in urban residential neighborhoods makes possible the intense political activity, the intricate organizational life, and the stable political loyalties of the highly developed political organizations. So, too, do the problems of the cities and the presence of the unassimilated minorities there. Intensive campaigning and regular contact with the voters—the usual signs of strong and vigorous party organization—make far less sense in rural America. Party nominating and electioneering differ there, and so do the incentives for party activity. It is not surprising, then, that the acmes of party organization have been reached in urban, especially metropolitan, centers.[39]

Differences in Political Cultures

The expectations citizens have about party organization differ. Persistent canvassing by committeepersons and their no-nonsense questions about voter preferences may be taken as a matter of course in some quarters but not in others. Similarly, patronage and the political organization founded on it may be respectable in some states or localities but not in others. What may seem to be a benevolent party organization in Chicago may offend a good many sensibilities in down-state Illinois. These differences in political culture tend to follow urban-rural lines, but there are also regional and social-class differences in norms and expectations for the parties.

Differences in Two-Party Competitiveness

Unquestionably, the greatest number of defunct party organizations occur in the long-term minority parties. The Republican parties of the Deep South until the 1950s served for a long time as a classic illustration.[40] Badly demoralized and shorn of both influence and hope, the minority party easily lapses into organizational feebleness. It can provide none of the rewards—tangible or intangible—that induce individuals to give their time, skills, or money to a party organization. Its activists often lack influence, even respectability, in the community.

---

[39]See Frank J. Sorauf, *Party and Representation* (New York: Atherton, 1963), especially Chap. 3. For a somewhat different approach to this issue, with results not altogether different, see Paul A. Beck, "Environment and Party: The Impact of Political and Demographic County Characteristics on Party Behavior," *American Political Science Review* 68 (1974): 1229–44.

[40]V. O. Key, *Southern Politics* (New York: Knopf, 1949), Chap. 13.

Differences in State Statutes

The statutory forms and regulations of some states are more burdensome than those of others. All other things being equal, a party is handicapped, for example, by a state law making it difficult to remove or replace an inactive party official. Particularly important are differences in primary laws, for they fundamentally affect the party's ability to decide which candidates will carry its label.

In a number of states with efficient party organizations (New York, Connecticut, and Michigan come to mind), the organizations still nominate candidates for statewide offices and for some local ones at conventions. The direct primaries of those states are among the least comprehensive in the country; in Connecticut, for example, the primary did not come into being until 1955. Consequently, the party still had a vital nominating role left to it—a purpose and a need for maintaining organizational capacity. Lockard wrote of the Connecticut parties before the primary:

> In the absence of a primary the opportunity for political advancement lay with the organization, not through independent appeals to the electorate in a primary election. Local organizations had reason to exist even where there was little hope of winning an election for their party, for there were state conventions biennially in which important decisions were made. In contrast to many states in which the primary has been employed, there has been no appreciable withering away of the party organization in local areas.[41]

V.O. Key argued, in fact, that the introduction of the direct primary into American politics in this century is primarily responsible for the atrophy of local party organization throughout the country.[42]

POWER AND DISCIPLINE IN THE ORGANIZATION

Organization implies discipline—at least enough discipline to coordinate its parts and to implement its decisions. It also implies some well-established system of authority for making those decisions. Many Americans have gone beyond these implications, however, and have imagined virtually authoritarian control within the party organization. Some leader, generally identified as the boss, has widely been thought to rule the party apparatus by a combination of cunning, bravery, and force of will. The boss, in fact, became something of an American folk hero, feared for his

[41]Duane Lockard, *New England State Politics* (Princeton: Princeton University Press, 1959), pp. 325–26.

[42]V. O. Key, *American State Politics* (New York: Knopf, 1956), Chap. 6.

ruthlessness and admired for his rascality and intrepid daring. He has been celebrated in the public arts,[43] and if he had not existed, it might have been necessary to create him, if only to justify the political cynicism of generations of Americans (see box).

Very few organizational leaders ruled absolutely by personal magnetism, tactical adroitness, or the use of sanctions. Even in the era of boss rule, the boss's power was shared with influential underlings, and the terms of that sharing were deeply rooted in all of the hierarchical traditions of the organization.

> The persistent attacks on "Boss rule" have misrepresented the nature of power in the old machine system. Power was hierarchical in the party, diffused in the way it is diffused in the army. Because the commanding general was powerful, it did not follow that the division generals were

[43]Note, for example, Edwin O'Connor, *The Last Hurrah* (Boston: Little, Brown, 1956); and Robert Penn Warren, *All the King's Men* (New York: Harcourt, Brace, 1946).

The Boss in Cartoon

American artists at the turn of the century caught, for all time, the enduring American view of the urban political boss. Thomas Nast's portrait of Tammany joined a moneybag head to the body of Boss Tweed. Walter Clark's image needs no explanation.

Thomas Nast, "The Brains." From
Harper's Weekly, October 21, 1871.
Metropolitan Museum of Art, New York.

powerless. Tammany district leaders were important men, and, right down to the block captain, all had rights.[44]

Yet in many of the classic political organizations, power and discipline were greatly centralized and largely removed from the control of workers and activists in the wards and precincts. The local leader had his rights, but they were bounded by the greater rights and authority of his superiors.

Much of that centralization was possible because the foot soldiers in the ranks accepted the hierarchical system of authority. If they were Catholics, and many were, the party's hierarchy may have seemed as natural and inevitable as that of the Church. Furthermore, their goals were clear and simple. If they sought patronage jobs, they cared little about what else the party did or did not do. More recently, however, party activists have come to demand a voice in the affairs of the party. A good portion

[44]Nathan Glazer and Daniel P. Moynihan, *Beyond the Melting Pot* (Cambridge, Mass.: MIT Press, 1963), p. 227.

Walter Appleton Clark, "The Boss."
From *Collier's Weekly*, November 10, 1906.

From Ralph E. Shikes, *The Indignant Eye*
(Boston: Beacon Press, 1969), pp. 312, 321.

of the ideological fervor of the amateurs has been directed at reforming the party's authoritarianism and bossism. They are committed to the norms and imperatives of democracy, at least in part because of a higher level of education and political information. Their commitment to intraparty democracy also follows logically from their desire to move the party to ideology, because achievement of their own political goals hinges directly on the party's achievement of congruent goals. Thus, they must reform the American parties if they are to reform American society.[45]

It is not only participation, however, that is cutting into the discipline of the party organization. Discipline depends also on the ability of the organization to withdraw or withhold its incentives. Much of the discipline of the classic machine resulted from the willingness and ability of party leaders to manipulate the material rewards of patronage and preferment. A recalcitrant or inefficient committeeman sacrificed his public job or his hope for it. The newer incentives, however, cannot be given or revoked so easily. The party is only one among many organizations pursuing policy or ideological goals; and given the party's very imperfect control of its legislators, it may not even be the most efficient means to these ends. The ideologically oriented activist may find substitute outlets for his or her activities in interest groups or nonparty political associations, such as neighborhood associations, professional groups, or political action committees of one kind or another.

Whether or not irresponsible power has been a fact within the party organizations, the American political culture is haunted by the fear that a few men, responsible to no one, will control the selection of public officials and set the agendas of policymaking in "smoke-filled rooms." Understandably, the search for mechanisms with which to control that power has been a long and diligent one. The results fall into two broad categories: mechanisms that impose controls from outside the parties and those that look to internal controls.

External Controls

Political laissez-faire suggests that two competitive parties will set limits to each other's exercise of organizational power by their very competition. This argument directly parallels the argument of the self-regulating effects of economic competition in the free marketplace. If one party offers the electorate a shoddy political product or if it overprices its political goods, it will lose its political consumers to its competitor. Indeed, the current spread of two-party competitiveness may make that assumption more credible. One-partyism—monopoly of the political system—negates the automatic corrective action assumed in laissez-faire theory, however, and

[45]Wilson, *The Amateur Democrat*, Chap. 5.

some of the centers of greater organizational power are without serious two-party competition. Mayor Richard J. Daley and his Democratic machine, for example, won reelection in Chicago with 78 percent of the vote in 1975.

The states have generally preferred statutory controls on party power to the unseen hand of competition, but their disappointments have outnumbered their successes. In those states in which voters in the primary pick precinct committeepersons and other party officials, there are rarely contests for offices. Frequently, there is not even a candidate. In other states, the attempts to regulate the holding of party caucuses and conventions have not always guaranteed access to all qualified comers. The states have not been without their successes, however. In some of them, statutorily guaranteed access has opened party organization to competition by other factions and oligarchies or to reinvigoration by new party personnel. Moreover, in all of the states, the direct primary has at least forced the parties to face the scrutiny of voters on one key decision: the nomination of candidates for office.

Internal Controls

In his sweeping "iron law of oligarchy," Robert Michels declared 70 years ago, without qualification, that majorities within organizations are incapable of governing themselves. Organizations, he argued, are by their nature oligarchic or "minoritarian," for only the active minority has the experience, interest, and involvement necessary to manage the affairs of complex organizations.

> Organization implies the tendency to oligarchy. In every organization, whether it be a political party, a professional union, or any other association of the kind, the aristocratic tendency manifests itself very clearly. The mechanism of the organization, while conferring a solidity of structure, induces serious changes in the organized mass, completely inverting the respective position of the leaders and the led. As a result of organization, every party or professional union becomes divided into a minority of directors and a majority of directed.[46]

To the extent that we are all believers in the myths of the bosses, the smoke-filled rooms, and the deals between oligarchs, we are all disciples of Michels.

The kind of intraparty democracy that Michels lamented has little relevance, however, to the nonmembership, cadre organizations of the American major parties. Who are the participating members, the ineffec-

[46]Robert Michels, *Political Parties* (Glencoe, Ill.: Free Fress, 1949; originally published in 1915), p. 32.

tive majorities, here? The party in the electorate, which the states permit to choose some party leaders, are members in only the loosest sense. Only in isolated parts of the country have the parties developed bona fide membership organizations. There is, in the meaning of Michels, really no inactive majority within the American parties. The American party organization is made up entirely of activists—active in varying degrees, of course—who are reckoned as being "of" the party simply because they *are* active, as workers, officers, leaders, or even hangers-on. Control of party power, therefore, must come largely from within the party cadre. The relevant question is not really so much one of control as it is one of the distribution of power within the organizational leadership.

The distribution of power within most American party organizations can be described in Samuel Eldersveld's apt term *stratarchy*. It is "the enlargement of the ruling group of an organization, its power stratification, the involvement of large numbers of people in group decision-making, and, thus, the diffusion and proliferation of control throughout the structure."[47] Various levels of party organization operate at least semi-independently of other levels, even superordinate ones. Precinct committeepersons, district leaders, and even county officials freely define their own political roles and nourish their separate bases of party power. Thus, "although authority to speak for the organization may remain in the hands of the top elite nucleus, there is great autonomy in operations at the lower 'strata' or echelons of the hierarchy, and . . . control from the top is minimal and formal."[48]

What accounts for stratarchy and the failure of top party leaders to centralize organizational power in the hierarchy? Weighing against the pressures of a centralized party oligarchy are these factors:

— *Participatory expectations.* Large percentages of the new party activists—accustomed to being beneficiaries of the democratic ethos in their service or fraternal clubs—expect to find it also in their political party. Therefore, the organization may have to tolerate or even create intraparty democracy (or consultation) to maintain vitality, to lift morale, and to achieve cohesion.

— *Controls of lower party levels over higher levels.* The chieftains of the lower-level party organizations collectively make up the conventions or consultative bodies that select the levels of party officialdom above them. County chairpersons who choose state officers are forces to be reckoned with in the state party organizations. Similarly, precinct workers or delegates often form or choose county committees.

[47]Eldersveld, *Political Parties*, p. 99. The term *stratarchy* originally comes from Harold Lasswell and Abraham Kaplan, *Power and Society* (New Haven: Yale University Press, 1950).
[48]Eldersveld, *Political Parties*, pp. 99–100.

— *Internal competition.* Party organizations rarely are monoliths. They often embrace competing organizations or factions. Differences in goals and political styles produce continuing competition in the selecting of party officials and the mapping of party activities. In 1956 and 1957 in Wisconsin, at least some county party offices were contested in 39 percent of the Republican organizations and in 59 percent of the Democratic ones.[49]

Diffusion of power marks all but the exceptional party organizations. Top party leaders engage in much mobilizing and placating of support within the organization; their consultations with middle-level leadership are endless. Even the ward or precinct leader with a small electoral following and a single vote at an important convention must be cultivated. Above all, party leaders in the eras after those of "patronage and preferment" no longer command, for their commands no longer carry potent sanctions. They plead, they bargain, they cajole, and they reason—and they even learn to lose gracefully on occasion. They mobilize party power not so much by threats as by the solidarity of common goals and interests.

In a sense, the concerns over power, discipline, and control in American party organization seem increasingly misplaced and out of date. Whereas earlier generations may have worried about the excesses of party power, we increasingly worry about the weakness and withering of party organization. Many reformers have turned their energies from curbing the parties to saving them.

American party organizations probably have never commanded incentives and rewards at all equal to their organizational goals and ambitions. In that sense, they have been chronically "underfinanced." They never have been able to recruit the kinds of resources they would need in order to flesh out the party organization that the state statutes create. The thousands of inactive precinct workers and unfilled precinct positions testify to that poverty of incentive. The parties, therefore, have had no alternative but to tolerate organizational forms that have permitted them to live within their means.

[49]Leon D. Epstein, *Politics in Wisconsin* (Madison: University of Wisconsin Press, 1958), p. 90.

5

NATIONAL ORGANIZATIONS:
THE UNCERTAIN SUMMIT

So extreme have been the traditional observations on the decentralization of the American parties that one is tempted to dismiss them as empty rhetoric or pure hyperbole. One noted scholar of the American parties has written:

> Decentralization of power is by all odds the most important single characteristic of the American major party; more than anything else this trait distinguishes it from all others. Indeed, once this truth is understood, nearly everything else about American parties is greatly illuminated . . . . The American major party is, to repeat the definition, a loose confederation of state and local bosses for limited purposes.[1]

Is it possible, one wonders, that these disparate, often disorganized local party organizations are not subordinated to or coordinated by some higher party unit? Are the local and state organizations free to use the name and traditions of a nationwide political party for their own parochial interests without any control by the national party? Closer examination of the American parties reveals that what seems to be hyperbole has actually been a statement of reality. Power and authority in the party organizations reside largely in the states and localities, and that fact colors virtually every aspect of the parties' activities.

State and local party organizations of the major parties pick their own officers, nominate their candidates, take their own stands on issues, and raise and spend their own funds without much interference from any manifestation of the national party. What appears to be a pyramiding of state party committees into a single, integrating national party authority, therefore, is in reality nothing of the kind. Often, the national committees serve

---

[1]E. E. Schattschneider, *Party Government* (New York: Rinehart, 1942), pp. 129, 132–33 (emphasis omitted).

only as arenas for the bargaining and jockeying among the powerful local and state organizations and presidential candidates within the party. The authors of the leading study of the national committees pointedly chose to title it *Politics Without Power*.[2] Indeed, it has often been said that, in reality, there are no national parties, that what we blithely call the national parties are merely coalitions of jealous, wary, and diverse state and local party organizations.

In the late 1970s and early 1980s, however, there have been incontestable signs that the national committees are emerging into the light after 150 years of eclipse. Their resources and staffs are growing, and they are undertaking new roles and activities. They have become, in short, more active, vital, and influential. Yet there are far fewer signs of their attempts to limit the autonomy of state and local organizations. For the present, at least, there appears to be far more *nationalization* of activity in the parties than *centralization* of authority within them. The distinction may be a fine one, but it is essential in assessing the state of national party organization these days.

If it is indeed true that we see the first signs of national vitality in the parties, it is useful to ask what took them so long. Most other aspects of American life have long since been nationalized. The mass media bring the same reporters, TV images, and commentators into homes in all parts of the country. By any measure, government in the American federal system has been increasingly centered in Washington since the 1930s. Even the other two sectors of the party have been nationalized in the past few decades. The party electorates respond increasingly to national issues, to national candidates, and to national party symbols and positions. Attention now centers as well on the national parties in government; the president and the congressional leadership of the parties are more than ever the preeminent spokesmen for their parties. The third sector—party organization—has remained rooted in the states for a number of reasons: the state regulation of parties, the thousands of public officials chosen in the states, and the domination of local organization by those officials. All those local pressures still exist, of course, and they will continue to resist centralization of authority within the parties.

THE NATIONAL COMMITTEES
AND NATIONAL OFFICERS

Technically, the nominating convention each party holds midway in a presidential election year is the party's supreme national authority. The convention's role, however, rarely goes beyond the selection of presidential

[2]Cornelius P. Cotter and Bernard C. Hennessy, *Politics Without Power: The National Party Committees* (New York: Atherton, 1964).

and vice-presidential candidates and the formulation of party platforms. It does ratify the selection of national committee members, and it does specify the structure and powers of the national committee; but since the convention adjourns *sine die* (i.e., without setting a time for a future meeting) until four years later, it can exercise no continuing supervision over the national organizational apparatus of the party.

For years, the national committees of the two major parties were similarly composed. The drastic revision of the Democratic body in 1972 changed that (Table 5.1). The Democratic National Committee has now become twice the size of its Republican counterpart. More important, the Democrats have abandoned the confederational nature of the committee. Traditionally, each state had been represented in both national committees on an approximately equal basis, regardless of the size of its electorate or the extent of its support for the party. States, not populations or number of partisans, were represented, much as the United States and the Maldive Islands are represented equally in the United Nations General Assembly. That representational system overrepresented the state organizations of the smaller states, however, and it also gave roughly equal weight in the na-

---

TABLE 5.1   *Composition of Democratic and Republican National Committees: 1982*

	Number of Members
Democratic National Committee	
Chairperson and next highest ranking officer of opposite sex from each state and from D.C., Puerto Rico, Guam, Virgin Islands, Democrats Abroad	110
200 members apportioned to states, etc., on same basis as delegates to national convention (at least two per state, etc.)	200
Chairperson of Democratic Governors Conference and two additional governors	3
Chairperson of Democratic Mayors Conference and two additional mayors	3
Chairperson of Democratic County Officials Conference and two additional officials	3
Democratic leader and one other member from each House of Congress	4
Officials and representatives of National Committee and its auxiliaries	10
No more than 25 additional members	0–25
	333–358
Republican National Committee	
National committeeman, national committeewoman, and state chairman from each state and from D.C., Guam, Puerto Rico, and Virgin Islands	162
	162

tional committees to the winning and the losing parts of the party. The practical consequence was a strengthening of the conservative wings of both parties—chiefly the southern and western segments of the parties. The newly restructured Democratic National Committee, however, gives weight both to population and to party support. California, for example, has eighteen members on the committee, and Nevada has four.

Formally, the national conventions select the members of the national committees, but that action merely ratifies decisions made within the states. The state parties differ from one another in how they make their decisions; and in many states, the two parties choose their national committeemen and committeewomen differently. Among the four main methods—selection by state party convention, by the party delegation to the national convention, by the state central committee, and by election in a primary—the first (selection by convention) is the most popular in both parties. In this welter of selection processes, one point is worth noting. Although the parties' state organizations usually can control the selection of committee members when they are chosen by the state committee and by the state conventions, they are less effective when the selection is by primaries or by national convention delegates. Especially in states that choose delegates in presidential primaries, the delegation to the national convention may represent voter support of a momentarily popular candidate more than it represents the leadership of the state party. A number of Democratic delegations in 1972, for example, were composed of party newcomers and mavericks who were pledged to George McGovern. The old-line party leaders in those states had supported other contenders and thus were not delegates.

The chairpersons and other officers of the national committees do not have to be—and often are not—members of the committees. They are elected and removed by the committees. Immediately after the conventions, however, tradition recognizes the right of the parties' presidential candidates to name the national chairpersons for the course of the presidential campaign. The committees ratify their choices without question. Moreover, since the party of the president will continue to respect his choice of a national party chairperson after the election, only the committee of the "out" party actually selects its own national chairperson. The committees generally have much greater freedom to select other committee officials—vice-chairpersons, secretaries, and treasurers—many of whom come from the committee itself. In addition, both national committees select executive committees, which include the officers and from ten to fifteen other members of the committee.

Within this apparatus—supplemented, of course, by the national committees' permanent staffs—the chairpersons dominate. The full committees meet only two or three times a year, and occasionally even less than that. As Cotter and Hennessy report:

Collectively the national committee is not much more than a categorical group. . . . The national committee members have very little collective identity, little patterned interaction, and only rudimentary common values and goals.

Except for occasional meetings—largely for show and newsmaking purposes—the national committees may be thought of not so much as groups, but as lists of people who have obtained their national committee memberships through organizational processes wholly separate in each state.[3]

The other officers of the party are not especially influential, and the executive committees meet only a little more often than the full committees. Like the full committees, the executive committees are composed of men and women whose concern is state (and even local) organizational work rather than the building of a strong national party apparatus. Tradition-

[3]*Ibid.*, p. 39.

A Republican Chairman Departs: 1981–82

A national chairperson's lot is not usually a happy one when he or she chairs the national committee of the president's party. Richard Richards, chairman of the GOP National Committee from 1981 to 1983, shared what is becoming a predictable fate. Several newspaper accounts tell the story:

> The national chairman of the party of an incumbent President often has difficulty in finding a comfortable role. He is frequently accused of either following a President slavishly, or somehow obstructing him—a gripe often heard from White House staffs under both Democratic and Republican Administrations.
>
> The internal complaints about Mr. Richards focus more on what he has failed to do than on what he and other officials have accomplished in the nine months since the inauguration.
>
> "They're always in the planning stages of everything," complained one campaign expert who thought the necessary efforts to broaden the base of the party were being neglected.
>
> Adam Clymer, in *New York Times*,
> October 9, 1981

> "I expect to serve out my term," he [Richards] said. "I am not out of sync with the White House. I'm satisfied I have President Reagan's confidence."

ally, therefore, the national chairperson, with the permanent staff, has in effect been the national party organization.

In reality, the role of the national committees and chairpersons is flexible. If theirs is the party of the president, they may be little more than managers of the president's campaigns and builders of his political support. Indeed, during the Nixon years, the president and his staff managed his political matters, and Rogers Morton and Robert Dole, the Republican national chairmen, did little more than serve as liaisons between the president and party leaders around the country. In any event, relationships between a chairperson and the political operatives in the White House are invariably difficult (see box). In the party out of power, the chairperson and committee must often bind up wounds, heal intraparty squabbles, help pay debts from the losing campaign, raise new money, and revivify the party organization around the country. The chairperson of the opposition party may also speak for the party and as an alternative to the president's party.

As for the future, Mr. Richards said: "I won't speculate on that. I never planned on running for another term. I'll have to see how bloody I am at that time. I came here to do two years."

Mr. Richards denied suggestions circulated by a top Reagan political aide that Rich Bond had been installed by the White House as the new deputy chairman to keep an eye on the chairman.

"Rich Bond is my choice; he was not forced on me," Mr. Richards said.

From *New York Times*,
December 22, 1981

. . . Richard Richards said he would leave as Republican chairman when his term expired in January. 'The decision was mine,' said Mr. Richards, who then acknowledged that neither President Reagan nor any other top White House official had urged him to stay.
. . .

Mr. Richards cited press speculation that he was about to be dumped as a major factor prompting him to announce his plans four weeks before elections in which many party leaders fear the Republicans will lose much of the ground they gained in 1980.

"Every clerk in the White House thinks he can do my job better than I do," replied Mr. Richards when asked if he could explain repeated speculation that he was on his way out. "If I had my choice I would not have a political shop in the White House," he said.

From *New York Times*, October 5, 1982

As the role of the committee and its chairperson shifts, so, too, do the job specifications for a national party chairperson. Within the party of the president, he or she must be congenial to the president, representative of his ideological stance, and willing to be loyal primarily to the president. Ronald Reagan's choice in 1982 of his personal friend and fellow conservative, Senator Paul Laxalt of Nevada, to the new role of party general chairman is only the most recent bit of evidence to that effect. Within the opposition party, the chairperson will often be congenial to—or at least trusted by—the various factions or segments of the party. Frequently, he or she is chosen for ideological neutrality or for lack of identification with any of the individuals seeking the party's next presidential nomination. Experience in the nuts and bolts of party organization is also desirable. It is significant that the Democrats, after their catastrophe in 1972, replaced George McGovern's choice, Jean Westwood, with an old party "pro," Robert Strauss. As the job specifications vary, so do the hunting grounds for prospective chairpersons. Historically, the parties have most frequently found their chairpersons among state party leaders; lately, however, the parties have shown a tendency to select members of Congress (see Table 5.2).

TABLE 5.2 *National Committee Chairpersons of the Major Parties: 1961–83*

Name	Years	Political Position at Appointment
Democrats		
John M. Bailey	1961–68	State party chairman in Connecticut
Lawrence F. O'Brien	1968–69	U.S. postmaster general
Fred R. Harris	1969–70	U.S. senator from Oklahoma
Lawrence F. O'Brien	1970–72	Former national party chairman
Jean Westwood	1972	Active in McGovern preconvention campaign
Robert S. Strauss	1972–77	Democratic national treasurer
Kenneth M. Curtis	1977	Former governor of Maine
John C. White	1977–81	Deputy secretary of agriculture
Charles T. Manatt	1981–	Finance chairman of Democratic National Committee
Republicans		
William E. Miller	1961–64	U.S. representative from New York
Dean Burch	1964–65	Active in Barry Goldwater campaign
Ray C. Bliss	1965–69	State party chairman in Ohio
Rogers C. Morton	1969–71	U.S. representative from Maryland
Robert J. Dole	1971–73	U.S. senator from Kansas
George H. Bush	1973–74	U.S. ambassador to the United Nations
Mary Louise Smith	1974–77	Cochairperson of Republican National Committee
William E. Brock	1977–81	Former U.S. senator from Tennessee
Richard Richards	1981–83	Regional coordinator for Reagan campaign
Frank J. Fahrenkopf	1983–	Republican state chairman in Nevada

THE SUPPORTING CAST OF NATIONAL GROUPS

Clustered around the national committees are a set of more or less formal groups that also purport to speak for the party or for some part of it. Some of them are creatures of the national committees, but some are not. Taken together with the national committee in each party, they come close to constituting that vague entity we call the national party.

The Women's Groups

For a long time, both the Democratic and the Republican national committees have had women's divisions within their structures. In addition, both have had national federations of state and local women's groups: the National Federation of Democratic Women and the National Federation of Republican Women. Even though they are officially independent of the national committees, they are housed with them and work closely with them. In the past, they have been responsive to the cues of national party leaders, and it would not be easy to find instances of substantial independence on their part.

Within the past decade or more, the importance of these women's divisions and organizations has declined markedly. Women increasingly have entered regular leadership positions in the parties, and a woman has now chaired each party's national committee for the first time in history. Moreover, the percentage of women delegates to national party conventions rose sharply in both parties in the 1970s, and in 1982 almost half the members of the Democratic National Committee were women. Both parties have also eliminated the designated offices for women—the party "vice-chairwoman" positions, for example—that for so long confirmed their separate but unequal status. Quite simply, women now want a role in the regular party organizations, or else they prefer to become active in nonparty organizations, such as the National Women's Political Caucus. Certainly, they do not have in mind the docile role they have traditionally played in the parties.

The Youth Groups

The Young Republican National Federation and the Young Democrats of America both meet every other year to elect national officers and to debate and pass resolutions. "Young" in both instances means men and women to the age of thirty-five; in fact, the Democrats did not retreat from a maximum age of forty until 1971. Both federations traditionally have been represented in their party's national councils, and the major staff and funding for both is provided in substantial part by the senior party.

Unlike the women, the organized youth of both parties have been neither docile nor compliant. They often have taken stands and have supported candidates that embarrassed the senior party organization. The Young Republicans, for instance, had a long infatuation with Goldwater conservatism, continuing in it long after the regular leadership of the party had tried to reflect a more centrist position. In the late 1960s and 1970s, their loyalties turned increasingly to the conservatism of Governor Ronald Reagan of California. The Young Democrats often stood to the left of their senior party organization. In 1969, for instance, their national convention called for repeal of all legal limits on abortion, for liberalization of marijuana laws, for recognition of Cuba and Communist China, and for an "immediate and total withdrawal of all American troops in Vietnam." In recent years, however, the Young Democrats have turned to the center, reacting, perhaps, to the defeat of 1980.

The adoption of the eighteen-year-old vote and the youth activism of the 1960s and 1970s brought thousands of young people into the main business of the parties and made them less willing to accept the status of tutelage that the youth organizations imply. Many of them had staffed the Eugene McCarthy campaign in 1968, and many also went as delegates to the subsequent conventions of both parties. In any event, membership in all party youth groups has fallen off, and signs of apathy are everywhere. It is no exaggeration to say that the youth and women's groups are in good measure victims of the parties' willingness to involve those very individuals in their central business.

The Party's Officeholders in the States

Although they are not part of the official national organizations of their parties, the state governors invariably speak with authority in them. They have the prestige of high office and electoral success. Many lead or command the support of state party organizations. Many also head state delegations to the parties' national conventions, and a few inevitably contend for their parties' presidential nominations.

The organization of the gubernatorial presence in the national parties, however, is relatively recent. The Republicans were first. After the Goldwater defeat of 1964, the moderate Republican governors wanted primarily to create a counterweight to the party's conservatives. A few years later, they established a full-time Washington office with financial help from the party's national committee, but their influence waned after the Republican victory of 1968. Like many such groups within the national parties, the governors operate most tellingly in the power vacuums of a party out of power. By the 1970s, the Democratic governors, by then in the party of opposition, began to press for a role in national party affairs. By 1974, they had achieved that voice and had won representation, although in modest numbers, on the national committee. By the late 1970s and early 1980s, therefore, the governors of both parties had Washington offices and staffs. Their influence in the national parties, however, continued to vary inversely with their parties' presidential fortunes.

State legislators and local officials in both parties are organized; moreover, they are formally represented on the Democratic National Committee. It would be hard to argue, though, that they greatly influence the national business of either party.

The Capitol Hill Committees

In each house of the Congress, the members of the parties are organized in committees to promote the reelection of their members and the addition of new members to their ranks. The names of the four committees reflect the two houses and the two parties: the Democratic Congressional Campaign Committee, the National Republican Congressional Committee, the Democratic Senatorial Campaign Committee, and the National Republican Senatorial Committee.

Their increasing ability to raise campaign funds has brought them a new visibility. The Republican committees are by far the more affluent and active; together they raised and spent more than $60 million in 1982. Some of those funds went directly to candidates, but the larger part went for candidate recruitment, candidate training, and research on opponents and issues, and for dealing with the media, opinion polling, ads, and other campaign services. The Democrats now function in a similar but more modest way. In both parties, however, the committees of The Hill are vastly more active and effective than they were just 10 years ago. In resources and campaigning skills, they have begun to challenge the importance of the national committees of their parties. Their strength also protects them and the congressional party very well from threats by the national party organization.

Party Notables and Allies

Both the Democrats and the Republicans have a group of party notables whose celebrity entitles them to attention, even influence, within the national party. Often, they are distinguished citizens, former officeholders, captains of industry or labor, holders of famous names, or long-time contributors to the party treasury. Sometimes—as in the case of a distinguished Democrat, Averell Harriman—they are all those things at once. Sometimes the notables combine visibility in nonparty pursuits with loyalty to a party—the Hollywood contingents of the two parties are a case in point—but whatever the source of their celebrity, they share with all other notables an entrée to important circles inside and outside politics. It is a status that, party and profession aside, unites Paul Newman and Henry Kissinger, Edmund Muskie and Bob Hope.

Also clustered around the official committees of the Democratic and Republican parties are those group allies whose loyalty to one or the other party is so great as to identify them with the party in the public mind. They achieve that power in the national party for one or both of two primary reasons: their financial support of the party and the loyalty of substantial numbers of party activists to them. Organized labor, especially the AFL-CIO and its Committee on Political Education (COPE), certainly stands in that relationship to the Democrats. So do some of the liberal groups and associations in American politics, such as the Americans for Democratic Action. Conservative groups, stout in financial resources and closely in touch with the party's right wing, enjoy a close relationship with the Republican party. So, too, do business groups such as the U.S. Chamber of Commerce.

TWO PATHS TO POWER

At some point in the 1960s, a quiet revolution began in the Republican National Committee (RNC). The committee's chairman of those years, Ray Bliss, involved the committee more and more in helping state and local parties with the nuts and bolts of party organizational work. Chairman William Brock carried the work forward in the late 1970s, turning the national party into an extraordinarily effective service organization for the parties of the states and localities. Brock, more than anyone else, revived and strengthened the Republican national party by fashioning a new role for it.

The keys to success in finding the new role or mission were two: new money and mastery of the new campaign technologies. Using direct mail solicitations, which in turn used computer-based mailing lists, the Republicans began to generate ever higher levels of income. By the 1979–80 election cycle, the Republican National Committee, along with its subsidiary funds and committees, raised some $75.4 million. (The Democrats raised $6.3 million. Campaign finance is discussed more fully in Chapter 13.) Those resources have enabled the RNC and its affiliates to engage in programs of aid to candidates and local party organization without parallel in American party history. More than a dozen full-time regional coordinators cover the country. Their activities and those of the RNC generally are not limited to Congressional elections; for instance, the committee mounted an extensive program of support in 1980 to increase the size of Republican delegations in state legislatures in order to influence the tasks of reapportionment after the decennial census.[4]

[4]See Charles H. Longley, "National Party Renewal," in Gerald M. Pomper (ed.), *Party Renewal in America* (New York: Praeger, 1980); and John F. Bibby, "Political Parties and Federalism: The Republican National Committee Involvement in Gubernatorial and Legislative Elections," *Publius* (Winter 1979): 229–36.

TABLE 5.3   *A Comparison of Assets of the Democratic and Republican National Committees: 1982*

	Democratic National Committee	Republican National Committee
Number of paid staff members	100	450
Regional staffing	limited	full; organizers in all regions
Operating budget	$8 million	$38 million
List of past contributors	250,000 names	1,500,000 names

Note   Estimates of budgetary and support strength from both inside and outside the parties differ to a considerable degree. The estimates for 1982 here are, in effect, averages or approximations derived from a number of sources.

As for the Democrats, they found themselves badly overmatched in organizational and service capacity by 1982 (see Table 5.3). The good news for the Democrats was that they had dramatically improved their fundraising capacities and their activities in the states and localities since 1979 or 1980. The bad news was that the Republicans were far ahead of them in 1980 and that the Republicans, too, were increasing their strength and capacity. Whatever the degree of Democratic success in becoming a service party, there was certainly no doubt that the party, under the national chairmanship of Charles Manatt, had seen that as the only feasible course for party development. Indeed, the national Democrats made no secret of their attempt to mimic the Republican success.

That had not, of course, been the path the national Democrats took in the late 1960s and the 1970s. In the reforms that grew out of Eugene McCarthy's insurgent movement in 1968 and George McGovern's candidacy in 1972, the goal was something approaching an American version of the European membership party—more participation by party activists, less dominance by the party in government, and a greater commitment to issues and ideology. Appropriately, the Democratic National Committee (DNC) represented not state parties but numbers of party loyalists. Party rules required open, participant processes for the election of party officials and, particularly, delegates to its national conventions. Moreover, rules for the selection of delegates were designed to ensure that the delegates were as representative as possible of the diversity of the American people. In the course of these reforms, the DNC achieved some stunning assertions of national party power, including the triumph of national party rules over Wisconsin's open primary in the selection of delegates to the Democratic national convention.[5] Finally, to make the

---

[5]*Democratic Party of the United States v. La Follette*, 450 U.S. 107 (1981).

expression of policy preferences more regular and forceful, the party created the biennial conference to meet midway in the four years between national conventions.[6]

By the early 1980s, the national Democratic party had decided to alter its plans and move toward the Republican service model. All of its centralization of national authority on questions of representation and participation, even the overriding of the procedural preferences of state parties and state laws, had done little to win elections. Moreover, it had divided the party and had alienated a good part of the Democratic party in government, much of which was conspicuously absent from party conventions and midyear conferences in the 1970s. Thus, in the Manatt years, 1981 and after, the Democrats shifted course. The national committee adopted rules for the 1984 national convention that guaranteed a much greater representation of the party's leaders and officeholders. (See Chapter 11 for much more on delegate selection.) The midyear conference of 1982 was reshaped from an issue-stating "miniconvention" to a "leadership conference" whose chief emphasis was on party building. To map winning strategy, the party convened not a group of party ideologists but a strategy council representative primarily of party leaders and officeholders. In addition, in the 1980s, the party rushed to broaden the base of its fund raising and to provide the means and know-how to recruit candidates and revitalize local party organization. In short, the signs of change were everywhere, and what had been two models for national party strengthening were rapidly converging into one.

POWER AND AUTHORITY IN THE NATIONAL PARTY

It is clear that there has been a strengthening of the national parties in the last decade and that the most apparent and important strengthening has been in the activities that would regain some of the parties' lost roles in nominating and electing candidates. What is less clear is the extent to which that buttressing of the national parties has altered relationships within the parties: between national party and local organization and between national party and its president.

The State and Local Connection

The increased resources and activities of the two parties, without question, have led to greater visibility and presence for the national parties. The

[6]On Democratic reform, see Austin Ranney, *Curing the Mischiefs of Faction: Party Reform in America* (Berkeley: University of California Press, 1975); and William J. Crotty, *Decisions for the Democrats: Reforming the Party Structure* (Baltimore: Johns Hopkins University Press, 1978).

beginnings of national party institutional advertising is only one sign of that (see box). National personalities and nationally determined issues became more important. National party activity in 1982 certainly focused the congressional elections on the first two years of the Reagan presidency.

The extent to which that kind of nationalization of the parties has also led to a centralization of authority within them is less clear. The Democrats approach the service party role with far more experience than the Republicans have in drafting and enforcing rules for all parts and places of the party. Moreover, the structure of representation on the DNC can

---

The National Parties as Publicists

Nothing signals the nationalization of the parties as surely as their recent forays into TV ads that set national party themes and that involve them in party-centered appeals to the electorate. Ben Wattenberg, a syndicated columnist who approves the innovation, described some of the ads:

> The Republicans began changing things in 1978 by investing about $2 million in televised "institutional advertising." The institution was their party.
>
> By 1980, Republican party-based television spending was up to $9 million. One TV spot showed a Tip O'Neill look-alike running out of gas after decades of political promiscuity. Another featured an unemployed steelworker, a Democrat, switching to Reagan. The slogan was "Vote Republican—For a Change.". . .
>
> This year the Republicans will boost spending to $15 million on televised ads. Their ads repeat the political promiscuity theme and say "Give the Guy a Chance" and "Stay the Course."
>
> And, finally, in this campaign, a resuscitated Democratic Party has started to play. . . . [A] series of brilliant spots shows: the step-by-step mutilation of a Social Security card, a champagne-glass model of trickle-down economics where the voter with the tin cup doesn't get a drop, . . . and the good old Democratic steelworker, now savaged by Reaganomics, returning home, telling us how the Republicans paid him to do the ad in 1980, but this one is on the house.
>
> The Democrats have only a million dollars to spend on party-based ads this year; they may yet raise an additional million. Still, it's a start. It's about where the Republicans were four years ago, and it will grow.

> From *The Washington Post*, September 29, 1982
> (© 1982, United Feature Syndicate).

---

sustain and legitimize more centralized authority. The Republicans, on the other hand, remain a confederation of equal state parties; they are also, by political philosophy, more wary of centralized authority in any form. Philosophies and organizational formalities aside, however, it is difficult to imagine that the national subsidization of state and local party organizations and the national intervention into their nominations and elections will not be accompanied by *some* centralization of authority. However lightly and informally it is exercised, it is most likely that a national imprint on issues, on the kinds of candidates recruited, and on the way things are done organizationally will follow. Resistance in the state and local organizations might well be at the price of starvation. Those who pay the pipers more often than not call the tune.[7]

The Presidential Connection

When the party holds the presidency, the president's program and record become the party's. It is the president who interprets the party's platform and the mandate of the voters. His preferences, whether embodied in the formal measures of the State of the Union address or tossed off more casually at a press conference, impose a policy and a record on his party. He may consult the party chairperson or other party notables, but it is his decisions, his successes or failures, that form the party record.

Every president in recent memory has kept his national committee on a short leash, but the White House dominance of the national party reached its zenith in the presidency of Richard M. Nixon. The Watergate tapes reveal that the president's principal assistants, John Erlichman and H. R. Haldeman, were deeply involved in the decisions of the 1972 campaign—a campaign headed, in fact, by another member of the Nixon personal following, former attorney general John Mitchell. So marginal to the 1972 campaign were the Republican party bodies and officials that they remained ignorant and innocent of the wrongdoing and scandals of the campaign. Democratic presidents, too, have wanted the national committee under their control. Initially Jimmy Carter relied on a strong national chairman, Robert Strauss, perhaps because the president had come to Washington as an outsider in the Democratic party. After the Strauss chairmanship, however, relationships between the White House and the DNC settled into more usual patterns. Carter men held the chief positions at the committee, and in 1980 the president angered party people by diverting crucial DNC personnel and resources for his own reelection campaign.

[7]For a good description of the traditional relationships of state party leadership and the national parties, see Robert J. Huckshorn, *Party Leadership in the States* (Amherst: University of Massachusetts Press, 1976), Chap. 8.

By contrast, in those four long years after presidential defeat, a national party suffers an almost incessant jockeying for the right to lead. The defeated presidential candidate, depending on his ties and popularity within the party, may achieve an important voice in the party. Gerald Ford did, but Jimmy Carter did not. A strong and vigorous national chairperson may also succeed; those with substantial financial and organizational accomplishments are more likely to succeed. Most commonly, however, leadership of the "out" party falls to its leaders in the Congress. During the Reagan years, it is the Speaker of the House of Representatives, Thomas P. ("Tip") O'Neill, who more than any other individual symbolizes the national Democratic party. The visibility of the party's leadership in Congress is matched by the political support and power of its campaign committees. Above all, the congressional party, simply because its legislative responsibilities force it to take policy stands, formulates the party position and challenges the program of the opposition's president.

It seems safe to predict that strengthened national party committees will assume a more prominent party role in the party out of power. The same is true of their chairpersons. That much seems clear when one considers the Republicans under William Brock in the late 1970s and the Democrats under Charles Manatt in the early 1980s—but what of a strengthened party and its president? It seems likely that presidents will continue to worry about independent party voices and that they will want the new party power to be at their service. They will certainly want the party committees to mobilize behind their programs all those members of Congress they recruited, trained, financed, and helped elect. Also, if presidents are in their first term, they will very likely want to draw on the assets of the national party for their reelection campaigns. If presidents feared and used the national committees when the committees were weak, they have even more reason to do so when the committees are more formidable.

Those considerations seem to have been at play as the White House managed changes in the leadership of the RNC in late 1982 and early 1983. The director of the Reagan campaign in 1980, who was also a personal friend of the president—Senator Paul Laxalt—was installed in the new "general" chairmanship of the party. In apparent recognition of the need for full-time management of the committee, a Nevada associate of Laxalt, Frank J. Fahrenkopf, became the "regular chairman" of the party. The dual chairmanship, devised in the White House, was explained to the national committee by the administration's secretary of transportation, Drew Lewis:

> "With an incumbent President, the party chairman is dominated almost totally by the White House," Mr. Lewis said. "Unless the chairman is an insider, he's not going to be heard. Dick Richards had that problem.

Fahrenkopf may have that problem. But Laxalt can pick up the phone and tell the White House what he needs and be heard."

Under the new arrangement, Mr. Lewis said, the Republican National Committee will function as part of the "re-elect the President committee," although the organizations probably will have separate identities for technical purposes.[8]

The Limits of Party Power

Amid all the talk and reports of new strength in the national party organization, it is well to remember that in the American way of politics, there are still many limits to the strengthening of party organizations. We see in the national committees of the 1980s a kind of strength and power we have not seen in our past; however, compared to the national parties of the democracies of the rest of the world, they are less impressive. They are still cadre parties, and the recent backing away of the Democrats from a membership model confirms that fact. We are seeing, that is, the refinement and improvement—not the transformation—of cadre parties, at both the national and the state levels.

Whether one talks of local or national party organization in a cadre party, the organization remains largely subsidiary to the party in government. Thus, at the national level, the dominant party voice is that of the party's president or its leadership in the Congress. The strengthening of national party organization over the last decade has helped it regain some of its electoral role. Although that greater electoral role has given the national organizations new sources of leverage vis-à-vis the party in government, however, it has not yet enabled the organization to challenge its dominant position within the party. It is one thing to win elections, but it is quite another to discipline public officials and enact party programs.

Does the fading of the dream of the Democratic reformers of 1968 and 1972 mean that the Democrats have rejected the membership, participatory, issue-concerned party for good? Not necessarily—it simply means that the party found that its goals were not those of large numbers of people in the electorate and that, consequently, it could not easily win elections while pursuing those goals. Some of the institutions of a transformed party remain, however: the party constitution (the Democratic Charter), a representative national committee, the midterm conference, the participant local parties, and a reformed national convention. There also remains a large group of party activists with strong issue concerns, with deeply felt expectations for change and for their role in it, and with

[8]Howell Raines in the *New York Times*, January 29, 1983.

no fears of national party authority. Their time might very well come again.

A FINAL NOTE ON PARTY ORGANIZATION

We have come to accept large-scale organization as an important social reality in this century. In business, government, universities, and voluntary organizations, it is a time of complex social structures and of the bureaucrats who have become their symbols. We have every right to include the parties among them, but it is an inescapable fact that the parties, almost alone among our major social institutions, have resisted the development of large, centralized organization.

Even by the standards of the parties of the other democracies, the American party organizations cut an unimpressive figure. They lack the hierarchical control and efficiency, the unified setting of priorities and strategy, and the central responsibility we associate with large contemporary organizations. Instead of a continuity of relationships and of operations, the American party organizations feature only improvisatory, elusive, and sporadic structure and activities. Also, whereas the party organizations of the other Western democracies have had permanent, highly professional leadership and large party bureaucracies, the American organizations have generally done without a professional bureaucracy or leadership cadre.[9] One does not make a career in the administration of the American parties. The business of American party organization is still largely in the hands of part-time activists, which is perhaps to say that its business and its organizational relationships require no specialists and no full-time professional care.

One is compelled to wonder at the reasons for the stunting of American party organization. In part, it results from statutory limits and prescriptions. Traditional fears of political parties and party strength have certainly contributed as well. (There is little in American political values that would welcome an efficient or "businesslike" operation of the parties.) In large part, however, the underorganization of the American parties results from their fundamental character. They have been pragmatic electoral parties, involved chiefly in supporting candidates for public office and active mainly during campaigns. As such, they have long been led and dominated, not by career bureaucrats, but by public office seekers and holders. Perhaps, too, the degree of pragmatic flexibility to which Americans have carried their party politics rules out the routine and the

[9]On party bureaucracy, see the perceptive article by Charles E. Schutz, "Bureaucratic Party Organization Through Professional Political Staffing," *Midwest Journal of Political Science* 8 (1964): 127–42.

fixity of a large organization. Organization is to some extent routine and unchanging, and it is therefore more compatible with the party of unchanging ideology or principle than with one committed to the adjustments necessary for electoral success. Thus, the electoral preoccupations of the American parties have tipped the scales in favor of parties in government and against the party organizations.

III

The Political Party
as an Electorate

In very few party systems is the gulf between the party organization and the party in the electorate[1] as great as it is in the American party system. Unlike most of the parties of the European democracies, the American party organizations have not been able to integrate the party's most loyal supporters into the party organization. Throughout the 1960s and into the 1970s, the Italian Communist and Christian Democratic parties by themselves enrolled about 10 percent of Italian adults into party membership. Membership groups within the American parties, however, are very small and comparatively rare.

Nor have the American parties mounted any substantial programs to educate their loyal electorates into the programs and traditions of the party. American party organizations view even the most sympathetic voters as a separate clientele to be reinforced anew at each election. Those sympathetic voters, for all their protestations of loyalty to the party, also stand apart. They consider their obligations to the party amply filled if they support its candidates in a substantial majority of instances.

This party in the electorate, unlike the party organization, is largely a categorical group. There is no interaction within it, no structured set of relationships, no organizational or group life. Also, like any categorical group, it is an artifact of the way we choose to define it. There is common scholarly agreement, however, that the party in the electorate is characterized by its feelings of loyalty to or identification with the party. In the American political context, its people are the men and women who consider themselves Democrats and Republicans; they may even, in the loose

---

[1]The term was popularized by V. O. Key in *Politics, Parties, and Pressure Groups*, 5th ed. (New York: Crowell, 1964), p. 164. Key, however, attributed the term to Ralph M. Goldman.

usages of American politics, consider themselves "members" of one party
or the other. In practical, operational terms, they are the partisans who
answer either "Republican" or "Democrat" to such survey questions as,
"Generally speaking, do you usually think of yourself as a Republican, a
Democrat, an independent, or what?"[2]

The size of the American parties in the electorate depends on the measures we employ to determine them. The 1980 data of the Center for Political Studies (CPS) at the University of Michigan, for example, indicate
the following breakdowns of party identifications within the American
electorate:[3]

Strong Democrats	17.7%
Weak Democrats	23.0
Independents	34.5
Weak Republicans	13.9
Strong Republicans	8.5
Others (apolitical, other party, etc.)	2.3

If one groups all the partisan identifiers together, one defines two party
electorates that account for almost two-thirds of American adults (63.1
percent). A more reasonable alternative might be to accept only the
"strong" identifiers, totaling 26.2 percent of the American adults, as approximations of the two parties in the electorate.

Such estimates of the size of the party electorate, it should be emphasized, are exceptionally arbitrary. One can imagine other acceptable ways
of measuring the party in the electorate. One might, for example, identify
it with the party's regular voters, regardless of any loyalty they may or
may not declare. (In 1980, about 33 percent of the CPS's national sample
declared that they had always voted for the same party since they began
to vote.) There are good reasons, however, for preferring the criterion of
party identification. Strong party identifiers do tend to be the party's
faithful voters, but they are more than straight-ticket voters. They have
a degree of loyalty and emotional attachment to the party that substitutes
in some measure for the formal act of membership in a party system in
which membership is not common. They are also more apt to be active

---

[2]The question is the chief one the Center for Political Studies of the University of Michigan uses to determine party identification. The Gallup Poll (American Institute of Public
Opinion) uses the following similar question: "In politics, as of today, do you consider yourself a Republican, Democrat, or independent?"

[3]The identifications here were developed in response to the question in footnote 2 and
to a follow-up question that separated the partisan identifiers into strong and weak groups.
Independents were also asked a follow-up question to see if they leaned toward a party. The
results: Democratic independents, 11.4 percent; pure independents, 12.9 percent; Republican independents, 10.2 percent.

workers in the party. In short, the party identifiers bring fairly predictable votes to the party, but they also bring loyalty, activity, and even public support to it.[4]

Despite their expressions of party loyalty, the members of the parties in the electorate are fickle, and they sometimes waver in their support of the party of their choice. The party organizations and candidates know that even their electoral support cannot be taken for granted; other appeals and loyalties may occasionally override even the staunchest party loyalties. Also, some loyalists—probably a minority—express a loyalty that is little more than an empty formula. They may be Democrats or Republicans in the same sense that many individuals call themselves members of a religious denomination even though they have not stepped inside a church for years. For all of this, however, the members of the party electorates do vote for the candidates of "their" party and do support its public positions with a faithfulness far beyond that of the rest of the total electorate. They tend, in other words, to be the party regulars and straight-ticket voters. They are the men and women who, in the argot of Madison Avenue, display the greatest partisan "product loyalty."

For all its uncertainties, the party in the electorate does provide the party organization and candidates with a stable, hard core of electoral support. Its reliability releases the organization and its standard-bearers from the intolerable burden of convincing and mobilizing a full majority of the electorate in every campaign. The party in the electorate also performs additional services for the party. It is a reservoir of potential activists for the organization. Its members may also make financial contributions to the party, or they may work in a specific campaign. Those people who attend party rallies, who talk about politics and persuade friends, or who express any form of political enthusiasm in the community very probably come from its ranks. Its members are most active in perpetuating the party by socializing their children into loyalty to the party and possibly activity in it. In sum, they give the party an image and a presence in the community, and the most involved among them constitute something of an auxiliary semiorganization that supports the work of the loyal party organization.

The party in the electorate is an alarmingly diverse group, largely because the simple gesture of loyalty that defines it—a word or two in response to a stranger asking questions—means so many different things to different people. (Notice that we include people in the party electorate on the basis of their own attribution of attachment, not on the basis of actual voting, activity, or contribution to the life of the political party.)

---

[4]For an examination of the alternatives in identifying party adherents, see Everett C. Ladd and Charles D. Hadley, "Party Definition and Party Differentiation," *Public Opinion Quarterly* 37 (1973): 21–34.

Understandably, the boundaries of the party electorate are indistinct. Individuals also move freely in and out of it, either to or from the more active circles of the party organization or the less committed circles of the electorate at large.

A party in the electorate is more, however, than a categorical group or even a quasi organization. It is also an aggregate of cognitive images. It is, in other words, a system of impressions, or an object of opinion and judgment, *within* large numbers of individual voters. It is a loyalty or identification ordinarily so strong that it assumes a dominant position in the individual's political cosmos. In this sense, it is the party *in* the elector. It acts as a reference symbol, a political cue-giver, and a perceptual screen through which the individual sees and evaluates candidates and issues. Loyalty to a political party, therefore, is often a dominant factor in the subtle calculus by which the American political animal sees, reacts, decides, and acts. For voters and citizens, the political party of their cognitions may be far more real and tangible than any overt political activity or any observable political organization, because they react to what they believe and perceive. The political party of their perceptions may be only a loosely codified set of judgments and impressions of people, issues, and events, but for them it may be more real than the party of leaders, platforms, and organizations.

Since the American parties are still cadre parties without important membership contingents, the party in the electorate gives the party its mass popular character. It is to the party in the electorate that people generally refer when they speak of Democrats and Republicans. It is certainly to the party in the electorate that the casual observer refers when he says, for example, that the Democratic party is the party of the disadvantaged or that the Republican party is the party of the small towns. Many of the differences in the programs and the public images of the major parties spring from differences in the segments of the American electorate that they are successful in enlisting. In fact, the interplay between the appeals of the party (i.e., its candidates, issues, and traditions) and its loyal electoral clienteles—each one shaping and reinforcing the other—comes very close to determining what the parties are.

All of this is not to suggest that the rest of the American electorate is of less concern to the American party. At no time can a national party or its candidates find within its party electorate the majorities needed for election to office. Even though the voters outside the loyal party electorates have lighter commitments to party and issue, competition for their support is keen. The two American parties cannot, as can some of the parties of the parliamentary democracies, fall back on a safely committed and heavily ideological 15 or 25 percent of the electorate. They must mobilize majorities partly from vast, fluid, heterogeneous, often disinterested voters beyond the parties in the electorate.

The individuals of the American electorate, therefore, range along a continuum from heavy, almost blind commitment to a political party to total lack of commitment, not only to a political party but to *any* political cause or object. The competitive American parties do not ignore or take for granted any segment of that total electorate. The three chapters in Part III examine the electorate's variety and importance. Chapter 6 deals with the amorphous parties in the electorate, asking who the Democrats are and who the Republicans are. It is concerned, as suggested earlier, with the party electorate as a categorical group. Chapter 7 takes up the party *within* the elector—the party as a set of cognitive images. It deals with the impact of party loyalty or identification on the political behavior of the individual. Chapter 8 focuses on the legal and self-imposed restrictions on the total electorate that limit the parties' attempts to activate their loyalists and recruit new supporters.

6

THE LOYAL ELECTORATES

For millions of Americans who are unconcerned with the intricacies of party organization, the group of party loyalists we call the party in the electorate *is* the political party. Much of the written history of American parties and politics has reinforced that impression. It has recorded the successes of the parties, not in terms of party organization, strategy, or activity, but in terms of the enduring blocs of voters that support them. Thus, the parties have been defined at various times as parties of the East or West, the North or South, the city or country, the rich or poor, the white or black.

This visibility of the party in the electorate, even though it is only a loosely defined categorical group, is one of the major sources of its importance. Its interests and involvements contribute significantly to the public image of the party, and its political goals and values will inevitably be impressed on it. That impact, however, is matched by a second. Within the cognitive mechanism of American voters, loyalty to or identification with a political party has long been the single most important influence on their political behavior. It colors judgments of candidates and issues, and it guides decisions on how to vote.

TWO-PARTY DIVISIONS IN THE ELECTORATE

Since 1860, the two major parties have each enjoyed a period of long-run ascendancy. From 1860 through the presidential election of 1928, Republican presidential candidates won fourteen out of eighteen times. Their supremacy was broken only by the two victories of Grover Cleveland, each won by an eyelash margin, and by the two of Woodrow Wilson. Moreover, Wilson's initial victory in 1912 was built on less than 40 percent of the popular vote, a result of the fact that Teddy Roosevelt's Bull Moose candidacy split a sizable chunk of Republican votes from the regular Republican candidate, William Howard Taft. Furthermore, in this period the Democrats managed to set one record in futility; in the election of 1924, they won only 34.8 percent of the two-party popular vote for president.

Since the 1930s, the Democrats have enjoyed a period of similar dominance. Of the thirteen presidential elections from 1932 through 1980, the Democrats won eight, losing two to Dwight D. Eisenhower, two to Richard Nixon, and one to Ronald Reagan. Furthermore, in this period, the Republicans set two records of their own in futility. In 1936, they won only eight electoral votes, the smallest number for a major party in modern times, and in 1964 Lyndon Johnson rolled up a record 61.1 percent of the total popular vote at their expense.

The same two periods of dominance are reflected even more dramatically in party control of the two houses of Congress (Table 6.1). The very fact that the cycles of control of Congress follow those of the presidency so closely lends further support to the conclusion that these are cycles of *party* ascendancy. Since the Civil War, in fact, on only three occasions (1956, 1968, and 1972) did a winning president see the opposing party carry both houses of Congress in a year of his election.

Behind the striking dominance of the Republicans from 1861 to 1930 and the Democrats from 1930 to the present lies the great probability that each party was the majority party in the time of its ascendancy. That is, during the period of its successes, the dominant party commanded the partisan loyalties of a majority of Americans. Its loyal, supportive party in the electorate was large enough to guarantee victory in the great percentage of elections. The minority party could win only sporadically by overriding the dominant party loyalties with an uncommonly attractive

TABLE 6.1 *Partisan Control of the Houses of Congress, 1861–1931 and 1931–83*

	House of Representatives		Senate	
	Dems.	Repubs.	Dems.	Repubs.
1861–1931				
(37th–71st Congress)	12	23	5	30
1931–83				
(72nd–98th Congress)	25	2	22	5

TABLE 6.2 *Party Identification of American Adults: 1960–80*

Identification	Oct. 1960	Oct. 1964	Oct. 1968	Oct. 1972	Oct. 1976	Oct. 1980
Strong Democrats	21%	27%	20%	15%	15%	18%
Weak Democrats	25	25	25	26	25	23
Independents	23	23	29	35	36	35
Weak Republicans	13	13	14	13	14	14
Strong Republicans	14	11	10	10	9	9
Others	4	2	2	2	2	2

Source Center for Political Studies, University of Michigan; data made available through the Inter-University Consortium for Political and Social Research.

candidate or an especially salient issue. That the Republicans were such a majority party before 1930 we must take more or less on faith. More precisely, we make that assumption in a backward projection of what we have learned about the American electorate and the power of party loyalty through public opinion surveys since the 1940s.

With an amazing regularity, for the past generation, the American adult population has been preferring, identifying with, or expressing loyalty to the Democratic party.[1] Table 6.2 indicates the persistence of the Democratic party's superiority among the party identifiers.[2] It also illustrates the remarkable stability of party identifications in the United States—a stability so great in recent years that not even a popular president of the minority party, General Eisenhower, could jar it. Nor did Richard Nixon's sweeping victory in 1972 add any loyalists to the Republican ranks.

More important than the question of how many Democratic and Republican identifiers there are, however, is the question of who they are. From what educational backgrounds, what regions, what occupations, what religions, what social groups come the Democrats and the Repub-

[1]For the basic procedures and assumptions underlying this concept of party identification, see Angus Campbell et al., *The American Voter* (New York: Wiley, 1960). For a continuation of the analysis represented in *The American Voter*, see Norman H. Nie, Sidney Verba, and John R. Petrocik, *The Changing American Voter* (Cambridge, Mass.: Harvard University Press, 1976).

[2]The data of the Gallup Poll (American Institute of Public Opinion) are very similar, although the questions and categories are a little different:

	1960	1964	1968	1972	1976	1980
Democrats	47%	53%	46%	42%	48%	44%
Independents	23	22	27	31	29	30
Republicans	30	25	27	27	23	26

licans? On what bases of interest do the parties attract supporters and voters? Conversely, what experiences and values shape the decisions of Americans to align themselves with one party rather than the other? Why do some Americans identify with the Republicans and others with the Democrats?

THE ACQUISITION OF PARTY LOYALTIES

It is a commonplace among Americans to say that they are Democrats or Republicans because they were born to the party, just as one was born to Methodism, Catholicism, or Christian Science. The processes of political socialization begin early in life as the child begins to become aware of political parties and absorb judgments about them. He or she soon realizes that one of the parties is the family's party, that it is "good," that it is "our" party. Even in later life, many Americans recognize the early origins of their party loyalties:

> I'm a borned Republican, sister. We're Republicans from start to finish, clear back on the family tree. Hot Republicans all along. I'm not so much in favor of Eisenhower as the party he is on. I won't weaken my party by voting for a Democrat. . . .
>
> I was just raised to believe in the Democrats and they have been good for the working man—that's good enough for me. The Republicans are a cheap outfit all the way around. I just don't like the Republicans, my past experience with them has been all bad.[3]

Even though they do not often consciously indoctrinate their children into loyalty to a political party, parents are the first agents of political socialization in the American culture. Their casual conversations, their references to political events, and the example of their political activity are sufficient to convey their party loyalties to their children. So stable are the results that the intergenerational similarities in party loyalty persist even when the children reach adulthood (Table 6.3).[4] Furthermore, parents with consistent, reinforcing party loyalties are more likely to produce strong party identifiers among their children. Those without party loyalties or with mixed loyalties produce offspring who are more likely to be independents.[5]

[3]Angus Campbell, Gerald Gurin, and Warren Miller, *The Voter Decides* (Evanston, Ill.: Row, Peterson, 1954), p. 92.

[4]Campbell et al., *The American Voter*, p. 147.

[5]The high degree of intergenerational similarity in party identifications is explained in Paul A. Beck and M. Kent Jennings, "Parents as 'Middlepersons' in Political Socialization," *Journal of Politics* 37 (1975): 83–107.

TABLE 6.3 *Intergenerational Similarities in Party Identification: 1980*

Party Identification of Children[a]	Parties of Mother and Father				
	Both Democrat (N = 548)	Both Independent (N = 65)	Both Republican (N = 284)	Father Democrat, Mother Republican (N = 46)	Mother Democrat, Father Republican (N = 38)
Strong Democrat	32.3%	3.1%	3.5%	6.5%	10.5%
Weak Democrat	32.1	10.8	7.7	23.9	18.4
Independent	26.2	80.0	28.8	39.1	34.3
Weak Republican	5.5	3.1	35.6	21.7	15.8
Strong Republican	3.8	3.1	24.3	8.7	21.1

[a] The table omits individuals who did not answer, who had other party loyalties or no party loyalties, who could not identify their parents' loyalties, or whose parents formed another combination of loyalties (e.g., one parent apolitical).

Source Center for Political Studies, University of Michigan; data made available through the Inter-University Consortium for Political and Social Research.

That the acquisition of party loyalties comes surprisingly early and easily is also one conclusion of a study of schoolchildren in New Haven, Connecticut.[6] More than 60 percent of the fourth-grade children were able to state a party preference—a percentage, the author notes, that is close to the percentage shown by the data of the Center for Political Studies (CPS), University of Michigan, for the twenty-one-year-old to twenty-four-year-old segment of its national adult sample. In the fourth-grade sample, however, few of the children support their identification with much information about party leaders, issues, or traditions. Not until they are eighth-graders do they develop the supportive knowledge that permits party identification to become fully operative in the political world. At that age they begin, for example, to associate the parties with general economic interests or groups—with business or labor, with the rich or the poor.

The strong correlation of the child's party identification with that of his or her parents points to the family as a major socializer into party loyalty. It also suggests that both parents and children have the same experiences that shape party loyalties and that they perceive and react to them with the same values and the same perceptual mechanisms.

Individuals' party loyalties are also supported by a homogeneous environment of family, friends, and secondary groups into which no "alien" socializers threaten to intrude. Friends, associates, relatives, and spouses have the same partisan loyalties that they do. Some offspring, to be sure, do leave the parties of their parents. Those whose initial identification is weak are more apt to change, and when the parents identify with different parties or when their identification is not congruent with their social class—that is, when the political signals are mixed—their children are more apt to develop an identification with the other party.[7]

In part, the stability of these party loyalties results from the relative absence in the American political system of other agencies of political socialization that might challenge the early influences of the family. Schools often avoid political studies in the early grades, and the main conscious educational attempt at political socialization—the high school civics course—may not have the impact planned for it. One recent national study concluded that there is no evidence that such courses have a significant effect on the political orientations of the great majority of high school students.[8] American churches generally steer clear of partisan commit-

[6]Fred I. Greenstein, *Children and Politics* (New Haven: Yale University Press, 1965). See also Robert D. Hess and Judith V. Torney, *The Development of Political Attitudes in Children* (Chicago: Aldine, 1967), especially pp. 80–81.

[7]Arthur S. Goldberg, "Social Determinism and Rationality as Bases of Party Identification," *American Political Science Review* 63 (1969): 5–25.

[8]Kenneth P. Langton and M. Kent Jennings, "Political Socialization and the High School Civics Curriculum in the United States," *American Political Science Review* 62 (1968): 852–67.

ments—contrary to the willingness of many European churches, for example, to support the various Christian Democratic parties of Europe. The American parties themselves engage in very little direct socialization; they do not maintain the youth groups, the flourishing university branches (which may have offices, lounges, and eating facilities), the social or recreational activities, or the occupational organizations that their European counterparts do.[9]

Despite the stability of the initial party identification, the process of political socialization is not a single, one-time shaping of a lifetime of political orientations. At the least, it involves a series of reinforcements of the initial socializations. For many individuals, it means sharp breaks with old loyalties; in 1976, for example, 21 percent of a national sample of adults reported that they had changed party loyalties at least once in their lives.[10] Party identifications are loosened or altered during adulthood by cataclysmic events, such as the Civil War, the Great Depression of the 1930s, or the unrest and upheaval in social values in the 1960s and 1970s. Although changes in occupation alone seem not to affect party loyalty, a change in life-style, peer groups, or basic social attitudes often does. So, apparently, does an extended period of unemployment.[11] In short, beneath the stability of the aggregate totals of party identifications in the country, there are individuals moving in some direction across party lines at every moment.

Carrying a party identification from childhood to adulthood may, indeed, be a more complicated process than we had thought. Recent research suggests that the acquisition and maintenance of a party loyalty over a period of years may involve a number of processes. Initially, the individual acquires it, rather young, in a process of early socialization dominated by parents. Subsequently, the individual maintains or changes the identification in an increasingly complex set of adult experiences. At this point in the life cycle, adults have tested their party loyalties against political reality. They have evaluated the performance of their favored parties and party leaders, and they also have watched the performance of

---

[9]The new Democratic Charter promises new Democratic activity in this area. Article Nine sets up a National Education and Training Council and provides: "In order to encourage a lifetime of meaningful political participation for every Democrat, the National Education and Training Council shall attempt to reach every young citizen as they [sic] enter the electorate at 18 years of age." It remains to be seen if the Democrats can carry out those plans.

[10]Data from the surveys of the Center for Political Studies of the University of Michigan. For the late 1950s, the estimate was less than 20 percent; see Campbell et al., *The American Voter*, p. 48.

[11]Kay Schlozman and Sidney Verba, *Injury to Insult* (Cambridge, Mass.: Harvard University Press, 1979), Chap. 12.

[12]Morris P. Fiorina, *Retrospective Voting in American National Elections* (New Haven: Yale University Press, 1981), p. 102.

the "other party." Events and experience may reinforce those loyalties, but they may also undermine them. Thus, in Fiorina's words:

> . . . there is an inertial element in voting behavior that cannot be ignored, but that inertial element has an experiential basis; it is *not* something learned at mommy's knee and never questioned thereafter.[12]

Beyond the processes of acquiring and maintaining the party identification, there apparently is also a process of strengthening or intensifying the party attachment for some adults. Party loyalties are most strongly held by older adults, and they are the least likely to change them. That strengthening across the life cycle may reflect an ongoing process of reinforcement in decades of political observation or activity; it may also reflect the usefulness of a party loyalty as a cue that will simplify choice and cut the costs of political decision for older voters.[13]

SOCIAL CLASS AND PARTY IDENTIFICATION

The processes of political socialization do not, however, explain the distribution of party loyalties in the United States. They describe how rather than why an individual acquires his or her particular party loyalty. To some extent, explanations of socialization, resting as they do on parental influences, merely push the question back a generation.

The search for an explanation of these party loyalties should very likely begin with social class. It is probably true, as Seymour Lipset has asserted, that the principal generalization one can make about loyalties in the parties of the democratic world is that they are based primarily on social class.[14] We have referred to social class and to socioeconomic status, and a fuller explanation of the terms is probably overdue. Much of the literature uses the terms interchangeably (or almost interchangeably), but the preference here is for the latter term and its conventional abbreviation, SES. Socioeconomic status is simply the relative ranking of the economic and/or social deference the individual can command. Regardless of the rubric one chooses, however, status differences underlie the party electorates of the mature, industrial democracies with which one can most reasonably compare the United States. The class differences of industrial-

---

[13]On these points, see Philip E. Converse, *The Dynamics of Party Support* (Beverly Hills: Sage, 1976); Paul R. Abramson, "Developing Party Identification: A Further Examination of Life-Cycle, Generational, and Period Effects," *American Journal of Political Science* 23 (1979): 78–96; W. Phillips Shively, "The Development of Party Identification among Adults," *American Political Science Review* 73 (1979): 1039–54; and William Claggett, "Partisan Acquisition vs. Party Intensity; Life-Cycle, Generation, and Period Effects," *American Journal of Political Science* 25 (1981): 193–214.

[14]*Political Man* (New York: Anchor, 1963), p. 230.

ized economies, in other words, have generally superseded the older party lines based on ethnic, racial, religious, or regional differences.

The signs and marks of SES conflict are scattered throughout American history, even in the preindustrial decades. James Madison, one of the most knowing observers of human nature among the Founding Fathers, wrote in his famous tenth paper of *The Federalist* that economic differences are the most common source of factions.[15] Social and economic status differences clearly underlay the battle between the wealthy, aristocratic Federalists and the less privileged Jeffersonians. Then, almost a century later, William Jennings Bryan made the Democratic party the vehicle for the protests of the Grangers, the emerging Socialists, the Greenbackers, the Knights of Labor, and the Populists—all of them composed largely of the discontented and disadvantaged. Bryan ("the Great Commoner") came to the Democratic convention of 1896 as the voice of prairie Populism. He challenged the conservatism of Grover Cleveland in his celebrated attack on the gold standard and hard money: "You shall not press down upon the brow of labor this crown of thorns. You shall not crucify mankind upon this cross of gold." Stirred by the Nebraska prophet, the convention repudiated its conservative leadership and picked Bryan himself as its candidate. Despite his defeat, the Democrats twice (1900 and 1908) returned to him as their presidential candidate for the crusade against corporate wealth, eastern banking interests, and what Bryan liked to call the "plutocracy."

In many ways, Bryan and the Democrats of 1896 appear to have been the harbingers of modern American politics. Bryan captured the Democratic party for the rural and agrarian interests in their fight against the new industrial and financial interests. The Republicans became the party committed to the pursuit of industrialization. Woodrow Wilson's "New Freedom" and its reforms reflected the Democrats' identification both with agrarian interests and increasingly with urban, immigrant, industrial have-nots. In the suffusing prosperity of the 1920s, many of the class differences between the two parties were greatly muted, but in the elections of 1928 and 1932 they erupted again.[16]

The SES stamp on the parties became more vivid in the 1930s. The migration to the cities and the crushing poverty of the Great Depression were the events out of which Franklin Roosevelt rebuilt the Democratic party more firmly than ever as a party of social and economic reform. This reinforcement of the SES lines between the two parties was his "revolution" in party politics. His New Deal programs—labor legislation, so-

---

[15]See Madison's tenth *Federalist* paper: "The most common and durable source of factions has been the various and unequal distribution of property."

[16]See the excellent account of this section of American party history in Everett C. Ladd, Jr., *American Political Parties* (New York: Norton, 1970), Chap. 4.

cial security, wage and hours laws—solidified the Democratic party's image as the party of the relative have-nots. Even groups such as the blacks, long allied with the Republicans as the party of Lincoln, were lured to the Democratic banner; the strength of SES issues even kept them as allies of southern whites in the Roosevelt coalition. In brief, Franklin Roosevelt buttressed the class divisions of industrialism by adding to its conflicts the consequent response of government: the Welfare State. Its programs and expenditures heightened the stakes of socioeconomic status politics.[17]

All of this is not to argue that only socioeconomic status differences divided the major American parties in this century; but the evidence is very strong that SES did constitute an important and possibly the overriding difference between them. Only since the 1940s and the advent of reliable public opinion polling, however, has it been possible to make fairly precise and confident statements about the attitudes, the SES, the party identifications, and the votes of individual Americans. Much of our analysis of electorates before World War II, therefore, rests on indirect evidence.

The relationship between party and SES in the 1970s is apparent in the nature of the two party electorates in 1980 (Table 6.4). It is apparent in the data on occupation and income, and the relationship lurks even where it is not obvious. The implications of the partisan differences in educational levels, for example, cannot be taken at face value. There seems little reason to suspect that the intellectually liberating experiences of formal education lead young men and women overwhelmingly to the true path of Republicanism. It seems more reasonable to suppose that the positive relationship between years of education and Republicanism results from the intermediating SES variable (i.e., a higher percentage of upper SES parents send their sons and daughters to college, and the college degree leads to higher SES). Also, given the higher SES of Protestants in the United States, their relationship with Republicanism unquestionably reflects, in part, those status differences; and there certainly is no need to elaborate the enormous SES differences between whites and blacks in the United States.

Furthermore, to the extent that Americans see themselves in different social classes, those differences relate strongly to their party loyalties (Table 6.5). In the survey reported in Table 6.5, less than one percent of the

[17]Among the histories of the American parties, see Wilfred Binkley, *American Political Parties* (New York: Knopf, 1962); George H. Mayer, *The Republican Party: 1854–1964* (New York: Oxford University Press, 1964); William N. Chambers, *The Democrats: 1789–1964* (Princeton: Van Nostrand, 1964); Arthur M. Schlesinger, Jr. (ed.), *History of United States Political Parties*, 4 vols. (New York: Chelsea, 1973); Ladd, *American Political Parties*; and Ralph M. Goldman, *The Search for Consensus: The Story of the Democratic Party* (Philadelphia: Temple University Press, 1979).

TABLE 6.4   *Social Characteristics of Party Identifiers: 1980*

	Strong Democrat	Weak Democrat	Independent	Weak Republican	Strong Republican
Race					
White	14.3%	23.1%	37.0%	16.1%	9.4%
Black	46.7	28.3	19.9	1.7	3.3
Other	23.5	17.6	52.9	—	5.9
Occupation					
Professional	11.7	23.2	38.7	16.7	9.5
Manager, official	11.5	18.0	33.1	25.9	11.5
Clerical, sales	14.9	25.4	35.3	15.4	9.0
Skilled, semiskilled	20.8	24.2	38.8	10.0	6.3
Unskilled, service	15.0	28.3	40.2	9.4	7.1
Farmer	—	27.8	38.9	27.8	5.6
Other (retired, student, etc.)	22.1	23.1	32.7	13.0	9.1
Religion					
Protestant	18.6	22.6	32.9	15.3	10.6
Catholic	18.6	24.7	37.8	12.9	6.0
Jewish	27.5	45.1	23.5	2.0	—
Other (Orthodox, non-Christian/non-Jewish)	18.8	12.5	31.2	28.1	9.4
Education					
None through 8 grades	33.0	23.8	25.9	9.2	8.1
Some high school	24.6	28.4	33.6	7.3	6.0
High school graduate	15.3	24.4	38.7	14.2	7.2
Some college	13.1	21.6	38.7	16.2	10.4
Baccalaureate degree	11.7	18.7	34.0	24.6	11.1
Advanced degree	18.0	21.3	29.2	15.7	15.7
Family Income					
$0–$9,999	25.3	23.7	32.6	10.9	7.2
$10,000–$19,999	17.8	27.9	35.2	11.6	7.5
$20,000–$29,999	14.9	22.1	40.7	14.9	7.4
$30,000–$49,999	12.9	23.1	31.1	21.8	11.1
$50,000 and over	5.1	17.9	41.0	15.4	20.5

Note   Totals cumulate horizontally rather than vertically.

Source   Center for Political Studies, University of Michigan; data made available through the Inter-University Consortium for Political and Social Research.

respondents put themselves in either an upper or a lower class; they are therefore eliminated from the data. Within that simplified view of social classes in America, however, the partisan differences are abundantly clear. Republicans tend to see themselves as middle class, and Democrats are much more apt to consider themselves working class.

TABLE 6.5   *Social Class Perceptions of Party Identification: 1980*

Respondent's view of own social class	Strong Democrat	Weak Democrat	Independent	Weak Republican	Strong Republican
Working class	63.1%	56.0%	52.4%	38.3%	37.0%
Middle class	36.9	44.0	47.6	61.7	63.0

Note   Small numbers of respondents indicating "lower," "upper," and "other" classes have been excluded from the table.

Source   Center for Political Studies, University of Michigan; data made available through the Inter-University Consortium for Political and Social Research.

Yet the lines of SES difference between the American parties are less distinct than the parties' rhetoric and campaigns might lead one to expect. They are certainly less clear than comparable ones in European party systems. In a comparison of party identifiers in the United States and Norway, Campbell and Valen reported:

> In both countries the occupational distribution of identifiers differs among the parties. In the United States, the differences are rather small. The Democratic Party draws 30 per cent of its adherents from the white-collar occupations, 46 per cent from the blue-collar. The Republicans come 36 per cent from the white-collar occupations and 39 per cent from the blue-collar. The occupational differences are very much greater among the various Norwegian parties. Of the Labor Party identifiers 79 per cent are blue-collar workers, 17 per cent are white-collar; among the Conservatives the proportions are 19 per cent and 76 per cent.[18]

Even the two Norwegian parties of the center, whose ideologies are not primarily economic, are more distinctive in their division of occupational groups than are the American parties. Furthermore, SES differences between the two parties are deteriorating at an increasing rate. As recently as 1968, almost 60 percent of the unskilled and service workers identified with the Democratic party; by 1980, it was 43 percent.

Thus we approach the conclusion of most observers of the American parties—that socioeconomic status and party loyalty are not so closely associated in the United States as they are in a number of the other Western democracies.[19] Both American parties have within their loyal electorates an important number of representatives from upper, middle, and lower

[18]Angus Campbell and Henry Valen, "Party Identification in Norway and the United States," *Public Opinion Quarterly* 25 (1961): 514–15.

[19]See Robert R. Alford, *Party and Society* (Chicago: Rand McNally, 1963), Chap. 8.

status groups. Consequently, they find it difficult to formulate overt class appeals or to enunciate ideologies that reflect sharp class differences. The heterogeneity of their loyalists is perfectly consistent with the parties' pragmatic, relatively nonideological tone and with their mission as brokers among diverse social groupings. Thus, the lines of SES division between the major American parties are indistinct and overlapping, and although SES is one explanation of interparty differences, it is by no means the only one.

The weakness of SES differences between the two party electorates may result partially from the imperfect translation of SES differences into differences in party identification. Among the influences muting that translation, the following may be the most important:

— *The shifting SES lines of American federalism.* SES lines differ from state to state, and it is difficult and somewhat misleading to make aggregate, national comparisons using identical categories. The distribution of SES groups in Montana, for example, differs greatly from that in New York. Some large and powerful groups in New York— blacks, Jews, and urban unionists come to mind—are considerably less numerous and important in Montana. The parties of the two states, therefore, recruit electorates that differ greatly in SES composition. By the sheer necessity of remaining competitive, the Republicans of New York, for example, will amass a more heterogeneous electorate than the Republicans of Montana.

— *The suppression of SES differences.* Some state and local party leaders obliterate SES lines (with decreasing success, probably) by fostering an issueless politics of localism and loyalty to personalities. For years, the Democratic parties of the southern states were classic examples of determinedly non-SES parties. The ascendancy of non-SES issues such as abortion and nuclear disarmament also inevitably mutes SES issues and differences. Furthermore, American mores do not encourage the perception of class or socioeconomic status. Many Americans do not see class divisions or conflict in the American society; at most, they see themselves as members of a very broad and inclusive middle class.

— *The slowness of SES translation into politics.* The loyalties of party identification tend to respond only slowly to changes in SES. In fact, many party loyalties formed early as a result of family influences are responses to SES one or two generations late. Furthermore, party loyalties shaped as SES responses to depression, recessions, or prosperity may remain long after the events have passed.

ALTERNATIVES TO THE SES BASIS OF LOYALTIES

In view of the relatively weak SES divisions between the Democratic and Republican electorates, there clearly must be additional explanations for the distribution of party loyalties in the United States.[20]

Sectionalism

Historically, the greatest challenge to the SES interpretations of American politics came from the school that ascribed the primary differences between parties to sectional differences. The sectional theories held that the varying geographic areas or sections of the country had separate and deeply felt political interests, which when honored and favored by a political party, united large numbers of otherwise differing voters.[21] Thus, the sectional explanations spoke of the Republicans' and the Democrats' building of coalitions behind presidential candidates by joining the votes of one section to those of another.

Unquestionably, the most enduring sectionalism in American party history was that of the Democratic party in the South. Even before the Civil War, the interests of the South in slavery and in an agriculture geared to export markets had unified it. The searing experience of that war and the reconstruction that followed made the South into the "Solid South" and delivered it to the Democrats. United by historical experience and by a desperate defense of a way of life, the eleven states of the Confederacy cast their electoral votes for Democratic presidential candidates in every election from 1880 through 1924, except for Tennessee's defection in 1920. Al Smith's Catholicism frightened four of these states into the Republican column in 1928, but the Roosevelt economic programs reinforced the region's economic interests—and in no way greatly challenged its way of life—and brought the South back to the Democratic party for the four Roosevelt elections. Only with the successes of the Dixiecrat ticket in 1948 and the start of the civil rights movement did the South begin to move away from its traditional party loyalties.

Similarly, strong East-West differences have periodically marked American party conflict. In the years of the Republic, the fading Federalists held to an ever-narrowing base of eastern seaport and financial interests, while the Jeffersonians expanded westward with the new settlers. Jackson, too, pointed his party appeals to the men of the frontier, and the protest movements that thrust William Jennings Bryan into the 1896 cam-

---

[20]Nie, Verba, and Petrocik explore the group and demographic bases of the parties in Chapter 13 ("The Party Coalitions") of *The Changing American Voter*.

[21]For a somewhat different and excellent essay on the nature of sectionalism, see V. O. Key, *Politics, Parties, and Pressure Groups*, 5th ed. (New York: Crowell, 1964), pp. 232–33.

paign sprang from the agrarian discontent of the western prairies. Many of the Populists' loudest complaints were directed at eastern capitalism, eastern bankers, and eastern trusts. Indeed, the geographical distribution of the presidential vote of 1896 is striking affirmation of sectional voting (Figure 6.1).

The pull of sectionalism has declined steadily within the past several generations. The isolation and homogeneity of life in the sections have yielded to a nationalization of life and interests in the nation. Sectional loyalties have not completely disappeared, of course. Southern sectionalism awakened in a new guise in 1964 as five states of the Deep South supported Barry Goldwater, the Republican presidential candidate. They were the only states he carried beyond his home state of Arizona. Then, in 1968, George Wallace carried only five states on the American Independent ticket: Alabama, Arkansas, Georgia, Louisiana, and Mississippi. Elsewhere, however, sectionalism now appears to have receded into a secondary position in the development of political party loyalties.

In the 1970s and early 1980s, some observers of American politics thought they saw the emergence of a new sectionalism—that of the Sun Belt. Evidence for it is not strong, however. The Republicans have indeed improved their position in a number of the states of the South, Southwest, and West, but the result of that improvement has generally been to increase rather than diminish two-party competition. Moreover, the re-

FIGURE 6.1   *States Carried by the Democratic Party in the Presidential Election of 1896*

gional distribution of party loyalties in 1981 offers no support for the emergence of a Sun Belt section. A poll conducted by CBS and the *New York Times* in that year found 26 percent of the adults of the nation identifying with the Republicans, with 26 percent in the East, 28 percent in the Midwest, 25 percent in the South, and 23 percent in the West.[22]

In retrospect, it is difficult to say what force sectionalism had even at its zenith. The great difficulty with the sectional explanations is that the term *section* may simply be an obscuring shorthand for a geographic concentration of other identifiable interests—ethnic, economic, or possibly SES. Much sectional voting in the past, for instance, reflected conflicts among crop economies in the various agricultural sections. Thus, the central question is whether the sections themselves are the basic source of sectional interests or whether they are merely categories or concentrations of voters who identify with a party for other reasons. It means little to say that the Midwest supported Franklin Roosevelt in 1936 or that the West backed Eisenhower in 1956. To be sure, the South has been more than a descriptive category; its political behavior has been sectional in the sense of unified interests and an awareness of the region and its distinctiveness. The case for sectional explanations weakens greatly, however, as soon as one looks beyond the South.[23]

Urban-Rural Differences

For a considerable portion of the twentieth century, there was a conventional wisdom that, especially outside the South, the Democrats were the party of the cities and the Republicans were the party of the small towns and countryside—and it was probably so. The big-city political machines were overwhelmingly Democratic, and it was largely in the urban centers that the Democratic blue-collar workers and racial and ethnic groups lived. The Republican commitment to individual self-reliance and a limited role for government appealed to the less complicated ways of rural America. Beginning in the 1960s, however, the urban-rural division between the major parties became progressively blurred and muted. By the 1970s, there was only an indistinct division in which, although the largest metropolitan areas show some preference for the Democrats, there were no real differences by party in any of the other urban or rural categories. What differences remained could clearly be explained on other than urban grounds, especially on the obvious SES ones.

As the United States becomes increasingly urban and metropolitan—almost three-fourths of the American population in 1980 lived in some

[22]*New York Times*, March 1, 1981.

[23]For a study of the end of Southern one-partyism at the level of the individual voter, see Paul A. Beck, "Partisan Dealignment in the Postwar South," *American Political Science Review* 71 (1977): 477–96.

urban place or urbanized area—the question ceases to be one of urban versus rural America. It becomes one of distinction within the urban sectors, between different kinds of cities and different parts of metropolitan areas. Selective migration out of the older center cities promises to leave them ethnic, racial, and low-SES enclaves, thus inclined to be Democratic. Urban diversity and two-party competitiveness may move to the suburbs and the urban fringe areas.[24] Two related points seem clear, however, on urbanism and the division of the two-party loyalties. First, what differences there are along or within urban-rural lines are largely socioeconomic; as those SES differences in American party loyalties decline, so, too, will the urban-rural ones. Second, although a case can indeed be made that there are genuinely urban or rural or small-city interests in American politics, they have never stamped themselves on party loyalties.

Religion

Even when income, education, and occupation are held constant, Catholics and Jews tend to support the Democratic party and non-Southern Protestants tend to support the Republican party. Again, however, the statistical relationships are only that; they do not necessarily identify cause. Perhaps despite the holding of some SES factors constant, there remains an SES factor. A Jew of high income, lengthy formal education, and professional occupation (the usual formal characteristics of high SES) may be denied by prejudice the status he might otherwise expect. The same illustration applies to some Catholics, but not with the force it had a generation or two ago, when anti-Catholic bias was greater and when Catholic identification with the Democratic party was at its strongest.

Yet it does appear that religion—both as theology and as group identification—is involved here.[25] A Jewish internationalism and concern for social justice, rooted in the religious and ethnic traditions of Judaism, disposes many Jews to the Democratic party as the party of international concern, support for the state of Israel, and social and economic justice.[26] In the case of American Catholics, the tie to the Democratic party is in great part a tie of personalities and political organization. The political machines of the cities were traditionally led by Catholics, and their patronage and largesse often went to the newly immigrated Catholics from Europe. Furthermore, the roll call of Catholics in Democratic leadership extends beyond the local bosses. Virtually all the national chairmen of the Democratic party in the first sixty years of this century were Roman Cath-

[24]See also Benjamin Walter and Frederick M. Wirt, "The Political Consequences of Suburban Variety," *Social Science Quarterly* 52 (1971): 746–67.

[25]David Knoke, "Religion, Stratification and Politics: America in the 1960's," *American Journal of Political Science* 18 (1974): 331–45.

[26]Lawrence Fuchs, *The Political Behavior of the American Jews* (Glencoe, Ill.: Free Press, 1956).

olics. The Democratic party was also the party of the two Catholic candidates for the presidency: Al Smith and John F. Kennedy. The ties of Protestantism to Republicanism are less obvious, probably in part because of the enormous diversity of sects that Protestantism embraces. Very possibly, however, the theological individualism of more conservative Protestantism disposes individuals to Republicanism; at least, there has been a clear relationship in recent years between Protestant fundamentalism and political conservatism.[27]

Race

Not too long ago, the Republican party—as the party of Lincoln, the Civil War, and Reconstruction—was associated with racial equality in the minds of both black and white Americans. In the generation between 1930 and 1960, however, the wheels of racial politics turned 180 degrees. It is now the Democratic party, the Kennedy and Johnson administrations, and Democratic Congresses that blacks see as advancing racial equality and integration. Blacks identify with the Democratic party in overwhelming numbers and regardless of any other set of social characteristics. The 1980 data from the Center for Political Studies, University of Michigan, show that 75 percent of black adults identify with the Democratic party and only 5 percent with the Republicans. All indications suggest that Chicanos, Puerto Ricans, and American Indians also identify heavily with the Democrats.

Gender

In recent years, the votes and stands of adult women have begun to diverge from those of men. Women voted in about 6 percent larger numbers than men did for Jimmy Carter in 1980, for instance; and following the 1980 election, the differences between the sexes grew. Women were considerably less approving of President Reagan, and they differed from men on a number of issues beyond the specifically women's issues. Their position on those issues, moreover, was the Democratic (or anti-Reagan) position: supportive of a nuclear freeze and spending for social programs, and critical of increased defense spending. Understandably, this development began to concern Republican leaders. Up to 1983, however, there were no clear signs that these views and opinions were causing shifts in basic party loyalties. (For the record, in 1980, women were both more Democratic and more Republican than men, because they were significantly less in-

---

[27]The 1960 presidential election occasioned a spate of works on the religious factor in American party loyalties and voting behavior. See Scott Greer, "Catholic Voters and the Democratic Party," *Public Opinion Quarterly* 25 (1961): 611–25; and Philip E. Converse, "Religion and Politics: The 1960 Election," in Angus Campbell et al., *Elections and the Political Order* (New York: Wiley, 1966), pp. 96–124.

dependent.) Then, in mid-1983, results of several polls showed women shifting their loyalties from the Republican party to the Democrats. The New York Times/CBS News poll of late June 1983, reported in the *Times* of July 10, found women favoring the Democrats over the Republicans by 43 to 21 percent, while men were divided 32 to 25 percent in favor of the Democratic party. Concern about the gender gap within the Republican party increased predictably within the following weeks.

Traditionalism

Attachments to a political party need not be associated with an interest, a set of goals, or a group need. It is sufficient for some Americans that their party is the party of their parents, their friends, or their locale, or that it is the party of their fellow workers or fellow worshippers. For these party identifiers, it suffices to say, for example, "Everyone around here is a Democrat (or a Republican)." In some sections of the country, the prevailing homogeneity of party identification may still reflect the loyalties of the original migrants into the area. Southern Illinois, for example—settled by Democrats from the South—inclines to the Democratic party even today.[28]

Party Leadership and Personalities

Individuals may identify a political party with a particular leader or group of leaders within it. They may attach themselves to the Democratic party as the party of Franklin Roosevelt or John F. Kennedy, or to the Republican party as the party of Dwight D. Eisenhower or Ronald Reagan. For them, the party is little more than an extension of an attractive, compelling personality, and their loyalty to it is in great part loyalty to that personality. Such an explanation of party identification, however, is probably easily overestimated. Despite the magnitude of his victories and his personal popularity, President Eisenhower made little dent in long-run party loyalties, even of those Democrats who voted for him.

Issue Involvement

Well-informed citizens will possibly identify with a political party because of the policy positions it takes. For most of this century, for example, the Democratic party has been more willing than the Republicans to espouse American commitments abroad, beginning with entry into the League of Nations and continuing today over questions of foreign aid. Republicans, on the whole, have been more chary of foreign involvement, more na-

---

[28]For a discussion of these traditional loyalties resulting from patterns of migration, see V. O. Key, *American State Politics* (New York: Knopf, 1956), Chap. 8.

tionalistic, and more prone to isolationism. Other short-run policy differences may have had an equal impact. The issues of prohibition and the "noble experiment" of the Eighteenth Amendment have by now receded into the mists of American history. In the 1920s and 1930s, however, the question divided the two parties and probably some of their identifiers. The "drys," who supported the experiment, were largely in the Republican party, and most of its "wet" opponents were Democrats.

Recently, party identification seems most closely related to individual stands on the social issues—on questions concerning government programs that guarantee a minimum standard of living or security for all Americans. These are the issues of the Welfare State, the ones touching government medical care or insurance, guaranteed levels of income, social security, or welfare programs. Fundamentally, they are questions of the redistribution of wealth, for the government taxes income progressively to provide programs of greatest proportional advantage to lower income groups. They are SES issues, one might say, because they propose different benefits for people of different economic status.

Clearly, much of the partisan rhetoric and conflict of American politics runs along SES lines—whether it is a congressional debate over a poverty program or medicaid, a presidential proposal to cut spending, or a state or local clash over a sales tax. The American electorate, even in its distribution of partisan loyalties, responds to SES issues. The response comes, however, not as the response of specific social classes or groups, but from individuals who, for one reason or another, have come to hold attitudes or views about the role of government and its social responsibility for the less advantaged. Americans develop what appear to be SES sympathies that are not necessarily congruent with their own socioeconomic status. They may reflect some sympathy for the socioeconomic "underdog," some deference to the socioeconomic "overdog," or some identification with an earlier status of their own (Table 6.6). They may even be

TABLE 6.6   *Feelings of Party Identifiers and Independents toward the Poor: 1980*

Questions: Do you feel close to the poor? Response:	Strong Democrat	Weak Democrat	Independent	Weak Republican	Strong Republican
Yes	67.4%	42.0%	37.4%	28.2%	23.0%
No	32.6	58.0	62.6	71.8	77.0

Source   Center for Political Studies, University of Michigan; data made available through the Inter-University Consortium for Political and Social Research.

TABLE 6.7   *Relationship between Ideological Self-Perception and Party Identification: 1980*

Voter's description of own position[a]	Strong Democrat	Weak Democrat	Independent	Weak Republican	Strong Republican
Liberal	43.7%	31.2%	26.0%	11.6%	5.6%
Moderate	32.9	36.9	31.9	27.3	12.1
Conservative	23.5	32.0	42.1	61.0	82.3

[a] Individuals who were unable to describe themselves in ideological terms were not included.

Source   Center for Political Studies, University of Michigan; data made available through the Inter-University Consortium for Political and Social Research.

acting on some personal vision of the good society. Thus, the relationship is not always between socioeconomic characteristics and party identification; it may be between attitudes and party. In politics, after all, it is the operational attitude, not the origin, that is important.

The force of issues on party identification is more complex than all of this suggests. For one thing, the attitudes on SES-type issues are for many voters absorbed into broader liberal and conservative ideologies. As one might expect, there is a considerable correlation between self-described liberals and Democrats and, conversely, between conservatives and Republicans (Table 6.7). Second, we clearly see the rising importance of non-SES issues in recent elections—issues of the war in Vietnam, violence and crime (and thus "law and order"), racial and sexual equality, and the new moral issues, such as abortion and sexual freedom. Most of these issues cut across present party lines. Many of them have influenced a good many presidential votes in recent years. So far, however, they have not altered many party loyalties.[29]

PARTY IDENTIFICATION IN FLUX

Party loyalties in the American electorate are more fluid than ever. The old ties to socioeconomic backgrounds, and even to attitudes or preferences on SES issues, are declining. It becomes harder and harder to say to what factors party identification relates and from what more basic attachments it springs. Indeed, fewer and fewer individuals will declare their loyalties. There is some evidence that changes in loyalties are occurring more rap-

[29]Warren E. Miller and Teresa E. Levitin, *Leadership and Change: The New Politics and the American Electorate* (Cambridge, Mass.: Winthrop, 1976), pp. 213–14.

idly, and perhaps more casually, than ever. Even among those who still hold to some measure of party loyalty, that attachment seems to affect less and less of their political perception and behavior.[30]

The consequences of these changes for the American parties can scarcely be exaggerated. Since the stability of the two major American parties has been grounded in the party as a symbol or a cognitive image, the decline of that symbolic strength *within* the American voter poses the most serious threat imaginable to the parties and to their traditionally central position in American politics. The American party electorate has always been distinctive in that it has been defined primarily by that loyalty and not by loyalty to an ideology or a class position (in which the party is merely a means to those ends). What has been most important, in other words, is not the composition of the two parties in the electorate but the depth and the durability of the allegiances behind them. It is precisely this willing loyalty on the part of so many Americans that has undergirded the stability of the two-party system. As the quantity and quality of that loyalty declines, the change in the parties and in American politics will be fundamental.

Despite this fragility and instability, however, the force of party loyalties remains formidable. Short-term events and personalities affect these loyalties and then, often quite suddenly, lose their hold. The events of 1980 and after afford a fine example. In the immediate aftermath of the election of Ronald Reagan and the popular successes of his first year in the presidency, Republican party identifications began a surge that led some observers to expect the larger movement of a realignment. As the Reagan popularity waned, however, party identifications returned to their previous patterns. Thus, according to the data of the *New York Times*/CBS poll:

— 1980: Democrats, 53 percent; Republicans, 34 percent.

— 1981: Democrats, 49 percent; Republicans, 39 percent.

— 1982: Democrats, 52 percent; Republicans, 36 percent.[31]

It was not unlike 1952. The popular candidate and appealing policies of a minority party overcame the unpopular image of a president and administration of the majority party. In the end, however, the basic loyalties to party were, in the aggregate, far more stable than the short-term fortunes of specific candidates at specific elections.

As strong as residual party loyalties may be at any time, there is no reason to think they will last for all time. It is entirely possible that a major American military loss or a crippling international oil embargo would elevate defense or foreign policy issues to a new power in determining party

[30]This point and its ramifications will be examined in the next chapter.
[31]*New York Times*, April 25, 1982.

TABLE 6.8   *Percentage of Partisans and Independents in Two Age Segments of the American Electorate: 1980*

Party Identification	Voters Aged 18–29	Voters Aged 30 and over
Democrats	32.5%	45.0%
Independents	47.6	30.9
Republicans	19.9	24.0

Source Center for Political Studies, University of Michigan; data made available through the Inter-University Consortium for Political and Social Research.

identifications. It is equally possible that a serious depression or a galloping inflation would reawaken and sharpen the old SES divisions. The determinants of party loyalties are themselves shifting, complex, and vulnerable to change. When they shift radically, we have those great and rare rearrangements of party loyalties called realignments. Most recently, the events of the Great Depression of the late 1920s and 1930s established the SES coalitions that persist, though in weakened form, in the parties today. (Realignments will be discussed more fully in the next chapter.)

Of all the instabilities in the party electorates, none are more important than those that result from the entrance of new voters. The party loyalties of young adults increasingly have been shaped by the events and values of their own generation, while the power of the family as a socializer diminishes. Family life and relationships between the generations have changed dramatically in recent years, and the mass media and other sources of information to which high schoolers are exposed may well have broken the family's dominance over the initial acquisition of party identification.[32] For specific consequences, one need only look at the new voters who have entered the American electorate in the last decade. The percentage of voters between eighteen and thirty who call themselves independents is much higher than the percentage for the adult population as a whole (Table 6.8). Furthermore, the younger voters less and less translate their social status directly into a party choice.[33]

[32]For evidence of changes in the process of initiation into party identification, see M. Kent Jennings and Richard G. Niemi, "The Transmission of Political Values from Parent to Child," *American Political Science Review* 62 (1968): 169–84.

[33]See Paul R. Abramson, "Generational Change in American Electoral Behavior," *American Political Science Review* 68 (1974): 93–105.

Thus, as young voters enter the party electorate—or do not enter it—the shape of American party coalitions is slowly altered. The conversion of individuals from one party to the other has a similar effect. So, too, will any mobilization movement that makes voters out of some of the millions of nonvoters among American adults. Nonetheless, the result falls short of a realignment. Missing are the massive and radical shifts in party loyalties, the sharp alterations in the coalitions of voters making up the parties, that one associates with realignment. Instead, we have erosion and weakening in the status quo without the renewal or "fresh start" that realignment brings.

Thus, both change and stability mark the party electorates in the late 1970s and early 1980s. We have experienced no realignment, and thus there is long-term stability. The short-term changes, however, have been dramatic. There has been a persistent rise in the number of independents. The Democrats have lost support in the South as the Republicans have gained it there. The simple SES lines between the parties of a generation ago have deteriorated. Working-class identification has risen among Republicans, and the Democrats have attracted new support from the professional middle and upper-middle classes. Yet—to complicate matters further—by 1976 the pace of even these changes had slackened off. The SES lines seem now to have stabilized, and the growth of the independents seems to be leveling off.

In this pause in recent trends, the parties thus find themselves with exceptionally diverse, potentially fluid electorates. They are so diverse that the parties will surely find it difficult in the future to keep all parts of them happy. At the very least, their candidates will find it a challenge to unite them at any one election.

That the bases and divisions of the party electorates seem less and less clear is perhaps only an analytical nuisance. That only a shrinking percentage of Americans is willing to join a party electorate is a challenge to party politics as we have recently known them. The possibility, however, that the force of the party *within* the voters is weakening—that the effect of party loyalties on their political perceptions and decisions matters less—threatens the very future of the American two-party system. We now turn to that issue.

7

THE PARTY WITHIN
THE ELECTOR

The hyperactive world of American politics is difficult to understand, at best. The contests of parties and candidates, the overlapping layers of party organization, the hyperbole of political charge and countercharge may baffle even highly politicized and active party workers. The confusion is inevitably greater among the less experienced and involved members of the party electorate. Their best guide to this trackless political world is their party identification.

For individuals, therefore, the political party exists in two forms. Obviously, they can see the party of the real world—the party of conventions, candidates, campaigns, and organizations; but they also come to depend on a cognitive party—the party of attitudes, goals, and loyalties, the party *within the elector*. This party is an organizing point of view, a screen or framework through which individuals see political reality and in terms of which they organize it in their own minds. We all perceive the world about us selectively, and for the committed partisan—the member of the party electorate—party loyalty is the key to this selectivity. Because the party identification will very likely be the individual's most enduring political attachment, it serves as something of a political gyroscope, stabilizing political outlooks against the buffetings of short-term influences.

Before we discuss the influence of party identification, three general points should be established about party identification. First, it is remarkably unchanging, despite all the flux of American politics. The distribution of loyalists between the two parties has been very stable (see Table 6.2). For three decades, now, the Democratic identifiers have remained between 40 and 52 percent; and in recent polls, only one in four

Americans said that they had had different loyalties at any earlier times in their lives.[1]

Second, party identification is the major key to the political behavior of the American adult. Knowing that one fact about persons or groups tells us more about their political perceptions and political activities than any other fact. It is the single most important influence on the political behavior of the American adult.[2]

Third, party identification, still powerful though it may be, is less dominant today than it was ten or twenty years ago. In fact, according to the Center for Political Studies, the 1972 election was the first presidential election in its experience in which party identification was not the major factor in determining the outcome of the election. In addition, although party identification was again the major key to voting decisions in the 1976 elections, its importance eroded once again in 1980.

IDENTIFICATION, PARTY, AND POLITICAL ACTIVITY

The stronger the individual's party identification is, the greater is the probability that he or she will be active in politics generally and active in a political party in particular. Individuals with the strongest party identifications are more likely:

— To evince an interest in coming elections, to express a concern about their outcome, and to think that their outcome makes a difference. In 1980, for example, the "strong party identifiers" were almost two times more likely to be "very much interested" in the election campaign than were other American adults.

— To follow newspaper, magazine, television, and radio reports about politics or a campaign and to be present at the events of the campaign themselves.

— To talk with their friends about the election and to try to persuade them to support a party candidate.

To put these relationships in more general terms, the men and women whose political interest and activity place them within or very close to the

---

[1]Such survey questions, it should be remembered, require respondents to recall their degree of party loyalty as much as forty or fifty years earlier in their lives. Thus, the rate of error in the responses is probably greater than usual.

[2]This chapter is concerned only with party identification and its influences and impacts. It is by no means an attempt to deal with the entire range of American political or voting behavior.

activists of the party organization come in disproportionate numbers from the ranks of these strong identifiers.[3]

Short of activity in the parties, the strong party identifiers also see the parties in sharper terms than do the weak identifiers and the independents. They describe the parties as more committed to sharply differentiated liberal or conservative positions, and they are more apt to spot extremism in the other party (Table 7.1). They also are surer that there are important differences between the parties on specific policy issues.[4] In addition—and this is not very surprising—the party electorates tend to have stronger positive and negative views about the two parties and about their abilities to govern for the benefit of the nation.

Such relationships, by themselves, are no reason to leap to the conclusion that party identification alone produces greater party activity or a sharper issue image. Party activity—or any political activity, for that matter—appears to be the result of a complicated set of recruitment, access, incentive, and availability factors. That one of these factors is probably loyal commitment to a party seems clear. It is equally clear, however, that party identification is not the only condition necessary for party activity.

JUDGMENT OF CANDIDATES AND ISSUES

Party identification provides a perceptual predisposition—a screen through which the voter sees the candidates. "The stronger the voter's party bias, the more likely he is to see the candidate of his own party as hero, the candidate of the other party as villain."[5] In the 1960 presidential election, however, competing perceptual predispositions were at work. Catholics tended to perceive John F. Kennedy more favorably than did Protestants. Nonetheless, party identification kept its organizing power. When religious loyalties were held constant, party identification had its effect on the perception of Kennedy. When party identifications were held constant, the religious loyalty had *its* effect. When one says, therefore, that a candidate is attractive or compelling, one says something about the electorate as well as about the candidate.

The control that party identification exercises in the perception of can-

---

[3]Data on the political activity and involvement of party identifiers can be found in virtually all studies of American voting behavior. Among others, see Angus Campbell et al., *The American Voter* (New York: Wiley, 1960), especially Chap. 6; and Sidney Verba and Norman H. Nie, *Participation in America* (New York: Harper & Row, 1972).

[4]Gerald M. Pomper, *Voters' Choice* (New York: Dodd, Mead, 1975), Chap. 8.

[5]Donald E. Stokes, "Some Dynamic Elements of Contests for the Presidency," *American Political Science Review* 60 (1966): 23. The material in this paragraph is drawn from the Stokes article.

TABLE 7.1 *Perceptions of Party Identifiers and Independents about the Ideological Positions of the Democrats and Republicans: 1980*

	Strong Democrats	Weak Democrats	Independents	Weak Republicans	Strong Republicans
Perceptions of Democrats					
Extremely liberal, liberal	33.6%	21.3%	30.7%	40.8%	60.4%
Slightly liberal, moderate	38.9	49.5	49.2	49.7	33.7
Perceptions of Republicans					
Extremely conservative, conservative	56.0	46.5	48.3	44.3	53.4
Slightly conservative, moderate	22.7	36.8	39.7	47.6	39.8

Note The percentages in the table are based on the respondents' ranking of the parties; excluded are the individuals who were unable or unwilling to respond.

Source Center for Political Studies, University of Michigan; data made available through the Inter-University Consortium for Political and Social Research.

didates may be somewhat selective, however. In any event, that is the conclusion of a study of a sample of Detroit voters.[6] The partisan perception appears to extend to the candidates' political traits but not to such purely personal matters as his personality, appearance, or social characteristics (e.g., his religion). The partisan view of candidates is selective in another sense: it is not without limits. Before the 1972 election, for instance, Democrats joined Republicans in viewing Richard Nixon more favorably than George McGovern. Even so, it is important to remember that Democrats still had a less unfavorable view of McGovern than did Republicans. In the 1980 campaign—one in which, by earlier standards, neither candidate was received very favorably—Democrats took a far more charitable view of Jimmy Carter's presidency and his general capacity for leadership than did Republicans.

The impact of party identification on political issues is not as easy to determine as its impact on the perception of candidates. The candidate is a tangible person, but an issue is an abstraction, with far more subtle components. Nonetheless, one can easily show that the identifiers of the two parties take sharply defined positions on issues and on their perceptions of their parties' ability to deal with them. In 1980, for example, only 6 percent of the strong Democrats thought the Republicans better able to handle such economic issues as inflation and unemployment; only 3 percent of the strong Republicans thought the Democrats more capable. Such dramatic party-rooted differences are not always the rule, however, and when one shifts to large numbers of issues, differences between the loyalists of the two parties are less marked (Table 7.2).[7] Moreover, the correspondence between the individual's issue positions and those of his or her party appears to be weakening over time, even though partisans are more and more able to identify the issue positions of their parties correctly. Consideration of those trends leads, in turn, to some general thoughts about the power of party identification *within* the voter.

The metaphor of party identification as a perceptual screen may have a major flaw. It suggests that a one-way relationship exists between the individual and political reality, that the individual's party loyalty colors his or her perception of that reality. If Fiorina and others are right, however, in claiming that party identification is at least partly the result of retrospective evaluations of performance, then perception of candidates and issues can alter the party identification, too.[8] Thus, we confront a

[6]Roberta A. Sigel, "Effects of Partisanship on the Perception of Political Candidates," *Public Opinion Quarterly* 28 (1964): 483–96.

[7]Paul R. Abramson, John H. Aldrich, and David W. Rohde, *Continuity and Change in the 1980 Elections* (Washington, D.C.: Congressional Quarterly Press, 1982), Chap. 8.

[8]See the discussion in Chapter 6 on the formation of party loyalties, and, in particular, Morris P. Fiorina, *Retrospective Voting in American National Elections* (New Haven: Yale University Press, 1981).

TABLE 7.2 *Congruence between Party Identifiers and Issue Positions of Their Parties: 1980*

Individual's Position on issues closer to:	Strong Democrats	Weak Democrats	Independents leaning to Democrats	Independents	Independents leaning to Republicans	Weak Republicans	Strong Republicans
Democratic candidate	26%	23%	27%	20%	12%	10%	9%
Neutral	34	37	33	43	40	43	31
Republican candidate	40	40	40	37	48	48	60

Source Paul R. Abramson, John H. Aldrich, and David W. Rohde, *Change and Continuity in the 1980 Elections* (Washington, D.C.: Congressional Quarterly Press, 1982), p. 173 (part of Table 8.6).

terribly complex two-way process, in which the loyalty to party affects one's evaluations and yet those evaluations shape the way one views the parties. Even if one concedes that party identification is usually stable and basic enough to withstand a number of conflicting short-term observations and evaluations, it is clear that party loyalty is only a partial or inefficient perceptual screen. Perceptions hostile to it seem to escape its modifying effects and register on the individual. It is increasingly unlikely, then, that party loyalty within the voter is able to turn observations of reality into reinforcements of that very loyalty.

All of this seems to mean that the force of party loyalties as cognitive instruments, as shapers of political reality, has diminished. Party identification is less and less the master key to a unified, coherent, reinforcing set of political attitudes for millions of Americans. Because they can and do make their political evaluations without it, it is simply less useful and thus less important to them.[9] This erosion of the political party matches, perhaps even exceeds, the more obvious erosion reflected in the growing number of political independents. That is, even among people who cling to party loyalties, those loyalties seem to affect them less and less. Evidence of that fact is apparent in the looser relationships between party identification and preferences for candidates and issue positions. It is also obvious in the reduced likelihood that individuals will actually vote for the candidates of their party.

PARTY IDENTIFICATION AND VOTING

So powerful and stable has party identification been in the voting behavior of American adults that the Center for Political Studies (CPS) organizes its main typology of American presidential elections around the question of the role that party loyalties played in them. Thus, the CPS describes three chief election types:

1. The *maintaining* election, in which the party attachments of the recent past prevail without any great change or divergence. The elections of 1948, 1960, 1964, and 1976 would appear to be examples.
2. The *deviating* election, in which the basic distribution of party loyalties is not changed, but in which short-run forces (such as an attractive candidate or issues of great salience) cause the defeat of the majority party. The Republican successes of 1952, 1956, 1968, 1972, and 1980 are examples.
3. The *realigning* election, in which a new distribution of party loyalties

[9]On this point, see Martin P. Wattenberg, "The Decline of Political Partisanship in the United States," *American Political Science Review* 75 (1981): 941–50.

emerges and governs the outcome. The elections of 1928 and 1932 offer the most recent examples.[10]

The realigning elections are distinguished by "the presence of a great national crisis, leading to a conflict regarding governmental policies and the association of the two major parties with relatively clearly contrasting programs for its solution."[11]

Implicit in this typology is a trichotomy to which we have already referred. Scholars of voting behavior find it useful to break the influences on the voting decision into three main categories: party identification, candidate, and issues. Of the three, party identification traditionally dominated, not only because it had such depth and endurance but also because it affected perceptions and judgments of the other two. Only very appealing candidates and issues would overturn the power of the long-run party identification (in what would be a deviating election). The 1972 presidential election is a classic example. President Richard M. Nixon, the candidate of the minority party in party identifications, won over George McGovern, the majority party candidate, on two grounds: he was the more credible and respected of the candidates (in October 1972, that is), and his party's positions on such issues as the war in Vietnam were more acceptable to the majority of voters. It was the first time among recent elections in which the issues weighed at least as heavily as party identification in determining the votes of the electorate.[12]

The stronger the party identification, however, the less likely it is that the voter will be deflected from support of his or her party by the short-run appeals of candidates or issues (Table 7.3). Even in 1980, strong Democrats voted for Carter over Reagan by a margin of eight to one. Also, the stronger the identification, the more likely it is that the voter has supported the party consistently in the past (Table 7.3). Although there is an

[10]See Angus Campbell, "A Classification of the Presidential Election," in Angus Campbell et al., *Elections and the Political Order* (New York: Wiley, 1966), pp. 63–77. See also V. O. Key, "A Theory of Critical Elections," *Journal of Politics* 17 (1955): 3–18.

[11]Campbell, "A Classification of the Presidential Election," p. 76. For an extended debate on an alternative, four-part scheme, see Gerald M. Pomper, "Classification of Presidential Elections," *Journal of Politics* 29 (1967): 535–66, and Walter Dean Burnham, *Critical Elections and the Mainsprings of American Politics* (New York: Norton, 1970), pp. 32–33.

[12]A note of clarification is in order. When we speak of the power of party identification here, we speak of its ability to affect large numbers of vote decisions. It is possible for party identification to be the prime determining force in the sum of the vote decisions and yet, at the same time, for the majority party to lose an election (as in 1952 and 1956). The margin of such electoral victories is small, and the great majority of voters may still be responding to party cues. In 1972, however, there was both a minority party victory and an eclipse of the total effect of party loyalty in the electorate. On the 1972 election, see Arthur H. Miller, Warren E. Miller, Alden S. Raine, and Thad A. Brown, "A Majority Party in Disarray: Policy Polarization in the 1972 Election," *American Political Science Review* 70 (1976): 753–78.

TABLE 7.3 *Presidential Vote and Record of Past Voting among Party Identifiers Who Voted in 1980*

	Strong Democrats	Weak Democrats	Independents	Weak Republicans	Strong Republicans
Vote for President, 1980:					
Ronald Reagan	10.7%	32.8%	55.9%	85.6%	92.0%
Jimmy Carter	85.7	59.7	26.5	4.6	4.5
John Anderson	3.1	7.5	14.1	8.5	3.6
Other	0.5	—	3.6	1.4	—
Voted in all past presidential elections	47.1	38.6	39.1	52.4	56.9
Voted for same party since began voting	74.3	47.2	21.2	28.5	60.5

Note Figures exclude respondents who gave no answer or who did not vote.

Source Center for Political Studies, University of Michigan; data made available through the Inter-University Consortium for Political and Social Research.

important conceptual distinction between party identification and party voting, one clearly leads to the other.

The 1960 presidential race between Richard M. Nixon and John F. Kennedy affords a fascinating example of the clash of party loyalties with another potent set of social loyalties—those of religion. In this sense, Kennedy's Catholicism was more than an issue or a candidate; it was the stimulus for another, largely nonpolitical predisposition. We have already assessed the effect of those loyalties on the perceptions of Kennedy himself. Despite the strength of the religious loyalties, however, Philip Converse concluded, after an examination of voting in the 1960 election, that in casting their votes, "Protestant Democrats were more likely to behave as Democrats than as Protestants, and Catholic Republicans were more likely to behave as Republicans than as Catholics."[13]

With all that, however, it is an inescapable fact that party identification and actual vote increasingly are diverging in American politics. Voters split their tickets more often; that is, they vote for Democrats and Republicans in the same election.[14] Furthermore, in the one election about which we have the most information—the presidential election—voters increasingly are abandoning their party to vote for the candidate of the other party. That drift is in both directions, but the major movement is surely that of Democrats voting for Republican presidential candidates. From 1952 through 1980, there were eight presidential elections and, despite considerable Democratic majorities in party identifications, the Republican candidates won five of those eight. Clearly, short-term considerations of candidate and issue have been overriding residual party loyalties. In 1980, for example, the election was "a referendum on the Carter Presidency. . . . Dissatisfaction with the Carter administration's performance on the economy, concern over Carter's handling of Iran, and a consistent general dislike of the incumbent all contributed to the Reagan victory."[15] Thus, what we have traditionally called deviating elections are becoming almost "normal."

These observations on the impact of party identification on the voter largely reflect decisions in national or statewide elections. Party identification may have either more or less impact in state and local elections. Where voters have personal, face-to-face contact with the candidates in a rural county, their evaluation of the candidates may be so strong that it

---

[13]Philip E. Converse, "Religion and Politics: The 1960 Election," in Campbell et al., *Elections and the Political Order*, p. 123.

[14]Frank Feigert has argued persuasively that there is too much confusion over what scholars mean by ticket splitting; nonetheless, there is still strong evidence that, in whatever form one envisions it, it is on the rise. See his "Illusions of Ticket-Splitting," *American Politics Quarterly* 7 (1979): 470–88.

[15]Kathleen A. Frankovic in Gerald Pomper et al., *The Election of 1980* (Chatham, N.J.: Chatham House, 1981), pp. 113, 116.

overrides party loyalties. In addition, some voters may find the application of party loyalties inappropriate to the less partisan campaigns for local office, especially when the office appears to have little policymaking responsibility (e.g., the local clerk of the court or the registrar of deeds). On the other hand, voters in local elections may have to rely on the guidance of party even more than they do in national elections. In a large city, the voter who has to make choices on a long ballot of city, county, state, and other officers may have no alternative but reliance on the party label. In these elections, the voter's information on issues and candidates may be only a fraction of what it is in a presidential election.

THE MYTHS OF THE INDEPENDENT

That party loyalties should govern so much political behavior in a culture that so warmly celebrates the political independent is too striking a paradox to ignore. There is clearly some gap between myth and reality, and the problem is with the myth of the independent. Before the myth is finally put to rest, however, we perhaps ought to be clear about what myth we are burying.

If we mean by the term *independent* those Americans who prefer not to identify with a political party, then the myth *is* a casualty of survey research. Although it is true that self-styled independents split their tickets more frequently, wait longer in the campaign to make their voting decisions, and show a moderate level of interest in government generally, they fall short of the picture of the independent in most other respects. They are less concerned about specific elections than identifiers are, less well informed and less active politically. Also, they are more likely not to vote at a given election. In 1980, independents once again had a higher frequency of nonvoting than did party identifiers, and "pure" independents voted less often than independents who leaned toward one party or the other. They are, in short, less politically active, less informed, and less involved than party identifiers, especially the *strong* party identifiers.

There is no reason, however, why we cannot define the political independents in terms of their behavior or activity. In his last work, published posthumously, V. O. Key attempted to reclaim the independents from their current obloquy by dealing not with the self-styled independents but with voters who switched their party vote in a consecutive pair of presidential elections.[16] The picture of the American voter that emerged from American political folklore and from the new electoral studies, Key

[16]V. O. Key (with the assistance of Milton C. Cummings), *The Responsible Electorate* (Cambridge, Mass.: Harvard University Press, 1966).

thought, was not a pretty one; it was one of an electorate whose voting decision was determined by deeply ingrained attitudes, perceptions, and loyalties without its having grasped the major political issues and alternatives.

Key's search for electoral "rationality" centered, therefore, on the switchers—the voters who did *not* keep voting for the same party in consecutive elections. Key's switchers, by the usual criteria, came much closer to the image of the independent than did the self-described independents. He found their levels of political interest no lower than those of the "stand-patters" who remained firm in their voting allegiances. By his definition, of course, switchers are not nonvoters. Above all, they are marked by an issue-related rationality that fits well the usual picture of the independent. They agree on policy issues with the stand-patters toward whom they shift, and they disagree with the policies of the party from which they defect.[17]

It is the self-described independent, however—the one who voices no party preference—who is the subject of most scholarly inquiry; and the numbers of them among American voters have increased significantly. (See Table 6.2.) Indeed, among the electorate under age thirty, the percentage of independents approaches 50 percent. There are also signs that recent additions to the group have altered its composition. Many of the new independents are from higher educational and SES levels than the older ones, giving the independents a more heterogeneous social composition.

It is not surprising, therefore, that the behavior and attitudes of independents in presidential elections have shown some inclination to change. Recently, independents have been as interested in the general affairs of government and politics as weak party identifiers have been (Table 7.4). In 1968, the independents voted in the same percentage and were as attentive to the campaign as the party loyalists were. It may have been that the range of options in 1968—from Eugene McCarthy through George Wallace—drew them, if only briefly, into more sustained contact with American politics. In 1976 and 1980, too, independents voted at about the same rate as the weak partisans. More generally, we now seem to have

at least *two sets* of independents: "old independents," who correspond to the rather bleak classical survey-research picture, and "new independents," who may have declined to identify with either major party not because they are relatively politically unconscious, but because the structure of electoral politics at the present time turns upon parties, issues, and symbolisms which do not have much meaning in terms of their political values or cognitions.[18]

[17]A related concept of the independent as ticket-splitter is developed in Walter DeVries and Lance Tarrance, *The Ticket Splitter* (Grand Rapids: Eerdmans, 1972).

[18]Burnham, *Critical Elections and the Mainsprings of American Politics*, p. 127.

TABLE 7.4   *Levels of Interest in the Campaign and in Government and Public Affairs among Party Identifiers and Independents: 1980*

	Strong Demo-crats	Weak Demo-crats	Indepen-dents	Weak Repub-licans	Stong Repub-licans
Respondent "very much" interested in campaign	49.4%	24.6%	30.6%	37.6%	63.0%
Respondent follows government and public affairs "most of time"	32.8	18.7	24.4	27.4	46.0

Note   The data come from two separate questions; in each case, the responses reflecting the highest level of interest are reported.

Source   Center for Political Studies, University of Michigan; data made available through the Inter-University Consortium for Political and Social Research.

Even though the second group may not quite meet the criteria for the classic American independent, it comes closer than the independents did earlier.[19]

The independents have evolved, in other words, into a group as diverse as the party identifiers. More important, they increasingly tend to react as other American voters do to the political events and personalities around them. They occupy not a place outside American politics but rather a center ground between the two groups of partisans. The heavy vote that John Anderson drew in 1980 from independents of the center is illustrative (Table 7.3). Moreover, the independents who confess to leaning toward one party or the other are now clearly more like the weak party identifiers than they are like the independents who show no party leanings at all. In short, the political activities of independents now tend to be more a part of party politics than they were a generation ago.

THE LOYAL ELECTORATES IN CHANGE

The leaders of the party organizations scarcely know the men and women of the parties' loyal electorates. They know them largely in the same way

[19]William H. Flanigan and Nancy H. Zingale suggest another kind of diversity among independents, based on whether or not they lean toward one party or the other, in *Political Behavior of the American Electorate*, 4th ed. (Boston: Allyn & Bacon, 1979). See also Hugh L. LeBlanc and Mary Beth Merrion, "Independents, Issue Partisanship, and the Decline of Party," *American Politics Quarterly* 7 (1979): 240–56.

that political scientists do—in some abstract, aggregate profile. They know that members of the party in the electorate see the issues and candidates through party-tinted glasses. They know that the party electorate has a somewhat unified and reinforcing view of politics, that it is more likely to vote the party ticket, and that it is easier to lure into activity for the party or for a candidate. Party strategists know, in other words, that the party electorate is a hard core of party supporters. In a general, if vague, way, they see—as do political scientists—that party identification is a commitment that is often strong enough to affect other commitments and pervasive enough to color and codify perceptions of political reality.

Much of the strategy of American political campaigning is based on these assumptions about loyal party electorates. The general strategy is often to stimulate and reinforce the party loyalties of one's own partisans while making candidate and issue appeals to independents and partisans of the other party. When workers and union members threatened to bolt the Humphrey ticket in 1968, labor leaders drove hard to reinforce old labor loyalties to the Democratic party and to hammer at the issues of wages and employment that would reinforce those ties. (As it turned out, they succeeded in bringing a large number of strays back into the Democratic fold by election day.)

Furthermore, the size and composition of the two party electorates determine the more specific strategies. It appears that the present pattern of party loyalty requires, for example, that the Republicans minimize party-stimulating appeals, party identifications, and SES issues. Their hope, at present, rests with attractive candidates and nonclass issues. It is surely not coincidental that both Barry Goldwater in 1964 and Richard Nixon in 1968 and 1972 emphasized a large number of issues that met those specifications: crime and morality, local responsibility for civil rights and racial equality, defense and foreign policy, and the war in Vietnam. In 1980, Ronald Reagan did challenge the Democrats on their SES territory, especially by appealing to middle-class concerns about inflation and taxation; but issues of defense, foreign policy (e.g., Iran), and morality also occupied high places on his agenda.

So great has been the stabilizing force of these two great party electorates in American politics that it is hard to imagine what politics would be like without them. Because large numbers of people have had party identifications, because they have rarely changed them, and because those identifications have strongly governed their voting decisions, patterns of voting support for the two parties have been extremely stable. In election after election, individual voters have voted straight party tickets. The patterns of party support also have remained stable geographically. A party's pattern of state-to-state support (and county-to-county support within states) has remained steady election after election. When the votes have shifted—enough to tip balances of victory and defeat—they have shifted so evenly that they have not greatly altered those overall patterns of support. A party's state-to-state profile of support has been raised or lowered, but it has not changed greatly.

Only periodic party realignments—those shifts triggered by the conjunction of presidential elections and such cataclysmic events as panics, wars, and depressions—have jolted this long-term stability. At such times, a new pattern and distribution of party loyalties has been established, and it has persisted until the next realignment. Since the 1960s, however, we have experienced instability in the alignment of 1932 without achieving any realignment. Split-ticket voting is on the upsurge, self-described independents are at an all-time high, and those party loyalties that remain do not govern political judgments as they once did. The elections of 1964 and after—with the possible exception of 1976—saw the parties putting together coalitions of voters that bore little resemblance to the coalitions of their supporters in 1960 and in the twenty-five years before.

It is just possible that we are teetering on the edge of party realignment. A strong third-party movement—such as that of George Wallace—has usually preceded realignments in the past. A great many signs now point to a decline in the number of party loyalists and a decline in the power of the loyalties that persist. A number of observers have suggested that the Democrats may build a new coalition by combining the young, the disaffected, the minority groups, the disadvantaged, and a good portion of the successful and affluent. The Republicans would thus become the party of a working-class and middle-class conservatism—the party of middle America or the silent majority of whom Republican orators speak.[20]

It is even more likely, however, that we will not have realignment. We may well be seeing nothing more than the declining effectiveness and strength of party loyalties. In the past, we ignored the possibility that alignments might stay relatively fixed while their force declined. Scholars now refer to that possibility as "dealignment."[21] So weak and attenuated do party loyalties become, in fact, that many voters do not take them seriously enough to change. Others slip into independence; still others may even shift their loyalties to another party on an individual, ad hoc basis. The aggregate effect of such a dealignment, then, is a weakening of party loyalties, a gradual erosion of the existing alignment, and a persistent failure to achieve the sharp and dramatic voter shifts that characterized the realignments of the past.[22] It is a scenario that appears to describe well the present condition of American party politics.

[20]James L. Sundquist, *Dynamics of the Party System* (Washington, D.C.: Brookings, 1973).

[21]Everett Carll Ladd, "The Brittle Mandate: Electoral Dealignment and the 1980 Presidential Election," *Political Science Quarterly* 96 (1981): 1–25.

[22]Many of these themes are developed more fully in Burnham, *Critical Elections*, Chaps. 5 and 6.

Is no realignment possible, then, after an interim period of dealignment? Conventional explanations of how past realignments happened assume a massive shifting of voters from one party to the other. They are, in other words, explanations based on the conversion of large numbers of voters. Recent and careful analysis of the 1928–36 realignment suggests, however, that it did not happen quite that way. Kristi Andersen has argued persuasively that the realignment was largely the result of the infusion of new voters—new citizens, young voters, and those who were already enfranchised but had been inactive.[23] Clubb, Flanigan, and Zingale see a more complicated process, whereby the weak party attachments of new voters and of those already in the electorate are shaped and even changed by dramatic events, by strong political leadership, and by the individual voters' reactions to the way parties and officeholders perform in a crisis.[24] In their concept of realignment, voters and parties interact and react over some time; realignment results from the infusion of new voters, followed by their consolidation as loyal partisans, and also from the gradual, reactive conversion of older partisans.

If it is indeed true that realignments depend, even in part, on the identifications of first-time voters, realignment does not seem imminent under present conditions. New voters entering the party system now are largely young voters, who show a marked preference for not having any party identification. Furthermore, in recent decades, we have not had the kinds of crises or events that might disturb old loyalties or force the search for new alternatives. Alternatively, we have not had the staking out of new party positions or programs around which new alignments might coalesce.

> Opportunities for realignment and revitalization of the parties have occurred in the 1960s and, it appears, again in the 1970s. The fact that these opportunities went unrealized was the consequence of failures of leadership and perhaps of the intervention of unforeseen and uncontrollable events rather than of any incapacity of voters to orient themselves toward and to support political parties. Thus, we can only conclude that the possibility of partisan realignment and revitalization of the parties in any form is critically dependent upon the behavior of political leadership and the performance of government.[25]

[23]See Kristi Andersen, "Generation, Partisan Shift, and Realignment: A Glance Back to the New Deal," Chap. 5 in Norman H. Nie, Sidney Verba, and John R. Petrocik, *The Changing American Voter* (Cambridge, Mass.: Harvard University Press, 1976); and her *The Creation of a Democratic Majority* (Chicago: University of Chicago Press, 1979). For a contrary point of view, see Robert S. Erikson and Kent L. Tedin, "The 1928–1936 Partisan Realignment: The Case for the Conversion Hypothesis," *American Political Science Review* 75 (1981): 951–62.

[24]Jerome M. Clubb, William H. Flanigan, and Nancy H. Zingale, *Partisan Realignment* (Beverly Hills: Sage, 1980), especially Chaps. 4 and 5.

[25]*Ibid.*, pp. 293–94.

That, one should note, is the optimistic view. It is also the "political" view of realignment, for it recognizes the role of political leadership and political interactions in the reshaping of party loyalties.

The many signs of weakened party attachments are so apparent that it is impossible to miss them. The abundance of those signs, however, ought not obscure the fact that, for many Americans, some power does remain in party loyalty. Identification with a party is still the most potent cue for political choice in the American electorate. In much of the rest of the politically free world, people find their political cues elsewhere—in religion, race, class, ethnic group, or ideology. The dominant, fundamental loyalty to a party—and all that flows from that loyalty—has contributed greatly to the special character of American party politics. It has made it possible, for example, for the parties to be flexible and pragmatic. Therefore, whether such identification with a party continues to erode or whether we manage to revitalize it is more than a matter of mere academic curiosity. It concerns the very nature of American parties and American electoral politics.

8

THE AMERICAN ELECTORATE

Much of the history of political parties can be written in terms of their responses to expansion of the suffrage. The parties began as essentially aristocratic instruments for mobilizing very homogeneous and limited electorates, but as the electorates expanded, they altered their organizations and appeals to include virtually all adults. In multiparty systems in the Western world, new parties often rose to represent new groups admitted to the suffrage. The European Socialist and Labor parties, for example, organized the newly enfranchised industrial workers.

The stability of the American two-party system, however, has ruled out such an accommodation of new electorates. The two major American parties have had to expand their hospitality to new groups winning the right to vote. Since they are overwhelmingly electoral parties, any changes in the size, composition, or activity level of the American electorate affect them profoundly. From the electorate's total dimensions, they recruit their own, especially loyal party electorates and the workers, skills, and money necessary for party organizations and campaigns. Above all, they seek in the electorate the majorities they must mobilize if they are to win elections.

Unfortunately, it is not entirely clear just who constitutes the American electorate. Obviously, it consists of something less than the total number of American adults. The "something less" is generally the result of two kinds of limiting factors: (1) the restrictions placed on it (or, if one prefers, the definitions of it) by the states and (2) the unwillingness of eligible adults either to register or to vote. Just how and why these limitations operate, whom they affect, and the numbers they disenfranchise are not easy matters to settle.

If the American electorate—in either its legal or its self-defining (turnout) dimension—were an accurate sample of the adult American population, the issue of its dimensions would be far less important. The effective electorate, however, is nothing of the sort. It overrepresents some groups in the American society and underrepresents others. Because of the preferences of various groups for one party or the other, the composition and possible enlargement of the electorate are matters of differential advantage for the parties. Since American blacks identify largely with the Democratic party at present, for example, attempts to bring them into the American electorate affect the parties' loyal electorates and thus the patterns of their competition.

THE ELECTORATE: THE PROBLEM OF MEASUREMENT

After every presidential election, commentators on American civic values don sackcloth and ashes to note that, as usual, a relatively small percentage of American adults stirred themselves to vote. In 1968, for instance, a campaign of unparalleled cost and scope—and one that included the liveliest third-party candidacy in more than forty years—attracted only 61 percent of the potential electorate to the polls. Somewhat more lackluster two-way races in 1972, 1976, and 1980 attracted only 55.5, 54.3, and 53.2 percent voter turnouts. The lowest turnout figures in 1980 were 35.4 percent for the District of Columbia and 40.7 percent for South Carolina; the highest were 70.6 percent in Minnesota and 68.6 percent in Idaho.[1]

These and similar turnout percentages, regardless of the elections that happen to be involved, depend on two categories of data—one fairly reliable and the other highly suspect. Because of the generally accurate counting and reporting of vote totals that prevail in most localities, the figures on actual turnout (the number of voters voting) are fairly reliable. The base figures of total possible voters (on the basis of which the turnout percentages are calculated) are questionable, however. Whether the base is called total voters, potential voters, or the potential electorate, it usually turns out to be a total of all persons of voting age in the states (by count of the United States Census Bureau). Thus, the widely quoted 53.2 percent turnout for the 1980 presidential election was computed on such a base of some 162,761,000 "potential voters."

Such reckonings of so-called potential voters are essentially misleading because they fail to take into account the restrictions on the suffrage other than age. Nor do they consider the number of voters made ineligible to vote by their failure (where required) to go through the administrative processes of registration. The reasonable remedy, therefore, is to substitute

---

[1]These data and many others in this chapter are from *Statistical Abstract of the United States: 1981*, 102nd ed. (Washington, D.C.: U.S. Bureau of Census, 1982).

for the concept of potential voters some measure of *eligible* voters; but that figure is precisely what is so hard to come by.

The outer limits of the American electorate are not hard to determine. The electorate can be no larger than the number of adults of at least age 18 in the country and no smaller than the number of actual voters. The two necessary intermediate figures, however—the number of eligible voters and the number of eligible voters actually registered—are the ones that are so elusive. In 1980 terms, the puzzle is this:

1. The *potential electorate* (all persons aged 18 years and older)— 162,761,000
2. The *eligible electorate* (persons aged 18 and older who meet voting requirements)—?
3. The *registered electorate* (all eligible voters who are registered to vote)—?
4. The *turnout* (the persons who actually vote; here, the vote for president)—86,589,000

The fourth figure divided by the first produces the conventionally cited 53.2 percent turnout for 1980. Until we have the intervening figures, the easy availability of the number of total adults (the potential electorate) will dictate the use of that figure, and we will continue to manufacture inaccurately low, and unflattering, turnout percentages.

The size of the effective American electorate results from the impact of forces both internal and external to the individual. The external influences include the legal restrictions of the states, their application by the administrative machinery of the states, and the informal restrictions of economic and social sanction. The internal influences are the values and goals, the motivational levels, the role perceptions, and the sense of civic responsibility within the individual. The external definitions of the American electorate are clearer because they are more tangible, and we turn to them first.

LEGAL DEFINITION OF THE ELECTORATE

The decentralizing influences of federalism touch almost every important aspect of American electoral politics, and the electorate itself is no exception. The definition of the electorate over the past 150 years has expanded through the curiously American interlacing of national and state action. The chief expansions have been these:

1. In the early nineteenth century, the states themselves gradually repealed the property and tax-paying qualifications for voting by which they had so severely restricted the male suffrage. By 1860, there re-

mained no states that required property holding and only four that required substantial tax paying as a condition for voting. About a century later, the Supreme Court, and then the Twenty-fourth Amendment, finally ended even the small poll tax as a requirement for voting.

— By the mid-1870s, women began to work through the states for their right to vote; in 1890, Wyoming became the first state to grant the full franchise to women. Progress slowly bogged down, especially in the eastern states, and women shifted their hopes to the United States Constitution. The Nineteenth Amendment, forbidding states to deny the vote on grounds of sex, was finally ratified in 1920.

— The expansion of black suffrage began by state action in some of the states of New England before the Civil War, but it culminated after the war with the passage of the Fifteenth Amendment. Congress and the federal courts, from that time to the present, have periodically attempted to enforce its clauses on some reluctant states.

— In the 1960s, young people met with varied success in their attempt to lower the voting age to eighteen or nineteen by state constitutional amendments. Then, in June 1970, the United States Congress passed a law extending the suffrage to eighteen-year-olds in both state and federal elections. Less than half a year later, the Supreme Court decided by a five to four vote that the act was constitutional as it applied to federal elections but unconstitutional as it applied to state and local elections. Congress then passed and sent to the states for ratification an amendment to the Constitution lowering the age to eighteen for *all* elections. That amendment, the Twenty-sixth Amendment, was ratified by 1971.[2]

None of the major expansions in the American electorate, therefore, was accomplished without national limitations on the power of the states to define the electorate.[3] Undoubtedly, however, it was the intention of the Founding Fathers to vest control over the electorate in the states. At least that was the outcome they attempted to ensure by Article I, Section 2, which provides that, for the elections to the House, "the electors in each state shall have the qualifications requisite for electors of the most numerous branch of the state legislature." That was as much as they said on the suffrage in the entire Constitution. No more was necessary, for senators were to be elected by state legislatures, and the president and vice-

[2]The Supreme Court decision was in *Oregon v. Mitchell*, 400 U.S. 112 (1970). The chief section of the amendment states: "The right of citizens of the United States, who are eighteen years of age or older, to vote shall not be denied or abridged by the United States or by any state on account of age."

[3]For background on the early development of the American electorate, see Chilton Williamson, *American Suffrage: From Property to Democracy* (Princeton: Princeton University Press, 1960).

president by a genuinely deliberative electoral college. As for the selection of electors to the electoral college, Section 4 of Article I stipulated that each state was to "appoint in such manner as the legislature thereof may direct, a number of electors. . . ." When the Congress and the states converted the election of senators to a direct and popular election, they wrote into the Seventeenth Amendment the same formula that applies to the House: "The electors in each state shall have the qualifications requisite for electors of the most numerous branch of the state legislature."

Thus, contrary to the traditions of other countries and even of other federal systems, the formulation of voting requirements was left to the states. The inevitable result was the absence of a uniform national electorate, even for national elections. The constitutional authority of the United States government, therefore, has been limited until very recently to the passive role of saying in four amendments that the states could not deny citizens the vote solely and explicitly on grounds of race or color (Fifteenth), sex (Nineteenth), failure to pay a tax (Twenty-fourth), or age (Twenty-sixth). Furthermore, the Fourteenth Amendment's equal protection clause ("no state shall make or enforce any law which shall . . . deny to any person within its jurisdiction the equal protection of the laws") was interpreted by the Supreme Court to prevent a state from discriminating against blacks in defining its electorate. Presumably, that same clause would similarly protect ethnic, religious, occupational, regional, or other social groups in the unlikely event that a state should deny the suffrage to, say, Presbyterians, Italian-Americans, or government employees.

In recent years, however, the national government, through both the Congress and the Supreme Court, has expanded its role in defining the American electorate. By ordinary statute—rather than by constitutional amendment—the Congress extended the vote to younger voters in federal elections; banned literacy, understanding, and character tests for registration; and waived residence requirements for voting in presidential elections. The newly expanded congressional authority appears to rest on the Supreme Court's interpretation of Article I, Section 4, the section on the control of congressional elections.[4] The Court itself has expanded its own powers in the application of constitutional guarantees, that expansion culminating in 1972 in its decision sharply restricting state residence requirements.[5]

---

[4]Section 4 of Article I is as follows: "The Times, Places, and Manner of holding Elections for Senators and Representatives, shall be prescribed in each State by the Legislature thereof; but the Congress may at any time by Law make or alter such Regulations, except as to the Places of choosing Senators." Every reader can be his or her own constitutional expert in deciding whether questions of suffrage are what the Founding Fathers had in mind in writing this section of Article I.

[5]*Dunn v. Blumstein*, 405 U.S. 330 (1972). For a full and excellent study of the legal and constitutional issues involved in defining the electorate, see Richard Claude, *The Supreme Court and the Electoral Process* (Baltimore: Johns Hopkins University Press, 1970).

Between the constitutional territory of the states and that of the nation there is a tiny no-man's-land, the District of Columbia. For almost all of American history, the citizens of the District have remained voteless, even in their own local affairs. Since the passage of the Twenty-third Amendment to the Constitution in 1961, however, the voters of the District of Columbia have had three votes in the electoral college. They also elect a nonvoting delegate to Congress and a series of local officials on the authorization of the Congress.

THE AMERICAN ELECTORATE TODAY

Despite their freedom under the Constitution, the states have developed legal definitions of the suffrage that are surprisingly similar. In part, the negative controls of the constitutional amendments have hemmed them in. So, too, have the political pressures for universal adult suffrage, the examples of other states, and increased supervision by the Congress and the Supreme Court. In any event, it is now possible to deal with the state definitions of the suffrage in a small number of categories.[6]

Minimum Voting Age

As recently as the 1968 elections, all but four states fixed the minimum voting age at twenty-one. Thanks to the 1970 Voting Rights Act and the Twenty-sixth Amendment, however, the minimum age became eighteen for all elections, beginning in 1972.

Citizenship

All states now require that voters be citizens of the United States. As surprising as it may now seem, in 1900 eleven states still permitted aliens to vote, although some states required that the individual had begun to seek American citizenship. In 1926, Arkansas, the last state to capitulate, closed off the alien suffrage. More than any other single factor, the end of mass and open immigration into the United States signaled the end of the vote for noncitizens.

Without any doubt, the requirement of citizenship is the major legal barrier to voting for adults now living in the United States. In 1980, 5.4 million aliens registered with the Justice Department; that figure was only 2.9 million in 1960 and 4.2 million in 1970. Of that 5.4 million aliens who reside legally in the United States and register annually, 27 percent lived

[6]For a general survey of state laws defining the electorate, see Constance E. Smith, *Voting and Election Laws* (New York: Oceana, 1960).

in California and 15 percent in New York state in 1980. In addition, there are millions of illegal aliens living in the country; the most reliable estimates put that number at 4 to 5 million in the years around 1980. Thus, by the most conservative reckoning, there are at least 10 million adults living in the United States who are ineligible to vote by reason of their foreign citizenship.

Poll Taxes

Until 1964, five states—Alabama, Mississippi, Texas, Vermont, and Virginia—continued to require payment of a poll tax (i.e., a head tax or a per capita tax) as a qualification for voting.[7] The tax amounted to only one or two dollars a year, but its disenfranchising effect was often increased by stipulations that it be cumulative, that it be paid well in advance of the election, or that the taxpayer keep the receipt and present it at the polling booth. In 1964, however, the Twenty-fourth Amendment to the Constitution invalidated tax paying as a condition for voting in national elections. A year later, in the Voting Rights Act of 1965, the Congress legislated a finding that poll taxes in *any* election are discriminatory. In interpreting that law, the Supreme Court noted that a state violates the Constitution "whenever it makes the affluence of the voter or payment of a fee an electoral standard."[8]

Residence

For most of the history of the Republic, the states were free to require that citizens live in the state and locality for a certain period of time before they could vote. Indeed, most states devised three-layer residence requirements: a minimum period of time in the state, a shorter time in the county, and an even shorter period in the local voting district. Traditionally, the longest residence requirements were those of the southern states (where they disenfranchised migrant and mobile farm labor), but long waits for eligibility were not uncommon elsewhere. In 1970, the median residence requirement among the fifty states was one year in the state, three months in the county, and one month in the voting district.[9]

Substantial residence requirements began to crumble in the 1950s and 1960s, however, largely in response both to the demands of a physically mobile society and to its rising democratic expectations. States lowered

[7]In Vermont, the poll tax was a qualification for voting only in local town affairs; the state repealed it early in 1966.

[8]The 1966 case was *Harper v. Virginia State Board of Elections*, 383 U.S. 633 (1966). On the poll tax generally, see Frederic D. Ogden, *The Poll Tax in the South* (University: University of Alabama Press, 1958).

[9]*Book of the States 1970–71* (Lexington, Ky.: Council of State Governments, 1971).

their residence requirements, and many also set up even lower requirements for newcomers wishing to vote in presidential elections. In 1970, Congress settled the latter issue by establishing a national uniform residence requirement of thirty days within a state for voting in a presidential election. Then, in 1972, the Supreme Court struck down Tennessee's one-year residence requirement for voting in state and local elections, indicating a strong preference for a thirty-day limit. The Court later accepted a fifty-day requirement, but in doing so it noted that such a period "approaches the outer constitutional limit."[10] Consequently, almost half of the states have dropped residence requirements altogether, and most of the rest have fixed them at one month.

Disqualifications

Virtually all the states restrict the suffrage for reasons of crime or mental incompetence. Institutionalization for insanity or severe mental illness temporarily removes an individual from the suffrage in all states; and in the great majority of states, so do convictions for certain categories of crimes, the most common being felonies and electoral corruption. The disqualification for mental illness is generally limited to the time of illness or incapacity. The disqualification for felonies, however, lasts indefinitely in some states, even after release from prison. Only gubernatorial pardon or some formal administrative or legislative action will restore the franchise.

Literacy Tests

In early 1965—before passage of the Civil Rights Act of that year—twenty states required that an applicant for registration demonstrate his or her literacy. Often, the test, especially when it was administered by an election clerk, constituted little more than a test of the applicant's ability to scrawl a signature. In other states, applicants proved their literacy by filling out application forms for registration. In a few states, the test was more substantial. The New York comprehensive test, drafted and administered by educational authorities, included questions to test the reader's understanding of brief expository paragraphs. (In Alaska, applicants could demonstrate their facility in English by either reading or speaking it.) Furthermore, it was customary for literacy to mean literacy in English; only Hawaii offered an alternative—Hawaiian.

Associated with these literacy tests were tests of understanding or interpretation. Originally, the states intended them as alternatives to literacy tests. If individuals could not read or write, they might qualify for the franchise by demonstrating their ability to explain some aspect of the

---

[10]*Dunn v. Blumstein,* 405 U.S. 330 (1972); and *Burns v. Fortson,* 410 U.S. 686 (1973).

governmental system or some section of the state constitution. In other states, such as Louisiana and Georgia, the local voting registrar could permit an illiterate person to register if the registrar was convinced that the individual was of "good character." Mississippi, home of the interpretation test, required interpretative ability in addition to literacy and good character. Local voting registrars selected one of the 286 sections of the state constitution for the applicant to read and interpret; the registrar, of course, was the judge of the adequacy of the interpretation.

In the Voting Rights Act of 1970, Congress suspended the use of literacy, understanding, and character tests anywhere as a prerequisite for registration to vote. It reasoned that, regardless of the states' various intentions, the tests had worked discriminatorily against minority groups. The Supreme Court agreed.

Federal Lands

Traditionally, the states have refused to recognize citizens living on federal reservations—military posts, national parks, and veterans hospitals, for instance—as citizens of the state for the purpose of voting. Only three states—California, Utah, and West Virginia—give such citizens a vote. Hence, the great majority of Americans who live on one or another of the 5,000 separate pieces of land over which the national government exercises exclusive jurisdiction are without a vote. The one exception is the District of Columbia.

THE SPECIAL PROBLEM OF MINORITIES

Throughout the preceding paragraphs runs a repeated theme—the special limits placed on racial and ethnic minorities. Take the case of American blacks. Residence requirements penalized them for poorly paid jobs as itinerant farm laborers, jobs that often prevented them from educating their children. Nor is it unfair to say that black disenfranchisement is a major reason why the poll tax persisted in the South, why residence requirements were more stringent in the South, why criminal disqualifications are broadest in the South, and why literacy, interpretation, and understanding tests were most common in the South.

Even beyond all these explicit limitations, however, blacks traditionally found themselves blocked by the administration of registration and election law. Endless delay, unavailable registrars, niggling technicalities, and double standards were their greatest barriers in recent years. In 1965 hearings of the United States Civil Rights Commission documented the problem in ample detail. Charles C. Humpstone, staff attorney of the Commission on Civil Rights, reported on the leniency of registrars in Issaquena County, Mississippi, in evaluating the interpretations of white applicants:

> A number of inadequate answers were accepted. For example, one white applicant, asked to interpret section 35, which reads, "The senate shall consist of members chosen every 4 years by the qualified electors of the several districts," wrote only, "equible wrights" . . . and passed.

Mrs. Mary Oliver Welsh of Humphreys County, Mississippi (who was on old-age assistance and receiving government surplus commodities), recounted her attempts to register to vote:

> Well, when I went to register, the registrar asked me what did I come down there for. I told him "to register." He said "Register? For what?" I told him, "To vote." He said "Vote? For what?" And I told him I didn't know what I was coming to vote for. He hollered at me and scared me so, I told him I didn't know what I came to vote for. I was just going to vote. . . . He told me I was going to get in trouble, and he wasn't going to give me no commodities. That's what he said.[11]

These extralegal barriers were in many ways the highest. They were, at least, the most elusive, the least predictable, and ultimately the most demoralizing. Also, along with physical and economic intimidation, they were the hardest to stop.

In the beginning, the struggle for the black franchise began in the classic American way as a constitutional issue. For years after the end of Reconstruction, in fact, the states and the United States Supreme Court played a grim game of constitutional "hide and seek." The states would devise a scheme of disenfranchisement, the Court would strike it down, and the states would find another—ad infinitum. The states sometimes were careful not to disenfranchise poorer whites along with the blacks—hence their devising of grandfather clauses, which automatically registered all persons whose ancestors could vote at some specific date before the ratification of the Fifteenth Amendment. The manic quality of this constitutional chase is perhaps best illustrated by the white primary cases. The white primary was simply a party primary in which blacks were forbidden to vote; it arose at a time in which the candidate who won the Democratic primary in southern states was assured of victory in the general election against an enfeebled Republican party. It finally expired, but only after twenty-one years of litigation and five cases before the United States Supreme Court.[12]

---

[11]*Hearings before the U.S. Civil Rights Commission, I* (held in Jackson, Mississippi, February 16–20, 1965), pp. 49, 53, 95–96, 131–32.
[12]The end of the white primary is recorded in *Smith v. Allwright*, 321 U.S. 649 (1944).

Court action is not nearly so well adapted, however, to dealing with informal administrative evasions. Increasingly, the most useful remedies are legislative and administrative—a fighting of fire with fire. The civil rights acts of 1957, 1960, 1964, 1965, and 1970 (some are also called voting rights acts) all make this kind of attack on discrimination against black would-be voters:

— The *attorney general* has been authorized to seek injunctions against individuals who prevent blacks from voting in primaries or general elections. In instances in which he can convince a federal court that a "pattern or practice" of discrimination exists in a district, the court may order registration and send federal registrars and observers to the area.

— The *Justice Department* has acquired authority to supervise voting procedures in states and counties in which less than 50 percent of potential voters voted in the most recent presidential election. Any changes in voting procedures (such as in election districts) must be approved by the attorney general or by the United States District Court in the District of Columbia. The attorney general may also send registrars and observers there.

— *Local registrars* have come under greater regulation and control. They must keep voting and registration records for twenty-two months, and they must not apply voting requirements unequally. Nor are they permitted to seize on immaterial errors or omissions in the application process as a reason for refusing registration.

It would be both inaccurate and unjust to treat all the states of the South as if they were of a single piece. They vary in racial ratios, in socioeconomic characteristics, in political traditions, and in the legal and extralegal barriers they raised to black voting.[13] Some of those differences are reflected in the different registration percentages—both black and white—shown in Table 8.1. Also, one should keep in mind that black registration and voting percentages in the rest of the country were and still are below those of whites. Whatever the variations and the history, however, black registrations in the South now approach those of white southerners and of blacks elsewhere.

Unquestionably, the major instrument in the lengthy fight for the black franchise has been the 1965 Voting Rights Act. Its life was extended in

---

[13]See the articles on black voter registration in the South by Donald R. Matthews and James W. Prothro, *American Political Science Review* 57 (1963): 24–44 and 355–67. See also H. Douglas Price, *The Negro and Southern Politics* (New York: New York University Press, 1957).

TABLE 8.1   *Registration by Race in States Covered by the Voting Rights Act of 1965: 1960 and 1980*

State	1960		1980	
	White	Black	White	Black
Alabama	63.6%	13.7%	81.4%	55.8%
Georgia	56.8	29.3	63.0	48.6
Louisiana	76.9	31.1	74.8	60.7
Mississippi	63.9	5.2	98.9	62.3
North Carolina	92.1	39.1	70.1	51.3
South Carolina	57.1	13.7	58.5	53.7
Virginia	46.1	23.1	62.2	53.2

Source   Statistical Abstract of the United States: 1982–83 (103rd ed.). All data come from the Voter Education Project of Atlanta. No explanation for the improbably high percentage of registered white adults in Mississippi accompanies the data.

1970, 1975, and again in 1982. Certainly, a major portion of the changes recorded in Table 8.1 results from it.[14] Gone by now is the systematic exclusion of blacks from the electorate by administrative delay or discrimination. Significantly, the frontier of discrimination has shifted from preventing black voting to limiting the successes of black voting. In fact, in the debate over the extension of the act in 1981 and 1982, the major issue was the inclination of governmental bodies to dilute black voting power or limit the opportunities for blacks to choose black officeholders by such changes as shifts to at-large local elections, legislative redistricting to divide black voters among a number of districts, or annexation of white suburbs to offset black majorities in the cities or towns. Any such change must be approved ahead of time, and the Justice Department's basis for rejecting a change was broadened somewhat in 1982.

Congressional concern for other minorities began officially in 1975. In the extension of the Voting Rights Act in that year, the Congress broadened its protection to include linguistic minorities. All the powers of the federal courts, the attorney general, and the Justice Department to assure access to the ballot were extended to any political subdivision in which more than 5 percent of the adults belong to a linguistic minority and in which more than half of the adults failed to register or vote in the preceding presidential election. Those districts were also required to provide

---

[14]For a full review of progress and problems under the Voting Rights Acts of 1965 and 1970, see the report of the U.S. Civil Rights Commission, *The Voting Rights Act: Ten Years After* (1975). It is uncommonly well organized and well written, especially for a report of a governmental commission.

bilingual voting materials and officials. This affected all of Texas, Arizona, and Alaska; substantial parts of Colorado, New Mexico, California, and Florida; and isolated counties in other states. Obviously, the largest of the linguistic minorities are the Spanish-speaking Americans, but the act also extends to American Indians, Alaskan natives, and Asian-Americans.

THE CUMULATIVE EFFECT

The voting requirements of the fifty states whittled down the 1980 American electorate well below the 162,761,000 persons of voting age (Table 8.2). The true "eligible" total was probably more than 14 million below the figures usually used to compute voter turnout percentages. Most ineligible persons were resident aliens, institutionalized individuals, residents on federal lands, or those unable to meet even modest residence requirements. With that estimate of eligible voters, then, one can say that 76.7 percent of eligible voters were registered in 1976 and 76.3 percent in 1980. Moreover, in those two years, 77.1 and 76.7 percent of registered voters actually voted. The cumulative effect of the failures to register and the failures to vote then yield turnout percentages of 59.1 percent for 1976 and 58.5 percent for 1980. It is thus clear that there are two equally important points at which the nation loses voters: the failure to register and the failure to vote.

The slow decline in the percentage of eligible voters actually registering over the past decade or more is all the more striking when one considers the attempts of a number of states to make it easier to register. States are increasingly adopting mail registration—twenty states and the District of Columbia by 1982—and several of them send registration forms even

TABLE 8.2   *The American Electorate: 1980*

	1976	1980
1. Potential electorate	150,127,000	162,761,000
2. Eligible electorate	138,000,000	148,000,000
3. Registered electorate	105,837,000	112,945,000
4. Voting electorate (turnout)	81,556,000	86,589,000

Source   For categories 1, 3, and 4; *Statistical Abstract of the United States: 1981* (102nd ed.). Data in category 2 were estimated by the author.

to persons who do not request them. (The United States is still some distance from those European countries in which voters are registered automatically without the voters requesting it or aiding the process.) Beginning in 1976, two states, Minnesota and Wisconsin, began to register voters on election day right at the polling place. In 1982, in fact, Minnesota registered 239,000 new voters at the polls. In 1972, the United States Senate killed a bill for a national system of voter registration by postcard in a close vote won by a coalition of Republicans and southern Democrats. The proposal of President Jimmy Carter in his first term to permit national registration on election day also came to naught, even though a careful scholarly study estimated that such a move would increase voter turnout by 10 percent.[15] It is clear, nonetheless, that the newest frontier in the expansion of the American electorate is the registration process.

TURNOUT: POLITICAL VARIATIONS

The attention and interest of American voters flag as they face the four-year cycle of American politics, and many of them respond only to the elections of greatest prominence. Probably no electorate in the democratic world is more frequently called to the polls than the American electorate. Within a four-year cycle, it confronts national, state, and local elections for legislative and executive officeholders (and for the judiciary in a majority of the states), not to mention elections for school boards and assorted other local authorities. Most of these elections are preceded by primaries; and initiatives, referenda, and even an occasional recall election further complicate the calendar. Thus, whereas British voters may go to the polls only twice in a four- or five-year cycle—once for a parliamentary election and once for the election of local officials—civic obligation may call their beleaguered American counterparts to the polls for six to ten primaries and general elections.

Size of Constituency

Voter participation varies substantially with the size of the constituency. It is generally greatest in presidential elections and smallest in local elections. Although the voting percentage in presidential elections now runs between 50 and 60 percent (of all the adults of voting age), it is less for gubernatorial elections that come in the nonpresidential years. The congressional elections, too, draw considerably fewer voters in the years between the presidential elections (see Figure 8.1). A relatively high turn-

---

[15]Steven J. Rosenstone and Raymond Wolfinger, "The Effect of Registration Laws on Voter Turnout," *American Political Science Review* 72 (1978): 22–45.

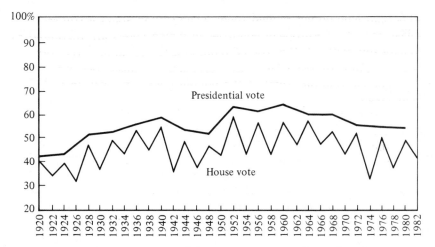

FIGURE 8.1 *Percentage of Adults Voting in Presidential and Congressional Elections: 1920–82*

Sources Statistical Abstract of the United States: 1981 (102nd ed.) and newspaper accounts of 1982 elections.

out of 40.3 percent for the 1982 Congressional elections was still 13 percent below the figure for 1980. In elections limited to local officials, turnout drops even further.

The reasons for this phenomenon are not hard to imagine. The more intense campaigns for the presidency and the governorships unquestionably spark greater voter interest and involvement. The personalities are famous or at least well known, and the issues seem more momentous. Furthermore, party fortunes are involved and party loyalties are inflamed— contrary to the case in many nonpartisan local and judicial elections. To put it very simply, one should hardly be surprised that a presidential election in which two national political figures and two national parties engage in a three-month mass-media campaign draws three or four times more voters to the polls than does a nonpartisan judicial campaign in which the candidates talk discreetly and a bit dully of the efficient administration of the courts. The wonder is that it is not eight or ten times the number.[16]

The Neglected Primary

Throughout the United States, voting in primary elections generally falls far short of that in general elections. It is not unusual for primary turnouts to be half or less of the turnouts in general elections—more precisely, only

[16]See, for example, Howard D. Hamilton, "The Municipal Voter: Voting and Non-Voting in City Elections," *American Political Science Review* 65 (1971): 1135–40.

20 or 25 percent of the adults of voting age (the so-called potential electorate). Even when looking at gubernatorial primaries in which both parties had contests, Jewell and Olson found an average turnout of 31.3 percent of all adults between the late 1940s and 1980. Turnouts were considerably below that average in the Northeast and Midwest and above it in the West.[17]

Among primaries for the same office, turnout tends to increase under two circumstances. It increases with competition in the primary—and the usually lively campaign that attends a contested primary. It also increases sharply within the dominant party of one-party states. In the southern one-party states, voter turnout in the Democratic primary historically exceeded even the voter turnout of the general election.

Issues and Referenda

Elections to decide issues—chiefly referenda and constitutional amendments—do not attract the same turnout as ordinary elections do. Even when these issues are on the ballot of a regular election, fewer voters choose to vote on them than for the candidates at the top of the ballot. Very possibly, the absence of a personal clash in these questions reduces their interest and immediacy. Perhaps, too, their frequent complexity confuses many would-be voters. Having made these general statements about issue elections, however, we should note that voter turnout for referenda fluctuates greatly. Emotionally charged and relatively clear issues—such as referenda on property taxes, equal rights for homosexuals, or the sale of alcoholic beverages—will attract far more voters than esoteric questions of bonding authority or reorganization of state administrative agencies.

The Political Factor

Although turnout does vary among different kinds of elections, other political influences also affect it. Interparty competition in a constituency— whether it is a state or a council district in a city—also increases voter turnout. Furthermore, it does so even when all differences in SES characteristics of the electorate and all historical voting trends in the district are held constant.[18] Understandably, voters seem to be stimulated politically by the excitement of closely contested elections and by the fact that

---

[17]Malcolm E. Jewell and David M. Olson, *American State Political Parties and Elections*, rev. ed. (Homewood, Ill.: Dorsey, 1982), pp. 128–29.

[18]C. Richard Hofstetter, "Inter-Party Competition and Electoral Turnout: The Case of Indiana," *American Journal of Political Science* 17 (1973): 351–66. Virginia Gray, however, finds a much weaker relationship between turnout and changes over time in competition in "A Note on Competition and Turnout in the American States," *Journal of Politics* 38 (1976): 153–58.

their votes may well affect the outcomes. Conversely, there is little appeal in trying to undo a foregone conclusion.

TURNOUT: THE PERSONAL EQUATION

Turnout can also be explained from the point of view of the individual citizen. He or she bears the burdens and the costs of voting—costs not in cash, but in energy, attention, time, and self-esteem. For the individual, the decision to register or not to register, to vote or not to vote, involves his or her personal political goals, values of civic responsibility (the "good citizen" factor), awareness of political alternatives, and feelings of political effectiveness. For the nonvoter, the many and varied costs of voting very likely outweigh any total of satisfactions or achievements that the act of voting brings. Indeed, for the nonvoter, the act of voting is often a threatening act. For adults whose political cues are mixed—those, for example, who were raised as Democrats but had Republicanism urged on them by persuasive spouses—the necessity of voting threatens a personal turmoil. Similarly, the uneducated and unsophisticated voter may very well find the imposing facade of the voting machine more than a little intimidating. (Conversely, for many habitual voters it is *nonvoting*, with its attendant feelings of guilt and irresponsibility, that is threatening.)

Even though the nonvoting trap has two steps—failure to register and failure to vote—most scholars do not make a distinction between them.[19] Logic, of course, makes some distinction. Illness or bad weather as explanations for nonvoting (see box) would seem to relate to the election day decision not to vote rather than to the prior failure to register. Beyond logic, however, we tend to look at a single set of explanations.

The explanations begin with an identification of the nonvoters. They tend to be young, poor, and uneducated. Perhaps the most careful study of nonvoting singles out low level of education as the major social correlate of nonvoting.[20] It used to be true that women voted less frequently than men, but with the changes of recent decades on the place and role of women, that difference has virtually disappeared. Because whites, on the average, have a higher income and educational level than racial minorities, they vote more frequently, but differences of race disappear if one

[19]For an exception, see Robert S. Erikson, "Why Do People Vote? Because They Are Registered," *American Politics Quarterly* 9 (1981): 259–76.

[20]Raymond E. Wolfinger and Steven J. Rosenstone, *Who Votes?* (New Haven: Yale University Press, 1980). See also Jae-On Kim, John R. Petrocik, and Stephen N. Enokson, "Voter Turnout Among American States: Systemic and Individual Components," *American Political Science Review* 69 (1975): 107–23, with a supplementary comment following it by Douglas D. Rose.

Nonvoting and the Public Service Ad

The advertisement below appeared as a full page in the *New York Times* the day before the 1977 local elections in that city (Monday, November 7, 1977). It carried no title or heading, and indeed, it hardly needed one. Barney's is a clothing store in New York City.

THE NEW YORK TIMES. MONDAY NOVEMBER 7, 1977

I only vote for President.
The polls are too far away.
I don't want to be called for jury duty.
I had to work late.
I was too tired when I got home.
It's raining.
I didn't know I had to register.
I have a headache.
I hate making decisions.
Whenever I vote, they lose.
I forgot.
Tuesday's my bowling night.
I hate waiting on lines.
The voting booth gives me claustrophobia.
I didn't know where to vote.
My company doesn't give me off.
I was out of town.
There's no one to watch the kids.
I broke my glasses.
The polls were closed when I got there.
I hate crowds.
The Knicks were playing.
I'm moving anyway.
My car broke down.
Everyone knows who's gonna win.
I had a doctor's appointment.
When was the election?
I already voted in the primaries.
I had to study for a test.
It was my vacation day.
My vote won't make the difference.

A collection of the classics from Barney's.
Polls will be open tomorrow from 6:00 AM to 9:00 PM

holds income and educational levels constant. After SES explanations, the next most powerful factor in accounting for nonvoting is youth. For a long time, voters under thirty-five have voted in below-average numbers, but they have increased substantially as a portion of the American electorate since the 1960s.

To describe the nonvoter is not necessarily to explain why he or she fails to vote. Chiefly, the explanation seems to hinge on individual attitudes, roles, and perceptions. Young, poor, and less educated people know less about government and politics. They tend to know less about the candidates and issues, and they are less likely to have strong loyalties to a political party. They feel less strongly than regular voters do about the duty to vote, and their feelings of political effectiveness (efficacy) are lower. They are more apt to have feelings of powerlessness, alienation, and anomie. Rarely sharing in the prosperity or esteem of the community, they believe that they are not influential in it and that those people who are influential care little about what they think or want.[21] In short, nonvoters in the United States are part of a larger group of political nonparticipants and apathetics—that is, the citizens who abstain from all forms of political activity, whether it be voting, discussing politics, working for a candidate, joining a political organization, or attending political speeches or events.[22]

The preceding factors are the sources of nonvoting within the cognitions and psyche of the citizen. In addition, there are important deterrents in the mechanisms of registration and voting—the so-called structural factors. The sheer difficulty of registering and voting imposes heavy costs of all kinds on many Americans. Where these burdens differ within the United States, they help to explain state-to-state variations in turnout. The fact that Minnesota leads states in voter turnout, for example, is certainly related to the fact that it is one of the two states that permit registration at the polling place on election day. Furthermore, the increase of these structural burdens over time explains at least some of the concomitant increase in nonvoting in recent decades. Richard Boyd, for instance, argues that the growth of the number of elections, both primaries and general elections, on the average citizen's calendar over recent decades accounts

[21]On political efficacy, see Angus Campbell et al., *The American Voter* (New York: Wiley, 1960), pp. 96–110; and on the related subject of political cynicism, see Robert E. Agger, Marshall N. Goldstein, and Stanley A. Pearl, "Political Cynicism: Measurement and Meaning," *Journal of Politics* 23 (1961): 477–506. A *New York Times*-CBS poll in 1976 found that feelings of powerlessness were much more strongly associated with nonvoting than was distrust of or disillusionment with government (*New York Times*, November 16, 1976). For a more impressionistic view, see Arthur T. Hadley, *The Empty Polling Both* (Englewood Cliffs, N.J.: Prentice-Hall, 1978).

[22]For general observations on political activity, see Lester W. Milbrath and M. L. Goel, *Political Participation*, 2nd ed. (Chicago: Rand McNally, 1977).

in part for lowered levels of voting.[23] All these structural burdens, collectively, go a long way in explaining the differences between American turnout percentages and those of European countries that have automatic registration, very few elections, and voting on Sundays or holidays.

When the thoughts of Americans concerned about nonvoting turn to reform, they usually turn to the structural factors. After all, they are easier to repair than the psyches and attitudes of individuals. Thus, we have recently seen campaigns to make voter registration easier by increasing the numbers of registrars, by using postal registration, or by permitting registration at the polls. Other reformers would make the act of voting easier by scheduling elections on Sundays or for twenty-four-hour or two-day periods. Others advocate voting by mail; their case got a boost in 1981 when the city of San Diego conducted a referendum by mail on the building of a downtown convention center. City officials proclaimed it was far less expensive than an ordinary special election, and 62 percent of the registered voters voted—a percentage about twice the size of the turnout at earlier special elections. (The bond issue for the convention center, incidentally, was roundly defeated.)

Finally, individuals otherwise not inclined to vote can be mobilized into voting by political organizations. When political party organizations flowered in the wards and precincts of America, one of their major activities was the registering of new voters and the turning out of all voters on election day. Organized labor has spent millions of dollars in the past forty or fifty years doing the same thing; recently, too, a few corporations have begun low-key programs of voter activation. Similarly, the Voter Education Project of the Southern Regional Council succeeded in registering large numbers of southern blacks in the 1960s, and now the Southwest Voter Registration and Education Project is working to bring Chicano citizens to the polls. Organized attempts to stimulate voting, in other words, have succeeded historically in overcoming the margins of citizen apathy, especially for voters new to the political system.

CONSEQUENCES FOR THE POLITICAL PARTIES

The American parties must operate, therefore, within an American electorate that constantly shifts in size and composition—but one that, regardless of its momentary size and composition, is never a sample either of the full American adult population or of that segment of it eligible to vote. Much of the strategy of the parties in pursuing their goals, especially the contesting of elections, must take account of those facts.

[23]"Decline of U.S. Voter Turnout: Structural Explanations," *American Politics Quarterly* 9 (1981): 133–60.

Long-range Consequences

The long-run consequences for the parties of changes in the electorate spring from basic changes in its legal definitions. Since electorates in democracies expand rather than contract, the changes invariably result from the addition of new groups to the eligible electorate. Most recently, the American parties have absorbed two major groups: previously disenfranchised American blacks and young citizens between eighteen and twenty-one.

All the SES characteristics of the black electorate have predisposed it to the national Democratic party. Three-fourths of the black electorate identifies with the Democratic party, and the Democratic black vote from 1964 through 1980 has hovered around the 90 percent mark. The major impact of the expansion of black voting opportunities after 1965 was, of course, felt more dramatically in some states than in others. In Texas, for example, the combination of the abolition of the poll tax and the passage of the 1965 Voting Rights Act—plus some vigorous registration drives among blacks and Chicanos—added well over 400,000 voters between 1964 and 1968. Not accidentally, perhaps, the Humphrey-Muskie ticket carried Texas in 1968.[24]

The impact of the young voters entering the electorate for the first time is more complex. They are somewhat more Democratic than the rest of the population, and they are also much more frequently ideological liberals, regardless of party preference. They are also more likely to be independents, to split their tickets, and, indeed, not to register or vote in the first place. In 1972, the class of newly eligible voters (aged eighteen to twenty-four) was larger than ever because of the lowering of the minimum voting age, beginning in that year. More than 25 million young voters entered the electorate at that time, and approximately half of them voted. That eighteen- to twenty-four-year-old group preferred George McGovern over Richard Nixon by a margin of 51 to 49 percent. Nixon won 66 percent of the votes of voters aged twenty-five and over. President Carter took only 51 percent of the under-twenty-five two-party vote in 1976, however, and 41 percent in 1980.[25]

Long-run consequences for the parties also stem from changes in the composition or distribution—rather than the size—of the American electorate. Population growth and migration offer an example. The parties of Alaska, Arizona, California, Colorado, Florida, Maryland, and Nevada all faced increases in state populations in excess of 25 percent between 1960

---

[24]On black voting and nonvoting, see Donald R. Matthews and James W. Prothro, *Negroes and the New Southern Politics* (New York: Harcourt, Brace, 1966).

[25]Gerald M. Pomper, *Voter's Choice* (New York: Dodd, Mead, 1975), p. 93. The 1976 and 1980 data are from the Center for Political Studies of the University of Michigan.

and 1970. Similarly, the aging of the American population creates a larger group of over-sixty-five voters in each successive presidential election. Again, the important point is that these shifts and growths are differential; the groups (and their goals) added in each case are not a sample of the entire American electorate.

One more striking datum should suffice to conclude these remarks about the consequences of voter participation and nonparticipation for the parties. There were still some 50 million adults of voting age in 1980 who were not registered to vote—whether for reasons of disqualification or their own unconcern. Those adults are widely considered more likely recruits for the Democratic party than for the Republicans. Therefore, legislation that would expand the electorate in any way—by permitting registration at the polls, for instance, or by making illegal aliens eligible for citizenship and thus for the suffrage—has partisan implications. Legislation to begin national election day registration indeed became a partisan issue in the Congress in 1977, with liberal Democrats supporting it and conservative Democrats and Republicans in opposition.

The most basic of all the consequences of voting and nonvoting concerns the distribution of political influence in the American political system. Citizens who fail to register or vote deny themselves a potent voice in American politics, and the implications of that loss are all the more serious when the nonvoters differ markedly from the voters. In the words of one observer:

> If those at the lower end of the status ladder do not protect their interests at the polls, there is little incentive for their elected officials to protect their interests in Washington. And the common use of campaign surveys must give candidates an all-too-accurate appraisal of the shifting preferences of the electoral universe, even if the changing composition of that universe has escaped conscious detection. Unless current trends are reversed, the disadvantaged members of American society are likely to find themselves playing an increasingly marginal role in the American political system.[26]

Yet that observation must be tempered by the finding of Wolfinger and Rosenstone that nonvoters, despite their social backgrounds, tend not to have very different views on the issues from those of voters.[27] What their political views and goals might be if they were mobilized into the American electorate is the fundamental question, however, and on that point scholars are of necessity reduced totally to speculation.

---

[26]Thomas E. Cavanagh, "Changes in American Voter Turnout, 1964–1976," *Political Science Quarterly* 96 (1981): 63.

[27]*Who Votes?*, Chap. 6.

Short-range Consequences

In addition to the long-range consequences of changes in the basic structure of the eligible electorate, the political parties must react to the short-range consequences of changes in turnout from election to election. Since increases or decreases in turnout are unlikely to benefit all parties and candidates equally—because nonvoters as a group have different political characteristics from voters (Table 8.3)—these matters, too, have potent political consequences. The increasing or decreasing of voter turnout and the exploiting of variations in turnout between various elections frequently become focal points in party strategy.

The conventional wisdom of American politics has it that big turnouts favor the Democrats. There is little room to quarrel with the underlying truth of that maxim. The greatest percentage of nonvoters in the United States comes from the groups ordinarily disposed to the Democratic party. It is for this reason that effective registration or get-out-the-vote campaigns are thought to help the Democrats more often than not. The maxim explains the money and manpower that organized labor spends in registration campaigns. It explains the ancillary maxim that rainy weather is Republican weather. It also suggests why, in some states, Republicans prefer an electoral calendar in which the gubernatorial elections are held in the nonpresidential years and therefore in a smaller electorate that is a bit more favorable to Republican candidates.

Despite the general truth of the maxim linking big turnouts with the Democrats, the relationship is more subtle and complicated. Dwight D. Eisenhower, for example, won the presidency as a Republican in two high-

TABLE 8.3   *Comparison of Voters and Nonvoters in the 1980 Presidential Election*

	Presidential voters	Presidential nonvoters
Percentage male	44.9%	38.2%
Percentage white	88.3%	83.8%
Median age	44	33
Median education	High school grad	High school grad
Percentage "very much interested" in campaign	44.8%	13.2%
Percentage identifying as "independent"	32.0%	43.9%

Source   Center for Political Studies, University of Michigan; data made available through the Inter-University Consortium for Political and Social Research.

TABLE 8.4   *Presidential Candidate Preferences of Nonvoters: 1952–80*

	1952	1956	1960	1964	1968	1972[a]	1976[a]	1980[a]
Would have voted Democratic	52%	28%	51%	80%	45%	35%	57%	51%
Would have voted Republican	48	72	49	20	41	65	43	34
	100%	100%	100%	100%	86%[b]	100%	100%	85%[c]

[a] The 1972, 1976, 1980 data are the preferences of respondents who said before the election that they did not intend to vote in the election.

[b] Fourteen percent would have voted for George Wallace's American Independent Party.

[c] Nine percent would have voted for John Anderson, and 6 percent would have voted for a minor party.

Source   Angus Campbell et al., *The American Voter* (New York: Wiley, 1960), p. 111. (Campbell's table has been updated by survey data from the University of Michigan's Center for Political Studies.)

turnout elections, and the nonvoters in 1956 also were disposed to the Republican candidate (Table 8.4). The Eisenhower success and that of Richard Nixon in 1972 seem to force a clarification. High turnout works to a Democratic advantage only in elections in which party loyalty is a chief or overriding factor. A heavy turnout may be stimulated by a candidate (Eisenhower) or by issues (as in 1972) that work to Republican advantage. Especially since the nonvoter is less partisan, he or she may be more responsive to the momentary, dramatic appeal of issue or candidate. Therefore, the maxim works best in elections or party systems in which SES factors underlie the division of party loyalties and in which party loyalties remain the key factor in the decisions of voters.[28]

Party strategists cannot fail to consider the likely voting electorate as they prepare their campaigns. They nourish the often fragile hope that turnouts can be affected selectively and differentially, and they attempt, therefore, to mold the size and makeup of the participating electorate itself in the campaign. When they must contest a primary election, they may hope by discreet and selective campaigning to minimize the turnout—for (generally) the smaller the turnout, the larger will be the proportion of it accounted for by the party's own loyal electorate. In general elections, the strategists may try to concentrate campaigns in areas of known party strength, thus maximizing that turnout. Individuals planning a congres-

[28]For a similar analysis, see James DeNardo, "Turnout and the Vote," *American Political Science Review* 74 (1980): 406–20.

sional career always confront the fact that they will seek reelection by different electorates in alternate elections—the large turnout of the presidential election followed by the smaller turnout of the midterm elections two years later.

THE BROADER ISSUES

The democratic ethos assumes the desirability of full popular participation in the affairs of democratic self-government. The case for democracy itself rests on the wisdom of the widest possible sharing of political power and political decision making within the society. It is precisely this ethos that is offended by the relatively low voting percentages of American adults. The affront to the democratic ethos seems all the greater in view of the fact that voting percentages are higher in countries that Americans would like to think have less stable and responsive democracies.

Widespread nonvoting also casts some doubt on the effectiveness with which the political parties—the political organizations primarily concerned with contesting elections—manage to involve the total eligible electorate. Presumably, the parties, heralded so often as the instruments of democratic politics, should maximize political participation in the American society. The political parties themselves are, after all, the political organizations that developed to mobilize the new democratic masses. All of their capabilities are directed to recruiting large political aggregates, and much of the case for their superiority as political organizations rests on that ability.

Clearly, the record of the parties in mobilizing and involving the American electorate is mixed. We can cite many examples of effective competition for the support of new groups entering the electorate. In various areas, the two parties of the South, despite the strength of old racial mores, have recently made room for black voices in party councils and have made more moderate appeals to the new black electorate. Even so, the hands of the parties are not completely clean. They often appear not to relish the challenges of new voters, especially those of low status. The experience of political power has made them (especially their parties in government) sympathetic to the comfortable status quo of two-party competition. They do not welcome the uncertainties that a radical alteration in the electorate would bring. The party in government, which will have to make the changes in the formal definition of the electorate, has won office with the support of the electorate as it now exists, and it is understandably not anxious to alter it greatly. Not unexpectedly, then, in the history of women's suffrage and the end of black disenfranchisement, the parties were not in the vanguard of either movement to expand the electorate.

Do the parties also carry a share of the responsibility for the voluntary disenfranchisement of the American nonvoter? They have been blamed for suppressing participation by failing to interest large numbers of Americans in the dialectics and personalities of politics. E. E. Schattschneider, for example, argued that the rituals and choices of American politics are virtually meaningless to 35 million nonvoters.[29] The trouble with Schattschneider's thesis is its assumption that nonvoters are rational, informed, and careful surveyors of the political scene who decide that it is irrelevant to their goals. All that we know about the American nonvoters indicates quite the contrary. Our data on nonvoters suggest only what they are, however, not how they happened to become what they are. Thus, it is possible to argue that the political parties are one of a number of important political and social institutions that fail to educate and involve various sectors of the American society.

Therefore, the American parties work within a somewhat homogeneous active electorate. That electorate reduces the totality of political conflict and the range of political interests to which the parties must respond. The parties find it easier to be moderate and pragmatic because the electorate to which they respond is largely settled in and committed to the present basic social arrangements. Compromise and tactical movement come more easily when the effective electorate is homogeneous and agrees on fundamentals. In brief, although it has been fashionable to say that the moderate, pragmatic, nondoctrinaire American parties are the result of an electorate that agrees on the fundamental questions, it is probably also true that the pragmatic, majoritarian parties in a two-party system do not easily draw into their ambit the low-status, alienated, dissident individuals who are not a part of that moderate consensus.

[29]E. E. Schattschneider, *The Semi-Sovereign People* (New York: Holt, Rinehart & Winston, 1960), Chap. 6.

IV

The Political Parties in the Electoral Process

The contesting of elections unites, however briefly, the disparate and fragmented American parties. The choice of a presidential candidate and the following campaign bind the state and local parties into a fleeting coalition with the national party. A statewide election similarly focuses the activities and energies of local organizations and leaders within the state. Furthermore, any election joins the three party sectors into a grand alliance of the party elites and the party clienteles. The contest for public office is the one time in the life of the party when all its sectors are united in the pursuit of their varied goals.

The pursuit of victory in elections unites the party for a number of reasons. The election is the event that elevates the business of politics to a visibility that stimulates even the less concerned members of the electorate. The candidates personify and simplify the difficult choices of American politics. Furthermore, the recruitment of resources for the party organization depends on the party's establishment of the likelihood, or at least the possibility, of electoral victory. In the long run, the incentives that lure resources to the party flow only to those parties that win. Only from electoral victory come the patronage jobs, the triumph of an interest or an ideology, and even the social and psychological rewards of politics.

Since the American parties are parties that must win elections, they must mobilize majorities in the electorate. The conventional references to the American parties as electoral parties are, however, a little too glib and hackneyed. For one thing, these references imply that the parties carry out their electoral activities with ease. To the contrary, the party organizations find it difficult to control the selection of candidates, to take stands on issues, to fix campaign strategies, even to raise money. Those aspects of election politics are controlled, in the name of the whole party, by its candidates—its party in government and the candidates hoping to join it.

In many parts of the country, in fact, the party candidates have organized their own campaigns, recruited their own workers, hired their own campaign advice, and raised their own campaign funds. If it is true that the party in government controls the central, most visible activities of the party (at the expense of a frustrated party organization), can the party organizations reasonably achieve the goals set by their activists?

At the same time that the party stages an internal competition over the control of its electoral strategies, it also faces the competition of other political organizations. They also increasingly seek their political goals in the electoral processes. Over the past twenty years, the nonparty political organizations—the interest groups, party factions, personal followings, campaign committees, ideological organizations—have taken aggressive, overt roles in the nomination and election of candidates. It is not uncommon now to read newspaper accounts of the electoral activities of trade unions, ad hoc campaign organizations such as the Ford for President Committee, public relations firms, reform groups such as the National Women's Political Caucus, and the more than 3,300 political action committees.

The continuing contest for influence in American electoral politics raises questions about the very role and viability of the parties. The outcomes of the competition for the election role within the parties and between parties and other political organizations determine, in great measure, what the parties are and what they do in the political system. Throughout the coming chapters there also runs a related theme: the impact of political institutions on the nature of the parties. Nowhere are the effects of political institutions on the parties clearer than in the electoral processes. The direct primary, for example, touches every attempt the parties make to control the nomination of candidates. In fact, it is the primary that so often turns the control of nominations from the party organization to the candidates themselves or to other political organizations.

In the chapters in this section, we will observe two sets of distinctions for the sake of orderly exposition. The first is the common distinction between the nominating of the parties' candidates and the contesting of the general election.[1] Even though the distinction between the two parts of the electing business can be arbitrary and misleading, it is analytically useful. The use of this distinction does not deny that we are describing a single process. Elections may be lost or won in the earliest prenomination steps to encourage candidates, and the nature of the nomination often depends on the ultimate changes for electoral victory.

---

[1]Within the past several years, Louisiana has broken the tradition of separate nomination and election steps. For races other than those for the presidency and Congress, it now holds a single election. All candidates of all parties run in it and are designated by party on the ballot. If one candidate wins a majority of the vote, he or she is elected to the office. If not, the top two candidates, regardless of their party, face each other in a runoff election.

TABLE IV.1   *Comparison of Steps in the Nomination-Election Processes in the United States*

	Prenomination	Nomination	Election
Presidential elections	Selection of delegates to national convention by state party action or presidential primary	By national party convention	By plurality vote within the states, and by majority of votes in electoral college
Other American elections	Access to primary ballot by petition, request, or party action	By direct primary or (in a few cases) by convention	By plurality vote at a general election

The two chapters dealing with the nomination and election of the American president reflect the second distinction. The contest for the presidency is a special case and must be so treated. Although the direct primary dominates the formal nominating machinery for almost all American public offices, the convention it replaced still functions in the nomination of presidential candidates. The special election machinery of the electoral college also sets the presidential election apart from the simpler plurality elections that prevail elsewhere in American politics (Table IV.1).

Thus, Chapters 9 and 10 describe the modal patterns of American electoral machinery and politics. Chapters 11 and 12 deal with the fascinating and peculiar processes by which presidents are chosen. The final chapter of this part discusses the recruitment of the most important resource for the contesting of elections—money.

9

THE NAMING OF THE
PARTY CANDIDATES

Few Americans realize how indigenously American the direct primary is. Having devised it and adopted it almost universally for the nomination of candidates, they seem unaware that the rest of the world has not followed their lead. The point is important, not because American political naiveté is unusually great, but because it underscores the special, even unique, aspects of American politics and political parties. No other single factor goes so far to explain the differences between the American parties and those of the other Western nations as the direct primary. It has forced on the parties a different set of strategies in making nominations, in contesting elections, and in attempting eventually to maintain responsibility over their successful candidates in office.

In the irresistible advance of the direct primary in the twentieth century, no state has been untouched. The great majority of states employ it in all nominations, and the rest use it in most. For the present, it suffices to say that by the direct primary (or, more simply, the primary), we mean a special election in which the party electorate chooses candidates to run for public office under the party label. At a subsequent general election, the total electorate then makes the final choice from among the nominees of the parties.

Even though the nomination does not formally settle the electoral outcome, its importance is great. The major screening of candidates takes place at the nomination; the choice is reduced to two in most constituencies. Especially in areas of one-party domination, the real choice is made at the primary. Moreover, the nominees of the party bring their images and visibility, their priorities and positions on issues, to the party. In the eyes of many voters, they *are* the party. Their quality and ability also determine, to a considerable extent, the party's chances for victory in the general election.

ADVENT OF THE DIRECT PRIMARY

At the beginning of the twentieth century, the direct primary was in use only in scattered communities in scattered states. For the first 110 years of the Republic, first the party caucus and then the party convention dominated the nomination of candidates for public office. Each gave way successively under the criticism that it permitted, if not encouraged, the making of nominations by self-chosen and irresponsible party elites. Finally, the primary triumphed on the belief that in a democracy, the greatest possible number of party members ought to take part in the nomination of the party's candidates. Above all, the history of the evolution of nominating methods in the United States is a story of the progressive victory of the values and symbols of democracy.

Formal systems of nomination developed in the United States along with and as a part of the development of the party system. In fact, parties as parties (rather than as legislative associations) developed and evolved largely as nominators of candidates for public office. At the end of the eighteenth century, local caucuses met to select candidates; and frequently, caucuses of like-minded partisans in legislatures met to nominate candidates for governorships and other statewide offices. Similar congressional caucuses met to nominate presidential and vice-presidential candidates. Whatever their form, the caucuses were self-selected. There was no machinery, no procedure for ensuring even the participation of all the major figures in the party. The Jacksonians attacked the caucus relentlessly as an aristocratic device that thwarted popular wishes. "King Caucus" was indeed an ample target.

In 1832, the Democrats met in a national convention for the first time and, appropriately, nominated Andrew Jackson for the presidency. From then on, the convention system quickly triumphed along with Jacksonian popular democracy, whose values it shared. It dominated the making of nominations for the rest of the nineteenth century. Broadly representative at its best, the nominating convention was composed of delegates chosen by the local party organizations. Even though they were representative in form, however, the large and chaotic conventions were scarcely that in reality. Both in the picking of delegates and in the management of the conventions, the fine, guiding hands of party leaders were too obvious and oppressive. Party insurgents, unhappy with bossism at the conventions and with the alliance of the bosses and "the interests," belabored the convention system with considerable fervor and cunning. The Progressives led the movement, and their journalistic allies, the muckrakers, furnished the often shocking, often piquant, corroborative details.[1]

---

[1]For the story of the convention system and the early years of the direct primary, see Charles E. Merriam and Louise Overacker, *Primary Elections* (Chicago: University of Chicago Press, 1928).

The cure offered by the Progressives—the direct primary—comported easily with their democratic norms. It was an article of faith among them that to cure the ills of democracy, one needed only to prescribe larger doses of democracy. Appropriately, it was one of progressivism's high priests, Robert M. La Follette, who authored the country's first statewide primary law in Wisconsin in 1902 (see box). In the next fifteen years, all but four states had adopted the primary, at least in part. In 1955, Connecticut capitulated and became the last state to adopt it.

Although the primary was designed to reform the nominating processes by "democratization," many of its supporters saw in it an instrument for crippling the political party itself. For them, the primary was an attempt to cut back the power of the parties by striking at their chief activity as a party organization: the nomination of candidates. The party organization had done the nominating under the caucus and convention systems, but primaries took from it the control of who would run under the party name and symbols. Regardless of the motives of the enactors of the

---

La Follette and the Primary

No one has captured the rhetoric and fervor of the movement for the direct primary as well as its leader, Robert M. La Follette, governor and then United States senator from Wisconsin. Writing in his autobiography, in the chapter "Struggle with the Bosses," La Follette reports a speech of his in February 1897 at the University of Chicago. Here are some excerpts from the conclusion:

> Put aside the caucus and convention. They have been and will continue to be prostituted to the service of corrupt organizations. They answer no purpose further than to give respectable form to political robbery. Abolish the caucus and the convention. Go back to the first principles of democracy; go back to the people. Substitute for both the caucus and the convention a primary election . . . where the citizen may cast his vote directly to nominate the candidate of the party with which he affiliates. . . . The nomination of the party will not be the result of "compromise" or impulse, or evil design—the "barrel" and the machine—but the candidates of the majority, honestly and fairly nominated.

> Robert M. La Follette,
> *La Follette's Autobiography*
> (Madison: R. M. La Follette,
> 1913), pp. 197–98.

---

primary laws, there is little doubt that the laws badly hurt the power of party organizations.

The quick success of the direct primary happened during the years of the greatest one-partyism in American history. In the early years of the twentieth century, sectionalism was pervasive, and one party or the other dominated the politics of many states. One-partyism made the nomination of the dominant party crucial. Although the failings of the conventions might be tolerated when a real choice remained in the general election, they could not be borne when the nomination of one party was equivalent to election. The convention could choose the weariest party hack without fear of challenge from the other party. Thus, the Progressives, who fought economic monopoly with antitrust legislation, fought political monopoly with the direct primary.

VARIETIES OF THE DIRECT PRIMARY

The primaries of the fifty states are usually divided into three categories, differing chiefly in the way they define the party electorate that can vote in them and in the way they ascertain party preferences.

The Closed Primary

The closed primary—found in thirty-eight states and the District of Columbia—requires voters to declare their party affiliation so that they may vote only in the primary of their own party. In most of these states, voters specify their party affiliation when they register. Then, at the primary election, they are given only the primary ballot of their party so that they may choose among their fellow partisans who seek nomination. They may always change their party affiliation on the registration rolls, but most states require that this be done sometime ahead of the date of the primary. Iowa and Wyoming permit a change of party registration at the polls.

In the other closed primary states, voters simply declare their party "membership"—or, more accurately, their party attachments or preferences—when they go to the polling place. They are then given the primary ballot of their party. In some states, their declarations can be challenged by one of the party observers at the polls; they may then be required to take an oath of party loyalty. Some states require voters to affirm that they have voted for the candidates of the party in the past; some demand that they declare themselves sympathetic at the moment to the candidates and principles of the party; and others ask nothing at all. Needless to say, the secrecy of the ballot makes it impossible to challenge the worth of such pledges.

The Open and Blanket Primaries

In the nine states of the open primary—Hawaii, Idaho, Michigan, Minnesota, Montana, North Dakota, Utah, Vermont, and Wisconsin—the voter votes in the primary without disclosing any party affiliation or preference. On entering the polling booth, voters are given either ballots for every party (one of which is selected in the privacy of the booth) or a consolidated ballot on which the part with the party of the voter's choice is selected. A voter may not, however, participate in the primary of more than one party.

The distinctions between open and closed primaries are easy to exaggerate. Too simple a distinction ignores the range of nuances and varieties within the closed primary states, which, after all, do account for 82 percent of the states. In Illinois, for example, voters do not register as members of a party; at the polling place, they simply state their party preference and are given the ballot of that party—no questions asked. Because Illinois voters must disclose a party preference before entering the voting booth, their primary is generally considered closed. One would be hard put, however, to argue that it is much different from an open primary in operation.[2]

The blanket primary—found in Alaska, Louisiana, and Washington—goes one step in freedom beyond the open primary. Not only do the voters not need to disclose any party affiliation, but they are free to vote in the primary of more than one party: that is, they may choose among Democrats seeking nomination for one office and among Republicans seeking another nomination (Figure 9.1). In more puritanical days, it was called the "free love" primary.

✗   Among these forms of primaries, the party organizations clearly prefer the closed primary with party registration prior to the primary. It pays greater respect to the right of the party itself to make nominations by limiting the party's primary electorate to its own party electorate. Prior registration of party affiliation also gives the parties an added bonus: published lists of their partisans. It is not quite that simple, however. Party registration is, at best, an approximation of party loyalties at the moment. People are slow to change their party affiliations, and the party totals lag behind the pattern of voting. Furthermore, the registration figures of the majority or leading party tend to be swollen by conformists and by a few

[2]Some authorities distinguish between open and closed primaries on the question of whether or not there is party registration (rather than freedom to choose one's party in the secrecy of the polling booth). This criterion inevitably yields a larger number of open primaries.

"political strategists," who register in a party solely to vote in its crucial primary.

The parties would gladly accept these uncertainties, however, in preference to what they regard as the more serious perils of the open primary. (The blanket primary enjoys even less favor.) Party leaders levy two charges against the open primary: crossing over and raiding. The terms are sometimes used synonymously, but a distinction can be made between them. Crossing over is the participation by voters in the primary of the party they do not generally support or feel a loyalty to. It is a drifting across party lines in search of the excitement of a primary battle. Raiding is an organized attempt on the part of one party to send its partisans into the primary of the other party in order to foist the least attractive candidates on it.

That crossing over happens in open primary states is beyond doubt. Consider the case of primary contests in Wisconsin, cradle of the open primary and home of an especially rambunctious political tradition. It is also the state in which the open primary has been most thoroughly studied. Survey data on two gubernatorial primaries in the 1960s put the crossover vote at between 6 and 8 percent of the primary voters. It was much higher, however, in the state's presidential primaries of the same period—an average of about 20 percent of the voters in the presidential primaries from 1968 through 1980. Crossing over was doubtless kept to a minimum in the gubernatorial primaries by the need to stay in one's party's primary to decide other party contests. Since the presidential primaries involve only one contest, no such constraint was present in those cases. Lost in the concern about crossing over is the much more frequent case of independents— voters with no party loyalty—who vote in the primary of one party or the other and help determine the party's nominees. In a real sense, they are no more a part of the party's electorate than are the loyalists of another party.[3]

As for organized raiding, there is little evidence to suggest that it is more than a worrisome myth. Every party fears that voters drifting to the other party's primary will develop bad voting habits. Furthermore, the party must also be watchful lest the migration from its primary permit its contests to be settled by unrepresentative minorities. In other words, a party has every reason to encourage its loyalists to remain and vote in its primary. One recent study explored the possibility that individual voters

[3]Austin Ranney, "Turnout and Representation in Presidential Primary Elections," *American Political Science Review* 66 (1972): 21–37; David Adamany, "Cross-over Voting and the Democratic Party's Reform Rules," *American Political Science Review* 70 (1976): 536–41; and Ronald D. Hedlund, Meredith W. Watts, and David M. Hedge, "Voting in an Open Primary," *American Politics Quarterly* 10 (1982): 197–218.

FEDERAL

U. S. SENATOR Vote for One	SLADE GORTON	Rep. 2 ➡
	WARREN G. MAGNUSON	Dem. 3 ➡
	JAMES SHERWOOD STOKES	Dem. 4 ➡
	JAMES LEVITT	Soc. Wkrs. 5 ➡
	WILLIAM "Mac" McCALLUM	Rep. 6 ➡
	BARRY W. McCLAIN	Rep. 7 ➡
	JOHN "Hugo Frye" PATRIC	Dem. 8 ➡
	LLOYD E. COONEY	Rep. 9 ➡
	RICHARD K. KENNEY	Libertarian 10 ➡

REPRESENTATIVE IN CONGRESS District 5 Vote for One	JOHN SONNELAND	Rep. 15 ➡
	THOMAS S. FOLEY	Dem. 16 ➡
	GEORGE W. BIBLE	Rep. 17 ➡
	MEL TONASKET	Rep. 18 ➡
	I. E. "Mac" McCRAY	Rep. 19 ➡

STATE

GOVERNOR Vote For One	DUANE BERENTSON	Rep. 21 ➡
	PATRICK SEAN McGOWAN	Rep. 22 ➡
	BRUCE CHAPMAN	Rep. 23 ➡
	DIXY LEE RAY	Dem. 24 ➡
	MARY NELL BOCKMAN	Soc. Wkrs. 25 ➡
	JOHN SPELLMAN	Rep. 26 ➡
	CAROLINE (Hope) DIAMOND	Dem. 27 ➡
	LOUISE A. SALUTEEN	Rep. 28 ➡
	JIM McDERMOTT	Dem. 29 ➡
	DOUGLAS P. BESTLE	Dem. 30 ➡
	ROBERT L. BALDWIN, Sr.	Dem. 31 ➡
	JEF JAISUN	Dem. 32 ➡
	LLOYD G. ISLEY	Dem. 33 ➡
	RABBINE MATTHEW SUTICH	Rep. 34 ➡

STATE (Continued)

LIEUTENANT GOVERNOR Vote for One	JOHN A. CHERBERG	Dem. 40 ■
	JOHN WILLIAM LYNCH	Rep. 41 ■
	RICHARD E. VAN HORN	Rep. 42 ■
	WILLIAM M. TREADWELL	Rep. 43 ■
	CHET G. HAWLEY	Dem. 44 ■

SECRETARY OF STATE Vote for One	EVELYN F. ASHLEY	Dem. 46 ■
	KEN CAPLINGER	Dem. 47 ■
	RON DOTZAUER	Dem. 48 ■
	PATRICIA GENTRY BONNIFIELD	Dem. 49 ■
	RALPH MUNRO	Rep. 50 ■
	KENT PULLEN	Rep. 51 ■
	JOHN P. NAGLE	Dem. 52 ■
	JOHN O'HAGAN McKEE	Dem. 53 ■
	VICTOR A. MEYERS, JR.	Dem. 54 ■

COUNTY

COUNTY COMMISSIONER District 1 Vote for One	WALTER C. COYLE	Rep. 116 ➡
	EUGENE "Gene" KELLY	Dem. 117 ➡
	WILLIAM R. SMITH	Rep. 118 ➡
	H. WILSON KERNS	Rep. 119 ➡

COUNTY

COUNTY COMMISSIONER District 2 Vote for One	HARMON F. JOHNSON	Rep. 120 ➡
	BILL R. SNELL	Dem. 121 ➡
	DON THOMAS	Rep. 122 ➡

COUNTY COMMISSIONERS APPEAR ON THE
OFFICIAL BALLOT ONLY IN THEIR OWN
DISTRICT IN THE PRIMARY ELECTION

STATE

SUPT. OF PUBLIC INSTRUCTION Vote for One	FRANK "Buster" BROUILLET	Non-Part. 135 ■
	NEIL TALMAN BURDETTE HELGELAND	N.P. 136 ■
	JOSEPH T. RHYMES	Non-Partisan 137 ■
	RICHARD A. FULLER	Non-Partisan 138 ■

Judges of The Supreme Cou

Position 1 6 Year Term Vote for One	ROBERT F. UTTER	Non-Partisan 140 ■
	DAN CLEM	Non-Partisan 141 ■
Position 2 6 Year Term Vote for One	JAMES M. DOLLIVER	Non-Partisan 143 ■
Position 3 6 Year Term Vote for One	FRED H. DORE	Non-Partisan 145 ■
	EDWARD P. REED	Non-Partisan 146 ■

COURT OF APPEALS

JUDGE Division 3 District 2 Vote for One	DALE M. GREEN	148 ■

Judges of the Superior Cour

Position 1 4 yr term, Vote 1	JAMES B. MITCHELL	151 ■
Position 2 4 yr term, Vote 1	YANCEY RESER	152 ■

FIGURE 9.1   *The Washington "Blanket" Primary Ballot: 1980*

STATE (Continued)

ASURER One	ROBERT S. O'BRIEN	Dem. 59 ➡
	HARRIS HUNTER	Dem. 60 ➡
	MARILYN B. WARD	Rep. 61 ➡

DITOR One	ART WUERTH	Rep. 63 ➡
	ROBERT B. KEENE, JR.	Rep. 64 ➡
	ROBERT V. "Bob" GRAHAM	Dem. 65 ➡

EY AL	JOHN ROSELLINI	Dem. 67 ➡
	JOHN MILLER	Ind. Cand. 68 ➡
	BILL NEUKOM	Dem. 69 ➡
	KENNETH O. EIKENBERRY	Rep. 70 ➡

One	FRED KAUL	Rep. 71 ➡
	JIM McCABE	Dem. 72 ➡
	MICHAEL C. "Mike" REDMAN	Dem. 73 ➡

STATE (Continued)

COMMISSIONER OF PUBLIC LANDS Vote for One	BERT COLE	Dem. 78 ➡
	LARRY MALLOY	Rep. 79 ➡
	WILLIAM F. BAILEY	Rep. 80 ➡
	WAYNE T. MADSEN	Dem. 81 ➡
	CLARICE L. R. PRIVETTE	Rep. 82 ➡
	RAY KOON	Dem. 83 ➡
	RICHARD L. ROBERTSON	Rep. 84 ➡
	LARRY S. BENNETT	Rep. 85 ➡
	PATRICK PARRISH	Dem. 86 ➡
	J. E. CONIFF	Dem. 87 ➡
	BRIAN J. BOYLE	Rep. 88 ➡

INSURANCE COMMISSIONER Vote for One	RICHARD G. (Dick) MARQUARDT	Rep. 90 ➡
	JOHN T. TAYLOR	Dem. 91 ➡
	LEO J. KRANTZ	Dem. 92 ➡
	JAMES E. HOFFMAN	Dem. 93 ➡
	JOE DAVIS	Dem. 94 ➡

LEGISLATIVE

STATE SENATOR District 16 Vote for One	JEANNETTE HAYNER	Rep. 97 ➡

STATE REPRESENTATIVE Position 1 Vote for One	GENE STRUTHERS	Rep. 100 ➡
STATE REPRESENTATIVE Position 2 Vote for One	RICHARD "Doc" HASTINGS	Rep. 102 ➡
	DOROTHY (Dot) MILLER	Dem. 103 ➡

CITY OF WALLA WALLA

cial Election - Proposition No. 1

Submitted by the City of Walla Walla

AGE TREATMENT PLANT IMPROVEMENT
BONDS, $3,500,000.00

City of Walla Walla, Washington, issue its
obligation bonds to make necessary capital
r improvements to the Sewage Treatment
the City by issuing its general obligation
the principal sum of $3,500,000.00, said
bear interest at the rate of not to exceed
annum, to mature in from two to twenty
m date of issue, and to be paid both princi-
interest out of the annual tax levies to be
on all the taxable property within the City
imitation as to rate or amount, all as pro-
Ordinance No. A-3123 of the City.

**Bonds,
YES - 155 ♦**

**Bonds,
NO - 158 ♦**

**LOCAL ELECTIONS WILL APPEAR
ONLY IN THE AREA ELIGIBLE
TO VOTE ON THEM**

COLUMBIA MOSQUITO CONTROL DISTRICT

Special Election - Proposition No. 1

Submitted by Columbia Mosquito Control District

EXCESS LEVY FOR GENERAL FUND

Shall the Columbia Mosquito Control District of Walla
Walla County levy a general tax upon taxable property
of the Mosquito Control District in the sum of
$55,000.00 an estimated $.23 per one-thousand dollars of assessed valuation?

**Levy,
YES - 174 ♦**

**Levy,
NO - 177 ♦**

SAMPLE PRIMARY ELECTION
BALLOT

County of Walla Walla

State of Washington

September 16, 1980

**TO VOTE, FOLLOW THE EASY
STEPS OUTLINED HERE.**

1. Using both hands, insert your ballot card in the slot. Insert your ballot
card as far as it will go, positioning the two holes over the red pins on the
voting device. Turn to the first ballot page.

2. Using the voting stylus, record your vote by punching the hole indicated
by the arrow for the candidate or measure of your choice. Continue turning
the ballot pages and vote your selection of candidates or measures. Be certain
that you vote all ballot pages.

3. Lift your ballot from the red pins and remove it from the voting device.

NOTE TO VOTERS: Due to the "rotation" of candidates required by state law,
the candidates may appear in a different sequence in your precinct election day.

**Compiled by C. Lynn Smith
Walla Walla County Auditor**

★ C ⬛⬛ 526

may engage in such strategic voting, but no substantial evidence of it turned up.[4]

PRIMARIES: RULES OF THE GAME

The distinctions discussed in the last few pages concern the basic types of primaries. The following paragraphs elaborate on their refinements.

Access to the Primary Ballot

First of all, the states must deal with the problem of how a candidate gets on the primary ballot. Most states permit access to the ballot by petition (called nomination papers in some states). State statutes fix the number of required signatures—generally, either a specific number or a percentage of the vote for the office in the last election. In some cases, it is sufficient for the would-be candidates to present themselves to the clerk of elections and pay a usually modest fee. Finally, a few states put candidates on the ballot if they have formal party support. In Colorado, for example, any seekers after nomination who poll 20 percent or more of the endorsement vote at party conventions are automatically placed on the primary ballot.

Even such mundane matters as access to the primary ballot have consequences for the parties. (The easier access is, the easier it is for crank or dissident candidates to engage the party-supported candidates in costly primary battles.) Such arcane matters as the number of signatures a petition must have, therefore, may materially affect the number of primary contests in a state.[5]

Cross-filing

Until 1959, California, alone among the states, permitted candidates to enter both major party primaries—a practice called cross-filing. In 1946, while it was in full flower, Earl Warren won both party nominations for

---

[4]Alan Abramowitz, John McGlennon, and Ronald Rapoport, "A Note on Strategic Voting in a Primary Election," *Journal of Politics* 43 (1981): 899–904.

[5]Access to the ballot, along with all other aspects of election law, is receiving greater attention by the United States Supreme Court these days. Undoubtedly, the effect of this scrutiny in the long run will be to make candidacy easier. In 1972, for example, the Court invalidated a Texas law requiring candidates to pay both a flat fee for candidacy and a share of the cost of the election. The total charges had run as high as $9,000 for a candidate. *Bullock v. Carter*, 405 U.S. 134 (1972). In March 1974, the Court also overturned the California scale of filing fees. It did not prohibit filing fees per se, but the justices ruled that states using them must provide an alternative means of access to the ballot (such as a petition) for candidates unable to pay the fee. *Lubin v. Panish*, 415 U.S. 709 (1974).

governor; in the general election, Warren, a Republican, ran without Democratic opposition. Bowing to criticism that cross-filing destroys a party's responsibility for its candidates and, in fact, destroys the basic assumption of nominations by a political party, the state legislature abolished it. The closest remaining practice is New York's willingness to permit cross-filing if—and the "if" is a big one—the second party approves. Since the two major parties do not often approve, New York has had few instances of candidates running on both Democratic and Republican tickets. In 1981, the mayor of New York, Edward Koch, did run successfully for reelection as the candidate of both major parties. The major parties are friendlier, however, to the idea of their candidates also running on the ticket of an appropriate minor party. Thus, one sees quests for two-way nomination on Democratic and Liberal party ballots or on Republican and Conservative party tickets.

Run-off Primaries

Finally, some states have tried to cope with primaries that are settled by less than a majority of the voters. In cases in which candidates are nominated by only 35, 40, or 45 percent, most states simply hope that the general election will produce a majority winner. The District of Columbia and nine states, all from the South and its borders, have run-off primaries, however, if the winner in the regular primary wins less than 50 percent. In these second primaries, the two candidates with the highest vote totals face each other. This southern institution reflects the period of Republican impotence in which the Democratic nomination was, in effect, election and in which intense Democratic factionalism often produced three, four, or five serious candidates for a single office. Much more recently, another center of one-party domination, New York City, has begun run-off primaries if no candidate in the primary wins 40 percent of the vote. Iowa and South Dakota have approached the same basic problem with a fresh solution: if no primary candidate gets 35 percent of the votes cast, a party convention meets and selects the party's candidate.

The Nonpartisan Primary

Although it is of lesser importance in a book on American political parties, the nonpartisan primary is the means of nominating most judges, thousands of local officials, and even the legislature of Nebraska. As the nominating system that must accompany a nonpartisan election, the nonpartisan primary puts all candidates for the office on one ballot on which no party designations appear. The two candidates receiving the highest number of votes at the primary become the candidates for the nonpartisan general election. Although there are no party labels on the ballot, the party affiliations of various candidates may be well known. Party organizations may even endorse and support candidates, especially in nonpartisan mayoralty and city council elections. In such cases, the distinction between a partisan and a nonpartisan primary may remain only for the voters who have inadequate political information.

THE LINGERING CONVENTIONS

The convention as a device for nominating candidates faded quickly under early inroads by the direct primary. Decline has not meant death, however, and as of now, the convention as a nominating device retains firm control over a significant number of public offices.

Many states exempt the minor parties from the direct primary. The states are not anxious to incur the financial expense involved, and realism suggests that minor party nominations are not especially important anyway. Moreover, parties such as the Prohibition and Socialist Labor parties have enough difficulty finding even one candidate to run a futile race. Depending on state law, their candidates may be chosen by party convention or simply by petition. In the one-party days of the South, it also became common to give Republican parties the option of making their nominations in party conventions rather than in the primary.

Furthermore, a minority of states still keep some offices (usually statewide ones) out of the direct primary. In Michigan, for example, nominations for all statewide offices except governor are made at party conventions. Until very recently, New York parties chose their statewide candidates in state conventions, in which the ideological and geographic factions of the parties were propitiated and possibly even unified. In 1967, however, New York replaced convention nominations with a system that permits the state committees of the parties to designate their candidates. Other would-be candidates may then challenge the committee's choices in a statewide primary.

Connecticut, the last state to embrace the primary, did so without a conspicuous show of affection. The Connecticut primary is, like New York's, a challenge primary. Each party holds conventions to nominate candidates, and if no other candidate challenges the party nominees, they go directly on the ballot of the general election without an intervening primary. In the event of a challenge, a primary is held, but the challenger must have sought nomination in the convention, must have amassed at least 20 percent of the convention votes, and must later have filed nomination petitions. The first statewide primary took place in 1970, fifteen years after the adoption of the Connecticut primary.

Why did the convention survive in some of the states? It remained in a few states that have strong, centralized party organizations and a political culture more accepting of the role of parties as robust, self-contained political organizations. As Lockard has written of Connecticut:

> Why such protracted and successful resistance? Connecticut is not immune to political innovation. Although it may be known as "The Land of Steady Habits," it has nonetheless adopted an imposing array of progressive legislation, particularly in matters of labor law and social welfare. Still, matters of party concern are different—at least in Connecticut. For Connecticut parties are different from those of most other states; they are strong, centralized, and highly competitive with each other. The character of Connecticut party leadership—the power it has and the generally responsible manner in which it uses its power—constitutes the main reason why advocates of the primary made so little progress in Connecticut.[6]

In other words, strong, centralized parties can protect the sources of their strength—for in politics, too, "them that has, gets." Convention nomination enables the parties to bargain within the party—to reconcile internal differences and to maintain a control over candidates and officeholders. It is no coincidence that in a state such as Connecticut, in which parties as parties still control nominations, party cohesion in the state legislature is about the strongest in the United States.

THE THREAT OF THE DIRECT PRIMARY

The direct primary does not often substantiate the parties' worst fears, but occasionally it does. In 1962, a political novice from Cleveland with the promising name of Kennedy (Richard D.) managed to win the Democratic nomination for Ohio congressman-at-large in an eleven-cornered primary contest. Not only was he a novice with no support in the Democratic party, but he had run in the primary on a frankly segregationist program. A shocked Democratic party announced that it would not support him in the general election, and Democratic Governor DiSalle said he could not vote for him. Only nominally a Democratic candidate, Mr. Kennedy lost badly in the general election to Robert A. Taft, Jr., the Republican nominee.

Although such a disaster befalls a party only rarely, the primary often causes it many lesser inconveniences, disruptions, and problems. Consider the threats the primary makes to the well-being of a political party organization:

— For the party that wants to influence nominations, the primary greatly

[6]Duane Lockard, *Connecticut's Challenge Primary: A Study in Legislative Politics* (New York: McGraw-Hill, 1960), p. 1.

escalates the costs of politics. Supporting candidates in a contested primary is almost always more expensive than holding a convention.

✳ By curbing party control over nominations, the primary denies the party a powerful lever for ensuring the loyalty of its officeholders to the party program. If the party cannot control or prevent the reelection of a maverick officeholder, it really has no effective sanction for enforcing loyalty to its programs. (The power of European parties to deny renomination to their recalcitrant parliamentarians contributes substantially to party discipline in the parliament.)

✯ The primary permits the nomination of a candidate (1) hostile to the party organization and leadership, (2) opposed to the party's platforms or programs, or (3) out of key with the public image the party wants to project—or all of the above! At worst, it may permit the nomination under the party label of an individual who will be, intentionally or not, a severe embarrassment to the party.

— The primary creates the distinct possibility that the party will find itself saddled with an unbalanced ticket for the general election. In the hypothetical case of an electorate divided into X (50 percent), Y (30 percent), and Z (20 percent)—with X, Y, and Z representing regions, races, religions, ethnic or national groups—the voters at the primary may select all or most of the candidates from X. (We are assuming considerable bloc voting, but that assumption, after all, lies behind party attempts to balance tickets.) Party leaders unquestionably would think that a sprinkling of Ys and Zs would make a stronger ticket.

— Party activists also fear that the primary may produce a losing candidate for the party. The nominee may have appealed to only a shade more than half of the dedicated 20 or 30 percent of the electorate that votes in the party's primary. Such a candidate may be poorly equipped to make the broader appeal necessary in the general election.

In addition, the primary exacerbates party rifts, splits, factions, feuds—or whatever the headline writers choose to call them. It often pits party worker against party worker, party group against party group.

> A genuine primary is a fight within the family of the party—and, like any family fight, is apt to be more bitter and leave more enduring wounds than battles with the November enemy. In primaries, ambitions spurt from nowhere; unknown men carve their mark; old men are sent relentlessly to their political graves; bosses and leaders may be humiliated or unseated. At ward, county, or state level, all primaries are fought with spurious family folksiness—and sharp knives.[7]

[7]Theodore H. White, *The Making of the President 1960* (New York: Atheneum, 1961), p. 78.

The resulting wounds are often deep and slow to heal. The cost to the health and strength of the party is considerable. Furthermore, there is substantial evidence that the candidate who wins a contested primary will fare less well in the election.[8]

Not even the gloomiest Cassandra expects all these misfortunes to result from any given primary or even from a series of them. They are distinct possibilities for any party, however, especially a relatively weak and passive one. The parties recognize the danger, but they recognize, too, the futility of a direct assault on the primary. Thus, in the best American tradition of "joining 'em if you can't beat 'em," some parties have set out to control the primary. Others have lacked the will or the strength to do so. Still others have lost ground to local political cultures that disapprove of a party role in the primary. The result is a range of party responses to the primary that extends from no response at all to complete party domination.

THE PARTY ORGANIZATION FIGHTS BACK

One axiom and a corollary deriving from it govern party strategy in the primary. The axiom is simple to the point of truism: The surest way to control the primary is to prevent competition with the party's choice. The corollary is equally clear: The party must act as early as possible in the preprimary jockeying of would-be candidates if it is to choke off unwanted competition.

Within some party organizations, a powerful party leader or a few party oligarchs make the preprimary decisions for the party organization—or it may be a party executive committee or a candidate selection committee. If their sources of information are good, they will know who intends to run and who is merely considering the race. They may arbitrate among them, or they may coax an unwilling candidate into the primary. If they command a strong and winning organization, their inducements to the nonfavored candidates to withdraw may be considerable. They may

[8]The search for the effects of a contested (and thus divisive) primary has led to a substantial scholarly literature. On the effects on the party organization, see Donald B. Johnson and James R. Gibson, "The Divisive Primary Revisited: Party Activists in Iowa," *American Political Science Review* 68 (1974): 67–77; and John Comer, "Another Look at the Effects of the Divisive Primary," *American Politics Quarterly* 4 (1976): 121–28. The research reports on the effect in the general election are divided. For the argument that it does lessen the chances of victory in the election, see Robert A. Bernstein, "Divisive Primaries Do Hurt: U.S. Senate Races, 1956–1972," *American Political Science Review* 71 (1977): 540–45. For the opposite view, see James E. Piereson and Terry B. Smith, "Primary Divisiveness and General Election Success: A Reexamination," *Journal of Politics* 37 (1975): 555–62; and Richard Born, "The Influence of House Primary Election Divisiveness on General Election Margins, 1962–76." *Journal of Politics* 43 (1981): 640–61.

be able to offer a patronage position or a chance to run in the future. Such control of nominations by the party organization and its leadership—a control not at all easy to achieve under the American primary election—is the norm in most of the parliamentary democracies of the world (see box).

This informal and often covert selection of candidates—communicated to the party faithful by the "nod" or by the "word"—has been replaced within more and more parties by representative, publicized party conventions. A few states have formalized them; but in those cases, state law usually prevents an unqualified endorsement. Colorado laws provide that all candidates who poll more than 20 percent of a convention endorsement vote shall go on the primary ballot in the order of their vote percentage. Utah directs the parties to nominate two candidates for each office. Conversely, a few states attempt by law to minimize the possibility or the power of endorsing conventions. In 1963, California prohibited party organizations from "officially" endorsing candidates for office.

In some states, however, party endorsing bodies act informally and

---

Nominating the Candidate, British Style

In common with most of the parties of the European democracies, the local organizations of the British parties control the selection (the "adoption") of their candidates for Parliament. As the following report indicates, it is a nomination system that also can present problems for the parties. Indeed, there is probably no nomination process that can save a divided party from itself.

> Fred Mulley is 63 years old. The son of a common laborer, he left school at 18 to go to work as a clerk, then served as a sergeant in World War II, spending almost five years as a German prisoner of war.
> Since then, he has earned an honors degree at Oxford, pursued economic research projects, qualified as a trial lawyer and shaped a highly successful political career. For 32 years, he has been the Member of Parliament for Sheffield Park; he has served as Defense Minister, as Transport Minister, and, from 1974 to 1975, as chairman of the Labor Party. A classic example, as one of his friends put it, "of the bright, worthy, slightly gray member of the postwar meritocracy."
> In the past, a man like Mr. Mulley, who represents a solidly Labor constituency, could have been sure of holding onto his seat in

extralegally—that is, without the laws of the state taking notice of them. In Minnesota, for example, both the Republican party and the Democratic-Farmer-Labor (DFL) party (the state's version of the Democratic party) hold conventions to endorse candidates for statewide office and Congress. In some parts of the state, chiefly the urban areas, they also endorse local candidates and candidates for the state legislature. The instruments of endorsement, the conventions, grow out of the local ward and precinct caucuses mandated by state law. The required vote for endorsement, set by party rule, is 60 percent within both the GOP and the DFL. The party endorsement, however, is strictly unofficial. The endorsee must still go through regular procedures to get on the primary ballot, and the ballot does not note the endorsement.[9]

If a primary contest does develop despite all plans and strategies, the party then falls back on its resources in conventional ways. It may urge party committeepersons to help the anointed candidates circulate nomi-

[9]On Minnesota, see G. Theodore Mitau, *Politics in Minnesota*, 2nd ed. (Minneapolis: University of Minnesota Press, 1970).

---

the House of Commons until he retired or died. Instead, he was humiliatingly ousted this week by his constituency—the latest and most prominent victim of the changes within his party that have shifted it sharply to the left and caused the emergence of the Social Democratic Party. . . .

Several years ago, Tony Benn, the leader of the Labor left wing, began campaigning for a series of changes in the party's rules. One of them, finally approved 18 months ago, is only now beginning to take effect in the toppling of Mr. Mulley and others on the right of the party. The change set up a process called reselection, which requires that every M.P. be renominated by his constituency party before each election.

Previously, M.P.'s in safe seats were almost automatically reelected, and they had relatively little to fear from their usually undermanned but in some cases fiercely militant constituency parties.

Mr. Mulley was challenged in Sheffield Park, a section of the Yorkshire steel-making city, by Richard Caborn, a 37-year-old left-wing member of the European Parliament. Mr. Caborn won, putting Mr. Mulley's political career to an end and infuriating the embattled right of the party, which believes that such ousters threaten what little credibility Labor has retained through months of infighting.

R. W. Apple, Jr., in *New York Times*,
March 5, 1982.

nating petitions and leave the other candidates to their own devices. It may make available to the chosen ticket money, know-how, party workers, and the party bureaucracy. It may print advertisements announcing the party endorsees or may issue handy little reference cards that the forgetful voter can take right into the polling booth. On the day of the primary, the party organization may help get the party's voters to the polls. Whether the party organization acts overtly or covertly in the primary campaign depends both on the local political culture and on the candidates' own appraisals of it. The party and/or the candidates may feel that voter sensitivity to party intervention (i.e., bossism) may dictate that the candidates appear untouched by party hands.[10]

It is impossible to write authoritatively of the frequency of party attempts to manage or influence American primaries. Practices vary, not only from state to state but within states, and descriptions of local party practice are hard to come by. One is probably safe in generalizing that the most common nominating activity is the recruiting of candidates to seek the nomination. County party leaders in Wisconsin and Oklahoma have freely conceded that they encourage qualified candidates to seek office. Yet they have not widely attempted to perform the more demanding recruitment activities; only 10 percent of the Wisconsin chairpersons, and less than that in Oklahoma, have tried to dissuade would-be nominees.[11] The result is that, in most parts of the country, the political party is only one of a number of agencies seeking out and supporting men and women to run for office. It shares their recruitment with local business, professional, farm, and labor groups, with civic and community associations, with ethnic, racial, and religious organizations, with interest groups, and with officeholders.[12]

There are some party organizations, however, that *do* control the recruitment of candidates and the other preprimary processes. Generally, they are the parties that also intervene in the primary itself. A study of legislative elections in Pennsylvania constituencies in the late 1950s found that party organizations regularly attempted to influence the outcome in

---

[10]There have always been dark intimations of another party tactic in the primary—"dummy" candidates. These are candidates induced by the party to enter an already contested primary in order to divert and divide the support of the unendorsed candidates. The tactic has undoubtedly been employed in American politics, but probably with an incidence far below some suspicions.

[11]Leon D. Epstein, *Politics in Wisconsin* (Madison: University of Wisconsin Press, 1958), p. 93; Samuel C. Patterson, "Characteristics of Party Leaders," *Western Political Quarterly* 16 (1963): 348.

[12]The interaction may also be reciprocal and complex. J. David Greenstone has illustrated Democratic party influence on trade union endorsements for congressional seats in "Party Pressure on Organized Labor in Three Cities," in M. Kent Jennings and L. Harmon Zeigler (eds.), *The Electoral Process* (Englewood Cliffs, N.J.: Prentice-Hall, 1966), pp. 55–80.

74 percent of the primaries. In 56 percent of them, the interventions in the primary were public and explicit.[13] Such determined attempts to control the primary are not necessarily the norm in other parts of the country, however. County chairpersons in Kansas, Nebraska, North Dakota, South Dakota, and Iowa disclosed a few years later that they do not participate in Pennsylvania-style activities in the primaries. Some 40 percent of them said that they never openly supported a candidate in a primary contest, and about two-thirds of them declared that their party organizations never endorsed candidates before a primary.[14] Just what kind of party relationship to the primary was or is now typical across the United States is anyone's guess.

The role that the party organization takes before and during the primary election appears to be a function of a number of factors. First, all data point to a greater party role in urban and metropolitan areas. The political ethos of the cities seems to be more tolerant of party action in the primary; furthermore, the cities are also the sites of the strong and virile party organizations.[15] Second, at least one study indicates that party intervention in the primary is most probable in areas of two-party competitiveness. In one-party areas, the majority party may tend to be smugly confident or may be dominated by incumbent officeholders. The minority party tends to be helpless, and primary contests within its ranks are rare.[16] Finally, scattered evidence suggests that party control of the primary is more common within the Democratic party, even when one controls for urban-rural differences. Commentators on the styles and images of the two parties have often noted the more aggressively partisan style of the Democrats and the "nonpartisan," middle-class style of the Republicans. It is very possible that these differences affect their approaches to the direct primary.

CANDIDATES AND VOTERS IN THE PRIMARIES

What the parties can accomplish in the primaries depends to a considerable extent on the candidates and on the electorate. They are often the parties' unwitting allies. To put it simply, the primaries are more "manageable" because serious candidates do not often contest them and because the vast majority of voters do not vote in them. Very possibly, one or both

[13]Frank J. Sorauf, *Party and Representation* (New York: Atherton, 1963), Chap. 5.

[14]Marvin Harder and Thomas Ungs, "Notes Toward a Functional Analysis of Local Party Organizations," paper presented at the 1964 meeting of the Midwest Political Science Association.

[15]Sorauf, *Party and Representation*, Chap. 5; Harder and Ungs, "Notes Toward a Functional Analysis."

[16]Patterson, "Characteristics of Party Leaders."

of these conditions is of the party's making; the absence of candidates, for example, may reflect the skill of the party's preprimary persuading and dissuading. Regardless of cause, however, the result tends to be a nomination politics of a limited scope more easily controlled by aggressive party organization.

The Candidates

Simple countings will confirm that, in every part of the United States, large numbers of primary candidates win nomination without contest. In the 1958 primaries for Pennsylvania legislative elections, for example, 66.2 percent were without contest; and 45 percent of the legislative primaries in Ohio in 1948 were not contested.[17] In Wisconsin from 1966 through 1972, 58.9 percent of state legislative primaries were not contested. More recently, in 1978, a study of state legislative primaries in fourteen states found that a median of 53 percent of the Democratic primaries and 83 percent of the Republican primaries had no contests.[18] (Competition appears to be much more plentiful, however, for the more prestigious statewide offices.) In a survey of gubernatorial primaries in thirty-five nonsouthern states from 1950 to 1980, Jewell and Olson found that the major parties had contests for the gubernatorial nominations 73 percent of the time.[19]

In the aggregate, competition in American primaries (measured by the number of contestants) is greater under certain rather predictable circumstances. First, competition tends to flourish in primaries of the dominant party. In other words, competition tends to increase as the party's electoral prospects do; aggregately, it is greatest between the two parties of a district when they are closely matched. Second, competition tends to be more robust in the Democratic party than in the Republican party. Third, competition thrives in primaries in which no incumbent officeholder is seeking nomination. Finally, competition increases in the absence of effective party control or endorsement.

There are also other factors influencing competition: the attractiveness of the office and the ease of getting on the ballot, for example. The chief factor, however, is probably the party's prospects for victory in the general election; large numbers of Americans do not fight for the right to go down to almost certain defeat. As for the power of the incumbent to discourage competition, it is one of the ironies of the primary. The pri-

[17]Sorauf, *Party and Representation*, p. 111; and V. O. Key, *American State Politics* (New York: Knopf, 1956), p. 178.

[18]Craig H. Grau, "Competition in State Legislative Primaries," *Legislative Studies Quarterly* 6 (1981): 35–54.

[19]Malcolm E. Jewell and David M. Olson, *American State Political Parties and Elections*, rev. ed. (Homewood, Ill.: Dorsey, 1982).

mary puts a premium on the popular appeal and exposure that often only the well-known incumbent can muster. As a result, it fosters the conditions that diminish its own effectiveness.[20]

The Voters

If competition is scarce at the primaries, so are voters. All evidence points overwhelmingly to one cardinal fact about the voting behavior of the American electorate at primaries: it does not vote. Even the study of gubernatorial primaries (1950–80) that identified a relatively high incidence of contested races found modest turnout levels. In all of the states in that period, only 31.3 percent of adults aged eighteen and over voted in the primaries.[21] Turnouts for uncontested primaries or for those involving only local races and normally placid judicial races often fall considerably below half of the turnout at the following election.

Even though the primary electorate is small, it does have some special characteristics. A substantial sector of it generally comes from party loyalists and activists. Primary voters, as one might expect, also have higher levels of political interest and higher educational attainments. Conventional political wisdom has also held that primary voters represent more extreme ideological positions than those of the party's full electorate. Ranney and Epstein's recent studies in Wisconsin, however, disprove that assumption for that state.[22] Yet it is probably true that primary voters generally are more concerned with ideologies and issues than nonvoters are. Hence, although the ideological position of the primary voters may not differ, the intensity of their commitment to it may.

Even this generally interested electorate often lapses into unpredictable voting behavior. For large numbers of voters in the primary, the choice is more difficult than the one at the general election. Since all the candidates come from the same party, party loyalties cannot guide the voters' decisions—nor can any reaction to "ins" and "outs." The primary campaign is brief, the candidates are not well known, and the issues, if any, are often unclear. Therefore, the voters' choice is not so well structured or predictable; the presence of an incumbent in the race may be the

[20]On the factors that promote or suppress competition in the primaries, see Sarah M. Morehouse, "The Politics of Gubernatorial Nominations," *State Government* 53 (1980): 125–28; Harvey L. Schantz, "Contested and Uncontested Primaries for the U.S. House," *Legislative Studies Quarterly* 4 (1980): 545–62; and Richard J. Tobin and Edward Keynes, "Institutional Differences in the Recruitment Process: A Four-State Study," *American Journal of Political Science* 19 (1974): 667–92.

[21]Jewell and Olson, *American State Political Parties*, p.129.

[22]Austin Ranney and Leon D. Epstein, "The Two Electorates: Voters and Non-Voters in a Wisconsin Primary," *Journal of Politics* 28 (1966): 598–616; and Austin Ranney, "The Representativeness of Primary Electorates," *Midwest Journal of Political Science* 12 (1968): 224–38.

only continuing, stabilizing element. Consequently, many voter decisions are made right in the polling booth; the effect of the ballot position and the success of candidates with famous names indicate that. Small wonder, then, that parties are never confident in primaries and that public opinion pollsters prefer not to predict primary outcomes.

There has been one great exception to all the generalizations on competition and voter turnout in American primaries: the South. From the end of Reconstruction to the years right after World War II, the South was securely and overwhelmingly a one-party Democratic section. For most offices, therefore, winning the Democratic nomination was tantamount to winning the office itself. The effective competitive politics of the southern states thus centered in the Democratic primary. Furthermore, voting in the Democratic primaries was structured in ways unknown in the rest of the country. The Democratic parties of the southern states developed fairly stable, identifiable factions centering on specific interests, regions, and personalities. The southern Democratic factions best known in the rest of the country have been those centering on great family dynasties—the Byrds in Virginia, the Talmadges in Georgia, and the Longs in Louisiana. To the extent that voters could identify candidates as representatives of one faction or another, they had a set of cues and a source of political information quite rare for a primary election. As the Republican party builds strength and competitiveness, however, the Democratic primaries in the South are gradually losing their special flavor and character.

THE DIRECT PRIMARY AFTER SIXTY YEARS

More than sixty years have now passed since the addition of the direct primary to American politics. Thousands of candidates have waged the necessary primary campaigns, and millions of weary voters have puzzled over obscure choices and no choices whatsoever. What difference has it all made? Has the primary democratized the nomination process by taking it out of the hands of party oligarchs? Has it materially increased popular participation in the selection of candidates for public office?

Basically, the democratic hopes behind the direct primary falter on the lack of competition and low voter turnout. There must be participation—both by candidates and by voters—if there are to be meaningful choices based on meaningful alternatives. The primary, however—by its nature—tends to diminish such participation. The need for broad public appeal, the cost of a contest, and the sheer difficulty of getting on the primary ballot discourage candidacies. In addition, the multiplicity of primaries, with their unstructured, confusing, and unclear choices, probably reduces both the quantity and the quality of voter participation. Clearly, if mass participation in the nominating processes was a goal of the re-formers who initiated the primary, their hopes have not been realized.

The 1980 primaries for the United States House of Representatives in all the nonsouthern states illustrate the amount of choice afforded American voters in one set of primaries (Table 9.1). In only 42 percent of the primaries was there any competition at all. More significantly, in only 21 percent of them was there enough competition to prevent the winner from winning by a two-to-one margin. Moreover, Table 9.1 pinpoints the presence of incumbents as a major inhibitor of primary competition. (It also indicates, again, the tendency toward a greater degree of competition in Democratic primaries.) All in all, the opportunities for popular choice in these congressional primaries were considerably limited. If one were to include the South, the precentages would be further diminished.

Second, if one purpose of the primary was to replace the caucuses and conventions of the party organizations as nominators, the primary fails when it falls under the sway of those organizations. Even if the party cannot eliminate primary competition, it can sometimes defeat it. It may

TABLE 9.1   *Competition in Primaries for the House of Representatives in the Non-South: 1980*

Primaries	Degree of Primary Competition			
	Uncontested	One Candidate	Some Competition	Close Competition[a]
Democratic with incumbent	—	113 (62.8%)	52 (28.9%)	15 (8.3%)
Democratic without incumbent	—	65 (45.1%)	31 (21.5%)	48 (33.3%)
Democratic, uncontested	3	—	—	—
Republican with incumbent	—	88 (79.3%)	16 (14.4%)	7 (6.3%)
Republican without incumbent	—	97 (47.8%)	39 (19.2%)	67 (33.0%)
Republican, uncontested	13	—	—	—
Totals	16 (2.4%)	363 (55.5%)	138 (21.1%)	137 (20.9%)

Note   The South consists of Alabama, Arkansas, Florida, Georgia, Louisiana, Mississippi, North Carolina, South Carolina, Tennessee, Texas, Virginia.

[a] "Close Competition" here means that the winner won by less than a two-to-one margin over the closest competitor.

Source   Richard M. Scammon (ed.), *America Votes 14* (Washington, D.C.: Governmental Affairs Institute, 1981).

command the money, symbols, and organization essential for primary victory. The party organization also often commands the chief political loyalty of a major share of those who vote in the primary. If only 30 or 40 percent of registered voters vote in the primary, some 15 or 20 percent will be sufficient to nominate a candidate. Parties count on the fact that a substantial part of that group is likely to be loyalists who respond to the cues of party leaders or endorsements. Thus, strong party organizations able to mobilize voters, money, and manpower are still very effective determiners of primary outcomes.[23]

For a variety of reasons, however, the parties control the primaries only imperfectly. The sheer size of the task deters some of them. The Jacksonian tradition of electing every public official down to the local coroner has confronted them with numerous contests. The expense of supporting a number of candidates—not to mention the expenditure of organizational energy—forces many organizations to be selective in their primary interventions. In other instances, parties stand aside because a role in the primary would threaten their internal harmony and cohesion. They may be paralyzed by the fear that their activity in the primary will open new wounds or heat up old resentments. Still others are stymied by their own weakness or by local political cultures that resist party activity as a violation of the spirit of the primary.

Yet to argue that the primary has not fulfilled the most optimistic hopes is not to argue that it has had no effect. In competitive districts—especially when an incumbent has stepped down—voters often do play the kind of role the reformers envisioned. Also, even for a strong party organization, the primaries set tangible limits. Many no longer find it possible to whisk just any "warm body" through the nomination process. The direct primary perhaps can best be thought of both as creating a veto body that passes on the work of party nominators and as affording an opportunity for intraparty dissidents to take their case to the party's electorate.

Finally, let us consider the more general impact of the primary on the political parties. V. O. Key argued that the primary leads to one-partyism by increasingly drawing both the voters and the attractive, prestigious candidates to the primary of the dominant party. Little by little, the majority party becomes the only viable instrument of political influence and the minority party atrophies, a victim of "the more general proposition that institutional decay follows deprivation of function."[24] The burden of

[23]See, for example, Phillip Cutright and Peter H. Rossi, "Party Organization in Primary Elections," *American Journal of Sociology* 64 (1958): 262–69.

[24]V. O. Key, "The Direct Primary and Party Structure," *American Political Science Review* 48 (1954): 24; the same argument reappears in Key's *American State Politics*, Chap. 6.

opposition is then shifted to contests within the primary of the majority party. However persuasive this argument may be, it is as yet unproved. One-partyism has receded in recent years, and much of what remains of it can be explained in terms of changes in the characteristics of the American electorate. It is more likely that the direct primary has caused a general atrophy in party organization—in dominant as well as minority parties. Strong, centralized party organization remains in those states in which conventions either nominate candidates or make systematic, crucial preprimary endorsements.[25]

Furthermore, the direct primary unquestionably has altered the distribution of power within the party. When one speaks of party control of nominations, one means control by the party organization, and any weakening of that control obviously weakens the organization and enhances the power of the party candidates and the party in government. Their ability, especially as incumbents, to defy the organization's wrath and to win primary battles frees them from its discipline and, indeed, often calls them to positions of party leadership. In fact, the inability of the party organization in the United States to control the party in government (as it does in so many other democracies) begins with its failure to control its nominations. The direct primary undercuts the ability of the party organization to recruit to public office those partisans who share its goals and accept its discipline.

The goal of the Progressives and the other proponents of the primary was to substitute the party electorate for the party organization as the nominator. With the primary, they thwarted the organization's quest for its own goals. Instead of achieving any genuine mass control of party nominations, however, they shifted the control from the elites of the organization to the elites of the party in government. They succeeded in multiplying the party oligarchies rather than in democratizing them.

Finally, the direct primary has buttressed the prevailing decentralization of power in the American parties. So long as the candidates or incumbents can appeal to a majority of local primary voters, they are free from the control and discipline of a state or national party. Even so powerful a president as Franklin Roosevelt in 1938 met his greatest political defeat in trying to purge a number of Democratic senators and representatives in their local Democratic primaries; only one of his conservative targets was defeated. The primary plays on local loyalties and appeals to the local electorate, and its localism puts it beyond the control of a central party organization.

---

[25]On the relationships among party, mechanism of nomination, and primary competition, see Andrew D. McNitt, "The Effect of Preprimary Endorsement on Competition for Nominations: An Examination of Different Nominating Systems," *Journal of Politics* 42 (1980): 257–66.

10

THE CAMPAIGN FOR ELECTION

The formidable Democratic party organization of Pennsylvania had long had a reputation for winning primaries and general elections. At the outset of the campaign in the gubernatorial primary of 1966, few observers gave any chance to Milton Shapp, a Philadelphia industrialist who was challenging the organization's candidate, a thirty-four-year-old lawyer and state legislative leader, Robert B. Casey. In what was billed as a battle of "exposure versus organization," however, the Shapp campaign employed some 7,000 spot radio commercials, thirty-four half-hour television shows on prime time, an assortment of thirty or so pamphlets and leaflets, more than sixty campaign headquarters across the state, and a mailing of one large brochure to a million and a half voters. The total cost of the primary campaign, financed in large part from Shapp's personal fortune, ran over a million dollars. Shapp won the primary.

The use of polls, direct mailings, and television—even campaign pictures with well-known athletes, who were paid up to $500 for the picture taking—continued into the general election. Shapp lost that contest, however, to Republican Raymond Schaefer. After it was all over, a reflective Robert Casey observed about the campaign he had lost:

> Politics is changing tremendously. The old ways no longer work. From that election, I learned that these days you need a combination of two things. First, the traditional grass-roots effort, the telephoning and the door-knocking. But more than that, you have to do what he did. You have to use the new sophisticated techniques, the polling, the television, the heavy staffing, and the direct mail. You can't rely any more on political organizations. They don't work any more. These days, who wants a job in the courthouse or with the highway department? Why, the sons of courthouse janitors are probably doctors or professional men. You can't

233

give those jobs away any more. We're at the tag end of an era in Pennsylvania.[1]

The Shapp campaign in 1966 was managed by a young, professional campaign manager, Joe Napolitan, who went on in 1968 to help run the Humphrey presidential campaign. In 1970, Shapp finally succeeded in winning the Pennsylvania governorship, without the help of Napolitan, after again defeating Casey in the primary.

Stories such as this one—typifying the clash of old and new campaigning—were news in the 1960s and the early 1970s. They heralded a great change, a watershed, in the contesting of American elections that we increasingly take for granted by now. It is clear to us in the 1980s that the new professional managers, media specialists, pollsters, and advertising and public relations people have become a new and powerful force in American political campaigning. It is equally clear that they are replacing the party organization as the major planners and executors of campaigns. As one urbane former candidate has put it:

> With mass media which use a common language that everyone can read, people no longer need party workers to advise them how to vote. When a citizen can see and hear the candidate on a screen at home, and read news, written by the best journalists from a variety of points of view, about the candidate's public and private life, he does not heed what is told him by the precinct captain on his block. The media have done to the campaign system what the invention of accurate artillery did to the feudal kingdom—destroyed the barons and shifted their power to the masses and the prince. A candidate now pays less attention to district leaders than to opinion polls.[2]

The argument, briefly, is that the party organization has become technologically obsolete—that it has been superseded by newer, more efficient, and more timely avenues and techniques of campaigning. Therefore, the argument continues, the party organization has lost an important measure of control over the contesting of American elections and, ultimately, over its candidates elected to public office.

These new campaign politics take place, however, within a limiting context of legal regulation and definition. Prior to a discussion of campaigning and changes in it, therefore, it is necessary to discuss the shape of the electoral process. The strategies of the electoral game make sense only if one first understands the game itself.

---

[1]*National Observer*, September 26, 1966.
[2]Stimson Bullitt, *To Be a Politician* (New York: Anchor, 1961), p. 65.

THE ELECTORAL INSTITUTIONS

Each part of the legal framework, each rule of the electoral game, places a strategic limit on the campaign. Each adjustment in any one rule may affect one party or candidate more than another. Thus, the framework is much more than a neutral presence in the campaign and election.

Political parties around the world have been quick to realize the possible advantages to be gained by careful, selective tinkering with election law. The major American parties are no exception. Americans, however, have generally tinkered more with the size and shape of the electoral districts; gerrymandering is a peculiarly American art form. The rest of the American electoral rules have remained surprisingly stable. The kinds of repeated electoral tinkerings common in Europe—the shifts to systems of proportional representation and back again and the experiments with run-off elections, for instance—have not been common here.

The Secret Ballot

The American ballot is now uniformly secret, but it was not always so. Until the late nineteenth century, the oral vote was common in many states and jurisdictions. The voter simply stated to the electoral officials which candidates he preferred. During the nineteenth century, the oral vote was gradually replaced by ballots printed by the parties or candidates. The voter brought the ballot of his candidate or party to the polling place and deposited it in the box. Since the ballots were by no means identical, his vote was often apparent to observers.

The secret ballot was introduced as a way of curbing election corruption, especially vote buying; with a secret ballot, the corrupter could never be sure the vote would be delivered. Called the Australian ballot after the country of its origin, the secret ballot quickly swept the day. By the beginning of the twentieth century, its success was complete, and it remains the practice today. The ballot is printed at public expense by public authorities, and it lists all candidates for office on its single, consolidated form. It is distributed at the polling places only to bona fide voters, who then mark it in the seclusion of a voting booth.[3]

Increasingly, especially in large American cities, the voting machine is replacing the paper ballot. It does not, however, alter the basic form and premises of the Australian ballot; only the mechanics of voting are different. The voter faces the machine within a small, draped enclosure

[3]Jerrold Rusk found that the introduction of the Australian ballot was accompanied by a sharp increase in split-ticket voting. See his article, "The Effect of the Australian Ballot Reform on Split Ticket Voting: 1876–1908," *American Political Science Review* 64 (1970): 1220–38.

and votes by moving levers next to the names of candidates or parties. A master lever formally records the votes and at the same time opens the drapery for the voter to leave. The advantages of the voting machine, its makers assert, are its long-run reduction of election costs and its speed and accuracy in counting votes. It also thwarts certain forms of ballot box stuffing and dishonest counts.

Forms of Ballots

There are two types of ballots in use in the United States. Fewer than twenty states use the *office-block* ballot, which groups the names of the candidates according to the offices they seek (Figure 10.1). In the majority of states, the *party-column* ballot prevails. It is so named because the candidates of each party are listed together in a vertical column; the names of all candidates for the same office fall in horizontal rows (Figure 10.2). Thus, only in the party-column ballot are the candidates of each party grouped so that the voter can perceive them as a party ticket. By their very nature, of course, nonpartisan elections employ the office-block ballot.

All evidence indicates that the parties are correct in their belief that the party-column ballot encourages straight-ticket voting (i.e., voting for all of a party's candidates for all the offices being filled at the election). The amount of straight-ticket voting also hinges, however, on the presence or absence on the ballot of a single square or circle (or a single lever on machines) by which the voter can, in one fell swoop, cast a vote for the entire ticket. These squares or circles appear on two-thirds of the party-column ballots, but only Pennsylvania includes one on the office-block ballot. Thus, the format of the ballot can affect the way the voter sees the electoral contest and the nature of the choices in it.[4]

Three other aspects of ballot forms deserve mention. First, almost every ballot makes some provision for voters to write in the names of persons not listed on the ballot. The success of write-in candidates is so rare, however, that it is hardly a real question in American politics. Senator J. Strom Thurmond of South Carolina was initially elected in 1954 as a write-in candidate, but one political scientist has referred to that election as "one of the seven wonders of American politics," noting that "nothing of the sort had ever happened before in the history of the country."[5]

Second, the order in which candidates' names appear in the office groupings on office-block ballots may affect the outcome of the election. American voters have shown a notorious disposition to vote for the first

---

[4]For these data on ballot forms in the various states, I am indebted to the researches of George C. Roberts.

[5]William Goodman, *The Two-Party System in the United States*, 3rd ed. (Princeton: Van Nostrand, 1964), p. 440.

name on a list of candidates.[6] The issue of ballot position is actually greater in primaries, in which a number of names in the same party compete for voter attention. Some states respond to the problem by asking candidates to draw lots for first place; others list incumbents first. Still others rotate names; if there are three candidates, for example, each occupies first place on a third of the ballots. In the general election, the issue is really one of *party* position—first place for the party's candidates on the office-block ballot or the left column on the party-column ballot. The states frequently give the preferred position to the majority party in the state.

Finally, the American ballot is and has always been a long ballot. To be sure, its length cannot be controlled merely by electoral or ballot law. It reflects the American tradition of electing, rather than appointing, a great number of state and local officials: judges, coroners, surveyors, sheriffs, jury commissioners, superintendents of public instruction, assessors, public utilities commissioners, clerks of the courts, party committeepersons, auditors, and comptrollers. The major observable effect of the long ballot, especially in the office-block form, is voter fatigue.[7] Many voters, either tiring or despairing, do not vote in contests that appear at the bottom of the ballot. Partial voting (drop-off) of this sort can be as high as 20 or 30 percent of the voters at a given election.

Structure and Rules of the Choice

Overwhelmingly, American elections are governed by the twin principles of single-member constituencies and plurality election. In other words, we elect only one person per constituency to a city council, to the House or Senate, to the local mayoralty. The candidate who gets the most votes (i.e., the plurality), even if it is not the majority of 50 percent plus one, is elected. Even in cases of multimember districts—two-, three-, or four-member state legislative districts or at-large elections of local councils or commissions—the principle is not altered.[8] The voter casts the same number of votes as there are officials to be elected from the district, and the plurality principle still governs. In a two-member state legislative district, for example, each voter casts two votes; and the two candidates with the greatest number of votes are the winners.

The American states have experimented scarcely at all with the systems of *proportional representation* (PR) that so often enchant the other

---

[6]Donald S. Hecock and Henry M. Bain, *Ballot Position and Voter's Choice* (Detroit: Wayne State University Press, 1957); and Delbert A. Taebel, "The Effect of Ballot Position on Electoral Success," *American Journal of Political Science* 19 (1975): 519–26.

[7]Jack L. Walker, "Ballot Forms and Voter Fatigue: An Analysis of the Office Block and Party Column Ballots," *Midwest Journal of Political Science* 10 (1966): 448–63.

[8]For a good survey of the effects of various types of districts, see Howard D. Hamilton, "Legislative Constituencies: Single-Member Districts, Multi-Member Districts, and Floterial Districts," *Western Political Quarterly* 20 (1967): 321–40.

238

FIGURE 10.1   *The Office-Block Ballot:*
The Nebraska General Election Ballot, 1982

SAMPLE BALLOT

General Election, November 2, 1982

Senatorial Ticket

FOR UNITED STATES SENATOR

Vote for ONE

- [ ] Jim Keck .... Republican
- [ ] Edward Zorinsky .... Democrat
- [ ] Virginia Walsh .... By Petition

Congressional Ticket

FOR REPRESENTATIVE IN CONGRESS
FIRST DISTRICT

Vote for ONE

- [ ] Doug Bereuter .... Republican
- [ ] Curt Donaldson........... Democrat

FOR REPRESENTATIVE IN CONGRESS
SECOND DISTRICT

Vote for ONE

- [ ] Hal Daub .... Republican
- [ ] Richard M. Fellman .... Democrat

FOR REPRESENTATIVE IN CONGRESS
THIRD DISTRICT

Vote for ONE

- [ ] Virginia Smith .... Republican

State Ticket

FOR GOVERNOR

Vote in ONE Square Only

- [ ] Charles Thone
  Governor
  Roland A. Luedtke } Republican
  Lieutenant Governor

- [ ] Bob Kerrey
  Governor
  Don McGinley } Democrat
  Lieutenant Governor

- [ ] ....
  Governor
  ....
  Lieutenant Governor

FOR MEMBER OF THE
STATE BOARD OF EDUCATION
SEVENTH DISTRICT

Vote for ONE

- [ ] Daniel G. Urwiller
- [ ] Gerald L. Clausen

FOR MEMBER OF THE
STATE BOARD OF EDUCATION
EIGHTH DISTRICT

Vote for ONE

- [ ] William C. Ramsey
- [ ] Eileen Dietz

FOR MEMBER OF THE LEGISLATURE
SECOND DISTRICT

Vote for ONE

- [ ] Calvin F. Carsten
- [ ] Boyd Linder

FOR MEMBER OF THE LEGISLATURE
FOURTH DISTRICT

Vote for ONE

- [ ] Gary E. Hannibal
- [ ] Bev Laing

FOR MEMBER OF THE LEGISLATURE
SIXTH DISTRICT

Vote for ONE

- [ ] Gayle L. Stock
- [ ] Peter Hoogland

FOR MEMBER OF THE LEGISLATURE
EIGHTH DISTRICT

Vote for ONE

- [ ] Wayne Hohndorf
- [ ] Vard Johnson

FOR MEMBER OF THE LEGISLATURE
TENTH DISTRICT

Vote for ONE

- [ ] Carol McBride Pirsch
- [ ] James S. Beutel

FOR MEMBER OF THE LEGISLATURE
TWENTY-EIGHTH DISTRICT

Vote for ONE

- [ ] Chris Beutler
- [ ] John W. Butler

FOR MEMBER OF THE LEGISLATURE
THIRTIETH DISTRICT

Vote for ONE

- [ ] Patricia S. Morehead
- [ ] Gordon C. Bud Pettit

FOR MEMBER OF THE LEGISLATURE
THIRTY-SECOND DISTRICT

Vote for ONE

- [ ] Sharon V. Apking
- [ ] Donald Eret

FOR MEMBER OF THE LEGISLATURE
THIRTY-FOURTH DISTRICT

Vote for ONE

- [ ] Rod Johnson
- [ ] Ted Regier

FOR MEMBER OF THE LEGISLATURE
THIRTY-SIXTH DISTRICT

Vote for ONE

- [ ] Roy E. Lundy
- [ ] Lorraine Langford

FOR MEMBER OF THE LEGISLATURE
THIRTY-EIGHTH DISTRICT

Vote for ONE

- [ ] Tom Vickers
- [ ] Phillys Person Lyons

FOR MEMBER OF THE LEGISLATURE
FORTIETH DISTRICT

Vote for ONE

- [ ] Jim Wolf
- [ ] John W. DeCamp

Vote for ONE

Allen J. Beermann .... Republican

FOR AUDITOR OF PUBLIC ACCOUNTS

Vote for ONE

Ray A. C. Johnson .... Republican

Darl A. Naumann .... Democrat

FOR STATE TREASURER

Vote for ONE

Kay A. Orr .... Republican

Orval Keyes .... Democrat

FOR ATTORNEY GENERAL

Vote for ONE

Paul L. Douglas............. Republican

Ernest W. Chambers .... By Petition

FOR PUBLIC SERVICE COMMISSIONER
FIRST DISTRICT

Vote for ONE

Harold D. Simpson .... Republican

Ralph D. Johnson .... Democrat

FOR PUBLIC SERVICE COMMISSIONER
THIRD DISTRICT

Vote for ONE

Duane Gay .... Republican

James Elby Fochman .... Democrat

Non-Political Ticket

FOR MEMBER OF THE
STATE BOARD OF EDUCATION
FIFTH DISTRICT

Vote for ONE

Bill Marshall

FOR MEMBER OF THE
STATE BOARD OF EDUCATION
SIXTH DISTRICT

Vote for ONE

Fred A. Lockwood

FOR MEMBER OF THE LEGISLATURE
TWELFTH DISTRICT

Vote for ONE

Jerry Koch

Chris Abboud

FOR MEMBER OF THE LEGISLATURE
FOURTEENTH DISTRICT

Vote for ONE

Ron Withem

Thomas D. Doyle

FOR MEMBER OF THE LEGISLATURE
SIXTEENTH DISTRICT

Vote for ONE

James E. Goll

Shirley A. Schmidt

FOR MEMBER OF THE LEGISLATURE
EIGHTEENTH DISTRICT

Vote for ONE

Harry B. Chronister

John E. Pokorny

FOR MEMBER OF THE LEGISLATURE
TWENTIETH DISTRICT

Vote for ONE

Glenn A. Goodrich

Jan Harrington

FOR MEMBER OF THE LEGISLATURE
TWENTY-SECOND DISTRICT

Vote for ONE

Francis Sand

Lee Rupp

FOR MEMBER OF THE LEGISLATURE
TWENTY-FOURTH DISTRICT

Vote for ONE

Harold F. Sieck

Dorris Marnhouzen

FOR MEMBER OF THE LEGISLATURE
TWENTY-SIXTH DISTRICT

Vote for ONE

Don Wesely

Jim Brown

Vote for ONE

James E. Pappas

Corinne J. Jochum

FOR MEMBER OF THE LEGISLATURE
FORTY-FOURTH DISTRICT

Vote for ONE

Rex Haberman

FOR MEMBER OF THE LEGISLATURE
FORTY-SIXTH DISTRICT

Vote for ONE

David M. Landis

Stanley L. Heider........... By Petition

FOR MEMBER OF THE LEGISLATURE
FORTY-EIGHTH DISTRICT

Vote for ONE

William E. Nichol

Roger L. Green

FOR REGENT OF
UNIVERSITY OF NEBRASKA
THIRD DISTRICT

Vote for ONE

Don Dworak

Margaret Robinson

FOR REGENT OF
UNIVERSITY OF NEBRASKA
FOURTH DISTRICT

Vote for ONE

Robert J. Prokop

Nancy Hoch

FOR REGENT OF
UNIVERSITY OF NEBRASKA
FIFTH DISTRICT

Vote for ONE

Robert R. Koefoot

James N. Morton

FOR REGENT OF
UNIVERSITY OF NEBRASKA
EIGHTH DISTRICT

Vote for ONE

James H. Moylan

Sharon Donnermeyer Jackson

GENERAL ELECTION, TUESDAY, NOVEMBER 2, 19

COUNTY OF   , STATE OF MICHIGAN

NAMES OF OFFICES VOTED FOR:	DEMOCRATIC PARTY FDR / JFK ◯	REPUBLICAN ◯
STATE GOVERNOR AND LIEUTENANT GOVERNOR VOTE FOR NOT MORE THAN ONE	Governor and Lieutenant Governor JAMES J. BLANCHARD MARTHA W. GRIFFITHS	Governor and Lieutenant Governor RICHARD H. HEADLEE THOMAS E. BRENNAN
SECRETARY OF STATE VOTE FOR NOT MORE THAN ONE	Secretary of State RICHARD H. AUSTIN	Secretary of State ELIZABETH A. ANDRUS
ATTORNEY GENERAL VOTE FOR NOT MORE THAN ONE	Attorney General FRANK J. KELLEY	Attorney General L. BROOKS PATTERSON
CONGRESSIONAL UNITED STATES SENATOR VOTE FOR NOT MORE THAN ONE	United States Senator DONALD W. RIEGLE, JR.	United States Senator PHILIP E. RUPPE
REPRESENTATIVE IN CONGRESS, DISTRICT VOTE FOR NOT MORE THAN ONE	Representative in Congress	Representative in Congress
LEGISLATIVE STATE SENATOR, DISTRICT VOTE FOR NOT MORE THAN ONE	State Senator	State Senator
REPRESENTATIVE IN STATE LEGISLATURE, DIST. VOTE FOR NOT MORE THAN ONE	Representative in State Legislature	Representative in State Legislature
STATE BOARDS MEMBERS OF THE STATE BOARD OF EDUCATION VOTE FOR NOT MORE THAN TWO	Member of the State Board of Education CARROLL HUTTON / Member of the State Board of Education BARBARA ROBERTS MASON	Member of the State Board of Education RONALD G. ERICKSON / Member of the State Board of Education JACQUELINE McGREGOR
MEMBERS OF THE BOARD OF REGENTS OF UNIVERSITY OF MICHIGAN VOTE FOR NOT MORE THAN TWO	Board of Regents, University of Michigan SARAH GODDARD POWER / Board of Regents, University of Michigan THOMAS A. ROACH	Board of Regents, University of Michigan ROCKWELL T. GUST, JR. / Board of Regents, University of Michigan ELLEN M. TEMPLIN
MEMBERS OF THE BOARD OF TRUSTEES OF MICHIGAN STATE UNIVERSITY VOTE FOR NOT MORE THAN TWO	Trustee of Michigan State University JOHN B. BRUFF / Trustee of Michigan State University BOBBY D. CRIM	Trustee of Michigan State University LAURA HEUSER / Trustee of Michigan State University GEORGE A. McMANUS, JR.
MEMBERS OF THE BOARD OF GOVERNORS OF WAYNE STATE UNIVERSITY VOTE FOR NOT MORE THAN TWO	Board of Governors, Wayne State University MICHAEL EINHEUSER / Board of Governors, Wayne State University MILDRED JEFFREY	Board of Governors, Wayne State University NANCY BOYKIN / Board of Governors, Wayne State University SAM TRENTACOSTA
COUNTY COUNTY COMMISSIONER, DISTRICT	County Commissioner	County Commissioner

Form No. P-881

FIGURE 10.2   *The Party-Column Ballot: The Michigan General Election Ballot, 1982*

INSTRUCTIONS—To vote a straight party ticket make a cross (X) in the circle under the name of your party. Nothing further need be done. To vote for a candidate not on your party ticket, make a cross (X) in the square ☐ before the candidates name:

NOTE: Candidates for governor and lieutenant governor must be voted for as a unit, and the vote cannot be split.

If two or more candidates are to be elected to the same office, and you desire to vote for candidates not on your party ticket, make a cross (X) in the square ☐ before the names of the candidates for whom you desire to vote on the other ticket, and strike out an equal number of names on your party ticket, for that office.

If you do not desire to vote any party ticket, do not make a cross (X) in the circle at the head of any ticket, but make a cross (X) in the square ☐ before the name of each candidate for whom you desire to vote.

If you desire to vote for a candidate not on any ticket, write or place the name of such candidate on your ticket opposite the name of the office.

> **Before leaving the booth, fold the ballot so that the face of the ballot is not exposed and so that the numbered corner is visible.**

American Independent Party of Michigan ⚹	LIBERTARIAN PARTY	SOCIALIST WORKERS PARTY	WORKERS LEAGUE	TISCH Independent Citizens Party	INDEPENDENT CANDIDATE
◯	◯	◯	◯	◯	
Governor and Lieutenant Governor JAMES O. PHILLIPS / DeLOYD G. HESSELINK	**Governor and Lieutenant Governor** DICK M. JACOBS / STEVEN J. FURR	**Governor and Lieutenant Governor** TIM CRAINE / ELIZABETH ZIERS	**Governor and Lieutenant Governor** MARTIN P. McLAUGHLIN / RUTH KEEDY	**Governor and Lieutenant Governor** ROBERT E. TISCH / CLAIR WHITE	**Governor and Lieutenant Governor**
Secretary of State JOHN L. WAGNER	**Secretary of State** BRIAN R. WRIGHT	**Secretary of State**	**Secretary of State**	**Secretary of State**	**Secretary of State**
Attorney General	**Attorney General** ROBERT W. RODDIS	**Attorney General**	**Attorney General**	**Attorney General**	**Attorney General**
United States Senator DANIEL ELLER	**United States Senator** BETTE ERWIN	**United States Senator** STEVE BEUMER	**United States Senator** HELEN HALYARD	**United States Senator**	**United States Senator**
Representative in Congress	**Representative in Congress**	**Representative in Congress**	**Representative in Congress**	**Representative in Congress**	**Representative in Congress**
State Senator	**State Senator**	**State Senator**	**State Senator**	**State Senator**	**State Senator**
Representative in State Legislature	**Representative in State Legislature**	**Representative in State Legislature**	**Representative in State Legislature**	**Representative in State Legislature**	**Representative in State Legislature**
Member of the State Board of Education JOHN P. SANTUCI, JR.	**Member of the State Board of Education** FREDERICK J. DECHOW	**Member of the State Board of Education**	**Member of the State Board of Education**	**Member of the State Board of Education** CARMEN BRADLEY	**Member of the State Board of Education** PEGGY GOLDMAN FRANKIE
Member of the State Board of Education RUTHANN A. WAGNER	**Member of the State Board of Education** DENISE KLINE	**Member of the State Board of Education**	**Member of the State Board of Education**	**Member of the State Board of Education**	**Member of the State Board of Education**
Board of Regents, University of Michigan ANTHONY V. GIAMANCO	**Board of Regents, University of Michigan** LOUIS GOLDBERG	**Board of Regents, University of Michigan**	**Board of Regents, University of Michigan**	**Board of Regents, University of Michigan**	**Board of Regents, University of Michigan**
Board of Regents, University of Michigan GERALDINE A. SANTUCI	**Board of Regents, University of Michigan** ALAN KURCZYNSKI	**Board of Regents, University of Michigan**	**Board of Regents, University of Michigan**	**Board of Regents, University of Michigan**	**Board of Regents, University of Michigan**
Trustee of Michigan State University ORLANDO J. BURIA	**Trustee of Michigan State University** STEPHEN PATRICK O'KEEFE	**Trustee of Michigan State University**	**Trustee of Michigan State University**	**Trustee of Michigan State University**	**Trustee of Michigan State University**
Trustee of Michigan State University HOWARD H. HATT	**Trustee of Michigan State University** TIMOTHY R. OREN	**Trustee of Michigan State University**	**Trustee of Michigan State University**	**Trustee of Michigan State University**	**Trustee of Michigan State University**
Board of Governors, Wayne State University WILLIAM J. LAUBSCHER, JR.	**Board of Governors, Wayne State University** RICHARD M. FERRELL	**Board of Governors, Wayne State University**	**Board of Governors, Wayne State University**	**Board of Governors, Wayne State University**	**Board of Governors, Wayne State University**
Board of Governors, Wayne State University JAMES H. WAGNER	**Board of Governors, Wayne State University** THOMAS W. JONES	**Board of Governors, Wayne State University**	**Board of Governors, Wayne State University**	**Board of Governors, Wayne State University**	**Board of Governors, Wayne State University**
County Commissioner	**County Commissioner**	**County Commissioner**	**County Commissioner**	**County Commissioner**	**County Commissioner**

Printed by Authority of the County Election Commission.

democracies of the world. In these systems, which are of necessity based on multimember constituencies, the voter casts his or her vote for a party slate of candidates. The parties then share the seats according to the percentage of the votes they polled. In a five-member legislative district, for example:

Party A	58% of vote	3 seats
Party B	21% of vote	1 seat
Party C	16% of vote	1 seat
Party D	5% of vote	—
	100% of vote	5 seats

The possible refinements are virtually limitless in PR systems, but those endless complexities need not concern us here.[9] What is important is the political result of proportional representation of any form. First, it encourages minor political parties by giving them a share of the elective offices. Receiving 10 or 20 percent of the vote will rarely win any public offices in the plurality elections of American politics; but in several European countries, it wins parliamentary seats and cabinet positions for a number of parties. Second, proportional representation strengthens the hand of the party vis-à-vis its candidates. In strict party list systems especially, the party fixes the order of the party list. To return to the illustration of the five-member district under simple PR, the leaderships of parties A, B, C, and D draw up party lists of five candidates. By placing candidates first on the party list, the leaders of parties A, B, and C virtually place them in public office; by placing them fifth, they consign them to defeat. The prevailing single-member, plurality structure of American elections, on the contrary, reinforces both the two-party system and the independence of candidates and officeholders.

In a few instances, however, American states and localities have experimented with various exotic electoral systems. New York City adopted a variety of proportional representation from 1938 to 1947, with a resulting growth and representation of minor political parties (Table 10.1). The system was abandoned in 1947 after tension with the Soviet Union made the representation of the local Communist party intolerable for many New Yorkers. Perhaps the classic case of electoral exoticism has been Illinois' cumulative voting system. From 1870 to 1980, the lower house of the Illinois legislature was elected from three-person constituencies. To facilitate representation of the minority party (of the two major parties), the voter could cast his or her three votes in any one of four different ways: all three for one candidate, one and a half for each of two, one for each

---

[9]For an excursion into some of the complexities, see Wolfgang Birke, *European Elections by Direct Suffrage* (Leyden: Sythoff, 1961). See also Douglas W. Rae, *The Political Consequences of Electoral Law* (New Haven: Yale University Press, 1967).

democracies of the world. In these systems, which are of necessity based on multimember constituencies, the voter casts his or her vote for a party slate of candidates. The parties then share the seats according to the percentage of the votes they polled. In a five-member legislative district, for example:

Party A	58% of vote	3 seats
Party B	21% of vote	1 seat
Party C	16% of vote	1 seat
Party D	5% of vote	—
	100% of vote	5 seats

The possible refinements are virtually limitless in PR systems, but those endless complexities need not concern us here.[9] What is important is the political result of proportional representation of any form. First, it encourages minor political parties by giving them a share of the elective offices. Receiving 10 or 20 percent of the vote will rarely win any public offices in the plurality elections of American politics; but in several European countries, it wins parliamentary seats and cabinet positions for a number of parties. Second, proportional representation strengthens the hand of the party vis-à-vis its candidates. In strict party list systems especially, the party fixes the order of the party list. To return to the illustration of the five-member district under simple PR, the leaderships of parties A, B, C, and D draw up party lists of five candidates. By placing candidates first on the party list, the leaders of parties A, B, and C virtually place them in public office; by placing them fifth, they consign them to defeat. The prevailing single-member, plurality structure of American elections, on the contrary, reinforces both the two-party system and the independence of candidates and officeholders.

In a few instances, however, American states and localities have experimented with various exotic electoral systems. New York City adopted a variety of proportional representation from 1938 to 1947, with a resulting growth and representation of minor political parties (Table 10.1). The system was abandoned in 1947 after tension with the Soviet Union made the representation of the local Communist party intolerable for many New Yorkers. Perhaps the classic case of electoral exoticism has been Illinois' cumulative voting system. From 1870 to 1980, the lower house of the Illinois legislature was elected from three-person constituencies. To facilitate representation of the minority party (of the two major parties), the voter could cast his or her three votes in any one of four different ways: all three for one candidate, one and a half for each of two, one for each

[9]For an excursion into some of the complexities, see Wolfgang Birke, *European Elections by Direct Suffrage* (Leyden: Sythoff, 1961). See also Douglas W. Rae, *The Political Consequences of Electoral Law* (New Haven: Yale University Press, 1967).

INSTRUCTIONS—To vote a straight party ticket make a cross (X) in the circle under the name of your party. Nothing further need be done. To vote for a candidate not on your party ticket, make a cross (X) in the square ☐ before the candidates name.

NOTE: Candidates for governor and lieutenant governor must be voted for as a unit, and the vote cannot be split.

If two or more candidates are to be elected to the same office, and you desire to vote for candidates not on your party ticket, make a cross (X) in the square ☐ before the names of the candidates for whom you desire to vote on the other ticket, and strike out an equal number of names on your party ticket, for that office.

If you do not desire to vote any party ticket, do not make a cross (X) in the circle at the head of any ticket, but make a cross (X) in the square ☐ before the name of each candidate for whom you desire to vote.

If you desire to vote for a candidate not on any ticket, write or place the name of such candidate on your ticket opposite the name of the office.

Before leaving the booth, fold the ballot so that the face of the ballot is not exposed and so that the numbered corner is visible.

No.

American INDEPENDENT Party OF MICHIGAN ○	LIBERTARIAN PARTY ○	SOCIALIST WORKERS PARTY SWP ○	WORKERS LEAGUE ○	TISCH INDEPENDENT CITIZENS PARTY ○	INDEPENDENT CANDIDATE
Governor and Lieutenant Governor JAMES O. PHILLIPS DeLOYD G. HESSELINK	*Governor and Lieutenant Governor* ☐ DICK M. JACOBS STEVEN J. FURR	*Governor and Lieutenant Governor* ☐ TIM CRAINE ELIZABETH ZIERS	*Governor and Lieutenant Governor* ☐ MARTIN P. McLAUGHLIN RUTH KEEDY	*Governor and Lieutenant Governor* ROBERT E. TISCH CLAIR WHITE	*Governor and Lieutenant Governor* ☐
Secretary of State JOHN L. WAGNER	*Secretary of State* ☐ BRIAN R. WRIGHT	*Secretary of State* ☐	*Secretary of State* ☐	*Secretary of State* ☐	*Secretary of State* ☐
Attorney General	*Attorney General* ☐ ROBERT W. RODDIS	*Attorney General* ☐	*Attorney General* ☐	*Attorney General* ☐	*Attorney General* ☐
United States Senator DANIEL ELLER	*United States Senator* ☐ BETTE ERWIN	*United States Senator* ☐ STEVE BEUMER	*United States Senator* ☐ HELEN HALYARD	*United States Senator* ☐	*United States Senator* ☐
Representative in Congress	*Representative in Congress* ☐	*Representative in Congress* ☐	*Representative in Congress* ☐	*Representative in Congress* ☐	*Representative in Congress* ☐
State Senator	*State Senator* ☐	*State Senator* ☐	*State Senator* ☐	*State Senator* ☐	*State Senator* ☐
Representative in State Legislature	*Representative in State Legislature* ☐	*Representative in State Legislature* ☐	*Representative in State Legislature* ☐	*Representative in State Legislature* ☐	*Representative in State Legislature* ☐
Member of the State Board of Education JOHN P. SANTUCI, JR.	*Member of the State Board of Education* ☐ FREDERICK J. DECHOW	*Member of the State Board of Education* ☐	*Member of the State Board of Education* ☐	*Member of the State Board of Education* ☐ CARMEN BRADLEY	*Member of the State Board of Education* ☐ PEGGY GOLDMAN FRANKIE
Member of the State Board of Education RUTHANN A. WAGNER	*Member of the State Board of Education* ☐ DENISE KLINE	*Member of the State Board of Education* ☐	*Member of the State Board of Education* ☐	*Member of the State Board of Education* ☐	*Member of the State Board of Education* ☐
Board of Regents, University of Michigan ANTHONY V. GIAMANCO	*Board of Regents, University of Michigan* ☐ LOUIS GOLDBERG	*Board of Regents, University of Michigan* ☐	*Board of Regents, University of Michigan* ☐	*Board of Regents, University of Michigan* ☐	*Board of Regents, University of Michigan* ☐
Board of Regents, University of Michigan GERALDINE A. SANTUCI	*Board of Regents, University of Michigan* ☐ ALAN KURCZYNSKI	*Board of Regents, University of Michigan* ☐	*Board of Regents, University of Michigan* ☐	*Board of Regents, University of Michigan* ☐	*Board of Regents, University of Michigan* ☐
Trustee of Michigan State University ORLANDO J. BURIA	*Trustee of Michigan State University* ☐ STEPHEN PATRICK O'KEEFE	*Trustee of Michigan State University* ☐	*Trustee of Michigan State University* ☐	*Trustee of Michigan State University* ☐	*Trustee of Michigan State University* ☐
Trustee of Michigan State University HOWARD H. HATT	*Trustee of Michigan State University* ☐ TIMOTHY R. OREN	*Trustee of Michigan State University* ☐	*Trustee of Michigan State University* ☐	*Trustee of Michigan State University* ☐	*Trustee of Michigan State University* ☐
Board of Governors, Wayne State University WILLIAM J. LAUBSCHER, JR.	*Board of Governors, Wayne State University* ☐ RICHARD M. FERRELL	*Board of Governors, Wayne State University* ☐	*Board of Governors, Wayne State University* ☐	*Board of Governors, Wayne State University* ☐	*Board of Governors, Wayne State University* ☐
Board of Governors, Wayne State University JAMES H. WAGNER	*Board of Governors, Wayne State University* ☐ THOMAS W. JONES	*Board of Governors, Wayne State University* ☐	*Board of Governors, Wayne State University* ☐	*Board of Governors, Wayne State University* ☐	*Board of Governors, Wayne State University* ☐
County Commissioner	*County Commissioner* ☐	*County Commissioner* ☐	*County Commissioner* ☐	*County Commissioner* ☐	*County Commissioner* ☐

Printed by Authority of the County Election Commission.

241

TABLE 10.1 *Effects of Proportional
Representation in the New York City
Council Elections: 1945*

Party	Percentage of Vote	Council Seats
Democratic	59	14 (61%)
Republican	15	3 (13%)
American Labor	10	2 (9%)
Communist	9	2 (9%)
Liberal	7	2 (9%)
		23 (100%)

Source Belle Zeller and Hugh A. Bone, "The Repeal
of Proportional Representation in New York City—
Ten Years in Retrospect," *American Political Science
Review* 42 (1948): 1132.

of three, or two for one and one for another. Before the election (and the
primary), party committees in each of the constituencies determined
whether the party in the district would offer one, two, or three candidates
for the three seats. They often decided to contest cumulatively only a total
of three seats (one party offered two candidates and the other party only
one), leaving the voters of the district no choice in the general election.
In 1980, the voters of Illinois, by a margin of more than two to one, accepted a constitutional amendment that replaced cumulative voting with
single-member districts.[10]

Date of Election

In 1845, the Congress took up its constitutional power to determine the
dates of presidential and congressional elections (Article I, Section 4; Article II, Section 1). It provided that all states would select their presidential
electors on the first Tuesday after the first Monday of November and that
the same date would be used for electing members of Congress unless a
state's constitution provided otherwise. For many years, Maine chose to
hold congressional elections in September, but all fifty states now use the
November date. Since considerations of economy dictate that the states

[10]The amendment also sharply reduced the size of the legislature. For a full and perceptive report, see "The Cutback Amendment," a special report of *Illinois Issues*, published
by Sangamon State University (1982).

hold state and local elections at the same time, they have widely accepted the same date. Thus, a uniform election date prevails, even though the rationale for the date, chosen originally to follow the fall harvests, seems less and less convincing in an urban nation. No such uniformity on primary dates exists, however. Some come in April and May, some not until September. Consequently, a general election campaign may be six months or more in some states and two or less in others.

Election Day

The states and localities set the hours and places of elections. In most communities, the polls remain open for about twelve or thirteen hours; they open between 6 and 8 A.M. and close at 7, 8, or 9 P.M. The polls usually are located in a public building—a school, a firehouse, a city hall—although they may be found in barbershops, auto showrooms, and private homes in some communities.

In each voting district, usually called the precinct, the administration of the polling place is in the hands of a group of publicly appointed judges, inspectors, or commissioners, as they are variously called. They check the voters' registration, give them ballots or see them into the voting machine, and make sure their votes are cast. Often, they remain after the polls have closed to count the ballots, although centralized counting exists in some jurisdictions. The parties or candidates usually have the right to appoint poll watchers to oversee the administration of the balloting and the counting of the ballots.

Voting machines greatly facilitate the counting, of course. Final totals are simply read off a set of dials. In precincts without machines, however, the job is still a laborious one, often extending into the small hours of the morning. Weary polling officials, often after twelve hours of work at the polls, must decipher unclear marks and apply the often complicated state law on what constitutes an invalid ballot. Does a check mark, for example, suffice as a substitute for an X? In some states it does, and in some it does not. In a few close cases, the count may be challenged, and a partial or total recount of the ballots may result. The 1962 Minnesota gubernatorial election was in doubt for four months while a special three-man court supervised bipartisan counting officials in a recount of every paper ballot cast in the state. The Democratic candidate finally emerged a ninety-one-vote winner. That and other recounts have testified to three conclusions about the marking and counting of ballots. First, there has been little or no dishonesty documented. Second, honest errors in counting and recording do occur; for example, 10s become 100s, digits are inverted, the two parties' totals are reversed. Third, a significant number of voters do not mark their ballots correctly. In the 1962 election in Minnesota, for example, 389 voters voted (invalidly) for two candidates for governor, more than enough to decide an outcome that hinged on ninety-one votes.[11]

Absentee Voting

Most states have some provision for voting by people unable to come to the polls because of illness, travel, service in the armed forces, studies, or an occupation that takes them away from home. There is little uniformity, however, in the details of the provisions for absentee voting. Some states permit it only for specific reasons, some permit it only for certain elections, and some permit it only if the person has left the boundaries of the state. Congress had been under pressure to ensure the serviceman's right to an absentee ballot in the face of the reluctance of some states to provide one, and in 1975 it granted citizens living overseas the right to register and vote in federal elections in the state in which they last lived.

POLITICAL CONSEQUENCES
OF ELECTORAL LAW

Perhaps the chief impact of American political institutions on the politics of campaigning has been to focus attention on the candidates rather than on the parties. The American electoral process is relatively free from such institutions as parliamentary-cabinet government or proportional representation, which encourage the voter to see electoral contests in terms of the greater fortunes and future of political parties. On the contrary, such details of electoral law as the office-block ballot tend to structure the electoral choice as a series of contests between individual candidates and not as a single, multifaceted campaign between two great parties. Nonpartisan elections have even further reduced the visibility of the party in elections.

The specific components of the electoral system, therefore, do more than ensure efficiency or good government, preservation of democratic norms, or protection against vote frauds. They carry grave consequences for the parties and for campaign politics in general. They may affect the voting behavior of the electorate in the following ways:

All evidence suggests that the office-block ballot discourages *straight-ticket voting* and that the party-column ballot encourages it.[12] So, too,

[11]On recounts, see Ronald F. Stinnett and Charles H. Backstrom, *Recount* (Washington, D.C.: National Document Publishers, 1964); and Samuel J. Eldersveld and A. A. Applegate, *Michigan's Recounts for Governor, 1950 and 1952: A Systematic Analysis of Election Error* (Ann Arbor: University of Michigan Press, 1954).

[12]Angus Campbell et al., *The American Voter* (New York: Wiley, 1960), p. 276.

do other electoral details, such as the presence of a party circle or square on the ballot.

— *Voter fatigue* (or roll-off), the tendency to vote in only some of the contests on the ballot, appears to be in large part the result of the ballot itself. It is greater in areas that use the office-block ballot, and it tends to be greater the longer the ballot is.

— Every ballot form discourages *write-in voting*, but some discourage it more than others. It is especially difficult on most voting machines; and even so small a detail as whether or not the state permits the use of stickers as a way of writing in a candidate's name may be significant.

Such impacts on the voting responses of the electorates to whom the parties and their candidates must appeal obviously affect the parties and their campaign strategies.

The electoral system, however, may have an impact on the parties and campaign strategy beyond its effect on the voters. The states may limit the access of minor parties and their candidates to the ballot by requiring that they file petitions with large numbers of signatures. Most important, the details of American electoral law often do not touch the parties or candidates equally. If voting machines confuse less well educated, lower SES voters, and if office-block ballots encourage greater voter fatigue (roll-off) among less-educated voters,[13] then the disadvantages may accrue more to the Democratic party. If the state refuses absentee ballots to travelers, whether on business or pleasure, the disadvantages may strike mainly the Republicans. Any ballot form that facilitates party-ticket voting works to the advantage of the majority party in the constituency. Prime ballot position helps the incumbent and the majority party; so do designations of incumbency printed on the ballot. Even the hours and places for polling may have some marginal benefits for one party or the other.

Just how aware the parties and state legislators are of the possible advantages in refining electoral law is not easy to say. It is always difficult to establish the motives of legislators, especially when those motives may not be of the highest type. Occasionally, however, an attempt is just too persistent, too transparent, not to reveal the motives of party or political advantage. Jack L. Walker, for example, comments on the evolution of the ballot form in one state:

> In the state of Ohio the ballot has been changed six times during the twentieth century, and in each case the Republican majority tried to gain an advantage for itself by tampering with the election machinery. In 1940 Governor Bricker tried to avoid the influences of F.D.R.'s "coattails" by calling a special session of the legislature which approved a sep-

[13]Walker, "Ballot Forms and Voter Fatigue," makes the latter point.

aration of the ballot carrying national races from the one on which state and local races appeared. Bricker reasoned that if a normally Republican voter who was determined to vote for Roosevelt had to use a second ballot in state races he would be less likely to vote a straight Democratic ticket (the ballots were later consolidated once again to capitalize on Eisenhower's coattails). In 1949 over $85,000 was spent in a campaign to substitute the Office Block ballot for the Party Column ballot in an effort to save Senator Robert Taft from defeat in the bitter 1950 election. . . . The Taft forces thought that by eliminating the party lever they would substantially reduce the number of straight Democratic votes and thus increase the Senator's chances among normally Democratic, working class voters. Key quotes Taft as claiming that the change "was responsible 'for something between 100,000 and 200,000' of his total majority of 430,000."[14]

Finally, in one way above all—the drawing of constituency lines— the American parties have tried repeatedly to steal an advantage in electoral politics. Traditionally, there have been two general tactics: constituencies of unequal populations and gerrymandered districts. The first and more obvious of the two—districts of unequal populations—simply involved stretching the popular vote of the majority party by putting fewer people in districts in its strongholds than in districts located in the other party's areas of strength. In the past, the heavily populated districts were usually in urban areas, working to the disadvantage of Republicans in the South and Democrats elsewhere. In 1962, however, the Supreme Court put an end to these inequities. As the courts have applied the "one man, one vote" rule to constituencies of all varieties, they have closed off a classically American way of exploiting the rules of the electoral game.[15] The consequences of reapportionment depend on the specific districts being reapportioned. In the one kind of district that had earlier been the most seriously malapportioned, however—the state legislative district—reapportionment has, on the whole, increased Democratic representation.[16]

More subtle and less easy to detect, the gerrymander survives unimpaired. It consists of one party's drawing district lines in such a way as to use its own popular vote most efficiently while forcing the other party to use its vote inefficiently. That goal can be achieved in one of two ways: either by dividing and diluting pockets of the other party's strength to prevent it from winning office, or (if the other party's strength is too great for dilution) by bunching its strength into a few districts and forcing it to

[14]*Ibid.*, pp. 448–49.

[15]Especially for the political ramifications of apportionment, see Malcolm E. Jewell (ed.), *The Politics of Reapportionment* (New York: Atherton, 1962).

[16]Robert S. Erikson, "The Partisan Impact of State Legislative Reapportionment," *Midwest Journal of Political Science* 15 (1971): 57–71. See also Timothy G. O'Rourke, *The Impact of Reapportionment* (New Brunswick, N.J.: Transaction, 1980).

win elections by large, wasteful majorities. Frequently, but not always, the resulting constituencies, instead of being compact and contiguous, have bizarre and fanciful shapes (see box). (The term *gerrymander* was coined in the early years of the Republic to describe a salamander-shaped congressional district drawn in Massachusetts when Elbridge Gerry was governor.) Which party reaps the advantage of the gerrymander depends entirely on which party controls the legislature that draws the district lines.[17]

Lately, however, state legislatures have progressively lost some control over the redrawing of those district lines. Federal district courts have taken an increasingly active role in the task, in response to suits charging legislatures with evading constitutional standards of equality. Approximately a dozen states were redistricted by court-adopted plans after the 1980 census. At the same time, the Justice Department rejected the reapportionment plans of nine states, some of them several times, under the authority conferred by the Voting Rights Act to screen proposed electoral changes in certain states to protect the voting rights of minorities. The political consequences of these shifts of control over redistricting are predictable. In some states, the voting power of racial and ethnic minorities has been enhanced; in others, the weaker of the two major parties has been strengthened. Furthermore, the courts and the Justice Department are far less inclined than state legislative majorities to gerrymander for party advantage and to protect the districts of incumbents. They are also more willing, in many instances, to draw district lines across the lines of civil subdivisions (e.g., counties) and thus across the lines of local party organization. The result is to make it harder in yet another way for party organizations to maintain a role in electoral politics.[18]

CAMPAIGN STRATEGY

The folk wisdom about all aspects of American politics is more than ample, but on the subject of campaign tactics it is overwhelming. Much of it has been brought together into little books on campaigning that read

---

[17]For an objective measure of gerrymandering, see Ernest C. Reock, Jr., "Measuring Compactness as a Requirement of Legislative Apportionment," *Midwest Journal of Political Science* 5 (1961): 70–74.

[18]The various pressures for equity in districting have forced some states to give up some of their multimember legislative districts for single-member constituencies. The consequences of that shift are explored in Keith E. Hamm, Robert Harmel, and Robert J. Thompson, "Impacts of Districting Change on Voting Cohesion and Representation," *Journal of Politics* 43 (1981): 544–55.

like modern how-to-do-it manuals.[19] Since many of the recent books have been written by advertising and public relations specialists, much of the wisdom has a modern tone. Candidates are advised on dress and makeup for TV, and there is a good deal of emphasis on catchy phrases and slogans.

There is much of value in the received wisdom about American campaigning. Generally, it represents the distillation of concrete experience. Yet it suffers from two deficiencies that themselves are generally warnings about the crafts of political campaigning. The conventional wisdom seems to suggest, first of all, that most political campaigns are run on a master battle plan adhered to with almost military discipline and precision. In reality, most American political campaigns lurch along from one improvisation to another, from one immediate crisis to another. They are frequently underorganized, underplanned, and understaffed; consequently, they often play by ear with a surprising lack of information.

The folk wisdom also suggests that there are principles of good campaigning that have an almost universal applicability. In truth, however, optimum campaign strategy depends on a great number of variables, and the only general rule is that there is no general rule. Strategy will vary with:

- *The skills of the candidate:* Does he or she project well on television, at a press conference, or at an informal coffee hour?
- *The nature of the constituency:* Is it several square miles of urban slum or 30,000 square miles of prairie?
- *The office being sought:* Is it a city councillorship, or perhaps a judgeship that will call for a more restrained campaign?
- *The nature of the electoral system:* Is the ballot partisan or nonpartisan? Is the general election two or six months after the primary?
- *The party organizations in the constituency:* To what extent can their organized resources be counted on? What can they do?
- *The availability of political resources:* What manpower, skills, and money will be available, and when?
- *The nature of the electorate:* What are the voters' political norms, party loyalties, perceptions of issues and candidates? What political styles and tactics do they approve? What turnout and voting record do they have?

[19]For some recent examples of the how-to-do-it genre, see Edward Schwartzman, *Campaign Craftsmanship: A Professional's Guide to Campaigning for Elective Office* (New York: Universe, 1973); Joe Napolitan, *The Election Game and How To Win It* (Garden City, N.Y.: Doubleday, 1972); and Dick W. Simpson, *Winning Elections: A Handbook in Participatory Politics* (Chicago: Swallow, 1972). A more scholarly approach is represented by Robert Agranoff, *The Management of Election Campaigns* (Boston: Holbrook, 1976).

Electoral Cartography in New Jersey

The census of 1980 compelled the New Jersey legislature to redraw the boundaries of the state's congressional districts. The state had had fifteen members in the House of Representatives before 1980, but after that it was entitled only to fourteen. Even if its number of representatives had not changed, redistricting would probably have been necessary if only to reestablish the population equality of the districts.

The post-1980 New Jersey districts (see map) struck most observers as a classic gerrymander. The reptilian shape of many of the boundaries seemed to be an earmark of a classic gerrymander. So also did the fact that a Democratic legislature had fashioned nine Democratic districts (and only five Republican districts) in a state that was by other measures closely divided between the two major parties. The state's Republican members of Congress challenged the districting in the federal courts, and eventually the United States Supreme Court in 1983 (*Karcher* v. *Daggett*, 103 S. Ct. 2653) held the plan unconstitutional in a 5–4 decision. The Court invalidated the New Jersey districts, however, simply on the grounds of population variation from district to district. A variation of seven-tenths of one percent from the average, the Court thought, violated its clear demand for "precise mathematical equality."

The *New York Times*, pleased though it was at the outcome, remained editorially convinced that the New Jersey redistricting had been an obnoxious gerrymander. The day after the decision in the case, its editorialist wrote:

> The Court did not call its political map an unconstitutional gerrymander. . . . But unquestionably the Justices looked with dismay at the silhouettes of a football running back, a swan, a fish hook and a donkey in the New Jersey plan's Fourth, Fifth, Seventh, and Thirteenth districts. As our colleague William Geist noticed, the creation "includes serpentine districts that overlap bodies of water; slither through as many as eight counties in search of Democratic voters; hang together precariously by thin membrances of land . . . to avoid including popular Republicans in districts earmarked for Democratic victories."

> From *New York Times*, June 23, 1983.

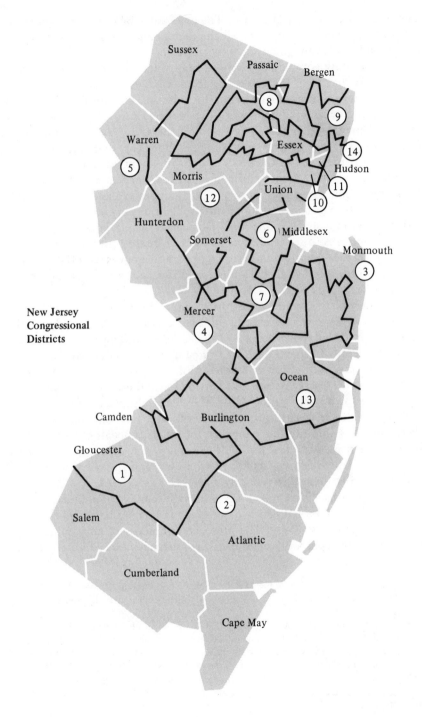

New Jersey
Congressional
Districts

There are other factors, of course. The chief early task of campaign strategists is the sober evaluation of all the factors and of the consequent demands and limits they place on the campaign.

It is not only campaign situations that differ. So, too, do candidates and the way they "see" the voters and the campaign. Candidates generally seem to believe that campaigns do affect election outcomes, and most of them are tireless campaigners who—not entirely sure of what will work in the campaign—spend every available hour and resource trying every conceivable stratagem. One study suggests, however, that candidates differ in their perceptions of the kinds of appeals voters respond to. Winning candidates saw voters as more influenced by issues and candidates, whereas losers saw them as more responsive to party appeals. Candidates may differ even in their understanding of the problem of putting together a majority. The same study found that Democratic candidates tended more than Republicans to see coalitions as built of interest groups and organizations rather than individuals.[20] If campaign strategy is essentially a matter of problem solving, then candidates differ in their understanding of the problem.

The nub of the strategic task in a campaign is selectivity in the expenditures of scarce time, energy, and resources in order to achieve the maximum effect on the electorate. The candidate and his or her managers must decide how to spend each unit of campaign resources so that it will return the maximum number of votes. Will they work on areas normally loyal to the other party in hopes of cutting losses there, or will they hammer at their own party strongholds? They must also decide how to tailor their appeals to different parts of the electorate. For some of the voters, there must be stimuli to party loyalty; for others, appeals of issue or personality are necessary. The problem is to know the variety and diversity of the voters, the likely bases of their decisions, and the ways of reaching and stimulating them differentially.[21]

All these decisions must be made within the context of political reality, and the political characteristics of the election race probably set the chief limits of campaign strategy. The presence or absence of an incumbent in the race and the competitiveness of the constituency exceed all other con-

[20]John W. Kingdon, *Candidates for Office* (New York: Random House, 1968). It is very possible that the different perceptions of group politics reflect real differences in party traditions.

[21]A number of writers have suggested that the problem of campaign strategy can be approached through maximization models such as those of game theory; for example, see John H. Kessel, "A Game Theory Analysis of Campaign Strategy," in M. Kent Jennings and L. Harmon Zeigler (eds.), *The Electoral Process* (Englewood Cliffs, N.J.: Prentice-Hall, 1966), pp. 290–304. For a more general approach to campaign strategy, see Lewis A. Froman's essay, "A Realistic Approach to Campaign Strategies and Tactics," in the same volume, pp. 1–20.

siderations in significance. Those two factors, perhaps, determine whether there is a possibility of victory. They affect the ability of the candidate to recruit workers and resources, to line up the support of groups (which usually have a taste for joining winners), and to attract the attention of voters.[22] In other words, the fact that a candidate is an incumbent running for reelection in a competitive district or a nonincumbent of the losing party in a noncompetitive district, for example, sets some major limits on campaign strategy before the imaginations of the candidate and his or her advisors even begin to work.

Finally, the very nature of the office being sought places important constraints on the nature of the campaign and its strategies. The most visible campaigns are those for the most visible and important offices— for governorships, for major city offices, for the Congress. Candidates for them tend to have name recognition already, and the attention given to the campaign increases it. They can raise large sums of money for splashy media campaigns aimed at reaching the mass of voters. The great majority of campaigns in the United States, however, are far less visible. Candidates whose names are hardly household words and whose campaign resources are modest must run far less ambitious campaigns. They must seek different ways to reach the voter, in fact. One study finds, for example, that such candidates tend to campaign indirectly—that is, to rely on the building of voter support through intermediary devices, such as the endorsement of better known political figures or the support of organized groups, whether of the party or not.[23]

THE NEW CAMPAIGNING

Within less than a generation, changes amounting to a revolution have altered much of American political campaigning. The skills of the mass media specialists have brought new persuasive techniques to bear on the American electorate—with attendant fears that presidents and lesser officials are now sold to the electorate much as Madison Avenue sells a new mouthwash or toothpaste. With the new techniques have also come the new technicians—the campaign management specialists, a new breed of sophisticated, hard-headed advisors who, as political mercenaries, deploy their troops and artillery for a suitable fee.

Professional campaign consultants emerged in California in the 1930s and matured in that state's politics after World War II. (It is one more bit of evidence for the belief that America's future seems to begin in Cal-

---

[22]See David A. Leuthold, *Electioneering in a Democracy* (New York: Wiley, 1968).

[23]Susan E. Howell, "Local Election Campaigns: The Effects of Office Level on Campaign Style," *Journal of Politics* 42 (1980): 1135–45.

ifornia.) In the last few decades, the archetype of the professional campaign consultant has been Spencer-Roberts, Inc., a firm that came to fame
in a number of California contests, especially Ronald Reagan's primary
and general election campaigns for the governorship in 1966 and 1970. By
1968, Spencer-Roberts was also working in a number of congressional
campaigns, employed and paid by the Republican Congressional Campaign Committee. After a falling-out with the Reagan forces, Stuart Spencer resurfaced in 1975 as the manager of Gerald Ford's campaign for the
Republican presidential nomination. Spencer resurfaced again in 1980 to
give emergency aid to the Reagan campaign for the presidency after it had
begun to founder. In the words of two chroniclers of the 1980 campaign:

> Spencer is one of these politicians—there are a handful in each
> party—who seem to have computers just behind their eyes. When a sit-
> uation arises, they are already programmed instantly to recognize and
> assess political ramifications of various courses of action. They can tell
> how other politicians will react, how the press is likely to behave, how
> the voters will respond. Big-time campaigns are rarely successful without
> someone like that at the elbow of the candidate, and Stuart Spencer was
> the obvious choice here.[24]

While Spencer was growing and prospering, so, too, were other political consultants: David Garth, Robert Goodman, John Deardourff, Joseph Napolitan, Matt Reese, and Robert Squier, among many. Some of
them came from the worlds of advertising and public relations, others from
political work of one kind or another. By 1980 or so, there were approximately 300 of them, and about 200 were members of the American Association of Political Consultants. Not only have they prospered in
American politics, they have also begun to export American campaign expertise to the rest of the democratic world. They have been retained to
manage electoral politics in an estimated twenty-five to thirty countries.
In 1981, for example, two American campaign professionals managed the
opposing campaigns of Menachem Begin and his party and Shimon Peres
and his party in the Israeli parliamentary election.

Campaign firms and specialists come in all sizes and shapes. Some are
experts in the use of the mass media, especially in buying time and in the
production of thirty- or sixty-second political advertisements. Some can
provide organizational skills, sometimes even lists of local party people and
possible volunteer workers; they can organize rallies, coffee parties, phone
banks, and hand-shaking tours of shopping centers. Some provide lawyers
and accountants to steer the campaign away from legal shoals and to speed
the reporting of campaign finance to the appropriate regulatory bodies.

---

[24]Jack W. Germond and Jules Witcover, *Blue Smoke and Mirrors: How Reagan Won
and Carter Lost the Election of 1980* (New York: Viking, 1981).

Some are publicists who write speeches and press releases; some sample public opinion; and some are very skilled in raising money. Some can offer virtually all of those services. It is a profession of both specialists and generalists, of both contractors and subcontractors. In it there is a scope and a skill for every candidate's need.[25]

New Sources of Information

The development of modern social science has opened up new sources of information and knowledge to the candidate. Computers and data-processing systems permit a party to keep records about constituencies and to process that information rapidly. Carefully kept records usually yield a faster and more accurate answer to how the twenty-first ward went four years ago, for example, than even the most conscientious party workers can. Wily parties and candidates have similarly used the scholarly data and findings on the demographic bases of Republican and Democratic strength. The managers of John F. Kennedy's presidential campaign commissioned a simulation of the 1960 electorate as an aid to campaign planning. The simulation attempted, with the aid of computers, to coordinate and correlate knowledge about the American electorate and to project the effects that various events of the campaign might have on it.[26] Other candidates have computerized records of canvassing so that they can quickly compile lists of voters to contact on election day.

No new avenue to political knowledge has been more fully exploited than the public opinion poll. It may be employed at the beginning of a campaign to assess the political issues uppermost in the minds of voters. Early polls can also develop candidate profiles—information about how the voting public views the two opponents. If it is found that voters think a candidate too bookish or intellectual, he or she may be sent to plowing contests, athletic events, or a weekend fishing trip. Polls can also indicate whether the campaign ought to capitalize on party loyalties or whether the candidate would be better advised to ignore an unpopular party or candidate at the top of the ticket. During the campaign, a poll or two can chart its progress and indicate where time and resources ought to be concentrated in its waning days.

---

[25]Among the many recent books on the subject, see Robert Agranoff (ed.), *The New Style in Election Campaigns*, 2nd ed. (Boston: Holbrook, 1976); the introductory essay by Agranoff is especially useful. See also Sidney Blumenthal, *The Permanent Campaign* (New York: Simon and Schuster, 1980); Larry J. Sabato, *The Rise of Political Consultants* (New York: Basic, 1981); and Dom Bonafide, "Are You Planning to Run for Office? Then a Political Consultant Is a Must," *The National Journal* (January 16, 1982): 101–104.

[26]Described in Ithiel de Sola Pool, Robert P. Abelson, and Samuel Popkin, *Candidates, Issues, and Strategies* (Cambridge, Mass.: MIT Press, 1964). A fictionalized version can be found in Eugene Burdick, *The 480* (New York: McGraw-Hill, 1964).

Parties and candidates have not been uniformly willing to avail themselves of such new techniques. Much of the knowledge thus far accumulated, especially about voting behavior, derives chiefly from presidential campaigns and elections and has only limited applicability. Also, many of the techniques are beyond the resources of local campaigns. The difficulty runs deeper, however. American political campaigns, despite popular impressions to the contrary, have rarely been run on a solid base of information. Thousands of party organizations around the country never have kept even basic voting data by precincts, wards, townships, cities, and counties. Thus, such a shift to the "new knowledge" involves a basic commitment to knowledge itself, as well as a willingness to bear the costs of acquiring knowledge.

New Techniques of Persuasion

Campaigns are basically exercises in mass persuasion, and the commercial arts of persuasion have increasingly been applied to them. There was a time when strong party organizations were the great persuaders in American campaigns. Changes in the organizations and in American politics, however, have diminished that role. Party organizations do not control votes and turn them out as they once did. It is left increasingly to candidates to do their own persuading of voters.

Predominant among the new persuasive techniques is the use of the mass communications media. Frequently, now, a candidate takes the time and effort to address a rally or meeting largely in the hope that it will produce a news report or a brief film clip on the local TV news. (Of course, the question of whether it produces a news report is not left to chance; the staff prepares news releases and copies of the speech for the local media.) Early in the campaign, candidates may vie to commit choice TV time and billboard space for the concluding weeks of the campaign. As the campaign progresses, the candidates' faces, names, and slogans blossom on billboards, newspaper ads, radio and TV spot announcements—even on lawn signs, automobile bumpers, and construction fences.

For the offices for which the new campaigning is most appropriate, television has become the major medium of persuasion. Time on TV may consume as much as 60 to 75 percent of the campaign's funds; since senate campaigns routinely cost at least a million dollars and congressional races cost in the $200,000 to $400,000 range, the sums are considerable. In the early and inexpensive days of television, candidates bought large chunks of time for entire speeches (oldtimers still remember Adlai Stevenson rushing the conclusion of a speech as the thirty- or sixty-minute segment ran out), but this is no longer done. Increasingly, the political message is compressed into the thirty- or sixty-*second* spot advertisement. The writing, the filming, and the placing of those messages (after the pro football game?

before the evening news?) become a major part of the campaign; so does the ability to raise the necessary money for it. Thus, what was a long, stem-winding speech by the candidate in a sweaty hall fifty or sixty years ago is now a few carefully crafted visual images and a very simple text put together by professionals.

At the same time, high-speed computers have brought the postal service back to the center of the campaign. They produce personalized, targeted letters by the millions (see box). They are effective both for campaigning and for fund raising; the well-written letter seeking money is indeed also an appeal for the candidate seeking the funds.

> Long gone, of course, are the days when a direct mailer began a form letter with an awkward "Dear Mr. Smith," printed in different type, usually above or below the line. Now, the "computer" types each letter individually, using the receiver's name throughout the text, in exactly the type of the letter body. If a letter to a Congressman is suggested, the computer knows the name of that representative by the person's zip code.
>
> The one thing direct mail letters are not is dispassionate. "You've got to have a devil," said Mr. (Roger) Craver. "If you don't have a devil, you're in trouble.". . .
>
> "You need a letter filled with ideas and passion . . . It does not beat around the bush, it is not academic, it is not objective."[27]

Gradually building a list of contributors and supporters—a list that can be returned to with good results—is also building for the political future. It is one of the many advantages an experienced and veteran campaigner enjoys.

All of this is not to argue that the traditional campaign techniques are obsolete. Handshaking on the streets and in the stores, speeches before anyone who will listen, endorsements by local groups and party organizations—all the old ways are very much alive. The new campaigning is too expensive for many candidates; a minute of prime TV time for a political spot announcement can easily cost $500, and a large billboard in a good city location may well cost that much per month. Also, these techniques are inefficient for many local candidates, because the radio, television, billboard, and newspaper space they purchase is wasted in great part on readers, viewers, and listeners who cannot vote for them.

TO WHAT EFFECT THE CAMPAIGN?

Many candidates—whether their campaigns are old or new style—have wondered about the impact of a campaign's sound and fury. The barrage

---

[27]E. J. Dionne, Jr., in the *New York Times*, September 7, 1980.

The New Campaigning:
The Next Frontier

Changes in campaigning in recent years have followed closely the development of new technologies in communication. The technology is already at hand for a new refinement in the ways of reaching voters—the targeting or narrowing of political messages in the campaign. A candidate can, in fact, mount a number of campaigns, each one aimed or targeted at one segment of the electorate. The technologies in question are computer-based mailings and new modes of television transmission.

> New York Republican Lewis Lehrman mailed out 3 million letters during the last week of the campaign before the Nov. 2 election that almost made him governor, according to the campaign manager for the winner, Democrat Mario Cuomo.
>
> Upstate independents with Republican leanings got one letter; downstate independents leaning Democratic received another. Jewish voters were sent a letter saying "Lew Lehrman speaks our language." Catholic voters got one saying Cuomo opposes tuition tax credits and "favors taxpayer funding for unrestricted abortion on demand." . . .
>
> One of the most sophisticated such efforts in the country took place in the Virginia congressional district directly across the Potomac River from the U.S. Capitol where former congressman [Herbert] Harris challenged incumbent [Stan] Parris.
>
> Parris sent out 1.3 million copies of 53 different letters. One went to firemen, another to policemen, another to lawyers, another to teachers. A letter to Alexandria voters said Parris obtained money to repair the deteriorating Woodrow Wilson bridge.
>
> Bill Peterson in *The Washington Post*,
> November 17, 1982.

of words and pictures is staggering, but is anyone listening or watching? Do the spot commercials, the literature, even the canvassing make any difference in the ultimate voting decision? No one really knows for sure.

Logical deduction leads to some plausible and probably reliable answers. We know that American voters expose themselves to a campaign with great selectivity. First of all, they tend to surround themselves with friends, literature, mass media reports, and even personal experiences (such as rallies and meetings) that support their perceptions and loyalties. Furthermore, they tend to perceive what they are exposed to in terms of stable, long-term loyalties, the most stable of which is their loyalty to a political party. Therefore, what we think of as a campaign may to some extent be two campaigns—one party and its candidates shouting at their

The FCC is about to award hundreds of new "low power television" licenses, and direct broadcast satellites may be operating by 1986, sending as many as 20 TV channels directly from space to small rooftop receivers.

This wave of outlets is creating the economic base for "narrowcasting." The big three networks will survive and will continue to aim at mass audiences, but dozens of new services will spring up for narrow audiences. Already, the new economics has spawned networks dedicated to news, sports, weather, movies, culture, health, Hispanics, Jews, blacks, the elderly, and the young.

Until now, politicians used TV to send short messages to large audiences. The new TV will mean longer messages for smaller audiences. When we watch the narrowcasting networks, we may see campaign ads and news programs showing candidates advocating bilingual education on Spanish channels, defending Social Security on channels aimed at the elderly, or playing football on sports channels. Politicians will find the all-news channels particularly fertile ground—viewers with enough appetite for news to watch it continuously will be good prospects to contribute, volunteer and vote.

The greatest impact may be on congressional and local campaigns. A candidate running in Lansing, Mich., for example, has to pay at least $500 for a 60-second ad on a regular TV station, and most of that money is wasted because the station covers half the state. The same commercial on the local cable system costs $30 and reaches just Lansing residents. Ads are new to cable, but they will be universal in a few years.

Richard M. Neustadt in *The Washington Post*,
March 14, 1982.

supporters and the other party and its candidates doing the same. Thus, a good deal of American campaigning has the effect of stimulating, activating, and reinforcing given political predispositions; far less of it achieves any political conversions. Much of the campaigning, too, is directed as much at getting people out to vote as at influencing their voting decision.

We can also make some deductions about the impact of campaigns just from the data we have about the exposure of the voter to the campaigns. Only a minority of the American adult public reports being contacted by a party worker in presidential election campaigns. Only 24 percent, for example, reported being approached by one of the parties in the 1980 campaign. Only 8 percent went to a political meeting, rally, or dinner during the 1980 campaign. Media exposure, on the other hand, reaches the great majority of the electorate. Significantly, 86 percent of the respondents watched at least one program about the 1980 campaign on TV.[28]

Therefore, the American electoral campaign is carried on by limited means within limited ranges of attention and perception. Even if it does reach voters, the campaign may not dent their fixed and stable loyalties to a candidate, party, or attitude. Moreover, events outside the campaign—wars, depressions, inflation—may have a far greater impact than the campaign itself has on voting decisions. Therefore, one cannot expect even the most dazzling campaign to achieve a full measure of persuasiveness, for it is directed to a political universe and not to a college debating society.

Beyond these generalizations, documenting the impact of a campaign is extremely difficult. For one thing, there are all manner of methodological difficulties. What we call the campaign is a congeries of events and activities; some of them are the activities of the parties and the candidates, and some are not. Consequently, it is difficult to say what part of the total impact can be attributed to any part of the campaign or its context. It is also difficult to determine what part of the campaign the individual voter has been aware of and how he or she has perceived it.

Have we, then, no empirical knowledge of the effects of the campaign? Two studies have indicated that personal contacts activate politically apathetic voters more often than mailed propaganda does, and that door-to-door canvassing is more successful in affecting voting decisions than telephone calls are.[29] The settings of both studies, however, were local elections, in which voter turnout and information were low. Other research has shown, in varying degrees of conclusiveness, that traditional precinct work by party committeepersons does have an impact on voting, producing a 5 to 10 percent change in the expected or usual party vote. The research suggests, further, that the effect of precinct work may well be greater in local elections than in media-centered presidential elections. In local elections, there are apt to be fewer alternative cues and sources

[28]The data in this paragraph come from the Center for Political Studies of the University of Michigan; they were made available through the services of the Inter-University Consortium for Political and Social Research. Since the postelection interviews were secured with a reduced subset of the original sample, it is probable that these percentages overstate the experience of the total electorate.

[29]Samuel J. Eldersveld, "Experimental Propaganda Techniques and Voting Behavior," *American Political Science Review* 50 (1956): 154–65; and John C. Blydenburg, "A Controlled Experiment to Measure the Effects of Personal Contact Campaigning," *Midwest Journal of Political Science* 15 (1971): 365–81.

of information.[30] Those conclusions are buttressed by another set of findings—that precinct canvassing in a presidential campaign increases turnout but has little effect on voter choice.[31] Finally, recent research has found
that active local party organization (before, during, and after the campaign) is associated with a vote increase over the expected norm,[32] and
that specific strategic decisions in campaigns (in this case, the decision of
some Republican congressional candidates not to associate themselves with
Barry Goldwater in 1964) also have an effect on the vote.[33]

To summarize briefly, there are indications that the campaign is more
successful in stimulating turnout than in affecting votes. (If that is the
case, the implications favor campaigning only among one's probable supporters.) Furthermore, the efficacy of only one kind of campaigning—
face-to-face personal contact—seems established, and that appears to be
successful only under limited circumstances. We know very little about
the effectiveness of other techniques, much less about their comparative
value. We also have some evidence that campaign strategies do matter.
Furthermore, we have considerable evidence that scholars have a very difficult time measuring the events and techniques of the campaign and an
even harder time accounting for their impact on the electorate. The techniques of evaluation have in no way kept up with the techniques gener-
ating the new campaigning.

THE PARTY ORGANIZATION'S ROLE

The campaign for the House of Commons in Great Britain is in the hands
of party agents based in the local constituencies. The parties employ the
agents, train them in the direction of campaigns, and place them in the
individual constituencies as managers of the local campaigns for Parliament. English law buttresses their authority by making them legally responsible for the observance of all election laws and for the management
of all money spent in the campaigns. (The parties, therefore, are guaranteed a guiding role in the parliamentary campaigns.\

[30]Phillips Cutright and Peter H. Rossi, "Grass Roots Politicians and the Vote," *American Sociological Review* 23 (1958): 171–79; Daniel Katz and Samuel J. Eldersveld, "The
Impact of Local Party Activity upon the Electorate," *Public Opinion Quarterly* 25 (1961):
1–24; and Raymond E. Wolfinger, "The Influence of Precinct Work on Voting Behavior,"
Public Opinion Quarterly 27 (1963): 387–98.

[31]Gerald H. Kramer, "The Effects of Precinct-Level Canvassing on Voter Behavior,"
Public Opinion Quarterly 34 (1970): 560–72.

[32]William J. Crotty, "Party Effort and Its Impact on the Vote," *American Political
Science Review* 65 (1971): 439–50.

[33]Robert A. Schoenberger, "Campaign Strategy and Party Loyalty: The Electoral Relevance of Candidate Decision-Making in the 1964 Congressional Elections," *American Political Science Review* 63 (1969): 515–20.

Nothing, either of law or of tradition, however, assures the party organizations a place in the American campaign. They must compete constantly for a role in it, just as they fought to control the nominations. Their adversaries in this struggle are the candidates, the personal campaign organizations they create, the new professional managers of campaigns, and the new financiers of election campaigns. Although the realities of American politics force candidates to run under party symbols that will help them attract the votes of a party electorate, nothing forces them to let the party organization control or even participate in their campaigns.

In some parts of the country, however, the party organization still retains assets that make it indispensable to the campaign. If it can command the armies of local workers, it can provide the candidate with a campaign vehicle (or medium) that ensures success but costs very little. These organizational campaigns occur chiefly in one-party urban areas, in which parties control primaries and voters habitually vote the party ticket in the general election. Canvassing and turning out the vote are still relevant there. Furthermore, the urban candidate is much more likely to have been nominated by the party organization through its control of the primary and thus to be its creature in the general election campaign.

In other races for public office, neither party organizations nor the new campaign professionals reign—the candidate is in control. Some candidates, indeed, are as suspicious of the new practitioners as they are of the party organization. In the words of the campaign manager of a successful congressional candidate:

> During our first campaign, some fellows from big P.R. outfits who live out here came around and volunteered their time and their talents. We talked with them and looked at the campaign material they'd put together, and we were scared witless. As far as they were concerned, facts and statistics were simply things to be changed. . . . Basically, the P.R. approach is different. Politics has a deeply negative quality. We're convinced that most people vote against somebody. . . . And that's what we concentrate on—making them vote against our opponent. The P.R. crowd feel they have to sell something positively. . . . We believe in being amateurish. Our brochures look as if they were got up in our basement. But the P.R. men want to put out four-color brochures with dazzling artwork and their idea of how the Gettysburg Address should have read.[34]

These candidate-run campaigns tend to rely on a campaign organization composed of friends, followers, and nonparty groups. They often involve people who are chary of party ties or who think of themselves as of the other party. Such campaigns enable the candidate to draw support by

---

[34]Richard Harris, "How's It Look?" *New Yorker*, April 8, 1967, p. 63. The article presents an excellent case study of a congressional campaign that relied neither on party organization nor on the new techniques and specialists.

Political Humor: Campaigns

A significant portion of the best political cartooning these days deals with American campaigns for public office. It is interesting, perhaps even revealing, to speculate why that should be so. Maybe cartoonists focus on campaigns because they are the most visible part of our politics. Perhaps, though, it is because they find an intrinsically humorous, even absurd, side to contemporary campaigning. Whatever the explanation, this example appeared in the pages of *The New Yorker*.

"Issue-oriented didn't work for beans."

Drawing by Stevenson; © 1976 The New Yorker Magazine, Inc.

personality and charisma. They are also appropriate in scale and skills to the less visible, less publicized races for local office. For these campaigns, there is no reason why the candidates or their managers cannot decide to make limited use of some of the new campaign crafts.

Behind the struggle of the candidate and the party organization for control of the campaign there is a basic truth: their interests never completely converge. The candidate, unless he or she has been dragooned to fill a ticket in a lost cause, takes the candidacy seriously. Even the longest shot among candidates tends to think he or she will win; the degree of ego involvement in the campaign almost demands it. The party, on the other hand, wants to be selective in its use of campaign resources. It may see some races as lost and thus may be glad to turn these candidates loose for their own independent campaigns. Party organizations want to set overall priorities and allocations of scarce resources; they want to eliminate the inefficient and uneconomical parts of the campaign. Furthermore, the party organization wants to activate party loyalty, and candidates may not care to do so. The organization may also want to protect a platform and a program, help a presidential or gubernatorial candidate, or win control of a legislature, but these may not be the goals and interests of individual candidates.

To be sure, there are potent advantages to a party-led series of campaigns on behalf of an entire ticket.[Such planning can eliminate the embarrassment and futility of two candidates' competing for audiences in the same small town.]The party organization can distribute campaign literature for a number of candidates at the same time. Also, it alone can mount the major election-day activities: setting up operation headquarters, providing cars and babysitters, checking voter lists to alert nonvoters late in the day, and providing poll watchers to oversee the balloting and counting. Efficiency and integration of the campaign, however, often threaten the interests of specific candidates. Although the party organization may prefer to raise money and prevent unseemly competition for the political dollar, an individual candidate may well believe he or she can raise more individually. Also, although the party may prefer billboard posters that celebrate the full party ticket of candidates, some among them may prefer to go it alone.

This distance, even estrangement, between candidate and party organization is also apparent in the expectations of candidates and party officials. In many parts of the country, neither group expects the party organizations to run the campaigns. Kingdon found that only a minority of Wisconsin candidates saw the party organization as the most important member of their campaign coalition. A slightly higher percentage saw interest groups as the most important.[35] In addition, there is at least some

---

[35]Kingdon, *Candidates for Office*, Chap. 3.

evidence that state party chairpersons do not think of themselves as campaign managers.[36]

In this battle for control of campaigning, the party organizations have historically been disadvantaged by the very nature of American elections. The sheer number of offices to be contested has forced the parties to surrender control by default. Electoral institutions, from the direct primary to the office-block ballot, have been on the side of the candidates. Now, recent revolutions in the ways of campaigning threaten to set the parties aside further. New sources of political information, political expertise, and political communication are available to the candidate, and so, too, are the sources of money to pay for them. Party organizations have long specialized in a kind of campaigning and voter activation that seems increasingly outmoded at a time of dazzling campaign technologies and campaign expenditures in six and seven figures.

It is an old American principle, however, that "if you can't beat 'em, you join 'em." Some state party organizations—and, increasingly, the two national party committees—have begun to raise the money and to provide the expertise necessary to compete with the new campaign industry. The operation of the Republican National Committee in supporting local candidates for state legislatures has become something of a model:

> The RNC has sponsored about 120 training seminars this year, where candidates and their campaign managers learned the fine points of how elections are won. The seminars included information about polling, how to target key precincts for campaign work, developing good radio and newspaper advertising, scheduling and staffing.
>
> A special RNC operation has been set up to allow candidates to conduct polls for as little as $250. Volunteers do the interviewing. Their raw data is then fed into the RNC computer in Washington, which tabulates and analyzes the results. Often, the state or national party will pick up the modest cost of the survey.[37]

By demystifying the wizardry of the new professionals, by teaching candidates how to do the job themselves, and by providing the new wizardry when necessary, the party organizations stand a decent chance of recap-

[36]On this point, two studies report virtually opposite conclusions. In 1970, Charles W. Wiggins and William L. Turk reported that, in a list of five roles, state party chairpersons gave last place in importance to the one described as "helping manage campaigns of state candidates"; see "State Party Chairmen: A Profile," *Western Political Quarterly* 23 (1970): 329. Robert Huckshorn, however, in *Party Leadership in the States* (Amherst: University of Massachusetts Press, 1976), found that chairpersons of both parties rated "campaign strategist" and "campaigner" responsibilities in the top third of a list of thirteen responsibilities. It may be that the respondents saw an important difference between managing campaigns and participating and strategizing in them.

[37]*Congressional Quarterly Weekly Report*, October 25, 1980, pp. 3188–92, at p. 3189.

turing some of the political ground they have lost over the past generation. If they do, however, only a battle will be won. The struggle between the party in government and the party organization within the American parties will go on.

The battle between the party organizations and the parties in government thus intensifies over the control of nominations and election campaigns. If the American parties are indeed electoral parties, then whoever controls the picking of candidates and the staging of campaigns controls the parties. At stake here is not only pride, but the fruits of victory. In the old days, the activists of the party organizations were satisfied with electoral victory by itself, for their goals were largely satisfied by public office per se and by the patronage and preferments that flowed from it. The new activists, however, seek much more than mere victory; they seek candidates and officials who will pursue specific issues and policy options after victory. Thus, to achieve their goals, the workers of the party organizations need to assert greater control over the party's candidates and officeholders at the very time when it becomes harder and harder to do so.

The new campaigning works against the party and the party organization in another way. It reinforces the development of personalism in politics. It is the candidate, not the party, who is "sold." The image transmitted by TV and the other media is of a person, not of the abstraction known as a political party. The campaign techniques, therefore, foster a tie between candidate and voter—a new personalism in politics—in which the role of party loyalty is less important. The new campaign techniques, thus threaten to displace the party *within* the voter as well as the party organization in the campaign.

By controlling their own nominations and elections, candidates are free of party organizational dominance and free to pursue their own relationships with their constituencies and their alliances with nonparty organizations. The failures of the party organizations enhance the competitive positions of other groups that want to play electoral politics and influence public policy. At stake in the battle, therefore, are the control and health of the political parties and the very nature of representative government in the United States.

11
PRESIDENTIAL POLITICS: THE PRELIMINARIES

It has often been said that the American presidency is the most demanding job in the world. Its size and responsibilities reflect, in part, the power and concerns of the government of the United States. They also reflect the unique institution of the presidency itself, for the United States is the only major power of the world that chooses a chief executive from a national constituency in free, competitive elections. As if to match the prodigious demands and responsibilities of the presidency, we have evolved a process of nomination and election to that office that, for sheer length, expense, and gaudy extravaganza, is without peer in the world. It commands front-page coverage in most of the world's newspapers, and in the United States alone, media coverage reaches enormous proportions. Approximately 120 million Americans watched at least some part of the Reagan-Carter campaign debate on television in 1980.

The quadrennial American presidential campaign has indeed become the focal point of all American politics. Its results radiate out to affect other elections; strong presidential winners, for example, carry other candidates into office on their coattails. Its candidates and rhetoric tend to shape party loyalties and identifications, and its regular four-year calendar is the basic pulse of American politics. The presidential election is also the great centralizing moment in American politics, the centripetal force against all of the decentralizing, centrifugal tendencies. It is the influential hour of the parties as national parties. Also, for many American citizens who are often apathetic to local elections, its salience and prominence make it virtually the whole of American politics.

Appropriately, this singular campaign and election pivots around two singular American political institutions: the nominating conventions of the summer before the presidential election and that constitutional anachronism, the electoral college. They combine to create a presidential politics of baroque complexity and an electoral process that remains an insoluble puzzle to many of the world's observers. It is a politics that is, to say the least, peculiarly American.

THE RULES OF THE PRESIDENTIAL GAME

If the American president and vice-president were elected directly by a simple plurality of the American electorate, presidential politics would be vastly different—and vastly simpler. The presidential constituency, how-ever—the one national constituency in American politics—is not com-posed simply of all American adults. It is a complicated constituency from which is chosen an eighteenth-century deliberative body that no longer deliberates. Like any formal electoral system, this one gives a special form to the political competition that goes on within it.

The electoral college as it is set down in the Constitution rests heavily on the structure of American federalism.[1] Each state receives a number of electors equal to its total representation in the two houses of Congress. In other words, to each state's fixed quota of two senators one adds the num-ber of the state's representatives in the House. The votes of the states in the electoral college, therefore, extend from a fixed minimum of three (two senators and one representative) to an open-ended maximum, cur-rently the forty-seven of California. In addition, since the ratification of the Twenty-third Amendment, the District of Columbia has had three electoral votes. Thus, the total membership of the college presently is 538, the sum of the membership of the Senate (100), the House (435), and the three votes of the District of Columbia.

The Constitution further provides that the president and the vice-pres-ident must be elected by an absolute majority of the votes of the electoral college. At present, that would be 270 votes. Should the electoral college not be able to elect a president by this absolute majority, the Constitution has provided for what is, in effect, a superelectoral college. The election of the president would then be settled by the House of Representatives, which would choose among the three candidates with the greatest number of votes in the electoral college. Although each state delegation in the House is to decide whom its state will support (and is not bound by the popular vote of the state), however, each state would have only a single vote in the balloting. The emergency procedure was employed twice in the early 1800s but has not been required since then. The procedure's drastic re-distribution of political power to the less populous states would today threaten seriously the assumption that presidents ought to be elected by majorities (or at least pluralities) of voters.

---

[1]Article II, Section 1, as amended by the Twelfth and Twenty-third Amendments.

The framers of the Constitution intended the electoral college to be a genuinely deliberative body. The choice of a president, argued Alexander Hamilton,

> should be made by men most capable of analyzing the qualities adapted to the station, and acting under circumstances favorable to deliberation, and to a judicious combination of all the reasons and inducements which were proper to govern their chioce. A small number of persons, selected by their fellow-citizens from the general mass, will be most likely to possess the information and discernment requisite to such complicated investigation.[2]

Not all the Founding Fathers were as fearful of direct popular election as Hamilton was, but the majority seemed to have accepted the wisdom of selection by a body of respected notables. The transformation of the electoral college began, however, with the rise of political parties. In the states, slates of electors began to run pledged to support a party's presidential and vice-presidential candidates. In other words, the ties of party loyalty assured voters that a vote for a specific set of electors was, in effect, a vote for party candidates. As soon as pledged slates became widespread, the electoral college ceased to function as an independent body. Thus, the electoral college today is perhaps the world's most important governmental body that has neither meetings nor choices. In most states, the electors meet briefly over lunch or dinner in the state capitol to register their vote formally. Some official of the state then transmits it to the president of the Senate in Washington, and the collective preferences of the electoral college are recorded without the inconvenience of a single meeting of the college as a whole.

Party slates and the party loyalty of those on them have had another transforming effect. The desire of parties to maximize support for a full slate of electors has encouraged the states to make the popular election of the electors an all-or-nothing race. A plurality edge for a party, whether of a few votes or of many thousands of votes, carries all the state's electoral votes. This winner-take-all principle, in turn, has had two consequences. First, it has forced the parties and the candidates to appeal to the voters of the large, competitive states that have the big, indivisible blocs of electoral votes. To fail to carry Wyoming or Delaware, with their three electoral votes each, is not a major loss. To fail to win in New York (thirty-six electoral votes) or in California (forty-seven), however, is a major setback. The parties tend, therefore, to pick presidential candidates from the large, pivotal states and to beam a great portion of the campaign at them. Second, the winner-take-all arithmetic increases the possibility that the loser in the national popular vote could be elected the new president. That

---

[2]*The Federalist*, number 68 (New York: Modern Library, 1937), pp. 441–42.

result can occur if a candidate wins some state blocs of votes by narrow margins and loses others by landslides.[3] Since the Civil War, two men have been presidential losers even though they led in the popular vote: Samuel J. Tilden in 1876 and Grover Cleveland in 1888.[4]

Although party ties have robbed the electoral college of its deliberative quality, they have not made it completely automatic and predictable. Electors in most states are not legally or constitutionally bound to vote for the presidential candidate under whose name they have run. Five times since World War II, individual electors, at the "moment of truth," have abandoned the candidate to whom they were pledged. A Virginia Republican bolted the Nixon slate in 1972, for example, to vote for the candidate of the Libertarian party; and in 1976, a Ford elector in Washington voted for Ronald Reagan.[5] (All electors honored their pledges in 1980.) Rebellious state parties may exploit this lack of a binding tie for their own purposes. They may deny the voters of their state the chance to vote for their party's national candidates by running either a different slate of candidates or an unpledged slate under the state party label. In 1948, for example, J. Strom Thurmond, the Dixiecrat candidate for president, appeared on the ballots instead of Harry S. Truman as the Democratic candidate for the presidency in a number of southern states. Mississippi Democrats in 1960 and Alabama Democrats in 1960 and 1964 ran unpledged slates of electors under the Democratic party label. A combination of party decentralization and state control over the presidential ballot, therefore, limits the development of a national, popular election of the American president.

Each of these characteristics and consequences of the electoral college

---

[3]As an example, consider the problem of three states with equal voting population and equal electoral vote:

State A: Population of 2,000,000 and ten electoral votes
           Democratic vote: 900,000
           Republican vote: 1,100,000
State B: Same population and electoral vote
           Democratic vote: 950,000
           Republican vote: 1,050,000
State C: Same population and electoral vote
           Democratic vote: 1,300,000
           Republican vote: 700,000

Here the Republican candidate leads in the electoral vote, twenty to ten, whereas the Democratic candidate leads in the popular vote by 300,000.

[4]Depending on how one counts the Alabama popular vote in 1960 for both pledged and unpledged electors, a case can be made that Richard Nixon won the popular vote in 1960 while losing the vote in the electoral college. See Lawrence D. Longley and Alan G. Braun, *The Politics of Electoral College Reform*, 2nd ed. (New Haven: Yale University Press, 1975).

[5]The Virginia elector, *mirabile dictu*, was chosen the Libertarian candidate for the presidency in 1976!

has produced a body of criticism and reform proposals.[6] One school of thought, concerned about the college's artificiality and the possibility of a "minority" president, has sought to abolish it in favor of a direct, popular election of the president. Others, alarmed by the system's emphasis on the indivisible big-state votes, have proposed various systems of dividing the electoral votes of the state: most of these proposals involve either dividing the electoral vote proportionally according to the candidates' percentages of the popular vote or electing some or most of the electors in the congressional districts of the state. (Maine, for example, decided in 1972 to choose two of its four electors in the state's two congressional districts. Thus, the party that carries the state will get two at-large electors, but the loser could conceivably carry one of the districts.) Still others have sought to check the uncertainty of the college's operation—the possibility of unpledged slates, of state ballots without a national candidate, of local slates intended solely to deadlock the electoral college, and of electors who abandon the candidates to whom they are pledged. Yet, despite a torrent of polemics and tomes of argumentation, operation of the college remains untouched. It changes today only as it has in the past—by custom, tradition, and state law.

Behind all the attempts to reform or abolish the electoral college lie broader questions of political power and ideology. In defining the national constituency of the president and the vice-president, the electoral college first of all enhances the political power of the large, urban, industrial states that have the large blocs of electoral votes. In other words, the college creates a presidential constituency that is markedly different from the sum of all the congressional constituencies. Because of the equal state representation in the Senate, regardless of population, the political power of the rural and small-city electorates is magnified in the Congress. In the past generation, the presidents, as a result of the nature of their national constituency, have usually espoused the liberal social and economic programs favored by the people of the urban areas. The desire of political conservatives to reduce the power of the large, urban, industrial states lies behind some of the attempts to alter the college, especially those proposals that would divide the electoral votes of the individual states;[7] and the desire to preserve that power lies behind a great deal of the opposition to change.

The second issue behind reform of the electoral college is no less than

---

[6]On the electoral college generally, see Neal R. Peirce and Lawrence D. Longley, *The People's President*, rev. ed. (New Haven: Yale University Press, 1981); Wallace S. Sayre and Judith H. Parris, *Voting for President* (Washington, D.C.: Brookings, 1970); and Longley and Braun, *The Politics of Electoral College Reform*.

[7]On this point and also for a general review of the impact of the electoral college, see Allan Sindler, "Presidential Election Methods and Urban-Ethnic Interests," *Law and Contemporary Problems* 27 (1962): 213–33.

direct, popular democracy itself. In the last 130 or 140 years, the electoral college has evolved into something very close to a de facto popular election of the presidency. That same period has also seen the spread of democratic norms and a constant broadening of the suffrage. Some of the proposed reforms try to protect the will of the majority either by institutionalizing the popular election of the president and vice-president or by preventing individual electors or state parties from thwarting popular will. Into this category fall both the attempts to abolish the college entirely and the less drastic proposals to limit state party control over the ballot choices and to force electors to vote for the candidates they had pledged to support. On this point, the opponents of change in effect deny the presence of a problem; in every presidential election since 1888, the leader in the popular vote has indeed won in the electoral college.

Finally, the debate over reform touches the future of the two-party system. Much of the impetus for reform in the 1970s came from George Wallace's attempt to deny Hubert Humphrey and Richard Nixon a majority of electoral votes in 1968 and thus to give himself a bargaining role either in the electoral college or in the "one state, one vote" ballot in the House. Opponents of abolition claim, however, that although direct election of the president would end that kind of minor party strategy, it would encourage the growth of minor parties and independent candidates. They focus on provisions in direct election amendments that provide for a run-off apparatus of some kind—another election or selection by a joint session of Congress—if no candidate receives 40 percent of the popular vote in the election. The possibility of such a run-off, they argue, combined with a direct, national popular vote, would be an even greater inducement to third parties.

Thus, although fair representation, the will of the majority, and the health of the two-party system are goals beyond serious debate, disagreement persists about what meaning they should have in practice and about what way of selecting a president will best achieve them.[8]

FIRST STEPS TOWARD THE NOMINATIONS

The national conventions of the two major parties conclude the complicated process of nomination. It is very difficult to say, however, just when

[8]There are two paradoxes in this debate. The first involves the third-party effect. Generally, the electoral college discourages smaller parties, if only because their support is so difficult to translate into electoral votes. A "larger" small party, however, especially one whose strength is regionally concentrated, can use the electoral college for its own strategic purposes. The second paradox concerns the effect on the smaller states. The informal political consequences of the electoral college lead to big-state arithmetic and thus to some slighting of candidates from and campaigns in the smaller states. Formally, however, the electoral college, by including the Senate's equal representation in the formula, overrepresents the small, usually rural states.

that nominating process begins. For some especially ambitious and far-sighted politicians, it may have begun in their own career planning some six or eight years before. Within the party defeated in a presidential election, jockeying for the next nomination begins the morning after that defeat. In a more traditional sense, the nomination process begins as the advance men and women for would-be candidates straggle into New Hampshire and Iowa to enter their candidates in the earliest of the processes in which convention delegates are chosen.

The preconvention part of the nomination process concerns the selection of delegates to the conventions. The major would-be candidates within each party seek delegates bound to them—or at least committed or inclined to them. Conversely, heads of state delegations often want delegates to remain uncommitted so that their bargaining power will remain unexpended until the convention meets. Typically, however, the party organizations do not really control the picking of delegates to their own conventions. State legislatures decide the crucial matter of how the convention delegates will be chosen—whether by a presidential primary, by a convention or committee of the party, or by a combination of the two.

Apportionment and Selection of Delegates

The national parties determine the number of votes and delegates each state will have in the Democratic and Republican national conventions. For the first time in a long while, the numbers of votes and delegates to the two national conventions in 1976 were identical. The Democrats, in particular, had a long earlier tradition of permitting state parties to send more delegates to the national convention than the number of their assigned votes, with the inevitable result that some delegates cast bizarre fractions of a single vote.

To assign the number of votes to each state, the national committees or conventions of the parties—whichever makes the decision—employ a more than usually complicated formula. The 1980 Republican convention, for example, was chosen according to this formula:

— Each state received six at-large delegates.

— Each state received three delegates from each of its congressional districts.

— Each state that had a Republican governor and/or senator received an additional delegate.

— Each state whose congressional delegation was at least 50 percent Republican received an additional delegate.

— Each state that gave the 1976 presidential candidate its electoral vote received a number of additional delegates equal to four and one-half plus 60 percent of the state's electoral vote (rounded to the next whole number).

— The District of Columbia received fourteen at-large votes, Puerto Rico eight, the Virgin Islands four, and Guam four.

The same formula will probably be used by the Republicans for their 1984 convention. The Republicans thus strongly favor the areas of heavy Republican strength, and they continue the tradition of overrepresenting the less populous states. Indeed, the 1976 formula was adopted over the strong opposition of about one-third of the 1972 convention delegates, who wanted to increase the representation of the urban, populous states. Those are the states of moderate Republican strength, however, and the apportionment of convention delegates in both parties tends to reflect the dominant ideologies within the parties.

That was how both parties apportioned their convention delegates for many years—in formulas that represented the states equally, with some modification by bonus delegates for recent electoral success. Beginning in 1972, however, the Democrats began to depart from that tradition; and by the 1980s, the structure of their convention differed markedly from that of the Republicans. They now represent more heavily the different populations of the states; the seven most populous states had 36 percent of the convention delegates in 1968 but 45 percent in 1980. They also began to represent the strength of Democratic voting more dramatically than the Republicans were able to do with the bonus delegates. In 1984, for the first time, the Democrats will seat, *ex officio,* about 550 of the party's officers and public officials. That group of delegates will include about 60 percent of the Democrats in the Congress.

For years, the national parties, in preparing for the conventions, had stipulated only the number of delegates the states would have. It was always left to the states or their parties to decide how the delegates would be chosen. Beginning in 1972, the Democrats ended that tradition, too. They began to control a number of the other aspects of delegate selection. Now the rules of the convention require each state party to file affirmative action goals for representing all groups in its delegation to the convention in proportion to their strength in the Democratic electorate in the state. The rules also stipulate that 50 percent of each state's delegation be women. In addition, the rules for 1984 require that, in selecting delegates to the convention, the states:

— Limit participation in primaries and caucuses to Democratic voters who will declare their party preference (thus ruling out selection in open primaries).

— Hold their primaries and caucuses largely within a period between the first Tuesdays of March and June 1984 (thus setting limits to state legislatures that wanted to move their state primaries or caucuses to earlier dates).

— Require that all would-be delegates be identified either by their presidential preference or as uncommitted (thus banning primaries such as New York's for selecting delegates).

— Allocate delegates to reflect "fairly" the strength of the various presidential contenders in the state (thus ending winner-take-all elections of delegates in the states).

So ended local autonomy over the selection of delegates to national conventions. Taken as a whole, the Democratic reforms have been a stunning and unprecedented assertion of the authority of the national party.[9] They are, moreover, an assertion of authority not only over the state parties, but over the states themselves. The Supreme Court has upheld the power of the national party to refuse to seat delegates chosen under a state law—such as Wisconsin's open primary—of which it disapproves.[10]

The Presidential Primaries

The number of states that choose their convention delegates in presidential primaries continues its steady climb. In 1968, only fifteen states and the District of Columbia elected some or all of their convention delegates in ways that offered voters of the state some opportunity to express a preference for the presidential nominee of the party. Together, the delegates from these states and the District of Columbia cast 47 percent of the votes at the Democratic convention and 46 percent at the Republican convention. In addition, Alabamans elected unpledged delegates to the Democratic convention. By 1980, the total of such states had jumped to thirty-five states and the District of Columbia. More than three out of every four delegates at the conventions came from them.[11] Furthermore, with the addition of Texas in 1976, there are primaries in all ten of the most populous states.

To speak blithely of presidential primaries, however, is an oversimplification. No two are identical. The major source of their variety lies in their two-part character: they can be devices for selecting delegates to the national conventions, and they can give voters a choice among contestants for the party's nomination. On the basis of how they combine or divide these two separate functions, the assorted presidential primaries fall into

[9]For a full account of the early steps in the Democratic reform of delegate-selection procedures, see Austin Ranney, *Curing the Mischiefs of Faction* (Berkeley: University of California Press, 1975). Many of the political implications of the reforms are explored in James I. Lengle and Byron Shafer, "Primary Rules, Political Power, and Social Change," *American Political Science Review* 70 (1976): 25–40.

[10]*Democratic Party of the United States v. La Follette*, 450 U.S. 107 (1981).

[11]The following fifteen states did *not* have presidential primaries in 1980: Alaska, Arizona, Colorado, Delaware, Hawaii, Iowa, Maine, Minnesota, Missouri, North Dakota, Oklahoma, Utah, Virginia, Washington, and Wyoming. Some states held primaries for only one party.

four categories: primaries in which only delegates are chosen, those in which the voters may show only a presidential preference, those that integrate the two features, and those that provide for separate delegate selection and presidential preference polls. (See Figure 11.1 for a sample ballot).

1. *Delegate selection only.* Only in New York, and only for the Republicans in that state, is the primary solely a vehicle to elect delegates to the national conventions. The ballot has only the names of the men and women who seek to be delegates. In practice, though, many of the would-be delegates have committed themselves informally to a presidential contender, and they circulate word of those commitments in the campaign. New York Democrats must choose their delegates in other ways, since this primary does not meet their national party's requirement that would-be delegates declare their presidential preferences or their status as unpledged or uncommitted delegates.

2. *Presidential preference only.* In states such as Indiana and North Carolina, the presidential primary is nothing more than a presidential preference poll. The voters are confronted by the names of their party's worthies who have entered the primary, and they merely indicate their preference regarding who should represent the party in the November presidential contest. State committees or conventions of the parties then pick the delegates to the respective national conventions. Those delegates, however, are usually required to support the candidacy of the winner of the state's presidential poll.

3. *The two elements combined.* A number of states—California, Ohio, and South Dakota among them—combine the presidential poll and the election of delegates by a simple device: the delegates pledge themselves to support specific candidates for the party's nomination. That pledge and the name of the national candidate are linked with the delegate's name on the ballot. In some states, every delegate's name on the ballot is associated with a presidential candidate; for example, a statement under each name might read, "Pledged to support John Smith for president." Other states provide that a full slate of delegate-candidates be listed on the ballot under the name of the presidential candidate to which the slate is pledged. On the California ballot, only the names of the presidential candidates appear; a vote for one of them automatically elects the slate of delegates pledged to that candidate.

4. *The two elements separated.* The remaining states—the largest number of them—and the District of Columbia include the two features of the primary but separate them. In these states, the ballot has a presidential preference poll in which the party's hopefuls compete for the favor of partisans within the state. In a separate section of the ballot, voters choose delegates to the conventions. Confusion and diversity of prac-

FIGURE 11.1 *Sample Ballot from the Republican Presidential Primary in New Jersey: 1980*

VOTE → HERE

The Polling Place for this Election District is—
Church of The Good Shepherd/Christ Chapel
497 Godwin Avenue
Polls Open 7 A.M. to 8 P.M. (D.S.T.)
FIRST ELECTION DISTRICT
Borough of Midland Park
SEVENTH CONGRESSIONAL DISTRICT
BERGEN COUNTY, N.J.   JUNE 3, 1980

PRIMARY ELECTION SAMPLE BALLOT
—INSTRUCTION TO VOTER—

FIRST OPERATION—Move Control (Lever or Switch) to Right which will Close Curtain and will Unlock Machine so you can vote.

SECOND OPERATION—Turn levers until ⊠ Mark appears at right of each Candidate's name for whom you intend to Vote and Leave ⊠ Mark Showing.

To Vote in Personal Choice Column, open the slide and write or paste in name.

NOTE—Leave Levers in voted position with CROSSES SHOWING. Then move Curtain Control (Lever or Switch) to Left which will record your vote.

CANDIDATE'S NAME

Carl R. Hartman County Clerk

		REPUBLICAN Column 1	REPUBLICAN Column 2	REPUBLICAN Column 3	REPUBLICAN Column 4	REPUBLICAN Column 5
PERSONAL CHOICE						
1	Member of the House of Representatives (VOTE FOR ONE)	Republicans for Responsible Government MARGE ROUKEMA				
2	Choice for President (VOTE FOR ONE)	RONALD REAGAN	GEORGE BUSH			HAROLD E. STASSEN
3	Delegates-At-Large To The National Convention (VOTE FOR SIX)	Regular Republicans for Reagan DAVID F. NORCROSS	George Bush for President RAYMOND BATEMAN	Moderate Republican Alternative JEFFREY M. ORBACH	Wiley for Congress Republican GLORIA B. KEMPF	Let's Fight Corruption Today JOSEPH T. DEVINE
4		Regular Republicans for Reagan RAYMOND J. DONOVAN	George Bush for President PETER H.B. FRELINGHUYSEN	Moderate Republican Alternative ANTHONY P. SCALCIONE	Wiley for Congress Republican FRANCIS J. COURT	Let's Fight Corruption Today DOROTHY L. DEVINE
5		Regular Republicans for Reagan MATTHEW J. RINALDO	George Bush for President ELEANOR S. TODD	Moderate Republican Alternative DAVID M. BROWN	Wiley for Congress Republican CAROLYN S. McCALLUM	
6		Regular Republicans for Reagan PHILIP MATALUCCI	George Bush for President EUGENE McCAFFREY	Moderate Republican Alternative ELIZABETH R. MACHOL	Wiley for Congress Republican ANDREW W. BANICK	
7		Regular Republicans for Reagan BENJAMIN H. DANSKIN	George Bush for President JANE BURGIO		Wiley for Congress Republican FREDERICK W. RICHARDS	
8		Regular Republicans for Reagan JOHN K. RAFFERTY	George Bush for President THOMAS J. SHUSTED		Wiley for Congress Republican RICHARD D. ILNICKI	
9	Alternate Delegates-At-Large To The National Convention (VOTE FOR SIX)	Regular Republicans for Reagan OLIVIA PANELLE	George Bush for President ROBERT A. WHITE	Moderate Republican Alternative MICHAEL L. PRIGOFF	Wiley for Congress Republican GREGORY A. BILSKY	
10		Regular Republicans for Reagan KATHRYN M. CHRISTIANSEN	George Bush for President BARBARA SMOYER	Moderate Republican Alternative LESLIE K. ROSS	Wiley for Congress Republican PATRICIA A. PLECHNER	
11		Regular Republicans for Reagan HAZEL GLUCK	George Bush for President NANCY SCHLUTER	Moderate Republican Alternative BROCK DAVID STOVALL	Wiley for Congress Republican RICHARD F. SCOTT	
12		Regular Republicans for Reagan EUGENE LISS	George Bush for President MARGARET HAGER	Moderate Republican Alternative MICHAEL MIELCHEN	Wiley for Congress Republican JOHN FREDERICKS	
13		Regular Republicans for Reagan MARIE MUHLER	George Bush for President RICHARD H. BAGGER	Moderate Republican Alternative DANIEL LICHTBLAU	Wiley for Congress Republican JOSEPH S. SUCHOWIECKI	
14		Regular Republicans for Reagan WILLIAM E. McCANN	George Bush for President HORACE PETERS	Moderate Republican Alternative ELIZABETH P. KOHN	Wiley for Congress Republican BARRY D. PEACOCK	
15	District Delegates At-Large (VOTE FOR ONE)	Republicans for Responsible Government JOHN F. INGANAMORT	George Bush for President HARRY RANDALL, Jr.	Moderate Republican Alternative ALICE D. HECHT		Republican Party Uncommitted CHARLES J. FREERICKS
16	Alternate District Delegates-At-Large (VOTE FOR ONE)	Republicans for Responsible Government CARL MARGGRAFF	George Bush for President MARGARET R. PATTERSON	Moderate Republican Alternative BRUCE BODNER		
17	District Delegates To The National Convention (VOTE FOR THREE)	Republicans for Responsible Government THOMAS H. BRUNIOOGE	George Bush for President RICHARD J. VANDER PLAAT	Moderate Republican Alternative RUTH PARSEKIAN		
18		Republicans for Responsible Government ROBERT N. GUIDO	George Bush for President HAROLD M. ZULLO	Moderate Republican Alternative ADAM P. BROWN		
19		Republicans for Responsible Government GARRETT W. HAGEDORN	George Bush for President WILLIAM T. SHEASBY	Moderate Republican Alternative STEVEN CLOTHIER		
20	Alternate District Delegates To The National Convention (VOTE FOR THREE)	Republicans for Responsible Government JOHN W. MARKERT	George Bush for President MICHAEL BUCHSBAUM	Moderate Republican Alternative TONI L. GOLDFARB		
21		Republicans for Responsible Government MICHAEL P. RINKO	George Bush for President GILBERT R. FREEMAN	Moderate Republican Alternative BARBARA J. STEVERT		
22		Republicans for Responsible Government CLAUDIA ROSS	George Bush for President CAROLE BLATCHFORD			
23	Members of the Board of Chosen Freeholders (VOTE FOR THREE)	Republicans for Responsible Government ARCHIE F. HAY				
24		Republicans for Responsible Government ROBERT P. PALLOTTA				
25		Republicans for Responsible Government JOHN E. ROONEY				
26	Members of the Council (VOTE FOR TWO)	Republicans for Responsible Government CLARENCE A. KNYFD				
27		Republicans for Responsible Government RONALD J. LE VINE				
28						
29						
30	County Committee (Male) (VOTE FOR ONE)	Republicans for Responsible Government CORNELIUS A. PONTIER				
31	County Committee (Female) (VOTE FOR ONE)	Republicans for Responsible Government ADELE W. MC KIM				

277

tice, however, surround the relationship between the two parts. In only some of the states do the results of the preferential polls bind the selected delegates. In the rest of the states, the polls are only advisory.

In outline, then, these are the presidential primaries, but there are still other differences among them. First, in some states, the convention delegates are elected from the state at large; in others, they are chosen from the individual congressional districts; and in still others, they are elected from both. Such a seemingly minor variation, however, can have major political consequences. The chances of a divided state delegation (and its attendant intraparty squabbles), for example, are much greater when delegates are chosen by congressional district. Nonetheless, the rules of the Democratic party that forbid statewide winner-take-all elections have fostered greater selection of delegates by district.

Second, some states elect in their primaries all the delegates the parties will send to the conventions, and some elect only some of them. In Pennsylvania, for example, a quarter of the delegates are chosen by the parties' state central committees. Such provisions have helped meet one of the parties' major objections to the presidential primary by permitting them to make sure that the important leaders of the state organizations go as delegates to the national convention.

Third, the states vary on the issue of whether a presidential hopeful must consent to being involved in the state's primary. Most states, but not all, require the candidate's approval (or permit his or her disapproval) before his or her name may be entered in a presidential preference poll or before delegates run as pledged to that candidate. In Oregon, the primary law entrusts to a state official the delicate decision of putting on the preference poll the names of *all* candidates "generally recognized in the national news media" to be candidates for the presidential nomination. A similar decision in Wisconsin is entrusted to an eleven-person committee made up largely of the leadership of the two major parties. The purpose clearly is to make it less possible for potential candidates to avoid some of the primaries and thus diminish competition and interest in them.

Fourth, the presidential primaries differ in the nature of the commitment of the pledged delegates. In some cases, the pledge of a delegate to support a certain candidate for the nomination is buttressed only by enthusiasm for the candidate, by a personal code of honor, or by a sense of the political value of integrity. In other states, delegates are required by law to take a pledge of loyalty to the candidate. Wisconsin, for instance, specifies by law the content of the pledge:

> I will, unless prevented by the death of the candidate, vote for his candidacy on the first ballot; and vote for his candidacy on any additional ballot, unless released by said candidate, until said candidate fails to receive at least one-third of the vote authorized to be cast; and that, there-

after, I shall have the right to cast my convention vote according to my own judgment.[12]

Finally, whereas thirty-three states and the District of Columbia have closed primaries, Wisconsin and Michigan hold open primaries. The possibility that voters who would normally support Democratic candidates at the general election will drift into the Republican presidential primary creates additional uncertainty and unpredictability for the candidates. There is no danger that Republicans will drift into the Democratic primary, because, in deference to national party rules, the Democrats no longer select their delegates in these open primaries.

Delegates Chosen by the Party Organizations

The presidential primaries are dramatic and are reported in the most intricate detail. Nonetheless, the parties of approximately a third of the states choose delegates by assorted internal party processes. Those processes are usually combinations of local caucuses followed by regional and statewide conventions. Generally, the regional conventions choose a fixed and equal number of delegates, and the state convention selects the remainder from the state at large. In a few states, some or all of the delegates are chosen by the state central committee of the party.[13]

For years, the selection of delegates in the nonprimary states was relatively invisible. The events of 1976, however, changed all that. A virtually unknown seeker after the Democratic nomination, Jimmy Carter, vaulted himself into serious candidacy by a strenuous campaign in Iowa that netted him both media attention and about 30 percent of the state's Democratic delegates. Within the Republican party in that year, Gerald Ford and Ronald Reagan emerged from the primaries almost deadlocked in the delegate count, and they consequently turned all of their considerable persuasive efforts toward the remaining state conventions and uncommitted delegates. As a result, the nonprimary states probably will never be invisible again, and party officials in them will find it harder to keep their delegations uncommitted. Also, since the Iowa selection process begins with caucuses in late February, it can fairly be said that the "great

---

[12]*Wisconsin Statutes*, Chap. 8.12. For a general study of the presidential primaries, see James W. Davis, *Presidential Primaries: Road to the White House* (New York: Crowell, 1967).

[13]The mechanics and politics of choosing convention delegates are discussed more fully by Gerald Pomper, *Nominating the President: The Politics of Convention Choice* (Evanston: Northwestern University Press, 1963), Chap. 3. On preconvention strategies, see Nelson W. Polsby and Aaron B. Wildavsky, *Presidential Elections*, 4th ed. (New York: Scribner's, 1976). For a study of the politics of electing convention delegates in a state convention, see Richard G. Niemi and M. Kent Jennings, "Intraparty Communications and the Selection of Delegates to a National Convention," *Western Political Quarterly* 22 (1969): 29–46.

delegate hunt" now begins there, rather than in the New Hampshire primary a week or two later.

THE POLITICS OF SELECTING DELEGATES

The politics of winning a presidential nomination obviously depends on enlisting the support of a majority of the delegates at the national convention. The strategies of the presidential aspirants differ, however, in how and when they make their move for delegate backing. As front-running candidates increasingly attempt to influence the selection and instruction of delegates—as they try to wrap up the nomination before the convention convenes—the significant part of the politics of nomination shifts to the preconvention phase. The intensive preconvention campaign for delegates begun by John F. Kennedy in 1960 accounts largely for the fact that every nomination in the 1960s and 1970s was won on the first ballot of the conventions of both parties.

Although candidates for their party's nomination increasingly feel the need to "sew up" the nomination before the convention meets, they still have a number of strategic choices in the preconvention campaigns for delegates. They have to decide whether or not to enter the fray, which states to contest, and what pace or timing to adopt for their campaigns. Their choices will depend on a number of factors, among them:

— *The presence or absence of a president.* When presidents are eligible for another term, they usually can arrange their own renomination. Even a weakened president such as Jimmy Carter in the late 1970s had little difficulty in brushing back the challenge of Edward Kennedy in 1980, and Ronald Reagan's failure to declare his intention by late 1983 kept a number of prospective challengers at bay.

— *The number of candidates and their strength.* A leading candidate has no alternative but to go all out in the preconvention campaign; if he does not, he risks an erosion of confidence among his supporters. A candidate with less support in a crowded field, on the other hand, may stay back and start more slowly, betting on the failures of some of the front-runners or deadlock among them.

— *The resources of the candidates.* Candidates can enter only those state delegate campaigns for which they have the necessary resources in personnel and money. Also, last-minute campaigns, such as Nelson Rockefeller's in 1968, can be undertaken only by candidates with the resources of a Rockefeller.

— *The electoral and party strength of the candidate.* Candidates obviously prefer not to enter races in the states in which they are weak; if they must, they will likely concede defeat and then minimize its impact by doing little campaigning in the state and telling the press that they will regard anything more than 20 percent of the vote as a "moral victory." More than voters, they need the support and work of some party activists in the states in which they expect to win. The heavy support for Hubert Humphrey of most Democratic party workers and officials was perhaps the greatest disadvantage Eugene McCarthy faced in his attempt to win the Democratic nomination in 1968.

— *The weaknesses of the candidate.* In 1960, John F. Kennedy entered the presidential primary in Protestant West Virginia to prove that his Catholicism would not prevent him from winning a presidential campaign. Any candidate may be forced to greater preconvention activity to counter a popular impression that he cannot campaign effectively and successfully.

All these decisions are made, of course, in the context of the rules set down by the two national parties and the various states. Thus, more resources will be needed, for example, to organize and contest a state primary that chooses delegates by congressional district than one that elects at large in the state. Moreover, these rules of the game differ from party to party. Since Democrats require a "fair reflection" of candidate strength in the selection of pledged delegates, no front-running candidate risks a total defeat in any state any more. In the California Republican primary, however, it is still possible for a candidate to get 45 percent of the votes in the nation's most populous state and still come away without a single delegate.[14]

Of all the strategic imperatives, none is stronger than the need to win early. The strategy of staying back in the pack and making a run in the final stretch is less and less feasible. Victories in the early primaries and caucuses get attention in the mass media and name recognition in the wider public. They create credibility for the campaign and make it easier to raise money; and, above all, they create that mysterious psychological advantage, momentum. Early victories, in short, bring the support and resources that increase the likelihood of later victories. Victors in the early stages thus become increasingly difficult to overtake, and so the pressure increases to spend much, work hard, and do well in the early stages of the delegate hunt. Front-runners must do so to keep the support of their voters and financial backers; other candidates must do so to keep the front-runners from opening insuperable leads. Thus, among the Republicans in 1980, what began as a field of seven leading contenders was narrowed to

[14]On all these strategic considerations, see John H. Aldrich, *Before the Convention* (Chicago: University of Chicago Press, 1980).

a field of three (Reagan, Bush, and Anderson) by the end of the second week of the presidential primaries with the withdrawals of Robert Dole, Howard Baker, John Connally, and Phillip Crane. On the Democratic side, Jimmy Carter built up an early delegate lead that Edward Kennedy was never able to overcome, despite the president's falling prestige.

These considerations of timing have not been lost on other participants in presidential politics. The states, not wanting the selection of their delegates to come in the less influential later stages of the process, have moved their caucuses and primaries forward to the early weeks of the campaign. They increasingly have bunched them in the weeks immediately following the New Hampshire primary; in fact, at least ten state primaries and caucuses now be held a week after the New Hampshire opener, on what is called "terrible Tuesday." In addition, large national groups have begun to endorse candidates before the caucus and presidential primary season even begins. In October of 1983, for example, the AFL-CIO threw its support behind Walter Mondale in the hope that its endorsement and the campaign help that accompanied it would help him secure the Democratic nomination for the presidency. If such endorsements become more common practice, we shall have opened a brave and new era of pre-preconvention politics.

The state party organizations and leaders also have interests at stake in the selection of delegates, and their interests often run counter to those of the aspiring presidential nominees. For the local and state parties, a hotly contested selection of delegates is often an occasion for intraparty conflict. In 1968, battles between Eugene McCarthy and Hubert Humphrey for Democratic delegates—both in primaries and in state conventions—created rifts in the party that have been slow to heal. George McGovern's fight for Democratic delegates in 1972 reopened many of these splits in the Democratic party. The McGovern candidacy—heavily supported by the young, female, minority, and very liberal segments of the party—won little favor among the staid and traditional leaders of many of the party organizations. Moreover, a state party organization (or one of its leaders) may want to pursue its own goals at the convention. It may want to preserve its bargaining power to affect the platform, to win a cabinet seat for a notable of the state party, to affect the vice-presidential choice, or just to enhance its value in the presidential nomination. Its interests may also be the parochial ones of a state party; a number of state Democratic parties, for example, were cool to Kennedy in 1960 for fear of losing the votes of Protestants in the state and thus hurting the party's ticket for statewide office.

Historically, the state parties protected their interests by selecting delegates uncommitted to any candidate. The bargaining power of such a delegation enhanced the power of the state party at the convention. The ability of the parties to engineer the selection of an uncommitted delegation fades with each year, however. As the nationally prominent candidates intensify the preconvention campaign, delegates pledged to them simply have greater appeal to the voters and party workers. Moreover, for delegates to remain uncommitted while one of the contenders for the nomination is locking up a majority of the convention votes is to squander all influence over the nomination and perhaps also some influence over the business of the convention. In a process dominated by the candidates, refusing to take sides carries considerable risk.

PRIMARY VERSUS PARTY SELECTION

Apart from the interests of parties and candidates, however, has it really made any difference whether delegates to the national conventions have been chosen by primaries or by party processes? Do the 75 percent of the delegates chosen by primary behave any differently than those chosen through party bodies? Do the presidential primaries have an impact on the nominations commensurate with the time and money spent in them?

Not too long ago in American politics, the processes of delegate selection were sharply bifurcated. In the states of the presidential primaries, a more open, popular, candidate-centered politics worked to the advantage of well-known personalities and generally helped insurgents in the party. In the other states, the party organization controlled delegate selection and could apply, with few exceptions, tests of party acceptability both to delegates and ultimately to the seekers after the party's nomination. Estes Kefauver in 1952 and 1956 and Eugene McCarthy in 1968 used the primaries to challenge the party apparatus for the nominations. They failed, as did all other challengers with little support outside the primary states. They failed if for no other reason than that there were not enough primaries; the delegates selected in the primaries were 40 percent or less of the total. Before the 1970s, the party nominees invariably fell into two categories: those, such as Hubert Humphrey, who mixed victories in primary and nonprimary states, and those, such as Wendell Willkie in 1940 and Adlai Stevenson in 1952, who entered no primaries and who won nomination in brokered conventions.

As the differences between the primary and nonprimary processes have diminished since the 1970s, however, the situation has changed. On the one hand, it is now necessary for a successful candidate to win many primary victories, and it is possible to succeed by winning only (or very largely) primary victories. That is so if for no other reason than that close to 80 percent of the convention delegates are now chosen in primaries. On the other hand, the comparison between primary and nonprimary selection is losing its importance simply because the politics of choosing delegates is now more similar in all states, primary and nonprimary alike.

TABLE 11.1   *The Carter and Reagan Preconvention Successes in Primary and Nonprimary States: 1980*

	Percentage of Delegates Elected in Primaries	Percentage of Delegates Chosen in Party Processes
Democratic delegates pledged to Jimmy Carter	62	72
Republican delegates pledged to Ronald Reagan	81	76

National candidates, media coverage, and more open and better publicized processes make for one long but continuous and homogeneous preconvention politics. As a result, the chief contenders for the party nominations tend to do about as well in the primary states as they do in the states that choose delegates by party processes (see Table 11.1). The pervasive shift to a more open, mass politics has also touched these presidential preliminaries.

To be more specific, comparisons of the two delegate selection processes reveal fewer differences than one might expect. The primaries do, indeed, involve four or five times more partisans. About 30 percent of voting-age adults vote in the primary states taken together, whereas caucus turnouts in nonprimary states rarely reach more than 8 or 9 percent. In both cases, however, the participants are drawn heavily from the strong partisans. That seems self-evident in the nonprimary states, but it is also true in the primary states. In 1980, for example, the data of the Center for Political Studies indicate that whereas adults who identify strongly either as Democrats or Republicans voted at a 53 percent rate in the presidential primaries, only 31 percent of other adults did. Furthermore, with the opening of selection processes in the nonprimary states, the participants in those states now have a range of options comparable to those in primary states, and the popular support of would-be candidates is as fairly represented as it is in the primary states.[15]

Still, the primaries maintain their special role and appeal. Their expansion continues to illustrate the way we view presidential nominating politics. Because of their openness to the voters, their results confer great

[15]These arguments are made effectively and at far greater length by Thomas R. Marshall, "Caucuses and Primaries: Measuring Reform in the Presidential Nomination Process," *American Politics Quarterly* 7 (1979): 155–74; see also his book, *Presidential Nominations in a Reform Age* (New York: Praeger, 1981). For an interesting study of the unrepresentativeness of primary electorates (and the consequences of it), see James I. Lengle, *Representation and Presidential Primaries* (Westport, Conn.: Greenwood, 1981).

legitimacy on the winners. Victories acquired in primaries may still be more important for these symbolic purposes than for the number of delegates acquired. The primaries also provide an opportunity for candidates to show their appeal and to build a following, and to show their stamina and adaptability under various pressures. Cruelly, too, they help weed out the nonviable candidates. As Lyndon Johnson discovered in 1968, disappointing results in the primaries may even help drive an incumbent president from office.

A SYSTEM IN NEED OF REFORM?

The briefs against both the presidential primaries and the party selection of delegates are long and weighty. In fact, they seem to outweigh the briefs in favor of each process to the extent that the observer might easily conclude that, once again in American politics, one must choose between the lesser of two evils.

The broader question of reform of the delegate-selection process inevitably begins with a hard look at the presidential primaries. The case against them is impressive:

1. They consume an enormous amount of time, energy, and money before the presidential campaign has even begun. Leading contenders for the nomination often run through a series of primary campaigns from February through June, arriving at the party convention personally and financially exhausted.

2. They put a tremendous premium on the well-known, familiar name—and thus often on the financial and other resources necessary to build that political familiarity. They also give an advantage to the candidates who have free time; members of Congress find it increasingly difficult to maintain a campaign schedule. Consequently, the existence of primaries makes it difficult for the party to consider less-known or reluctant candidates, or even those otherwise occupied.

3. Their importance may easily be distorted out of all perspective. In the mass of publicity surrounding the primaries, candidates and voters alike often fail to assess them soberly. The nation's first and most influential primary, in fact, is held in a state (New Hampshire) that has less than one-half of one percent of the nation's population.

4. Victory in the primaries is won by plurality vote and, if the competitors are numerous, often by a small plurality. George McGovern won the Democratic primary in Wisconsin in 1972 with only 30 percent of the vote.

5. The presidential primaries frequently result in internal divisions in state party organizations, in warring delegations to the national con-

ventions, and in delegates not representative of the party organization and leadership in the state. Like any other primary, they take an important party process out of the control of the party organizations and thus weaken them.

The presidential primary is, indeed, an institution that only the voters love.

On the other hand, the charges against party selection of a state's delegates rest on the traditional complaint about party processes—that they are too easily controlled and manipulated by a handful of party oligarchs. In any event, that has been the charge of the reformers in the Democratic party since 1968. Furthermore, in the nonprimary states, the party electorates and even some of the party activists are excluded from the crucial first step in picking a president. Also, it is undoubtedly true that, in these states, the would-be presidential nominees have had to fight for the access and visibility they enjoy in the presidential primaries. A number of state parties would still prefer to send uncommitted delegations to their national conventions.

Debating points aside, however, we seem to be in the middle of a great revival of interest in the primaries. After a period of disenchantment, the states are returning to them with the enthusiasm they had fifty years ago.[16] Increasing media coverage has spotlighted the role of the primaries in the nomination process; and their basic rationale—the twin democratic norms of mass popular participation and fear of party oligarchies—seems more powerful than ever. Most important, the states *think* the primaries are becoming more important. Clearly, some states are venturing into the primaries for the first time to increase their own political leverage. (In the case of some of the new southern primaries, at least some state legislators see them enhancing the power of the South in national presidential politics by forcing all candidates to be tested—and possibly tarnished—in those states.) No reform movement can ignore, therefore, the presently secure place of the primaries.

If we cannot live without the primaries, is it possible that we might learn to live more comfortably with them? The most drastic reform proposal of recent years was to do away with the national nominating conventions altogether and to choose the presidential nominees in a single national primary. A consideration of that proposal will follow an assessment of the conventions in the next chapter. If one assumes the survival of the nominating conventions, however, is no change possible in the way we select delegates to them? Probably the most realistic proposal has been to group primaries by four regions, with a few weeks separating the four

---

[16]On the early development of the presidential primaries, see Louise Overacker, *The Presidential Primary* (New York: Macmillan, 1926). In 1916, at least twenty-three states had some sort of presidential primary.

election days. (Most proposals also make some arrangement for rotating the dates of the regional elections so that no region finds itself permanently last.) Bills embodying those proposals have had little success in the Congress. A few states, however, have begun to work with their neighbors for primaries on the same day; the problem with such ad hoc groupings is that all of them want a date that is earlier rather than later in the primary season. The necessary elements of spacing and rotation can probably be achieved only by national legislation.[17]

Even at these early stages of presidential politics, one sees the beginning of the repetition of an old theme in American politics. It is difficult for the party organizations to control the presidential nomination, just as it is difficult for them to control other party nominations. In part, the presidential primary weakens organizational control and shifts it to the candidates. In part, too, the organizations are weak because they have no means of uniting or coordinating their own preferences prior to the nominating conventions. Thus, candidates with comparatively rational and unified national strategies increasingly find it easy to take the initiative from individual state party organizations in this phase of presidential politics. To the extent that they are able to win the commitments of enough delegates to capture the nominations, they and the party in government capture the nomination before the party organizations ever gather themselves together to act as a national party at the convention.

---

[17]In general, the best accounts of recent preconvention politics (and of the conventions and campaigns as well) are those of Theodore H. White in his four volumes on the 1960, 1964, 1968, and 1972 elections. See *The Making of the President* for those years, all of them published in New York by Atheneum in the first years after the elections. The events of the 1976 election are also recounted in Jules Witcover, *Marathon* (New York: Viking, 1977). The 1980 story is told by Jack W. Germond and Jules Witcover in *Blue Smoke and Mirrors: How Reagan Won and Why Carter Lost the Election of 1980* (New York: Viking, 1981).

12

PRESIDENTIAL POLITICS:
THE CRUCIAL DECISIONS

That cynical observer of American politics, H. L. Mencken, especially loved the challenge of reporting a national nominating convention. After ruminating on the Democratic convention of 1924 and the 103 ballots it took to nominate John W. Davis, the Sage of Baltimore wrote:

> There is something about a national convention that makes it as fascinating as a revival or a hanging. It is vulgar, it is ugly, it is stupid, it is tedious, it is hard upon both the higher cerebral centers and the *gluteus maximus*, and yet it is somehow charming. One sits through long sessions wishing heartily that all the delegates and alternates were dead and in hell—and then suddenly there comes a show so gaudy and hilarious, so melodramatic and obscene, so unimaginably exhilarating and preposterous that one lives a gorgeous year in an hour.[1]

Former President Dwight D. Eisenhower felt the irritation without experiencing the exhilaration. The conventions, he said, were "a picture of confusion, noise, impossible deportment, and indifference to what is being discussed on the platform." He dismissed the banner-waving demonstrations that typify the carnival gaiety of the conventions as "spurious demonstration[s] of unwarranted enthusiasm."[2]

Indeed, scarcely a convention goes by without evoking a number of tongue-clucking appraisals. Calls for convention reform come as regularly as the conventions themselves. Yet the national conventions persist—the chief holdout against the domination of American nominations by the direct primary. How is it that so maligned an institution has so successfully resisted the pressures of change? Has it become an indispensable political

---

[1]Malcolm Moos (ed.), *H. L. Mencken on Politics* (New York: Vintage, 1960), p. 83.
[2]*The New York Times*, June 29, 1965.

institution? Even while offending the canons of taste and decorum, has it really managed to function effectively as a recruiter of presidents?

THE STRUCTURE OF THE CONVENTION

The conventions are the creatures of the parties themselves. They are subject to no congressional or state regulation, and even the federal courts have been reluctant to intervene in their operation. Responsibility for them falls to the national party committees and their staffs, although an incumbent president inevitably influences the planning for his party's convention.

Planning for the quadrennial conventions begins several years before the event. The first harbinger of that work comes with the selection of the host city. That choice reflects a vast number of considerations, from the size of the financial package the bidding cities offer to such usual convention matters as available hotel space. Political considerations enter, too. For 1976, the Democrats selected New York as their site, partly as an affirmation of the American city; and the Republicans chose Detroit for 1980 at least partly to broaden their support among urban and minority voters.

Months before the convention, its major committees emerge. Like all other major American institutions, both political and nonpolitical, the conventions function, in part, through committees. Generally, there have been four important ones:

Credentials. The credentials committee accepts the credentials of delegates and alternates and makes up the official delegate list of the convention. Its prickliest duty is deciding contests (between two delegates or slates vying for the same seats) and challenges (of the qualifications of any delegate or alternate, or, indeed, of any delegation).

Permanent organization. This committee selects the permanent officials of the convention—the permanent chairperson, secretary, and sergeant at arms, for example. Generally, its work provokes little controversy.

Rules. This committee sets the rules of the convention, particularly the specific procedures for selecting the presidential nominee. The main procedures have been fixed for some time, but the committee struggles at every convention with rules such as those governing the length and number of nomination speeches, the number of nondelegate demonstrators that will be permitted on the convention floor, and the method of polling delegations should controversy arise within them.

Platform (or Resolutions). This committee's chief responsibility is to draft the party's platform for action by the convention. It holds open hearings to receive the ideas of citizens, party activists, and the potential presidential nominees.

Early appointment of these committees is necessary if only because they begin to function before the convention convenes. Platform committees, especially, begin to scour the party and the nation for ideas several months before the convention opens.

The first three of these committees—credentials, permanent organization, and rules—make decisions that define the structure and procedures of the convention. They often have enormous impact on the important decisions the convention makes on the nominees or the platform. In the 1976 Republican convention, the Reagan forces proposed a rule change to force presidential contenders to announce their vice-presidential choices *before* the selection of a presidential nominee. Ronald Reagan had already announced his running mate (Senator Richard Schweiker of Pennsylvania), and the move was clearly designed to embarrass and weaken the candidacy of Gerald Ford. The proposal was narrowly defeated, and the nomination roll call that gave the nomination to Ford was anticlimactic. In 1980, the supporters of Senator Edward Kennedy sought to repeal the rule forcing delegates to support the candidate to whom they were pledged in hopes of picking up some wavering Carter delegates at the convention. The Carter forces beat back the challenge, and the president won renomination on the first ballot. It is precisely because procedural battles such as these so affect the distribution of power at the conventions that state parties, the candidates, and the ideological camps within the parties work so hard to win representation on the committees.

In recent years, the decisions of the credentials committees have had the greatest repercussions. The 1952 contest for the Republican nomination between Senator Robert Taft and General Dwight Eisenhower hinged in great part on the battle over delegates from Georgia, Louisiana, and Texas. The credentials committee voted to seat the pro-Taft delegates from the three states; but, in scenes of recrimination, the convention as a whole seated the pro-Eisenhower claimants. If Senator Taft had had the votes of those contested delegates, he would have led Eisenhower on the convention's first ballot. In 1972, George McGovern's quest for the Democratic nomination was aided by the convention's decisions to seat the California delegates loyal to him and not to seat the Illinois delegation loyal to Mayor Daley and the local party. In fact, in that convention, more than a dozen credential disputes received full floor debate. It was something of a modern record.

A somewhat different problem in credentials plagued the Democratic conventions after World War II: the unwillingness of some southern state delegations to take the delegate loyalty oath, a pledge to support the candidates and platform of the convention. In 1948, delegates from Mississippi and Alabama marched out of an evening session of the convention after northern liberals nailed a strong civil rights plank onto the platform. Many of those delegates and their state parties later supported the Dixiecrat party ticket or, worse, put the Dixiecrat slate on their state presidential ballot as the ticket of the Democratic party. The loyalty issue in the Democratic party was supplemented in the 1960s by charges that delegate-selection processes in some southern states were not fully open to blacks. In 1968 and 1972, the regular Mississippi delegation (and half of the Georgia regulars in 1968) were replaced by challengers loyal to the national ticket. The two Mississippi parties negotiated a merger in 1975, however, and a single, integrated, loyal delegation has represented Mississippi since then.[3]

Finally, to complete the organization of the convention, the national committee selects the temporary chairperson, who usually delivers the extravagantly partisan keynote address. His or her qualifications are only two—an aloofness from the major contestants for the nomination and a telegenic oratorical style—but the candidates are many. They may remember that Alben Barkley's oratorical flights in praise of the Democratic party won him the vice-presidential nomination in 1948.[4] Even at lower levels of ambition, however, the assignment is an ideal showcase, one that does no politician's political future any harm.

The description of the formal structure of the convention fails to convey anything of its ambience, however. Born of a rough-and-tumble political tradition and related to the institution of the boisterous convention in other areas of American life, the national party conventions have been part carnival, part "fling at the big city," and part (a large part, actually) serious party conclave. At one and the same time, they mix well-rehearsed demonstrations of enthusiasm with serious thought about presidential stature, the military precision of floor managers with the aimless amblings of ordinary delegates, perfunctory afternoon oratorical fillers with the often eloquent messages of the party worthies. If television has now made them somewhat more sedate, they can still offer moments of raw political excitement unmatched in the rest of American politics.

THE DELEGATES

The combination of large numbers of delegates and equally large numbers of alternate delegates produces gargantuan conventions. There will be

[3]On the issue of the loyalty oath, see Abraham Holtzman, "Party Responsibility and Loyalty: New Rules in the Democratic Party," *Journal of Politics* 22 (1960): 485–501.

[4]For a contrary case, they may remember that General of the Army Douglas MacArthur disappointed his supporters by failing to light any fires with his keynote speech before the Republicans in 1952.

3,850 delegates to the Democratic convention in 1984, and to that total must be added several thousand alternates. The Republicans will have approximately 2,000 delegates. The national committees are under tremendous pressure from the state party organizations to increase the number of delegates. Party people in the states cherish the prestige of attending a convention, and the experience of being a delegate is also likely to stimulate them to work in the campaign that follows. Large convention size is also increasingly the price of representing the large, populous states in some reasonable ratio to the representation of the small ones. Finally, big conventions create a mass rally atmosphere for television coverage. Especially when the convention is certain to renominate an incumbent president—as the Democrats did in 1964 and the Republicans did in 1972—the rally aspects of the convention replace its nominating duties.

The delegates to the Democratic and Republican conventions have never been a cross section of American citizens. Whites, males, the well-educated, and upper income groups have been overrepresented to some degree. There have also been differences between the two parties. Democratic delegations have had more Catholics, Jews, and trade unionists, the Republicans more Protestants and businessmen. Recently, however, both parties have attempted to broaden the representativeness of their delegations, with the Democrats making by far the greater change since 1972. The waning of some of those pressures is apparent in the 1980 data on delegates (see Table 12.1); inevitably, too, the concerns over representation shift from decade to decade. In 1982, the Democratic National Committee urged its state party organizations to recruit more delegates and other party participants of "low and moderate income." (The median income of delegates to the Democratic and Republican conventions in 1980 was $37,000 and $47,000, respectively.)[5]

Ideologically, the delegates are more committed, more aware of issues and issue positions, than the ordinary voters of their party. They also tend more to the ideological poles than do the electorates of their parties. In 1980, for example, 46 percent of the Democratic delegates considered

[5]On convention delegates, see Jeane Kirkpatrick, *The New Presidential Elite* (New York: Russell Sage Foundation and Twentieth Century Fund, 1976). Kirkpatrick's book is the most ample and most sophisticated study in the scholarly literature of any set of convention delegates, and it is also one of the best studies of women activists in party politics. For other studies of the 1972 and 1976 delegates, see John W. Soule and Wilma E. McGrath, "A Comparative Study of Presidential Nomination Conventions: The Democrats of 1968 and 1972," *American Journal of Political Science* 19 (1975): 501–17; Joseph H. Boyett, "Background Characteristics of Delegates to the 1972 Conventions: A Summary Report of Findings from a National Sample," *Western Political Quarterly* 27 (1974): 469–78; Thomas H. Roback, "Amateurs and Professionals: Delegates to the 1972 Republican National Convention," *Journal of Politics* 37 (1975): 436–67; and John S. Jackson III, Jesse C. Brown, and Barbara L. Brown, "Recruitment, Representation, and Political Values: The 1976 Democratic National Convention Delegates," *American Politics Quarterly* 6 (1978):187–212.

TABLE 12.1   *Percentage of Blacks, Women, and Young People Serving as Delegates to Democratic and Republican Conventions: 1968–80*

Year	Blacks		Women		Under 30	
	Dem.	Repub.	Dem.	Repub.	Dem.	Repub.
1968	7%	2%	13%	17%	4%	1%
1972	15	3	40	35	22	7
1976	11	3	33	31	15	7
1980	15	3	49	29	11	5

Source   Adapted from Table 2.2 of Thomas R. Marshall, *Presidential Nominations in a Reform Age* (New York: Praeger, 1981), p. 46.

themselves liberals, but only 21 percent of all Democrats did. (The other options were moderate and conservative.) Some 58 percent of Republican delegates allied themselves with conservatism, as against 41 percent among Republicans in the entire nation.[6] That same ideological commitment is also apparent in the willingness of recent conventions to break with the tradition of pragmatic compromise and to choose frankly ideological candidates such as Barry Goldwater, George McGovern, and Ronald Reagan. The ideological gap between convention delegates and the party's voters results both from the differences between activist and nonactivist and from the way in which the apportionment of delegates at the conventions overrepresents the areas of the party's weakness across the country and thus overrepresents some of the party's electors. Ironically, as Jeane Kirkpatrick has concluded, reforming the party conventions has not made them more representative of the views and values of the parties in the electorate. To the contrary, the "reformed" Democratic delegates of 1972 were less representative than the "unreformed" Democratic delegates of 1968 or the Republicans of 1972.[7]

Actually, the differences among the delegates of a single convention may be as significant as the differences between any two party conventions. A number of observers noted the much larger number of clergymen and academics among the McCarthy-Kennedy-McGovern delegates than

[6]Data from a poll conducted by the *New York Times* and CBS News, reported in the *New York Times*, August 13, 1980. See also John S. Jackson III, Barbara L. Brown, and David Bositis, "Herbert McClosky and Friends Revisited: 1980 Democratic and Republican Elites Compared to the Mass Public," *American Politics Quarterly* 10 (1982): 158–80.

[7]Kirkpatrick, *The New Presidential Elite*, Chap. 10. See also James I. Lengle, *Representation and Presidential Primaries* (Westport, Conn.: Greenwood, 1981).

among the delegates as a whole in the 1968 Democratic convention.[8] The McCarthy delegates also tended in their style and approach to politics to be "amateurs," similar to those taking over some of the urban organizations; the Humphrey delegates were more likely to be "professionals." In other words, the McCarthy delegates were more attracted by programs and issues, more insistent on intraparty democracy, less willing to compromise, and less committed to the prime importance of winning elections. Similar differences carried over to the Humphrey and McGovern delegates in 1972. Delegates pledged to Ronald Reagan in 1976 and 1980 were more often motivated by ideology than were the other delegates to those conventions. Thus, the delegates differ not only in their candidate preference but also in their political styles, their reasons for being active, and their political values and outlooks.[9]

As interesting and important as the individual delegates are, the most significant unit of the conventions, historically, has been the state delegation. Delegates room together at the same hotel and share their experiences with each other; they also often share the same goals and outlooks. They caucus periodically, and they are often bound together by loyalty to the same candidate or party leaders. They share loyalty to the same state party. The only challenge to the supremacy of the state delegation as the basic grouping of delegates comes from the new caucuses of blacks, women, Latins, senior citizens, and farmers, among others. They are more common and better organized in the Democratic conventions, but in neither party's convention have they yet become major factors in the important convention decisions. Candidate groupings and state delegations remain the chief building blocks for convention coalitions.

THE BUSINESS OF THE CONVENTION

The convention begins in low key, with stiff formalities and the business of organization. It warms up with the keynote address, tries to maintain momentum and expectation through consideration of the platform, and

---

[8]Theodore H. White, *The Making of the President 1968* (New York: Atheneum, 1969), p. 272. The White volumes, beginning with the 1960 election, are the major chronicles of recent presidential politics. For an earlier period, similar data are available in Paul T. David, Ralph M. Goldman, and Richard C. Bain, *The Politics of National Party Conventions* (Washington, D.C.: Brookings, 1960).

[9]John W. Soule and James W. Clarke, "Amateurs and Professionals: A Study of Delegates to the 1968 Democratic National Convention," *American Political Science Review* 64 (1970): 888–98. For a report on "purists" and "professionals" in 1972, see Dennis G. Sullivan, Jeffrey L. Pressman, Benjamin I. Page, and John J. Lyons, *The Politics of Representation: The Democratic Convention 1972* (New York: St. Martin's, 1974). See also Kirkpatrick, *The New Presidential Elite*, and Thomas H. Roback, "Motivations for Activism Among Republican National Convention Delegates," *Journal of Politics* 42 (1980): 181–201.

reaches a dramatic peak in the nomination of the presidential and vice-presidential candidates. This general format remains basically the same convention after convention. Television coverage has necessitated some rearrangement into a more compact convention, with the events of major interest reserved for prime evening transmission time, but the tempo of the convention is still governed by the pace of business, and not by any dramatic considerations.

Aside from the rites of nomination, the approval of the platform is the convention's chief business. The platform committees begin hearings long before the convention opens, so that the platform will be in draft form for convention hearings. Those hearings before and during the early phases of the convention are often spiced by the appearance of leading contenders for the nomination. The finished platform is then presented to the convention for its approval. That approval is not always pro forma; the platform has occasioned some of the most spirited recent convention battles. In 1968, the forces supporting Hubert H. Humphrey engaged the McCarthy delegates in a virtually unprecedented three-hour floor debate over what the platform would say about the war in Vietnam. The Democrats' discussion of the 1972 platform touched on subjects new to platform discourse (e.g., abortion and gay rights) and set a record for the longest discussion of a platform in American convention history.

Few aspects of American politics so openly invite skepticism, even cynicism, as do the party platforms. They are long and prolix; they often run to ten or fifteen times the length of the Declaration of Independence. Furthermore, they are not often read; the congressional party generally ignores them, and even presidential standard-bearers reserve the right to disagree with them. Basically, the problem is that platforms are the instruments of ideology, and the two major American parties really have no total political philosophy that unites their followers. The American party platform, rather than being a statement of the party, is much more likely to be a string of pragmatic stands on quite separate issues, one not necessarily related to another.

Rather than a statement of continuing party philosophy, the platform is really a manifesto of the majority that happens to control the convention in that year. Thus, the conservative wing of the Republican party that supported Ronald Reagan in the Republican convention of 1980 was strong enough to drop the party's historic commitment to the Equal Rights Amendment from the 1980 platform. Since the party's presidential nominee generally controls the convention, the platform ordinarily has also been a reflection of his views. When it has not been, nominees have either changed the platform or have gone their own way. In 1960, Richard Nixon, clearly about to receive the Republican nomination, bowed to the criticisms of the draft platform by the party moderates, rushed to New York to confer with their spokesman, Governor Nelson Rockefeller, and then hurried back to Chicago to force revisions on an unhappy committee. In 1980, a Democratic convention somewhat unenthusiastic about the man it was about to nominate forced the contenders for the nomination to state in writing any objections they had to the platform. President Carter noted reservations about clauses on the public funding of abortions and about the denial of party support to candidates not supporting the ERA. Some feminist delegates were unhappy, but the event did not seriously threaten his renomination.

Part of the cynicism about the platforms grows from the impression that they are exercises in semantic virtuosity. The words and phrases used are sometimes intended to obfuscate rather than clarify, for phrases that mean all things to all people achieve compromises of a sort. Vague or artful as the platforms may be, however, they do take stands on some issues, and they are not identical. In recent years, they have differed over social security, labor-management relations, farm price supports, medicare, racial integration, and war and peace in Vietnam. Above all, the platforms are campaign documents in which the parties pick their issues and positions selectively to promote the assembling of a majority coalition. The party platform is important, its leading scholar says,

> but not as an inspired gospel to which politicians resort for policy guidance. It is important because it summarizes, crystallizes, and presents to the voters the character of the party coalition. Platform pledges are not simply good ideas, or even original ones. In their programs, Democrats and Republicans are not typically breaking new paths; they are promising to proceed along one or another path which has already become involved in political controversy. The stands taken in the platform clarify the parties' positions on these controversies and reveal the nature of their support and appeals.[10]

Finally, the platforms are what they are largely because they are drafted and approved in conventions mainly concerned with picking a presidential candidate. Every convention vote tends to become a test of the strength of the various candidates, and votes on the platform are no exception.[11]

FINDING A PRESIDENTIAL CANDIDATE

The pièce de résistance of the convention—the selection of a presidential candidate—begins as the secretary intones the litany of the states: Ala-

---

[10]Gerald Pomper, *Elections in America* (New York: Dodd, Mead, 1968), p. 201.

[11]All the party platforms are available in one volume: Donald B. Johnson, *National Party Platforms, 1840–1976* (Urbana: University of Illinois Press, 1978). For a broad discussion of platform making, see Paul T. David, "Party Platforms as National Plans," *Public Administration Review* 31 (1971): 303–15.

bama, Alaska, Arkansas. . . . As each state is called, the head of the state's delegation responds in one of three ways: by placing the name of a candidate before the convention, by yielding the state's position in the roll call to another state to make a nomination, or by passing. As the secretary progresses through the states, the contenders for the nomination are entered, each one by a formal speech of nomination and shorter seconding speeches.

It is at this point that, traditionally, the conventions reached back to a nineteenth-century political style. The speeches of nomination rolled out in great Victorian periods, often seeming to be parodies; seconding speeches, carefully chosen to provide a cross section of the party, were frequently vest-pocket versions of the main speech. After each set of nomination speeches, the supporters of the nominee, usually augmented by young, tireless nondelegates, snaked their way through the crowded aisles of the hall, singing, chanting, and waving banners and signs for almost an hour.

The first modifications of those hoary traditions began with the advent of television, for the endless hijinks often pushed the most dramatic portions of the convention out of prime evening time. What had seemed colorfully old-fashioned in the hall looked grotesque or vulgar on the TV screen. The Democrats, spurred again by the reform impulses springing from their 1968 convention, made further inroads in 1972. They banned all floor demonstrations, shortened nomination speeches drastically, and made the nomination of favorite-son candidates—noncontenders with support in only one delegation—vastly more difficult.

Once all the names have been presented to the convention, the task of settling on a single presidential nominee begins in earnest. The secretary of the convention starts again through the states (and the District of Columbia, the territories, and the dependencies), asking each delegation to report its vote. If no candidate wins the necessary majority of votes, the convention presses on to a second ballot. A number of nominations have been settled on the first ballot, but in 1924 the Democrats plodded through 103 ballots in sultry New York's Madison Square Garden before nominating John W. Davis. (That record number of ballots resulted, at least in part, from the Democratic rule, abandoned in 1936, that required that the nominee be supported by two-thirds of the delegates.) Since 1952, no nomination contest in either party has consumed more than one ballot (Table 12.2). Furthermore, since 1948, the conventions have averaged only two candidates who polled more than 10 percent of the convention votes on any ballot (Table 12.2).

The casting of the votes takes place in a context of some of the most compressed political activity in all of American politics. Even before the opening of the convention, representatives of the various contenders have stalked uncommitted or wavering delegates across the country by mail,

TABLE 12.2   *Number of Ballots Required to Nominate and Number of Candidates Polling 10 Percent of Votes in Democratic and Republican Conventions: 1948–80*

	Democratic Conventions		Republican Conventions	
Year	Candidates Polling over 10 %	Number of Ballots	Candidates Polling over 10 %	Number of Ballots
1948	2	1	3	3
1952	4	3	2	1
1956	2	1	1	1
1960	2	1	1	1
1964	1	1	2	1
1968	2	1	3	1
1972	2	1	1	1
1976	2	1	2	1
1980	2	1	2	1

Source   Data from *Congress and the Nation* (Washington, D.C.: Congressional Quarterly, 1965), and from newspaper accounts of conventions from 1968 to 1980.

phone, and personal visit. Once the convention opens, the process is stepped up. Of the 1960 Kennedy organization, Theodore H. White has written:

> In all, some forty delegate-shepherds were assigned each to a particular state delegation that was theirs to cultivate; each was given packets of name cards listing the assigned state delegates by name, profession, hobby, children, wife, peculiarity, religion, and sent out to operate. They were instructed, as they found shifts in any delegation, to report such changes to a private tabulating headquarters in Room 3308 at the Biltmore; and there, every hour on the hour from Friday through balloting day, a new fresh total, accurate to the hour, was to be prepared. For five days, the shepherds were told, they were not to sleep, see their wives, relax, frolic or be out of touch with 8315. Each morning, for the five Convention days from Saturday to the Wednesday balloting, they were to gather in Room 8315 for a staff survey at nine A.M., then disperse to their tasks.[12]

Such organizational thoroughness has rarely been seen at conventions before or since, but front-runners generally know they must win quickly. The only strategy the other candidates can employ is to join in a coalition

[12]White, *The Making of the President 1960* (New York: Atheneum, 1961), p. 157.

to prevent a first-ballot victory. That imperative can join—however temporarily—men of such divergent views as Nelson Rockefeller and Ronald Reagan, who tried unsuccessfully in 1968 to prevent the first-ballot nomination of Richard Nixon.

If the convention has passed through an inconclusive ballot—and not one has done so in thirty years—negotiations renew with even greater intensity. The leading candidates must take care to prevent a chipping away of their supporters—a genuine danger if they fail to increase their votes on a second or third ballot. New support comes most easily from minor candidates or uncommitted delegates, since delegates bound to candidates are too loyal to those commitments to be lured away.[13] A favorite-son candidate faces the delicate decision of whether to cast his lot with a front-runner or to hold tightly and maintain (either alone or in concert) a defensive action.[14]

Following the naming of the presidential nominee, the secretary begins the roll call ritual again—usually on the next day—to select a vice-presidential nominee. Conventions uniformly ratify the choice of the presidential candidate. Rebellions flash occasionally but always fail; in the Democratic meetings of 1944, for instance, the supporters of Vice-President Henry Wallace tried futilely to resist the decision of President Roosevelt to replace him with Harry S. Truman. Once in recent years, the presidential candidate did not indicate his preference. Adlai Stevenson convulsed the 1956 Democratic convention by opening the vice-presidential choice to the convention; Senator Estes Kefauver was selected on the second ballot.

The method of selecting vice-presidential candidates has recently elicited a crescendo of criticism. It is not so much that they are hand-picked by the presidential candidate but that the decision is made by a tired candidate and tired advisors in so short a span of time. Yet, of the six different men who were presidential candidates from 1960 through 1972, three had been chosen as vice-presidents in the hurly-burly of an earlier convention. Moreover, the withdrawal of the initial Democratic vice-presidential nominee in 1972 (Thomas Eagleton) and the eventual resignation of Vice-President Spiro Agnew in the following year gave the unease about vice-presidential selection a new impetus. Little has changed, however. Ronald Reagan did pick a vice-presidential running mate before the 1976 Republican convention, but the decision was motivated, most observers agree, by the politics of nomination rather than by any desire to reform the process of picking vice-presidents. In 1980, Reagan picked his running mate in the usual way and at the usual time.

---

[13]David, Goldman, and Bain, *The Politics of National Party Conventions*, p. 379.

[14]On the strategies of presidential politics generally, see Nelson W. Polsby and Aaron B. Wildavsky, *Presidential Elections*, 4th ed. (New York: Scribner's, 1976).

THE "AVAILABILITY" OF PRESIDENTIAL NOMINEES

There is a bland and misleading term in American politics that describes the personal, social, and political characteristics the parties seek in their presidential nominees. If an individual possesses the right attributes, he is said to be *available*. Contrary to its popular use, the word in this idiomatic sense has nothing to do with the candidate's willingness to be a candidate; one can assume, in that sense, that every native-born American adult is available for the presidency.

The concept of availability sums up the qualities the parties believe make a politically appealing and acceptable candidate. In part, the canons of availability reflect the distribution of political power in presidential politics. It is said, for instance, that the presidential candidate must come from a large state—that is, from a state with a large electoral vote that he can be presumed to carry. From 1896 to the present, only five of the twenty-six men originally nominated for the presidency by a convention came from the smaller states. Nineteen came from eight large states: seven from New York, four from Ohio, three from California, and one each from Illinois, Michigan, Texas, Massachusetts, and New Jersey. One came from Minnesota and one from Georgia, states that would appear to be "in between." None of the five from the smaller states—Landon of Kansas, Davis of West Virginia, Bryan of Nebraska, Goldwater of Arizona, and McGovern of South Dakota—won the presidency.[15]

In part, too, the concept of availability is a codification of widely held expectations in the American electorate of what a president should be. It is an aggregate of the characteristics the parties think the American electorate would vote for in a presidential candidate. Some years ago, it was commonly said that for a person to be considered seriously for the office, he had to be a personal success in business or public life; happily married and blessed with an attractive family; a reasonably observant Protestant; a white male in his late forties or fifties; of Anglo-Saxon or north-north-western European ethnic background; and the product of small city or rural life.

Although there is considerable validity in such a list as a description of past presidential nominees, projecting such requirements into the future would be dangerous. The lore of acceptability shifts with changes in social attitudes. Adlai Stevenson, a divorced man, was nominated in 1952 and 1956; an urban and Catholic candidate, John F. Kennedy, was nominated in 1960. Those nominations probably indicate, at least in part, the declining social stigma attached to divorce, the life of the big city, and Ca-

---

[15]If one uses the 1980 electoral vote as a measure, none of the seven large states referred to here had an electoral vote smaller than fourteen, and none of the small states had one greater than seven. Minnesota had ten, and Georgia had twelve.

tholicism in contemporary America. In coming decades, changing attitudes about women and blacks in public life will probably also strike the white male qualification from the formula of availability.

Related to the issue of availability, but somewhat different, is the question of career pattern. Although not all presidential candidates have had prior governmental or officeholding experience, most have. Thus, the question arises of what positions provide the better jumping-off points and training for the presidency. What public positions grace a man with an aura of governmental success and competence and yet give him a good base for building party and public support? From 1900 through 1956, nineteen different men ran for the presidency on the Democratic and Republican tickets; eleven of them had been governors (McKinley, Theodore Roosevelt, Wilson, Hughes, Cox, Coolidge, Smith, Franklin Roosevelt, Landon, Dewey, and Stevenson). Only two, the luckless Harding and Harry Truman, had been senators. It had come to be a commonplace in American politics that the Senate was the graveyard of presidential ambitions. Senators, it was said, were forced to cast too many politically sensitive votes and risk too many political enemies. They also were thought to lack the opportunities for national popularity and image.

In 1960, 1964, 1968, and 1972, however, all eight nominees had been senators and none had been a governor. In the presidential politics of 1972 and after, in fact, even a majority of the unsuccessful seekers for presidential nominations were senators or former senators—Birch Bayh, Henry Jackson, Edward Kennedy, Edmund Muskie, Howard Baker, and Robert Dole. In 1976, Representative Morris Udall mounted the first challenge from the House of Representatives in a long time, and President Gerald Ford had been a leader in the House for years before his appointment to the vice-presidency. Representatives John Anderson and Philip Crane followed in 1980. In 1983, the Democrats' front-runners for 1984 both come from careers in the Senate—Walter Mondale and John Glenn. Thus, despite the gubernatorial route of Jimmy Carter and Ronald Reagan, candidates now come heavily from the Congress, especially from the Senate. Undoubtedly, members of Congress find it easier now to keep themselves in the public view, especially with their ready access to the media. Also, the very nationalization of American politics may have convinced large numbers of Americans that coping with issues of national importance in the Congress is a good apprenticeship for the presidency. The governors, on the other hand, have found themselves in serious political difficulties in recent years. Problems of taxation and budgeting, abortion and capital punishment, law and order, and legislative reapportionment—as well as the more conventional political conflict resulting from the spread of two-party competitiveness—have impeded many political aspirations.[16]

[16]For another approach to availability, see John H. Aldrich, *Before the Convention* (Chicago: University of Chicago Press, 1980).

Finally, convention delegates consider the personal qualities of the contenders and their abilities to meet the demands of the presidency. They do so, however, in the context of loyalties to specific candidates and often, too, to specific ideologies. In other words, the standards for presidential timber are not universally agreed on. Furthermore, delegates may find a dilemma in the fact that the qualities that ensure effective performance in office are not necessarily those that win it in the first place. Difficult as such evaluations of presidential candidates are, they are far less likely to be made in the speed and confusion with which vice-presidential candidates are found.

CONVENTIONS: YESTERDAY AND TODAY

It is unlikely that small bands of national kingmakers bargaining in smoke-filled rooms ever did control the national conventions to the extent that popular myth has it. Even the celebrated negotiations at the Republican convention of 1920—in the course of which Warren G. Harding emerged—took place in a convention deadlocked by other candidates with large popular and delegate followings. Whatever power the kingmakers may have had in the past, however, it is declining rapidly. In that and in a number of other important ways, the national nominating conventions are not what they were a generation or two ago.

New Preconvention Politics

More nominations are decided on the first convention ballot these days, and the chances of a party's picking an unknown candidate diminish. This is all the result of a new style of campaigning for delegates, which was ushered in, perhaps, by the 1960 preconvention campaign of John F. Kennedy. More effective organization, greater resources, jet planes, polls, and expanded media exposure all permit it. The press services keep count of the number of delegates committed to various candidates, and the pollsters periodically report the state of public enthusiasm for them. Both candidates and delegates have fuller information about the entire nomination politics before they get to the convention than they ever did before. Delegates are more likely to be committed to a contender before the convention opens. Consequently, the crucial bargaining and trading of support, the committing of delegates, and the weeding out of candidates take place increasingly at the preconvention stages. The heart of presidential politics now precedes the conventions.

New Centers of Power

To some extent, political power has shifted away from the state and local party leaders, who at one time came as ambassadors to the convention for the purpose of negotiating within a fragmented, decentralized party. Power in the parties in the mid-twentieth century is less decentralized as national issues, national candidates, presidents, and congresses dominate the political loyalties and perceptions of voters. National party figures and national concerns—and party identifications shaped by national politics—have cut into the autonomy of state parties and leaders. So, too, has the increased power of potential candidates in the convention, power that is largely a product of their preconvention successes in rounding up delegates. Therefore, we find in many recent nominating conventions a tension among the old and new centers of power. In 1968, both Richard Nixon and Hubert Humphrey were supported by the leaders of the states and localities; their major challengers, Nelson Rockefeller and Eugene McCarthy, staked their campaigns on national issues and sought their support in a broader national public.

As ideologies and issues become more important in the parties generally, they structure more and more of the choices in the conventions. Ideological factions or tendencies thus become new centers of power. The battle for the Democratic nomination in 1972 clearly was a battle between the liberal and moderate centers of gravity within the party. In the Republican party, those ideological clusters were evident in the contest for 1976, and they were also geographically clustered (Table 12.3). The same division persisted, though less dramatically, in the 1980 contest between George Bush and Ronald Reagan. The post-1968 reforms have made issue and ideological differences even more likely and predictable within the Democratic party. In response, the party's national committee voted to seat some 550 Democratic party and public officials as delegates to the 1984 party convention in the hope of restoring some of the lost power of the party's traditional leaders.

The New Media Coverage

The mass media have increasingly turned the conventions into national political spectaculars, intended as much for the national audience as for the delegates in attendance. Party officials have given key roles to telegenic partisans, have speeded up the pace of business, and have virtually eliminated serious business from daytime hours. The strategic moves of major candidates, the arrival of powerful figures in the party, and the defection of individual delegates are reported fully. Even the formerly secret hagglings of platform and credentials committees are done in the public eye. For the party, then, television coverage offers a priceless opportunity to

TABLE 12.3   *Regional-Ideological Divisions in the Republican Party: The Choice of a Candidate for the Presidency in 1976*

Delegates Pledged to:	Delegates from:	
	Northeast and Midwest	South and West
Gerald Ford	945 (77%)	191 (19%)
Ronald Reagan	277 (23%)	790 (81%)
	1,222 (100%)	981 (100%)

Note   These data are only for the forty-eight states of the continental United States and the District of Columbia. The Northeast and Midwest states (in addition to the District of Columbia) are these: Connecticut, Delaware, Illinois, Indiana, Iowa, Kansas, Kentucky, Maine, Maryland, Massachusetts, Michigan, Minnesota, Missouri, Nebraska, New Hampshire, New Jersey, New York, North Dakota, Ohio, Pennsylvania, Rhode Island, South Dakota, Vermont, West Virginia, and Wisconsin.

reach voters and party workers and to launch its presidential campaign with maximum impact. Thus, the media spotlight shifts the role of the convention—not completely but perceptibly—from the conduct of party business to the stimulation of wider political audiences. Yet there is a paradox and a problem with the contemporary convention. Just when media attention to it is at its greatest, the convention has lost its excitement and suspense; we increasingly know who will win the presidential nomination before the proceedings begin. It is little wonder, then, that media reporters, straining for excitement, are more than willing to blow out of proportion whatever conflict or rumors they can find.

Media coverage is thus a two-edged sword, and its results are not always the ones the parties want. Television's capacity to relay so dramatically the scenes of violence in Chicago's streets and parks during the Democratic convention of 1968 provided an embarrassing counterpoint to the deliberations of the party within the convention hall. Media exposure is also problematic in other ways. The availability of prime evening time encouraged issue enthusiasts in the 1972 Democratic convention to debate the platform far longer than the media-oriented schedule provided. As a result, George McGovern began his acceptance speech at 2:48 A.M. before a TV audience reduced to one-fifth of what it had been earlier in the evening. Occasionally, the media even manage to participate directly in party decisions. While Ronald Reagan was trying to persuade former President Gerald Ford to be his vice-presidential candidate at the 1980 Republican convention, Ford granted an interview to CBS anchorman Walter Cronkite live on national TV. In their discussion of Ford's conditions for accepting the nomination, Cronkite used the phrase "co-presidency," and when Ford did not demur, the phrase came to summarize the commitments Ford was seeking from Reagan. By so framing the terms of the demands, one of TV's respected elders made the reaching of an agreement more difficult, perhaps even impossible.[17]

The conventions have therefore lost some of their freedom and deliberative character. Genuinely brokered conventions and last-minute compromise candidates seem now to belong to the past. The unlikelihood of lightning striking the unknown statesman does not, of course, signal the end of the convention. In some years, at least, delegates may have to choose from among a small number of candidates who have established themselves in the preconvention stages. When the choice must be made among these well-known hopefuls, it will be made by a freer, more open bargaining that involves the majority of delegates as well as the prominent bosses and kingmakers.

The conventions simply reflect, as never before, a heterogeneous mix of political roles and expectations. There are the old state and local leaders, representing the interests of their party organizations, and now there are also new national party leaders, national officeholders, and powerful candidates with blocks of loyal delegates. Old organizational styles also mix incongruously with new styles of media-based politics; professional party leadership rubs elbows with volunteer, amateur party activists. The old electoral pragmatism—the traditional convention emphasis on picking the winning candidate—clashes with the unwillingness of the ideologists to compromise. In reflecting all these conflicts, the conventions only mirror the broader conflicts and divisions of American party politics. Nonetheless, the stresses and strains that result are debilitating.

Taking a broader overview, one may put the matter of change another way. Aided by media-reported campaigning and by the results of periodic polling, the entire process of nominating a president has fallen under the spell of a national, popular democracy. More and more people are becoming aware of the candidates and the choices before the party, and more and more of them are formulating views about those choices. Therefore, nominating an unknown candidate today is doubly dangerous—first, for the seeming affront to the popularly supported contestants and, second, for the handicap of running an unknown candidate against the well-known candidate of the other party. Even the style, manners, and seriousness of the convention are under a new mass popular scrutiny. To the

[17]For fuller studies of the impact of television on the conventions, see Herbert Waltzer, "In the Magic Lantern: Television Coverage of the 1964 National Conventions," *Public Opinion Quarterly* 30 (1966): 33–53; and David L. Paletz and Martha Elson, "Television Coverage of Presidential Conventions: Now You See It, Now You Don't," *Political Science Quarterly* 91 (1976): 109–32.

extent that secretive or apparently manipulated party conventions are incompatible with the democratization of the presidential nominating process, they have had to change.[18]

Although change and declining power may beset the conventions, the parties are not about to abandon them. They will gladly make the compromises that are necessary to shore up the conventions' credibility. Even in its altered condition the national convention of the 1960s and 1970s is

[18]William Lucy found that, in most recent instances, eventual presidential nominees had been leaders in the opinion polls even before the presidential primaries. He suggested that the linkages between mass opinions and convention outcomes have been more direct than we suspect; see "Polls, Primaries, and Presidential Nominations," *Journal of Politics* 35 (1973): 830–48.

From Dross to Banality:
The Media Touch

No recent commentator has seen through the pomposities and absurdities of American politics more clearly than John Kenneth Galbraith. Economist and diplomat, Galbraith is also a gifted raconteur and satirist. In his memoirs, he reflects on the demise of the national nominating conventions and on the desperation of the media in trying to make something important of them:

> These vast ceremonials are now a bloated corpse. Candidates, as we know, are selected in the primaries or in the local caucuses and state conventions. There cannot be two separate arrangements for performing the same task and so it is the preconvention selection that counts. . . . But now fraud enters. A semblance of life is breathed into the corpse by delegates who, having been elected or selected and having traveled to the great event, wish to believe they are doing something. In this wish they are abetted by the press, which is enjoying an expense-paid reunion and a carnival untaxing to the mind, and above all by television commentators whose livelihood is involved, as also their reputation for raising banality to an art form:
>
> "How would you rate the applause for this speech, John?"
>
> "Average for this stage of convention proceedings, I'd say, David."
>
> Lester Markel, the long-time Sunday editor of the *New York Times*, once told me that he looked forward confidently to the day when the *Times* would send one man to a national convention and tell him not to file more than fifteen hundred words.
>
> John Kenneth Galbraith, *A Life in Our Times*
> (New York: Houghton, Mifflin, 1981), pp.
> 377–78.

too precious an institution to surrender. It is the only real, palpable existence of a national political party. It is the only occasion for rediscovery of common traditions and common interests, the only time for common decision making and a coming together to celebrate old glories and achievements. It stimulates the workers and contributors to party labors, and it encourages party candidates in the states and localities. Its rites may not mean a great deal to the majority of Americans passively peering at the TV screen (and a bit sullen about missing the summer reruns), but they do mean something to the men and women of the party organization. The conventions are, in short, a vital, integrative force in the life of the American national parties.

It is not surprising that the parties have resisted the various proposals for a national presidential primary advanced over the past several generations. Such a primary would replace the nominating conventions with a national primary for nominating the presidential and vice-presidential candidates. Its rationale is the general rationale of the direct primary. The objections to it are considerable. First of all, there are the practical problems: a uniform national date, the provision of a run-off primary if candidates are not to be chosen by small pluralities, and the implications of such a primary in open primary states. There is, too, the staggering burden in time and resources that a nomination campaign in fifty states would place on the parties and candidates. (Very possibly, too, a national primary would encourage a lengthy preprimary politics, in which the leading contenders would seek the endorsement of the state organizations.) Above all, however, most scholars and political leaders are not convinced that a national presidential primary would result in the selection of more able candidates for the presidency. It might well result in the nomination of those candidates best able—with money and personal charisma—to mount an effective mass-media campaign. From the party's point of view, it might also result in the nomination of candidates less likely to unify the party or appeal to its activists.[19]

THE PRESIDENTIAL CAMPAIGN

Tradition has long dictated that the presidential campaign open in early September. After the July or August conventions, the presidential and vice-presidential candidates rest and map strategy for the approaching campaign. Then it all begins with the Democratic candidate's traditional opening speech on Labor Day, often in an industrial center. (Jimmy Carter, however, chose to open both his 1976 and 1980 campaigns in the South.)

[19]For a defense of the convention, see Aaron Wildavsky, "On the Superiority of National Conventions," *Review of Politics* 25 (1962): 307–19.

The campaign for the presidency is in many ways the generic American political campaign "writ large." Its main problems and tasks are different in degree but similar in kind. The candidate and his campaign managers must still print literature and flyers, contract for ads and media time, schedule travel and speeches, put together an integrated campaign organization, and amass the necessary research. The candidate also faces similar strategic choices. On what mixture of appearances or radio-television speeches will he rely? What timing will he adopt—the full-speed-from-the-beginning strategy of Kennedy in 1960 or the pointed, paced buildup favored by Nixon in the same year? Will he play primarily on the appeal of the party, of the candidate ("I like Ike," "All the way with LBJ"), or of issues and ideology (Barry Goldwater: "In your heart you know he's right")? Also, like candidates all over the country, he faces problems in presenting himself to voters: Nixon's reputation for deviousness; Johnson's for the ruthless exercise of power (arm-twisting); Humphrey's for garrulousness; McGovern's for radicalism; Carter's for "meanness"; and Reagan's for misinformation.

Yet many of the usual campaign problems are heightened by the nature of the presidential office and constituency. The candidate's problem of keeping posted on how the campaign is going, on his progress with the electorate, is tremendous. The expanse of the country, the variety of local conditions, and the candidate's isolation from the grass roots make any kind of assessment difficult. In this dilemma, the presidential candidates have increasingly relied on professional pollsters to supplement the reports of local politicians. That expanse of the continent plus the length and pace of the campaign put exceptional physical strains on the candidate. The jet airplane adds to the strains by making more and more travel possible within a few months. Virtually every presidential candidate comes to election day on the fine edge of exhaustion. Perhaps these developments in the presidential campaign can best be illustrated by the changes of a century. During the 1860 campaign, Abraham Lincoln never left Springfield, Illinois. During the 1960 campaign, the two candidates together traveled more than 100,000 miles and gave almost 600 speeches.

There are, however, some important ways in which the presidential campaigns are really quite different from others in American politics. The most significant difference concerns their financing. Beginning in 1976, presidential candidates had the option of accepting federal campaign funds if they would raise and spend no other money. Both candidates chose that option in 1976 and 1980. Aside from money spent on their behalf by separate individuals and by national party committees, each of the candidates was limited in 1980 to the $29.4 million public grant. In one fell swoop, they were released from the heavy burden of fund raising. In return for that advantage, of course, the presidential candidates did have to scale back their campaigns. The $58.8 million they received together was considerably less than the 1972 candidates had spent. (The details and implications of public financing of campaigns will be explored at greater length in the next chapter.)

The electoral college and the nature of the American parties also give a special shape to the presidential campaigns. Because of the electoral college, presidential candidates allocate their time and resources in a special way. In all other American constituencies, candidates can pick up useful votes in their areas of weakness, even in areas they will lose. In the electoral college, though, the candidate gains only if he wins a plurality of the vote in a state. Presidential candidates generally pick a group of states, they feel they can carry and then devote their time to those states. As a result, presidential campaigns have tended to be concentrated in the close, two-party states, with the candidates largely avoiding each other's areas of strength. Moreover, when there is a credible third contender—as John Anderson was in 1980—candidates have to adapt to the possibility that the third candidate will win a few states' votes in the electoral college, thus making it harder for one of the major party candidates to win the necessary majority. [John Anderson's lack of a regional base of support reduced that possibility in 1980.]

The rambling, decentralized character of the American parties creates special problems for the campaign, chiefly in its organizational aspects. Neither the presidential campaign staff nor the national committee controls the whims and activities of the state parties. Most candidates work pragmatically (and inefficiently) through the maze of state and local organizations, finding useful leaders and contacts as best they can. In 1964, however, Barry Goldwater made the best-known and best-chronicled attempt to establish a single national organization with direct lines of authority and a comprehensive campaign plan (down to vote quotas for each precinct in the country).[20] Most presidential candidates rely on a mixture of personal campaign organization—usually drawing on their preconvention organizations in the states—and regular party officials and staffs in the states. Incumbent presidents organize their campaigns out of the White House and with a national committee dominated by their loyalists.

The Nixon administration carried domination of the presidential campaign to new lengths in 1972. Its instrument, innocently entitled Committee for the Reelection of the President, came to be known by the not-so-innocent acronym CREEP. It was a long step beyond the usual presidential campaign organization in two ways. First, its leadership was limited to personal loyalists of the president; at the outset, at least, it had very few people with any experience in the Republican party. Second, it

---

[20]For two good reports on 1964 campaign organization, see Karl A. Lamb and Paul A. Smith, *Campaign Decision-Making* (Belmont, Calif.: Wadsworth, 1968); and John H. Kessel, *The Goldwater Coalition* (Indianapolis: Bobbs-Merrill, 1968).

was controlled by the president's closest aides in the White House; thus, there was virtually no separation of the campaign and the government. Beyond all that, CREEP achieved a kind of sordid immortality by spawning the major case of corruption in presidential politics in American history. Most of its unwholesome activity actually took place before the nominating conventions and included, *inter alia*, the break-in and attempted bugging of Democratic National Committee offices (in the Watergate complex), the keeping of intelligence files on Democratic candidates, a vast series of "dirty tricks" in the presidential primaries (e.g., a bogus billboard in Florida purporting to be sponsored by Democrat Edmund Muskie and urging "More Busing"), and the collecting and spending of illegal and unreported campaign funds. All in all, the committee's activities helped to bring down a president and contributed to an already hefty cynicism about the ethics of campaigning in the United States.[21]

RADIO, TELEVISION, AND THE THIRD ESTATE

For several special reasons, presidential campaigns depend more heavily than most others do on campaigning through the mass media—radio, newspaper, and television ads and appearances:

— Media exposure costs dearly, and presidential candidates command larger sums of money than other candidates. (In 1980, the presidential candidates spent close to $40 million on mass media advertising.)

— Media exposure is more efficient for presidential candidates. They have none of the usual problems of paying for an audience that lies partly outside their constituency.

— The presidential candidates have a more receptive audience for a media-centered campaign. The voter who wouldn't pass up a TV quiz show for a congressional candidate may do so for a presidential aspirant.

— The size of the presidential constituency dictates that use of the media is the only practical way for the candidate to reach large numbers of voters. The alternative, especially as the states become more competitive, is an exhausting travel schedule.

Thus, the dependence of presidential campaigners on the media grows, and there is no end in sight. To a greater extent than in most other campaigns, the masters of the media—public relations specialists, pollsters, ad

---

[21]What we have come to call, collectively, the Watergate affair also involved abuses of executive and presidential power far beyond the 1972 campaign.

agencies, TV production experts—form a new political elite in the presidential races.[22]

No candidate can escape the exposure the media provide. A good deal of it will come without cost or effort. Every speech or foray, no matter how trivial, will be reported. Some of this kind of exposure can be controlled, however. Barry Goldwater's campaign managers, for example, persuaded him to forgo press conferences during the 1964 campaign so that he would not be goaded into rash and ill-considered retorts. In their commercial uses of the media, the candidates have full control. Candidates may choose their form of exposure—whether it will be full speeches or spot announcements. The former run the danger of boring voters; the latter have been criticized for "merchandising" presidents. In 1968, for instance, Richard Nixon developed a novel TV format. He appeared in ten hour-long programs in which he answered questions from panels of six or seven usually friendly questioners. An enthusiastic studio audience of carefully chosen Republicans watched and cheered.[23]

Something of an apogee in the trend toward media-centered presidential campaigns was reached in the presidential debates of 1960, 1976, and 1980. In 1960, the television networks contributed free time for the debates when the Congress waived the equal time rule and thus freed them of the necessity of granting time to minor party candidates. In 1976 and 1980, the League of Women Voters Educational Fund sponsored the debates, and the networks simply covered them as public events. (In 1976, there was also an unrelated vice-presidential debate between Walter Mondale and Robert Dole.) The impact of such debates is not easy to measure. Most observers and scholars of the 1960 debates thought they did more for John Kennedy than for Richard Nixon. At the least, they enabled Kennedy to close the publicity gap between himself and the better-known vice-president and to establish his credibility as a possible president. Indeed, the size of the audience—at least 125 million viewers saw the Carter-Reagan debate in 1980—marks the debates as a unique opportunity for a candidate. Moreover, the composition of the audience is as remarkable as its size. Candidates perpetually face the problem of speaking largely to their supporters, but the debates bring each candidate before the partisans of the other party and before the self-defined independent and undecided voters.

Such media confrontations are not without their traps and pitfalls, however. President Gerald Ford unquestionably hurt himself and his campaign in 1976 by asserting publicly that there was no Soviet domination

---

[22]For an excellent study of the media in a presidential campaign, see Jeff Greenfield, *The Real Campaign* (New York: Summit, 1982).

[23]For a generally acerbic account, see Joe McGinniss, *The Selling of the President 1968* (New York: Trident, 1969).

From a Dictionary: "Campaign Promises"

There is an amazing amount of American political folklore that we are in danger of losing as the oral tradition dies and as interest in things political wanes. William Safire, newspaper columnist and former presidential speechwriter, has brought together a good deal of it in *Safire's Political Dictionary* (New York: Random House, 1978). It is a dictionary in that it provides definitions and has alphabetical entries, but Safire uses the dictionary form for recording a great deal of additional folk and historical material. Here is his entry under "Campaign Promises":

> *Campaign Promises*   pledges made by a candidate to gain certain things for his constituents after election.
>
> This is probably the oldest form of politicking since elections began. Said a sign on a first-century Roman wall: "Genialis urges the election of Brutius Balbus as duovoir (commission member). He will protect the treasury." A candidate's promises, like a party platform, are rarely taken as literal commitments. Often they seem part of a game in which candidates out-promise each other, accuse each other of making rash promises and cite the opposition's unfilled promises left over from previous elections.
>
> Occasionally a particular promise takes on major—even historic—importance. One such was Dwight Eisenhower's pledge to go to Korea if elected in 1952. But for the most part, Bernard Baruch's admonition seems valid. "Vote for the man who promises least," said Baruch. "He'll be the least disappointing."
>
> The classic campaign-promise story is recounted by Senator Russell Long (D.-La.) about his uncle, Governor Earl Long. He had promised voters the right to elect their local sheriffs, but once in office, went in the opposite direction. When a delegation came to "Uncle Earl's" office to protest, Senator Long tells the author, "Uncle Earl told his right-hand man, 'I don't want to see 'em—you see 'em.' His aide said, 'What'll I tell 'em?' And Uncle Earl said, right out, 'Tell 'em I lied!' "

of East Europe. No amount of explaining and clarifying could repair the damage to his ethnic support and to his reputation for experience in matters of foreign policy. In 1980, the experience and easy informality of Ronald Reagan with the visual media clearly put his opponent at a disadvantage in the debate. So risky are the debates, in fact, that some presidential candidates have not been willing to participate. Lyndon Johnson was far ahead in 1964 and was disinclined to chance a debate. Having once been burned, Richard Nixon ruled out debates in 1968 and 1972.[24]

Much of the media's attention to the campaign is the ordinary attention they give to "news." By reason of selection and commentary, however, the images the media select have a life and character of their own. For one thing, the media cannot help drawing attention to themselves and to the facts of their own coverage of the news. The reporters inevitably become participants. Moreover, the mass media tend to be more interested in the election race itself than in the substance of any differences between the parties and candidates. In the words of Thomas Patterson:

> In 1976 the coverage centered on the race. The principal subjects were the status of the contest and the candidates' strategies and campaign efforts. Moreover, the issues that the news emphasized in 1976 were not the ones stressed by the candidates. Although the candidates concentrated on general and coalition appeals, journalists preferred lively, controversial issues. Increasingly, election news has come to reflect journalistic values rather than political ones.[25]

Jeff Greenfield came to similar conclusions after observing the media in 1980. His verdict on that year was even more dramatic: "The failure to cover consistently and conscientiously the struggle among competing views about the nature of government—which was at the heart of the real campaign—effectively helped disenfranchise the voter by stripping him of a reason to care about the outcome."[26]

Presidential campaign politics is thus both typical and atypical of American campaigning generally. On the one hand, the sheer magnitude of the office and its national constituency puts a special stamp on the campaign for the presidency. It is also contested within a special nomination process and with the unique constraints of the electoral college. On the other hand, the campaigns for the presidency grow out of the same norms, styles, and traditions that shape other American campaigns. Thus, the art of presidential campaigning is also the basic art of American political campaigning—the art of defining the various audiences of the campaign and reaching them as efficiently and effectively as possible.[27]

[24]On the debates of 1960, see Sidney Kraus (ed.), *The Great Debates* (Bloomington: Indiana University Press, 1962). For the effect of those in 1976, see Douglas D. Rose, "Citizen Uses of the Ford-Carter Debates," *Journal of Politics* 41 (1979): 214–21.

[25]Thomas E. Patterson, *The Mass Media Election* (New York: Praeger, 1980), p. 176.

[26]Greenfield, *The Real Campaign*, p. 26 (Emphasis removed).

[27]For a thoughtful essay on the presidential campaigns generally, see Stephen Hess, *The Presidential Campaign*, rev. ed. (Washington, D.C.: Brookings, 1978).

THE NATIONAL PARTY

If there is a national party in the United States—despite all the influences that fragment it into fifty state parties and innumerable local ones—it must materialize as the parties contest the one national election in American politics. It must be able to function as a national party and to identify some goals and interests beyond those of the state and local parties. Does the quadrennial race for the presidency, then, see the emergence of a national party? The answer is both yes and no.

Even during presidential elections, the localism of American political organization is apparent. The incentives of patronage and preferment, of political career and social advantage, depend on winning state and local elections and maintaining an effective state party organization. The goals and incentives of party activists, however, appear to be shifting from these locally rooted incentives to ones of issue, interest, and ideology. These incentives tend to be national, since the great public policy concerns with which they are involved are national concerns that will be resolved largely by national political institutions. The party worker, therefore, must look to national politics—to the election of a president and a Congress—for the achievement of these goals. That trend is probably matched by an increasingly national focus within the loyal party electorate. The political information and goals of American voters, as well as their party identification, are increasingly dominated by the personalities and issues of national politics.

Thus, there are forces making for a national party and forces resisting one. The conventions themselves illustrate that ambivalence. In some states, the state organizations may be strong enough to send to the convention delegates who will protect the interests of the state party. In other cases, the delegates may be loyal primarily to a would-be candidate and committed to support him, regardless of the competing interests of the state party. The result is an unstable amalgam of state-oriented and national-oriented presidential politics.

With the state party organizations and delegates thus divided between local and national outlook, the national party is easily dominated by the presidential candidate and his followers. His is the major organization with purely national goals and incentives. Frequently, the party activists whose incentive to action is a national personality or a national ideology find their best avenue to national political involvement in the campaign organizations or the personal followings of the present or potential presidential candidates. Thus, what is loosely called the national party is largely the party of the presidential candidate. His main problem in presidential politics, in fact, is to override and unite all the local, separatist interests and loyalties within the party. He must nationalize the attention of voters and the activities of party activists for at least the brief time of the presidential campaign.

The politics of nominating and electing a president also creates a national image for each party. What the party does in nominating a candidate and what the candidate does in the campaign put a stamp on the party, give it a profile and salience for millions of Americans. For them, the business of presidential politics defines what the party is, what it stands for, and who its supporters are. The creation of that image of the national party is, then, one of the major stakes of the presidential nomination and campaign. In this sense, the Watergate sins of CREEP in 1972 attached to the Republicans, even though the major sinners had few ties to and little experience in the Republican party organization. Ronald Reagan's conservatism in 1980 became the conservatism of the Republican party.

Thus, the American party is something of a hierarchical hybrid. It combines a decentralized organization with a politics in which the focuses—party identifications, personalities, and issues—are increasingly national and centralized. Taken as a national entity, the American party is an illogical, even contradictory mixture of a decentralized party organization and an increasingly centralized party in government. In that contradiction lies a major reason for the significance of the presidential election.

13

FINANCING THE CAMPAIGNS

At some time in the future, it may be possible to draw up a great balance sheet for the parties, in which all the resources they recruit—manpower, skills, and money—are balanced against all the resources they spend. We would then know the sources and the value of all party resources and the costs and activities on which they were spent. That kind of total input-output accounting, however, is beyond us at the moment.

The resources gathered by the parties fall into two main categories: those of the party organization and those of the party in government (Table 13.1). The discussion in Chapter 4 on the recruitment of manpower and skills into the party organizations approached the question of resources for the organizations. It dealt almost exclusively, however, with their principal resource: the efforts of active individuals. The party's candidates and public officials—the party in government—also recruit and spend political resources for their campaigns for election. They increasingly need cash, however, rather than volunteer labor. This chapter is primarily concerned with that money.

Again, in the best of all possible scholarly worlds, we might be able to account for all the contributions to campaigns for nominations and elections—to account, that is, for all the hours of work, all the goods, all the skills and expertise, and all the cash contributed. Difficult as they may be to identify, however, the cash contributions are easier to total than the others, and this chapter will be largely limited to them. Although that limitation is forced by sheer lack of information, one can build a substantial rationale for it at the risk of seeming to make a virtue of necessity. Whereas the work of the party organizations has largely employed valuables other than cash (e.g., goods and services), the campaign activities of the party in government have been based mainly on cash contributions (Table 13.1).

The increasing importance of money as a political resource can be easily documented. There is abundant evidence scattered throughout this chapter that the cash inputs into American political campaigning have risen steeply. As candidates free themselves from the control of campaigns by the party organization, they need cash to pay for the information, skills, and manpower that the party organizations once furnished for no charge (other than a mortgage on their political loyalties). It is doubtful that the noncash resources are increasing, at least at such a pace.

HOW BIG IS THE MONEY?

A forbidding secrecy long veiled the budgets of parties and candidates. Contributors were hesitant to be identified publicly, and candidates feared public disapproval of even the most modest expenditures. The reform legislation of the nation and the states in the 1970s, however, forced an unprecedented reporting of contributions in federal campaigns and in those of most states. As a result, we now have more information on campaign finance than we ever had before or ever dreamed of having. Where once the problem was secrecy, it is now a flood of data.

Alexander Heard and Herbert Alexander, the most authoritative sources on the sums of money spent on campaigns in the last generation or so, have estimated total campaign expenditures in every presidential year from 1952 through 1980 (see Table 13.2). By their calculations, those expenditures—for all offices at all electoral levels, including both nominations and general elections—have increased almost ninefold between 1952 and 1980. Just from 1976 to 1980 they more than doubled. Of the approximately $1.2 billion spent in 1980, a bit more than half went to the

TABLE 13.1 *Total Party Resource Needs*

	Party Organization	Party in Government
Type of resource	Predominantly noncash contributions (especially manpower)	More cash than noncash contributions
Purpose	General expense of maintaining the organization	Largely for election campaigns
Schedule	Continuous	Periodic, at elections

TABLE 13.2   *Total Campaign Expenditures for All Offices in Presidential Years: 1952–80*

Year	Sum Expended	Percentage Increase over Previous Election
1952	$140 million	—
1956	$155 million	10.7
1960	$175 million	12.9
1964	$200 million	14.3
1968	$300 million	50.0
1972	$425 million	41.7
1976	$540 million	27.1
1980	$1.2 billion	122.2

Source   Data from Alexander Heard and Herbert Alexander; see text footnote 1.

presidential and congressional races, a bit less than half to all state and local elections.[1]

It is not surprising that the most expensive campaign for public office in the United States is that for the presidency. Just winning the party nomination—that is, the right to run—may cost $20 million. Even with the restrictions on spending that were a condition of accepting public funding, the seekers after the Democratic and Republican nominations in 1980 spent $106.6 million. Jimmy Carter paid out $18.5 million, and Ronald Reagan spent $19.8 million; the biggest spender among the unsuccessful candidates was George Bush at $16.7 million. All of that, to repeat, was spent before the conventions ever named their candidates.

The presidential campaign raises the ante conspicuously (Table 13.3). Even a third-party candidacy is increasingly expensive; George Wallace spent more than $7 million in 1968, and John Anderson spent $14.4 million in 1980. Before the advent of public financing in 1974, Richard Nixon set records in his successful campaign in 1972 by spending about $68 million. Since all four major party candidates in 1976 and 1980 accepted public financing, they also accepted the condition that they spend only the

[1]The data from 1952 and 1956 come from Alexander Heard, *The Costs of Democracy* (Chapel Hill: University of North Carolina Press, 1960). Those for 1960 through 1980 are from Herbert E. Alexander's six studies: *Financing the 1960 Election* (Princeton: Citizens' Research Foundation, 1962); *Financing the 1964 Election* (Princeton: Citizens' Research Foundation, 1966); *Financing the 1968 Election* (Lexington, Mass.: Heath, 1971); *Financing the 1972 Election* (Lexington, Mass.: Heath, 1976); *Financing the 1976 Election* (Washington, D.C.: Congressional Quarterly, 1979); and *Financing the 1980 Election* (Lexington, Mass.: Heath, 1983).

public funds. Thus, in 1980 Carter and Reagan each spent $29.4 million. John Anderson was free to spend $14.4 million because he had not yet qualified for public funding. (He did so by getting more than 5 percent of the popular vote, and he thus received $4.2 million in public monies after the election.) Since the public funding limits are indexed to the cost of living, the expenditure levels in 1980 were considerably higher than they were in 1976. Even so, the Nixon record will be broken only when some candidate does not accept public financing and manages to raise a lot of private money—or, alternatively, after inflation has raised the spending limits a great deal higher. (The totals in Table 13.3 include more than the expenditures of just the major party candidates.)

It is difficult to generalize about the cost of a race for the Senate, but it is not unheard of for a candidate to spend more than several million dollars. In 1982, in fact, the two senatorial candidates from the nation's most populous state, California, spent more than $9 million in pursuit of a seat in the Senate. Republican Pete Wilson, the winner, paid out $5.2 million, and loser Edmund (Gerry) Brown spent $4 million. More typically, Senate races in fairly competitive states may cost several million dollars; the *average* senatorial candidate of the two major parties in 1982 spent $1.3 million. It is possible, of course, for a firmly entrenched senator from a small state to spend considerably less. It is no easier to generalize about the costs of House campaigns, except perhaps to say that they cost somewhat less than those for the Senate. Two Democrats led the House candidates in spending in 1982: Adam Levin of New Jersey's seventh district at $1.2 million, and Barney Frank of Massachusetts' fourth district at $1.1 million. Only Frank was successful. At the other end of the scale,

TABLE 13.3   *Total Spending by Candidates, Parties, and Groups in Presidential Elections: 1960–80*

Year	Amount	Republican Percentage of Two-Party Expenditures
1960	$19.9 million	49
1964	$24.8 million	63
1968	$44.2 million	65
1972	$103.7 million	67
1976	$88.7 million	56
1980	$142.9 million	61

Source   Herbert Alexander, *Financing the 1980 Election* (Lexington, Mass.: Heath, 1983).

it is possible for secure incumbents to get by on less than $100,000; in 1980 more than a quarter of the victorious candidates did so. The average race of major party candidates for the House in 1982 cost about $155,000. Costs also fluctuate erratically in successive congressional campaigns. It is not unusual for a new member of the House to spend much more beating the incumbent than he or she will spend in the first defense of the office two years later.[2]

Beyond these quests for national office are the thousands of campaigns for state and local offices. Hard information is rare, and generalizations are questionable. Many of these campaigns involve almost unbelievably small sums. Each year, hundreds of candidates win office in the United States in campaigns that involve cash outlays of a few hundred dollars; on the other hand, the mayoralty campaign in a large American city may cost a candidate and his or her supporters several hundred thousand dollars. Campaigns for governor of the larger states often exceed $500,000. Governor John D. Rockefeller 4th, a Democrat from West Virginia, spent almost $12 million to win reelection in 1980; it was probably the most expensive nonpresidential campaign in the history of American politics. Campaigns for referenda in California, the home of the most elaborate noncandidate campaigns, have been known to exceed a million dollars. The various groups on both sides of the 1978 California referendum on property tax reduction (Proposition 13) spent well over $2 million.

The levels of campaign spending, therefore, are related to a number of factors. Clearly, the importance of the office and the size of the constituency are significant factors. Important, also, is the degree to which the party organization controls campaigning and uses its own apparatus as the chief campaign vehicle. The competitiveness of the race also affects levels of spending. A pair of major party candidates will generally spend more when and where the election outcome is uncertain.[3]

To repeat, all of these figures reflect only cash outlays. Therefore, they do not reflect the true economic costs of the campaign. Volunteer workers contribute time for canvassing, typing envelopes, phoning voters, writing press releases, and dozens of other campaign jobs. Nor do these totals include the costs of campaigning borne indirectly by the public treasuries. In cities and states with old-style patronage systems, the city halls and

---

[2]These data and other figures for specific elections and/or years in this chapter come from the Federal Election Commission, either from its summaries in press releases or from its final and full reports, the general titles of which are *FEC Reports on Financial Activity: 1979–1980* and *1981–1982*.

[3]For a fuller development of these points, especially competitiveness, see David Adamany, *Financing Politics* (Madison: University of Wisconsin Press, 1969). Adamany's study is the best one on party finance in a single state (Wisconsin). Most of its findings parallel those of Alexander at the national level; that is, the patterns and relationships that prevail nationally also prevail in the main within Wisconsin.

county courthouses and all their employees may be a vortex of campaign activity for the weeks before elections. (Certain in-kind contributions to the campaign—the loan of an airplane or free printing, for example— must be reported as contributions under federal law.) Heard suggests that these additional contributions, exclusive of party-time volunteer labor, would add another 5 percent to the campaign bill; the value of contributed labor seems greater, but it is virtually impossible to estimate.[4] One might venture the opinion, however, that these noncash expenditures form a larger chunk of local campaign costs and that, with a shift from party organization campaigning (noncash) to media campaigning (cash), the percentage of noncash costs is, on the aggregate, declining.

The most important question about the "big money," however, is whether it is getting bigger. Heard, writing in 1959, plotted the rises in costs from 1940 through 1956 and concluded that the 54 percent increases in that period were no greater than the increases in the price level—that is, no greater than the increases in the general cost of living.[5] Since then, however, the increases have far exceeded the rise in the price level. Between 1956 and 1972, the aggregate sums increased by 174 percent, while the price level rose about 54 percent. Most observers attributed the rise in campaign costs to a greater dependence on the technology of campaigning: jet travel, opinion polling, computer management of data, and reliance on the media. From 1972 to 1976, however, the total increase of 27 percent was less than the approximately one-third increase in the cost of living over the four years because of the new limits that accompanied public funding of the presidential campaigns. From 1976 to 1980, the increase was 122 percent, only 47 percent of which was attributable to inflation.

These, then, are preliminary answers to the question of how big the political money is. Unanswered is the more difficult question of how big it *really* is—how big it is when measured by relative values and utilities rather than by the fixed measure of the dollar sign. In the American economy of 1980, the $1.2 billion spent on election campaigns represented less than .05 percent of the gross national product. Since campaigns are a grand exercise in communication and persuasion, one is tempted to compare their costs with those of advertising campaigns. In 1980 in the United States, all advertising for all products consumed $54.5 billion, a figure 45 times the costs of all of our election campaigns in that year. The $1.2 billion that those election campaigns cost was just about the same as the costs of advertising for toiletries and toilet goods in the nation that year. It also matched the advertising budgets of Procter and Gamble, General Foods, Philip Morris, and General Motors put together.

[4]Heard, *The Costs of Democracy*, p. 372.
[5]*Ibid.*, p. 376.

NONCANDIDATE SPENDING

So far, we have been talking exclusively of candidate spending, but the candidates and their committees spend only part of the money consumed by American campaigning. Party committees and nonparty groups, especially political action committees, also account for substantial sums. To approach the question of noncandidate spending, it is best to look at all expenditures in a specific election. The entire presidential campaign of 1980—from earliest prenomination spending through the general election in early November—affords a useful illustration (Table 13.4).

As Table 13.4 indicates, the major party candidates spent $185.1 million of the $275 million spent in the presidential politics of 1980, part of it in the prenomination campaigns and part in the general election campaigns. The other categories of expenditure are less obvious and may well

TABLE 13.4 *Costs of Nominating and Electing a President; 1980*

	Amount ($000,000)	
I. Prenomination		
Spending by candidates for major party nomination	$106.3	
Independent expenditures	2.8	
Communication costs	0.9	
Spending by minor party candidates	1.2	
Miscellaneous expenditures	0.9	
		$112.1
II. Conventions		
Republicans' expenditures	$5.1	
Democrats' expenditures	4.2	
		$9.3
III. General Election		
Spending by all candidates	$78.8	
Party committee spending	32.0	
Expenditures by labor, corporations, associations	16.8	
Independent expenditures	10.6	
Communication costs	1.7	
Costs of complying with regulations	3.0	
		$142.9
Miscellaneous unreported expenses		10.7
Grand total		$275.0

Source Adapted from Table 4–7 in Herbert Alexander, *Financing the 1980 Election* (Lexington, Mass.: Heath, 1983), p. 111.

bear some fuller explanation. The major party organizations and their committees spent substantial sums on their national conventions and directly in the general election. Individuals and nonparty groups also made substantial independent expenditures—expenditures on behalf of or in opposition to a candidate made without the knowledge or cooperation of any candidate or party. A few individuals made such independent expenditures in 1980, but the overwhelming majority of them were made by political action committees (PACs). In fact, of the $13.4 million in independent expenditures in all stages of the presidential campaign, PACs supporting Ronald Reagan spent more than $12 million. The communication costs noted in Table 13.4 refer to expenditures made by organizations to urge their workers or members to vote for a particular candidate; labor unions account for approximately 90 percent of the $2.6 million reported. Finally, Herbert Alexander has estimated the general expenditures of labor unions, corporations, and membership associations in "nonpartisan" voter mobilization—largely in voter registration and get-out-the-vote programs—at $16.8 million for the election. (That figure is an estimate because such expenditures do not have to be reported to the Federal Election Commission or to state agencies that regulate campaign finance.) Again, labor accounts for the largest part of the expenditure.

Similar analyses of congressional campaigns are also possible with the data of the Federal Election Commission. Campaigns for nomination and election to the two houses of the Congress went on simultaneously with the 1980 presidential campaigns. All parties' candidates for the Congress spent $242 million in the primaries and general election. In addition to that total, however, party committees spent $9.2 million "on behalf of" candidates of their parties for election. (That figure is above and beyond the contributions that party committees made directly to candidates.) The party committees in question are primarily the four so-called Hill committees: the Democratic Senatorial Campaign Committee, the Democratic Congressional Campaign Committee, the Republican Senatorial Campaign Committee, and the Republican Congressional Committee. Finally, $3.7 million was spent in communication costs and independent expenditures. As in the presidential campaign of 1980, labor led in communication costs, and conservative, pro-Republican PACs dominated the independent expenditures. Of the $2.3 million in independent expenditures, $1.9 million went either for a Republican candidate or against a Democratic candidate. More than a million of that $1.9 million total is accounted for in the negative campaigns of the National Conservative Political Action Committee against six liberal Democrats running for reelection to the Senate. On the matter of expenditures for voter registration and get-out-the-vote campaigns, there are no estimates. In any event, those activities are rarely focused on congressional elections; efforts to "get out" a vote usually are geared to a full party ticket or a presidential candidate.

Thus, when one looks beyond candidate expenditures in campaigns, the major participants who emerge are individuals, groups (especially PACs), and party organizations. Although individuals and groups do spend directly in campaigns, most of their political resources go in contributions to candidates and thus are spent by the candidates. (Those contributions will be discussed at greater length in the next section of this chapter.) Only the party organizations and their finance committees maintain a major financial role in campaigns in addition to their contributions to candidates. An extended word about them is appropriate here.

In the morass of data about party spending in American politics, only one conclusion is clear: Republican party committees are now raising and spending much more than the Democrats are. In 1980, for example, national, state, and local Republican party committees raised $169.5 million, while Democratic committees raised only $37.2 million. That is a ratio of almost five to one. Moreover, the ratio lengthened in 1982, with the Democrats raising $39 million and the Republicans $214.9 million.

Figures on receipts are misleading in various ways, however. Considerable portions of funds received go for administrative, overhead, and fund-raising costs. Direct-mail solicitation of contributions, on which the national party committees increasingly depend, have high costs of solicitation per dollar raised. Furthermore, some of the receipts go to state and local campaigns. Since the availability of state reports and data vary so greatly, it is virtually impossible to estimate those state and local expenditures precisely and thus to separate them from overhead costs. All of that notwithstanding, in view of the great differences in receipts between the two parties, one can safely say that Republican committees spend more in the states than the Democrats do.

The picture of spending in national elections is far clearer. Those expenditures are of two kinds: direct contributions to candidates and expenditures on behalf of candidates. In 1980, Republican committees outspent Democratic committees in the congressional races by a margin of about two and a half to one (Table 13.5). Even if one looks only at the two campaign committees of each party in the Congress (i.e., the Hill committees), their receipts and expenditures are similarly disparate. The Democrats raised $4.5 million in 1979–80 and contributed $1.1 million to candidates; they also spent $0.6 million on behalf of Democratic candidates. The Republican figures for the same year show $51.9 million in receipts, with $2.4 million in contributions and $6.4 in expenditures on behalf of Republican candidates.

Thus, although the candidates of the two major parties for the presidency and for the Congress spend approximately equal sums, that equality vanishes when one adds the expenditures of other political actors. The Republican advantage in party spending is clear and overwhelming for

TABLE 13.5 *Expenditures of National Party Committees in the 1980 Congressional Elections*

	Amounts ($000,000)	
	Democrats	Republicans
I. Contributions to candidates		
National committees	$1.3	$3.7
State, local committees	0.4	0.8
II. Expenditures on behalf of candidates		
National committees	4.6	11.6
State, local committees	0.4	0.8
Totals	$6.7	$16.9

the moment. (Such party fortunes do change suddenly, though; Democratic committees outraised and outspent the Republicans for much of the 1960s.) The weight of independent expenditures, in both presidential and congressional races, was also on the side of the Republicans in 1980 and 1982. Yet it is hard to know how many of those expenditures to chalk up in the Republican column. They were made independently of Republican candidates and committees and of their campaign plans and strategies. Indeed, they may have achieved Republican goals very imperfectly; in 1982, the National Conservative Political Action Committee (NCPAC) targeted thirteen incumbent Democrats for defeat but succeeded in only one race (the defeat of Senator Howard Cannon of Nevada). By election time, in fact, some observers saw NCPAC opposition as a boon to a Democratic campaign. The communication costs of heavily Democratic organized labor present similar problems; they, too, are made apart from party candidates, and their effectiveness is similarly unclear. Finally, do we throw the "nonpartisan" voter registration and voter activation campaigns into the calculus? On the surface, they are nonpartisan, but the unions, corporations, and associations that mount them usually do so in the confidence that they are mobilizing voters strongly in favor of one party or ideological preference. Therefore, the toting up of partisan advantage must be done in the face of poor information and shaky assumptions. If one sweeps aside all these doubts and problems and assigns all campaign expenditures to the party they were intended to help, the Republican advantage in the 1980 presidential campaign, for example, was $65.2 million to the Democrats' $54.3 million. Republican aggregates were similarly greater in the congressional elections of 1980 and 1982.

SOURCES OF THE FUNDS

Candidates raise their campaign money from five sources: individual contributors, political action committees, political parties, the candidates' own resources, and public funds. There are no possibilities beyond those five. All candidates—and anyone who proposes reform in the American system of campaign finance—are limited to them.

Individual Contributors

It is one of the best kept secrets in American politics that the individual contributor still dominates campaign finance. In the 1980 congressional elections, individual contributions amounted to 57 percent of the receipts of the congressional candidates. The reforms of the 1970s did, indeed, end the era of the genuinely big contributors—the so-called fat cats—but those wealthy felines have been replaced by large numbers of individuals willing to give smaller sums. Of the approximately $188 million the congressional candidates in 1980 raised from individuals (including themselves), only $47.5 million was raised in contributions of $500 or more.

Over the years, the parties and the candidates have devised all manner of ways to entice the political contributions of individuals:

1. *Personal solicitation.* Personal visits, phone calls, and conversations with the candidate or the candidate's workers raise substantial sums. Since most of the solicitation of the "fat cats" before 1974 was done as a matter of personal acquaintance, this form of solicitation was the preferred and most effective one in that era.

2. *Mail solicitation.* Aided by computerized mailing lists and printers and the ability of the machines to "personalize" letters, the parties, PACs, and candidates now increasingly raise funds by mail. It is a method of solicitation well adapted to the important search for small contributors. That quest depends on expansion of the lists of party and candidate contributors, and computers and high-speed data-processing machines easily read borrowed lists, sort subsets of them (by zip code, for example), and amend them to include new prospects and cull out the unpromising names.

3. *Dinners.* Surprisingly, part of the structure of American campaign finance rests on a foundation of banquet chicken, mashed potatoes, and half-warm peas. For a ticket price of between twenty and several hundred dollars, a contributor has dinner in a large hall, listens to endless political exhortations, rubs elbows with the party elite, and—if the price warrants it—observes a "name" guest, who gives the major speech. The sums raised are significant; a senator or a prominent member of the House may well net more than $100,000 from such an

occasion. The parties themselves have also traditionally employed the dinner as a fund raiser. The Lincoln Day dinners of the Republicans and the Jefferson-Jackson Day dinners of the Democrats are traditional events all around the country.

④ *Other diversions.* Taking their cue from the success of dinners, money raisers have begun to rely also on similar occasions: cocktail parties, receptions, theater parties, even trips to concerts or horse races. Along with the political dinner, these occasions have in common a general American fondness for raising money for all kinds of purposes with benefit events. Similarly, the candidates and parties have used auctions, art shows, and telethons to raise money. (Jimmy Carter raised $328,000 in a telethon early in his campaign for the presidency; beamed throughout Georgia, the telethon was called "Spend Valentine's Day with Jimmy Carter.") Indeed, these examples suggest an important observation: we tend to raise political money in many of the same ways we raise money for the arts and charities in American society.

⑤ *Patronage.* Although patronage is passing from national politics, it still yields contributions in some states and localities in which the holder of a public job is expected to make a political contribution at campaign time. In Indiana, the state's patronage holders long were called the "Two Percent Club," because the size of their contributions was not left to their discretion. Crude as such a system may seem, it comes close to governmentally financed campaigns in some localities. In addition, patronage workers often are expected to make substantial noncash contributions to candidates and parties through their political work in the campaign and throughout the year.

Such a catalog does not exhaust the rich ingenuity with which individuals are parted from their money for political purposes. In 1960, Syracuse Democrats offered trading stamps (at a rate higher than that of the supermarkets) for contributions. In 1968, many George Wallace rallies were graced by a blonde activist who bestowed kisses for $20 contributions; the Wallace forces were said to have raised greater sums, however, by passing an old fashioned yellow "suds-bucket."

Political Action Committees

Political action committees (PACs) are political committees that are connected with neither parties nor candidates but raise and spend money to influence election outcomes. The great majority of PACs are the creature of a sponsoring parent organization; that is, they are PACs of corporations, labor unions, and membership associations. Some, however, have no sponsoring organization; these are most likely to be ideological PACs of the right or the left. The PACs spend their money in three different ways: they transfer it to parties or to other PACs, they spend it independently to support or oppose candidates, and they give it to candidates. Since the first route (transfers) is negligible, and since we have already discussed independent expenditures, the concern here is with the PACs as contributors to the candidates.

In 1974, there were only 608 PACs operating in national elections, but by 1982 that number had grown to 3,371. A number of influences account for that growth. The decline of the parties and the advent of a more fragmented, issue-centered politics fostered it. So did the reform legislation of the post-Watergate years. The Federal Elections Campaign Act of 1974, for example, in its zeal to limit the big individual spenders of American politics, put the limit on individual contributions far below that for the PACs (see the discussion of contribution limits later in this chapter). Furthermore, decisions of the federal courts and the Federal Election Commission made clear the legality of PACs and confirmed the right of sponsoring organizations to pay their administrative and overhead expenses. (Their political funds, though, must be collected and kept separately in what federal statutes call a "separate segregated fund"; under federal law, the sponsoring corporation or labor union may not use its regular assets and revenues for political expenditures.)

For all the bad press the PACs have received recently, they do not dominate American campaign finance. In the 1980 congressional elections, for instance, all PACs accounted for only 26 percent of the receipts of all candidates for the Congress. That percentage rose to approximately 28 percent in 1982. The PACs thus contribute about half of what individual contributors give to congressional candidates. Furthermore, their contributions come from all points along the political spectrum. Of the $83.1 million that PACs gave in 1982 to congressional candidates, corporate PACs contributed $27.4 million, association PACs gave $21.7 million, labor PACs accounted for $20.2 million, and the PACs without sponsoring organizations gave $10.7 million. (The PACs of cooperatives and corporations without stock account for the rest.) Those recent figures, however, reflect a shift in the relative strength of the categories; labor PACs, the first to organize, were the PAC leaders as recently as 1976. Finally, one must keep in mind that the totals of $55.2 million in PAC contributions in 1980 and $83.1 million in 1982 far exceeded the $2.2 million and $5.2 million they spent in independent expenditures on congressional races in those years.

Candidates pursue the PACs just as sedulously as they pursue individual contributors. Both parties' congressional and senatorial campaign committees put their candidates in touch with PACs likely to be sympathetic to their causes. Candidates and their campaign managers also track the PACs at first hand, assisted by the directories and information services that list PACs by their issue positions, the size of their resources, and their previous contributions. Incumbent members of Congress also invite the PACs or lobbyists of their parent organizations to fund-raising parties in Washington, at which $200 to $500 gets the PAC people hors d'oeuvres, drinks, and legislative gratitude. On the other hand, the PACs also take the contributing initiative. Unlike most individual contributors, they are in the business of making political contributions, and they don't necessarily wait to be asked.[6]

Political Parties

In addition to all of their spending on party business, on running party conventions and other party processes, on behalf of party candidates, and for the general party ticket in campaigns, the parties also contribute funds to candidates. They accounted for $6 million of the $248.8 million that all congressional candidates raised in 1980. That 2.4 percent still becomes only 6.1 percent if one adds the $9.2 million the parties spent on behalf of candidates. That almost insignificantly low percentage begs comment for at least three reasons. First, it suggests how much more money the parties will have to raise and spend before they can reestablish a major role for themselves in American electoral politics. Second, it contrasts sharply with the substantial role of parties in financing and running campaigns in the other democracies of the world. Finally, modest though those sums are, they come predominantly from the party committees in the Congress. The congressional party in government, at least, relies heavily on its own financial instruments rather than on those of the party organizations.

The Candidates Themselves

No government agency, either national or local, easily makes available any data on the candidates' use of their own fortunes and those of their immediate families. Various scholars estimate it at about 10 percent of the receipts of all congressional candidates.[7] Of all the sources of campaign funds, this one is the most unevenly distributed. The average figure is greatly inflated by the self-financing of a few relatively wealthy candi-

---

[6]On PACs, see Michael Malbin (ed.), *Parties, Interest Groups, and Campaign Finance Laws* (Washington, D.C.: American Enterprise Institute, 1980), and Frank J. Sorauf, "PACs in American Politics: An Overview," a background paper printed in *What Price PACs?* (New York: Twentieth Century Fund, 1984).

[7]See, for example, Tables 6 and 7 in Joseph E. Cantor, *Political Action Committees: Their Evolution and Growth and Their Implications for the Political System* (Washington, D.C.: Congressional Research Service of Library of Congress, 1982). Although it is primarily about PACs, the Cantor study brings together a good deal of data on campaign finance generally.

dates. John Heinz, for example, spent $2.5 million of his own fortune (out of a total expenditure of about $3 million) in his 1976 senatorial race. In 1982, a Democrat from Minnesota, Mark Dayton, spent $7.1 million in an unsuccessful bid for a seat in the Senate; $6.8 million of it came from the candidate and his family. (Dayton is the scion of a large mercantile family; his wife is a direct descendant of John D. Rockefeller.) In fairness to Dayton and other affluent candidates who would doubtless prefer to broaden their base of financial support, it is true that individual contributors avoid giving to candidates whom they think do not "need" their money.

Public Funding

Finally, for some American campaigns, public funding is available if the candidate wishes to claim it. Claiming it, of course, also means accepting spending limitations as a condition of receiving the money. Public monies are most conspicuously available for the presidential campaigns; in 1980, public matching funds for preconvention contenders, subsidies for the national conventions, and grants to Carter, Reagan, and Anderson totaled $100.6 million, or somewhat more than one-third of the $275 million total costs in that election (see Table 13.4). There is no public funding of congressional elections, although it has been proposed in most congressional sessions since 1974. Bills to institute it did pass the Senate in 1973 and 1974, but parallel proposals have never come close to passing the House. Although the actual general election campaigns of the major party candidates for the presidency were fully funded by the federal treasury in 1976 and 1980 ($29.4 million for each in 1980), public funding in the fifteen states that have it tends to be less generous and less widely accepted. In the 1980 state legislative elections in Minnesota, for example, only two-thirds of the candidates accepted public funding, and public funds constituted less than 20 percent of the total receipts of all candidates.

The preceding paragraphs have focused largely on the national funding experience. The picture in the fifty states is, as usual, both confusing and unclear. All evidence suggests that national patterns generally prevail in state and local election campaigns. Individual contributors are the most important source of campaign funds, followed by PAC contributions and then, at greater distance, by party and personal funds. Two modifications to that pattern should be noted, however. Individual contributions become relatively more important in local campaigns, since the interest of parties and PACs in those campaigns is less lively. Second, candidates in the localities are also more limited in the ways in which they raise money; fund-raising experts are usually beyond their means, for example, and the practicalities rule out such techniques as telethons and mass mail solicitation.

Ultimately, all campaign funds in American politics come from individuals. They pay the taxes (or divert the tax payments) that provide public funding, and they contribute the dollars that parties and PACs have available for their contributions. They also contribute enormous sums directly to candidates. How broad, then, is individual participation in American campaign finance? Approximately 11 percent of the sample of Americans in the Center for Political Studies survey of 1980 reported having given money in the campaign to a party, a candidate, or a PAC. In the same year, about 29 percent of taxpaying Americans diverted a dollar of their tax liability ($2 for married persons filing jointly) to the federal fund from which the presidential campaigns are financed. What is one to conclude? First of all, the 11 percent figure probably overrepresents contributions by some amount; even the most careful polling systematically overrepresents political activity to some degree.[8] Second, even with modified estimates, the verdict is mixed. On the one hand, such levels of participation indicate a funding base broader than that of the rest of the world's democracies. The special American tradition of voluntarism extends to our politics. On the other hand, the low figures, on the tax checkoff especially, suggest a widespread refusal by some Americans to come to grips with the options in the funding of campaigns. Large numbers of Americans will not contribute voluntarily, and they accuse the wealthy candidate who finances his or her own campaign of buying the office. They are inclined to accuse candidates who rely on large contributions from PACs of selling out to special interests, yet they do not find public funding an acceptable alternative either. One can only suppose that they subscribe to a "stork theory" of campaign funding.

REFORM AND REGULATION

For a long time, the regulation of campaign finance in the United States was a jerry-built structure of assorted and not very well integrated federal and state statutes. Periodically, reformers attempted to bring order out of that legislation and at the same time to strengthen legal controls over the raising and spending of campaign money. A new episode of reform was under way in the early 1970s when the Watergate scandals broke over the country. The result in 1974 was the most extensive federal legislation on the subject in the history of the Republic.

The 1974 law, as many laws are, was set down on an already existing web of legislation, superseding some of it and supplementing some of it. Some of it, in turn, was invalidated by the United States Supreme Court

[8]In addition to overreporting, the wording of the survey question on contributions to political action groups may have led some respondents to report nonpolitical dues and contributions.

in late January 1976. It was then supplemented by amendments passed in the late 1970s. The resulting structure of federal legislation falls into two main categories: the limitations on campaign contributions and spending and the provisions for setting up a system of public funding of national politics.

Limitations on Contributions and Expenditures

The chief provisions of existing federal law are these (see Table 13.6 for a summary):

1. _Restrictions on sources of money:_

✳ Each individual is limited to a contribution of $1,000 per candidate in primary elections, $1,000 per candidate in the ensuing general election, $5,000 to a political action committee, and $20,000 to a national party committee. The contributor is also limited to a total of $25,000 in all such contributions in any one calendar year.

✳ Political action committees are limited to contributions of $5,000 to any candidate in any election if they qualify as "multicandidate committees" by making contributions to at least five candidates.

✳ Corporations and labor unions themselves may not contribute. (They may, however, set up political action committees and pay their overhead and administrative costs.)

✳ Federal employees may not solicit funds from other federal employees on the job. The same limitation also applies to state or local employees whose activities are financed by federal loans or grants.

The new limits on the size of contributions in the 1974 legislation have already curbed the role of the very large contributor. Even with the loopholes (and the possibility that all adults in a family can contribute within the ceiling), there is no possibility that we will ever again see gifts of the magnitude of Clement Stone's $2 million-plus to Richard Nixon in 1972 or Stewart Mott's million-plus to McCarthy in 1968 and then again to McGovern in 1972. The Motts and Stones will be unlimited only in their personal, independent efforts on behalf of candidates (e.g., newspaper ads). The contributions of political action committees have already become more important, as have small contributions from individuals and the personal funds of wealthy candidates.

2. _Restrictions on expenditures:_

✳ If presidential candidates accept federal subsidies for the prenomination and general election campaigns (see following discussion for details),

TABLE 13.6   *Limits on Campaign Contributions under Federal Law*

Contributor	Limit on Contributions			
	To Candidate or Candidate Committee (per election)	To National Party Committee (per year)	To any Nonparty Committee (per year)	Total Contributions (per year)
Individual	$1,000	$20,000	$5,000	$25,000
Political action committee	$5,000[a]	$15,000	$5,000	no limit
Party committee	$5,000[a]	no limit	$5,000	no limit

[a] If the political action committee or the party committee qualifies as a "multicandidate committee" under federal law by making contributions to five or more federal candidates, the limit is $5,000. Otherwise, it is $1,000.

Source   Adapted from Federal Election Commission, *Campaign Guide for Corporations and Labor Organizations* (January 1982), p. 51.

they must agree to spend no more than the sum of the subsidies. They are therefore limited to $12 million before the convention and $20 million after it (in 1974 dollars). Thus, with the correction for rises in the consumer price index, the limits were $17.7 million and $29.4 million in the 1980 elections. (In addition, national party committees may collectively spend up to two dollars per voter in the presidential election campaign; that allowance totaled $4.6 million in 1980.) If presidential and vice-presidential candidates accept the public subsidies, they are also limited to expenditures of no more than $50,000 of their own or their family's money on the campaigns.

The 1974 law's limits on spending in House and Senate campaigns were the chief casualties of a Supreme Court decision in 1976.[9] The challengers to the statutes—an unlikely coalition extending from Senator James Buckley and *Human Events* to Eugene McCarthy and the New York Civil Liberties Union—had argued that restrictions on campaign expenditures infringed the rights of free speech and political activity. The Supreme Court agreed. Expenditure limits, therefore, are permissible only when they are a condition of the voluntary acceptance of public subsidies. Congress could thus reinstate the expenditure limits on its own campaigns only as part of a plan for subsidizing them. Candidates, of course, would have

[9]*Buckley v. Valeo*, 424 U.S. 1 (1976).

to be free to reject the subsidies, as the presidential candidates are. (The restrictions on contributions make rejecting subsidies a hazardous option, however, for the presidential contestants.)

3. Requirements for accounting and reporting:

All contributions to a candidate must go through and be accounted for by a single campaign committee.

Each candidate must file quarterly reports on his finances and then supplement them with reports ten days before the election and thirty days after it.

All contributors of $200 or more must be identified by name, address, occupation, and name of employer.

The publicity provisions of earlier legislation had not been notably effective. Reports were sketchy at best and missing at worst. The new legislation has improved the quality of reporting, however, by centralizing candidate responsibility in a single committee, by creating a new public interest in reporting, and by setting up an agency (the Federal Election Commission) to collect the data and make them available.

Public Funding of Presidential Campaigns

Although the Congress has not yet been willing to fund its own challengers from the public treasury, it has embarked on a program of public support for presidential candidates. The 1976 elections marked the inauguration of this program.

Candidates seeking their party nominations were aided only if they first passed a private funding test. They had to raise at least $5,000 in contributions of $250 or less in each of at least twenty states. If they so established their eligibility, public funds matched every contribution up to $250, to a total of $7.4 million (the 1980 figure). In addition, each of the major parties received $4.4 million to offset the costs of its national nominating convention.

Provisions for funding the election campaign are somewhat simpler. Candidates may draw on a public fund for some or all of their expenses up to the $20 million ceiling. (That $20 million figure is in 1974 dollars; it is recalculated for each presidential year according to rises in the consumer price index.) Minor parties fare less well. They receive only a fraction of the $20 million maximum, and then only *after* the election and after they have received at least 5 percent of the vote. (If they drew at least 5 percent of the vote in the previous election, they can receive their payment before the election. Thus, John Anderson received $4.2 million after the 1980 election and will be entitled to a comparable sum before the 1984 election if he or his party chooses to run.) The section dealing with minor parties has received a major part of the criticism directed at the 1974 statute. Critics charge that it will enfeeble minor parties, certainly making it hard for them to reach major party status and, in view of the need to pay cash for many campaign expenses, making it hard for them to finance even a modest campaign.[10]

First Results: 1976 through 1982

The largely new structure of federal regulation and subsidy worked a number of changes in its first applications. Although any conclusion based on so short an experience must be tentative, the main results of the new legislation appear to be these:

— Obviously, the 1974 law achieved its stated and explicit purpose of lowering the scale of presidential campaign expenditures and ending the role of the giant contributors to both presidential and congressional campaigns. At the same time, alternative sources of money— PACs, wealthy candidates, and small contributors—became more valuable and plentiful in the campaigns for Congress.

— As expenditure ceilings were lowered for the 1976 presidential campaign, the patterns of spending changed. Candidates cut down less on media advertising and travel costs but cut down more on other advertisements (e.g., billboards), organizers and professional staff, and the traditional paraphernalia of campaigns—buttons, leaflets, and bumper stickers, for example. Tighter planning and setting of priorities became the order of the day in presidential camps; by general agreement, there was less activity in the smaller states, for instance.

— Most observers thought the new subsidies and expenditure limits helped Jimmy Carter to the White House. The preconvention grants obviously help the less well known candidate, especially the one with a limited financial base. The grants and limits in the presidential campaign have erased the usual GOP advantage in spending and have prevented affluent campaigns from developing a late media blitz that conceivably could carry a close election.

— Regulation and the 1976 Supreme Court decision have clearly stimulated the growth of independent expenditures. Moreover, the clear favoring of Republican causes in those expenditures has introduced a new source of inequality into campaign finance.

— More generally, we are learning that the system of campaign finance operates as if it were a great hydraulic apparatus. If one narrows a pipe or closes a spigot in one part, one creates greater pressure and flow in other parts.

[10]For an evaluation of this and other public funding plans, see David W. Adamany and George E. Agree, *Political Money* (Baltimore: Johns Hopkins University Press, 1975).

In one important way, however, the experience did *not* have the result many expected. It has not yet led to public subsidies for elections to Congress. The main issues here were two. First, there was a good deal of concern about voter reaction—a concern that voters would view subsidies as an improper use of tax monies or as a congressional raid on the treasury for its own advantage. (The lack of public support was evident in the polls.) The second issue concerned a possible "goring of oxen." A few members of Congress grumbled that they would be encouraging their own opponents, but the Republicans and many observers thought the plan would further entrench the incumbent Democrats. What scholarly evidence there is on the point suggests that there is, indeed, a significant relationship between a challenger's level of expenditures and his or her ability to give an incumbent a close race.[11]

State Regulation and Financing

To the maze of federal legislation must be added the even more complicated fabric of state regulation. The states have long set at least some limits to campaign activity. Most states, for example, have some law prohibiting certain election-day expenditures; all states prohibit bribery and vote buying; and some prohibit such practices as buying a voter a drink on election day. Most states also require reporting of campaign contributions and expenditures. In general, however, state regulations have never achieved even the modest effectiveness of the old federal legislation.

The Watergate scandals spurred a new round of state legislation after 1972. New state legislation on campaign finance was often set in a broader framework that included legislation requiring registration by lobbyists, open meetings by government bodies, and disclosure of the personal finances of public officeholders. Consequently, by the 1980 campaigns, virtually every state had a disclosure statute that forced reports on campaign giving and spending. (North Dakota was the single exception.) Many of the states that had long had such requirements tightened them up after Watergate. At the same time, a record number of states—about 30 of them—either adopted or refurbished limits on the expenditures that candidates could make. Since the 1976 decision in *Buckley v. Valeo*, of course, they are unenforceable even if they have not been formally repealed.

In the 1980s, then, the picture in the states is as follows. Virtually all states compel disclosure of some sort. A total of twenty-five states and the District of Columbia place some limits on contributions; the other twenty-five states place no limits on them. Although direct contributions from

[11]Stanton A. Glantz, Alan I. Abramowitz, and Michael P. Burkhart, "Election Outcomes: Whose Money Matters?" *Journal of Politics* 34 (1976): 1033–38; and Gary Jacobson, *Money in Congressional Elections* (New Haven: Yale University Press, 1980).

corporate and union treasuries are banned by federal law, only twenty-four states so limit corporations and only ten prohibit direct union contributions. Overall, therefore, the states are less severe in their restrictions than the federal government is. A minority of states, however, have ventured further into public funding than the Congress has. There are fifteen states with operating programs of public funding; of them, seven give the public funds directly to candidates, but eight make the payments to political parties. In the latter case, the parties are free to either use the money for their own expenditures or parcel it out to deserving candidates. Because of the party-building implications of such programs, they are the ones that party organizations elsewhere are watching most closely. Fifteen states also permit taxpayers to claim deductions or tax credits on their state income tax returns for contributions they have made to political campaigns. In grand total, twenty-two states and the District of Columbia have either public funding or a tax break for contributors, or both.[12]

The burst of post-Watergate legislative activity in the Congress and the states has not put the question of reform to rest, however. Pressures for new regulations follow changes in the patterns of campaign finance. The growth of the PAC role has spawned a new set of proposed remedies: reduced limits on PAC contributions to candidates, a new limit on the total dollar amount congressional candidates could accept from PACs, and, ultimately, public finance, with its condition of limits on how much the candidate can raise and spend. Similarly, the growth of independent expenditures, especially in national politics, has spurred the search for limitations on them. At the least, the reformers would like to tighten the statutory definition of independence to eliminate the possibility of coordination between candidate or party and the independent spender. At least two considerations now slow the course of additional reform, however. First, unless the Supreme Court retreats from its position in *Buckley* and subsequent cases, the reform options are sharply limited. By holding limits on expenditures unconstitutional, for example, the Court sharply limits the feasible ways for capping the costs of campaigning or independent spending. Second, campaign finance has increasingly become a partisan and ideological issue, with liberals and Democrats favoring new restrictions and conservatives and Republicans opposing them. It would thus appear that substantial reform at the national level would be difficult or unlikely unless the Democrats controlled both the Congress and the presidency.[13]

---

[12]Data drawn from Herbert Alexander, *Financing Politics*, 2nd ed. (Washington, D.C.: Congressional Quarterly, 1980), Chap. 7. See also Ruth S. Jones, "State Public Campaign Finance: Implications for Partisan Politics," *American Journal of Political Science* 25 (1981): 342–61.

[13]For a survey of reform issues, and for a review of recent literature on them, see David Adamany, "Money, Politics, and Democracy: A Review Essay," *American Political Science Review* 71 (1977): 289–304.

BROADER CONSIDERATIONS AND PROBLEMS

Recent developments in campaign finance directly reflect the recent changes in American campaigning. As the new campaigning shifts from a noncash economy of volunteer labor to a cash economy of vastly greater magnitude, and as campaigns shift from party control to candidate management, the effects on the amounts of money raised and the ways it is raised are obvious. If cable TV or any other revolution in communication further changes campaigning, it is safe to predict that there will be accompanying changes in campaign finance.

Nothing illustrates the tie between the shape of campaigning and the nature of campaign finance better than the rise of mass media campaigning over the last several generations. In the presidential election of 1948, there were no expenditures for television; twenty years later, however, the campaigns of Richard Nixon and Hubert Humphrey together spent $13.5 million just for television time. By 1976, Jimmy Carter and Gerald Ford— under the constraints of spending limitations and forced to set severe spending priorities—spent about half of their available public money for media expenditures. That percentage rose above 60 percent in 1980, as Ronald Reagan's campaign spent $17 million on all media advertising and production and Carter spent $19.5 million; in both instances, the greatest share of those amounts went to TV. On the other hand, where media campaigning is inappropriate, especially in local elections, the entire scale of funding is lower and the pattern of expenditures is sharply different. It is as if we were developing two different styles of campaigning, with two different systems of campaign finance to accompany them.

The status quo in American campaign finance also raises a series of questions about power and influence in the American democracy. Indeed, no subject raises such questions as predictably as political money. The first is the basic question of influence in the parties and electoral processes. Political contributors have political goals and incentives, just as do activists who contribute their skills and labor to the party organization or to a candidate's campaign. Large numbers of Americans wonder what kinds of demands or expectations accompany their financial contributions. Money is obviously a major resource of American politics, and its contributors clearly acquire some form of political influence. What is not yet clear is the nature of the influence and the differences, both quantitative and qualitative, between it and the influence that results from nonmoney contributions to the parties and candidates.

It is not easy to specify with certainty the goals or incentives that motivate the financial contributor. Very likely they come from the same range of incentives that stir the activist to contribute his or her time to the party organization: patronage, preferment, a political career; personal, social, or psychological satisfactions; and an interest, issue, and ideology. Unquestionably, the chief incentive is the combination of interest, issue and ideology—the desire, that is, to influence the establishment or administration of some kind of public policy. The concentration of PAC contributions on incumbent members of Congress is a case in point. The contributor's desire may be for direct access or for the ear of the powerful. More commonly, it is only a desire to elect public officials with values and preferences that promise a sympathy for the goals of the contributor. Thus, the demands of the contributor are largely indirect; certainly, very few contributors seek a direct quid pro quo.

Second, in addition to the issue of influence on policy, there is the question of power within the party. The status quo in American political finance supports parties in government and helps them maintain their independence from the party organizations. So long as candidates and officeholders continue to finance their own primary and general election campaigns, they block the organizations' control of access to public office. Unquestionably, the reluctance of Congress and state legislatures to disturb the present patterns of political finance grows, in large part, from their satisfaction with the political independence these patterns ensure them. Despite the spate of reforms of recent years, candidate spending—as opposed to party organization spending—remains entrenched. The candidate, rather than the party, raises and spends large sums of money. Even in the sorties into public financing of campaigns, the funds go to candidates (not to party organizations) in half of the states. To be sure, there has been some indirect support of a party role—the federal legislation permitting party committees to spend beyond candidate expenditure ceilings, for example—but it is far less than would be necessary to establish strong and disciplined parties with sanctions over their candidates and officeholders.

Third, reform in campaign finance, like all other party reform, never affects all individuals and parties alike. It works to some people's advantage and to others' disadvantage. The cumulative effect of the reforms of the 1970s will surely be to diminish the influence of wealthy contributors and to make the "little" contributor more valuable than ever. (In that respect, one ought to note, however, that it is hardly certain that one contributor of $10,000 actually made more effective demands on the recipient than 100 contributors of $100 will.) New influence and access also accrue to the technicians who can raise small gifts as well as to group contributors and incumbents. Also, some advantages clearly accrue to candidates who can raise substantially greater sums than their opponents can. Concern over the effect of unequal cash resources cuts two ways, however. Some of the support for public funding comes from those who see it as a way of equalizing resources and thus eliminating unfair advantages; but cash is not the only resource a candidate needs. Incumbent officeholders have all manner of other advantages over challengers—staffs, media access, and name recognition, for example—and challengers may well need to have a cash advantage if they are to have a chance of winning and if elections are to remain competitive.

The American way of campaign finance reflects the American way of politics. Campaign costs reflect the vastness of the country, the many elective offices on many levels of government, the localism of American politics, and the unbridled length of our campaigns for office. The domination of spending by candidates reflects our candidate-dominated campaigns and, more generally, the dominance within American parties of the party in government. The importance of the mass media in major American campaigns speaks volumes about the media themselves, while it also reflects the sheer size of our constituencies. By contrast, campaign finance in Great Britain involves far smaller sums more firmly in the control of the party organizations. In Britain, however, there is free time on the government-run BBC and a long-standing tradition of the "soft sell" in all forms of public persuasion. Moreover, the British election campaign runs for only about three weeks, and the average constituency in the House of Commons has less than one-fifth as many people as the average American congressional district. Most significantly, there is no larger constituency, no office with a constituency as vast as most American states, not to mention the American presidency's national constituency.

Aided by institutions such as the direct primary and the office-block ballot and supported by their ability to recruit the campaign resources they need, the American parties in government thus largely escape the control of party organizations. In many states and localities, indeed, they dominate them—but at what price? Certainly, there is the price of a loss of cohesion as a party in government—for example, in the loss of a unified presence as party representatives in American legislatures. Certainly, too, there is the price of a weakening of party organization, not only vis-à-vis the party in government, but also internally, in terms of its ability to achieve the goals of its activists. Finally, nowhere in the life of the parties is the competition between party in government and party organization any clearer than in the competition for campaign funds and campaign control. As the costs of campaigning rise and as all participants are forced to shift to a cash economy of enormous magnitude, the future is with the sector of the party with access to those cash resources. So far, the advantage is clearly with the candidates and officeholders.

V
The Party in Government

The charge that the American parties cannot govern is an old one, and few scholars of American politics have made it as pungently as E. E. Schattschneider:

> Yet, when all is said, it remains true that the roll calls demonstrate that the parties are unable to hold their lines on a controversial public issue when the pressure is on.
>
> The condition . . . constitutes the most important single fact concerning the American parties. He who knows this fact, and knows nothing else, knows more about American parties than he who knows everything except this fact. What kind of party is it that, having won control of government, is unable to govern?[1]

In campaigns, each political party tries to convince the American electorate that it does matter that it, rather than the opposition party, wins office. Can it matter very much, however, when the parties in Congress are so easily fragmented in votes on important issues? In the roll call votes in 1982, for instance, in which a majority of one party disagreed with a majority of the other party, the average Democrat in Congress voted with the party only 72 percent of the time, and the average Republican only 71 percent.[2]

Yet, in the face of this and other evidence that the American parties do not and cannot govern, it remains true that party lines, however loosely drawn, are the chief lines in American legislative voting behavior. There is a degree of party cohesion in the roll calls of Congress and the states that cannot be lightly dismissed. Furthermore, recent research suggests

[1]E. E. Schattschneider, *Party Government* (New York: Rinehart, 1942), pp. 131–32 (Emphasis removed).

[2]*Congressional Quarterly Almanac* 38 (1982): 20–C.

that the party winning the presidency even succeeds in carrying out a good portion of its party platform.[3]

The evidence on party government in the United States thus points in a number of directions. It suggests that the parties do not fail entirely in enacting their programs into public policy. Yet it betrays the frequency with which officeholders of the same party disagree on matters of public policy. It also suggests that an individual's assessment of the parties' ability to govern depends on how and to what extent he or she expects the parties to govern.

Some distinctions are important here. We are talking of *party* government, not merely the governing and policymaking of officeholders elected on party tickets. Certainly, men and women who seek legislative or executive office do intend to govern, to take their responsibilities seriously, but that is not the issue. We are talking about the ability of public officials of the same party to enact the programs of their party. Furthermore, since it is *party* government about which we speak, which parts of the party do we expect to set the policy by which the party will govern— all three sectors, the party organization, or just the party in government? If the latter, would it be the entire party in government, or is it possible that the executive party has propensities and abilities to govern different from those of the legislative party?

It is well to remember, too, that although the three sectors of the party are brought together in the search for power at elections, each has its own goals and motives. The activists of the party organization may seek to translate a program or ideology into policy, but they may also seek patronage jobs, other forms of reward or preference, the sensations of victory, or the defeat of a hated opposition. The party's voters may be stimulated by an issue, a program, or an ideology, but they also respond to personalities, to incumbency ("time for a change"), to abstract and traditional loyalties to a candidate or party, or to the urging of friends and family. The candidates and officeholders seek the office, its tangible rewards, its intangible satisfactions, and its opportunities to make public decisions. The important point is that none of the three sectors is committed wholly—or possibly even predominantly—to the capture of public office for the purpose of enacting party policies into law.

The classic American statement on party government (or party responsibility) was made in the late 1940s by a committee of the American Political Science Association in a report entitled *Toward a More Responsible Two-Party System.*[4] The report argued that the American parties ought to articulate more specific and comprehensive policy programs,

---

[3]Gerald M. Pomper, *Elections in America* (New York: Dodd, Mead, 1968), Chap. 8.

[4]The report was published in New York by Rinehart in 1950. It also appears as a supplement to the September 1950 issue of *American Political Science Review.*

nominate candidates pledged to those programs, and then see to it that their successful candidates enact the programs while they are in office. In other words, the major parties ought to serve as the mechanisms through which American voters can choose between competing programs, and through which the winning majority of voters can be assured of the enactment of its choice.

In such terms, the question of party government (or responsibility) concerns not just the nature of the parties but the nature of American democracy itself. If the parties were to become policy initiators, they would assume a central representative role in the American democracy. They would bring great, amorphous majorities in the American electorate into alliance with groups of officeholders by means of some kind of party program or platform. They would forge a new representative link between the mass democratic electorate and the powerful few in government. To put the issue another way, responsible parties would bring electorates closer to the choices of government by giving them a way to register choices on policy alternatives. Those choices might be partly before the fact (in the mobilization of grass-roots support behind proposed programs) and partly post facto judgments on the stewardship of two different, distinguishable parties in government. In both cases, the proposal is an attempt to restore initiative and significant choice to the great number of voters.

The critics of such proposals for party government have concentrated on one insistent theme: the nonideological, heterogeneous, and pragmatic nature of the American parties. They argue that agreement on and enforcement of a coherent policy program is very difficult, if not impossible. Recently, of course, the party organizations are more oriented toward programs and ideology—and thus toward the uses of governmental authority for specific policy goals. There was a time when the activists of the party organization contested elections largely for the spoils at stake: jobs, contracts, honors, access, and other forms of special consideration. It made little difference to them what uses public officeholders made of the governmental power in their hands. That time is passing. As more and more citizens are attracted to the party organizations and electorates for reasons of policy, important intraparty pressure builds for some degree of party responsibility.

Discussion of more programmatic and disciplined political parties leads always to the European parties, especially those of England. Parliamentary institutions foster the kind of legislative cohesion and discipline—the sharply drawn party lines—that the advocates of responsible parties have in mind. Party organizations in Britain and on the continent, especially those of the parties of the left, also seek to enforce the party's program on its legislators. In some cases, they have succeeded—in many of the socialist and communist parties, among others. In others, they have not, but even in these cases the national party leaders speak powerfully for the party's program. One often sees a concerted effort on the part of the party in government (all of which sits in Parliament) and the party organization to carry out a program that was adopted with the help of the party members at an earlier party conference. Indeed, so strong is party discipline in the legislative process in some European countries that scholars complain about the decline of parliaments, and journalists write darkly of "partyocracy." Ironically, in these circles, it is not uncommon to hear envious talk of the flexible, nondogmatic American parties and the uncontrolled and deliberative American legislatures.

The European experience is important for perspective and comparison. It is also important because the European variety of party government, with its focus on parliamentary discipline, has dominated the thinking of many Americans about party government. Any change in the American parties toward greater responsibility, however, will probably follow no European route. The role the parties now have in American politics and the roles toward which they move will be as uniquely American as the institutional complex of American federalism, separation of powers, and electoral processes. Given the power of the executive in American government, its ability to convert party goals or platforms into public policy may be as important as the legislature's.

Beyond this question of the party's contribution to the making of public policy—to the organizing of majority decisions in a democracy—there is another one: the question of the impact of winning office and making policy on the political party. The achievement of party goals (the goals of all three sectors) depends directly on the holding of governmental power—but in what way? To put it bluntly, what does governmental power do for the parties? What kinds of rewards does it generate for the men and women who have invested so much in politics and the party? How does it contribute to the health and vitality of the party and its various sectors?

The first two chapters in this part examine the present role of the political party in the organization and operation of the three branches of government. They are primarily concerned with the degrees of party direction or party cohesion in legislative and executive policy decisions. In short, they deal with the impact of internalized party loyalties and external party influences on public officials. The third chapter in this part faces the general question of party government—its desirability and its possibility. It also addresses the question of whether the new programmatic orientations within the parties create conditions hospitable to the development of party government.

14

PARTY AND PARTISANS
IN THE LEGISLATURE

The political party assumes an obvious, very public form—yet a very shadowy role—in American legislatures. The parties organize majority and minority power in the legislatures, and the legislative leaders and committee chairpersons are usually party oligarchs. Yet, despite the appearance and panoply of party power, voting on crucial issues often crosses party lines, not to mention party pledges and platforms. The party in many forms dominates the American legislatures; yet the effect of party effort and loyalty is often negligible. On this paradox turns much of the scholarly concern and reformist zeal expended on American legislatures.

The character of the American legislative party has been deeply affected by the American separation of powers. In a parliamentary regime, such as that of Great Britain, a majority party or a multiparty coalition in the Parliament must cohere in support of the cabinet (and its government), thus creating a constitutional presumption and pressure on behalf of unity within the legislative party. When the parliamentary majority no longer supports the cabinet, a political adjustment follows. Either reorganization of the cabinet or a reshuffling of the legislative coalition supporting it ensues, or else the Parliament is dissolved and sent home to face a new election.

No such institutional and constitutional pressures weigh on American legislators. They may divide on, dispute with, or reject executive programs, even if the executive is of their own party, without dire consequences. In American legislatures, the party role is not institutionalized as it is in parliaments. The American legislature may not run so smoothly without party cohesion and discipline, but it can run, and executives survive its faithlessness.

PARTY ORGANIZATIONS IN LEGISLATURES

In forty-nine of the state legislatures and the Congress, the members come to their legislative tasks as elected candidates of a political party.[1] The ways in which they form and behave as a legislative party, however, differ enormously. In some states, the legislative party scarcely can be said to exist; in others, it dominates the legislative process through an almost daily regimen of party caucuses. Parties in most of the state legislatures and in the Congress, however, fall comfortably in the territory between these two poles.

Parties in the Congress

Party organization in the United States Congress stands as something of a benchmark for observations of the American legislatures because it is the best known of the legislatures. Both parties in both houses of Congress meet at the beginning of each congressional session to select the party leadership: a party leader, a whip, a party policy committee, for example. In addition, the party meetings (called caucuses or conferences) present their candidates for the position of Speaker of the House or president pro tempore of the Senate, and they set up procedures for the appointment of party members to the regular committees of the chamber. In effect, then, the basic unit of party organization, the caucus or the conference, begins the business of organizing the chamber. From its decisions rises the machinery of the party as a party (the leaders, whips, policy committees) and the organization of the chamber itself (the presiding officer and the committees).

In short, the organization of the two parties and the organization of the House and Senate are melded into what appears to be a single fabric of organization (see Figure 14.1). The organizational system appears to work better in organizing the two chambers, however, than in organizing the parties for action as parties. When the party caucuses or conferences do meet on important issues during the session, they only rarely undertake to bind the individual members. Indeed, they do not even meet regularly during the session. Moreover, the policy committees set up in the Reorganization Act of 1946 have not succeeded as broadly based instruments of party policymaking or strategy setting, even though they were created for the "formulation of overall legislative policy of the respective parties," as the act puts it. One study found that they lacked any internal agreement on party policy and that, instead of being a collective party leadership, they had lapsed into the practice of representing the assorted blocs and

---

[1] The Nebraska legislature is chosen in nonpartisan elections.

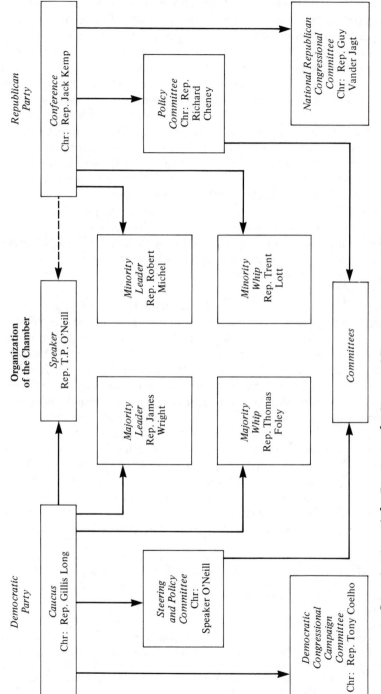

FIGURE 14.1 *Organization of the Parties in the House of Representatives: 1983*

wings of the party.[2] Despite the original hopes, the policy committees have operated primarily as advisory groups and channels of communication between party leaders and influential figures and the full party membership.

Dissatisfaction with leadership control of the policy committees breaks out periodically, especially among the liberal Democrats. In 1963, in an attack on the "Senate Establishment" Senator Joseph Clark (Pennsylvania) included strictures about conservative and leadership domination of the Democratic Policy Committee.[3] (In the same year, the overthrow of Representative Charles Halleck, the Republican leader, by Representative Gerald Ford was accompanied by an increase in the number of younger Republicans on that party's policy committee in the House.) In the reform of party machinery in the 1970s, the House Democrats formed a new Steering and Policy Committee, with elected representatives from the caucus. Since 1975, it has at least begun to function as the party's committee on committees. Moreover, some years earlier, the Democratic liberals of the House had formed a policy committee of their own: the Democratic Study Group. The DSG does some staff research, takes policy stands, and represents the liberal views of its members. It has even developed its own whip system.[4]

To the extent that there is party policy in the houses of Congress, then, it is largely set by the party leadership. The floor leaders and the powerful figures of the party consult widely throughout the party, but the final codification of party policy, the sensing of a will or consensus, rests primarily on their judgment. If they are of the president's party, their actions and decisions are limited by his legislative program and his influence within the Congress. Within the nonpresidential party, the leadership in the House and Senate may act not only without a continuing check by the legislative party but also without a continuing check by any party organ or spokesperson. Senate party leaders such as Lyndon Johnson and Everett Dirksen, and Speaker of the House "Tip" O'Neill, in fact, established themselves as spokesmen for both the legislative and the national parties.[5]

What emerge as the decisions and priorities of the party leadership, however, are not really "party policy"—except in the sense that they are voiced by leaders of the legislative party. They are, rather, an amalgam

[2]David B. Truman, *The Congressional Party* (New York: Wiley, 1959), pp. 126–30.

[3]Joseph S. Clark, *The Senate Establishment* (New York: Hill and Wang, 1963).

[4]See Arthur G. Stevens, Arthur H. Miller, and Thomas E. Mann, "Mobilization of Liberal Strength in the House, 1955–1970: The Democratic Study Group," *American Political Science Review* 68 (1974): 667–81.

[5]More generally, on party leadership in the Congress, see Ralph K. Huitt, "Democratic Party Leadership in the Senate," *American Political Science Review* 55 (1961): 333–44; Randall B. Ripley, "The Party Whip Organizations in the United States House of Representatives," *American Political Science Review* 58 (1964): 561–76; and William J. Keefe and Morris S. Ogul, *The American Legislative Process: Congress and the States*, 5th ed. (Englewood Cliffs, N.J.: Prentice-Hall, 1981), Chap. 9.

of or a negotiated compromise among the goals of the senior party members (who hold committee power), the party leaders themselves, the rank and file of the legislative party, and (in one party) the president. They rarely flow from any national party program or platform. They speak, instead, of the powers and perquisites of the legislature, the need to support or oppose a president, and the demands of the legislative constituencies. The party leaders, in other words, do not enforce a prior party policy: they make policy for and with their fellow legislators in an ad hoc way. Their party policy is purely that of the legislative party. In view of the party leadership's brokerage role in making the policy, therefore, it is mandatory that party leaders come from the mainstream, the dominant wing of the party.[6]

Parties in State Legislatures

Among the state legislatures are those in which daily caucuses, binding party discipline, and autocratic party leadership make for a party far more potent than exists in the two houses of Congress. There are also state legislatures, however—especially those of the traditional one-party states— in which party organization is perceptibly weaker than it is in the Congress. Even in states that have a complete apparatus of party organization, the parties fail more frequently than the congressional parties to make the apparatus operate effectively. The party caucuses in Congress at least maintain cohesion in their initial organizational tasks; they always agree on candidates for the presiding officers. State legislative parties periodically find themselves too divided by factionalism or ambition even to organize the legislature. In some states with comparatively weak legislative parties, such as California, coalitions across party lines to elect legislative leaders are not rare. They happen occasionally, however, even in states with greater party strength, such as Illinois (see box) and New York. In 1965, the Democrats of New York, though a numerical majority in both houses of the legislature, could not agree on a single set of leadership candidates. After a hiatus of a month, during which the legislature could conduct no business, Republicans decided to support one of the Democratic factions and thus elected leaders for both chambers of the legislature.

In a one-party state, the party caucus has little excuse for being. Disagreement over organization, leadership positions, and policy issues in these states usually falls along factional lines within the party or along the lines of followings of powerful personages. In the heyday of the Long dynasty in Louisiana, one Democratic faction adhered to the Longs and others supported their opponents. In this particular case and in others,

---

[6]Robert L. Peabody, *Leadership in Congress* (Boston: Little, Brown, 1976), Chap. 16.

Party Deadlock in Illinois

The reputation for contentiousness in Illinois Democratic politics is not without foundation. In part, it reflects a historic Chicago–downstate division; and in part, it also reflects divisions among the many ethnic and racial groups that make up such an important part of the Illinois Democrats. One of the leading authorities on state legislative politics writes:

> In 1975 it took the Democrats in Illinois 93 ballots before they could elect a speaker of the house, and they needed Republican help to do so. Then in 1977 Democrats in the Illinois senate were divided into several factions, each of which was backing one of three candidates for president of the chamber. A majority, including most of those from Chicago, was behind one candidate; a group of downstate dissidents was supporting another; and the blacks in the house were in still another camp, insisting that in return for their support a black Democrat get the post of assistant majority leader. Democratic dissidents held out, hoping to win Republican votes on the floor. The struggle lasted longer than a month, and was not resolved until 186 ballots had been taken on the senate floor. The candidate of the majority faction of the Democrats finally won, with the candidate of the dissidents receiving the post of assistant leader.
>
> Alan Rosenthal, *Legislative Life: People, Process,*
> *and Performance in the States* (New York: Harper
> & Row, 1981), pp. 155–56.

factional lines built on personal and family followings coincide with differing regional loyalties. Alternatively, the legislative caucuses in one-party states may reflect ideological lines; from 1910 to the 1930s in Wisconsin, for example, the La Follette Progressive Republicans organized one legislative caucus, the conservative Republicans another, and the very feeble Democrats a third.

Party leadership in the state legislatures assumes a number of forms. The traditional floor leaders and whips exist in most. In others, the Speaker of the House or a spokesperson for the governor may mobilize the party's legislators. State party officials, unlike the relatively powerless national party officials vis-à-vis Congress, may have a powerful voice in the legislative party. As Lockard reported of the heyday of party control in the Connecticut lower house:

> The "outside" party leaders are in daily attendance at the capitol and can be seen in corridor conferences with the great and small alike. Each

party chairman sits in on his respective party policy conferences and not infrequently he is the real leader of the conference. With few exceptions the men who reach the party pinnacle of the state chairmanship can expect (and they certainly receive) proper deference from their fellows in the legislature.[7]

Whatever their relationship with state party leaders may be, however, the legislative leaders enjoy enormous power in the day-to-day workings of the legislature. Their influence on party caucuses is great, and they do not often have to contend with steering or policy committees in state legislatures.

It is probably reasonable to say that the range of extremes in party influence in state legislatures in recent years is narrowing. Jewell and Patterson write about one state:

> For many years the classic example of a powerful caucus was found in New Jersey, where the majority party caucus in each house met daily and decided which bills would be passed and which would die. . . . The power of the caucus was so great that the standing committees had no significant functions and seldom met. In recent years, however, the caucuses in both houses have reduced the scope of their activities, and now take action only on a limited number of bills designated by the leaders as party policy measures. As a consequence, the committee system in the New Jersey legislature has begun to develop some independent authority.[8]

As the strong party discipline of a few states dissipates and as two-party competition brings legislative parties to states that had not known them, practice in the states becomes more similar, more homogeneous.

THE EFFECTS AND INFLUENCE OF PARTY

The shape of party power is clearly evident in American legislatures—but power for what? Is it power for organizing party support for a set of party programs or merely for parceling out the perquisites of legislative office? Or does the legislative party seek both policy and perquisites?

Effects in the Congress

The parties in the United States Congress have amply illustrated over the last century that they can impose party sanctions on only one issue: the

---

[7]W. Duane Lockard, "Legislative Politics in Connecticut," *American Political Science Review* 48 (1954): 167.

[8]Malcolm E. Jewell and Samuel C. Patterson, *The Legislative Process in the United States,* 3rd ed. (New York: Random House, 1977), pp. 159–60; the authors also cite an unpublished paper by Alan Rosenthal and the Eagleton Institute of Politics, "Studies of the New Jersey Legislature" (New Brunswick, 1970).

failure of a member of the legislative party to support its presidential candidate. Representatives or senators can freely vote against the party's platform, majority, or leadership—or against the program of their party's president. They risk punishment, however, if they undercut their party's presidential candidate. In 1925, the Republican caucus in the Senate expelled Senators La Follette, Ladd, Frazier, and Brookhart after they had supported La Follette and the Progressive ticket in the 1924 elections. That decision also robbed the four senators of their Republican committee assignments and seniority.

Expulsion from the party is very rare, however. Even the greatest displeasure in legislative parties rarely leads to more than a stripping of seniority or committee assignments. In 1965, the Democratic caucus in the House took all committee seniority from two southern Democrats who had supported the Republican presidential candidate, Barry Goldwater, the year before. In 1968, the same fate befell Representative John Rarick, a Democrat from Louisiana, for supporting George Wallace. In early 1983, the Democratic caucus removed Representative Phil Gramm from his seat on the House Budget Committee; in the view of his Democratic colleagues, Gramm, a conservative Democrat from Texas, had given too much support to the Reagan budget in the session that ended in 1982. (Gramm, a leader of the Democratic "boll weevils," a group of conservative members of the House, resigned his seat shortly thereafter and was elected to it as a Republican in a special election some weeks later.) It is no accident, of course, that all of these instances of discipline occurred in the Democratic caucus of the House. The House Democrats, largely because of greater divisions and greater power in the hands of the caucus itself, have sought a far greater degree of discipline than have any of the other three legislative parties in the Congress.

Beyond these relatively infrequent disciplinary actions, the party organizations in Congress rely on informal pressure of one sort or another. If they are of the president's party, they convey the president's wishes and with them the president's influence and sanctions. In other instances—not frequently, indeed—legislative leaders report and transmit the feelings of party leaders outside the Congress. Chiefly, however, they depend on their own legislative leverage. They may give the choicest committee assignments to the most loyal members of the party. The favors they give—the help in passing favorite bills or the additional office space, for example—can cultivate a measure of party support. So, too, can their political help to their fellow legislators; party leaders give political speeches and raise campaign funds at least in part for that purpose.[9] When party leaders fail in their attempts to maintain party unity in the legislature, it is not so

[9]See Barbara Sinclair, "Majority Party Leadership Strategies for Coping with the New U.S. House," *Legislative Studies Quarterly* 6 (1981): 391–414.

much for lack of leverage as for the strength of the pressures from the local congressional constituencies. The chief limit to their success is always the need of the individual member of Congress to satisfy a constituency in order to win reelection. When party and constituency conflict, responsiveness to the folks back home usually outweighs the calls for party unity in Congress.

Attempts to build party discipline in Congress have also been undercut in the past by the power of the committees and by a tradition of seniority that awards committee chairmanships to legislators of longest service. The independence of the committees places them, as a system of influence, squarely in opposition to any influences that the parties might exert. Seniority as a key to power in the committees puts a premium on getting reelected rather than on party loyalty or regularity within the Congress. Thus, attempts by a legislative party to reform seniority and the committee system—such as those of the House Democrats in the 1970s—are nothing less than struggles for control of the business of the Congress. The Democrats of the House succeeded by modifying the power of committee chairpersons and also by establishing the principle that the party caucuses would vote every two years to approve the continuance in power of every committee chairperson. As a result of the reforms, three Democratic chairmen who had held their positions by reason of seniority were deposed in 1975. As committee power was diminished, one barrier to the influence of party organization was lowered.

Effects in the State Legislatures

In some state legislatures, party leadership and organization operate far more effectively than they do in the Congress. Positions of party leadership and committee power much more frequently go to legislators loyal to the party and to its programs. Furthermore, either the party leaders, the party speaking through a periodic caucus decision, or the party's governor or state committee may expect the legislators to support the party program or stand on a particular issue. It is not surprising that state legislators look to party leaders for cues and direction much more frequently than do the members of Congress.[10] For excessive lapses of party loyalty, state legislators may suffer sanctions that would be inconceivable in the United States Congress. Their influence may wane in the legislature, and they may ultimately lose positions of power. In a patronage state, they may find that the applicants they sponsor fare less well than formerly. They may also find in the next election campaign that they no longer receive campaign

[10]Eric M. Uslaner and Ronald E. Weber, *Patterns of Decision Making in State Legislatures* (New York: Praeger, 1977).

funds from the state or local party or, worse yet, that the party is supporting competitors in the primaries.

Clearly, the parties in some of the competitive, two-party state legislatures have advanced the art of discipline far beyond its state in the Congress. The reasons for their success tell us a good deal about the building of party power in legislatures.

Absence of competing centers of power. In the Congress, the committees traditionally have been the centers of legislative power. A vast amount of the real business of the Congress goes on in them. They are the screens that sift through the great mass of legislative proposals for those relatively few nuggets of legislative metal. The result is the creation of important centers of power in the Congress that owe nothing to the parties and that do not necessarily reflect the party organization or aims. (In fact, one can argue that since seniority and its power accrue to members of Congress from noncompetitive, one-party areas, they are definitely unrepresentative of the party in the country at large.)

In the states, on the other hand, legislators accumulate less seniority (turnover is greater), and deference to seniority in allocating positions of power is far less common. A 1950s survey of the state legislatures concluded that seniority "figured prominently" in the selection of committee chairpersons in only fourteen senates and twelve lower houses in the states.[11] The parties in the states are freer to appoint their loyalists to positions of legislative power; the committees and other legislative agencies of the states generally operate as instruments of party power in a way unknown in the Congress.

Patronage and preferences. Patronage and other forms of governmental preference still exist in some states to a far greater extent than they do in the national government. Especially in the hands of a vigorous and determined governor, these rewards may be potent inducements to party discipline in state legislatures. Legislators who ignore their party, if it is the party of the governor, may not be able to secure the political appointments that their constituents and local party workers have been waiting for. Conversely, the loyal and faithful party legislator is amply rewarded. In the Congress, little such patronage remains with which to induce party discipline. Its last, gaudy twilight came in the early 1930s, as Franklin Roosevelt mustered what remained of the federal patronage and told his patronage chief, Postmaster General James A. Farley, not to dole out the jobs until the voting records were in from the first congressional session.

Influence of the state party organization. State party organizations exert far greater control over state legislators than does the feeble national

[11]Belle Zeller (ed.), *American State Legislatures* (New York: Crowell, 1954), p. 197.

committee of the party over the members of Congress. In the states, the party organization and the legislative party are far more likely to be allies. State party leaders may inhibit the political ambitions of party mavericks or deny them advancement within the party, especially in states in which they can control the nomination processes. They may even prevail on local parties to deny renomination to those who are disloyal. Indeed, state party leaders may occupy positions of legislative leadership; powerful figures such as the former Democratic Speaker of the California Assembly, Jesse ("Big Daddy") Unruh, combined state party influence with legislative leadership. Lockard reported that Republican legislators in Rhode Island had "a policy committee comprised of important senators, a few representatives, the state party chairman, and a few members of the state central committee."[12] By contrast, the national political party is relatively powerless in dealing with its congressional parties. Even so powerful a party figure as Franklin Roosevelt was unable to purge a group of conservative Democrats for failing to support his program. Members of Congress are protected by decentralized party power. State legislators are not.

Electoral dependence of state legislators. State legislators are far more dependent on the local and state party for nomination and election than are the members of Congress. Also, what the local party has given, it may take away. Representatives and senators build their own political organizations, their own coteries of local supporters, and their own sources of campaign financing. State legislators, however, are less well known and therefore more dependent. In some states, the parties control the election of state legislators to such an extent that these positions approach an elective patronage, which the party awards to loyal toilers in its organizational ranks. (About 70 percent of the candidates for the Pennsylvania House of Representatives in the election of 1958 had held some party office.)[13] Even where control of elections is less certain, a lack of party support creates unwelcome campaign problems.

Greater political homogeneity. Greater party cohesion in some state legislatures also reflects the greater homogeneity of state parties. Although a legislative party in Congress reflects the full range of differences within the nation, that same party in any given state embraces a narrower spectrum of interests and ideologies. This greater political homogeneity of the states produces legislative parties in which the ranges of differences and disagreements are smaller and in which there are fewer sources of internal conflict. The political culture of the state also is more homogeneous and, in some cases, more tolerant of party discipline over legislators than the

---

[12]W. Duane Lockard, *New England State Politics* (Princeton: Princeton University Press, 1959), p. 218.

[13]Frank J. Sorauf, *Party and Representation* (New York: Atherton, 1963), p. 86.

national constituency is. Legislative party strength has traditionally flourished, for example, in the northeastern part of the country (Rhode Island,
Connecticut, Pennsylvania, New Jersey, for example), the states of party
organizational strength, patronage, weak primaries, and, one infers, a political culture tolerant of political muscle.

PARTY COHESION IN LEGISLATIVE VOTING

Party organization in Congress and the state legislatures—with caucuses,
leaders, whips, and policy committees—is only the most apparent, overt
manifestation of the party in the legislature. Its efforts on behalf of party
unity and discipline among its legislators are tangible, if difficult to document. Party influence in legislatures, however, is broader and more pervasive than the enforcing activities of the organized legislative party. Party
in a broader, more figurative sense may also operate "within" the legislator as a series of internalized loyalties and frameworks for organizing his
or her legislative decisions. To speak of party only in the organizational
sense of leaders and caucuses, therefore, is to miss the richness and complexity of party influence on the legislative process.

The political party is only one of a number of claimants for the vote
of a legislator on any given issue. The voters of the home constituency
make their demands, too, and so do the more ideological and militant
workers of the party back home. Nor can the wishes of the president be
easily dismissed. To all of these pressures one must also add those of interest groups, financial contributors, friends and associates in the legislature, and the legislator's own system of beliefs. Happily, all or most of
these pressures point in the same direction on many issues. When they do
not, party loyalty understandably gives way from time to time.

Although no single legislative decision is in any sense typical of the
work of even one legislature, an illustration of the cross-cutting influences
may be useful. The continuing financial crisis of New York City came back
to the Congress in 1978. To enable New York to sell its bonds—and thus
to avert bankruptcy—the Congress agreed to guarantee up to $1.5 billion
of the city's bonds. The vote for passage in the Senate was 53–27, with
Democrats voting 35–12 and Republicans 18–15. Both parties were therefore in the majority, with the Democrats providing more support for a bill
that had the support of a Democratic administration. At the same time,
the vote also illustrated how easily the parties in the Senate fragment under constituency and regional-ideological considerations. Only three senators from the urban, industrial states of the Northeast and the Midwest
voted against the bill. In the southern, southwestern, mountain, and western states, however, the vote totaled sixteen for the bill and twenty-four
against.

Illustrations aside, however, the cumulative consequences of party influence can be gauged only by looking at all of the roll calls in a legislative session. The ability of a party to maintain cohesion among its members over a session is, after all, the ultimate operational test.

Incidence of Party Cohesion

Answers always depend on the wording of the questions and so it is with the question of the cohesion or discipline the American parties generate in legislatures. The answer depends to a considerable extent on the definition of the term *cohesion.*

One more or less classic measure of party cohesion in legislatures has been the party vote—any legislative roll call in which 90 percent or more of the members of one party vote yes and 90 percent or more of the other party vote no. By such a stringent test, party discipline appears frequently in the British House of Commons but far less often in American legislatures. Julius Turner found that from 1921 through 1948, only 17 percent of the roll calls in the House of Representatives met such a criterion of party discipline. In the 1950s and 1960s, it dropped steadily to about 2 or 3 percent. Recently, in the British House of Commons, the percentage of party votes averaged very close to 100 percent.[14]

Although the "90 percent versus 90 percent" standard discriminates between British and American party cohesion—indeed, between parliamentary and other systems—it is too stringent a standard for comparisons within the American experience. Scholars of the American legislatures have opted for less demanding criteria. Whatever criterion one accepts, it may be used to describe both the overall incidence of cohesion in the legislatures and the party loyalty of individual legislators. In other words, one can make statements about the percentage of instances in which the majority (or 80 percent) of one party opposed a majority (or 80 percent) of the other. One can also figure the percentage of times that an individual legislator votes within his or her party when party opposes party. In their study of American legislatures, Jewell and Patterson have collected data from various other studies and sources on party cohesion in state legislatures, drawing on a number of these measures of party cohesion. Table 14.1, based on their data, indicates the enormous variation in party cohesion in the decisions of a number of state legislatures. It also illustrates the high degree of cohesion in the urban, two-party states of the northeastern section of the country.[15]

[14]Julius Turner, *Party and Constituency: Pressures on Congress,* rev. ed. by Edward V. Schneier (Baltimore: Johns Hopkins University Press, 1970), pp. 16–17.

[15]See also Table 1 of the study by Hugh L. LeBlanc, "Voting in State Senates: Party and Constituency Influences," *Midwest Journal of Political Science* 13 (1969): 36.

TABLE 14.1   *Party Cohesion in Nonunanimous Roll Calls in Selected State Legislatures*

	Percentage of Roll Calls with Majority vs. Majority		Average Index of Cohesion (Median Session)[a]			
	Senate	House	Senate		House	
State and Year(s)			D	R	D	R
Pennsylvania (1959)	82	29	82	90	—	—
Massachusetts (1959, 1965)	74	72	78	77	53	73
Ohio (1959–69)	74	51	84	83	61	66
Iowa (1965–74)	49	55	79	70	72	70
Illinois (1959)	27	—	75	63	—	—
Utah (1965)	8	20	60	52	70	65
New Mexico (1951–59, 1963)	24	20	42	53	42	57

[a]The Index of Cohesion is a simple measure whereby one subtracts the percentage in the minority from the percentage in the majority; hence, if 75 percent of a party are together in a vote, the index is 50.

Source   Data from Malcolm E. Jewell and Samuel C. Patterson, *The Legislative Process in the United States*, 3rd ed. (New York: Random House, 1977), pp. 384–85.

By similar measures, the degree of party cohesion in the United States Congress falls somewhere between the extremes of party cohesion among the states. In recent years, the two houses of Congress have been pitting majorities of Democrats against majorities of Republicans in 30 to 50 percent of the roll calls. Within those votes in which party majority opposed party majority in the 1970s, the average Index of Cohesion was in the range of 30 to 35, substantially below the score of most state legislatures.[16]

Occasions for Cohesion

Cohesive voting among members of the same legislative party is greater on some issues and questions than on others. Studies in the Congress and in the state legislatures find that three kinds of legislative concerns are most likely to stimulate high levels of party discipline: those touching the interests of the legislative party as a group, those involving support of or opposition to an executive program, and those concerning the socioeconomic issues and interests that tend to divide the party electorates.

The interests of the legislative parties as parties—as interest groups,

---

[16]See the note under Table 14.1 for an explanation of the Index of Cohesion.

one might say—often spur the greatest party unity in legislatures. The range of such issues is broad. It includes, especially in two-party legislatures, the basic votes to organize the legislative chamber. In the Congress, for example, one can safely predict 100 percent party cohesion on the early-session votes to elect a Speaker of the House and a president pro tem of the Senate. Discipline runs high in the state legislatures over issues such as patronage (and merit system reform), the laws regulating parties and campaigning, the seating of challenged members of the legislature, election and registration laws, or the creation or alteration of legislative districts. Whatever form these issues take, they all touch the basic interests of the party as a political organization. They threaten some aspects of the party status quo: the party's activists, its internal organizational structure, its system of rewards, its electorate, it electoral competitiveness.

Second, legislators of a party rally around the party's executive, or they unite against the executive of the other party. Perhaps the reaction to an executive program is not so predictable as it is in a parliamentary system, for American presidents freely court the support of the other party. Nonetheless, it is a significant partisan issue even in the American context. *Congressional Quarterly* periodically measures the support that each legislative party gives to the president on issues that he has clearly designated a part of his program (Table 14.2). This executive-oriented cohesion in the Congress and in the state legislatures reflects a number of realities of American politics. It may result from the executive's control of political sanctions—patronage in some states, personal support in fund raising and campaigning, or support of programs for the legislator's constituency. It also results from the fact that the executive increasingly symbolizes the party and its performance. Legislators of the president's party or the governor's party know that they threaten their party and their own political future if they make the party's executive appear ineffective.

Finally, legislative cohesion remains firm on some policy issues, especially those that bear directly on the socioeconomic interests of the electorate. Especially in those states in which the SES foundations of party loyalties produce an issue-oriented politics, this fact is not surprising. Such issues include labor-management relations, aids to agriculture or other sectors of the economy, programs of social security and insurance, wages and hours legislation, unemployment compensation, and relief and welfare programs. In the oversimplification of American politics, these issues involve the welfare state, the whole complex debate over government responsibilities that we sum up in the liberal-conservative dualism. On issues, for example, that the AFL-CIO's Committee on Political Education (COPE) considered a test of labor-liberal positions in 1981–82, the Senate Democrats supported the COPE position 69 percent of the time, the Senate Republicans 17 percent of the time. Such substantial cohesion, however, does not obscure the fact that senators differ in the degree of their

TABLE 14.2   *Percentages of Times That Members of Congress Supported Bills from the President's Program: 1966–82*

Party of the President	Year	Senate Democrats	Senate Republicans	House Democrats	House Republicans
Democrat	1966	57%	43%	63%	37%
Democrat	1967	61	53	69	46
Democrat	1968	48	47	64	51
Republican	1969	47	66	48	57
Republican	1970	45	60	53	66
Republican	1971	40	64	47	72
Republican	1972	44	66	47	64
Republican	1973	37	61	35	62
Republican	1974	39	56	44	58
Republican	1975	47	68	38	63
Republican	1976	39	62	32	63
Democrat	1977	70	52	63	42
Democrat	1978	66	41	60	36
Democrat	1979	68	47	64	34
Democrat	1980	62	45	63	40
Republican	1981	49	80	42	68
Republican	1982	43	74	39	64

Source   Data from *Congressional Quarterly Almanacs* for each year.

personal support. In the same session, Republicans varied from a high of 67 percent (Mathias of Maryland) to a low of zero (shared by Armstrong of Colorado, Lugar and Quayle of Indiana, and Simpson of Wyoming). Among the Democrats, there were three perfect scores of 100 percent (Cranston of California, Dodd of Connecticut, and Levin of Michigan) and a low score of 28 percent (Stennis of Mississippi). The highs and lows were almost exactly reversed in the scores of the U.S. Chamber of Commerce.[17]

To single out these issues is not to imply that they are the only instances of party cohesion. In the Congress, for example, issues of federalism and states' rights also produce partisan voting.[18] The structure of the choice itself may encourage or discourage cohesion. In the Congress (and probably in the states, too) party discipline seems to be easier to maintain on the complex, almost invisible procedural issues that come before the chamber. Apparently, the simple, substantive questions attract publicity and thus attract the attention and activities of nonparty pressures. In the

[17]*Congressional Quarterly Weekly Report*, July 3, 1982.
[18]Turner, *Party and Constituency*, Chap. 3.

House of Representatives, at least, party leadership finds its task easier when it is working on an obscure issue.[19]

The Constituency Basis of Cohesion

Party cohesion in legislative voting is greatest in those states with competitive, two-party politics. One-partyism in a state legislature invites the disintegrating squabbles of factions and regional or personal cliques within the dominant party. The South, therefore, has been the region of the least cohesive legislative parties. This is perhaps to labor the obvious, however; the very concept of cohesive parties and party government presumes two healthy, competitive parties locked in the struggle to make public policy.

Party cohesion, furthermore, is at its maximum in the legislatures of urban, industrialized states (see Table 14.1). The key here—and perhaps the key to the entire riddle of legislative party cohesion—is in the types of constituencies the parties represent. In these urban, industrial states, the parties tend to divide the constituencies along urban-rural and SES lines, and they develop an issue-oriented politics that reflects those lines. Party cohesion in the legislature, therefore, reflects the relative homogeneity of the interests and constituencies the party represents. It also reflects, of course, the fact that the other party represents a different configuration of interests in different constituencies. Moreover, the legislators of one party usually have different backgrounds and life-styles from those of the legislators of the other party; that is, differences in their own values and experiences reinforce the party differences in constituencies. Thus, in such state legislatures, an attempt to revise an unemployment compensation program will put two cohesive parties in sharp opposition, with the pro-labor and promanagement sides each reinforced by their roots in their home districts and by their own lives and values.

There do exist urban, industrial states with relatively little legislative party cohesion. California has become the most famous example. California's two parties represent districts that, by the usual SES measures, are fairly mixed. The Democratic party, for instance, has an important rural wing, a possible result of the long-time overrepresentation of rural areas in the state legislature. In other words, in California, each party represents a relatively heterogeneous set of constituencies. In such states—and more commonly in the less urban states—there probably is no single, sharp dualism of interests on which to develop clearly marked grass-roots differences between the parties.

Within the legislature of a particular state, the degree of any individual legislator's party loyalty also appears to be related to constituency

[19]See Lewis A. Froman and Randall B. Ripley, "Conditions for Party Leadership: The Case of the House Democrats," *American Political Science Review* 59 (1965): 52–63.

characteristics. Party cohesion is greater among those legislators who represent the typical or modal constituency, when typicality or modality is measured by some index of SES or urbanness. In MacRae's study of the Massachusetts legislature, for example, Republicans tended to represent districts with a high rate of owner-occupied housing; Democrats tended to come from areas in which fewer people owned the homes they lived in. Republicans from low owner-occupancy areas and Democrats from high owner-occupancy districts—that is, legislators from districts not typical of those their party generally represented—tended to be the party mavericks on roll calls.[20] This kind of analysis—pointing to the influence and limitations of constituency loyalties—is based on the assumption that each party has typical districts that differ primarily in SES interests. In short, we appear to be examining here the same constituency effect on the individual legislator that we saw working on entire legislative parties a few pages back.[21]

The Other Bases of Cohesion

Clear and unmistakable though the constituency bases of party regularity may be, they do not explain all party cohesion in the state legislatures. The parties as operating political organizations account for some. Daily caucuses, state party representatives roaming the legislative corridors, and the party pressures of a vigorous governor do count for something. Even though it is difficult to measure their influence, few observers of the state legislatures deny it. Whatever actual organizational pressure the legislator feels, however, probably comes from the state party, the party in the executive, or the legislative party itself. It rarely comes from the local party, which, if it makes any demands at all, generally makes them on purely local, service issues. The varying strengths and capacities of constituency political parties may affect legislators' relationships with their constituencies, but they seem not to affect their votes at the state capitol or in Washington. The local party is much more concerned with matters of local

[20]Duncan MacRae, "The Relation Between Roll Call Votes and Constituencies in the Massachusetts House of Representatives," *American Political Science Review* 46 (1952): 1046–55. See also Thomas A. Flinn, "Party Responsibility in the States: Some Causal Factors," *American Political Science Review* 58 (1964): 60–71.

[21]For a useful exploration of the relationship between party cohesion and constituency variables, see LeBlanc, "Voting in State Senates," pp. 44–53. There is also considerable evidence to suggest that constituency differences lay beneath the high degree of party cohesion in the United States Congress at the turn of the century. See David W. Brady and Phillip Althoff, "Party Voting in the U.S. House of Representatives, 1890–1910: Elements of a Responsible Party System," *Journal of Politics* 36 (1974): 752–75.

interest and its own perquisites than it is with questions of state or national policy.[22]

Party regularity may also be related to the political competitiveness of the legislator's constituency. Legislators from the unsafe, marginal districts with finely balanced parties are more likely to defect from their fellow partisans in the legislature than are those from the safer districts. To be sure, it is likely that many of these marginal districts are the districts with SES characteristics atypical of the parties' usual constituencies. Marginality may also be a product, however, of the organizational strength of the opposing party or the appeal of its candidates, which in turn forces the legislator to be more than usually sensitive to the constituency.[23]

Finally, as obvious and even banal as it may seem, parties must cohere in order to get the business of the legislature done. If bills are to be passed and the public's business done, majorities must be put together. Putting together those majorities is the prime task of the party leadership of the majority party. In truth, that leadership is far more likely to be concerned with the smooth operation of the legislative body than with the enactment of some stated party policy. It is also persuasive and influential at least in part because it dominates the group life of the legislative party and controls access to its esteem and camaraderie.[24]

In summary, the northeastern states provide the prototype of the state legislatures with greatest party cohesion. They are largely competitive, two-party states. Drawing on urban-rural lines and the SES differences of a diverse population, their major parties represent fairly homogeneous and markedly differing clusters of constituencies. Those differences give rise to a politics of issue and even of ideology, which is reinforced, in turn, by the similar dimensions of national politics. These are also the states with old-line, vigorous party organizations and party control of nominations. Here, too, one finds that the hardship politics of favors and patronage has armed the parties with impressive arsenals of sanctions and rewards. Organizational strength also carries over into the legislative chambers, where

---

[22]David M. Olson, "U.S. Congressmen and Their Diverse Congressional District Parties," *Legislative Studies Quarterly* 3 (1978): 239–64.

[23]The scholarly evidence on this point is very mixed. A recent article by Barbara S. Deckard makes a strong case for the argument that there is no relationship between electoral marginality and party disloyalty in roll calls; the article also summarizes a good deal of the recent literature on the point. See "Electoral Marginality and Party Loyalty in House Roll Call Voting," *American Journal of Political Science* 20 (1976): 469–81.

[24]Some observations of state legislatures and the logic of coalition theory suggest that the size of the legislative party itself would have some effect on party cohesion, that the smaller the margin of the majority, the greater would be the pressure on it to cohere. Eric M. Uslaner finds no such relationship in the Congress in "Partisanship and Coalition Formation in Congress," *Political Methodology* 2 (1975): 381–414.

The Case for Party Discipline

Legislators often chafe under pressure from party leaders to support a party position. Even those who accept the need for party discipline do not often accept it with more than resignation. The following statement, clearly an exception, comes from an anonymous member of the Connecticut General Assembly:

> "A lot has been said about the importance of parties in the Assembly and by and large what they say is true. I was a little amazed that I really didn't have the freedom to vote as I wanted on some legislation. It wasn't that I found myself in disagreement with my party very often but it was assumed after the caucus that I would fall in line and there were implied sanctions that might be imposed if I didn't. Actually, though, it's not as bad as it sounds. You do have the opportunity to speak in the caucus. If you have good reasons, and you are honest about it, you can vote in opposition to a party position. There are also many issues where there is no party position and you are completely free. In retrospect I think that strong party organizations in the legislature are a good thing. It is an efficient way of running the legislature, it facilitates the process of compromise, and it enables you to run on a party record. It takes a little while to get used to the fact that you seem to be subordinate to some higher force within the Assembly. But eventually most of us come around to the view that we can't operate as 177 individuals and parties are the best way to get the job done."
>
> Wayne R. Swanson, *Lawmaking in Connecticut: The General Assembly* (Washington, D.C.: American Political Science Association, 1972), p. 13; quoted in William J. Keefe and Morris S. Ogul, *The American Legislative Process*, 5th ed. Englewood Cliffs, N.J.: Prentice-Hall, 1981), p. 270

regular caucuses and the apparatus of party discipline are often in evidence (see box). Here, also, party differences and party conflict have a greater salience for the individual legislator (and for the individual voter). In a now-classic study of four state legislatures, the legislators were asked to indicate the kinds of conflict that were important in their legislature; 96 percent of the members of the New Jersey lower house designated party conflict as important; comparable percentages for Ohio, California, and Tennessee were 49, 26, and 23 percent, respectively.[25]

[25]John C. Wahlke et al., *The Legislative System* (New York: Wiley, 1962), p. 425.

It is not easy to bring the United States Congress into this discussion of the conditions that lead to cohesion in legislative voting. There is nothing among the state legislatures to which the Congress can be compared. Perhaps it is because of the unique scope of its politics and its powers as a legislature that it does not lend itself to the relatively simple generalizations we have made about the state legislatures. The members of Congress come from fifty different political systems, not one, and the diversity of the constituencies and constituency politics they represent may be too great for a continuous, simple set of party battle lines. The parties in Congress have a more complex pattern of party cohesion than do the state legislative parties. Because of the special case of the South, the Democratic party achieves varying degrees of cohesion on various issues. The Republicans often manage a greater cohesion on foreign policy issues than on the conventional welfare state issues of domestic politics. Not until one narrows the members of Congress to the non-Southerners do the constituency bases of party cohesion appear.[26]

LEGISLATIVE PARTIES AND PARTY GOVERNMENT

Even though party cohesion in American legislatures falls far short of the standards of some parliamentary parties, it remains the most powerful determinant of roll call voting in American legislatures. Party affiliation goes further to explain the legislative behavior of American legislators than any other single factor. Legislators' normal disposition seems to be to support the leadership of their party unless some particularly pressing consideration intervenes. All other things being equal (i.e., being quiescent and not demanding), party loyalty usually gets their votes.

Yet, despite the relative importance of party cohesion, the fact remains that most American legislative parties achieve only modest levels of cohesion. Party lines are often obliterated in the coalitions that enact important legislation. Interest groups, powerful governors, local political leaders, the mass media, influential legislative leaders—all contend with the legislative party for the ability to organize legislative majorities. In this system of fragmented legislative power, the legislative party governs only occasionally. It often finds itself in conflict with other party voices in the struggle to mobilize majorities in the legislatures. Governors or presidents, as party leaders and expounders of the party platform, may find themselves repeatedly at odds with legislators of their party whose roots are deeply implanted in local, virtually autonomous electorates.

[26]Lewis A. Froman, *Congressmen and Their Constituencies* (Chicago: Rand McNally, 1963). See also David R. Mayhew, *Party Loyalty Among Congressmen* (Cambridge, Mass.: Harvard University Press, 1966).

Thus, the fragmenting institutions of American government once again have their impact. With the separation of powers, there is no institutionalized need for party cohesion, as there is in the parliamentary systems. Two recent studies of Canadian parties suggest, indeed, that the presence of a parliamentary form primarily accounts for the greater cohesion of legislative parties in Canada.[27] It is possible for government in the United States to act, even to govern, without disciplined party support in the legislature. In fact, at those times when one party controls both houses of Congress and the other the presidency—or one controls both houses of the state legislature and the other the governorship—it would be difficult to govern if high levels of cohesion behind an a priori program *did* prevail in each party.

Even where one finds party cohesion or discipline in an American legislature, however, party government or party responsibility need not result. Cohesion is a necessary but not sufficient condition of responsibility— and there's the rub. The American legislative party tends to have only the most tenuous ties to the various units of the party organization. The legislative parties of Congress do not recognize the equality—much less the superiority—of the party's national committee. Many state legislative parties similarly escape any effective control, or even any persistent influence, by their state party committees. Nor do the legislative parties have a great deal of contact with local party organizations. Many legislators depend on personal organizations for reelection help, and even those who rely on the party at election time receive no advice from the party back home during the legislative session. Local party organizations do not often sustain enough activity between elections to keep even the most fleeting supervisory watch over their legislators.

The American legislative party, therefore, has often found it easy to remain aloof from and independent of the party organization and its platforms and program commitments. The legislative party creates the major part of its own cohesion, employing its own persuasions, sanctions, and rewards. What discipline it commands generally serves a program or a set of proposals that originates in the executive or within the legislative party itself. Only rarely is the legislative party in any sense redeeming earlier programmatic commitments or accepting the overriding discipline of the party organization. As a legislative party, it is politically self-sufficient; it controls its own rewards to a considerable extent. In some cases, it also attempts to control its own political future; the party campaign committees of both houses of Congress are good examples. So long as the members

---

[27]Leon D. Epstein, "A Comparative Study of Canadian Parties," *American Political Science Review* 58 (1964): 46–59; and Allan Kornberg, "Caucus and Cohesion in Canadian Parliamentary Parties," *American Political Science Review* 60 (1966): 83–92.

of the legislative party can protect their own renomination and reelection, they can keep the rest of the party at arm's length.

This freedom—or irresponsibility, if one prefers—of the legislative party grows in large part from its unity and homogeneity of interests in a total party structure where disorder and disunity prevail. Even if local party organizations were to establish supervisory relationships with their legislators, no party responsibility would result unless those relationships were unified and integrated within the state as a whole. In other words, there exists no unified political party that could establish some control over and responsibility for the actions of its legislative party. There is only a party divided geographically along the lines of American federalism, functionally along the dimensions of the separation of powers, and politically by the differing goals and commitments its various participants bring to it.

At the most, therefore, the American legislative parties are tied to the rest of their parties by some agreement on an inarticulate ideology of common interests, attitudes, and loyalties. In many state legislatures and in the United States Congress, the mute ideology of one party and its majority districts differs enough (even though roughly) from that of the other party to promote the tensions of interparty disagreement and intraparty cohesion. These modal sets of interests and attitudes—we most often give them the imprecise labels "liberal" and "conservative"—may or may not find expression in platforms, and they may or may not be articulated or supported by the party organizations. Legislative parties may even ignore them in the short run. Nonetheless, they are there, and they are the chief centripetal force in a political party that has difficulty articulating a central set of goals for all its activists and adherents. Whether this inarticulate ideology can produce a measure of party responsibility is another question, however, and it will wait until the considerations of Chapter 16.

15

THE PARTY IN THE EXECUTIVE
AND JUDICIARY

The American involvement of the executive and the courts in party politics stems in considerable part from the traditions of nineteenth-century popular democracy. The belief that democratic control can best be guaranteed through the ballot box led to the long ballot, on which judges and all manner of administrative officials (from local coroners to state auditors) were elected. Popular election led easily to party influences in those elections. At the same time, the tenets of Jacksonian democracy supported the spoils system and the value of turnover in office, justifying the use of party influence in appointments to administrative office. Thus, in the name of popular democracy, the access of parties to the executive and judicial branches was established to an extent quite unknown in the other Western democracies.

It is one thing for the political party to influence—or even control—the recruitment or selection of officeholders. It is quite another, however, for it to mobilize them in the exercise of their powers of office. The parties have had only limited success in mobilizing American legislatures. The pertinent question here is whether they have had equal success with the executive and judicial branches. In other words, in the decisions that affect us all, has it made any difference that the men and women making them have been selected by a party? Does the pursuit of public office by the political parties serve only their internal organizational needs for rewards and incentives, or does it also promote the enactment of party programs and platforms?

THE EXECUTIVE AS A PARTY LEADER

The twentieth century has been a century of mass political leadership, both in the democracies and in the dictatorships of the world. In the democracies, electorates have expanded to include virtually all adults. At the same time, the revolutions in mass media and communications have brought political leaders closer than ever to the electorates. In the United States, these changes have culminated in the personal leadership of the presidency in the twentieth century—a trend summed up merely in listing such names as Wilson, Roosevelt, Eisenhower, and Kennedy, names that signify both executive power and a personal tie to millions of American citizens. Not even the post-Watergate reaction against the "imperial presidency" is apt to reverse the trend. Even the parliamentary systems and their prime ministers have been energized by the growth of personal leadership. It is no longer true that the British prime minister is merely "first among equals" in the cabinet, for British election campaigns increasingly center on the potential prime ministers.

Unquestionably, one major ingredient of executive leadership in the United States has been leadership of a mass political party. When Andrew Jackson combined the contest for executive office with leadership of a popular political party, he began a revolution in both the American presidency (and governorship) and the American political party. The presidency ceased to be the repository of elitist good sense and conservatism that Hamilton hoped it would be and became, slowly and fitfully, an agency of mass political leadership. Ultimately, it was the president rather than the Congress who became the tribune of the people in the American political system. Popular democracy found its two chief agents—a popularly elected leader and a mass political party—merged in the American chief executive, the power of the office reinforced by the power of the party.

It is easy to speak glibly of the American chief executive as the leader of a party. The specific components of leadership are more elusive, however, for the president and governors rarely are formal party leaders. National and state party chairpersons hold that responsibility. The chief executive's role as party leader is really a subtle, complex combination of a number of overlapping partisan roles. Among them, certainly, are the following.

Party Leader as Representative of the Whole Constituency

James MacGregor Burns has written of an American four-party system composed of the two "presidential parties" and the two "congressional parties."[1] Even if one does not see the basic divisions of the American party system in executive-legislative differences, however, it is evident that the two branches represent different constituencies. The national constituency the president represents differs from the sum total of the congressional

[1]James M. Burns, *The Deadlock of Democracy* (Englewood Cliffs, N.J.: Prentice-Hall, 1963).

constituencies. Whereas the congressional constituencies are local and particularistic ones that (especially in the Senate) collectively overrepresent the rural areas of the country, the president's constituency overrepresents the large, urban, industrial states on which the electoral college places such a premium. His constituency is more concerned with the problems of the big cities, their industrial workers, and the racial and ethnic minorities that live in them. It is a constituency that often makes its incumbent more "liberal," more committed to government responsibility for solutions to social problems than the congressional party is. Furthermore, since his is the only truly national constituency—especially in contrast to the localism of the congressional party—the president or the presidential candidate is the only candidate of the national party. Apart from the party's national convention, he is its only manifestation.

Many of the same observations may be made of the American governors. They, too, represent the entire state in contrast to the local ties of the state legislators. Other public officials may also have statewide constituencies (the constitution writers of the states have seen fit to elect treasurers, attorneys general, and state insurance commissioners), but unlike these less known fellow executives, the governor embodies the party on the statewide level. He or she is the political executive and is so recognized by the voters of the states. Like the president, most governors must make political and policy records appealing to the voters of the entire state, and, like him, they embody concern for the problems of the whole constituency.

Party Leader as Organizational Leader

At the same time, the American executive may choose to be concerned with the organizational affairs of his political party. Some, like President Eisenhower in the 1950s, may choose not to be. A president such as Lyndon Johnson, however, drew on years of experience in American politics to involve himself in the Democratic National Committee and, through it, in state and local party politics.

The opportunities for organizational leadership, however, are generally greater for governors than for the president. Their constituency and political power coincide with a viable level of party organization. In the state party organization, there is an organization worth leading and capable of being led. Not all governors assert themselves in positions of party leadership, of course. They may have no taste for party organizational leadership, or they may even represent a dissident faction within the party. Many governors do lead, however. Their control of the state patronage and executive appointments establishes them as party leaders, since they control a considerable portion of the party's rewards. Many governors establish themselves as important forces in the state party organization, its campaigns, and its fund raising. Some, too, still represent the state parties in national party circles as party spokespersons or as leaders of their state delegations to the national party convention.

The president's greatest influence in the business of the party organization rests in his control of the national party committee. Its chairperson must be acceptable to him, and he is free to shape the committee's role, even if only to turn it into his personal campaign organization. Presidents' relationships with state and local party organizations, however, have become increasingly attenuated. Presidents are less and less willing to put their executive appointments to the political uses of those party organizations. They are now virtually unwilling to do the kind of "party building"—strengthening of state parties and their leadership—that presidents did routinely early in the century. As a result, the national committee and state party organizations of the president have lost virtually all of their role in making executive appointments to the president's immediate White House staff.[2] Presidents now use their appointments for governing and for protecting their own political positions.

To find a way through all the thickets of party politics, presidents do not usually rely on the national committee or its officers. Earlier in this century, presidents used the cabinet position of postmaster general as the post for an advisor knowledgeable in the intricacies of the party's many organizations. Franklin Roosevelt relied on James Farley, and Dwight Eisenhower chose Arthur Summerfield; each had extensive party organizational experience, and each served simultaneously as the national party chairman. This was the tradition that Lyndon Johnson honored in 1965 by appointing Lawrence O'Brien, his predecessor's shrewdest political counselor, as his postmaster general. Now that the postal service is reorganized and the postmaster general no longer sits in the cabinet, political advisors hold positions on the White House staff. In the case of Jimmy Carter, they were largely his trusted early supporters from Georgia, and in the Reagan administration they are largely former associates from the Reagan governorship in California.

Party Leader as Electoral Leader

The common sense of the executive's role as electoral leader is that executives, by their successes or failures and by their popularity or lack of it, affect the electoral fortunes of other office-seekers of their party. One sees, for example, a strong correspondence between the fortunes of presidents and their parties. Lyndon Johnson's landslide victory over Barry Goldwater in 1964 was accompanied by a sharp upturn in Democratic fortunes in congressional elections (see Table 15.1). That landslide also swept Dem-

[2]Roger G. Brown, "Party and Bureaucracy: From Kennedy to Reagan," *Political Science Quarterly* 97 (1982): 279–94.

TABLE 15.1   *Johnson Landslide of 1964: The Impact in the House of Representatives*

Year	Percentage of Vote Cast for Democratic House Candidates	Percentage of Democrats in House	Percentage of Vote Cast for Democratic Presidential Candidate
1962	52.5	59.3	
1964	57.2	67.8	61.1
1966	50.9	56.8	
1968	50.0	55.9	42.7

Source   Data from *Statistical Abstract* (1968).

ocratic parties to power in the states. North Dakota Democrats won a house of the state legislature and half of the state's congressional delegation for the first time in history. In Iowa, the Johnson sweep turned that state's congressional delegation from six Republicans and one Democrat to six Democrats and one Republican.

How one explains these relationships between presidential fortunes and party success, however, is less a matter of common sense and more a matter of scholarly analysis. The traditional explanation has employed the old metaphor of presidential coattails. Presidents ran "at the top of the ticket," the explanation goes, and the rest of the party ticket came into office clutching and clinging to the sturdy coattails of the successful presidential candidate. (Nineteenth-century dress coats did have tails.) The trouble with that graphic explanation is twofold. First, it tends not to distinguish between presidential-led sweeps and those led by the party itself. In 1964 terms, does one attribute those pervasive Democratic victories to the influence of Lyndon Johnson or to the awakening of Democratic party loyalties? Second, since the president is not on the ballot in the midterm congressional elections, his coattails are, strictly speaking, not there for the grabbing. One has to think of presidential influence in those elections in other terms.

Fortunately, we have another measure of presidential impact: popularity. As measured by the opinion pollsters, it is generally some index of satisfaction or dissatisfaction, approval or disapproval, with presidential performance. In the early 1980s, for example, the Gallup organization phrased the question this way: "Do you approve or disapprove of the way Ronald Reagan is handling his job as President?" In the years of the mid-

TABLE 15.2   *Relationship between Popularity of President Reagan and Vote Intentions of Voters before the 1982 Congressional Elections*

	Percentage Approving Reagan's Conduct of the Presidency	Percentage Intending to Vote for Republican Congressional Candidates
June 1981	59	45
October 1981	56	41
January 1982	47	39
April 1982	43	36
July 1982	42	35
September 1982	42	36

Source   Gallup polls for the months indicated.

term congressional elections, the intention of voters to vote for candidates of the president's party fluctuates during the campaign with the level of their approval of how the president is managing the presidency (Table 15.2). Moreover, that relationship has been apparent in presidencies going back more than twenty years before the Reagan presidency. Clearly, then, the president's influence as an electoral leader extends beyond his coattails and into elections in which he is not on the ballot.

As surprising as it seems in view of the realities of recent American politics, there are signs that the effects of presidents on elections are not as great as one might imagine. Two recent studies indicate that the presidential coattail effect may not be as great now as it was a generation ago.[3] The authors of both studies agree that the reduction is related to decreased competitiveness in the congressional elections, a result, in turn, of the increased ability of incumbent senators and representatives to entrench themselves in office. Other scholars also suggest that the popularity of a president has a relatively small effect on the outcome of the midterm elections. Again, the explanations center on the increasing ability of incum-

[3]George C. Edwards III, *Presidential Influence in Congress* (San Francisco: Freeman, 1980); and Herbert M. Kritzer and Robert B. Eubank, "Presidential Coattails Revisited: Partisanship and Incumbency Effects," *American Journal of Political Science* 23 (1979): 615–26. On the subject generally, see also Warren E. Miller, "Presidential Coattails: A Study of Myth and Methodology," *Public Opinion Quarterly* 19 (1955): 353–68; Charles Press, "Presidential Coattails and Party Cohesion," *Midwest Journal of Political Science* 7 (1963): 320–35; and Milton C. Cummings, *Congressmen and the Electorate* (New York: Free Press, 1966).

bents to curry the favor of their constituents and assure their reelection.[4] (It is hard to know how many of these conclusions one can confidently extend to the American governors, since virtually no research has been devoted to governors' impacts on the candidates of their parties.)

Where does all of this leave the American president as electoral leader of his party? Clearly, first of all, the impact of his popularity and his coattails is not what it once was. That fact reduces both an important aspect of his party leadership and an important source of his influence over the Congress. Furthermore, given the distribution of party loyalties in the United States, the coattails of an executive of the Republican party will be especially weak. The landslide elections of Dwight Eisenhower in 1956 and Richard Nixon in 1972 did increase Republican representation in the Congress, but they did not prevent Democratic control of the House in both years. The presidential impact has hardly vanished, however. Even if presidential influence accounts for only small percentage shifts in the total vote (Table 15.2), small shifts convert into substantial numbers of seats in the Congress. In fact, a shift of about 3 percent generally means the addition or subtraction of some 20 to 25 seats in the House. Also, voters do continue to evaluate presidential performance. There is evidence, in fact, that voters who disapprove of presidential performance vote in larger numbers in midterm elections than those who approve, and that their negativism leads them to prefer the other party and its candidates.[5] (Such a phenomenon would also explain why the party of the president traditionally loses seats in the Congress in the midterm election.) Finally, it is also very likely that perceptions and evaluations of the president (and governor) affect the way individuals view the parties. Executive programs are party programs, and the successes and failures of executives are party successes and failures. For a public that views politics chiefly in personal terms, a president or a governor is the personification of the party.

Imposing as these ties between the chief executive and the party may be, they are not without real and tangible limits. First of all, the executive may be limited by his own political experience and taste for political leadership. Some presidents and governors do not want to lead a party, or they do not think it proper for an executive to do so. Even those who do want

[4]Lyn Ragsdale, "The Fiction of Congressional Elections as Presidential Events," *American Politics Quarterly* 8 (1980): 375–98; and Thomas E. Mann and Raymond E. Wolfinger, "Candidates and Parties in Congressional Elections," *American Political Science Review* 74 (1980): 617–32.

[5]Samuel Kernell, "Presidential Popularity and Negative Voting: An Alternative Explanation of the Mid-term Congressional Decline of the President's Party," *American Political Science Review* 71 (1977): 44–66. See also James E. Piereson, "Presidential Popularity and Midterm Voting at Different Electoral Levels," *American Journal of Political Science* 19 (1975): 683–94.

to be party leaders may find that the representational demands of the office—the pressures to be a president or governor of "all of the people"—
limit their partisan work and identification.

Presidents and governors also may lead only part of a party. Governors
from one-party states, for example, often lead only a party faction. Executives also may share leadership of the party with other partisans. Presidents who are not especially secure in national party affairs may find the
more experienced leaders of the congressional party asserting major leadership in the national party. Governors also may find senators and representatives of their party pressing parallel leadership claims over the state
party. These legislators and state party leaders may fear that the governor
will use party control for his or her own political ambitions.

Nonetheless, the president heads, and occasionally even unifies, the
national party. He dominates the national committee and the rest of the
national organization, and, through a combination of his powers of office
and his party leverage, he often exerts enough mastery of the legislative
party to speak for the party in government. Most important, perhaps, for
millions of American voters he is the symbol of the party, its programs,
and its performance. The national constituency is his, and his nomination
and campaign are the chief activities of the national party. They are the
only activities with any visibility. Within the state parties, the governors
have the same unifying, symbolizing role, and they, too, have their leverage on legislative parties and state organizations.

Therefore, it is no exaggeration to speak of the American parties as
executive-centered coalitions.

> The party primacy of the chief executive lies not only in his advan-
> tage in establishing himself as the party leader in the state or nation, but
> also in the difficulties facing any alternative leader in attempting to do
> more than limit the impact of his titular status. The loose structure of
> the party is a coalition which necessarily centers on the chief executive,
> even though his influence within this coalition may vary widely depend-
> ing on his skills and opportunities. No other source of party leadership
> has the legitimacy or the range of sources of influence.[6]

Even in the party out of power, the executive office and its opportunities
dominate. Opposition to the other party's executive and his coalition, as
well as planning for the next election's assault on the office, provide the
chief unifying focus. Moreover, it is the headless quality of the party out
of power that most typifies its melancholy condition.

To some extent, the executive-centered party is a coalition of the ex-
ecutive-dominated party in government with the party in the electorate.

[6]Judson L. James, *American Political Parties* (New York: Pegasus, 1969), pp. 163, 169–
70.

That alliance, of necessity, bypasses the party organization. The identi-fications and loyalties of voters are not to the party organization but to the party symbols, the meaning for which comes largely from executives and their programs. The men and women of the party in government often build their own supporting organizations and thus bypass the party or-ganizations in their quest for office. As an example, one need only mention once again the fatal strategy of Richard Nixon in 1972. Even in the use of patronage, executives maximize support for their programs and their own political futures rather than maintaining or rebuilding the strength of the party organization.

Once in office, executives generally put the leverage they derive from their position as party leaders into the business of governing, rather than into any concern for the party as an organization. The president, for ex-ample, finds himself without sufficient constitutional powers to hold his own in the struggles of the American separation of powers. Indeed, if the proverbial man from Mars should obtain a copy of the United States Con-stitution, he could not imagine from its niggardly grants of power to the president what the office has come to be. American presidents, faced with that shortage of formal powers, have had to rely heavily on their extra-constitutional powers. They derive an important portion of those powers from party leadership.

PARTY LEADERSHIP AND LEGISLATIVE RELATIONS

The American chief executive does not possess a large area of policymaking autonomy. Aside from the president's primacy in the fields of defense and international relations, little major policymaking power is reserved for the American executive. What impact the executive is to have on the making of policy or on the enacting of a party program must come about through the formal actions of the legislature. In this pursuit of policy by influenc-ing a legislature, the president and the governors turn repeatedly to the ties of party.

The coordination of legislative and executive decision making under the aegis of a political party is not easily accomplished, however. Between 1961 and 1969, only thirteen states (Idaho and South Dakota were the only two states of the thirteen outside the South or its borders) did not experience at least some period in which one house of the legislature was of a party different from that of the governor. The reasons for those di-vided regimes are several: overlapping terms of office, differing constitu-encies, the impact of a politics of personality and localism, and legislative gerrymandering. At such times, the executives have no choice but to min-imize partisan appeals. In view of the closeness of the party division in many legislatures and the unreliability of some legislators of their own party, they must also curry the favor of some legislators of the opposing party. Thus, the president and the governors follow a mixed strategy: partisan appeals and sanctions for their own party and nonpartisan or bipartisan politics for those of the opposition.

The role of the president vis-à-vis the Congress is too well known to bear a great deal of repetition here. Presidents rely on their nonparty sources of leadership, of course—their prestige and persuasiveness, their command of the communications media, their own attention and favors. Overtly or not, they also use their identification with the party, the lingering patronage, their ability to influence coming elections. Members of the president's party know that if they make him look bad, to some extent they also make themselves and their party look bad. That awareness surely accounts for their rallying around a presidential veto despite their own legislative preferences (Table 15.3). Nor can they escape the fact that the president heads the party ticket when he runs and that his performance becomes the party's record when he does not. In fact, members of Congress who benefited in the past from presidential coattails are more likely to support the president's program than those who did not. Legislators thus appear both to anticipate and to react to presidential leadership at the polls.[7]

There are signs, however, that the president's party leverage in the Congress is diminishing. The impact of presidential coattails and presidential influence on congressional elections is dropping off. Incumbent members of Congress are increasingly secure in their constituencies. The quantity and the closeness of the competition they face are not as great as they were a decade ago. A congressional politics of cultivating the constituency by greater attention to its interests and increased services to individual constituents secures these legislators' political futures and isolates them from the electoral influences of the presidency.[8] As they lose party leverage, then, presidents are forced back on the nonparty components of their influence. Inevitably, their role as party leaders seems less important to them.

Governors, on the other hand, are frequently in a position to exercise far greater and more direct party organizational power over the legislators of their own party. In many states, their legislatures are unbound by the traditions of seniority, and governors may take an active part in selecting committee chairpersons and influential party floor leaders at the beginning of the session. They often view the party's legislative leaders as "their"

---

[7]J. Vincent Buck, "Presidential Coattails and Congressional Loyalty," *American Journal of Political Science* 16 (1972): 460–72; and Jeanne Martin, "Presidential Elections and Administration Support Among Congressmen," *American Journal of Political Science* 20 (1976): 483–90.

[8]See, for example, Morris P. Fiorina, "The Case of the Vanishing Marginals: The Bureaucracy Did It," *American Political Science Review* 71 (1977): 177–81.

TABLE 15.3   *Republican Vote on Vetoed Bills in Congress: 1973 and 1976*

Bill and Chamber (Year)	Vote on Original Passage		Vote on Veto	
	Republican Vote	Percentage Supporting Nixon or Ford Position	Republican Vote	Percentage Supporting Nixon or Ford Position
Vocational Rehabilitation Act—Senate (1973)	35–2	5	10–31	76
Water-Sewer Program— House (1973)	105–48	31	24–161	87
OMB Confirmation—Senate (1973)	16–17	52	14–22	61
OMB Confirmation—House (1973)	20–164	89	18–167	90
Cambodia Bombing Halt— House (1973)	63–120	66	53–133	72
Public Works Employment— House (1976)	62–71	53	56–82	59
Public Works Employment— Senate (1976)	20–16	44	12–25	68
Aid to Day Care Centers— Senate (1976)	18–16	47	11–26	70
Hatch Act Revisions—House (1976)	49–93	65	22–113	84

Source   Randall B. Ripley, *Congress: Process and Policy*, 3rd ed. (New York: Norton, 1983), p. 210.

leaders, chosen to steer their programs through legislative waters. Governors may attend party caucuses and may even direct the strategy of the party's legislative leaders. They may also lead powerful, ongoing state party organizations. To cross them may be to run the risk of falling from party favor; a legislator's career in the legislature, not to mention his future ambition, may be at the mercy of a determined, politically skillful governor. In short, the average governor has far greater control over party rewards and incentives than a president does. On the other hand, in the symbolic aspects of party leadership a governor probably exerts less influence than a president. Since governors are less visible and salient than presidents, their coattails and prestige are likely to be less potent than those of presidents.

PARTY POWER AND ADMINISTRATIVE POLICY

Administrative agencies now regulate vast areas of the economy—the air-
lines, atomic and nuclear energy, radio and TV, for example—under only
the vaguest legislative mandates. Even the question of tariff barriers, long
the occasion for protracted congressional politicking, has largely been del-
egated to the president, the State Department, and the Tariff Commission. Obviously, then, any concept of party responsibility or party
government cannot be restricted to legislatures. The administration clearly
shapes policy in its applications, and, to be effective, party programs require sympathetic administrative leadership.

There are substantial limits, however, on the executive's ability to
unify an administration and hold it responsible to a party program:

1. The legislature may place administrative positions outside executive
control by stipulating terms of appointment that last beyond a president's or governor's term, by limiting the executive's power of removal, or by placing policymakers under merit system and tenure. It
may extend a special legislative protection to others. So potent were
the legislative supporters of the late director of the Federal Bureau of
Investigation, J. Edgar Hoover, that he was independent of presidential authority.

2. Special precautions may also be taken to thwart partisan control of
an administrative agency. Federal agencies such as the Securities and
Exchange Commission, the Federal Trade Commission, and the Civil
Aeronautics Board are headed by five-person commissions or boards,
but not more than three of the members of each board may be of the
same political party. (Republican presidents often meet that formal
bipartisan requirement by appointing conservative Democrats, and
Democrats seek out liberal Republicans.)

3. In a number of states, the top administrative positions, like the gubernatorial office, are filled by election. At worst, that places members of both parties—a Republican governor and a Democratic state
treasurer, for example—in an uncomfortable alliance. Even if the offices are filled by candidates of the same party, they are often politically and constitutionally independent. In Minnesota, for example,
eleven different men held the governorship between 1930 and 1969.
In that same period, there were only two auditors, four secretaries of
state, and six treasurers. Thus, the governor may confront a number
of entrenched "executive parties" on entering office; they may even
be there when the governor departs.

4. Furthermore, American executives suffer some diminution of political
power as their terms approach a predetermined end. The Twenty-

second Amendment to the United States Constitution limits the presidential term to between eight and ten years, and a majority of the states limit the gubernatorial time in office.

Finally, political realities may force executives to share the instruments of party leadership with others. Senatorial courtesy and other political considerations guarantee that the Senate's confirmation of presidential appointments will be more than pro forma. Also, in forming a cabinet, the president cannot ignore the feelings and aspirations of groups within the party that contributed to his victory.

Establishing control of the executive branch, however, is far more complex than simply putting fellow partisans into positions of power. The chief executive faces essentially the same problem in enforcing party discipline on administrative subordinates that a party leader in the legislature faces. In both cases, the problem is loyalty to and the power of a constituency. Just as the legislators identify with the problems and outlooks of the citizens they know and represent, so administrators often identify with the problems and outlooks of the groups and individuals with which their agencies deal. Also, just as legislators must depend on the folks back home to protect their political careers, top-level administrators know that the support of client groups is their best personal political protection and the only protection for an agency, its mission, and its budget. In this way, the Veterans Administration enjoys the protection of the American Legion and the Veterans of Foreign Wars, and the Environmental Protection Agency depends on the support of organized naturalists and environmentalists. Only with the greatest difficulty does the pressure of party loyalties and party sanctions overcome the power of these administrative constituencies. In the executive as well as the legislative branch, the party has less to give and less to take away than the constituency does.

Only in that part of the administrative establishment closest to the chief executive is there the possibility of party responsibility. At these top administrative levels, the appointee often has been politically active and has associated actively with a political party. He or she has very likely come to recognize the claims of the party organization and has developed a commitment to party goals and programs. The cabinet of a president such as Ronald Reagan (see box) suggests the extent to which the political party remains a reservoir of talent, even a recruiter of talent, for modern administrations. It is undoubtedly true that presidents no longer are as explicitly partisan as they once were in their cabinet appointments, that they no longer use them as rewards for party service or as symbolic rewards to some part of the party. Presidents increasingly draw on individ-

The Reagan Cabinet and Republican Politics

From what one can piece together from their biographies in newspaper and reference sources, it appears that only one member of the first Reagan cabinet—Secretary of the Treasury Donald Regan— had no prior experience as a Republican officeholder, either elected or appointed, or as an official or activist of the Republican party. On the other hand, at least seven of the thirteen cabinet members had been delegates to a Republican national convention at one time or another, and three of them (Smith, Baldrige, and Lewis) had been members of the Republican National Committee or its finance committee.

	Previous Partisan Appointive or Elective Office	Previous State Party Activity	Previous National Party Office
Alexander M. Haig	X	X	
Donald T. Regan (Treasury)			
Casper W. Weinberger (Defense)	X	X	
William T. Smith (Justice)		X	X
James G. Watt (Interior)	X		
John R. Block (Agriculture)	X		
Terrel H. Bell (Education)	X		
Malcolm Baldrige (Commerce)		X	X
Raymond J. Donovan (Labor)		X	
Richard S. Schweiker (Health and Human Services)	X	X	
Samuel R. Pierce (Housing and Urban Development)		X	
Andrew L. Lewis (Transportation)		X	X
James B. Edwards (Energy)	X	X	

uals with experience in the areas of policy they will administer.[9] At the same time, however, presidents largely find their appointees among those who have earlier held public office as members of the party or who have experience in the affairs of the party itself. Their political careers and their values and commitments have in some significant degree been shaped by their political party.

When one looks a step below in the administrative structure to the assistant secretary level, however, party and governmental experience dwindles. These are individuals most often chosen for their skills and experience in administration and only secondarily for their political credentials. In the selection of many of them, the role of the party organization may not have extended beyond determining whether they were politically acceptable (i.e., inoffensive) in their home states. Yet they continue to come largely from the party of the president. Although these positions no longer serve so frequently as party patronage, the party link is still there to guarantee a commitment to a common political outlook.[10]

For what purposes, then, do executives use the executive party and their leadership role in it? Their power and influence go chiefly for the tasks of governing, of meeting their executive decision-making responsibilities. Only secondarily can they attend to the goals and interests of the party organization. Many governors use some chunk of their patronage purely for party goals, and presidents may use cabinet appointments to assuage and satisfy the need for recognition of various groups or factions within the party. Such concessions may satisfy the political demands of the party and build party cohesion, but they may also thwart the executive or administrative goals of the president. Ultimately, chief executives need whatever party loyalty and cohesion they can build for their own programs and, if they are in their first term, for their own reelection. It is the goals of the office, not of the party, that they pursue.

THE MYSTERIOUS CASE OF THE JUDICIAL PARTY

Nothing illustrates the difficulties of evaluating the party in office quite so clearly as the examples of cohesive party voting in American appellate courts. Several recent studies point to the presence of party-rooted blocs in state appellate courts in cases such as those involving workers' compensation. Another broader study, cutting across a number of states, found

[9]Hugh Heclo, "Issue Networks and the Executive Establishment," in Anthony King (ed.), *The New American Political System* (Washington, D.C.: American Enterprise Institute, 1979).

[10]Dean E. Mann, *The Assistant Secretaries* (Washington, D.C.: Brookings, 1965); and Brown, "Party and Bureaucracy."

that Democratic and Republican judges differ significantly in the ways they decide certain types of cases. Democrats on the bench, for example, tend to decide more frequently for the defendant in criminal cases, for the government in taxation cases, for the regulatory agency in cases involving the regulation of business, and for the claimants in workers' compensation, unemployment compensation, and auto accident cases.[11] To be sure, no one suggests that the incidence of party cohesion in judicial decision making approaches that in legislatures. It appears only in certain types of cases; and the amount of disagreement within an appellate court that can be explained by party division falls far below the amount of legislative division that can be explained by partisanship. Yet there is party cohesion in the American judiciary.

It may infrequently happen that an American judge is swayed by some subtle persuasion of his or her political party. If it does happen, though, it doesn't happen frequently enough to explain party cohesion in the courts. The explanation rests in the different sets of values, even the different ideologies, that the major parties reflect. Quite simply, judges of the same party vote together on cases for the same reasons of values and outlook that led them to join the same political party. In other words, two judges will vote together on the issue of administrative regulation of utilities because of deep-seated values they share about the relationship of government and the economy. Those same values or perceptions led them some years earlier to join the same political party, or they were developed out of experience in the same political party.

The impact of the party on the decision-making processes of the judiciary, therefore, is indirect. It stems largely from the role of the party as guarantor of its members' commitments. This should not surprise anyone, for the appointment of judges in the United States traditionally has taken the values and attitudes of judges into account. Although we have only recently accepted in any overt way the notion of judicial lawmaking—the notion that, in some instances, judges have options and that in making these choices they may reflect, in part, their own prior experiences, perceptions, and values—we have acknowledged it implicitly for

[11]On the general subject of party blocs or voting affinities among justices of the same party, see Sidney Ulmer, "The Political Party Variable on the Michigan Supreme Court," *Journal of Public Law* 11 (1962): pp. 352–62; Stuart Nagel, "Political Party Affiliation and Judges' Decisions," *American Political Science Review* 55 (1961): 843–50; Glendon A. Schubert, *Quantitative Analysis of Judicial Behavior* (Glencoe, Ill.: Free Press, 1959), pp. 129–42; and David W. Adamany, "The Party Variable in Judges' Voting: Conceptual Notes and a Case Study," *American Political Science Review* 63 (1969): 57–73. Similar differences in decision making in the federal judiciary are reported in Sheldon Goldman, "Voting Behavior on the United States Courts of Appeals, 1961–1964," *American Political Science Review* 60 (1966): 374–83.

some time. President Theodore Roosevelt, considering a replacement for Justice Horace Gray on the Supreme Court, wrote Senator Henry Lodge to inquire about a certain Judge Oliver Wendell Homes of the Massachusetts Supreme Court:

> In the ordinary and low sense which we attach to the words "partisan" and "politician," a judge of the Supreme Court should be neither. But in the higher sense, in the proper sense, he is not in my judgment fitted for the position unless he is a party man, a constructive statesman, constantly keeping in mind his adherence to the principles and policies under which this nation has been built up and in accordance with which it must go on.
>
> Now I should like to know that Judge Holmes was in entire sympathy with our views, that is, with your views and mine and Judge Gray's, just as we know that ex-Attorney General Knowlton is, before I would feel justified in appointing him. Judge Gray has been one of the most valuable members of the Court. I should hold myself as guilty of an irreparable wrong to the nation if I should put in his place any man who was not absolutely sane and sound on the great national policies for which we stand in public life.[12]

Congress, too, has often implicitly examined such issues in approving appointments to the federal judiciary. In 1969 and 1970, the Senate rejected two appointees to the Supreme Court (Clement Haynesworth and G. Harrold Carswell) at least partly because of the general conservatism of their views on race and labor.

Whether or not it should be within the province of a president or a governor to consider such matters in proposing judicial appointments, the appointee's political party loyalties serve as some indication of his or her values and attitudes. Indeed, it is one of the reasons that, in the last century, American presidents have appointed judges largely from their own parties. They have generally chosen more than 90 percent of their appointees from their own partisans, and in every case, from Cleveland through Carter, the percentage has been above 80 percent (Table 15.4).

In the presidency of Jimmy Carter, the appointment of federal judges was transformed briefly. The Carter administration instituted judicial selection committees to recommend several names to the Justice Department for appointment to the courts of appeal. Moreover, senators were strongly encouraged to form similar panels for district court vacancies, and a majority of them did. The result of the Carter reforms was to diminish the power of senators—and thus of state party organizations—in the process

---

[12]The Roosevelt letter is quoted more fully in Walter F. Murphy and C. Herman Pritchett, *Courts, Judges, and Politics* (New York: Random House, 1961), pp. 82–83.

TABLE 15.4   *Percentages of Judicial Appointments from the Party of the President: Grover Cleveland through Jimmy Carter*

Cleveland	97.3	F. Roosevelt	96.4
Harrison	87.9	Truman	90.1
McKinley	95.7	Eisenhower	94.1
T. Roosevelt	95.8	Kennedy	90.1
Taft	82.2	Johnson	94.6
Wilson	98.6	Nixon	92.4
Harding	97.7	Ford	81.2
Coolidge	94.1	Carter	93.1
Hoover	85.7		

Source   Data from Evan A. Evans, "Political Influence in the Selection of Federal Judges," *Wisconsin Law Review* (May 1948), pp. 300–51; Harold W. Chase, *Federal Judges: The Appointing Process* (Minneapolis: University of Minnesota Press, 1972); and Sheldon Goldman, "Carter's Judicial Appointments: A Lasting Legacy," *Judicature* 64 (1981): 346–50.

of appointing federal judges and to achieve the Carter goals of increasing the numbers of women and minorities on the federal bench. Although the usual 90 percent or so of the Carter appointees were of the president's party, there is good reason to think they were less active Democrats than might otherwise have been chosen. The Reagan administration has not required the selection commissions, but a number of senators have continued to use them. Thus, as the power of senatorial courtesy fades in these appointments, so does the possibility of their use as party rewards.

In the majority of the states, the judiciary is not appointive; it is filled by either partisan or nonpartisan elections. In the partisan elections of seventeen states, judges are elected as members or candidates of a party, and one can reasonably suspect that their party ties represent certain generalized value positions. The state parties vary greatly, however, in the active ways they contest these elections. In a few states, the party organizations make primary endorsements and actively support energetic partisans for the judgeships. Other state parties pay far less attention to judicial elections; in some cases, the same candidate will run on both party tickets—often with the endorsement of the state bar association.

Party pressures and activities are far less obvious and important in nonpartisan elections. Regardless of the election process and the politics, however, a judge still may come to the bench with the values that a party represents, and party lines may even be apparent in the divisions of a nonpartisan judiciary.[13] Judicial terms tend to be so long that many elective judgeships become appointive. Death often takes a nonpartisan judge from the bench in midterm, and the vacancy is filled before the next election by a gubernatorial appointment. The political considerations attending such appointments may then prevail, and with the advantage of even a brief period of incumbency, the appointee usually wins a full, regular term at the next election.

The point, then, comes down to this. There is no way to eliminate the values and preferences, the important frames of reference, that judges bring to their work. Judges have been men and women of the world; they know the issues of their times and the ways the parties relate to them. Furthermore, given the tradition of political activity of the American lawyer, there is a good chance that the judge has had some active, political party experience. Beyond this, the political party has an opportunity for active and overt influence in the selection process through the initiatives of governors or the president of the party or through the usual processes of a partisan election. In these selection processes, the party has the opportunity to achieve two goals: the selection of judges who are sensitive to the values for which the party stands, and the appointments of deserving (and qualified) lawyers for service to it.

In some instances, the relationship between judge and party may extend beyond the politics of appointment. In some parts of the country, the local district or county judge sometimes still retains hidden ties to local politics. In a few American counties, he is the *éminence grise* of the party, slating candidates behind the scenes, directing party strategy, arbitrating among the conflicting ambitions of the party's candidates. Moreover, the local administration of justice occasionally opens new reservoirs of patronage for the party. The judge who is a loyal member of a political party may parcel out guardianships, receiverships in bankruptcy, and clerkships to loyal lawyers of the party. In a 1966 battle in New York for the Democratic nomination for a judgeship in Manhattan's surrogate court, it developed that in the preceding year, the surrogates had issued 428 guardianships, with lawyers' fees running into many millions, in that one borough of the city alone. Many commentators and journalists, and many party officials, believe that such appointments go chiefly to attorneys active in the party ranks.[14]

---

[13]Even in a state in which judges are chosen on a nonpartisan ballot, partisan blocs may be apparent in some kinds of issues. In Minnesota, for example, the state supreme court in recent years has shown a high degree of party cohesion in two celebrated "political" issues: an important question of procedure in the early stages of the recount of the state's 1962 gubernatorial election and the question of the authority of the governor to veto a legislative reapportionment.

[14]On judicial patronage, see Herbert Jacob, *Justice in America* (Boston: Little, Brown, 1965), pp. 87–89.

How is it that the tie between the judiciary and the parties is so substantial in the United States? The factors are complex and mixed. The phenomenon of the elective judiciary, compounded by the political appointment process, is one factor. Then, too, there is no career vocation, no special training process or examination for the judiciary; any lawyer can be a judge. By contrast, in many continental European countries, the career of judging requires special preparation, study, and apprenticeship, and one enters it by special civil service examination. In the American context, then, the additional factor of the dominance of our politics by the legal profession is free to operate. Lawyers are everywhere in American political and public life, and many of them hope for ultimate reward in appointment to the bench.

CONCLUSION

Surprisingly, the influence of the political party on the executives and judiciaries of the American political system differs in degree but not in kind. The main avenue of party influence is indirect, and in both cases it stems from the kinds of commitments and values that membership in a party— or loyalty to one—represents. It depends, in other words, on the ideological impact or presence of the party *within* the men and women who hold administrative or judicial office.

Furthermore, in both the executive and the judiciary, one observes the conflict between the policy purpose—even when pursued within the limits of judicial propriety—and the demands of the party organization. The administrative position and the judgeship are two of the few available positions with which to reward party leaders, and the party is not anxious to have them pass to party "nobodies." In the filling of positions in both branches, however, one sees again the struggle between the party's own important need for organizational incentives and the need to recruit people who can best meet the responsibilities of governing. It is a struggle the parties are slowly but certainly losing.

16

THE QUEST FOR
PARTY GOVERNMENT

Political parties are everywhere in American legislatures and executives, and even in American judiciaries. All American executives, all American legislatures but one, and about half the American judiciaries are selected in processes that weigh heavily the party affiliation of the office seeker. Moreover, the appearances of party power are plentiful in the party leaders and whips of the legislatures and in the clearly partisan cast of many executive appointments. Even the elemental struggle between government and opposition, between ins and outs, largely follows political party lines in the American system. Yet, despite the trappings and portents of power, the American major parties do not govern easily. They find it hard to mobilize cohesive groups of officeholders behind programs and ideologies to which their organizations, activists, and candidates have committed themselves.

The discontent with this inability of the American parties to govern is an old one within academic political science.[1] The dissatisfactions, however, are with more than the American parties. They extend to the entire American political system and its fragmented centers of authority, its tendency to blur political alternatives and differences, and its built-in barriers to strong and vigorous governmental initiatives. The critics, many of them admirers of the cohesive parties in the British Parliament, have long hoped that by joining electoral majorities and officeholders to party programs, they could surmount the diffusion of power in the American polity. The 1950 report *Toward a More Responsible Two-Party System*[2] gave the con-

---

[1] Austin Ranney, *The Doctrine of Responsible Party Government* (Urbana: University of Illinois Press, 1962).

[2] Committee on Political Parties of the American Political Science Association, *Toward a More Responsible Two-Party System* (New York: Rinehart, 1950).

troversy its major recent stimulus. The ensuing academic controversy has slowly simmered down, but it is by no means quiet today.

While the controversy over party responsibility and party government has embroiled academic political science for the past generation, a parallel concern has agitated the world of political parties. From the ideologically oriented activists in both parties have come wails of dissatisfaction with the issuelessness of American politics and the tendency of the major parties to take similar centrist positions. They complain, much as Lord Bryce did some seventy years ago, that the American parties are as similar as Tweed-ledum and Tweedledee (see box). In 1964, the Republican conservatives inveighed against the "me-too-ism" of the party's liberals and moderates; in working for the nomination of Barry Goldwater, they pleaded for "a choice, not an echo." Eight years later, the major ideological pressures were from the left; the New Left and a coalition of the young, the disadvantaged, and the disaffected spearheaded a movement that won the 1972 Democratic presidential nomination for George McGovern. This movement, too, rejected the American status quo and the centrist politics of the established leadership of the Democratic party.

At first blush, it may seem that the ivory tower controversy over party responsibility does not have a great deal to do with the development of distinct programs for the parties. In any event, one would not ordinarily expect such a conjunction of academic debate and popular political controversy. The two questions are to a great extent the same, however. The groups of scholars who favor party government (or responsibility) and the ideologues of the left and right in American politics both want the major American parties to present more specific and differentiated programs. Both groups also want the parties to govern by carrying their programs into public policy. To the extent that such goals require some degree of consensus on basic values and long-term philosophies, they both also want greater ideological clarification and commitment within the parties.

THE LOGIC OF THE RESPONSIBLE PARTY

Despite the nomenclature, the doctrines of party government (or party responsibility) are only secondarily concerned with political parties.[3] They

[3] A word of semantic elaboration may be helpful here. Even though the two terms, *party government* and *party responsibility*, are used synonymously here, some authors make distinctions between them. Party government denotes leadership by a major political party in the important decision-making processes of government. For some observers, the concept of party responsibility is more than party government in that it suggests party government in which there is, additionally, responsibility to a priori party programs and to the voters who have chosen officeholders loyal to them. For others, however, party responsibility is less than party government; it identifies a degree of party program and discipline greater than presently exists but perhaps not great enough to provide cohesive majorities with which to enact party programs.

Tweedledee and Tweedledum

It has become a commonplace to compare the similarity of the Democratic and Republican parties on issues to those two identical little fat men in Lewis Carroll's *Through the Looking Glass*, Tweedledee and Tweedledum. Carroll borrowed their names from an earlier English poet, John Byrom, but it was his adoption of them in 1872 that secured their modern fame. James Bryce, later Lord Bryce, was apparently the first to use them to describe the American parties; he did so in his *American Commonwealth* (1888). Some years after Carroll's masterpiece, Tweedledee and Tweedledum also developed a stereotyped appearance, complete with schoolboy caps—doubtless the creation of some influential illustrator. After all these years, the twins are alive and well in American politics, as witness the cartoon below. It carried no caption, except perhaps the words on the briefcase that identify the visitor as a "pollster." Ironically, the artist is Charles Addams, best known for his ghoulish and gothic imagination.

Drawing by Chas. Addams; © 1975 The New Yorker Magazine, Inc.

are fundamentally doctrines of democratic government—or, more precisely, doctrines that advocate one particular variety of American democracy. Much of the debate over them has been over the kind of democracy we are to have. The whole movement for party government, in other words, has sprung from discontent over what some scholars have seen as the ills of American democracy.

The proponents of party government begin with a belief in strong, positive government as a necessary force for the solution of problems in the American society and economy. Like so many of the advocates of positive government in the context of the American separation of powers, they see a need for strong executive leadership if the whole complex governmental apparatus is to move forward with vigor and with a semblance of unity. Yet they know all too well that the institutions and traditions of American government diffuse and divide governmental power in ways that prevent the generation of aggressive and responsive governmental programs. Theirs is the old complaint that American political institutions—suited, perhaps, for the limited, gingerly governing of the eighteenth and nineteenth centuries—are far less adapted to the present century's need for positive government action. Clearly, decentralized political parties, each of them divided by a vast diversity of interests and points of view, only accentuate the problem of diffusion. In a sense, therefore, doctrines of party responsibility are attempts to bind American politics and government into a cohesive and integrated whole of the kind more typical of parliamentary government.

A second thread of argument runs through the political diagnoses of the proponents of party government: concern for the minuscule influence of individuals in a mass, popular democracy. Contemporary government becomes complex and remote, and individuals find it hard to have the time, attention, and political knowledge for an active role in it. They find it especially difficult to assess what their elected representatives have been doing in public office. Into the political void resulting from their ineffectiveness and ignorance rush well-organized and well-financed minorities—local elites, interest groups, party bosses, or political action committees. Consequently, so the argument goes, important decisions frequently are made by public officials and organized minorities without the participation or even the post hoc judgment of the great majority of individual citizens. Individuals drift from one meaningless decision to another; they do not know what the candidates stand for when they first elect them, and they have no standards or information for judging their performance in office when they come up for reelection.[4]

---

[4]See Ranney, *The Doctrine of Responsible Party Government*, Chaps. 1 and 2, for an analysis of what party government presumes about democracy.

This sense of alarm about the American democracy is by no means limited to the proponents of party government. It is a more or less standard critique from those quarters of American life committed to the liberal confidence in the usefulness of a broad governmental role and to the liberal belief in the rationality and desirability of citizen involvement in a popular democracy.[5] What sets the school of party government apart is its reliance on the organizing and consolidating powers of the competitive political party. A reconstructed (and responsible) pair of political parties, it is hoped, would bring together masses of voters behind meaningful party programs and candidates loyal to them and then would hold their elected candidates to the obligation of carrying those programs into public policy. The responsible political party thus would bridge the gulf between the disoriented individual and the complex institutions of government. It would also bind the divided institutions of government into an operating whole.

In essence, these are proposals for the reinvigorating and animating of popular democratic institutions through the prime organizing role of the political party. Why use the political party for so crucial a role?

> As mobilizers of majorities the parties have claims on the loyalties of the American people superior to the claims of any other forms of political organization. They have extended the area of popular participation in public affairs enormously and have given elections a meaning and importance never before thought possible. . . . Moreover, party government is good democratic doctrine because the parties are the special form of political organization adapted to the mobilization of majorities. How else can the majority get organized? If democracy means anything at all it means that the majority has the right to organize for the purpose of taking over the government.[6]

Only the parties, their supporters believe, are stable and visible enough to carry this representational burden. As the only completely political organization and the only one with a public or semipublic character, the political party alone has the capacity for developing the essential qualities of responsibility.

The call for responsible political parties, therefore, is a call for political parties with new capacities and new goals. Specifically, the responsible political party must:

① Enunciate a reasonably explicit statement of party programs and principles.

---

[5] I am using the word *liberal* here in the sense it is used in contemporary American politics. The liberal position favors popular, participatory democracy and positive government. Conservatism, on the other hand, generally connotes a preference for limited government and for the wisdom of political leaders and elites.

[6] E. E. Schattschneider, *Party Government* (New York: Rinehart, 1942), p. 208.

2/ Nominate candidates loyal to the party program and willing to enact it into public policy if elected.

3/ Conduct its electoral campaigns in such a way that voters will grasp the programmatic differences between it and the opposing party and make their voting decisions substantially on that basis.

4/ Guarantee that public officeholders elected under the party label will carry the party program into public policy and thus enable the party to take responsibility for their actions in office.

The entire argument, therefore, rests on replacing individual or group responsibility for governing with responsibility of the political party. Concern for developing and enacting programs must infuse all relationships within the party and all steps in the contesting of elections. As the report of the committee of the American Political Science Association argues in its very first paragraph:

> While in an election the party alternative necessarily takes the form of a choice between candidates, putting a particular candidate into office is not an end in itself. The concern of the parties with candidates, elections and appointments is misunderstood if it is assumed that parties can afford to bring forth aspirants for office without regard to the views of those so selected. Actually, the party struggle is concerned with the direction of public affairs. Party nominations are no more than a means to this end. In short, party politics inevitably involves public policy in one way or another.[7]

The whole idea of party government is policy- and issue-oriented. It is concerned with capturing and using public office for predetermined goals, not merely for the thrill of winning, the division of patronage and spoils, or the reward of the office itself. The winning of public office becomes no more than a means to policy ends.

Despite the persuasiveness of the advocates of party government, there still remains a sizable platoon of American political scientists and political leaders who are definitely unconvinced.[8] The journals of American political science, in fact, were dotted with rejoinders for several years after the publication of the report of the Committee on Political Parties in 1950. Their collective case against party government and responsibility divides into two related but independent arguments: the *undesirability* of party government and its *impossibility* (or at least its improbability). Although

---

[7]Committee on Political Parties, *Toward a More Responsible Two-Party System*, p. 15.

[8]The literature critical of the concept of party responsibility is a large one. Pendleton Herring's *The Politics of Democracy* (New York: Rinehart, 1940) presented an early view against the reformers. A recent article by Evron Kirkpatrick refers to a great portion of the writing on the subject; see "Toward a More Responsible Two-Party System: Political Science, Policy Science, or Pseudo-Science?", *American Political Science Review* 65 (1971): 965–90.

the two points are related, both logically and polemically, one does not have to make both in order to venture one.

On the grounds of undesirability, the skeptics argue across a number of fundamental issues of political philosophy. They fear that party government would stimulate a more intense politics of dogmatic commitment—one in which the softenings and majority building of compromise would be more difficult. They fear, too, that by making the political party the prime avenue of political representation, the advocates of party government would destroy the richness and multiplicity of representational mechanisms in the American democracy. Interest groups and other non-party political organizations, they feel, are necessary means of political representation in a large and heterogeneous polity. Channeling the representation of such a diversity of interests into the party system would overload two parties and risk the development of multipartyism. Furthermore, the skeptics are concerned lest party government destroy the deliberative quality of American legislatures, for legislators would cease to be free, independent men and women and would become the mandated representatives of a fixed party position. In short, they fear what European critics often call "partyocracy"—the domination of politics and legislatures by a number of doctrinaire, unyielding political parties, none of them strong enough to govern and none willing to let others govern.

On the related grounds of realism (i.e., the question of possibility and probability), the critics of responsible parties have argued:

1. The American voter remains insufficiently involved in issues to be coaxed easily into viewing politics and electoral choices in programmatic terms.

2. The complexity of American society and the diversity of interests it generates are too great to be expressed in the simple set of alternatives a two-party system can frame.

3. The parties themselves are too diffuse and decentralized—too lacking in central disciplinary authority—ever to take a single national position and then enforce it on their holders of public office.

4. The institutions of American government stand in the way at a number of crucial points. The direct primary, for example, makes it difficult for the parties to choose nominees loyal to their programs, and the separation of powers (and bicameralism) often prevents the control of all executive and legislative authority by a single party.

In other words, the model of the responsible, governing political party appears to the critics to demand too much of the American voters, of the parties themselves, and of the institutions of American government.

If the major American parties are to meet the demands and roles of party government, they must find some way to overcome their egregious disunity. The problem is really one of uniting the party organization, the party in the electorate, and the party in office in active and responsible support of a party program—despite their different political goals, different political traditions and interests, and different levels of attention, information, and activity. Three sources of the cohesion or unity necessary for party government seem to be at least logically possible:

1. Cohesion may be promoted by *constitutional imperatives*. The parliamentary system demands that the majority party maintain cohesion in the legislature—and to a lesser extent in the electorate and the party organization—if it is to stay in office. In the United States, the constitutional fragmentation of authority brought about by federalism and the separation of powers is, in fact, the root of the problem at hand.[9]

2. Cohesion may also be promoted by *organizational discipline.* A strong party organization may impose its discipline and cohesion on balky partisans in office if it can control renomination to office.[10] The American direct primary, however, makes that a hard task. Alternatively, powerful party leaders or executives may enforce discipline through the manipulation of the rewards they control (patronage, preference, access to authority, etc.). The value of these rewards is shrinking, however, and political ethics in the United States no longer easily accept an enforced toeing of the line. Although the available rewards and a tolerant political culture permit this kind of discipline in a few American states and localities, it is impossible in many others.

3. Finally, the cohesion may be produced "naturally" by an all-pervasive, intraparty *agreement on ideology or program*. All three components of the party may reach some consensus on a basic party ideology or program—or at least on a "silent ideology" of commonly held interest. The activists and identifiers of the party would then achieve a cohesion arising from common philosophy and goals, and their cohesion, to a considerable extent, would be a result of internalized and self-enforced commitment to those goals. Distasteful external constraints and restraints would thus be less necessary.

Because it seems that only the third avenue to party government is a likely one for contemporary American parties, the issue of party government becomes one of ideological—or more nearly ideological—politics and

[9]See Leon D. Epstein, "A Comparative Study of Canadian Parties," *American Political Science Review* 58 (1964): 46–59.

[10]A highly centralized party such as the Indian Congress party can maintain control over nomination and renomination of candidates to the national Parliament and thus exercise a potent sanction upon those parliamentarians of the party who break party discipline. In 1957, for example, the national Parliamentary Board of the party, the agency that selects and approves the candidates for local constituencies, declined to renominate almost one-third of the party's incumbent members of Parliament.

parties. A pervasive ideological commitment appears to be the necessary condition for cohesion, which in turn is a necessary condition for responsible governing parties. Organizational discipline may supplement and buttress the ideology, but it does not appear to be an alternative to it.

IDEOLOGICAL PARTIES IN THE UNITED STATES

The complaint of the American ideologist about the major American parties is an old and familiar one:

> The elections this November will prove totally irrelevant because the American electorate will have no substantive choice among the candidates. Naturally, there will be the traditional rhetoric about the "great liberal policies of the Democratic party" and the "great Republican tradition of fiscal responsibility," but if one pierces the rhetoric of each party, one sees that while each may say varying things, each pursues a common policy, i.e., the preservation of the status quo.[11]

If the complaint is clear, its author and occasion are not. The author could be from the political left or the political right, and the complaint might well have been made at virtually any national election since World War II. As it happens, it opened an article by a prominent spokesman of the New Left shortly before the 1966 congressional elections. From the conservative right came similar sentiments some years later:

> I favor the two-party system. But the two parties should represent distinct positions; the reason for the demise of the modern system has been too much sameness and liberal-financed convergence. . . . A "broad-based" party is possible and desirable. To be a "party," an interest, it must have discernible principles, not just a roost for "personalities," engaging or otherwise.[12]

The Democrats and Republicans are guilty, so the charges go, either of suppressing positions subscribed to by significant numbers of Americans or of failing to promote a wide-ranging debate on public issues. In other

---

[11]Edward M. Keating, "The New Left: What Does It Mean?" *Saturday Review*, (September 24, 1966), p. 25. The second paragraph of the essay is also illustrative:

"Republicans and Democrats in 1966 are snarling and snapping at each other, vainly attempting to deceive the voter into thinking that there are choices, not echoes, on the political horizon. This is to dissemble. Both parties know that neither will attempt to alter basic American policy, which, on the national level, is to obfuscate the social sickness that is consuming us all, and, on the international level, is intended to extend Americanism to the rest of the world by military blackmail."

[12]From Anthony Spinelli, "Hooray for the Two-Party System," *New York Times*, July 17, 1971.

words, they smother existing ideological differences and close off opportunities for others to develop.

Some academic and nonacademic reformers seek full-blown, total commitment to ideologies in the parties. Others, however, seek only bolder programs or issue positions from the parties. The differences between issue and program on the one hand and ideology on the other—and the relationship between them—lie at the heart of the problem. Some distinctions between them are probably overdue.

Terms such as *issues* and *programs* denote the stands that parties and politicians take on specific policy questions—on defense, foreign policy, medical care, labor-management relations, and protection of the environment. Traditionally, the parties, however hesitantly, have taken programmatic stands in their platforms. Presidents and presidential candidates take their stands in speeches, messages, position papers, and press conferences. *Ideology*, by contrast, denotes the broader values or philosophies that give rise to coherent sets of stands on issues. Liberalism or conservatism, to illustrate, provides an underlying structure of values that leads an individual to a logical, even predictable, position on a number of issues.

In a descriptive sense, it is unquestionably true that there are parties of issue (or program) and parties of more explicit ideology.[13] Certainly, not many of the reformers can hope to develop in the American political context the kind of total *weltanschauung*, the all-embracing concern, of an East European Communist party or an Asian Moslem party. Theirs is an ideology encompassing virtually all social relationships, and it spawns a politics of limitless scope and total involvement. Because of the general American agreement on basic institutions, differences between the American parties are not apt to involve disputes over the Constitution, the general outlines of the American economy, or the basic fabric of American society. Thus, ideological parties as one finds them elsewhere—especially in the bitter class politics of the European democracies—do not exist in the United States.

Indeed, it would be a mistake to draw the distinction too broadly between issue stands and ideology. Both are really points on the same continuous dimension; one blends into the other. Individuals take stands on specific policy issues, but those stands are often related to some more basic value or goal. Their disapproval of income taxation (or any taxation) may be related to their desire to toughen eligibility requirements for welfare programs. In other words, although few Americans develop total, all-encompassing ideologies, many do develop rudimentary, restricted ideologies, which at their minimum are little more than expansions of a single value or interest. The result is an ideology—or quasi ideology—in the sense

[13]Leon D. Epstein, *Political Parties in Western Democracies* (New York: Transaction, 1980), Chap. 10, distinguishes between parties of program and ideology.

that it guides the individual to a reasonably logical, interrelated set of positions on a group of issues.

The modest form of ideology one finds in American politics perhaps can be explored and explained in another way. The American parties have often differed on the major political issues of the moment. In recent years, their national platforms have differed over American foreign policy in the Far East, government medical insurance and aid for the unemployed, fiscal policy and the balanced budget, and government regulation of labor-management relations. Beneath these differences on the policy issues are the different constellations of attitudes, interests, and goals each party has embraced. In other words, each American party has developed a "silent ideology," based on the common interests of its activists and its party electorate. Its leaders are a group of like-minded men and women whose views on public issues separate them from the like-minded leaders of the other party.[14] Such a silent ideology stops short in only one main way from being an ideology in the more conventional sense; it is not usually codified or explicated—either by the party or by the individual voter—into a systematic, coherent, and consistent pattern of political values. The classic American political style focuses the party's attention not on fixed, abstract principles of ideology but on immediate, concrete issues of public policy.

All these distinctions and definitions are not merely an arid exercise in precision. Some kind or degree of ideology is implicit in every demand for party government. In a heterogeneous society of many conflicting interests, parties cannot take stands on ten or fifteen separate issues if there is no similarity among the coalitions on each issue. There must be some clustering of one group of voters on one set of issue positions and of another group on the opposing sides (see box). That alignment of voters along a single axis presumes, in turn, some kind of ideology, some basic commitments or values that connect separate issues into logical structures and govern stands on a number of them. Thus, call it what one will (the APSA report refers at several points to general party principles), greater programmatic commitment in the American parties depends on underlying values or philosophies to reduce the vast number of policy issues to one or a few dimensions. In the absence of constitutional pressures and sheer organizational discipline, there appears to be no other possible cohesive force for programmatic parties.

Although the American major parties have never been indistinguishable, attention to issues and even ideological concerns within the parties has risen over the last several decades. For example:

---

[14]Thomas A. Flinn and Frederick M. Wirt, "Local Party Leaders: Groups of Like Minded Men," *Midwest Journal of Political Science* 9 (1965): 77–98.

The Alignment of Voter Preferences in Ideological and Non-Ideological Parties

When the major lines of issue differences coincide in an electorate, one has fulfilled a necessary condition for ideological parties. If they do not, the result is important division *within* the parties as well as between them; nonideological parties that try to soften those internal divisions are the inevitable consequence. If one assumes the most simple case—only two parties and only two major issues—the following diagrams illustrate the two possibilities:

(1)

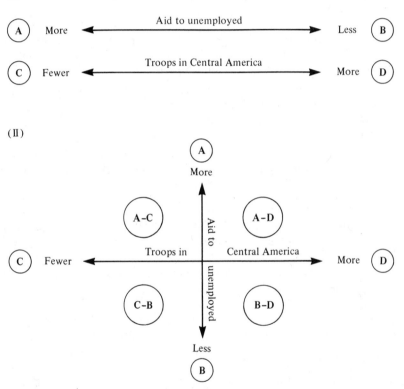

In Example I, the A–C voters form one cohesive party, and the B–D voters the other. Both parties can obviously sustain clear ideological (or issue) differences from each other. In Example II, the voters fall into four groups, guaranteeing that the two parties that absorb them will be divided. If one adds a third or fourth cross-cutting dimension (in three-dimensional space!), the problem for the two parties becomes far more acute.

— Men and women are increasingly being drawn to party work out of their involvement with issues and ideologies. The triumph of political ideas and values thus becomes a major incentive to party activity. To some extent, it replaces the older incentives of patronage and preference.[15]

— Ideologically motivated partisans formed ideological organizations both within and parallel to the party structure in the 1960s and 1970s. The club-style organizations of some urban Democrats are a case in point. The Republicans developed extra-party organizations (e.g., the Free Society Association and the Ripon Society), and groups such as the New Democratic Coalition grew up on the fringes of the Democratic party.

— The labels of liberal and conservative are freely accepted by increasing numbers of political activists, in contrast to the widely expressed belief of less than a generation ago that accepting the labels, especially the conservative label, was gross imprudence.

— In 1964, one of the major political parties chose an avowedly ideological candidate and wrote an unabashedly ideological platform. One observer termed it the end of the "reign of pragmatism" within the GOP.[16] A similar unwillingness to make the usual pragmatic compromises marked the unsuccessful campaign of Eugene McCarthy for the 1968 Democratic nomination and the successful pursuits by George McGovern in 1972 and Ronald Reagan in 1980.

There are other symptoms of the ideological renaissance. George Wallace ran programmatic campaigns for the presidency in 1968 and 1972. As a number of observers noted, he appealed to a cluster of goals and interests (an ideology?) that we often describe as populism, as well as to rather specific racial attitudes. John Anderson's issue positions in 1980 were less clearly defined, but part of his appeal was built on rejection of the policies of the major parties.

Most of these signs of increased ideological concern are visible chiefly among the activists of the party organization. What of the American voters, however, especially the less partisan electorate? It may very well be that the small core of party activists will bring their new involvement to a deaf or hostile public, that their "ideologizing" will only bore or alienate the majority of the electorate. Moreover, the issue of the differences in ideological concern between activists of the party organization and the electorate is not merely a scholarly one. The ideologists of American politics have long claimed that a horde of ideological voters is increasingly

[15]See Chapter 4.

[16]James Reichley, quoted by Theodore White, *The Making of the President 1964* (New York: Atheneum, 1965), p. 217.

alienated by parties unwilling or unable to give them clearly defined ideological alternatives. Are the American parties, then, reflecting a nonideological electorate or suppressing an ideological one?

IDEOLOGY IN THE AMERICAN ELECTORATE

In the late 1950s, the authors of *The American Voter* found that, by the most generous criteria, only about 15 percent of the American electorate employed an ideological framework of ideological terminology as either a primary or marginal means of evaluating parties and candidates.[17] That is, less than one in six American voters applied to the presidential politics of the time some ideological abstractions greater than a single issue or group of isolated interests. Beneath this thin stratum of ideologists and near ideologists, some 45 percent of the electorate operated on an interest-oriented level—a level that we have earlier called the level of the silent ideology. Their subideological preferences were nonsystematic projections of the interests of a group or the fervor of an issue position. They characterized the Democratic party, for example, as the party of the worker, the Republican party as the party of business or fiscal responsibility.

The 1950s, however, were years of consensus in American politics, a period in which increased affluence seemed to have produced a new politics to replace the SES politics of the New Deal and the 1940s. The consensus, however, was either illusory or short-lived. From 1960 on, it became clear that the scholarship of the 1950s had reflected a period of complacency in emerging policy disagreements.[18] By the 1970s, it seemed clear that the differences between Democrats and Republicans on major issues of public policy were increasing. The alternatives they represented were becoming clearer and clearer. Indeed, there was also some reason to think that they had also been clearer before the 1950s and that the soundings taken in those years merely represented a dip in the level of issue concern and awareness in the American electorate.[19]

As things have turned out, the late 1960s and the early 1970s were the high point of recent issue and ideological content in American politics.[20] Voters were more alert to and more informed about issues than they had

[17]See Angus Campbell et al., *The American Voter* (New York: Wiley, 1960), Chap. 10.

[18]John C. Pierce, "Party Identification and the Changing Roles of Ideology in American Politics," *Midwest Journal of Political Science* 14 (1970): 25–42.

[19]Everett C. Ladd and Charles D. Hadley, *Political Parties and Political Issues: Patterns in Differentiation Since the New Deal*, Vol. 1 of Sage Professional Papers in American Politics (Beverly Hills: Sage, 1973).

[20]See, for example, Gerald Pomper, *Voters' Choice* (New York: Dodd, Mead, 1975); and Norman H. Nie, Sidney Verba, and John R. Petrocik, *The Changing American Voter* (Cambridge, Mass.: Harvard University Press, 1976).

TABLE 16.1   *Percentages of Voters Perceiving Different Party Stands on Government Guarantees of Jobs: 1956–72*

	1956	1960	1964	1968	1972
Strong Democrat	73.0%	74.5%	80.3%	78.1%	86.9%
Weak Democrat	54.2	66.3	69.3	65.4	82.0
Independent	36.4	57.6	55.2	54.2	60.2
Weak Republican	50.3	50.5	61.3	64.1	76.8
Strong Republican	63.7	42.5	76.7	79.1	89.5

Source   Data from Table 8.2 in Gerald Pomper, *Voters' Choice* (New York: Dodd, Mead, 1975).

been. More important, they increasingly saw the two parties as presenting alternatives in the major areas of public policy (Table 16.1). Issue voting also reached new highs in the period. In the 1972 presidential election, issues assumed an importance equal to party loyalty in shaping voter choices. Democrats abandoned McGovern to vote for Richard Nixon because of his stands on the important issues.[21] Finally, there is some evidence, though disputed, that American voters also became more consistent in their issue stands, more able to relate their stand on one issue to their stand on another—in short, more ideological in their responses.[22] All in all, it appeared to most observers that the American electorate had moved to a new stage of politicization in which issues would count for more and party loyalties for less in American politics.

The developments of the 1964–72 period, however, were to be remarkably short-lived. It may have been that scholarship overestimated them, at least in part.[23] It is also clear, however, that the American electorate made one of its unexpected shifts following the events of the 1972 election. Voters no longer saw the differences between the parties so sharply, and their consistency in finding similar sides to related issues also declined.[24] Self-proclaimed liberals and conservatives no longer differed

[21]Arthur H. Miller, Warren E. Miller, Thad A. Brown, and Alden Raine, "A Majority Party in Disarray: Policy Polarization in the 1972 Election," *American Political Science Review* 70 (1976): 753–78.

[22]John L. Sullivan, James E. Piereson, and George E. Marcus, "Ideological Constraint in the Mass Public: A Methodological Critique and Some New Findings," *American Journal of Political Science* 23 (1978): 233–49.

[23]Michael Margolis, "From Confusion to Confusion: Issues and the American Voter (1956–1972)," *American Political Science Review* 71 (1977): 31–43.

[24]John R. Petrocik, "The Changeable American Voter: Some Revisions of the Revision," paper presented at the annual meetings of the American Political Science Association, September 1978.

as sharply as they once did, even on a number of social welfare issues. Also, as if to clinch the erosion of issue and ideology, Americans made their voting decisions in the 1976 presidential election as if it were 1956! That is, there was a marked decline in issue voting, and party loyalties governed more voting decisions than in any election since 1960. In 1980, party loyalties and candidate evaluations—especially the evaluation of Jimmy Carter's four years in the presidency—dominated voter choices in the presidential contest. To put it simply, both Carter and Reagan consequently "drew support from voters of widely varying views" on major policy issues.[25] Although he certainly was a conservative, Ronald Reagan was not elected *because* he was a conservative.

At the risk of more premature generalizing, it is beginning to look as though the American electorate periodically raises and lowers its concerns for issues. The salience of issues and ideologies reflects the events of the time and the extent to which campaigns and candidates play on such concerns. It is surely not a coincidence that the period of 1964 through 1972 featured the principled, issue-centered rhetoric first of Barry Goldwater in 1964 and then of Eugene McCarthy and George Wallace in 1968 and George McGovern four years later. By contrast, the Ford-Carter campaign of 1976 featured low-key appeals to trust and confidence and, indeed, a conscious avoidance of well-defined policy initiatives. It may even be true that after the intense politics of the late 1960s and early 1970s, American voters found, by 1976 and 1980, that politics were less compelling and important. The middle 1970s and early 1980s were, in short, a time of alienation and cynicism about politics, of conspicuous nonvoting, and of a muting of rhetoric in presidential campaigns. In retrospect, it seems not to have been a time for a national debate on issues or ideologies.

Moreover, not only does issue salience come and go—so also do specific issues. A whole set of social issues—abortion, racial integration, legalization of marijuana, for example—rose to prominence in the late 1960s. By 1976, though, Americans had returned their primary attention to the economic issues they had thought most important in earlier decades; although attention to the economic issues fell off in 1980, those issues still remained dominant. Although only 27 percent of American adults thought the economic issues—recession, unemployment, inflation—the most important issues in 1972, that percentage rose to 76 percent in 1976 and was at 56 percent in 1980. Conversely, foreign and defense policy achieved first importance for 31 percent of adults in 1972 but only for 4 percent in 1976. In 1980, the events in Iran and the rest of the world brought it back to 32 percent.[26]

[25] William H. Flanigan and Nancy H. Zingale, *Political Behavior of the American Electorate*, 5th ed. (Boston: Allyn & Bacon, 1983), p. 129.

[26] Paul R. Abramson, John H. Aldrich, and David W. Rohde, *Change and Continuity in the 1980 Elections* (Washington, D.C.: Congressional Quarterly, 1982).

These stories of trends and developments are simply stories. They record the rise and fall, the high and low points, of issue concern, but they do not tell us how high is "high" or how low is "low." Such determinations, of course, involve personal judgment and evaluation, but benchmarks are available. First, large numbers of Americans think of themselves as liberals and conservatives—indeed, the great majority do (see Chapter 6). In 1980, some 62 percent of American adults were prepared to accept some ideological label along the liberal-conservative dimension for themselves. The acceptance of such labels is easy, however, and tells us nothing of the intensity of the commitment behind it. There is also troubling evidence that those conventional labels mean different things to different individuals. The liberal-conservative dichotomy may suggest different views of the proper role of government to political scientists, but it suggests different views about social values and life-style to many other people. For some people, being "conservative" may mean more about dress, leisure pursuits, or religion than it does about politics and government.

If one looks, instead, at the ability of individuals to see the different issue positions of the two parties—and to see them correctly—one is applying a higher and probably a more appropriate standard. In 1980, considerably less than half of the American adults could correctly identify the Democratic and Republican positions on the basic question of government responsibility for insuring employment and an acceptable standard of living (Table 16.2), and this is the issue that best defines the liberal-conservative dimension in contemporary American politics. Even among those Americans who profess to have opinions on the subject, only about two-thirds perceive and identify the differing positions of the parties. At the very least, these data force one to view ideological self-identifications with some caution. In that same vein, John Pierce has found that the increase in the numbers of "conceptual" ideologues (those who perceive parties and issues in ideological terms) has not been matched by increases in numbers of "informational" ideologues (those who have specific information about the content of ideologies).[27] In other words, voters may think in ideological terms, but they may lack information about candidates and campaigns on the basis of which to make specific ideological choices.

The politics of ideology is abstract and remote, and it thrives with difficulty in the folksy, face-to-face politics of personal followings, family political traditions, and patronage and preference. In the increasing reliance on campaigning in the mass media, furthermore, all advantages are with the campaigns that stress personal appeal and punchy sloganeering. Most voters cannot sustain the interest or provide the intellectual sophistication that ideas demand; theirs is not the ideologist's view of American society. Once the short-term ideological stimulus has disappeared, the con-

---

[27]Pierce, "Party Identification and the Changing Roles of Ideology."

TABLE 16.2 *Perception of Party Positions on Issue of Government Responsibility for Jobs and Standard of Living: 1980*

| | Percentage Perceiving Democrats Holding Position that Government Should See to It That People Are Employed and Enjoying a Good Standard of Living[a] | | Percentage Perceiving Republicans Holding Position That Each Person Should Get Ahead on His or Her Own[a] | |
	Including "No Opinion" Responses	Without "No Opinion" Responses	Including "No Opinion" Responses	Without "No Opinion" Responses
Strong Democrats	43	69	39	69
Weak Democrats	34	59	34	61
Independents	41	70	36	63
Weak Republicans	45	78	36	60
Strong Republicans	53	75	47	64
Total	41	71	37	64

[a] In the two sets of columns, the percentages on the left are computed by adding those who had no opinion into the base; the percentages on the right in both sets reflect only those respondents able and willing to express an opinion on the issue.

Source Center for Political Studies of the University of Michigan; data made available through the Inter-University Consortium for Political and Social Research.

cern with issues abates. Thus, although an ideological minority within the parties and the electorate will see American politics largely in ideological terms, the American majority apparently will do so only under special circumstances. What is an easy and natural way to understand American politics for some is an unusual, even unnatural way for many others.

THE ANGUISH OF IDEOLOGY

In general, the uneven and uncertain rise of ideology risks a discontinuity between the ideological minority within the parties and the essentially nonideological majority in the electorate. At best, the full electorate is only sporadically given to ideologies. It responds selectively to issues, to be sure, but it also responds to a personality, a deeply felt personal interest, a campaign, a group loyalty, an ancient tradition. The parties and their candidates may respond to that gulf between the ideological minority and the nonideological majority with appeals on a number of levels—ideological arguments for some parts of the audience, nonideological arguments for others. Always, however, there is danger of alienating a majority irritated and ultimately repelled by a discourse they find obscure, irrelevant, and even fatuous.

Thus, the establishment of an ideological party is impeded, first of all, by the fact that only some Americans see party politics consistently in issue or ideological terms. It is important, also, that those ideological concerns are spread unevenly across American social classes. Because they are so strongly associated with higher levels of formal education, one finds them disproportionately among higher SES Americans. They are, in a sense, the political preoccupations of an affluent, well-educated, upper-middle-class elite in American politics for whom the abstractions and verbal content of ideology come easily. Thus, they increasingly tend to be the preoccupations and even the political incentives of the middle-class activists within each party's organization.

That gulf between an ideological elite of activists and a less ideological party electorate would pose problems for the parties in itself. That problem is made even more serious, however, by the fact that the party activists tend to take more extreme ideological positions than the party voters. Careful scholarly studies both of officials in the party organizations and of delegates to the two national parties found the electorates of both parties close to the center on the left-right continuum, with the activists of the Democratic party farther to the left and the Republican activists and officials farther to the right.[28] Moreover, the Republican officials-activists are farther away from their voters than are the Democratic officials—so far, in fact, that Republican voters are actually closer ideologically to the Democratic officials than they are to those of their own party. Thus, the activists and voters in the two parties differ both in the extent and in the position of their ideologies. Caught in the middle of these differences are the party candidates and officeholders. The only alternatives open to them—conflict with the party's activists, lack of candor with the electorate, or defeat at the next election—are hardly attractive. It is no wonder that the party in government so strongly resists fixed issue and ideological commitments within the parties.

Thus, a major American party, faced with the development of ideological activists, may develop an internal, private ideology or issue consensus at odds with the stance necessary to win elections. That divergence aggravates, in yet another way, the tensions and strains among the party organization, the party in government, and the party in the electorate.

[28]Herbert McClosky, Paul J. Hoffman, and Rosemary O'Hara, "Issue Conflict and Consensus Among Party Leaders and Followers," *American Political Science Review* 54 (1960): 406–27; Robert S. Montjoy, William R. Shaffer, and Ronald E. Weber, "Policy Preferences of Party Elites and Masses: Conflict or Consensus?" *American Politics Quarterly* 8 (1980): 319–44; and John S. Jackson III, Barbara L. Brown, and David Bositis, "Herbert McClosky and Friends Revisited: 1980 Democratic and Republican Party Elites Compared to the Mass Public," *American Politics Quarterly* 10 (1982): 158–80.

There are periodic eruptions of dissatisfaction among the conservatives of the Republican organization with the moderation of the party in office. Even so conservative a "moderate" as President Gerald Ford found himself rejected by many of the organization Republicans in favor of the more conservative Ronald Reagan. Reagan himself, as president in the 1980s, found that his brand of Republican conservatism was not conservative enough for the stalwarts of some Republican organizations.

Beyond these differences in levels of issue involvement and in distances from the political center, ideologies within each party differ from state to state and from region to region. A persistent ideological factionalism in both parties has been evident in the behavior of state delegations to the two national party conventions over recent decades. Within the Republican party, for instance, one can identify a group of state parties, largely of the North and Northeast industrial states, whose delegates, since 1940, have taken a consistently moderate or liberal position in votes at Republican conventions.[29] Other state Republican parties take consistently more conservative positions, and similar factionalism is apparent, too, within the Democratic party. Those differences obviously reflect the different economies and demographies of the states, as well as different state political cultures.[30] Thus, lacking any unifying structures, the two national parties speak in a babel of ideological voices. They have no annual party conference or other instruments for fashioning a party doctrine; their quadrennial platforms are instruments of the presidential campaign for votes rather than lucid declarations of party principles. In short, the national parties are structurally incapable of articulating, much less monopolizing, the ideological content of American politics.

Finally, to all of these divisive aspects of ideology one must add one more: the lengthening ideological agenda. In retrospect, perhaps a nostalgic retrospect, the debate spawned by the Goldwater candidacy in 1964 seems almost classic in its simplicity. Most of it turned on a single ideological dimension: the traditional liberal and conservative differences over the proper and useful role of government. It was strong, positive government and the welfare state versus very limited government and individual responsibility. By 1968 and after, the ideological dimensions were no longer simple. Cross-cutting issues of defense and foreign policy, of racial and sexual equality, of law and order, of personal morality and life-style, of energy and the environment, had all been posted on the nation's agenda. What was largely a unidimensional ideological politics in 1964 had become a multilayered politics of assorted issues in less than a decade. As

[29]David Nice, "Ideological Stability and Change at the Presidential Nominating Conventions," *Journal of Politics* 42 (1980): 847–53.

[30]Howard L. Reiter, "Party Factionalism: National Conventions in the New Era," *American Politics Quarterly* 8 (1980): 303–18.

James Piereson reminded the advocates of party responsibility, an increase in ideological awareness and involvement alone will not bring the changes they want; those increases must be accompanied by an ideological alignment along a dominant dimension. He found that there had been no such aligning of issue commitments between 1960 and 1976. The degree of alignment in 1976 was, in fact, less than that in 1956.[31] Thus the final irony: the growth of ideology itself thwarts the development of ideological political parties.

Ideology thus brings all manner of torments and problems to the American parties. For them, the question is not primarily whether they can become ideological parties, for they cannot. It is, rather, whether they can contain the new ideological commitment of their activists without it tearing them apart. The threat to the parties is, in part, one of factionalism, conflict, and splintering—the usual forms of intraparty bickering. Beyond that threat is another: greater numbers of ideologues threaten the party organizations with an inflexibility of goals that rejects the parties' traditional electoral pragmatism. Many delegates to the Republican convention of 1964 and the Democratic conventions of 1968 and 1972 were prepared to nominate candidates without greatly considering their electability. Some, indeed, preferred defeat with principle to victory with compromise. If the importance of the ideological goal of the party ever crowds out the electioneering role, then the parties themselves will be greatly altered. So, too, will most of American electoral politics.

PARTY RESPONSIBILITY AMERICAN–STYLE

The model of the responsible political party is an ideal. One does not look for it in reality, for no political system yet has developed the cohesion, discipline, and unity that its pure form demands. Even in Great Britain, home of the hopes of the American reformers, practice falls short of the model. Party cohesion in the British Parliament, though significantly greater than that in the American Congress, is by no means perfect. British cabinets and parliamentary parties, moreover, have long insisted that constitutional traditions forbid them to be bound by party decision or commitment. Even within the Labour party, historically committed to the binding discipline of party decisions, Labour prime ministers have made

---

[31]James E. Piereson, "Issue Alignment and the American Party System, 1956–1976," *American Politics Quarterly* 6 (1978): 275–308. It is interesting to speculate why, in view of greater issue salience, there should be no increase in alignment. The multidimensionality of issues during the 1964–72 period may be at fault. It may also be that the strength of party identification in the 1950s promoted acceptance of a partisan issue alignment as a consequence or derivation of loyalty to a party.

it clear that although a Labour government will consult with the party's national executive, it cannot be bound by it.

American practice is even further from the model. To be sure, one finds in some state legislatures a high order of party discipline behind or in opposition to a party program. The programs of principles, however, spring not so much from a party organization or from the decision of the electorate as from the initiative of the governor or the party's legislative leadership. What responsibility there is to the voters for their program is established at later elections, when the voters reward or punish their programmatic stewardship.[32] Even when sophisticated voters may be able to identify a past policy or decision with a party, such a quasi responsibility diverges from the model in one major way: there is little role in it for the party organization, since the legislative party or the executive originates the program and enforces discipline behind it. The responsibility rests not on the overt program of party activists and organizations but on the homogeneous interests of the voters, party leaders, and constituencies that support the legislative and executive parties. It is a cohesion and responsibility that springs essentially from the coalescing of common interests in electoral politics.[33]

Occasionally, under the stress of crisis or catastrophe, American politics approaches the model of party responsibility even more closely. In the presidential election of 1936, the Democrats and Republicans were identified with sharply differing solutions to the nation's economic woes. If their positions were not truly ideological, they were at least determinedly programmatic. The burdens of the depression may have focused voter attention on the hopes and remedies of policy to an unusual degree. Much of the campaign oratory centered on the Roosevelt program for social and economic change and on his opponent's charges that Roosevelt was proposing radical changes in the American polity and economy. The programmatic rhetoric and identification, combined with high voter attention, may well have produced something close to a mandate election and a mandated congressional contingent of Democrats. That election of 1936 suggests that the kind of ideology or programmatic concern necessary for "pure" party responsibility is a product of crisis conditions that have

[32]This is largely the point V. O. Key makes in *The Responsible Electorate* (Cambridge, Mass.: Harvard University Press, 1966). On the American voter's lack of the perceptions and decisions the goals of party responsibility would demand, see Donald E. Stokes and Warren E. Miller, "Party Government and the Saliency of Congress," in Angus Campbell et al., *Elections and the Political Order* (New York: Wiley, 1966), pp. 194–211.

[33]Richard C. Elling also makes the point that some degree of party responsibility is more likely in a "moralistic," issue-centered politics such as Wisconsin's than it is in the individualistic, patronage-oriented politics of Illinois; see "State Party Platforms and State Legislative Performance: A Comparative Analysis," *American Journal of Political Science* 23 (1979): 383–405.

prevailed only for short periods in American experience. It is also evidence that such periods of party government are understandably more likely after a new realignment has stamped fresh and vivid party loyalties on the American electorate.[34]

More common than the case of crisis-stimulated responsibility is the type of responsibility that results from presidential government. Strong presidential leadership, especially when aided by majorities of the same party in the Congress, produces a somewhat cohesive program that becomes the program of the president's party. Indeed, some presidents, such as Ronald Reagan, have been able to organize the enactment of large parts of the party platforms on which they ran for office.[35] Presidential government, of course, produces only the kind of post hoc responsibility that we noted earlier. It need not produce the kind of clear programmatic alternative the reformers want. (Platform differences between the two parties, although they can be observed, are not generally great enough to satisfy the same critics.) Presidential government does stamp some differences on the parties, however, and it does fashion points of reference for the approval or disapproval of voters.

Can one expect more than this of the American parties? There are any number of barriers to the achievement of party responsibility. To recapitulate both the earlier pages of this chapter and much of the earlier chapters of this book:

1. Even with the rise of ideological and issue concerns in the electorate, the American parties face severe tests and strains in converting themselves into ideological parties. The spread of issue involvements, in fact, further divides the parties as different groups and individuals within them attach themselves to different causes.

2. American electoral politics has developed in directions not easily compatible with party government. The parties have lost control of nominations—the strength of the direct primary guarantees that loss—and they find it increasingly hard to manage election campaigns and to establish election programs. The new campaigning and its new campaign finance have freed candidates and officeholders even more from the party organization. Even legislators who are at odds with the platforms of their party and the programs of their party's executive do not find it hard to survive.

3. The classic American institutions that divide the powers of government—federalism and the separations of powers—also divide the parties that would govern in them. Instances of executives of one party

---

[34]Barbara Sinclair relates these conditions to the immediate aftermath of the 1928–32 party realignment in "From Party Voting to Regional Fragmentation: The House of Representatives, 1933–1956," *American Politics Quarterly* 6 (1978): 125–46.

[35]Gerald M. Pomper, *Elections in America* (New York: Dodd, Mead, 1968), Chap. 8.

and legislatures of the other are not infrequent, and even bicameralism decreases the probability that one party will control a single legislature.

4. The weakness of American party organization is apparent to all observers. It does not involve large numbers of Americans—even the most political Americans—either as members or as officials or volunteer activists. Its eclipse by the party in government leaves it woefully short of the authority necessary to integrate a political party and to police its use of public office.

5. The American electorates increasingly resist giving loyalty to or taking cues from a party. The weakening of the party as a cognitive symbol matches the weakening of its organization. A more political, more sophisticated, better educated electorate takes its cues from a far broader range of sources.

In short, when the reformers began to urge a new and expanded role on the parties more than thirty years ago, they were forced also to argue for strengthened parties. More than a generation later, we find ourselves applying their plans and nostrums to parties that are even weaker. Talk of strengthening the parties in contemporary terms usually has little to do with party government. Even the optimists hope only to recapture the party role in electoral politics.

The breadth of the problem of converting the major American parties into prototypical responsible parties can perhaps best be gauged by looking at the scope of the reformers' proposals. The Committee on Political Parties of the American Political Science Association, for example, proposed the following:[36]

A massive shoring up of the national parties and their organizations. The committee recommended that the national conventions meet at least biennially and exercise greater control over the national committees. Above all, it suggested a national party council of some fifty members that would draft a platform for the national convention, interpret and apply it to issues between conventions, make "recommendations . . . in respect to congressional candidates" and about "conspicuous departures from general party decisions by state or local party organizations," provide a forum for "the discussion of presidential candidacies," and coordinate relations among national, state, and local party organizations.

---

[36]The direct quotations in the following paragraphs are from the report of the committee, *Toward a More Responsible Two-Party System*. Emphasis in the original has been eliminated. One of the members of the committee has also recently published some reflections on its work; see Evron M. Kirkpatrick, "Toward a More Responsible Two-Party System: Political Science, Policy Science, or Pseudo-Science?" *American Political Science Review* 65 (1971): 965–90.

A perfecting of the instruments of ideology. The committee proposed, in essence, that the platform mean something and that it bind the party officeholders and organizations. The platform ought to deal at least partially with the party's "permanent or long-range philosophy," and it ought also to be carefully prepared and systematically interpreted. "The party programs should be considered generally binding" on both officeholders and state and local parties.

An assertion of party control over the congressional party. To tackle so protean a task, the committee recommended both a consolidation of the present congressional party organizations into a single-party leadership group and the elimination of practices (such as the seniority system and the traditional power of the House Rules Committee) that undermine party discipline.

A remodeling of the American parties into membership, participatory parties. The committee's hope was perhaps best expressed in these words:

> With increased unity within the party it is likely that party membership will be given a more explicit basis. Those who claim the right to participate in framing the party's program and selecting its candidates may be very willing to support its national program by the payment of regular dues. Once machinery is established which gives the party member and his representatives a share in framing the party's objectives, once there are safeguards against internal dictation by a few in positions of influence, members and representatives will feel readier to assume an obligation to support the program.[37]

The committee's report ranged beyond these general points. It dealt with other barriers to party responsibility: the direct primary ("the closed primary deserves preference"), the electoral college (it "fosters the blight of one-party monopoly"), political finance, and barriers to full and meaningful adult suffrage (e.g., the long ballot). In short, it becomes clear that to achieve the goal of government by responsible parties, one would have to undertake a wholesale reconstruction not only of the American parties but of the American electorate and political environment as well.

Some other proponents of party responsibility, however, have been more modest in their goals. One of the most persistent, James MacGregor Burns, touches on many of the same themes as the ASPA Committee.[38]

---

[37]Committee on Political Parties, *Toward a More Responsible Two-Party System*, p. 70.

[38]See James MacGregor Burns, *The Deadlock of Democracy* (Englewood Cliffs, N.J.: Prentice-Hall, 1963), especially Chap. 14. Note, also, that Burns is dealing with the parties in terms of his own, somewhat different frame of reference, especially the distinction between the presidential and the congressional parties. See also Stephen K. Bailey, *The Condition of Our National Political Parties* (New York: Fund for the Republic, 1959).

He puts the same emphasis on the building of grass-roots, membership parties, the buttressing of the national party (the presidential party), and the reconstructing of a vigorous congressional party. He notes the same recognition of the need for change in the parties' political environment (e.g., the restrictions on adult suffrage and the status quo in political finance). Yet the reforms Burns suggests are less drastic and more realistic, even though their direction and their pinpointing of the causes of the present lack of responsibility are not greatly different. Perhaps Burns's relative moderatism springs, in part, from his recognition of an essentially Madisonian political culture that has not tolerated any one instrument—party or other—of national majoritarian political power.

For the immediate future, barring the special conditions of crisis, it seems likely that the American parties will continue their modest governing role—a post hoc responsibility for carrying out programs that generally promote the interests of the party's activists and loyal electorate. Neither the American parties nor the voters can meet the demands that the classic model of party responsibility would impose on them. Rather, the various sectors of the party are increasingly bound together by a commitment to a set of issue positions that separates the activists, candidates, and voters of one party from those of the other. In a loose, often distressingly imprecise sense, each of the two parties is a distinct group of like-minded men and women. That tentative and limited agreement on issues, reinforced by executive leadership of the party in government, may produce enough cohesion for a modest, variable degree of responsibility. Ironically, such a degree of party responsibility will be achieved without the central role—drawing up a program and enforcing it on candidates and officeholders—that the reformers planned for party organizations. It will be a party responsibility of the party in government, and that is a very significant difference.

Two things must be kept in mind regarding the relationship between party responsibility and the new ideological and issue concerns in American politics. First, such concerns, in their purest form, will very likely be limited to a minority of Americans. The ideological view is one pattern of perception that the party develops with one segment of the electorate. To the nonideological segment, the party continues to make appeals on other than ideological grounds—on a mixture of issues, traditions, interests, and personalities. Second, the salience of issues or even of ideologies is a consequence of events in the broader political context. American politics apparently reached one peak of issue salience in the 1930s, and the years from 1964 through 1972 may well have been another. In 1976 and after, the electorate was returning (but who knows for how long?) to an electoral politics dominated more by partisan loyalties and candidate evaluations and less by commitments on issues.

To conclude, parties in government govern for a great many goals and reasons. They want to satisfy the multiple and complex demands of the electorate. They want to meet the goals—also complex and contradictory—of the activists of the party organization. Furthermore, they have their own goals to meet, goals that range all the way from individual desires for power and the perquisites of office to their obligations to public office and service. In the aggregate, those various goals are extraordinarily complex. Although program or ideology is an important goal for many people in the parties in government, it does not necessarily dominate all others, just as it does not dominate the perceptions of the American electorate. The present extent of party government—that is, of the parties' ability to enact cohesive programs into public policy—probably reflects the present place of program and ideology in the total structure of the goals and incentives in American politics.

VI

The Political Parties: Role and Theory

Textbooks change with changes in the subjects they treat. Some years ago, the concluding chapters in books of this sort invariably discussed the place of the parties in the broader political system and in the smooth operation of American democratic processes and institutions. Those questions are still important and are almost obligatory. Political science has changed, however, in the last generation. Since World War II, political scientists have been caught up in explanations of the empirical behavior, institutions, and processes they study. That new commitment of the profession of political science thus creates a new expectation: the final theoretical essay.

The theoretical aspirations of political scientists vary greatly. The more confident and optimistic of them aspire to propositions that not only will explain past behavior but also will meet the higher test of predicting future behavior. Less hopeful ones are content with specifying major variables and relationships, with the understanding that the arrangement of them into a final, integrated theoretical pattern of explanations will have to await the collection of more observations and more explanatory fragments. The pages of these last two chapters will make it clear that the choice here is for the second, more modest, route. The development of theoretical statements about most political institutions and processes is in an early, rudimentary stage, and modesty becomes such a condition.

One begins the theoretical task by attempting to explain why the American parties are what they are and why they do what they do. One of the best strategies for this purpose is to observe changes in them over time. As the parties develop new activities, depend on new incentives, take new organizational forms, for example, one is naturally led to wonder how and why the changes came about. What changes in the parties' environment accompanied those changes in the parties? Is there a causal relationship between changes in the parties and those outside them? If the decline of patronage accompanies the decline of the old-style urban machine, does it *cause* the change in party organization? Or has the decline of the machine reduced the need for patronage and thus caused *its* demise? We learn much about the parties if we put the changes together into a pattern and adduce explanations for them.

Chapter 17 begins the analytical task by examining the changes presently under way in the American parties. It brings together the trends and changes that have been mentioned throughout the book and concludes with an explanation of those changes and a series of projections of what's ahead for the American parties. The central theme—already more than hinted at in earlier chapters—is that the major American parties have lost their powerful, predominant role in American electoral politics. Of necessity, we also face the questions of what produced that change and what electoral politics will look like in their release from party domination.

The last chapter, Chapter 18, carries the analysis beyond the specific changes presently abroad in the American parties to the level of parties in general and to the American parties in other periods of time. In that chapter, too, the theoretical problems and issues suggested by the contemporary changes will be brought together into some more general categories. The chapter will be concerned with changes in the parties' roles and activities within the larger political system. It concludes, in fact, with the proposal of a developmental approach to the parties, an approach suggesting that parties usually enjoy their heyday when electorates are less educated, less secure, and politically unsophisticated, and that as populations develop political knowledge and sophistication, the parties become less important to the mass electorate.

Theory may well be too pretentious a word for the tentative suggestions that follow. At least, their goal is a modest one: to raise the understanding of the American political parties beyond the level of analysis of specific events to a more general knowledge that provides insights into continuing trends and into groups of events or phenomena. After a journey through a book such as this, one at least ought to be able to explain why the American parties differ at any one time and from one time to another.

17

THE FUTURE OF THE
AMERICAN PARTIES

A great deal has turned sour for the American parties in the last few years. The late 1960s saw the decline of their prestige; and along with other institutions of American government and politics, they have borne a good deal of the blame for the general malaise and the decline in public confidence that beset American society. From all sides, critics blame the parties and the other institutions of the "system" for the ills they think afflict American government and politics.

Whether or not the parties deserve such disfavor depends in great part on one's estimate of the problems and progress of American society. Whatever current reputation the parties enjoy, however, their most fundamental problems predate the dip in public esteem. Their time of troubles had started by the 1950s and early 1960s. Furthermore, their troubles resulted more from long-run changes in American society and politics than from any recent events.

CHANGES IN THE THREE SECTORS

The American parties have long been characterized by the loose set of relationships that have bound the three party sectors together. That looseness, or lack of integration, is indeed one of their most fundamental signs. The party organization has not been able either to bring a substantial part of the party electorate into membership or to assert its leadership or discipline over the campaigns and policymaking of the party in government. It is not surprising, therefore, that the recent widespread changes in the parties have hit the three sectors quite differently.

The Party in the Electorate

The American electorate seems to be losing its long-run attachment and loyalty to the American parties. More and more American adults consider themselves independents rather than members of or identifiers with a major party. Even among those who profess a loyalty or attachment to a party, that attachment to a political party no longer dominates the decision on how to cast the vote, as it once did. Thus, we have a decline in both the quantity and the power of party identification in the American public. Since those changes are now more apparent in the eighteen- to thirty-year-old group, they will likely accelerate. The result, obviously, is a shrinking of the size of party electorates and an eroding of the quality of their loyalty. More serious than the loosening of identifications, of course, is the increasing rejection of politics altogether, evident, perhaps, in the declining confidence in the parties and the increased nonvoting of the 1970s and 1980s.

It has been the stability of party identification that has undergirded the stability of the two-party system. The unchanging adherence to the party as a reference symbol and an object of loyalties—and operationally as the key to the voter's decisions—has left no opportunities for a new party to gain a foothold in the electorate. It is not surprising, therefore, that the decline of party identification in the American electorate has been reflected in the victories of independents and third parties in increasing numbers since 1960. In 1968, independents and third-party candidates won seats in the Senate, an independent was elected governor of Maine, and George Wallace ran with amazing strength as a third-party candidate. Even the little-advertised independent candidacy of Eugene McCarthy for the presidency in 1976 drew more than 750,000 votes, and John Anderson attracted almost 6 million in 1980. Furthermore, ticket-splitting and non-party voting are on the increase. In 1972, for example, the voters in 45 percent of the congressional districts selected presidential and congressional candidates of different parties. Even in the less unusual politics of 1980, the comparable figure was 33 percent.[1]

If the American electorate is not responding so eagerly to its party loyalties, to what does it now respond? Some segments of it are attuned to the new appeals of program and ideology. The Goldwater campaign of 1964, the McCarthy and Wallace appeals of 1968, and the McGovern candidacy of 1972—along with those of many state and local issue-oriented candidacies—drew on and activated higher levels of issue aware-

---

[1]Gerald M. Pomper, *Voter's Choice* (New York: Dodd, Mead, 1975), p. 215. The 1980 data come from Norman J. Ornstein, Thomas E. Mann, Michael J. Malbin, and John F. Bibby, *Vital Statistics on Congress, 1982* (Washington, D.C.: American Enterprise Institute, 1982), p. 53.

ness. The Reagan candidacy of 1980 featured a return to frankly ideological appeals. For less sophisticated voters, the appeals that now register most effectively are those of candidate personality and image. The handsome faces, ready smiles, and graceful life-styles that television screens so fully convey attract some of the support that party symbols once commanded. Also, since candidates and issues change far more frequently than parties, the consequence is an increasingly unstable, less predictable pattern of voting.

The Party Organizations

In the party organizations, the machines have been passing from the scene, and with them their activists and incentives. Even the Daley organization in Chicago has suffered a series of humiliating defeats. Many organizations of all kinds no longer can depend on the patronage and preferments or the guaranteed election to public office that once recruited their full-time, vocational activists. Instead, they draw the better educated, part-time leadership, whose incentives more often incline to issues or ideology and who bring with them new demands for intraparty participation. Indeed, some among them increasingly reject the politics of compromise, accommodation, and pragmatism that resulted from the assumption that the capture of public office is the alpha and the omega of American politics. If their ideological goals are not satisfied—or even recognized—within the party, they may leave it for particular candidates or issue organizations.

Increasingly, too, the internal, intraorganizational processes cease to be under the organization's control. Under the force of growing participatory expectations, these processes are becoming progressively more public; the private sphere of the party organization shrinks accordingly. The direct primary began the process of taking decisions from the party organization, and some eighty years later it continues apace. Also, one can now see the "publicizing" of the national convention processes. The convention is no longer a device for the organization's deliberation and choice making. Its processes are public, and, more important, its options have been sharply restricted in recent years by the activities of the would-be candidates in the preconvention politicking. Even the preconvention scramble for votes increasingly moves from the hands of party organizations, as at least four-fifths of convention delegates are chosen in states with presidential primaries.

At the same time that they are undergoing internal changes, the party organizations are losing their capacity for controlling American electoral politics. No longer do they consistently control either nominations (thanks to the direct primary) or the politics of election campaigning. Candidates increasingly find themselves able to build their own campaign organizations, raise their own campaign funds, and go their own merry ways in the campaign. All the campaign assets they once received from the party organizations and their workers—skills, information, pulse readings, manpower, exposure—they now can get from pollsters, the media, public relations people, volunteer workers, or even by "renting a party" in the form of a campaign management firm. Especially because the party organizations have been unwilling or unable to provide the new arts for the candidates, they have waned in influence in the contesting of elections. Their fairly primitive campaign skills have been superseded by a new campaign technology, and more and more they are finding themselves among the technologically unemployed.

Furthermore, the party organizations remain decentralized in the face of the increasing centralization of life and politics in the United States. The electorate looks more and more to national political symbols and figures, but the party organizations remain collections of state and local fiefdoms. The national committees and the national conventions are loose confederations of powerful local organizations and, despite new signs of life in the national committees, seem destined to remain so. Even those assertive local organizations no longer prosper. They do not easily recruit full-time, concerned workers and leadership with the new incentives.

The Party in Government

The men and women of the party in government, freed from reliance on the party organizations by the direct primary, by access to the media, by independent sources of funds, and by supportive personal followings, increasingly establish a direct appeal to the voters. No longer able to rely so heavily on abstract party loyalties, they develop more personal appeals and rely on personal style, physical appearance, even what personal magnetism they can generate. They find, in many ways, that it is quite a different matter to be advertised by the media than by party canvassers.

The successful candidates are the parties' contingents in American legislative bodies. There, in direct relationship to the decline of party loyalties among voters and the decline of party organizations' power over legislators, they vote as legislative parties, with decreasing party cohesion. The instances in the Congress in which a majority of one party opposes a majority of the other in recorded roll call votes have been at an all-time low over the last several decades. Freed from the party demands of both voters and the party organizations, they are more vulnerable to the nonparty pressures—the local interests of the constituency, primarily. More important, perhaps, with the decline of competition (especially for incumbents) in congressional elections, they are not very vulnerable to anyone.

As the legislative party loses its cohesion and strength, the executive party rushes into the vacuum. Presidents and governors enjoy governmental power and leadership of the executive branch at the very time at which they increasingly represent the party and its programs to so many voters. They personify the party and give tangible content to its labels and symbols. In a period when many partisans seek programmatic goals, they alone formulate programs and control policy initiatives. Therefore, it is no exaggeration to speak of the parties as executive-centered coalitions. Nowhere is the phenomenon clearer than in the ability of presidents to dominate the national party organization of their parties, to give life and meaning to the symbol of their parties, and, with the help of federal subsidies, to mount campaigns free of obligation to the party organization.

This much is merely a summary of what has been said in greater detail in earlier chapters.[2] The changes cumulatively amount to a vast shift of power within the American political party from the party organization to the executive-led party in government.

The crucial fact, perhaps, is the progressive isolation of the party organization in the American political parties. The organizations had their days of glory in some of the larger cities, but they never succeeded in integrating any significant measure of the party electorate into the organization on a membership basis. Isolated from the electorate and without its broad-based support or participation, they have always been vulnerable to suspicions that they were run by irresponsible oligarchies. The smoke-filled room myths have never died, the cries of bossism are as alive at today's party conventions as they were at the turn of the century.

What assets the party organizations once had they are losing rapidly. They no longer control the chief incentives for political activity, as they did when it was patronage and preference that made the activists active. They no longer control the resources and technology of campaigning and of electoral politics. Also, they no longer invoke the feelings of party loyalty in their electorate. What kind of party is it, however, in which the party organization loses a preeminent or even equal position? Is not the party organization the only sector of the party that has more at stake than the winning of elections, that offers some possibility of life and principle beyond specific elections and even beyond electoral defeat?

In the American parties, in any event, a coalition of an executive-led party in government and a somewhat restive and fickle party electorate has resulted. The executive rather than the party organization controls and manipulates the party symbols. The alliance of the executive with the party electorate rides on the message of the mass media and political personalism; the organization as a channel of communication no longer matters so

---

[2]The "decline of party" literature is extensive. Its major recent contributors include Walter Dean Burnham, "Revitalization and Decay: Looking Toward the Third Century of American Electoral Politics," *Journal of Politics* 38 (1976): 146–72; Jeane J. Kirkpatrick, *Dismantling the Parties: Reflections on Party Reform and Party Decomposition* (Washington, D.C.: American Enterprise Institute, 1978); and Gerald Pomper, "The Decline of the Party in American Elections," *Political Science Quarterly* 92 (1977): 21–42.

much. That coalition is all the easier because party organization has been unable to centralize, whereas the other two party sectors have done so. Especially in national politics, that centralization or nationalization of party messages, cues, and personalities unites the president-led party in government and the large numbers of voters who react primarily to national issues and faces.

THE NEW CONTEXT: THE NEW POLITICS

These changes in the contemporary American parties are taking place in the context of broader ferments and upheavals in American politics and even in American society. Most of them matured in the middle and late 1960s. In an American society that believes change is invariably good and innovation always newsworthy, it was perhaps inevitable that the new politics would be called "the new politics." The term, however, is one of considerable variety and looseness, and one commentator's description of the new doesn't always match that of another. There is some consensus, however, that it includes these elements:

Concern for issues and principles. In substance, the new politics connotes a heightened concern for issues and ideology, often even such new issues as the environment, the war in Vietnam, and abortion. At a more abstract level, it also marks a commitment to values and principles in public policy and a concomitant reluctance to compromise them.

Increased citizen participation. The new politics exalts the mass participatory ethic to broaden the base of American politics. (It is opposed, of course, to elites, bosses, establishments, and all other forms of limited decision makers.) It demands a voice in government down to the local neighborhood level, and it is committed to more representative participation that includes women, minorities, and the disadvantaged. At a less active level, it pays new attention to mass opinion (e.g., the polls) and devices for citizen consultation. With some reason, therefore, it has been said that there is a new populism in the new politics.

Personalism and the "new individualism." In a rejection of institutions and structures, the new politics has put new value on the individual, whether as citizen, candidate, or officeholder. Candidates run for office on personal magnetism and govern on the basis of personal trust. It is a political style perfectly adapted to the messages of the mass media, except, perhaps, that the media easily trivialize the messages. The individual too easily becomes merely an image, a smile, a well-clothed appearance, or a celebrity. (On the subject of celebrity, one need only refer to professional athletes, astronauts, and film stars as public officials.) At the level of the individual voter, the new individualism translates into a new independence of parties and into a hesitation to make any form of collective action possible by moderating one's views or interests.

④ *Reformism and political skepticism.* The new politics has certainly been marked by skepticism, even cynicism, about traditional social and political institutions. It has questioned traditional processes (the "system") and traditional leadership (the "establishment"), and it has fueled a vigorous program of reform for the parties, presidential nominations, and campaign finance, among others.

⑤ *New techniques of campaigning.* From the early 1960s to the 1980s, the ways of campaigning for public office were revolutionized. The use of the media, advances in opinion polling, the development of computer-based information systems and mailing lists, and the rise of a new breed of campaign specialists transformed the search for major office in the United States. To pay for those new techniques, vastly greater sums of cash were required. Candidates who could raise them thus were free to run their own campaigns.

The new has not, to be sure, completely replaced the old. It joins the older political styles and modes in the mainstream of American politics. It is only part of a new amalgam, but it is an important part nonetheless. One need only look at the 1976 and 1980 elections and the candidacies of Jimmy Carter and Ronald Reagan for illustration. Both ran as critics of and outsiders to "Washington," and both traded heavily on personal appeal and trust. Reagan, furthermore, ran as an admitted ideologue, and Carter's campaign was substantially an exercise in the new populism.

Thus, for the parties, the advent of the new politics seems to mean a sharp division—in all three sectors—between old-style and new-style politics, and so between old-style and new-style activists. On the one hand, there are the upper-middle-class ideologues, the so-called amateurs, who demand a politics of differentiation, attention to issues and ideology, and a major participatory role in the party. On the other hand, there are the older, more traditional partisans, whose politics are centrist and consensual, whose incentives for activity are varied, and who are willing to accept the old modes of authority in the party organization. It was that difference that lay, in good measure, behind the battle in the Democratic party in 1972 between the McGovernites and their opponents, in the Republican party in 1976 between the Reagan and Ford forces, and in the Democratic party between the Carter and Kennedy supporters in 1980. It is a difference that underlies an increasing number of factional divisions in the parties, however, and it promises to remain with them for the foreseeable future.

The impact of the new politics on the political parties is readily apparent if one looks at one of its chief by-products: single-issue politics. The parties traditionally have been committed to the building of consensus and the fashioning of majorities—with all the compromise and pragmatism that implies in a complex society. They build those majorities to win elections, to organize cohesive legislative parties, and, in their fashion, to govern. Single-issue politics threatens all of that. It is, by definition, a commitment to an issue position that is so deep and principled that compromise is often ruled out. The single issues spawn political organizations in which activity for many of the new activists is more satisfying than activity in a political party. Loyalty to a single-issue position—and the rewarding or punishing of a candidate or officeholder on that basis alone— is quite different from the pragmatic acceptance of a number of candidates and issue positions that loyalty to a political party assumes. Perhaps most troubling of all for the parties, the organization of political activity single issue by single issue bespeaks, in the aggregate, a degree of politicization, a sheer quantum and intensity of political feeling, that the major American party cannot integrate or contain.[3]

Two caveats about the new politics and the changes in the parties must be entered, however. The first is merely that predictions about American politics are very perishable. Only a decade or so ago, there were many predictions of sweeping and fundamental changes in American politics, and the turmoil on the campuses and in the streets did, indeed, seem to promise major changes in other parts of American society. It also seemed that a new dawn of ideology had arrived for all time. The issues, causes, and enthusiasms that stir Americans, however, also shift with unexpected speed. Thus, the new politics and the contemporary phase in which the American parties find themselves may turn out to be, contrary to expectations, an interlude of no lasting force in American politics. One might note, for example, the steps to "de-reform" the Democratic National Convention of 1984.

Second, it is terribly important to realize that these developments in American politics are not of a single piece. They constitute no one movement or logical, coherent program. (Nor should we expect logic or consistency in a politics marked by a history of diversity and accommodation.) To some extent, they pull and tug against each other as well as against the traditions of the past. The commitments to issue and ideology flower

---

[3]It should be noted that single-issue politics has, to some extent, begun to develop within the parties. Feminist, prolife, ethnic, rural, minority, and labor caucuses can now be found within the national conventions, some legislative parties, and some state organizations.

simultaneously with an increase in personalism, life-style appeals, and media images. Not only is most of the personalism distinctly *not* issue- or policy-oriented, but in its most attenuated form—the concern for the profile, the smile, the hair, the clothes of the candidate—it is supremely nonpolitical. At its worst, ironically, it is less political than the reliance on party loyalties and identifications that it replaces. The choice made on the basis of party label certainly weighs more political factors than the choice made on the basis of the candidate's self-confidence in front of a TV camera.

THE DECLINE OF THE PARTIES

It is one of the comforting beliefs of the conventional wisdom that social systems contain their own self-adjusting mechanisms. The free-market, competitive economic system, which freely adjust prices and production to changes in supply and demand, offers a ready example. So, too, does the self-correcting system of checks and balances that generations have trusted to keep the American separation of powers in a well-tuned equilibrium. We have long had similar hopes for the party system. For the ills of unresponsiveness and dissatisfaction in the electorate, the cure is said to be a readjustment of party appeals (spurred by competition) and a consequent realignment of party loyalties in the electorate.

Is it possible that realignment may yet come as a response to the disaffection with the parties? Indeed, it is possible. The external symptoms that ordinarily precede a realignment are evident: third-party surges named Wallace and Anderson, for instance, the instability of the vote from one election to another, and the diluted effects of party loyalties on the voting of individuals. In short, the signs of realignment are all around us.

The realignment, however, is greatly overdue. Perhaps the most striking aspect of the 1968 and 1972 elections was the fact that, in the end, there was no realignment, that despite all the ticket-splitting, the old party identifications held and that, indeed, American voters returned to them in 1976 and 1980. Furthermore, an issue or ideological axis on which realignment might take place has not appeared. Alternatively, it may be that realignment cannot take place once the voters' confidence in the party system has slipped below a certain point. A considerable number of Americans may simply decide to rely on cues and political organizations other than the parties. Thus, they will have no incentive to change party loyalties; new nonparty symbols and loyalties will be added to the old party ties. Perhaps, too, our politics—at least for the moment—is too complex to produce the simple dualism, any dualism, around which voters can cohere in a new alignment. Most of the party realignments of the past formed along the classic lines of "ins" and "outs" at a time of national crisis.[4]

Even if the parties should find an issue and a catalytic event for realignment, however, it is by no means certain that realigning will restore the parties to their political preeminence. Realignment is no solution to the erosion of the party's organizational capacity to nominate and elect candidates. Nor is it any guarantee that large numbers of Americans will return to an unswerving partisanship or that they will again mark the straight party ticket. The truth is that a party realignment is only a readjustment of the parties to new cleavages in the society. It does not strengthen them per se. Moreover, it may even require the very kinds of confidence in party and need for party symbols that the American parties appear to be losing.

For the moment, therefore, a good many signs point beyond the cure of realignment to a decline of the parties generally and of party organizations in particular. Both the parties' dominance of our electoral politics and the stability of the two-party system have rested on the acceptance of the party label as a cue for action. Large numbers of voters now have cues and sources of information outside the parties. Many of them also are less and less inclined to accept the omnibus commitments that party loyalty implies. They want to pick and choose among issues and candidates. Party loyalty demands that they buy a whole collection of commitments; in effect, it asks them to divide the political world into two simple categories, ours and theirs. The simple, dichotomized choice that party loyalty within a two-party system demands no longer appeals to an educated, issue-oriented electorate. Knowing, confident, even assertive adults are less and less willing to surrender their selective judgment in favor of an unquestioning loyalty to party.

To look at it another way, the Republican-Democratic loyalties of the American two-party system actually require a politics of low intensity and moderate involvement in issues. The willingness of millions of voters to accept a diverse collection of candidates and issues assumes that they can compromise their feelings about any one of them. Loyalty to the party as a least common denominator can bind diverse populations into one party electorate only when the other lines that divide them are weaker. What happens, however, when large numbers of voters repeatedly feel more strongly about a candidate or an issue than they do about a party? What happens when large numbers of voters decide that they no longer need the ready-made, all-purpose, prepackaged judgment of a political party? Above all, what happens when that voter disenchantment takes place at

---

[4]On realignments, see James L. Sundquist, *Dynamics of the Party System* (Washington, D.C.: Brookings, 1973); Walter Dean Burnham, *Critical Elections and the Mainsprings of American Politics* (New York: Norton, 1970); and Jerome M. Clubb, William H. Flanigan, and Nancy H. Zingale, *Partisan Realignments* (Beverly Hills: Sage, 1980).

the same time that candidates find ways of communicating with voters outside the usual channels of the party organization?

It must be clear, however, that all of this is not to predict the imminent decline and fall of the political parties, American or otherwise. There is considerable danger of exaggeration when one draws a series of indicators into one concentrated argument. A good many of the necessary qualifications and counter-indicators get lost. There are, indeed, ample signs that the parties have and will continue to have a creative role in American politics, even if they no longer dominate the channels and resources of our electoral politics. There are hundreds of thriving party organizations, aggregate trends to the contrary notwithstanding. Lately, too, the national committees of the two parties have begun to stake out new campaign roles for themselves. There are still thousands of ardent party loyalists, and millions of voters still cast straight party tickets every four years. When we talk of today's decline, we do not mean death.

Furthermore, we ought not to assume that the decline will lead irreversibly and inevitably to death. On the contrary, there are signs that the decline of the parties is beginning to level off. The growth of the independents in the American electorate literally stopped between 1972 and 1980. Voters resorted to their party identifications in 1976, and to a lesser extent in 1980, with an old-time confidence. Legislative party cohesion (in those legislatures for which we have time-series data) seems not to be declining further. There are, after all, a good many traditional and institutional forces ensuring some role for the parties. They act collectively as a brake or a barrier against the infinite decline of the parties. It may well be that they are taking hold now and that the parties, consequently, are settling into a new and stable, if reduced, role in American politics.

Thus, the parties are alive, if not well, in America; but they will increasingly become a part of a richer, more diverse pattern of American politics. We may well see the repeated emergence of third parties as expressions of deeper discontent with the parties and with American society. Eugene McCarthy talked freely of a third-party attempt for the presidency in 1976 before settling on an independent candidacy. After his independent candidacy in 1980, John Anderson formalized his movement into a political party for 1984. Some scholars of American politics have also begun to reexamine the long-accepted case against multipartyism.[5] Moreover, other political organizations—interest groups, PACs, candidate organizations, ideological movements—have assumed a progressively greater role in the electoral politics the parties once dominated. The number of PACs active in national politics has increased from 608 in 1974 to 3,371 in 1982, and whereas their contributions accounted for 13 percent

---

[5]See, for example, Lawrence C. Dodd, *Congress and Public Policy* (Morristown, N.J.: General Learning, 1975).

of the funds that the general election candidates for the Congress received in 1974, PAC funds accounted for 27 percent in 1982. Quite apart from their direct expenditures in campaigns, a growing number of groups are also mounting registration and get-out-the-vote campaigns. Organized labor has been the traditional leader in those activities, of course, and the value of their voter mobilization efforts in the 1980 presidential and congressional elections may conservatively be valued at more than $20 million.[6]

In other words, the political organizations of today appear to have rediscovered the fundamental truth that political influence throughout the American political system flows from the election of public officials. So, especially, have the political parties. They appear now to be turning away from the membership organizations, the intraparty participation, and the explicit commitments to ideology that marked them in the 1960s and 1970s. They faced the great choice between ideology and issue on the one hand and pragmatic electoral politics on the other, and, led by the resurgence of the Republican National Committee, they appear to have made their commitment to electoral politics. Even the Democrats now seem willing to move away from some of the reforms of 1968 and after. The point can easily be overstated, of course. Where voters are politically more sophisticated and more committed to a set of issue positions, ideological activists will continue to control the party organization. In the aggregate, however, the thousands of organizations in each party seem to want to change their course back to electoral pragmatism.

Since the key to the revived electoral role is money, there has been a good deal of comment about the parties becoming "super PACs." In a sense, they are moving in that direction. To recapture or refashion a significant role in campaign politics, they must dispense cash or the new campaign expertise. They may combine that aid—also in the manner of PACs—with attempts to recruit or nominate candidates in the first place. Simply because they *are* political parties, however, they can more easily convert electoral success into some greater degree of cohesion in the party in government in support of an executive program. That is not the vision of the advocates of "responsibility," for it generates a capacity for governing out of the fashioning of electoral successes—and the obligation and gratitude that follow them—rather than out of the refining of party principles. That tension between electoral pragmatism and ideological commitment, however, is the enduring one for the parties. By adapting themselves to the new campaigning and trying to find a role in it, the

---

[6]Herbert E. Alexander, in *Financing the 1980 Election* (Lexington, Mass.: Heath, 1983), estimates that labor's registration and get-out-the-vote campaigns on behalf of Jimmy Carter alone cost $15 million.

parties have once again made their choice. Once again, apparently, it is to be a reaffirmation of the course of pragmatism.[7]

What seems likely, in other words, is a politics of greater fluidity and instability, carried on by a wider range of political organizations. The parties will exert their influence over nominations, elections, and policy-making, but so will other political organizations. In many instances, the personal candidate—aided by the media—will attract the voter loyalties and activist labors that the party organizations once did. The erosion of the one, stable, long-run loyalty in American politics will contribute to a politics more often dominated by the short-term influences of the charis-matic candidate or the very salient issue. In its volatility, its lack of con-tinuity, and its lack of predictability, the new electoral politics may increasingly resemble that of the one-party factional and personal politics in the American South in the 1930s and 1940s.[8] The diversity of goals in the American electorate, multiplied by the intensity of feelings about them, cannot easily be met even by two pragmatic, compromising political par-ties. Voters want more specialized cues for political choice and action, and the activists among them want to discriminate among the causes and peo-ple for whom they will work. The parties, in other words, are fighting to define a role, not the role, for themselves in American electoral politics.

AFTER THE REIGN OF THE PARTIES

Political life in the United States without the guiding dominance of two assertive political parties is not unthinkable. Much of our local politics has been nonpartisan in reality as well as in name for some time. A diminished role for the parties throughout much more of electoral politics, however, suggests impacts of a greater magnitude. The consequences, not only for the political processes but for the quality of American democracy, trouble many observers. Burnham has put the concern directly and simply:

> Political parties, with all their well-known human and structural short-comings, are the only devices thus far invented by the wit of Western man that can, with some effectiveness, generate countervailing collective power on behalf of the many individually powerless against the relatively few who are individually or organizationally powerful. Their disap-pearance as active intermediaries, if not as preliminary screening devices, would only entail the unchallenged ascendancy of the already powerful, unless new structures of collective power were somehow developed to

---

[7]On the financial role of the parties and on parties as "super PACs," see F. Christopher Arterton, "Political Money and Party Strength," in Joel Fleishman (ed.), The Future of American Political Parties (Englewood Cliffs, N.J.: Prentice-Hall, 1982), pp. 101–39.

[8]V. O. Key, Southern Politics (New York: Knopf, 1950).

replace them, and unless conditions in America's social structure and political culture came to be such that they could be effectively used.[9]

The American parties—and all others for that matter—mobilize sheer numbers against organized minorities with other political resources, and they do so in the one avenue of political action in which sheer numbers of individuals count most heavily: elections. Thus, the parties traditionally were the mechanisms by which newly enfranchised and powerless electorates rose to power. The old-style urban machine in the United States, for example, was the tool by which the recently arrived, urban masses won control of their cities from older, largely "Wasp" elites. In a more fluid politics of bargaining among a larger number of political organizations and millions more uncommitted voters, the fear is that the advantage will be on the side of the well-organized minorities that have other political resources.

The continued commitment to ideology in weakened parties may have additional elitist consequences. The educated, sophisticated, and involved political minority may impose a new kind of political tyranny on the less involved, lower SES segments of the electorate. It increasingly tries to impose an ideological politics that lacks salience and may indeed be incomprehensible to the less sophisticated. At the same time, it contributes to the decline of the most useful cue-giver, the major political party. The removal of the political party as an organizer and a symbol in our present nonpartisan elections helps upper SES elites, both of the right and the left, to dominate those politics.[10] The political party, in other words, is the political organization of the masses who lack the cues and information—as well as the political resources of status, skills, and money—to make a major impact on public decisions via other means. The diminished power of the parties makes the game of politics more difficult for them to play and win.

Finally, the continued decline of the parties would rob the political system of an important building of majorities. Although imperfectly, the major American parties have helped piece together majority coalitions. American presidents have enjoyed the legitimacy of majority coalitions most of the time, and the party majority in legislatures has at least permitted them to organize for action. With weakened parties, how are we to find majorities in a fragmented politics? Are we to rely on the personal appeals and promises of national candidates? Or do we face the kind of political immobility that has resulted elsewhere from the splintering of majorities into intransigent groups with deeply felt loyalties and senti-

[9]Walter Dean Burnham, "The End of American Party Politics," *Trans-action* (December 1969), p. 20.

[10]Willis D. Hawley, *Nonpartisan Elections and the Case for Party Politics* (New York: Wiley, 1973).

ments? To be sure, it is easy to overestimate what the parties traditionally have contributed to our politics, but the contributions, if more modest than many believe, are real and important. Certainly, a mature political system can and will work out its adaptations. There are, indeed, alternatives to stable, two-party systems that dominate electoral choice. The issue is whether they can pull together the separate pieces of American politics and political institutions as effectively as the parties have.

18

TOWARD A THEORY OF THE
POLITICAL PARTY

The political parties have never been able to contain the splendid diversity of American politics. Americans have always pursued many routes to influence—by dealing directly with public officials, by working through interest groups and other nonparty groups, by engaging in various forms of direct representation and demonstration, and by making choices through a political party. In other words, it has never been the case that all of our politics has gone on through the political parties. Indeed, the parties have never even monopolized our *electoral* politics.

It is important to keep the parties in a realistic perspective, because a good deal of scholarship on them attributes to them a role far more central and impressive than they have played in reality. It is as if the sheer pervasiveness of the party label in American elections and public office guaranteed a position of primacy for them. In reality, however, the American parties do not easily control nominations or elections, nor do they readily govern on behalf of party programs. Their place today in American politics is not easy to square with the view that considers them the "indispensable instruments of government,"[1] or even the originators of the American democracy.

Behind the attributions of a prime, central role to the parties is a false theoretical assumption, and that is what concerns us here. It is the assumption that the parties are causes rather than effects, that they are perpetually independent rather than dependent variables. They are said to cause, to shape, to produce. The fact that they themselves are caused, shaped, and produced is overlooked. Simply because the rise of the American parties accompanies the rise of democratic institutions and the ex-

---

[1]Committee on Political Parties of the American Political Science Association, *Toward a More Responsible Two-Party System* (New York: Rinehart, 1950), p. 15.

pansion of the adult suffrage, we cannot assume that they somehow "caused" the rise of democracy. Both political parties and American democracy arose more or less simultaneously from the interplay of the same general forces and conditions. Parties do, indeed, have an impact on political processes and institutions, but other political and nonpolitical forces, in turn, have effects on the parties. The parties are in and of the political system, and one cannot expect that they alone among political institutions can escape the influences that shape everything around them.[2]

The mission of this chapter, therefore, is to identify the reasons why political parties—especially the American parties—are what they are and why they have developed as they have. What shapes the particular structure of the parties, the relationships among their three sectors, and their various activities and roles in the political system? What accounts for changes in them over time, and for variations in them from place to place? Why do they differ from the parties of the other Western democracies?

What follows is not a full-blown, systematic explanation or a comprehensive and tidy wrap-up. Rather, this chapter is built around four analytical ways of looking at the parties. It can perhaps be said to be four fragments in search of a theory, for when we search for explanations about parties and party systems, we tend to break the problem into manageable parts. These four fragments, then, reflect four very common ways of looking at political parties. They are different perspectives—views of the parties from different sides or different analytical points of view.

I—THE IMPACT OF THE EXTERNAL ENVIRONMENT

In the first chapter we briefly discussed the major environmental influences that impinge on the parties (Table 18.1). Subsequent chapters have elaborated on these influences, especially on the ways in which they shape and mold the parties. The effect of the direct primary, for instance, on the parties' ability (inability, really) to control nominations was set out in great detail. So, too, was the effect of the separation of powers—and the absence, therefore, of parliamentary government—on the legislative party and the national committees.

In other words, the political parties are surrounded by a context, an environment, of the most varied sort. One can visualize it only imperfectly

---

[2]One very extensive attempt to treat the political parties as a dependent variable—as an effect rather than a cause—has been the persistent urge to reform them. Austin Ranney, in *Curing the Mischiefs of Faction* (Berkeley: University of California Press, 1975) describes the attempts with enormous insight. On the recent reform attempts within the Democratic party, see William Crotty, *Decision for the Democrats: Reforming the Party Structure* (Baltimore: Johns Hopkins University Press, 1978); and Nelson W. Polsby, *Consequences of Party Reform* (New York: Oxford University Press, 1983).

TABLE 18.1 *Major Categories of Influences in the Environment of the Political Parties*

Influences	Examples
1. Political institutions	Federalism, separation of powers, development of presidency
2. Statutory regulation	Legislation on campaign finance, structure of party organization
3. Electoral processes	Definition of franchise, the direct primary
4. Political culture	Attitudes about politics and the two-party system
5. Nonpolitical forces	State of economy, age distribution of population, use of TV

in two-dimensional images (Figure 18.1), but such an illustration at least helps to convey the comprehensiveness, even the oppressiveness, of the political world external to the parties. One point about Figure 18.1 needs to be elaborated a bit. The argument thus far might suggest an assumption that the direction of cause to effect runs exclusively from the environment to the parties—that the parties are always the dependent object or result of external, independent forces. That would be an overstatement of the relationship. Although the direction of the relationship is, indeed, primarily from environment to party, the parties do have some control over their environment. They do participate, for example, in the making of public policy on who votes, on the kinds of ballots voters use to mark their choices, and on the kinds of primary elections at which candidates will be nominated. They also shape, by education and by their own performance, public attitudes about the parties themselves and, more generally, about politics. Many more examples could be cited, of course.

The diagram of the political party within the broader spaces of Figure 18.1 should not go unnoticed either. It suggests a way of thinking about the parties—as an input-output mechanism. Parties both get and spend. They get in the sense that they recruit the inputs or resources that they need to function: money, skills, manpower, and loyalty. They spend in that they convert these resources into outputs or party activities: the contesting of elections, organizing of public officeholders, and propagandizing on behalf of issues or ideologies. All three sectors of the party, in their various ways, must mobilize resources, and all three generate results (outputs) in their special ways.

Thus, the political party in such a conception is first of all a conversion mechanism for changing resources and demands into goal-seeking activities. It must mobilize resources to maintain itself and undertake its activities. Obviously, a change in the statutes regulating campaign finance or a further contraction of patronage impinges on those efforts. The vitality

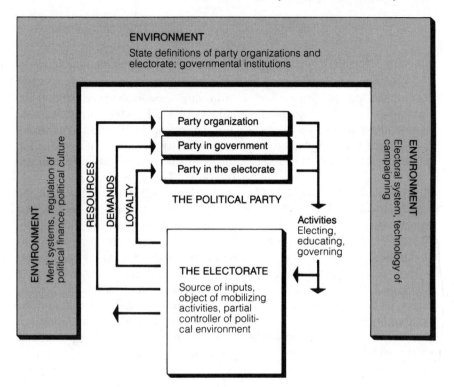

FIGURE 18.1 *The Political Party: Structure and Environment*

of the party organization, an essential element in the conversion mechanism, also depends on the network of state legislation that sets its outlines and powers. The outputs—the activities or functions—of the parties are similarly sensitive to changes in the environment. Any change in electoral law—whether it is the closing of a primary in one state or the abolition of the electoral college—clearly affects their electoral activities. The electorate itself is shaped by birthrates, patterns of education, and the spread of democratic and participatory expectations. Also, the demands the party activists and electorate bring to politics reflect issues of a war or a depression, for example, or alienation and trust in government.

There is a sense in which all the elements of their environment generate needs or demands on the parties. The concepts of "needs" and "demands" offer a way of viewing that environment. More precisely, they refer to the conversion or impact of the environment on the party. They are an elaboration of the connection between them. Thus, for instance:

— A parliamentary system operates in a specific way, and that operation "requires" or "needs" or "demands" certain kinds of parties and certain kinds of party capabilities and activities.

— As the new campaign experts broke the party's monopoly of the skills and information for contesting elections, candidates no longer "needed" the party organizations as they once did.

The use of *demands* and *needs* in this explanatory sense is simply another way of stating the cause-effect relationship. Some observers find these terms more comfortable intellectually than bald statements of cause;[3] but—and it is a big "but"—we also use the concept of demand in another, more direct way. We refer, for example, to the demand of citizens for government action of one kind or another or the demands of party activists for patronage or for a voice in party affairs. These are demands as *goals* of voters and party workers. Those individuals seek those goals, those demands, through the political party. The goals, too, are shaped by the broader political and social environment, just as the party is.

Obviously, the environment of the parties embraces an enormous range of components—from laws regulating the registration of voters in one state to the social-medical-technical forces affecting the national birthrate. Is it not possible to group the components into a manageable set of categories, or to establish some hierarchy of importance that will enable us to say that one element of the environment is more important than another? It is possible to do so to some extent, but that attempt should be postponed until we look at the other three theoretical fragments.

II—TWO TYPES OF PARTY STRUCTURES

Nothing characterizes the parties as political organizations quite so clearly as their three-part structure. Much of what they are, what they do, and how they do it is suggested merely by calling to mind that political parties include a party organization, a party in government, and a party in the electorate. It is not surprising that differences among the parties often come down to questions of the activities of the three parts or sectors and the various relationships among them. The relationships of the three sectors describe both a division of labor and a hierarchy of authority within the parties.

When measured by the roles and influence of their sectors, political parties in democratic regimes tend to fall into two main groups: those dominated by the party organization and those dominated by the party in government. The American parties are moving increasingly to the type headed by the party in government—that is, by the party's candidates and

---

[3]There is an old tradition in political science of avoiding direct statements of cause and effect. In fact, political scientists have developed an extensive vocabulary that avoids the word *cause* while suggesting causation; this vocabulary includes such nouns as *force, factor, influence, condition, determinant,* and *variable.*

officeholders. In their glory days at the turn of the century, one might have argued that they were organization-dominated, but no longer. The American party in government increasingly contests elections, controls the party image and reputation, and governs in office without important constraints or even contributions from the party organizations.

A party dominated by its organization differs in several very fundamental ways from the party led by its party in government (Table 18.2). The party controlled by the party in government, almost by definition, is a heavily electoral party. The concerns of the party's officeholders are in winning elections, and they establish both the priority of the electoral mission and their control over the resources and choices for it. Once elected, they govern in response to the need for securing reelection and for making a record of accomplishment in governance. The alternative—the party dominated by its organizational sector—is best typified by the parties of the European parliamentary democracies. The issue commitments or ideologies of the organization's activists assume a greater importance in the life of the party. They have such an impact within the party precisely because the organization speaks for the party, picks its candidates, and maintains some degree of leverage over its parliamentarians.

One can summarize many of the differences between the party models in terms of their ability to integrate their three sectors. In the organization-centered model, the three sectors are bound closely by ties of loyalty and discipline. A substantial part of the party electorate, in fact, joins the or-

---

TABLE 18.2   *Characteristics of Two Types of Political Party Structures*

Party Organization Dominates	Party in Government Dominates
1. Party in electorate assumes (in part) a membership role in the organization	1. Little or no membership component in party organization
2. Party organization controls nomination of candidates and much of election campaign	2. Party in government largely free from organizational control in nomination and election
3. Relatively high degree of cohesion in legislative party	3. Relatively low degree of cohesion in legislative party
4. High degree of integration of three sectors	4. Low degree of integration of three sectors
5. Unified by goals of party organization's activists	5. Unified by goals and programs of executive party
6. Activities substantially electoral, but programmatic as well	6. Activities almost exclusively electoral

ganization as members, and the debts of candidates for nomination and election assistance bind them to the party organization. The key to the organization-centered party lies in the ability of the organization to unite the party in government to it and to the goals of its activists. In the classic urban machine of patronage and preference, both sectors were united in the overarching goal of electoral victory and the electoral pragmatism it demanded. Alternatively, the two sectors might be united, as the "party responsibilitarians" argue, by loyalty to the same principles or issue positions. In the party controlled by the party in government, in contrast, everything depends on the pragmatic alliances of convenience at election time. The dominant party in government, indeed, is free to form alliances with nonparty organizations, such as interest groups, rather than working with its own party organization. The distance between the congressional parties and the national committees illustrates the point. The party in government establishes contact with the party electorates without relying greatly on the party organization.

Obviously, the differences between these two varieties of political party run to deeper, more basic issues. Ought a political party to be something more than the sum total of the candidates who choose to run on its label? At the very least, it seems unlikely that the party led by its party in government can provide the continuity and breadth that sets the party aside from other political organizations. The parties that are strong in their ability to dominate or monopolize certain forms of activity have been those led by the organizational sector. Only the party organization has the range of skills and resources, as well as the commitment to all party goals and even to the party itself, to fill this leadership role within the party. Only such a party can approach the model of the responsible party. Only strong parties that exert policy leadership as well as leadership in the recruitment of public officials—and in providing a stable cue to millions of voters—can augment or support the officeholder's responsibility to his or her electorate.

These two kinds of parties do not occur without reason or explanation. What differences are there in the different environments from which they come that will explain their differences? One can also put the question in more parochial terms. Since the American party is the archetype of parties controlled by the party in government, what accounts for the differences between American parties and parties dominated by their organizations?

Scholar after scholar has noted that the American party is not associated with parliamentary institutions and that the organization-dominated party is. The very nature of a parliamentary system demands discipline and integration of the parties; the American separation of powers does not.

2. American electoral law (primaries and the regulation of finance, for example) is all on the side of the party in government, giving it easy access to nomination and great freedom from the party organization in waging campaigns.

3. State regulation of and legislation on parties has placed a set of heavy constraints on the party organization; the reformist urge has indeed been heavily antiorganization in its goals. The states have imposed cumbersome forms and a weakening openness and permeability on the organizations, while making it difficult for them to develop large memberships.

To be sure, there are additional secondary and reinforcing explanations. The availability of the new campaign arts and technologies is clearly one. It has provided the party in government with an alternative to party organizations by destroying their monopoly over election campaigning. The new campaigning is available to parties everywhere, however, and one must ask why it has freed the parties in government in the United States but not elsewhere. The answer, of course, is that elsewhere there are parliamentary institutions and election legislation that limit the freedom of candidates and buttress the central, dominant role of the party organization.

III—THE SOCIAL PSYCHOLOGY OF THE VOTER

Among political organizations, the parties alone attach their names to candidates for public office. On the surface, the point appears to be trivial. On closer examination, however, one sees that it involves the willingness or need to respond to that label on the part of large numbers of Americans. Thus, the durability and special character of the parties result in great measure from the needs and perceptions of the American voters. In fact, political parties originated in large part from the need of voters for a guide, a set of symbolic shortcuts, to the confusing and often trackless political terrain. The labels, activities, and personages of the parties ran as a clearly perceptible thread through the jumble of political conflict and the baffling proliferation of American elections. When that cue giving also produced loyalties and identifications with the parties, when those loyalties were stable and enduring, and when they dominated so many voting decisions, the conclusion was inescapable that this pattern of reliance and loyalty was a primary determinant of the American political parties.

In other words, political parties are historically a reflection of the ability or inability of the electorate to cope with its responsibilities. Their symbolic importance, the value of their labels in elections, directly reflect the informational needs and problems of a new mass electorate. Those needs change over time, however. Note, for example, the reduced incidence of and reliance on party loyalties in the American electorate. Voters simply are better educated and better informed than they were sixty or eighty years ago. They are more involved and active in the affairs of politics— more "political" than they once were. They are also more often bombarded by nonparty political messages—especially those of the personalities and personal images that the mass media carry so effectively.

This is not to say that American voters no longer need cues or labels. Rather, they increasingly seek the mixed and different cues that the party organization cannot provide. The integrated party dominated by an organization suited an earlier American electorate seeking a single, consistent cue to a great many political decisions and judgments. As voters become more political, however, they are prepared to handle a wider range of political perceptions and loyalties and to sift through a greater variety of political messages. They may form an attachment to an issue or two— or to an entire ideology—and they are not prepared to surrender that loyalty or those loyalties to an overriding loyalty to a political party. Although they may find many of the candidates of "their" party perfectly acceptable, they refuse to accept party loyalty as a reason to favor all of its candidates. In short, voters increasingly want to pick and choose in their political decisions. The American electorates thus find the candidate-centered party better tailored to their preferences than the party dominated, integrated, and unified by a party organization.

In another, more general sense, too, parties reflect the political-psychological needs of voters. The rise of personalism in political campaigning is a case in point. It is easy—too easy—to attribute this personalism to the new campaign technology and reliance on the mass media. Behind the personalism is the need of many citizens for personal leadership, for flesh-and-blood embodiment of distant government, even for the vicarious ego strength of a confident public figure. Perhaps, too, the new personalism reflects a dissatisfaction with the parties (and other political organizations) as lifeless and impersonal abstractions.

IV—DEMOCRACY AND THE DEVELOPMENT OF PARTIES

It is abundantly evident that the origin and rise of the political parties is intimately bound up with the sweep and spread of democracy. The parties grew as the first mobilizers of electoral power while the electorates expanded. The relationship of the parties to democracy, however, extends beyond their origins and initial growth. Democracy presupposes a degree of citizen participation and choice. By definition, it involves a broad distribution of political power and requires organizational intermediaries to mobilize the political power of individuals in order to make it effective.

The entire development of the parties reflects these imperatives of democracy, and changes in the parties have mirrored changes in the very nature of democracy and its electorates.

The democracy of the mass political parties, however, is not necessarily democracy's pure or final realization. Democratic expectations, institutions, and processes change, and with them so do the parties. The political parties may have been essential, as many have suggested, during the initial politicization of the uneducated, economically disadvantaged masses. When education and affluence open new channels of political information and activity, however, competitors arise with new organizational forms, new appeals, and new political resources. We see the growth of a politics that is more issue-oriented, more committed to goals and values, and less pragmatic and compromising. The argument that only the parties can aggregate or mobilize political influence is no longer so convincing as it once was.

The relationship of the changes in the parties to those in the democratic processes is closer than one might infer from mere assertions that everything changes. In the United States and many of the other Western democracies, the changes in the parties occur in phases related to the development of democratic politics and modern political institutions. In all those changes, three phases are evident:[4]

1. Initially, the parties began in most of the Western democracies as parties of limited access and narrow appeal. Originated at a time of a restricted, aristocratic suffrage, they were limited in personnel, confined largely to electioneering, and closed to mass participation. This formative, premodern period in the American experience came before 1830 or so.

2. As the electorates expanded, the parties also expanded their organizational forms to include more activists and members. (Although the American parties resisted more than most the development of mass membership bodies, they were no longer largely legislative caucuses.) The parties dominated the political loyalties and even the political socialization of the new electorates. As the dominant political organizations of a citizenry marked by relatively low levels of political information and sophistication, they became the chief givers of political cues. In the American experience, of course, this stage of their development reached its zenith at the beginning of the twentieth century. (In many of the new nations of Asia and Africa, which began with virtually complete adult suffrage, the parties entered the second stage very quickly.)

[4]For another developmental approach to political parties, see Samuel P. Huntington, *Political Order in Changing Societies* (New Haven: Yale University Press, 1968), especially Chap. 7. His four stages seem to coincide with the first two here.

③ Finally, as electorates mature along with democratic processes, as political loyalties and interests become more complex, politics becomes more diverse and differentiated. The political party in this phase becomes merely *primus inter pares*. Its sole control of the mobilization of power ends amid growing competition from other political organizations. The party remains both a potent organization and a powerful reference symbol, but its total role in the politics of the nation diminishes.

These stages in party development reflect no organic growth or inherent life cycle. They are direct responses to changes in democratic processes and economic development, and they certainly do not appear to be limited to the United States. Parties in Western Europe, for example, are losing members and appear to be entering the third phase, too.[5] When an electorate reaches a certain point of politicization, party loyalties and parties themselves are no longer so useful as they once were.

Does such a developmental sequence foretell the continued decline of the parties? Are they merely the relics of a simpler political age? Such questions force speculation about the tomorrows of American society and politics. The best clue we have to that future is in the research on "postindustrial" politics. It suggests that something like the aforementioned stages two and three coincide with emergent and mature industrialism in the Western world. Those are times in which electorates are overwhelmingly concerned with issues of economic well-being and security. In the postindustrial world, affluence will be taken for granted and people will seek less material, life-style, "quality of life" goals: education, leisure, democracy, attractive surroundings, and social and moral freedom. Already, in fact, identifiable groups of voters with "postmaterial" values have appeared in the Western democracies and Japan, and, in one instance at least, they have launched a postindustrial party: the Greens of West Germany. At least in the early decades of postindustrialism, then, one might expect an even more active and participatory middle class, an even greater fragmentation and diversity in politics, and a greater potential for movements of change and reform. It is not easy to imagine a return to a dominant role for the parties in such a milieu.[6]

---

[5]Anthony King discusses this and related points in his excellent essay, "Political Parties in Western Democracies," *Polity* 2 (1969): 111–41.

[6]It is possible, of course, that not all voters in a society will come to take affluence for granted; one might then see a politics of bitter conflict between material and postmaterial values. On the subject of postindustrial politics, see, for example, Samuel P. Huntington, "Post-Industrial Politics: How Benign Will It Be?" *Comparative Politics* 6 (1974): 163–91; and Ronald Inglehart, *The Silent Revolution: Changing Values and Political Styles Among Western Publics* (Princeton: Princeton University Press, 1977).

WHAT SHAPES THE PARTIES?

Two main influences or sets of influences from the environments of the American parties meet to shape their outlines and dimensions. They are, first, those that define and mold the electorate and, second, those that set the basic electoral and governmental structures of the political system. They are not special influences that shape only the American parties. All scholarly evidence suggests that they set the outlines of the parties in all the Western democracies.

That these are the chief influences on the parties reminds us once again that the parties are, first and foremost, electoral organizations. They and their candidates contest elections, and their party labels furnish the electorate a variety of cues, symbols, and information. It is a small but very significant point that the party label appears with the candidate's name on the ballot. Thus, the parties are what they are primarily because of the ways in which they contest elections and relate to their successful candidates after election. It is true that some parties are more purely electoral in their mission than others, but in the Western democracies, the major parties are all electoral parties. It is that fact, indeed, that accounts for most of the differences between the major and the minor parties.[7]

The Definition of the Electorate

That first set of influences—the one defining the electorate—is in fact made up of a number of components. It includes the legal statements, both constitutional and legislative, that define which individuals will be in the electorate. It includes the social conditions that determine the numbers, the age distribution, the education, the affluence, and the other social characteristics of the electorate. It also includes the influences that shape the levels of political awareness and information, the attitudes and expectations, and the sheer political understanding of the electorate. What causes the cognitions of the adults in a society is a question far beyond the scope of this book. It is enough to take them as a major set of causes acting on the parties.

The nature of the electorate, in all of these facets, clearly changes over time. The changes in the Western democracies appear to be almost invariably in one direction—from lesser to greater politicization, from fewer to more democratic and participatory expectations, and from a limited to a larger or universal adult suffrage. All these changes are obviously interrelated, although they happen at different rates and sequences in different

---

[7]For a systematic attack on these explanatory problems, see Robert Harmel and Kenneth Janda, *Parties and Their Environments: Limits to Reform?* (New York: Longman, 1982).

political systems. Taken together, they constitute the rise of mass popular democracy, a process that began in the United States at the beginning of the Republic and has extended virtually to today. Only one trend in the American electorate appears to move in the opposite direction—rates of political participation, especially voter turnout. The recent downturn may be temporary, or it may signal a fundamental, long-term change in the electorate.

At this point in this long book, not much needs to be said about the specific ways in which the nature of the electorate impinges on the parties. It shapes the pattern of party loyalties and the reliance on the parties for political cues and information. It affects the nature of campaigns and candidates; it affects, too, the relationship of the officeholders with the parties and with their constituencies once they are elected. It is indeed a truism to say that the shape of electoral politics depends to a great extent on the nature of the electorate. Finally, it is the electorate from which the party activists are drawn, and changes in it change the personnel of the parties.

The Governmental and Electoral Institutions

The second cluster of influences on the parties includes the chief governmental institutions and constraints within which the parties work and to which they relate. Foremost within this cluster is the basic configuration of political institutions—federalism or unitary government, parliamentary forms or a separation of powers, the nature of the executive, and the extent of governmental authority. Second, it includes the myriad laws and constitutional provisions that define the election processes (and those for nominations, too, where that is a matter of public policy). Finally, there are the regulations of the parties per se and of the activities carried out under their labels. They run the gamut from laws creating party organizational structure to those regulating the spending of money in campaigns. Often, too, they merge almost imperceptibly into the legislation creating election machinery. Again, the impact of all this on the parties is an old subject. One need only reiterate, as examples, the effect on the democratic parties and party systems of the separation of powers, the impact on party organizations of the direct primary as a way of choosing party candidates, and the use of single-member districts rather than proportional representation from multimember constituencies.

These segments of the parties' environments change, too. Constitutions and electoral systems are often replaced, though not in the United States. If one compares the United States and Great Britain to the nations of continental Europe on this point, the contrast is striking. Although their constitutions change and adapt, there have not been any abrupt breaks with the past in the last 100 years in either Britain or the United States. In that time, however, France has launched five entirely separate republics, each one intended to be a break with, even a repudiation of, its predecessor. Similarly, large numbers of European countries have tinkered with various election systems, whereas Britain and the United States have stayed with plurality election from single-member constituencies. On the other hand, the American parties have been subjected to a range of legislation on themselves and their activities quite unknown anywhere else. The direct primary constrains their selection of candidates, for example; and state laws defining the party organizations have no parallel elsewhere. The effect, and in some cases the intention, of such regulation is to restrict the party organization and thus to favor the party in government. What is more, the reformist zeal behind much of this legislation lives on and has recently begun to work within the parties themselves. As an example, one need only mention the reform of the national party conventions.

These two sets of variables interact in a special way on the American parties to produce their rather different, special qualities. First of all, many of the important institutional-structural influences on the parties are rare or uniquely American: the direct primary, the separation of powers, the nationally elected executive, and the network of regulatory legislation on the parties. It is precisely these factors that are instrumental in shaping the American two-party system and in vaulting the parties in government to a dominant place in the American parties (at the expense of the party organizations). Second, although the first set of influences—those shaping the electorate—have changed over time both in the United States and in the other democracies, the second set has remained fairly constant in the United States. For that reason, changes in the American parties seem more directly related to changes in the specification and behavior of the American electorate.

There is also a third set of environmental variables that ought to be mentioned: variables of the nonpolitical environment. These are the events and trends beyond the political system that nonetheless shape our politics—the wars, international crises, recessions, economic prosperity, birth and mortality rates, energy shortages, and new moralities, for instance. Their effect on the parties, however, is not really *on* the parties. They define the policy issues of a time, and thus they shape the demands and goals that individuals try to achieve *through* the parties, whether as activists in them or simply as voters. They originate outside the parties and the political system, and they are to a great extent beyond their influence. The ultimate impact of these variables is beyond the parties. In other words, their effect is not primarily on the parties as conversion mechanisms but on the goals for which the mechanisms are employed.

After such an intensive look at the political parties and the influences that make them what they are, one ought to step back a bit and take a broader perspective. Political parties are not caused or shaped, not changed or modified, in a vacuum or in isolation. They contribute to a broader, aggregative politics, and, in a sense, they compete with other organizations and avenues for aggregating and representing large numbers of individuals. If there are other more effective ways for individuals to seek their political goals than through political parties, they will take them. If a relationship with a particular congressman and his attentive staff secures a social security check or access to federal contracts, why work through a party? If an interest group is more forthright and effective in opposing abortion or gay rights, why work through a party? What the parties are at any given time, therefore, is determined, in part, by the alternatives to them that are available. If those alternatives should be fostered by public policy—as the PACs have been by the federal campaign finance laws—the parties will be shaped, in a sense, by their competitors.

Indeed, the major problem for the American parties today arises from the increased differentiation of American aggregative politics. As the American electorate continues to develop more complex interests, it acquires more differentiated loyalties and responds to more complex and differentiated cues. It maintains identifications with parties, but it also responds to candidates and to issues, programs, and ideologies. It responds differentially to different elections and even to the choice between electoral and nonelectoral politics. The ultimate consequence is a more diverse, complex politics that no single set of loyalties, and thus no single set of political organizations, can easily contain.

Thus, the American parties find it increasingly difficult to be all things to all citizens. There probably will never again be a dominant, all-purpose political organization in our politics. The parties, especially, cannot easily meet the expectations of ideological politics and pragmatic electoral politics at the same time. Their symbols cannot continue to work their old magic on all elements of so diverse a political population. The new challenge for the parties in this fragmented politics is to fight, for the first time, for a place and a role in American politics—to cope with the fact that they do not have a guaranteed future.

Index

447

Acknowledgments

Table 2.1: Data from 1932 through 1960 from Donald E. Stokes and Gudmund R. Iverson, "On the Existence of Forces Restoring Party Competition," *Public Opinion Quarterly* 26 (Summer 1962): 162. Reprinted by permission.

Table 2.2: From John F. Bibby et al., "Parties in State Politics," Copyright © 1983 by John F. Bibby, Cornelius P. Cotter, James L. Gibson, and Robert J. Huckshorn, in Gray, Jacob and Vines, eds., *Politics in the American States: A Comparative Analysis,* 4th ed. Reprinted by permission of Little, Brown and Company.

Table 2.4: From Richard M. Scammon (ed.), *America Votes 14* (Washington, D.C.: Governmental Affairs Institute, 1981). Reprinted by permission.

Excerpt, p. 49: From Warren Weaver, Jr., "The Libertarian Alternative," *The New York Times,* January 22, 1980. Copyright © 1980 by The New York Times Company. Reprinted by permission.

Excerpt, p. 54: From *Blue Smoke and Mirrors* by Jack W. Germond and Jules Witcover. Copyright © 1981 by Jack W. Germond and Jules Witcover. Reprinted by permission of Viking Penguin Inc. and International Creative Management.

Excerpt, pp. 64–65: From H.G. Nicholas, "A Briton Considers Our Bewildering Party Apparatus," *The Reporter,* November 25, 1952, pp. 28–29. Reprinted by permission.

Excerpt, pp. 74–75: From Milton Rakove, *Don't Make No Waves, Don't Back No Losers* (Bloomington: Indiana University Press, 1975) pp. 120, 121, 122. Reprinted by permission.

Excerpt, pp. 90–91: From James D. Nowlan, *Inside State Government* (Urbana: Institute of Government and Public Affairs of University of Illinois, 1982). Reprinted by permission.

Excerpts, pp. 118–119: From *The New York Times,* October 9, 1981, December 22, 1981, October 5, 1982. Copyright © 1981, 1982 by The New York Times Company. Reprinted by permission.

Excerpt, p. 127: From *The Washington Post,* September 29, 1982. © 1982 United Feature Syndicate, Inc. Reprinted by permission.

Page 159: Data from *New York Times*/CBS poll, April 25, 1982. Copyright © 1982 by The New York Times Company. Reprinted by permission.

Table 7.2: From Paul R. Abramson, John H. Aldrich, and David W. Rohde, *Change and Continuity in the 1980 Elections* (Washington, D.C.: Congressional Quarterly Press, 1982), p. 173. Reprinted by permission.

Page 196: Advertisement courtesy of Barney's, New York.

Excerpt, pp. 222–223: From *The New York Times,* March 5, 1982. Copyright © 1982 by The New York Times Company. Reprinted by permission.

Table 9.1: From Richard M. Scammon (ed.) *America Votes 14* (Washington, D.C.: Governmental Affairs Institute, 1981). Reprinted by permission.

Table 10.1: From Belle Zeller and Hugh A. Bone, "The Repeal of Proportional Representation in New York City: Ten Years in Retrospect," *American Political Science Review,* 42 (1948): 1132. Reprinted by permission.

Excerpt, p. 250 and map, p. 251: From *The New York Times,* June 23, 1983. Copyright © 1983 by The New York Times Company. Reprinted by permission.

Excerpts, p. 257: From *The New York Times,* September 7, 1980. Copyright © 1980 by The New York Times Company. Reprinted by permission.

Excerpts, p. 258: From *The Washington Post,* November 17, 1982. Copyright © 1982 The Washington Post. Reprinted by permission.

Excerpt, p. 259: From *The Washington Post,* March 14, 1982. Reprinted by permission of the author.

Cartoon, p. 263: Drawing by Stevenson; © 1976 The New Yorker Magazine, Inc.

Table 12.1: Adapted from Thomas R. Marshall, *Presidential Nominations in a Reform Age,* Table 2.2, p. 46. (New York: Praeger, 1981). Reprinted by permission.

Excerpt, p. 312: From *Safire's Political Dictionary.* Copyright © 1968, 1972, 1978 by William Safire. Reprinted by permission of Random House, Inc.